T0305245

UNSTABLE GROUND

UNSTABLE
GROUND

UNSTABLE GROUND

The Lives, Deaths, and Afterlives
of Gold in South Africa

ROSALIND C. MORRIS

Columbia University Press
New York

Columbia University Press
Publishers Since 1893
New York   Chichester, West Sussex
cup.columbia.edu

Library of Congress Cataloging-in-Publication Data
Names: Morris, Rosalind C., author.
Title: Unstable ground : the lives, deaths, and afterlives of gold in South Africa /
    Rosalind C Morris.
Description: New York : Columbia University Press, [2024] |
    Includes bibliographical references and index.
Identifiers: LCCN 2024014908 | ISBN 9780231216111 (hardback) |
    ISBN 9780231216128 (trade paperback) | ISBN 9780231216128 (ebook)
Subjects: LCSH: Gold mines and mining—Social aspects—South Africa. |
    Gold miners—South Africa. | Gold—Social aspects—South Africa. |
    Gold—Economic aspects—South Africa.
Classification: LCC HD9536.S62 M67 2024 | DDC 338.2/7410968—
    dc23/eng/20240607
LC record available at https://lccn.loc.gov/2024014908

Printed and bound by CPI Group (UK) Ltd, Croydon, CR0 4YY

Cover design: Milenda Nan Ok Lee
Cover image: Clive van den Berg, *African Landscape: The Big Koppie*, 2019 (oil on
    canvas, 2.7m × 2.7m). Courtesy of the artist.

GPSR Authorized Representative: Easy Access System Europe, Mustamäe tee 50,
10621 Tallinn, Estonia, gpsr.requests@easproject.com

In memory of my mother and my father

*This book is for my students and is dedicated to
Yvette Christiansë* ◠

CONTENTS

PREFACE

Ground—Preliminary Definitions

(After the *Oxford English Dictionary*)

1. Past tense and participle of the verb (transitive), *to grind*. To reduce to small particles or powder by crushing between two hard surfaces.
2. Noun. *Ground*. The bottom or lowest part of anything.
3. In plural, the particles deposited by a liquid, dregs.
4. Noun. Base. Foundation.
   a. That on which a system, work, institution, art or condition of things, is founded;
   b. A fundamental principle;
   c. A circumstance on which an opinion, inference, argument, statement, or claim is founded, or which has given rise to an action, procedure, or mental feeling; a reason, motive. Often with additional implication: a valid reason, justifying motive, or what is alleged as such. *On the ground of*: by reason of; *on public (also religious, etc.) grounds*: for reasons of the nature specified.
5. Noun. The substratum over which other parts are laid.
   a. The chief or underlying part in a textile fabric;
   b. Any material, natural or prepared, which is taken as the base for working upon.
6. Noun. The surface of the earth, or part of it.
   a. The earth regarded as the surface upon which man and his surroundings naturally rest or move; frequently in prepositional phrases, as *along* (also *on, to*) *the ground*; *above* (also *underground*);

b. Figure in phrases; *to bring to the ground*: to cast down, overthrow, overcome, subdue; *to come* (also *go*) *to the ground*: to be overcome; to perish; so *to be dashed to the ground* (of hopes); *down to the ground*: completely, thoroughly, in every respect (*colloq.*); *from the ground up* (*colloq.*, orig. U.S.*)*, completely, entirely; "down to the ground"; *to get off the ground*, to make a successful start; *on the ground*, in situ, on the spot.

c. Regarded as the place of burial. *Above ground*: unburied, alive.

7. Noun. The earth contrasted with heaven.
8. Noun. The earth contrasted with the sea.
9. Noun. Area on the face of the earth. Especially in the phrases, *to break new ground, to gain ground, to give ground, to lose ground.*
10. Noun. With reference to possessor, denoted by a genitive noun or possessive noun:
    a. The portion of land belonging to a person;
    b. The space on which a person takes his stand (esp. in the phrases *to hold one's ground, to keep one's ground, to maintain one's ground, to stand one's ground*).
11. Noun. The soil of the earth. Also without article. Only in *mining*, except with descriptive adjective: *break ground*.
12. Noun. Technical, from telegraphy. The contact of an electric conductor with the earth; the escape of energy resulting from this.

Related Definitions—Underground

1. Adjective. Below the surface of the ground.
2. Carried on, taking place underground, as in underground mining.
3. In figurative context.
    a. Hidden, concealed, secret;
    b. Designating the activities of a group, organization, or its representatives, working covertly to subvert a ruling (often occupying) power.

A NOTE ON ORTHOGRAPHY AND CAPITALIZATION

Among the Bantu languages of South Africa, prefixes are used to modify nouns. The prefix "ama," "ma," or "bo" indicates people (for example, amaXhosa refers to the Xhosa people; Marashea is the name of a gang), whereas "isi," "se" or "tsi" indicates language or a type of person in the larger group. This protocol, however, has not always been observed in the literature of South Africa, especially during the colonial and Apartheid eras. When citing literature, I have retained the orthography and spelling as it appeared in the original text. When speaking of ethnic groups, and in colloquial discourse, the unmodified noun is generally used and may also be treated as an adjective: Xhosa (or Xhosa nation), Zulu, Shona, Sotho, and so forth. When statements are translated from South African languages, they are followed by a letter indicating the language of origin (X = isiXhosa, Z = isiZulu, N= isiNdebele, S/T = Sesotho/Setswana, T = Chitonga). The X indicates the lateral click common to isiXhosa and isiZulu but is also present in other South African languages. It is stereotypically described as the sound made to "encourage a horse" to move. The Q is an alveolar click.

Census categories and other nominations of racial groups changed significantly over the century and a half covered in this book. Black South Africans were variously denominated as Africans, n/Natives, b/Black, and c/Colored. Once again, when citing literature, I have retained the original spelling and categories. Black, used to refer to people, is not generally capitalized in contemporary South African literature, as is the case in the United States, where it indicates historically minoritized status. I have observed the South African convention, except when citing U.S. literature.

Apartheid (capitalized, as a proper noun) is used here to refer to the formal governmental dispensation enacted and overseen by the National Party, operative between 1948 and 1994. It is distinguished from the earlier regime of segregationism and, before that, colonialism, although these former modes of governance shared some of the separatist logic that would be radicalized and increasingly codified after 1948. In this book, I do not use the term "apartheid" (uncapitalized) to refer to a generalized logic of racialized separation, but almost always as the proper name of a South African form of governance.

The names of published authors and public persons are used in this text. Unless indicated otherwise, or in the form of acknowledgments, all other people have been given pseudonyms.

UNSTABLE GROUND

UNSTABLE
GROUND

CHAPTER 1

CLEARING GROUND

Time comes into it.
Say it.   Say it.
The universe is made of stories,
not of atoms.

—Muriel Rukeyser, "The Speed of Darkness"

All around us and our resting place
The stones are blind.
Their eye is in the talking dream
Whose lips are eternally opened
Emitting the rich fruits of fire
Telling the story of running men.

—Mazisi Kunene, "The Song of the Stone Clan"

August 5, 2018

Sky gnaws the earth. Or perhaps it is the other way around. The horizon is unstable. Clouds of dust the color of dried blood rise in tiny whirlwinds before settling, rising again, and then subsiding once more below an otherwise peerless sky. The wind moans in the ears, then whispers in the dusted leaves of the trees, and finally falls silent. The dust stings the eyes and coats the teeth with grit.

Into the morning air, burning grasses release a pungent odor and a paraffin haze settles on the horizon in a soft and poisonous cloak: the fragrance of the season before planting. It is winter deep in the southern hemisphere, but the sun, still low and throwing hard shadows, is already warm. On the horizon, the flat trapezoids of huge mine dumps furrowed by rain and time rise in a golden outline above a web of electric wires, pipes, and shacks topped with zinc roofs held in place by old tires and soda crates. Trucks and taxi-minivans crammed with bodies pass indifferently on the highway named for the reef of gold beneath the earth's surface.

Occasionally, a car pulls onto the pocked dirt sideroad and approaches, coming to a stop at the little rise where a group of women now stands a few meters from a corpse that has been brought up from beneath the earth. The car doors open, and men step down and gather in claques of outrage. Their eyes are on the police officers who pace the scene and on the young woman who answers their questions, the widow of the man whose lifeless body lays in this wind, shrouded by this dust the color of dried blood, beneath this paraffin-stained but peerless sky on an August day when the sun, still low, is throwing hard shadows.

This Call Cannot Be Completed

I had received news of an underground rockfall in the late afternoon two days earlier, on August 3. A young *zama zama* miner had apparently reached to hold onto a rock as he climbed upward, out of the "hole." It was loose.

"Pebbles and scree. And a shard note, thin, as the hour's message of comfort."[1]

Perhaps he mistook the rock for an overhang. Perhaps, as someone who had been working in this area for only two months, he did not recognize how unstable the earth is in these abandoned shafts. Perhaps, he had failed to test his hold. Perhaps, the rock had been newly loosened by blasting. Perhaps it was just fate calling the gambler.

"You can't judge a stone; can't judge a rock." Another young zama zama had spoken these cautionary words to me a year before the accident. "You may say it is strong, but it's not strong. [At any time, it] can collapse onto you and then you are no more," he added soberly.

The fickle rock fell, and with it, a small avalanche had descended on the man. He tumbled backward, headlong into the shaft, into the darkness of the underworld. The other men on his team could see that he had been buried up to his neck. Only his head protruded from the heap of stone. They had assumed he was dead, but in any case, they could not reach him. The rocks were unstable; the route back now blocked. Another path would have to be found or opened. The men thus proceeded to the shaft exit to tell the others and to arrange a rescue—of the corpse if not the man. They had done this before.

The bearer of the news was a gentle young man with the name of a Biblical king, one whose love of gold had led to a divine punishment: Solomon, whose kingdom was riven. Biblical names are common here, and Abrahamic myth interweaves itself with ancestral narrative to provide a palimpsest of reference and a dreamscape of community and divine judgment. These narratives overlay the text of gambling and the fateful encounter, which are encoded in the word, zama zama, meaning both to keep on trying and to gamble. And so, the prophetically named young man, a fellow gambler, made a call from his own phone to report the worst of luck, the end of the game. The news reached the young woman as a burdensome message from elsewhere that she could not refuse. The message came from both the past (the accident, her husband's death) and the future (a woman's unfolding life without her husband, more unimaginable than the life with him). It was an *arrivant*, in Derrida's sense of the term.[2] But its domain stretched beyond both for it included the subsumption of the man within an ancestral tradition that reached both backward and forward. Yet, access to this other world was also blocked. Without a body, without mourning rites, he would remain unmoored from the future community.

When the news came, relayed in person by a friend from the dead man's village, the young woman was at home in an informal settlement not far from the mines, caring for their six-month-old son. The dead man had left his phone with security guards as guarantee to cover the fees charged at the entrance of shafts in the ruins of industrial mines. The role of these guards is not merely to ensure that gangsters do not enter the mines to rob the zama zamas or press them into servitude, as they sometimes do; it is also to protect the mines and their illegal, itinerant scavengers from arrest by the police. Because he had not returned to pay the outstanding amount due, the dead man's SIM card and battery had been removed from his phone to cover his debt. With them had vanished both the possibility of using the phone and of retrieving the man's contacts in his home province—and especially of his family—for he was, like most of the people in this area, a migrant. His wife did not have a phone and did not know these numbers linking her husband to the world of his kin; they came from different points of origin and indeed from different countries—he from Zimbabwe, and she from Eastern Cape Province. The ransoming of the SIM card was therefore a second severance, one that interrupted the socialization and finalization of the first, namely the man's death. In its absence, time opened between the man's death and his natal family, extending the period of waiting that had begun when the miners first looked at their friend's fallen body. We may imagine that it also extended and radicalized the waiting of his parents and siblings, who had not seen him for years. This waiting, however, could not be measured by the hands of a clock.

The "reluctant minutes of the marathon day" added up and spilled into the night.[3] This waiting, the anxious experience of duration between the event

of death and its social recognition, was to be extended further.[4] The informal security guards who had confiscated the SIM card had refused to let the
man's friends return to the shaft before dark, on the grounds that they all—
guards and miners alike—would be arrested. Deterred by these seeming guard-
ians from retrieving the corpse in respectful service to grief and the ancestors,
the men were forced to wait for the next twelve hours. They passed the time
standing adjacent to the women, who were clustered in small groups from
shared villages. The women remained in place over the next day, quiet for the
most part, occasionally weeping, sometimes prognosticating about the young
widow's future, and sometimes complaining about the injustice of the police
who harassed them even in times of grief.

When darkness fell at last, the men took their leave from the women and
descended. They did what they always do when a man is killed underground.
They took poles and the jute sacks that would normally be used to carry
gold-bearing sand and made a litter for the corpse, binding his broken body in
a shroud between the lengths of wood. Then, sharing the body's dead weight
between them, they moved it up the narrow and broken passage and returned
to the surface, where they placed the limp body on the tawny grass. The orphic
journey of retrieval lasted more than twenty-four hours: "They took a path that
steep upright/Rose dark and full of foggy mist. And now they were within/a
kenning of the upper earth."[5] Throughout that long cold night, the women continued to wait. As the sun rose, only the young widow still hoped against hope
that the man who would be brought to them would be breathing and capable of
being restored. Alas, he could not answer her wish.

Warning, Danger Ahead: An Accidental Beginning

I arrived on the scene of these events a few hours later, called by friends in
the area who knew of my research and recent film work. The details that
I have just recounted are the result of the many conversations that followed,
some, although not all, with people I had never met before. On the hurried
drive from Johannesburg that day, I wrestled the fear that I would know
the man whose body was by then lying on the Highveld grasses. I had come
to know many zama zamas over the previous few years, and I hoped to be
spared that awful familiarity.

I had asked to be contacted in the event of an accident. When the call came,
the news confirmed what I had already known would occur—sooner or later.
Yet, it brought with it a primal regret and liberated a repressed fear of implication as well as the consciousness of magical thinking. As anthropologists who
have learned from E. E. Evans-Pritchard, an accident is almost invariably an
incitement to magical thinking.[6] It ignites the desire to find an explanation for

the singular event, quite beyond the general rules that make that event possible or even likely. Why him? Why was he there, then, when the rock fell on that day? Why not sooner or later? Why not someone else? Neither the explanation of technological failure or ruination, nor that of geological instability can answer such questions. "Time comes into it," as Muriel Rukeyser wrote.[7] Time comes into it as the medium and as the object of a narration that seeks to understand the singularity of the event. But the object of that narration is better understood as a question of timing rather than of time. What is desired by the one who is befallen by an event is some explanation for the simultaneity in spacetime of beings and forces that collide with fatal consequence. One word for this collision, when it is understood to be something more than an accident, is *fate*.

The accident is always an event, of course. But the mining accident is also a specific form and figure of eventfulness—that through which one may grasp something about traumatic experience more generally. Only as a figure—a figure at the limit of figuration, the figure of *an accident*—can the accidental be imagined as something to attend, for in its eventfulness, the accident will always be that which is missed, that which takes place at the limit of what can be known or anticipated. The figure of *an accident*—an automobile wreck or a collapsed rock face—is merely the screen on which the eventfulness of accident is displaced. This is why one gapes at it; its fascination is that of the inassimilable, of the unimaginable, of the limit transgressed. Still, one must ask: What kind of understanding depends on being present at an accident, the event of death, when it is a (technoindustrial) function and not merely an end of laboring life? Was the request to be notified a wish for knowledge? For its limit? For the transcendence of those limits? I cannot answer these questions, but they have accompanied me for much of my life—encrypted in childhood memory.

I still recall the few charged days of a childhood summer that were spent watching a competition between safety teams in the little Canadian mining town where I grew up. A relentless rehearsal for disaster is part of life in advanced industrial mining contexts everywhere in the world, and I have accompanied rescue teams in formal mines in South Africa as they scout the terrain in which they might have to work, should a rock face burst, or a train run off the rails, a carriage fall. Prepare for the accident to avoid death. That is the theme and implicit motto of these rehearsals and of virtually all occupational safety discourse in industrial contexts. But the dramaturgy of the accident also has a macabre attraction, quite beyond that discourse's utility. I recall that we (children) were horrified but also entranced by the staged accidents and the theatrically made-up bodies that were strewn across the schoolyard as the rescue teams demonstrated their skills and raced the clock that hung in surreal enormity above the proceedings. The protruding bone of the compound fracture, the ludicrous red of the painted blood, and the feigned cries and false silence of this strange death-play thrilled and repelled us by turns.

They gave us a banalized taste of the allegorical, that experience of transitoriness that Walter Benjamin discerned at the heart of the mourning play and of all industrial ruins.[8] And they assuaged our fear. For, to our euphoric relief, the actors in our proud theater of safety and rescue got up off their stretchers and wiped their wounds away when twilight fell and the whining hour of the mosquitoes arrived. Moreover, the siren that concluded the proceedings and that was tested every day seemed to announce the fact that nothing had really happened; indeed, that nothing would ever really happen. Until it did. And then it would be too late. Such is the nature of traumatic events in general. They are experienced as "too soon," and we therefore feel our responses to them are *belated*. They are the occasion of an experience of time *out of joint*. In such moments, one is often left speechless.

The insight that the accident or traumatic event can be understood as a missed encounter comes to us from Freud.[9] In his writings on the war neuroses, Freud observed the peculiar prevalence of mutism among veterans of armed conflict and, reflecting on this painful interruption of the subject's capacity for communication, came to understand trauma as an experience *at* as well as *of* representation's limits, one that would have to be encountered again and inscribed in what Lacan would later call a symbolic register before it could be accommodated—to not be forgotten but lived with. Until that happened, the sufferers of the symptoms would be subject to the effects of the event without being able to reflect on it and without being able put it behind them as part of their subjective history. Made incapable of this historicizing gesture by the sudden and overwhelming force of the event, the trauma would repeat in them—often in the form of flashbacks or nightmares—subjecting them to terrifying and disorienting repetitions. In Freud's readings, and in Lacan's later glossing, it is not merely the event that is terrifying but the fact of its recurrence, for the repetition also interrupts the presumptive linearity of historical experience. It plays havoc with the temporality of everyday causality, quotidian reason.

The term Freud developed to describe this predicament, in which a person is subjected to a prior trauma, which becomes constitutive as a result of an accumulating but retrospectively discerned force, is *Nachträglichkeit*. Belatedness. In this book, I gesture toward Freud's reading, and Fanon's rereading of Freud, as well as the orientation toward the ancestral, with the linked notions of *Nachträglichkeit* (or belatedness) and *Nachleben* (or afterlife). If the former designates a retrospective discovery of a determining force, the latter refers to the durational space or the afterward. The ancestral names an epistemic structure that can, on occasion, encompass both and accommodate the recurrent presentation of the dead in life as something other than a violation of reason's nature. This is not, however, a book about trauma per se, although many episodes of trauma are recounted in the following pages. Throughout this book, the concept of belatedness describes a broad historical predicament, one that has particular affective dimensions in many South African communities and especially in the unsettled spaces that I will later describe as "deindustrializing." Yet, it is not mere coincidence, or structural homology that makes mining and mine accidents the scene of experiences and expressions that are also poignantly visible among the survivors of war. The English term *mine* is itself a point of contact, or perhaps, the symptom of a conjuncture between industrial extractive processes and systemic violence of a sort that produces accidents. As Peter Szendy reminds us, *mine* is a term originally used to denote a concealed and explosive weapon. Only secondarily—belatedly?—did this term acquire its signification of a hole in the ground from which valuable resources may be extracted. In English, of course, mine is also a term signifying personal or private possession. So, beneath the woven text of underground mining are three terms: war, extraction, property. Erupting from them, as that which is over-determined and contingent, is the accident.[10]

* * *

By the time I arrived at the place where the corpse was laid out that August day in 2018, I had already passed two fatal traffic accidents. This was an unusually grim morning, but not unprecedented in this world of compulsive automobility.

Perhaps it was for this reason, perhaps because I arrived in the trembling penumbra of those pathos-filled but unremarkable catastrophes of automotive life, minute details of a newly intense, sensible world became focused in my mind. The litter with the enshrouded man was lain next to the unpaved road in a stubble of tawny grasses. Although the densely packed soil of this area appears to be dried-blood red when seen from a distance, it acquires an ochre hue when it settles in a thin layer on cloth or flesh. So, the litter, like the men who had borne it, seemed to be dusted with the color of the dead grasses on which the deceased man was laid out. One synonym for this color is gold. But to say so immediately requires qualification: dull gold, straw gold, dead gold, muted gold. Which is to say, not quite gold. But not quite yellow either.

The dead man's wife, modestly dressed in black with a dull-gray scarf wrapped around her head, waited with their infant wrapped in a canary yellow blanket. The baby was silent, even when the women wept. But nobody remarked this fact. His mother wrapped and unwrapped the blanket, then tucked it again around the baby's cherubic face at regular intervals, relinquishing her bundle to the other women when the police demanded her presence near the corpse. When the police finished questioning her and she finally agreed to leave her husband's body to return to her shack dwelling, she undressed the child and took the clothes in a neat ball to a nearby house. Why?, I asked. She had borrowed them to keep him warm in the long night, but now she had to return them to their rightful owners. With this poignant gesture, the hieroglyph of a poverty that denied her the means to even clothe her child while leaving her respect for property intact, she once again wrapped the naked boy in the yellow blanket, covering his legs and the umbilical hernia that testified to his medically unattended home birth. Like the bird in the proverbial coal mine, the bird-blanket was a flag of surrender above the mine. Too late. Too soon.

What Is Interred: Grounding Metaphors

How did we get here? They? I? We? What forces brought us to this "bleeding piece of earth"[11] on the Highveld, not far from the glittering skyline of Johannesburg, known colloquially as Egoli, the City of Gold? Along what paths of natural circumstance and technological overdetermination, economy, sociopolitical history, fear, and desire did we travel to arrive at this place where now, amid the ruins, a man lay dead after having been crushed in a mine that was ostensibly closed more than two decades ago? Where a woman now stood with other women in uncomprehending solidarity, on the side of a road that links Egoli to the sprawling industrial dreamscapes and broken remnants of the world's deepest mines. Where vengeance would be demanded. Where that same vengeance would be disavowed not only in gestures of polyglot alliance but also by virtue of sacrificial violence. What bonds of affection, what scars of enmity, what brittle structures of ethnic or racial difference and sexual hierarchy, what systems of opportunity and foreclosure explain the convergence of our wildly disparate itineraries at this threshold, where an accident occurs as an event in the chronicle of a death at once feared and foretold?

"Beyond these coins and seasons, then look back
When the black voices turn brilliant and call: Here!"[12]
How indeed did we get here? They? I? We?

Benjamin Wallet Vilakazi asked that question in his monumental versenarrative about these mines, *Ezinkomponi* (On the Mine Compounds) more than seventy-five years ago. The world described in that oft-quoted poem is "upside down," and one of the symptoms of this destructive inversion, beyond the forced regression that sees men turned into boys (as their white supervisors called them), is the fact that men *both* live and die while buried underground. The space of the grave and the space of work become almost indistinguishable. Indeed, in the languages spoken in this area, the same word is used for the mine and the hole in which a coffin is placed: *umgodi* or *igodi* (Z and X, N); *sekota* (SS).[13] Hence, Vilakazi's narrator asks his reader, as if in disbelief, "Have you seen buried men survive/Walking and seeing and staying alive?"[14] They do not only enter the earth when interred. Thus, the opposition between the above- and below-ground world loses its metaphoric capacity to distinguish the living and the dead. What the poem distills in its dense narrative form, then, is the fact that structural violence takes the form of relative exposure to accident, whether the kinds that led to the death of the zama zama described here or those that cause the slower unfolding wounds of the lung diseases that are linked to work underground: phthisis or pulmonary tuberculosis, silicosis, AIDS-related respiratory syndromes, and cancer.

About ten years into my apprenticeship to the fissured dream of self-transformation in post-Apartheid South Africa, I began to conceive of my research in terms of the idea of accident. I had been struck, during the previous decade, by how often, when asked about the enormous mines and the knotted clusters of towns and townships that surrounded them, people's narratives gravitated around the tale of one or another accident. It was as though they all followed the example of Peter Abrahams's novel, *Mine Boy* (1946), in which an accommodation to the relentlessness and the boredom of mine labor—"this mocking of a man by sand"—could only be stalled or interrupted by an awful event.[15] Sometimes, these narratives followed the pattern of epic and culminated in fantastic rescues and heroic survivals—in the aftermath of rock face bursts and the apocalypses of flood or fire or asphyxiation that followed. Sometimes, as with the sinkholes of Carletonville (the mining town in present-day Merafong), they were obsessively attached to the uncanny disappearance of people and objects into cavernous pits—at once like and unlike the mines—that opened without warning to swallow the aboveground world. Often, such narratives were suffused with Biblical references, and the idea of an incomprehensible but divine judgment was part of the telling. "He opened the bottomless pit, and smoke went up out of the pit, like the smoke of a great furnace; and the sun and the air were darkened by the smoke of the pit."[16] Equally often, the narratives of accident, of events that had arrived suddenly and beyond comprehension, were threaded or undergirded by a single concept or metaphor, which was itself woven into a multiplicity of related idioms: unstable ground.

Unstable ground. This phrase is an evocation of a corporeal sensation and a term describing terrestrial conditions; it is a reference to economic precarity and a future of as-yet unfathomable transformation. Sometimes, it can imply a vague sense of moral weightlessness. At other times, it suggests the labor necessary to establish new foundational principles to legitimate a novel order while also containing the excess energies that course through all social worlds and especially those that are in the throes of radical social transformation. Hence, the title of this book: *Unstable Ground: The Lives, Deaths, and Afterlives of Gold*. I intend for the phrase unstable ground to reverberate across many registers and indeed to resound beyond the vernacular discourses in which it originally became audible to me. These hoped-for reverberations should traverse material and geological, legal and philosophical, sociological and historical, and mediatic and aesthetic domains. I will begin with matter by way of word: let the reader's mind, eye and ear, feet, and innermost linings of the lungs conjure the "murmurs from the earth of this land, from the caves and craters/from the bowl of darkness."[17]

The auriferous rock (mainly quartz) of the Witwatersrand is famously nestled in porous dolomite ridges: it is a folded landscape that lies beneath the earth, lit only by artifice, and inhabited by the dead—fossils of ancient creatures that once populated an inland sea or lake formed by converging rivers, and the remains of men and, now, women, who have vanished in the mines and become both dust and spirit over the past century. Dolomite is soluble in water; thus, underground holes are "eaten out by water/and now filled with water."[18] Michael Cawood Green describes this geological fact, a condition predisposing the land to sinkholes and rock falls, in the following lines: "The tempting domesticity of its/Scoured surface smoothness,/Is eaten out from within by conflicts/Older than poetry."[19] It is not only geology, nor the ancient enmity suggested by Green, that dictates the fate of miners. It is capital-intensive, industrial mining itself.

In industrial operations in the area of which I write, taking pace as they do in a once-oceanic space, digging deep requires the evacuation of water from underground, lest the miners be drowned in the torrents that would rush in to fill the voids created by drilling—as sometimes happens. But this evacuation, the apparent solution to a problem, leaves the caverns empty, and therefore vulnerable to collapse. When that happens, the surface of the earth can also cave in to form a sinkhole. Sinkholes occur naturally, but they also can be caused by artificial dewatering. The material instability of the mined earth is then the first referent of my title. In part 2, I describe the histories, mythic structures, and memories of the famous sinkholes that afflicted Carletonville, a mining town not far from the scene with which I have commenced this introduction, during the 1960s. It was the point of my entry into research about the lives, deaths, and afterlives of gold in South Africa and southern Africa more generally. However, the mythification of that event, which was centrally woven into the tragic lore of the place in the local white imaginary, simultaneously occluded its many counternarratives among the municipality's black township residents. I try to show how these latter accounts, which form one part of at least two braided and racially perspectival narratives, was available to be mobilized during political struggles in the post-Apartheid area. In the early years of the democratic transition, the term *sinkhole* assumed an enlarged metaphoric range and was commonly invoked in descriptions of both economic unsustainability and new legislative gestures that local people experienced as destabilizing—as destabilizing as "forced removal" had been in the years immediately following the enactment of the *Group Areas Act* (1950) and the *Immorality Act* (also 1950, revised in 1957). The sinkhole figured this predicament in which the grounds of a predictable, although not necessarily easy existence, were taken out from beneath people. Imagery of unstable ground—of tremor, quake, and subsidence—was in this sense available to metaphorize political experience and the epistemological crises that attended it. As I hope to show, this process of translation and transposition also often works through forms of demetaphorization.

The phrase *unstable ground* has many other possible resonances and significances as well, and they animate various dimensions of this book. In addition to the geological associations and the political processes and conflicts that were metaphorized through reference to them, this locution can bespeak the relationship between figure and ground in an aesthetic sense or in terms of the system of visibility within which particular objects rise above and are apprehended against a surface or background that functions as the scene and condition of possibility for their appearance. This structure is not confined to an "art historical" discourse. Understood in terms of a figure-ground dynamic, the notion of *unstable* ground suggests an experience of the reordering of a representational system, including both its aesthetic and political dimensions. It does so in the sense that what was previously mere background intrudes on vision, soliciting the eye rather than fading away into an illusory second nature. It thus denotes a loss or at least a shaking up of prior axioms and perspectival systems.

In any period of political transformation, the task that confronts individuals and collectives is not merely the reorganization of the apparatus that condenses and distributes power, a process that not infrequently reduces itself to the mere appropriation of power by a new group that then maintains old structures and hierarchies, exclusions and marginalities. It also entails a reorientation of vision, or, as Jacques Rancière suggests, a new partition of the sensible.[20] New questions and new possibilities must be conceived on a horizon where they had not previously been discerned, even vaguely. When the figures and concepts that dominated thought in the past no longer function, when they recede into meaninglessness or dissolve (like dolomite) in the acid bath of moral opprobrium or more vigorous critical denegation, the ground of what had previously been normalized rises up and loses its status as background. In such moments, and I believe the early post-Apartheid era constitutes such a moment, destruction may assume its productive dimension and, in the best cases, unleash an energetic exploration and experimentation with new kinds of representation and new aesthetic forms. Beginning in the late 1990s and persisting into the present, South Africa saw a fluorescence of institutional and aesthetic experiments aimed at the creation of new modes of collective being and self-representation, some of them marked by a salvific aspiration and others by righteous antagonism: from the extrajuridical theater of the Truth and Reconciliation Commission to the transformation of Apartheid era prisons and sites of state power into museums and forums for democratic and national pedagogy, and from the creation of new political parties to the rise of militant unions challenging an entrenched labor aristocracy. Incendiary protests in shack settlements and rural townships, as well as on university campuses, expressed a profound if dispersed democratic ambition and, on occasion, an equally profound populist authoritarianism. They experienced, as their corollary, emergent literary movements devoted to the revival or invigoration of vernacular traditions and a burgeoning art scene of uncommon creativity.

Powers from Afar, Poetry from the Future

Not all forms of experimentation are liberatory, however. Nor is every departure from sedimented form enabling of more inclusive modes of collective life. And even if, as Foucault made clear, visibility and sayability are discontinuous domains, the tasks confronting thought in a moment of political transformation are not fully captured by analogy with visual representation.[21] Perhaps for this reason, Marx wrote of the need of "social revolution . . . to take its poetry from the future."[22] Marx formulated this elusive phrase in counterpoint and opposition to that famous theater of repetition in which the would-be revolutionary leaders of 1848 had attired themselves in the regalia of prior revolts, thereby displaying their incapacity to escape the past or invent something truly new. "Poetry from the future" is one name for a capacity to imagine otherwise. Today, in South Africa, as in so many places, revolution is often conceived as a denegation of prior orders. Ambition for the new has for many people surrendered to an aspiration for an improved version of what is, as the ideal of equality gives way to the dream of equal access to inequality. Lesego Rampolokeng accuses the covetous, consumer commodity-centered attitude of the newly enriched, and especially those enabled by the policy to promote black capital formation (Black Economic Empowerment, BEE) with lacerating satire: "they're grabbing the grabbing,/they're nabbing the verbing."[23] Nonetheless, in academic and public intellectual contexts, radical transformation is now discussed in the idiom of the "decolonization of consciousness." It is difficult to overestimate the enormity of this task, which Marx, a not always unsympathetic critic of religion, also described as an escape from the "superstition of the past." But the notion of superstition can no longer function as a mere foil for enlightened reason. Indeed, if the colonization of consciousness can be grasped as the origin of contemporary superstition, the opposite may also be said. Nonetheless, whether it can be emancipated from its derogatory connotations or not, what Marx implies, across the broad range of his writings, is that superstition is not merely a form of illusion that can be shucked off through acts of will; it is the affectively intense condensation of the epistemological structures and normalized modes of being that the past, as a system of inequality and oppression, bequeaths to its heirs. Some people would call this condensation culture, although culture is poorly understood if it is limited to its normative dimension. For all cultures include the capacity to think through counterexamples, to question and thus to critique what is—precisely because it is that which is learned.

Against this background, both critics and anthropologists are confronted by the question: How may we access not only the form of the learned but of the learning? And what might be the relationship between this question and that to which Marx offered his oblique formula about a poetry from the future? I pose these questions because they are demanded by the task that so many South Africans set for themselves in the struggle against colonialism, segregation, and Apartheid, and in the effort to forge a new society under a new constitutional dispensation. The extent to which that project succeeds depends on the transformation of education—a fact that became evident in the struggles over redemarcation in Khutsong (a township near the largest gold mines), as I shall argue in part 2. In that conflict, a drama that deserves to be called a tragedy, the problem of education was often reduced to the certification and even branding of examinations by provincial authorities. It was not only literature or even literacy, but rather the signature of power that oriented the school protests. Had the new struggle been thought of as a fight to learn how to read a poetry from the future, things might have turned out otherwise. And they may still do so. But this task has not yet been accomplished.

To speak of a poetry from the future is not to assume that all poetry has an oracular dimension. Nor does Marx privilege poetry as the medium of emancipated thought. As Andrew Parker has reminded us, Marx spoke of the revolutionary *poesie* of the future to designate the kind of invention that would be differentiated from the derivativeness of the bourgeois revolutionary thought that characterized the eighteenth century: "The social revolution of the nineteenth century cannot draw its poetry from the past but only from the future. . . . Early revolutions required recollections of the past world history in order to drug themselves concerning their own content. In order to arrive at its own content, the revolution of the nineteenth century must let the dead bury their dead. There the phrase went beyond the content; here the content goes beyond the phrase."

Parker argues that this formulation, "'poetry of the future' may figure the unprecedented as such," on the basis that Marx refers to *Poesie*, which generally encompasses all literary arts, rather than *Dichtung*, meaning, more narrowly, "poetry."[24] If poetry in the latter, narrower sense has or can have an emancipatory capacity, it is because, as a mode of enfleshed language at the threshold of the singular in which the abstractness of the sign and the material concreteness of the image converge and diverge, it opens onto multiplicity—the multiplicity of signification. The density of poetic language is the call for interpretation. This is why, the "attitude of poetry," including that of the past, and thus of tradition, "is capable of facing the tragic, the complex, the fantastic. . . . It is a technique that may provide the fierce and vivid spirit with its complexity, a many-sided resistance," as Rukeyser wrote in 1941.[25]

The future seemed bleak when Rukeyser penned those words, as it does once more. Poverty rates in South Africa have grown to desperate proportions (more than 55 percent in 2022);[26] xenophobic violence erupts with disquieting frequency, in that country as elsewhere; political authoritarianism and all the corruption and terror that go with it are discouragingly evident, locally as internationally; labor is threatened by capital in ways that have not been seen in decades; and precarity is the condition in which many migrants, but also citizens, now must find their way—in South Africa as around the world. The COVID-19 pandemic only intensified the conditions that were already arrayed in this manner. Popular discontent about these issues led voters to deny the African National Congress (ANC) a majority for the first time in 25 years, in the national elections of 2024. The subsequent formation of a multi-party coalition, or national unity government, has yet to yield substantial changes, but whatever it does will be shaped in part by the legacies of the extractive industries.

Rukeyser, whose *Book of the Dead* offers a poetic testament to the violence that mining had wrought on the bodies of workers in the United States during the 1930s, is often cited in the pages that follow. A fierce but patriotically American leftist, she offers a somewhat different reading of the question of "tradition" or "superstition" than does Marx, for whom "the tradition of all dead generations weighs like a nightmare on the living."[27] By contrast, she writes that "any age of life this earth produces—is lived in a rare and carnal dancing on the grave, the solemn beautiful dance over the home of the dead of the living mystery, the living truth."[28] No doubt, Rukeyser had something other than the ancestral traditions of migrant miners in mind when she wrote of the carnal dance on the grave of the dead. But, reflecting on the fate of the young man whose death occasioned the opening narrative of this book, a death among many others, I am inclined to agree with her. This book is an effort to bring into the foreground those who have been buried in the green mold of oblivion that has accompanied the long history of extraction in South Africa.[29] Per Rukeyser: "this earth of our learning is, rather than dust ground out of rock, the packed and leafdrift earth of centuries of falling lives, fallen under our feet, anonymous, the inarticulate centuries."[30]

In addition to the citations of scholars from various disciplines, and scraps of news and popular media, the pages that follow are often punctuated by poetry and literary prose: of praise poets and *lifela/difela* singers in South Africa; of classical (Greek and Roman) myth and Biblical tradition, both of which suffuse the thought and literary production of the region; of South African writers, from the early twentieth century to the contemporary era; and of the American and European modernists who wrote in and against the brutal experiments of twentieth-century technoindustrial life, which was also at the heart of the South African state and its natural resource-based economy. At times, these self-conscious texts are the objects of analysis. At other times, citations are embedded without comment in my text, as the poetic mediation that brings into articulateness an analysis or a sensibility that I am otherwise trying to convey more prosaically. I want these echoes of other writers, from other times and places, to haunt the reader's consciousness, with the firm belief that this mode of articulation—the precise, language-dense, and self-reflecting form of an utterance—can reorient the figure-ground relationships, focalizations, and conceptual schema with which anthropologists otherwise think the world.

I hope that the voices summoned here will surprise the reader into questioning rather than lull her into complacency with lyricism. To be sure, these voices come from different languages and literary traditions, some quite remote from southern Africa. As will become clear in the following pages, however, and as has been argued by historical anthropologists and literary critics for many decades, the dream of isolated islands of tradition, like the fantasy of national sovereignty, is an illusion (one also propagated by Apartheid ideologues). Transnational and transcontinental networks of capital, technology, ideology, and political form make up the factual ground on which a séance of critical anthropological, literary, and artistic response can be held. This is partly because the writers and those who aspire to communicate their truths in language are already conducting such a séance or have been forcibly inducted into its audience.

From Sol Plaatje's translations of Shakespeare, and his incorporation of the English bard's forms and narratives into his writings, along with references to Sherlock Holmes; to S. E. K. Mqhayi's anthropomorphizing ekphrases to the steam engines of Europe; and Benjamin Wallet Vilakazi's verse narrative about the compounds of the gold mines, in which Britain's industrial machinery is the recipient of improbable empathy because it is as enslaved as black labor, South African writers have been reading, drawing from, echoing and subverting, and being haunted by writers and speakers elsewhere. This includes those who entered or were raised in European language traditions and who self-consciously inserted themselves into the lineages of their literary production. Ntongela Masilela has excavated the genealogies of the New African movement's intellectuals, noting the stylistic influence and citational presence of Francis Bacon, John Milton, Alexander Crummel, and Thomas Carlyle, along with the Greek and Elizabethan dramatists, in the writings of people like Elijah Makiwane, R. V. Selope, Henry Selby Msimang, H. I. E Dhlomo, and Jordan Magubane.[31] Some of these writers will figure in the discussions to come. I think, too, of Njabulo Ndebele's wondrous rewriting of Homer's *Odyssey* from the perspective of the women who wait, with Winnie Mandela as Penelope.[32] I am guided by Sandile Dikene's refusal of literary quarantine: "Like the minds of Hughes/Black has many colours./Black is/Light and caramel sweet and blue/ Like Nesta/And Coltrane/Or Mozart or all of them in song./Black is/Red and deep scarlet/Like Pushkin."[33] I take the work of these writers as examples and models of intertextuality—and encouragements to further the conversation between so-called Western and African literary and critical traditions.

Those whose natal languages emerge from a precolonial heritage live with the effects of a governmental project that was descendent of, and oriented toward, Europe and that disseminated its traditions in and through its curricula. To the easy demand for a purgation of colonial remnants—which sometimes offers itself as a substitute for the more complex task of decolonization—South(ern) African writers, who are heirs to colonial missionization and education, and many who have followed in their wake, seem to say: "The dead have offered us lines of tradition, and emblems. We are free to choose from among them."[34] If, that is, they speak in a manner that illuminates the world and that thereby summons that which would otherwise go without saying (one of the formulae for doxa or culture) into the foreground of reflective thought and analysis. This freedom is circumscribed, of course. Nonetheless, the people with whom I have worked over the years in South Africa have repeatedly expressed a deep admiration for the kind of linguistic precision and artistry that realizes itself most fully in literary language. Mineworkers' love of wit and verbal dexterity, as well as their understanding of the mortifying powers of language, whether in witchcraft or merely humiliating jokes, and their deft, nearly acrobatic cross-lingual play has inspired my method of writing.

To cite poetry is not, however, to claim the place of the poet, or even that kind of philosophical poeticizing that Nietzsche attempted in his effort to make corporeal experience, and especially pain, the basis of a new and radical understanding beyond moral philosophy.[35] Nor do I believe that an ethnography can simply assume the form of poetry. Certainly, anthropologists have written poetry that is rooted in their more specifically ethnographic work. But the analytical rather than the expressive task of ethnography is also properly philosophical, even when it does not aspire to become, in a fully Kantian sense, philosophical anthropology. To invoke Theodor Adorno, its merit can be determined neither by its "manifestation of the thinker's subjectivity nor the pure coherence of the work," as would be the standard for judging an ethnography understood as poetry, or even novelistic prose.[36] Rather, its success is to be "determined in the first place by the degree to which the real has entered into [its] concepts, manifests itself in these concepts, and comprehensively justifies them."[37] An ethnography, and the theorization to which it gives rise, must serve the reality to which it is devoted, and which it must also attempt to understand as the product of a complex, if nonprogressive dialectical history: a becoming second nature (normality) of collective artifice, under particular conditions.[38] In this labor to understand, it is not enough to poeticize, even when poetry provides the effort with a means of expression. One needs also to uncover the means by which particular figures have been made to apprehend and grant significance to social facts and processes, while simultaneously concealing that significance and the power-ridden history of its conferral, in the imagery of (more or less) natural phenomena. By considering how the concept and the metaphors of ground and underground work in the world made by and for gold mining, this doubled and redoubling process can be approached.

Metaphor Is the Thing

Let me then return to the question of ground and of grounding, to the question of the underground. Obviously, too obviously perhaps, the underground can appear as the literal scene of mining, at least that kind of deep industrial gold mining that takes place in much of South Africa. This does not make it a natural scene; it is anything but given in or by nature. The "unnaturalness" of mining is why its excavation has been, for millennia and in diverse places, a royal concession, a guarded and secreted activity, a mythicized field. The activity of extraction has also been a punishment; a labor demanded of war captives and slaves; and, finally, a scene of scientific knowledge production, technological development, and financial investment. As Goethe's Mephisto says, in a play about the costs of a desire for money at a time when the substitution of paper currency for gold represented a possible loss of moral grounding, "pick it off the floor,/But Wisdom's skill is getting what's most deeply hidden/In mountain veins and in foundation walls/you'll find both coined and uncoined gold,/and if you ask who will extract it, I reply:/a man that nature has endowed with mighty intellect."[39]

Goethe had considerable experience with such questions, having overseen the reopening of the silver mines of Ilmenau in Weimar when he was appointed to the privy council of Duke Karl-August of Saxe-Weimar in 1782. He knew the difference between surface mining and underground excavation. Alluvial mining, that in which gold is gathered on the surface of the earth, from riverbeds and glacial fields, and that can indeed appear at times to be that which is merely raked up, is less common in South Africa. The geology of the Witwatersrand requires "Mind's power," but this term cannot be understood in an idealist sense; it includes both technological know-how and economic power, including capital and the organization of labor for the purposes of surplus value extraction. In South Africa, the famous depth of the gold deposits, often several kilometers below the surface, has both determined the nature of mining and provided an alibi for the forms of surplus value extraction deployed there— including those grounded in the racialization of labor. I draw from the rich literature generated by South African historians to rethink that history and the role that international finance capital played in its early development. Some of part 1 covers familiar ground, as it were, but it also aims at an alternative reading of the early history of deep-levels mining, one in which cyanide-based processes both enabled the transcendence of a geological obstacle (having to do with the specific nature of the quartz conglomerate in which gold was found) and redoubled and charged the metaphor of separation, such that even social separation could appear to be an entailment of technology. In the deployment of the cyanide process, I suggest, a technoaesthetics of separatism, and not merely of separation, was elaborated.

Beyond but not unrelated to its function as the name of a subterranean location, the underground is also a term of reference in political discourse, a name for oppositional, insurrectionary, and revolutionary forms of collective organization and practice. It is not incidental for what follows that the area in which my research was conducted, adjacent to some of the largest and deepest mines in the world, was also the birthplace of the National Union of Mineworkers (NUM), which, during the 1980s and 1990s, played a central role in the anti-Apartheid movement. When, following the student uprisings of 1976, the South African state began to intensify its violent repression of oppositional activity, the African National Congress Youth League (ANCYL) was forced underground. Seeking locations from which to launch its operations and recruit members, the Youth League and the armed wing of the ANC, *uMkhonto weSizwe* (MK), sent cadres into the area that was nearest to Soweto, westward along the sickle-shaped arc of the Witwatersrand. There, they were engaged in a kind of proxy warfare involving state and nonstate forces, ethnic gangs, private security, and internationally linked white supremacist movements. The effects of that conflict, including the enforcement of boycotts, were catastrophic for many people, and some of the violence and its traumatic effects resurfaced in the Truth and Reconciliation Commission that followed the end of Apartheid, as I discuss in part 2.

Years after its formation, the NUM, which had successfully agitated in favor of the transformation of working conditions on the mines in alliance with other unions and the ANC (acting on the belief that miners deserve "reward to match [their] service"[40]), would be the object of another insurrection. This one was to be led by an emerging union, the Association of Mineworkers and Construction Union (AMCU), which had been founded in 1998, as a result of factional disagreements within NUM. AMCU's seemingly sudden appearance on the horizon, as the figure of a new militancy, caught many by surprise. Its conflict with the NUM assumed an overtly violent form in 2012, when strikers at the Lonmin platinum mine in Rustenburg, some 125 kilometers from Carletonville, undertook what was deemed by the Chamber of Mines to be an illegal (because off-schedule) strike, contravening both the mine management of Lonmin and the aristocracy of the relatively bureaucratized NUM. The Faustian bargain, to which NUM was accused by AMCU of having become a bloody signatory, ended, as perhaps all such bargains end, with death. The horrifying murder of thirty-four mineworkers by police, and ten others by insurgents and party security forces, in a period of days in August 2012, shook the South African political world—not least because it was filmed by television journalists. Shortly thereafter, many of the mineworkers who were fired in the platinum sector as a result of their activism moved on or back to the gold-mining region to take up the struggle. There, within less than two years, AMCU assumed dominance in the former place of origin of NUM. Thus, the twinned history of an underground—including both a scene and a delegitimized but ultimately victorious political force—found itself contested if not fully supplanted by another. The many histories of this mutually metaphorizing underground, then, forms another referent for the title of this book. There are at least two others, and these are related.

The first of these concerns the efforts of the post-Apartheid regime to ground itself and produce the terms of the new state's legitimacy in the aftermath of a transition that had been centered in a critique of the previous state's legally founded racism. The anti-Apartheid movement did not, by and large, take the form of anti-statism, and if "ungovernability" became a strategy in the 1980s—especially in the region of which I write—anarchism was not a dominant strand of the movement, which encompassed a broad range of parties, trade unions, religious organizations, armed groups, and other highly bureaucratized structures. Yet, despite the continuity in political form (the administrative state), every foundational moment, every origin in the political domain, must confront the need to enunciate and establish the principles on which its new order will unfold. This is grounding in the political sense. It takes place after and beneath the space conjured in images from the poetry of the future.

As is well known, the transition to liberal democracy in South Africa, even if it initially appeared to take the form of single-party rule, was negotiated under terms of relative unfreedom; international finance and various organs of the international monetary order and its (un)civil society enforced a program of neoliberalization rather than more radical redistribution or nationalization, especially in the natural resource sector of the economy. The figure whose imprimatur authorized this strategy of initial but compromised decolonization was Nelson Mandela. His radiant and chiefly personality was made even more luminous by his quarter-century in prison on Robben Island, and his subsequent if recently questioned iconization, indeed his elevation to the status of cult object in a global imaginary of belated but pacific revolution, provided the sheltering image within which the poignant task of constituting new powers and grounding a new order had to be undertaken. In this sense, South Africa shared what had become evident in many other postrevolutionary regimes (irrespective of their ideological content, and their success or failure): the need to represent the legitimacy of a new regime when it could not rely on tradition or defer to the "already established" status of a constitution to secure either its right to rule or the right of its rule as representative of the people's will.

South Africa's admirable new constitution (1996) was rewritten and ratified *after* the first post-Apartheid elections, which were undertaken on the basis of an interim constitution (1993) and thus after Mandela's assumption of the presidential office. It was, then, in lieu of tradition's guarantee for the new regime's claim to represent the interests of the people that the new state adopted a single and singular figure in which to incarnate what was otherwise, as of yet, a mere assertion—one awaiting the test of time. In such circumstances, writes Alain Badiou, "it becomes crucial for there to be a *representation of the representation*, one that would be a singularity, legitimated precisely by its singularity alone. . . . one person, a single body, comes to stand for this superior guarantee, in the classical aesthetic form of the genius."[41] For a period, Mandela appeared to be such a genius, and for a while, his singular person secured the legitimacy of the new regime—until, that is, the ANC government's policies and practices could be reckoned in relation to the axioms and principles on which the new constitution claimed to ground the post-Apartheid order. That process of reckoning continues to unfold and extends toward the future as an exposure to, and perhaps a call for, critical judgment.

It is not merely because so much of this process of grounding the new regime implicates the mining sector and the powerful unions that arose on the Witwatersrand that I raise these issues by way of introduction. It is, rather, because, on this same ground, as it were, people talk volubly about the nature of the transformations that have occurred since the end of Apartheid. They have not only labored to effectuate the promised liberation at the level of local governance but also have fought among themselves over what such liberation ought to mean: for housing and education, public services and access to the judiciary, freedom from arbitrary arrest and police brutality, new wealth, and an end to corruption. They have exercised their judgments—in often conflictual manner—on the success and failure of what has happened thus far during the post-Apartheid era, vigorously protesting what have been perceived as merely self-interested decisions by a ruling party that has yet to fully represent and serve the common interests of all people. When, for example, the national ANC's executive committee determined to redemarcate municipal boundaries and transfer several of the mining towns and townships on the West Rand from the provincial jurisdiction of Gauteng to Northwest Province, residents of Khutsong, the largest township in the area, commenced incendiary protests, boycotted elections, and undertook what can rightly be termed a general strike. Although there were no actual mass deportations, opposition to the redemarcation (what, in the United States, would be called redistricting) was cast in an idiom drawn from the Apartheid era. It construed redemarcation as a "forced relocation," thereby invoking the specter of a literal movement to new ground as the means to represent what was experienced as a new and treacherous political disenfranchisement—a losing of ground in the space of expected freedom.

At various moments over the past two decades, people in this area—on many sides, for many reasons, and across racial and ethnic divisions—have asserted or implied that the post-Apartheid regime has not demonstrated through its members' practice that it has the moral ground on which to rule. One of the most powerful gestures by which the critique has been authorized has claimed for the gold-mining region and its workers a constitutive role in the national economy. Precisely because the gold mines were at the center of the modern nation's original, if violent founding, people say, those who work in, or who are heirs to those who have worked in, the mines should be granted a central place and relative share of both the fruits of that history and of the decision-making powers that have accrued to the victors in the anti-Apartheid struggle. In making this argument, grounded as it is on an idea of private property—if only the right to own the fruits of one's labor—these contestants of the new world order disclose the depth of their entanglement in and subjection to the axioms on which colonial and imperial, which is to say racial, capitalism are based. The story of that ongoing struggle, carried out in the shadow and under the compulsions of capitalism's double binds, is threaded across several of the chapters of this book, in a narrative process that implicates another one of the meanings of ground, namely the meshwork or surface on which a text(ile) is woven. My discourse is not independent of that produced by those whose words I sometimes quote. Their speech is not the mesh, nor mine the embroidered text(ile). When referring to narrative through the figure of text and textile in this sense, as a woven artifact of historical forces, I mean to imply a world in which language—beyond the opposition of speech and writing—functions as a force, one that possesses us more than we possess it.[42] This broad notion of language functions as the host of numerous historically existent languages—in this case, isiZulu, isiXhosa, isiNdebele, SeSotho, Setswana, Chitonga (from Zambia, to be distinguished from the Tsitonga spoken in South Africa), Shona, English, Afrikaans, and Mozambican Portuguese—that are neither isomorphic nor perfectly commensurable but that nonetheless often touch each other and allow for mutual recognition and understanding. Sometimes, too, this contact permits relations based in misrecognition and misunderstanding—and their refusal.

Stakeholders: On the Virtues of Slowness

An ethnography written on the basis of more than two and a half decades of field and archival research must account for the changes that have occurred during that period. Such an extended relationship does not produce more surety about "the way things are" in a given sociopolitical scene; rather, it cultivates a consciousness of the instability or transitoriness of phenomena. This is especially true in a world defined and characterized by migrancy, as is the case around the gold mines. But this is not a "longitudinal study" of a single and stable object. I first went to South Africa in 1996, partly to attend a conference and literary festival staged to accompany the opening of the Truth and Reconciliation Commission. I had many personal connections to the country: my father had gone to high school there and obtained a doctorate in geology at the University of the Witwatersrand; my parents had lived there briefly before my birth; one of my siblings was born there; my life partner was born and raised there. And I had studied with the preeminent anthropologists of the region while at the University of Chicago. Like many people of my generation, I was also actively supportive of the ANC's struggle to overturn Apartheid. I was deeply marked by the murderous events of 1976, when South African security forces fired on and killed unarmed school children protesting mandatory education in Afrikaans, killing several and forever transforming the movement.[43] It entered my consciousness through the Canadian Broadcasting Corporation's coverage of the massacre, and the searing photographic testimony of Sam Nzima, whose image of Mbuyisa Makhubo carrying the dead body of Hector Pietersen, with his sister Antoinette Sithole at their side, shocked the world. The dead student was my own age and the mournful cross-racial sympathies solicited by the image were transformative. Moreover, I felt great solidarity with the mining unions, seeing in them the righteous agent of social justice that my maternal grandfather, also an immigrant, an underground mineworker and trade unionist, had quietly embodied. But these facts had led me to avoid the country, rather than to visit it. When I went in 1996, it was the sheer creativity and apparent hunger for self-transformation, the courage and audacity of the social, political and aesthetic experimentation that I saw almost everywhere, that attracted me. Nor was I alone.

The Truth and Reconciliation Commission (TRC) had a magnetic allure for many journalists, scholars, anticolonial sympathizers and would-be critics of what appeared to be the first great experiment in postcolonial democratization in the post-Soviet era. It is remarkable to reflect on the literature generated by outsiders at that time, and it is difficult not to observe the alacrity with which many people, on the basis of relatively short periods of exposure, felt empowered to forecast the future, and not merely to describe the present or recent past of the country. Thus were delivered summary pronouncements on the success or failure of the TRC, its Christian or African nature, and the status of Ubuntu as a practice of African mutuality contrasted with both capitalist covetousness and the socialist materialism of the West; the nature of the country's political transformation and the disjuncture between its constitution's capaciousness and the narrower political commonsense of most people; the possibilities for multilingualism beyond ethnicization; the inevitability of economic crime and corruption; the rise (or decline) of racialized violence and its political significations; the failed state, the securitized state, or the precarious state; the ANC leadership's incapacity or refusal to address the HIV epidemic, explained through recourse to stereotypes of African masculinity or nostalgic accounts of supposedly traditional heteronormative families, and the neotraditionalist persecution of sexual minorities; South African exceptionalism and the specter of anti-black xenophobia; and Mandela's moral exemplarity and his party's compromises with neoliberalism. Some of these prognostications and judgments had more empirical bases than others. Some have proven to be painfully accurate, and some were made by people with long, deep, and devoted relations to the place and its people. But many of those who wrote such confident pronouncements did not wait or return to see what had become of the processes they diagnosed because they conflated history with the past. To an extraordinary degree, the country had functioned as a screen, a surface onto which the world could project its desires as well as its fears in shadow forms of either salvific or terrifying dimensions. And yet, and of course, history did not end.

Over the past two and a half decades, I have attempted to respond to the transformations that I have observed. As a result, my research has been dominated by different questions at different moments. These questions orient the chapters that follow, which, like the issues discussed, are woven together in a pattern whose overarching themes have been preliminarily elaborated in this introduction. As it happens, the region around the gold mines proved to be especially advantageous as a point from which to observe and to learn from the changes that continue to alter the social fabrics of South Africa and the region more generally. For reasons that I will try to describe, this scene became a particularly concentrated zone of social experiment, in all its hopeful and disappointing ways. From the crisis of the HIV/AIDS epidemic, to the boycotts of elections, from revelations at the TRC about the sexualized proxy wars fought between youth of the governing National Party (or Nasionale Party, NP) and the ANC, to the rise of new unions and political parties, from the contraction of the gold industry to the proliferation of informal migrant economies of scavenging in the ruins, from the creation of fantastically wealthy black entrepreneurs in the mineral sector, to the spectacular intensification of poverty: all of these phenomena assumed an acute form around the gold mines. It is therefore imperative to assert now what has perhaps been implicit in the foregoing, namely that this is not an ethnography of underground mining, so much as it is an ethnography of the worlds that gold made possible, or that were made in the pursuit of gold.

Or. Or, ore, d'or. Or I could put it another way. This book responds to two simple questions. It asks, "What has gold done to people? What has it made them do?" If these questions seem to be beholden to superstition, and even to fetishism, by granting gold a force capable of determining people's actions, it is because gold is such a fetish. I am not only referring to diggers, speculators, capitalists, or the people who descend into the earth to mine its ores. Nor I am

I referencing those who work in the ancillary industries that support mining—from bankers to the manufacturers of cyanide vats. Most of the people who live near mines do not ever enter them; they are shopkeepers and schoolteachers, council members and accountants, wives and children, domestic servants, custodians and gardeners, mechanics and gas station attendants, pastors and health practitioners, police officers and gangsters, sex workers, and nongovernmental organization volunteers. Or (and) they are part of the great precarious mass of the unemployed and the underemployed who live in shack settlements that crust the perimeter of the wounded landscapes where deep-level mining keeps the earth perpetually open. This book is an account of the lessons learned from these diverse and sometimes divided, still metamorphosing, and often transient assemblages.

As will become apparent in the pages that follow, gold possesses people—makes them "gold-minded"—in ways that lead them not only to sacrifice themselves or gamble their fortunes, to mortgage their property and pawn their valuables, but also to commit acts of great violence and unspeakable cruelty. It leads them to express their largesse with donations that plate the domes of civic buildings, churches, and mosques in gold leaf. There is an expression used by informal miners and many others in the area of which I write that captures this ambiguous force: "where there's gold, blood is there." When I first heard it, the young man who had uttered the words didn't wait for me to formulate my question before explaining, "because it's money." And, he might have added, money makes people do things. Or so it seems.

Trying Not to Run Aground

"This land is not the sweet home it looks,/Nor its peace the historical calm of a site/Where something was settled once and for all."[44] These lines come from W. H. Auden's *In Praise of Limestone* and are cited in Michael Cawood Green's verse novella about the catastrophic sinkhole that occurred on August 3, 1964, in Carletonville, one of the towns at the center of this world, exactly sixty-four years to the day before the accident with which I began this chapter. *Unstable Ground* is, in many ways, a book about matters that remain unsettled, about the subterranean forces—remnants and effects of traumatic historical processes—that persistently erupt into daily life and that seem to overdetermine much of what unfolds in the surface world. The legacies of colonialism, segregation, and Apartheid, and the specific technological conditions of deep-level industrial mining continue to structure the forms of life that inhabit and are inhabited by people in the region today. They ensure that the impending closure of the mines and the eventual demise of the gold industry in South Africa—eventualities that have been anticipated by mining engineers, actuaries, and scholars for

many decades but not fully assimilated in the consciousness, or the unconscious, of those who inhabit the artificially fabricated peri-urban spaces around
the mines—are experienced in the mode of both afterlife *and* belatedness.

It is in this haunted and belated space that the accident with which I began
this chapter occurred: in the ruins of one of the oldest mines on the Witwatersrand. I will return to that scene in the coming chapters and in concluding this book, where, among other things, I provide an understanding of the
ways in which the history of speculative finance capital has incited and even
demanded the forms of daily gambling that, today, go by the name of zama
zama. I shall conclude a discussion about the ways in which sacrificial violence
has been restituted in the spaces where the state has withdrawn its forces. But,
insofar as this world is one of "risk," as people there say, it is the kind of risk that
exceeds the aspirations of calculative reason and the containment strategies of
actuarialization. For, over and above the entire scene is the bedazzling promise of value and wealth unmoored from labor and immune to time's corrosive
forces, a form of value that is at once unperishable and constantly vanishing.
This value and medium of all other values, both alluring and conductive, is at
once hard (cash) and liquid (currency), a hedge against loss and an object of
desire in its own right. Such is gold: the monstrous doubled-headed surplus
machine gnawing at the dream of liberty with an ironically silver tongue. To
explain gold's allure requires more than recourse to an idea of cynical reason,
even if people do know the truth of gold's fetishistic status (and the violence
involved in its production) very well but, nevertheless, live in its thrall.[45] Capitalists and laborers, and nearly everyone I have spoken to in South Africa,
know that commodity gold is valuable only because of what is invested in it—
labor, capital, technology, and the total, still racialized organization of society—
but this does not shut down the dream machine that grants to gold that most
magical capacity, namely access to all that money can buy and to the possibility
of transformation and thus to otherness, alterity. This is because gold, a metal
of relative uselessness, is valuable by either precedent or fiat and by virtue of
an ancient and repeating set of phantasmatic investments that confer upon it
its symbolic radiance, its value-storing powers, and its capacities to function
as the instrument of conversion and value enhancement. It is in the halo of
these dreams, crisscrossing the centuries and backed by bloody force, that gold
achieves its status not only as an object but as an object *and* medium of desire,
becoming that for which people are prepared to gamble, sometimes to the point
of tempting Fate, which is to say Death. The different forms in which this dream
of transport enters the world of lived experience is, however, not always that of
alchemical myth, and often the ante must be paid by those who did not choose
the game. Invariably, but unequally, people have to pay to cross the threshold.
With this in mind, let me return to those ruins near the scene of the accident,
where, in the summer of 2017, I asked one of the long-term residents of the

zama zama community and an elderly inhabitant of the old mine compound, which had by then become a squatter camp, to narrate the space to me as part of a documentary filmmaking project.

I will call my seventy-one-year-old guide Virgil-Umholi, for it seemed to me at the time (as it does now) that he was a kind of guide through the labyrinths of dispossession, one who, though stranded there, seemed immune to the more profound humiliations that others had been forced to endure. Although he had lived near the mines most of his adult life, he had not worked underground; like Virgil in Dante's *Inferno*, he had seen what happened to those who paid the *obolus* and crossed into the underworld, but he had somehow managed to traverse that space not as a condemned soul but as a surviving witness.[46] At the time that I interviewed him, he had a room in an old cement barracks and thus was relatively protected from the elements—although the winter's cold and the summer's heat surely took their toll. His abode held a few pieces of sturdy furniture and the door to his dwelling locked. It also had a window, adorned (more than covered) with a lace curtain, so that, although small, the room was suffused by a thin, natural light during the daytime. Virgil-Umholi was unbowed by his age; he walked with a vigorous stride. As we meandered in the ruins, he explained how, during the days of the formal mine's operations, the space had been segregated by race and professional category, with foremen and workers sleeping in separate quarters. Women were not permitted except in designated areas and with the express approval of mine authorities, and only for short periods of time. Virgil-Umholi nonetheless remembered the days of the mine's functioning as ones of glorious abundance, if only relative to the extreme poverty of the present. And much of his nostalgia focused on food, as well as the social occasions that were associated with feasting: weddings and funerals, and the arrival of visitors from people's home villages. His eyes shone with delight when he described the sides of beef being unloaded from the supply trucks whose axels or breaks squealed with porcine shrillness as they pulled up to make their weekly deliveries; his mimicry of that sound made the dogs turn, as if frightened to find the air filled with the sounds, at once machinic and animal, of another time. Occasionally, Virgil-Umholi's dilatory reminiscences gave way to blunter, nearly aphoristic discourse, and a tone that was tinged with both anger and resignation. But mainly, his isiZulu speech, infrequently peppered with lexicalized English terms, was lucent with reverie.

Again and again, as Virgil-Umholi described the absented world, we encountered the memory of a gate. In the old man's recollection, the gates were always guarded. Only one of these myriad portals could be entered by the workers; the others were simply little theaters of power. He pointed out the now-overgrown paths where people had stood in line to pass through them, and almost seemed to believe that those waiting queues could still be seen, often urging me and the other man in our conversation to "look" and "see." Listening to recordings of these conversations again, I am struck not only by the closure of the gates but by a fragmentary remark that Virgil made when asked about these thresholds:

D-X: Was this another gate that led outside?
V-U: Yes, but this is another item here. It was not just leading you outside.
   It was a passage. It was a passage that led you to the other side.

Often, as we walked, Virgil-Umholi indicated that we were moving through a passage, and when he did so, he narrated the connection of adjoining spaces and the movement between them. A gate is a boundary to be crossed in a manner that testifies to one's right of entry, or, by contrast, it is a mark of exclusion and thus a threshold to be transgressed. A passage, however, is a conduit, a space of movement and of connection and conveyance. In his analyses of the Paris Arcades, Walter Benjamin notes modernity's "remarkable propensity for structures that convey and connect." In those alleys of illuminated consumption, he says, "iron construction . . . is on the verge of horizontal extension" while nonetheless retaining something of the vaulted hall and the vertical aspiration of Baroque sacred architecture.[47] In the Arcades, passage was not only a function but also a theme, linked to the movement of goods and money. It was a theater of display value precisely because it was also a theater of conveyance.[48] Passage and movement, movement as passage: these were the values of modernity understood as infinite mobility and thus as access to the objects of desire. Equally important was the fact that in them anything could be transformed into a consumable value, including waste. The Arcade, one notes, is coemergent in Benjamin's dialectical historiography, with the ragpicker and the scavenger.

Now, the architecture of passage is always also an architecture of separation. Separation is the flip side of connection. This ambivalence is what Virgil-Umholi narrated as he paused, again and again at gates, accounting for movement across the racialized space of Apartheid. For Virgil-Umholi, as for Benjamin, the logic of the passage becomes most visible in the moment of obstruction and ruination.

It is my belief that the underground mines of South Africa are usefully understood by analogy with the Arcades. Despite their subterranean darkness, their inaccessibility, and their lack of opportunities for consumption, they are precisely theaters of display value and spectacles of conveyance. They are illuminated by the fetish of gold, but it is not precisely gold that is on display in the mines. In those underground passages, the value that is placed on the altar of desire is not the consumer commodity produced en mass with technological methods, nor even the pure form of exchangeability that is gold, but rather it is technology itself. Images of that technology, which adorn corporate reports and nationalist historiography, solicit viewers through a complex mediatic display that is at once more extended and more dispersed than the shop window (although, as we know, the latter is also mediated in comparable ways). More-over, like the Paris Arcades, the mines redouble the catacomb. For, industrial technology is the congelation of dead labor—and this is independent of the fact that, in the mines, too, death is also a more literal stalker. In the end, what sustains the analogy between the mines and the arcades for the purposes of this book is not merely a parallelism of functions and forms of value, but the fact that the mines are now closing and that, in their ruins, that historical pas-sage of which Benjamin wrote becomes visible—again and anew. This is why I have commenced this book with a narrative account of events that took place in the wreckage rather than in still-operating industrial mines. Those events actualize Adorno's belated answer to the question that Benjamin penned in "Convolute O," of the *Arcades Project*: "Isn't there a certain structure of money that can be recognized only in fate, and a certain structure of fate than can be recognized only in money?"[49] Adorno's deferred answer is that "death [is] the absolute price of absolute value."[50] Gold is the figure and medium of that absolute value, and its pursuit has exacted an absolute price from many. If most people who live near gold mines do not enter them, they nonetheless live in their penumbra, are moved by its shimmering image, and are haunted by its magical promise of transubstantiation. It is the violent point of contact and conversion between the several orders of magical thinking that will be traced in the following pages and that will be discerned in the word-art of individual men and women, whether they be writers or so-called illiterate speakers of many-wounded mother tongues.

This book is organized into three parts. In part 1, "Groundwork," I recon-sider the early history of gold mining on the Witwatersrand, covering the period from its discovery to the beginning of the Apartheid era and the estab-lishment of communities around the deep-level mines of the Far West Rand. This early history is approached from the vantage point of the present in the era of these same mines' ruination. In this part, I attempt a doubled renarration of seemingly familiar terrain. One dimension of this renarration is summoned and enabled by the accounts, questions, and critiques of this history that are expressed by the current residents. The second dimension, provoked by the first, entails a reconsideration of the now taken-for-granted accounts of deep-level mining, the rationalities that oriented it, and the ostensible necessities of its forms of value production. In the five chapters that make up this part, I return to the notion of the gold rush and gold-mindedness, and the place of cyanide in the development of deep-level mining and the aesthetic and political economy of the segregationist state. My argument, briefly, is that cyanidation was linked to a transformation in the concept and value of superfluity, and that it provided the structure of grounding within which the idea of separation came to be aestheticized. Finally, I reconsider questions of cyclic labor migra-tion, and the gold industry's role in the production of an integrated system of state surveillance, asking how the pass system, and opposition to it, were integrated into a system of visibilities and a structure of recognition whose gradual unfolding led to an inversion of values, with documents coming to be perceived by migrants as a source of freedom rather than an instrument of disenfranchisement. In this part, I aim to understand this entire social economy of the early gold economy as one in which waste is increasingly incorporated into the value system, where it functions at both ends of a racialized aesthetic machine—as telos, as limit, and as the sign of that which cannot be limited.

Part 2 of this book, titled "The Deep," is oriented by long-term field research on the Far West Rand, and especially in Carletonville and its major township Khutsong. In this part, I consider the heyday of industrial deep-level mining from the perspective of its denouement in a period of rapid and often disorienting political transformation, extending the key terms of the previous section, namely: waste and superfluity, separation, movement without mobility, and dust and visible invisibility. This section of the book is especially concerned with understanding the transformations of life worlds through an analysis of key signifiers, supplementing the analysis of "ground" with "sinkhole," "accident," "reserve," and "tragedy" with the "mourning play." To grasp the movement or passage from one regime (Apartheid) to another (the post-Apartheid experiment in liberal democracy), I reflect on the genre of political tragedy and seek an alternative thread through the labyrinth. As Luce Irigaray has taught us, thought of the passage demands thought of sexual difference, and this section of the book takes up a thread introduced at the end of part 1, to address not only the ethnic and racial structures within South Africa's gold industries operated but also the forms of sexual and gendered difference that subtended them.

Part 3, "Surfacing," is devoted to a consideration of all the foregoing on the basis of several years of field research in an area in the Near West Rand where gold mining has been on the decline for several decades and where it is now on the verge of total ruin. This part of the book, foreshadowed by this introduction, considers the temporization of gold in the global economy (its fluctuations, rises and falls, prophesied disappearance, and fantastical resurgence) and the forms of radical precarity that accompany it in so many places but that are so acutely visible in the now-evacuated spaces of the compound pseudo-states. It features a kind of mirror image of part 1 and thus returns to the questions of waste and superfluity, speculation, and gambling. Here, the figures and values of the (il)liberal state are exposed in the silhouetted form of their absence. In the ashes of that burned-out ruin, there emerges one of the most terrifying legacies of Apartheid, namely a theater of ethnicized sacrificial violence, driven by statist impulses but entirely lacking in the mechanisms of recognition that it offers as compensation for its own violence. Alongside this séance of sovereignty's ghosts, however, I suggest that other forms of cosmopolitical society also have arisen in the ruins, sustained by a combination of fear, pleasure, and play in the always shifting terrain of the underground. These, and the often-arduous labors at self-transformation, as well as the hopeful visions of distributive democracy, offer a counterbalance to the resurgent terrors that erupt so frequently from the underground of South Africa's modernity.

Each part of this book starts in the contemporary period and then goes back or down to consider the contingent historic factors that informed without determining how we got here—they, I, and we. Each chapter is intended to generate the motive force for the subsequent descent. In this way, the book can be said to resemble a trip into the underground—if that it is, one bears in mind the limits of the metaphor by which the past is the ground of the future. The past, like the dead, sends messages in need of decipherment, while also exercising a force that needs to be exorcised. This book does not have a conclusion, but it does have an Afterword. I have been writing this book for too many years to believe that there is a history that can be grasped, thematized, and concluded upon. Such gestures of closure can be based on only the false assumption that history has come to an end or that it can be confined to matters of the past. As I write in the hiatus of my decades-long apprenticeship to the form of learning that is anthropology, I acknowledge that what appears in this moment to be an end may turn out in some as-yet-unforeseen future to have been a beginning, an interruption, a continuation, or simply a moment in a long, folded series of movements that, even when taken together, is neither the presence of history, nor the history of a present. Rather, it is the coming into being and the coming to pass of lives, deaths, and afterlives.

PART I

GROUNDWORK

GROUNDWORK

CHAPTER 2

LETTERS, RUIN

Migrancy's Remainders

And the gold of that land is good.

—Genesis 2:12

Wanderer
Of the homeless,
Wander on and let us go,
Let us go there to bondage,
To bondage where we go
Not to stay

—Anonymous Southern Sotho poem

n the beginning was the story of a word: word from home. And thus, word of a home left behind, of dislocation. That is how the question of migrancy and more permanent unsettlement was brought home to me—again. This question arrived not merely in the well-documented record of racializing legislation, coerced movements, and social disruption that historians of the South African mining industry have scrupulously assembled over the past half century or so. It was also audible as a remainder in the consciousness of those who, today, live in the afterlife of segregation and Apartheid's separatism, on the very grounds of the mines that summoned and legitimated these processes more than 125 years ago. If, however, this remainder is still audible today, it is because it emerges in a speech that bears within itself much that has never been explicitly articulated and much that resists conscious reflection. All of the elements of the spoken world—the rhyme that summons a memory, the inflection that recalls another's pronunciation, and the stuttering that betrays a trauma—are significant even when they do not communicate a symbolizable meaning.

The Stamp of Migrancy

The conversation with Virgil-Umholi with which I concluded the previous chapter was facilitated by another long-term resident of the same dispersed collective of squatters. The younger man, whom I will call Dante-Xolani, was an undocumented migrant from Zimbabwe, although he had lived in the area for almost two decades. He enjoyed a reputation as a trusted mediator when disputes arose, and he was the nodal point of innumerable informal networks that brought people and information from elsewhere.

The discussion that day vacillated between the past and the future, each crumbling wall or broken doorway a kind of architectural "madeleine" for the narrative. Unlike for Proust, however, the objects of desire whose images arose spontaneously from these fleeting sensuous encounters were special commodities. They were basic consumer goods: food, drink, and clothing. To be sure, their presence on the mine during a period that commenced in the late 1960s, seemed, for him, to be evidence of fantastic, if now vanished, abundance, but such plenty was limited and practically defined. Although he insisted that luxury goods and so-called fancy clothes had been available in the company stores and concessions, whose now-absented location he pointed out, he made no mention of radios, hi-fis, or television sets (after television was introduced into South Africa in 1976), of perfumed soaps and talc, of antimacassar, or of picture frames and table cloths. He said nothing of dining suites or bed sets. The trucks delivered coal twice a day, he claimed, and paraffin was cheap. But there were no Defy stoves in his account, no enamel pots to set upon their flames.[1] Indeed, Virgil-Umholi did not mention any of the consumer goods that were available, if only through hire purchase, in the nearby town, and that had formed the material tissue of township aesthetics and working-class respectability throughout the period of which he spoke. Virgil-Umholi's vision of plenty was a modest vista of need's satisfaction (as opposed to desire's fantasies), and his reveries were occupied primarily by elementary things—like winter coats, blankets, and spare batteries.

He almost never mentioned the people who purveyed these goods or the workers who served in the ancillary occupations of the compound. Other than his brother, who had worked here for decades, there was but one exception, one individual whose biography he narrated. It was the postman. This man, whose residence now stood vacant and overgrown by grasses, had been the courier who ferried messages from the nationally mediated outside world into the private pseudo-state of the mine compound: "He got the letters that came from the rural areas, from the post office. Yes, from the post. He delivered them right to the doorsteps. This was his place. He used to sleep here." Thus did Virgil-Umholi, his arm outstretched and pointing to the evacuated abode, introduce the compound Hermes, messenger of impossible communications and patron of travelers.[2]

It was difficult not to be moved by Virgil-Umholi's recollection of this enchanting medium. In the context of oscillating migrant labor, so crucial to the mining industry of South Africa, this moment of his discourse condensed an entire psychosocial structure in which individuals' attachments to their natal homes (*ekhaya*, meaning both home and rural village) were both stretched to the limit and somehow preserved. It was at once the supplement and the narrative transposition of a vast infrastructural network, including the railways and highways on which migrants continue to move and that sustained generations in the strange institution and double consciousness of what social scientists have called South Africa's peasant-proletariat.[3] Much of the scholarly literature on cyclic migration, and especially that written under the influence of structural Marxism or other forms of dialectical materialism, has been either focused on the political economic dimensions of this system, or, somewhat more rarely, it has turned to the subjective experience of migrancy to find evidence of a normative sense of belonging that is affixed to the value of a rural origin. On the one hand, these two typically distinct approaches were appropriate to the time in which the task of critique in South Africa demanded an analysis of the ruses by which cyclic migrancy functioned as a technique of governance that simultaneously repressed wages and excluded black subjects from access to urbanity and the forms of publicness that accompanied it (including full participation in the polis). On the other hand, these approaches responded to the empirical experience of people who were indeed confined to rural or pastoral spaces and villages when not working on or near the mines, and whose vacillations were nonetheless contained by a circuit that returned them to the peripheries. With the passage of time and the increasingly permanent settlement (or permanent unsettlement) of black South Africans in peri-urban spaces, the experience of the relation between so-called rural and urban spaces changed. Moreover, from the perspective of this changed circumstance, this earlier history—of movement and alienation, of split and ambivalent attachments, and of desires for the new and nostalgia for the old—becomes visible in a new light. It is possible, and I shall later argue, that the oppositional relationship between rurality and urbanity was sedimented in the townships around mines. This is not a mere matter of recoding or resignifying the past, but rather of thinking about it differently. Thus, in the charmed reflection of a postman's letter delivery, previously overlooked dimensions of the world suddenly flash up, not only to be seen but also to illuminate a previously inumbrated dimension of the lived reality that was the migrant system. On this basis, the letter and the postal system offer themselves as figures for the larger tasks of historical analysis and of the kind of reading that ethnography demands.

Virgil-Umholi's remarks about the postman's delivery of letters "right to the doorsteps," a phrase he repeated many times, almost reverentially, suggested something often overlooked in accounts of both letter writing in the histories of African literacy and the logic of the postal system more generally: namely, that the state-mediated structures within which letters circulate—as a strange kind of public secret and an equally strange form of territorialized address— are in some places also incarnated in an intimate encounter between otherwise unrelated people. This encounter between people who are not quite strangers (in Georg Simmel's sense of the term) has its own significance, quite beyond the relationship between the senders and receivers of letters.[4] Their habitual and routinized meetings—the salutations and friendly exchanges at the door- step; the queries about family members and shared gossip about neighbors; and the reports of police activities, corporate news, and strikes—can seem to enact a quality of small-town life. But in the urban and peri-urban spaces of the mines, their nature is rather different. Untethered from the totality of inhibit- ing forces that operate in more delimited communities of face-to-face interac- tion, they are not only consoling simulacra but also mediating figures in which the opposed worlds of the rural village and the urban meet and are (or rather, were) briefly but deceptively reconciled.

Such mediation is deeply desired, and it is also a source of exposure and vulnerability—especially when the recipient of the letter cannot read it. If Virgil-Umholi recalled the postman with fondness, the narrative of the postal hour of the mines is suffused with ambivalence in many other accounts.[5] Consider these lines from a Sotho *lifela* sung by Serame Thuhloane, first recorded in 1982:

> Illiteracy is a sad matter:
> Your letter is read by someone at the chimney.
> You know what? He laughs in front of the letter owner.
> He remarks, "As for your news, I understand it, sir:
> They report starvation,
> Lack of clothing, corn worms in the fields over there."[6]

Sefela is a genre of sung verse narrative that was created and developed by Sotho migrants to the mines, with *lifela* or *difela* indicating individual compo- sitions. As described with verve and insight by David Coplan, *lifela* are often practiced in competitive form. They are full of vivid descriptions and trenchant criticism of migrant life, and they are appreciated for their ribald jokes.

The historian, referring to the public reading of an intimate missive as a moment of "collaboration," will perhaps respond to such songs, whose oral performance underlines the very dilemma of the "sad matter" of alphabetic illiteracy, with an exploration of the complex simultaneity of literacy *and* illiteracy or of "constrained literacy" among migrant laborers.[7] She or he will remind us that people often have access to written culture even when they cannot themselves read or write (thanks to reading aloud)—a fact that is never captured by literacy statistics, any more than the nature of the literacy that is revealed by those statistics. Indeed, a rich if small body of scholarship addresses this very question, focusing on the fact that, from the earliest days, letters were an important part of life on the mines, given the centrality of migrant labor there. It played a special role in courtship and marriage as well as in the relationships between parents and children, despite low levels of alphabetic literacy. The significant role of amanuenses and the sometimes playful, sometimes conspiratorial practice of collective love letter writing, as well as the public reading of letters and the corollary disassociation of writing from interiority in the formation of a South African private sphere, have been well analyzed by Keith Breckenridge.[8] He notes that early labor recruiters for the mines complained of having to write hundreds and even thousands of letters for the men and to supply them with paper, envelopes, and stamps.[9] In fact, these items were budgeted as staples when labor recruiters drew up their estimates of costs for importing workers from China during the brief period of substitutional labor importation in the early twentieth century.

Almost all of these many thousands of letters have been lost or intentionally destroyed by their owners. But a few have entered the archive. The extant letters, including the bitter epistles between lovers and parents about the need for money, the humiliation of passbooks, and the longing for food, such as those collected by Isaac Schapera in depression-era Bechuanaland, have been read with impeccable fidelity by analysts who have sought the letters' origins and mode of creation, their social conditions of possibility, and the political consequences.[10] These are necessary and instructive pursuits. It is not the origin of the letter, however, nor its evidentiary function in an analysis of the past that interests me here. For, Virgil-Umholi's story about the postman demonstrates that the letter that comes from the past has not been left behind. The letter survives its sending, and this survival exceeds the matter of the paper object or the ink inscribed on its surface. It survives beyond the opposition of presence and absence, just as the experience of migrancy is irreducible to the question of presence or absence in one place or another.[11] In its survival, the story and thus the memory of the postman bears the stamp of migrancy as a force that displaces and decenters subjects, that fragments and doubles them, while installing loss in the innermost recesses of consciousness.

This sensation exceeds any particular loss, and even the accumulation of many losses. In this context, it is particularly notable that, in Virgil-Umholi's narrative, the letter appears only through the cipher of the postman, in whom it is displaced. This displacement permits it to signify the structure and psychic burden of the alienation accompanying migrancy as well as the partial transfer of social relations from one place to another. Moreover, the social connection emphasized by Virgil-Umholi does not lie at the origin of the letter's writing; his entire discourse is focused on the moment of *receiving* letters from the postal system's representative. This is the point of contact; it is the occasion that excites his narrative, which may partly explain his genial tone. For the story functions as a kind of allegory of connection and continuity in general, qualities that survive as abstractions precisely in the moment that they are threatened with destruction in actuality. In this allegory, the postman is the incarnation of that which has been transformed, although not entirely effaced: it is the world of face-to-face sociality, of actual connection. He is the signifier for and the embodiment of the migratory system and, in this respect, he provides the human visage or mask, and the mythic mediation for a historical process that was profoundly dehumanizing—even if migration could and would be appropriated by some (in the idiom of mobility) as a source of authority and as an object of desire.

To grasp the importance of the transposition within Virgil-Umholi's narrative, it may help to recognize just how bleak and desperate were many of the migrants' letters cited by Isaac Schapera and that others have described. "I am sick, my child, I have nothing to say except starvation," commences one such letter.[12] Many of the missives Schapera invokes were concerned with economic exigencies, or the erotic longing, fears of infidelity, and concerns about pregnancy that are made so acute by temporary absence.[13] But it is the anguish of the letters reporting deprivation and distress that stand in most obvious contrast to Virgil-Umholi's cheerful remembrance of the postman's deliveries. Another of the letters reads: "I myself am sick, I am suffering from an ailment of the chest . . . , I am unable to eat, and I am weakened by emptiness from hunger."[14] More recent examples of the *lifela* recorded by David Coplan are equally searing. Here is one by Tsokolo Lechecko, which describes the arrival of a "letter from my mother . . . the kindhearted mother." She solicits her son, "Come home, my child,/Come home and get married." But then the sweet memory gives way to caustic sarcasm:

> If poverty were contested,
> God would be tied up endlessly in court.
> We would sit in High Court against him. [People say]
> "Poverty is eliminated by hard work only."
> This is a lie; they deceive us.[15]

The possibility of justice becomes the farce of a courtroom, and the hope for a liberating judgment is absorbed by the specter of bureaucratic entanglement. The punchline remains, but the indictment of duplicity brings with it a recognition of having been duped. Such acid wit, which characterizes much of the verse narrative of this genre, has its less ludic counterpart in the more direct accusations of revolutionary poets like Peter Abrahams and Mazisi Kunene, who writes, "They have deceived themselves, they have deceived one another." Kunene's poem "White People" culminates with the derisive conclusion that "they are also scared!/They know they are like this because of the fairy tales/They tell the nations."[16] Such derisiveness is utterly absent in Virgil-Umholi's avuncular discourse. And he had long ceased moving back and forth between the compound and any home village elsewhere.

A certain pathos is evident in the fact that his affectionate memory of a vital relation was prompted by our sojourn in the ruins and that it recalled a time of extreme structural violence with the sense of its relative plenty. His nostalgia was not a valorization of the ruins. If Virgil-Umholi discerned a beauty in this vanished and vanishing world, it was of the sort that Walter Benjamin describes in the moment that the storyteller is displaced within the newly technologized order of information.[17] His concern, his narrative attention to the postman (rather than the letter writers) expressed a longing not for immediacy but precisely for mediation—for the sociality of the compound, however inhospitable was its material routine.

The postman of Virgil-Umholi's narrative is now dead; his house is a mere ruin. But even if he had been alive, his function would have become obsolete; it had been displaced by the cell phone in the mid-1990s when cellular technology had enabled people who had previously been unable to access the limited supply of landlines to partake of this telephonic revolution—if they could afford it. That development transformed the lives of migrants and the entire social field, in ways that must wait to be explored. Initially, it seemed to bypass the question of literacy and to tighten the temporal circuit within which communication occurs (texting changed this somewhat). It is in this context that the significance of the postman, as a sign of the past and perhaps pastness itself, and not merely of migrancy, emerges.

As it happens, Virgil-Umholi's narration of the postman's former presence in the compound was uncannily followed by a toddler crossing our path. Half clad in the evening chill, she was trailing behind her a damaged old custard-colored telephone: not a cellphone but a flat touch-tone device, in which the receiver was tethered to its base by a spiral cord. Virgil-Umholi regarded her with the kind of affection that his speech otherwise exuded when speaking of the postman. Although contemporary computer-based games are increasingly popular among the wealthy, the treatment of technology as a toy is, in poor communities like the one I am describing, a sign of its brokenness, its becoming useless.

Only when it is beyond repair can a phone become a toy. Cell phones promised a connection to surpass that of the face-to-face relation for which the postman had been a substitute. It promised something even better than that for which it was itself a surrogate. And this promise, whose structure has all the qualities of a fetish, in that it promised an even better version of what had been severed, was both nurtured in the space of massive social dislocation and seeded by global marketing fantasies that mobilized a romantic opposition between the city and the country.[18] In the mid-1990s, U.S. telecommunications companies urged cell-phone users to "reach out and touch someone."[19] And Vodacom, South Africa's largest network provider, echoed that pitch when it solicited its own clients with the adage, "You're always in touch," implying that social connection no longer required proximity and might even depend on relinquishing literal contact with the land(line). And cell phones arrived just in time, as it were. They were the timely technologies of a new dislocation: the time of freedom, which was also, it turned out, the time of the end of this mine and perhaps the beginning of the end of gold. Virgil-Umholi would say much about endings. But migrancy and unsettlement has lived on, sustained by the desire for gold and the desires that gold engendered. Their relation to capital has changed, however, and this fact demands an account and an accounting.

If I have lingered here with Virgil-Umholi's story of the compound Hermes, it is because he is not only the remembered emissary of news from home but also the cipher and metasign for a general structure at the center of which is migrancy. He is the bearer of, and a figure for, what Derrida has called the postal principle, which afflicts not merely the "literal letter" but also sociohistorical processes in general. Inscribed in and by language, they exceed their intended purpose, not merely because they are "delivered to a future that may transform, corrupt, or delete"[20] them, as Hägglund would have, but because, in addition to being real institutional forms and practices, they also have a phantasmatic dimension. In South Africa, this can be said of both the idea of gold and the concepts of racial difference on which Apartheid and the segregation that preceded it were erected and that, together, produced the regime of oscillating labor migration evoked in Virgil-Umholi's narrative. I want to now trace the history in which that phantasm was generated, and I want to do so in ways that demonstrate not only its economic roots and social entailments but also the development of a politico-aesthetic form in which the values and the structure of value in the gold economy, were given expression. That aesthetic was one in which the idea of separation was autonomized, reified, and valorized, in which the metaphoric translation of a social ideal was concealed in a technological form. Let us then return to the beginning, or the story of the beginning and the story of an ending. Once again, my purpose is to approach this history from a reframed perspective to think what has previously been occluded in this seemingly settled past.

No Return Address: Black Spots

"More than a hundred years, more than a hundred years." That is how Virgil-Umholi described the age of the complex where we met. The mine had opened in 1893. It was a fabulously promising undertaking from the perspective of its investors, and the Wernher, Beit, and Eckstein group who controlled it. But, in 1893, getting labor to the mines in the Transvaal was difficult, and Lionel Phillips, then president of the Chamber of Mines, complained that recruits from Cape Colony, where many had been working in the open pits of the diamond fields, had failed to keep up with the burgeoning demand. He noted that "although engaged at fixed wages and to work underground, the natives on their arrival here in most cases demanded current wages, and absolutely refused to go underground. A certain proportion of them, too, in spite of all precautions, bolted while on the road from Vereeniging to these fields."[21] Such reluctance was not part of Virgil-Umholi's discourse. For him, as for most of his contemporaries, the mines whose "millipede darkness"[22] had seemed to demand that they relinquish their humanity had healed into the normal order as that whose absence is felt as loss. In any case, it was Virgil-Umholi's word, grounded in his experience and validated by his age, that legitimated his discourse for contemporary residents—much more so than any recourse to archived title deeds or corporate reports, to which an historically minded anthropologist might turn for verification. In 2017, such "antiquity spoke in the language of stone."[23]

The transformation of this once-rich mine into a stage of destitution began to accelerate in December 1992, following violent interethnic conflict (specifically anti-Mozambiquan violence) in the mine's residential compound. Such conflict was all-too common during the last years of Apartheid when conflicts fomented by the state's security apparatus converged with the xenophobia that had been cultivated by Apartheid ideology. Subcontracted labor was seen by many to be undermining union efforts to achieve better compensation, and contracted workers often worked in ethnolinguistic groups.[24] The tension between union and nonunion workers, coded as ethnic difference, was also manipulated in the fight between African National Congress (ANC) and Inkatha Freedom Party (IFP) forces, and between ANC and NP forces—as will be discussed in part 2. It would be several years before the various transfers of ownership, temporary suspensions of activities, restarted operations with outsourced contract labor, and gradual reduction in activities, before this mine ceased operations altogether. At the end of Apartheid, residents who failed to pay rents in the larger dwellings were gradually evicted and, if they refused to depart, their property was removed. As time went on, residences were themselves dismantled to discourage squatters from occupying the place—a practice of seemingly vindictive excess whose interruption Virgil-Umholi credited to

Kaizer Matanzima, the one-time leader of the Transkei (now part of Eastern Cape Province[25]) whence many of the mineworkers hailed.

Virgil-Umholi's narration of that process was prompted by the outline of a foundation from which the walls had been entirely removed. All that remained was a flat cement slab. Dante-Xolani pointed to the ground and summoned its ghost.

> *D-X*: And here, was this a house?
> *V-U*: Yes, this was a house. People lived here. It was demolished when the mine closed down.
> *D-X*: You mean by the time the mine closed . . .
> *V-U*: Before that they used this house for renting, until the person who lived here failed to pay their rent. The white man who was here in the office decided that the houses must be destroyed, and then they were demolished.
>   Those people living back there who failed to pay their rent also had their houses destroyed. The person who . . . managed to put a stop to this was a man named Kaizer [Matanzima]. He helped put a stop to this, to the demolishing of houses here. The law was that, if you didn't pay—
> *D-X*: If you didn't pay the rent, they would demolish your house?
> *V-U*: That's why they demolished all those houses back there. Then Kaizer came through and said "No. This cannot happen." (Z)

Again and again, as we encountered a broken door or a scraped foundation, the story of the demolitions and of Matanzima's interventions was repeated. Partly, this repetition is a feature of this oral narrative mode of storytelling. Partly, too, it reflects the special nature of this intervention. Matanzima's status in South African history is ambiguous, at best: he was an ardent Xhosa nationalist and also an advocate of Apartheid, a man who was both capable of inspiring fear in the white nationalist government and of being deemed a lackey by ANC ideologues, including his cousin, Nelson Mandela. For Virgil-Umholi, he incarnated the virtues of a pastoral chiefly authority dedicated to the well-being not only of the Xhosa nation but of all disenfranchised residents of the mine compound.

Virgil-Umholi would vacillate between describing the cruelty of the eviction and the improbable care with which it was undertaken, as if to underline the fact that the procedure had been intended to announce to every spectator, and especially the other compound residents, that the objects of the household merited more delicate handling than did the people who would no longer be permitted to sleep there.

> *D-X*: So, were people staying in these houses, when they were demolished?
> *V-U*: When he demolished your house, he would take out your furniture first.
> *D-X*: And chuck them out?

V-U: He didn't chuck them out. He would place them neatly outside. And
remove the zinc roof and the electricity . . . using a machine. . . . you would
find what's left waiting for you outside on the ground.

D-X: Didn't they throw away your belongings?

V-U: No, you would find all your things in one piece. (Z)

The machine is here the mark and the instrument of total destruction, the telos
of dehumanization. This consists not only in the removal of those objects in
which psychic and social life had been vested. Even more than such expropriation, the machine effects (almost automatically) a deprivation of the future as
continuity in place. Its deployment aims to foreclose any future arrivals. After
the machine is brought to bear—to eliminate the roofing and the electricity—
there should be no hope of return, nor of anyone else taking over the residence. This is why Virgil-Umholi's narrative was bifurcated between the time
of destruction and the time of its afterward. But this latter time was suspended.
The ending of destruction stretched out, it was neither punctual nor complete.
In Virgil-Umholi's words, the historical predicament of post-Apartheid South
Africa seemed to condense itself as an endless ending, a deferred interruption.
Almost a stutter.

Virgil-Umholi walked as he spoke, moving forward with surety, as he stepped
deftly around the piles of rubble. "The demolishing of houses was stopped"
(by Matanzima), he repeatedly asserted. If this cessation of demolition did not
entail a restoration, and if it did not immunize anyone against eviction, it at
least seemed to put a limit on the company's capacity to generalize the exclusion
and to extend it forward in time. But even if, as the presence of squatters today
suggests, people did finally reoccupy the space, we may yet ask, Was the demolition actually terminated?

I have not been able find any record of Kaizer Matanzima's interference with
the mine management's practices of evictions. I have no reason to doubt it,
and such negotiations would surely have taken place *sub rosa*, but destruction
continued regardless. Following the mine's final closure, squatters, many of
them more recent immigrants to the area, ransacked its remaining ruins for
remnants of electrical cable, bricks, beams, and recyclable fixtures. That process continues, and one still sees young men sitting atop the walls of remaining
buildings with hammer and chisel, chipping the bricks from their plaster bed.
It is as if they have taken into themselves the destructive function that had
been performed by mine management in the era of evictions. The young men
are also radicalizing that function and attempting, perhaps, to redeem it; in
their refusal to submit to the question of who (still) owns the house, they enact
a disregard for all the laws of property that excluded them "more than a hundred" years ago. At the same time, they are repurposing these bricks, giving
them a second life and finding in the ruins a function for what had otherwise

been treated as waste. Such recycling is not a *return* to a primordial order of utility; it is the expression of a long history, whose specific development in the goldfields of South Africa shaped the ways in which waste has become a locus of value. That story, however, which is in some senses *the* story of gold, is still to come. Before then, the concluding narrative of this compound remains to be recounted.

The last operating remnant of the mine, its hospital, was burned to the ground in 2007, during protests against forced removals—not of renters whose bills were unpaid but of more recently arrived squatters. This destruction also took place in the mode of a violent mimesis. The squatters' outrage was provoked by the arrival of state agents, colloquially referred to as the "Red Ants," whose charge it was to remove occupants from land to which they had no legally recognized claim. According to Virgil-Umholi, they had been called in at the behest of the mine.

V-U: In 2007 . . . when there used to be shacks around here . . . there were shacks over there, and over here. . . . Then, there was a fight. And this place was burned down. Including the hospital.
D-X: And it was burned?
V-U: They burned it. The hospital was burned down.
D-X: Was the hospital burnt while it was still working?
V-U: What?
D-X: Was it working at that time?
V-U: Yes, it was working! It was working. The mine was closed but . . . the mine was closed but the hospital was working. . . . Even the office there was still working.
D-X: So, it was burned by the community?
V-U: Yeah, in 2007, because the informal settlement was unwanted.
D-X: So, they burnt the hospital. And they burnt the office.
V-U: Just like that.
D-X: Was this the office over here?
V-U: That one, there. It was burned by the community.
D-X: What was troubling the community for them to have burnt down the hospital?
V-U: When they burnt the hospital, they were upset that their shacks were being forcibly removed.
D-X: Oh, had they occupied the land by force?
V-U: They had occupied it by force. It was against the rules of the mine. This was mine property.

Their "fury poured out like fire."[26] The squatters, relatively recent arrivals in this world and still bearing the stigmata of the new immigrant, consumed as

much of this world as they could, down to its ashes. They did so without sacrificial reverence and without satisfaction. Only that made of stone and cement
remained of many structures. Some of these old buildings, roofs caved in and
walls crumbling, can still be seen. But often, Virgil-Umholi and Dante-Xolani
were pointing to entirely absented edifices, and the world of the pre-riot era
had thus to be conjured as a mirage. Walls rose, rooms appeared, phantom
doctors and nurses filled the offices, and the dream of care was like a wraith in
their midst. I looked without seeing the forms to which the two men alluded
with such certainty. Yet, many people in the neighborhood seemed to recognize these locations, as though they all had access to a vision in which the built
forms of time past were still physically present. It was a felt absence, like an
amputated limb.

Virgil-Umholi's explanation conceded the mine management's claim on
the property and, with piquant irony, granted the corporation its title to this
space while rendering the squatters, among whom he was now numbered, as
interlopers. The entire scenario reproduced in miniature the structure within
which mining capital had partnered with the state without, at the same time,
submitting to any form of accountability other than its shareholders. The history of this relation, which produced what I have called the pseudo-state of the
mine compound, and which enabled its unaccountable influence on the legislative process throughout much of South African history (thereby rendering the
state something like its own shadow), is recounted in the next section. Later,
we will want to consider the nature of the incendiary rage that it provoked and
that is so often represented in the press as self-destructive recklessness. Already
we can discern the contours of the awful repetition compulsion that it enacted,
and that sounded in the language of eviction (*ukuxoshwa*)], forced occupation
(*qhubeka*), and forced removal (*ukususwa*) or relocation. As for the language
of burning, it hissed in searing onomatopoeia: *shisa* (burn), *ukushisa* (to burn
[down]), and *bashiswe* (burned).

Since the 1960s, when the Group Areas Act began to be implemented with
mass evictions and forced relocations, it has not been uncommon to hear that
the townships were or are "on fire." And often, this is literally so; burning barricades were then, and are once again, the media of protest.[27] These intentional
fires are sometimes indistinguishable from those accidental conflagrations
caused by faulty wiring, spilled paraffin, and the wayward spark of cooking fire
or the smoldering ash of cigarette. But these terms and their cognates in related
languages do not only orient the discourse of material displacement caused by
actual fire, an all-too-common terror in shack settlements. They provide an
idiom in which all forms of political dislocation can be spoken. Their exchange
not only poses the question of historical causality but also reveals something
of the contradictions at the heart of the gold economy, contradictions that are
organized by the problem of the remainder.

Closed for Business

Virgil-Umholi and Dante-Xolani recounted the events at the compound with great animation. Separated by a generation, they spoke easily as they walked and recalled with nearly perfect unanimity the incidents that had accompanied the closure of the mine over whose grounds we were ambling. But the younger man, the lines on his face betraying his decades on the margins of survival, was intrigued by Virgil-Umholi's long-term recollections. He deferred to his elder's precise chronologies, but he was more circumspect about the enchanted vision of plenitude nurtured by the elder whom he respectfully addressed as either chief or grandfather. And he frequently but gently tried to catch the old man in a contradiction, or to elicit from him a recognition of the humiliations that time and, perhaps, the forces of repression, had buried.[28] He asked about the location of sleeping quarters and prodded the old man to acknowledge the segregation of black and white workers.

Surprisingly, after his initial paean to the mine's early largesse, Virgil-Umholi was quick to project the image of the open-air showers where black men had to bathe themselves in mortifying full view of each other and the management. The married residential facilities, which were among the prized ruins in which to squat, had had private ablution facilities, but this was not the case for the single-sex hostels. Listening to the recording of this conversation some months later, I recalled the famous image of Ernest Cole's scandalous exposé, *House of Bondage*, where a caption accompanying the image of naked black men, their faces turned to the wall, explains that "nude men are herded through a string of doctors' offices" as part of hiring inspections. I found myself flipping through the book's awfully revelatory pages. One of Cole's photographs features a small child in soiled clothes standing before a broken-down brick house. It bears the caption, "Child's home, in area declared as 'black spot,' has been destroyed."[29] The resemblance between that image, published in 1967, and the scene before me where the toddler had dragged her phone through the sand of a crumbled house, was so nearly complete that it took my breath away. And the reference to the conspicuously named "black spots," punctuating spaces that were designated for whites only but that were occupied by black South Africans and were thus subject to demolition, provided another example of Apartheid's survival in the democratic era. The ruins on which we walked were evidence of that. When we strolled past the now-defunct toilets, which had been located outside of the main living quarters, Dante-Xolani asked, "So, why couldn't they put a toilet inside the house, so if someone has diarrhea or something, they didn't have to go outside? . . . Was it because it was that time of Apartheid, and they knew there were just black people here?" Virgil-Umholi could only say that he had arrived after they had been installed.

Shit, and being treated like shit. A formless figure of disposability, shit is an obvious and even a clichéd signifier of wasted life, of life as waste. But if shit as waste is a metaphor, it also returns in processes that demetaphorize. It is the vacillation between these two processes that the entire history of the gold economy, including its racialization and eroticization takes place. In this context, one should note that the term or rather the knot of terms and concepts that are associated with waste, including excess, superfluity, and shit, are too often treated as mere synonyms, but they are concatenated by apposition more than by definition. It is important to disentangle these terms and their cognates in other languages, to clarify and comprehend their differences to understand how the wastage of some becomes the excess of others, even as the excess of some is based on the representation of others as prone to wasteful excesses, which is to say of not understanding the nature of value.

In his repeated insistence on talking about the toilets, and naming the shameful ailment that renders one incapable of the continence that is, everywhere in the world, a basic requirement of public decorum, Dante-Xolani took his leave from Virgil-Umholi and implied what Dante Alighieri poeticized, namely that to be "plunged in excrement . . . poured from human privies" (18.113) is an experience of ejection from society, and thus of the social abyss. In Alighieri's *Inferno*, this "abyss, a broad and yawning structure" (18.5) is among the lowest levels of hell, and, not incidentally, it is imagined as being like a mine of sorts: "it is made all of stone the color of crude iron" (18.1–2). I am not the first person to find echoes of Alighieri's hell in the undergrounds of mining, just as Alighieri was not the first to find a form for hell in the mines. Ovid, for example, referred to mines as the "bowels of the earth" long before it had become a descriptive platitude. He added that "riches couched and hidden deep in places near to hell" were "spurs and stirrers unto vice." And that gold was "more hurtful than the iron far," for, from it "came forth battle bold."[30] He would surely have read the Anglo-Boer War of 1899–1902 in these terms, as a war born of the desire for gold. For his part, Virgil-Umholi did not fully share this sense of gold's morally corrupting force, but the rhetoric that aligned the mines with excess, if not excremental waste, recurred in his speech and was punctuated by Dante-Xolani's question marks.

No doubt, it is in reference to the most primary bodily functions that people feel most exposed to the pressures and ravages of social institutions. Dante-Xolani's question, which seemed to embarrass Virgil-Umholi in its directness, made clear that the coercive institutions of the state, which on the mine compounds was both enabled and operated by the corporation, penetrated into this most intimate domain, a domain from which there was no escape.

What can it mean to distinguish between ideological and coercive apparatuses, as some theory of ideology does, when defecation is racially organized as the scene of an unevenly distributed vulnerability, fear, and public humiliation?[31]

It is not only young, malcontented radicals throwing bags of feces at politicians who have failed to deliver toilets to informal settlements, as happened in South Africa in 2013 and periodically recurs, that testifies to shit's power as a political signifier. The angry youth's gestures refuse the predicament to which they have been assigned, to be sure, but that predicament is not reducible to a lack of sanitation facilities. It is rage at the foreclosure of their desire to become more than what they are. Sanitation is merely one form of appearance of a structure in which people's capacity to exceed themselves and generate more than is necessary for mere existence is reduced to an excremental function. In this manner, a creative capacity is absolutized as a material fact, an organic automaticity. In this same representational structure, forms of expressing desire are signified as being wasteful, and people's ostensible failure to channel their capacities for excess into the creation of surplus value (for capital) are deemed a waste. Thus, at the turn of the twentieth century, deaths of black or, in the parlance of the day, Native workers, because of disease and accidents at the mines, were calculated by the industry's major labor recruiting body, the Witwatersrand Native Labor Association (WNLA), under the category of "wastage."[32] This term came to encompass workers discharged at the end of their contracts as well as those killed or absented by desertion and imprisonment. But it did not include those who were rejected outright by labor recruiters for reasons of illness—mainly phthisis, tuberculosis, and silicosis. Rather, it referred to a loss from within the body of potential productivity.[33] Waste in this sense is not simply a remainder, or a kind of superfluity—and thus it is not adequately captured by the concept of disposability; it is the specifically squandered residue of what might have become or generated value. It arises in time, in anticipation and disappointment of something more. This conceptual structure is as operative in the twenty-first century as it was in the early days of the mines' excited development. Thus, for example, when informal miners find that their samples have not delivered much gold, they speak first of low percentages and then of shit. Shit is the aftermath and the name of a failure—when effort does not convert into value, when labor bears no fruit.

This linkage of shit and failure is important, particularly in the racialized economy of the compound. Nor is failure reducible to that which is unused or used up. Capitalist society makes destruction a source of value in two ways: (1) through productive consumption (when one object is used up in the production of another),[34] and (2) in its distinction between voluntary and unwilled loss. "The coffee overboard," as Georges Bataille, remarks, is a failure. But giving and the voluntary disposal of wealth is something else: it is testament to a power of (human) nature's self-transcendence.[35]

One of the more spectacular recent symbols of that transcendence in the contemporary art world takes the form of a gold toilet. Maurizio Cattelan's infamous sculpture of a gold toilet not only makes visible the symbolic fecundity of shit but also is a figural apotheosis, exploding or conflating the dimensions of excess that otherwise operate and signify the social hierarchy. In a fabulous case of serendipity that nonetheless revealed the complex entanglements of the global economy, Cattelan's sculpture, titled *America*, was stolen just as I was writing the first draft of this chapter. The news came to me from the digital mediasphere: "Police are trying to recover a solid gold toilet made entirely of 18-carat-gold that was stolen Saturday Morning from Blenheim Palace in Oxfordshire, England, the stately home where former Prime Minister Winston Churchill was born."[36] Cattelan's sculpture may be titled *America*, in reference to President Donald John Trump's penchant for gold, and to whose White House it was offered before being installed at Blenheim Palace, but among the Zimbabwean migrants who scavenge for gold, it is Robert Mugabe's gold toilet that is often adduced as the emblem of Mugabe's corruption and betrayal of his revolutionary pretensions. The excessiveness of the gold toilet, where waste is normally disposed, derives not merely from its expense, which is both represented and grounded in the material of its fabrication, but by virtue of its symbolic condensation of a surplus that is lacking elsewhere because it has been stolen. It is a spectacle not of the generous squandering to which Bataille assigned the name *potlatch* (appropriating and mistranslating the name of an indigenous ritual feasting) but of theft. Theft is the third and absent term of Bataille's analysis, the necessary supplement to the dyad of failure and expenditure. For, those who have been deprived of that which could be either lost or dispensed with are condemned to a certain demetaphorization. They are condemned to literality and a reduction to waste.

The degree to which the bodily functions of excretion can be concealed, disciplined, and cloaked in ritual, and the related degree to which such processes can be valorized, is linked to claims on a relative cultural capacity—namely, to achieve distance from nature. Thus, the separation and distribution of ablution facilities and the exposure of the black workers' toilets materialized a commonplace racist presumption about black individuals' incapacity to leave nature behind. Such statements threaten to collapse beneath the weight of the most banal functionalism, to be sure. That risk assails both the anthropologist and those whose exposure to this reduction she would describe. So, it is critical to grasp the profundity and symbolic potentiality, the psychic power and affective intensities that attach themselves to this domain—where, as Bataille rightly discerned, reason does battle with matter, and where, too, the pitiful effort to assert white supremacy leads to the resentful and deluded imputation to others of the "non-logical difference" that is material life, the putrefying but also fecundating matter of life.[37]

When Dante-Xolani asked Virgil-Umholi whether the publicness of the toilets was related to the fact of Apartheid, he was addressing a relatively practical consideration—convenience or, indeed, inconvenience, in times of need, and the relative exposure to that need on racial grounds. Later, both he and Virgil-Umholi talked at length about the frustrations and humiliations, as well as the dangers, especially for women, of having to slog to unlit outhouses in the middle of the night, where the presence of a door could not be assumed. During the recently passed election cycle, the promise to install more and better toilets in the informal settlements around these mines had been a campaign pillar and, like many others, it had gone unrealized. Dante-Xolani's repetitive and ire-filled queries testified to the symbolic dimension of this organized lack, which had once been related both to the industry's contempt for black workers and to the inclusion of white workers, along with white capital, in the cultural–racial category of those who can take leave of their "baseness." That alliance would be defended as furiously by white workers as by white capital over the decades, and the insistence on maintaining a color bar within mine labor was the central issue animating the Witwatersrand strikes of 1914 and 1922, just as its overthrow was the central issue animating the black labor movement on the mines throughout the twentieth century. Dante-Xolani's recognition of this latter fact is implicit in his question about Apartheid, which ultimately privileged racial separation over class division, even as it worked to racialize class.

More than eighty years ago, Bataille argued that it was the "preliminary existence of a class held to be abject by common accord, as in the case of the blacks" that permitted the hypocritical (if limited) transfer of wealth from the upper to the lower classes of whites in the United States. And this gesture, he argued, was primarily aimed at attenuating the likelihood of a revolutionary violence that would dispense with those whose "contemptuous forms" had sought to exclude human nature, and to thereby rise above nature itself, but only by excluding others from this glorious status.[38] That letter also continues to be sent. To read Virgil-Umholi and Dante-Xolani's discourse in this way, and to describe the logic of the compound sanitation facilities in this manner, is *not* the same as stating, as some would have it, that black subjects, thus humiliated and made abject, came to dwell in the mode of *bare life*, or that the logic of disposability actually determined the consciousness of the compounds.[39] Everywhere, and most certainly in the discourse of these two men, we find evidence of desire's survival, of generosity's persistence. But most often, the escape from racism's efforts to effect *bare life* were legible in the remarkable and repeated resurgence of hope and a vision of future plenitude.

In response to Dante-Xolani's bitter cajoling, while beneath a clothesline of scrubbed but tattered t-shirts and denims, and as we were assailed by the rank odor of an open ditch running with sewerage, the elder man slowed his pace and began to speak. His words took flight in an imagination of future restoration:

V-U: Given that we're struggling, maybe there will be a change and the mines will reopen.

D-X: (apparently perplexed): Do you think the mines will reopen?

V-U: Yes. And there will be jobs.

D-X: Do you still hope that the mines will reopen? Because, they say there will be development in this area. (Z)

Dante-Xolani was referring to the fact that the municipal government had been holding discussions about a possible real estate development of the now-defunct spaces. This development would have constituted an alternative to the reopening of the mines, and, ideally, it would have entailed the remediation of the highly toxic environment. As it happened, a concession would soon be granted to an Australian mining entity (with South African partners), which would commence open-pit extraction nearby within the year, its remediation strategy seemingly limited to the removal of the tailings dumps that it was reprocessing for residual gold. But, like most other residents (and me), Virgil-Umholi was at that time unaware of these negotiations, and he was speaking dreamily about a reopening of formal operations, imagining it in opposition not to real estate development but to the informal scavenging that was then taking place on these grounds. This was not because he despised or feared the scavenging (he described the zama zamas as "wonderful" and repeatedly remarked their disciplined work ethic), but rather because he believed that stable employment and safety measures in the mines would be preferable to the terrifying risks and unrelenting precarity that afflicted everyone in the area.

With the perhaps distorted memory of the mines' more generous heyday, and with hope for the upgrading of the local infrastructure, but especially the sanitation facilities, Virgil-Umholi continued. As he did so, his discourse shifted again, and as he explained what had caused the closure of the mines, the tempo of his speech hastened as his voice grew powerfully indignant:

V-U: There's still a lot of money [mali] in the mines and . . .

D-X: There's still a lot of money?

V-U: There's still money in there. No. These mines were just closed when a black man came into power.

D-X: They just shut down.

V-U: They were upset because a black man was in power. And they shut down, just like that.

D-X: Oh, they shut down when they heard, freedom is coming.

V-U: Freedom. And they closed. (Z, the word *freedom* was spoken in English)

The simultaneity of political emancipation and economic destitution is a recurrent theme of Virgil-Umholi's perplexed lament, which poses a question in the form of an indictment. But this lament is not merely the idiosyncratic speech of an old man beholden to nostalgia.[40] It bespeaks a broad set of questions that have afflicted South Africa more generally over the past few decades, and it has lurked in the underground and the unconscious of the industry since its foundation.

Emerging from the violent histories of colonialism, segregation, and Apartheid in 1994, at the very moment when the mine in which we were walking closed down, South Africa was confronted with a set of unbearable and often contradictory and overdetermined needs, if not outright double binds. The formal dawn of the democratic era occurred in the aftermath of the collapse of the Soviet system and thus in the relative absence of external material and ideological support for a more collectivist alternative to the neoliberal policies that everywhere were on the ascent. In this context, pressure from big capital enjoyed the authority of history's Last Man, as Fukuyama had it, and could easily assert that "there is no alternative" to neoliberalism, as Thatcher had claimed.[41] The government of the new nation had to establish the terms of its legitimacy while developing policies and programs that could address extensive black poverty, with catastrophically high unemployment rates among black citizens, and high in-migration from the surrounding nations, which themselves were suffering economic collapse because of monetary crises, externally enforced debt burdens, political mismanagement, and ethnic conflict—not to mention the legacies of their dependency on migrant labor linked to South Africa's mining industries. Its revenue-generating tourism sector, especially its nature tourism, was often environmentally destructive and competed for resources, such as water and electricity, needed in poor communities. And it had to create solutions to Apartheid's awful legacy against the backdrop of an HIV/AIDS epidemic that was ravaging the poorest communities and decimating the generation of parents whose children would soon (and once more) become the burden of their grandparents, while also inciting fear and suspicion within communities. Beyond the psycho-social trauma that accompanied the epidemic, the material costs of responding to the health crisis, which was both slow and sometimes willfully ineffectual, would have been nearly insupportable even if the health infrastructure already existed to fully service the nation's population, and there were monetary resources available. But, of course, that sector was unevenly developed and racially differentiated, and those most afflicted were least able to access necessary diagnostic, prophylactic, and treatment services, even when these were rolled out many years later (see chapter 9). Much of a generation was lost in the chasm.

To make matters worse, the first ten years of the new dispensation also coincided with the lowest gold prices since 1980; they would not rise above that level until 2003. Revenues and taxes that might have been generated under more auspicious circumstances, as well as mine employment in the gold sector, which declined sharply during this early period of "freedom" (although the platinum sector grew), were thus not available to the new state, many of whose fiscal decisions (e.g., the purchase of armaments) worsened the crisis.

Thus, what had promised to be the best of times for the country's formerly disenfranchised citizens became, for many of those who did not already have savings or capital assets, the worst of times. And the ANC-led government's determination to pursue black capital formation (through policies like Growth, Employment, and Redistribution or GEAR, and Black Economic Empowerment, or BEE) rather than equity through redistribution surely exacerbated problems.[42]

Virgil-Umholi's speech does not allude to these phenomena in particular. It simply insists that the closure of the mines was gratuitous and that the current economic crisis is a function of highly self-interested political decisions and not a geologically overdetermined fact. This accusation is grounded in his unshakable belief in the residual abundance of the precious metal he believed was still buried in the earth.

The dream of gold's persisting amplitude seemed improbable in that desolate landscape, so long after the mines had closed. And yet, everywhere I looked, there were men entering and exiting the earth, or women grinding the stone that the men were bringing to the surface in plastic sacks that once had held rice or cornmeal. Some people who make their living scavenging in these ruins, including both the zama zamas and the crushers, speak of the possibility that gold is growing back, germinating in the recuperating earth of the now-quiet mines. Some even specify that this rejuvenation occurs according to a predictable temporality, after a period of seven years. And a few suggest that the earth is not merely the home of creaturely and spiritual life but also is itself animate. Others are more skeptical, scoffing at a belief in the earth's powers of fecundation. Instead, they call on both science and political economy when explaining that the gold that remains underground is plentiful enough for a man to extract when he has only his own body to sustain but insufficient to justify the significant investment that would be required for capital-intensive industrial mining. These skeptics know that they are mining the margins of payability. Still, the dream of a generous remainder persists, as Anita Parbhaker-Fox asserts in "Treasure from Trash: How Mining Waste Can Be Mined a Second Time."[43] This siren song of the industry recurs in the headlines of newspapers around the world, as much as in the colloquial discourse of scavengers on the mines of South Africa. This is partly because rising gold prices have made the recovery of even tiny bits of gold a source of sufficient revenue to justify at least individual labor. But it is also because of the ways in which gold has been made to function as the general form and signifier of excess. What the entire history of the gold industry shows is that abundance is a relative concept and, moreover, a phantasmic one; it was generated through the careful deployment of technological, financial, juridical, and social-administrative techniques, and in the fantasies arising therefrom.

We will now turn to the early part of that history in outline. This is not to verify (or contradict) the statements made by Virgil-Umholi or Dante-Xolani, nor to reduce their experiences and those of their communities to the mere effects of politico-economic structures. To the contrary, it is their formulations that allow for a reframing of the historiographical task and the analytic challenges that arise in the present. And it is their insistent gesture of self-historicization that begs the following exploration.

Much of what follows has already been addressed by historians of the gold industry. And I have relied heavily on their primary archival research. Nonetheless, the terms of the debate concerning deep-level mining and its relationships to social and political structures, and especially the racialization of this form of extractivist industrial capital have been significantly overdetermined by the mode-of-production narrative. And much has been lost, or at least sidelined in such readings. A tangential glance can still reveal a great deal. Indeed, one may yet "dig up" remnants in these margins, which, having been treated as incidental to the central narrative (typically either a mode-of-production narrative, or one of bourgeois individualist or workerist heroism), may turn out to have played a constitutive role in the phenomena whose exhaustion has been claimed by previous analysts.[44] My aim, therefore, is to re-excavate the early histories of deep-level mining to understand why the future history of the region of which I write took the form that it did, and why it was afflicted with the specific aspirations and nightmares that it was. These questions—what does gold do to people, and what does it make them do?—lead me to other questions—about the structures, associations, functions, uses, valuations, and histories of gold that give it this force and this capacity to make things happen. Gold is like that: like the golden frame with which Kant describes the ornamental excess that he claims distracts from the appreciation of real beauty, and that Derrida rethinks as a constitutive feature of the picture, the marker of a boundary between interiority and exteriority. It is both that which demands and that which is adduced as explanation. To pose the question of gold's force is thus to plunge headlong into a kind of abyss—an "abyss and satire of the abyss," writes Derrida—in which the question of priority, or causality, becomes unmoored form its ostensible opposition to the question of effect.[45] With respect to gold, nature and history (or culture, if one prefers), revolve around each other in a vertiginous spiral of alibi and explanation. But this does not mean that one should not make that descent.

CHAPTER 3

GOLD FOOLS

Or, What Is a Gold Rush?

Why do you hoard? Why do you squander?

—Dante Alighieri, *Divine Comedy*

If you think I see only profit in the gold I win, you are mistaken. I see in it the pleasures it procures for me, and I enjoy them to the full. They come too quickly to make me weary, and there are too many of them for me to get bored. I live a hundred lives in one. When I travel, it is the way an electric spark travels.

—Eduoard Gourdon, *Faucheurs de la nuit* [Reapers of the Night]

Virgil-Umholi emphasized that, when he arrived at the compound, it was already built, already old. His history is not an origin myth. Indeed, the origin of the compound is that which exceeds him, and which recedes into a past without measure. Nonetheless, it is extraordinary how often people do indeed tell and retell the story of the gold industry's origins in this area. After many decades of contestation, a sedimented narrative arose, one that is anchored in and by a proper name: Langlaagte. In this narrative, the first find on the Main Reef, as it would come to be known, was made in 1886 by an Australian digger named Harrison on Farm Langlaagte (which was actually four separate farms, the site of the strike being on land owned by Gerhardus Cornelis Oosthuizen[1]). This is perhaps the most oft-cited piece of the origin myth of the gold industry, and the ten-stamp mill that was initially set up at Robinson mine at Langlaagte in 1886 is still on display in the South African Institute of Mining and Metallurgy in downtown Johannesburg.[2] I say myth because, even though the narrative is composed of factual elements, the story attributes to them the power of firstness, and in so doing, it obliterates the conditions of possibility, the deeper histories, economies and phantasmatic structures that impelled the metal's pursuit—in the first place, as it were. Nonetheless, like thousands of others, I have often recalled this narrative of discovery while driving past the location that still bears the name on the route that links Johannesburg to Roodepoort—that is, Main Reef Road. In 2016, an accident in one of the shafts being worked by zama zamas at Langlaagte claimed the lives of an unknown number of men, and, in typical fashion, newspaper coverage of the story widely repeated that foundational myth, while describing the missing miners doing what "millions of men have done before [them]: seek[ing] their fortune deep underground in the gold mines that help to define South Africa."[3]

FORM OF APPLICATION FOR SHARES IN THE
DEEPKLOOF GOLD MINING COMPANY, LIMITED
(*To be Incorporated under the Limited Liability Acts of the South African Republic.*)

To _____

    Sir, _____Please enter _____ name for _____ Shares of £1 each in the above-named Company, and receive, herewith, cheque for £_____, being amount of the Deposit of 2s. 6d per Share in terms of the Company's Prospectus, on the basis of which I make this application; and I hereby engage to pay all Calls as required by Prospectus, also to sign the Company's Trust Deed when called upon to do so.

    Name in full _____ Signature _____
    Occupation _____ Address _____
    Date _____
Applications for Shares will be received Messrs.
FAIRBRIDGE and PETIT, Share Brokers, Port Elizabeth.[4]

3.1 Application for shares in the Deepkloof Gold Mining Company, Limited.

Seeking their fortune and seeking fortune. When it comes to gold, the idea of riches almost always is linked to serendipity, luck, or fate. The precious metal is not only resistant to rust, and thus permanently lustrous, but it seems resistant to the idea of labor. At least that is the story told by those who do not venture underground. Thus, the journalists' stereotypical description of motive among informal miners conflates the idea of a gold rush as it exists for prospectors, speculators, and capitalists, with the motive force for the men who have worked the mines throughout the past century and a half. It is somewhat at odds with the actuality of contemporary informal mining, although the dream of a big strike persists. It is entirely incorrect as a description of how and why the majority of mineworkers have entered those bowels to extract what Freud called "Hell's excrement" from the earth that is traced by Main Reef Road.

Many of the roads branching off or running parallel to Main Reef Road bear the names of minerals or mining-related activities: Platinum, Coal, Azurite, Uranium, Slate, Shaft, Smelt, Leader, and Reamer. And, of course, gold. There are Gold Streets and Gold Avenues everywhere in the mining towns of South Africa (and no doubt, elsewhere). There is the Golden Highway, the R533 that links Johannesburg with Vanderbiljpark, and Main Reef Road is a major transportation artery. Reading a map for the names of the areas that lie next to it is like looking at an historical index of all the mining companies and properties that came, within three decades of the Langlaagte strike, to dominate that always already transnationalized industry. These signs and the names they bear reveal a more general, one might even say deeper, truth. This is a scripted landscape.

Despite the fantasy of a fortunate discovery, people had been looking for gold in the Transvaal for some decades before the strike: Foreigners (Uitlanders), that is. Europeans. The "rush" preceded the discovery, which was intensified by it. This rush came from afar and when it arrived, it transformed the original residents and sojourners of these rolling grasslands into the *other* of colonial fantasy, evicting them from their life worlds even as it enabled the imperial economy to be realized by exporting the men and capital that it could no longer utilize in Europe.

Fevered desire is not always discerning, of course. People see gold everywhere. It colors the horizon at dawn, it lays on the grasses in the midafternoon, it glints in the waters of the dams that gather seasonal rains, and it fills the annals of poetry. As the adage goes, "all that glitters is not gold." The earth is also deceptive; you have to know how to read it. Early in my research in the town of Carletonville, some sixty miles from Langlaagte, a former (white) municipal official took me out onto the street in front of the spacious bungalow where he and his wife lived with their menacing guard dogs, and pointed to the tarmac that was sparkling under a blanching Highveld sun. That glitter, he said, was gold. He was a Christian man, and he might well have been quoting scripture.

"And the twelve gates were twelve pearls: every several gate was of one pearl: and the street of the city was pure gold".[5] He asked me if I believed him, about the sparkle being gold, and I laughed nervously before informing him that I was a geologist's daughter. I hoped I would know fool's gold when I saw it.

Since the very earliest days of prospecting for gold on the Witwatersrand, the risk of confusing mica or pyrite, two of the minerals often mistaken for the precious metal (and that sometimes occur in its vicinity), have hovered above its frenzied pursuit. This is not because of any geochemical proximity between gold and these minerals; it is rather a symptom of the desire for gold, of its hallucinatory projection onto other surfaces. In 1854, for a typical early example (for South Africa), a professional "goldspanner" who had joined the growing population of prospectors seeking their fortune in what was then the Transvaal Republic, tried to pawn off a thirty-pound bag of "yellow metallic powder mixed with flaky leaves" to a passing tourist, who, wary of the fantastical size of the offering, took only a few ounces for testing. The assay results showed it to be mica.[6] This episode was reported in the local newspaper, *The Friend*, at a time before the Transvaal government had developed a consistent policy for granting digging rights or recognizing claims. It demonstrated (or at least warned) that gold mining depended on sophisticated knowledge and technologies—knowledges and technologies that could contain the deceits that desire would otherwise beget or that unscrupulous swindlers might cultivate in more innocent gamblers. It was a lesson that Georgius Agricola had tried to impart to his readers already in the sixteenth century.

> Many persons hold the opinion that the metal industries are fortuitous and that the occupation is one of sordid toil, and altogether a kind of business requiring not so much skill as labour. But . . . a miner must have the greatest skill in his work, that he may know first of all what mountain or hill, what valley or plain, can be prospected most profitably, or what he should leave alone; moreover, he must understand the veins, stringers and seams in the rocks. Then he must be thoroughly familiar with the many and varied species of earths, juices, gems, stones, marbles, rocks, metals, and compounds. He must also have a complete knowledge of the method of making all underground works. Lastly, there are the various systems of assaying substances and of preparing them for smelting; and here again there are many altogether diverse methods.[7]

For good measure, Agricola added that "the miner should not be ignorant of philosophy, medicine, astronomy, surveying, arithmetic, architecture, and law."[8] By miner he did not mean mineworker, but rather the one (or group) that owned and operated the mine. The mere toiler of the soil—which phrase acquires an entirely new meaning in the mines, although the rhetoric of the field and harvest persist—was not of interest to him. Miners were men of money for Agricola. And already, in the sixteenth century, he discerned the advantage of joint ownership, the spreading of risks across several mines and even an investment strategy entailing the purchase of shares in adjacent mines of various stages of development toward production, including those for which the payability and even the presence of valuable ores might not yet be known— on the assumption that ore bodies would likely extend laterally beyond the shafts of known mines.[9] It is remarkable how much his strategy would be repro- duced by the financial houses of South Africa some four centuries later.

Agricola's treatise remained influential in European mining circles for more than two centuries after its writing. But the English translation had to await the labors of a man who made his fortune in gold mining, first in Australia, then in China, and finally through the recruitment of Chinese mining labor for the gold mines of South Africa between 1903 and 1908 (including for the very mine in which Virgil-Umholi and Dante-Xolani, were conversing).[10] Herbert Clark Hoover and his wife, Lou Henry Hoover, translated Agricola's treatise after he completed work in China as a director of the British-based gold mining entity, Bewick, Moreing and Co. (which had a consulting presence in South Africa), and the Chinese Mining and Engineering Company.[11] This same Hoover would later be president of the United State. The Hoovers had become aware of the history of dreamed and lost fortunes that had clouded the southern African horizon even before the discovery of gold on the Witwatersrand. Among early observers of these deluded prospectors, Thomas Baines, the adventurer art- ist who accompanied Livingstone on his journeys before authoring *The Gold Regions of South Eastern Africa* (1877), had written sternly that "it is sheer folly for men to leave the writer's desk, or the mechanic's bench, where some earn 12s. to 13s. per diem, and rush to this or that gold field on hearing of a splendid find—totally ignoring the lengthened search, the sore privation, the exhaust- ing toil, and the back-breaking disappointments the finders have endured before success rewarded them—and trusting in some vague manner to realize the same 'good luck' without the skill or perhaps the intention to labour with the same energy."[12]

As for the cautionary story in *The Friend*, it revealed the financial risks for those who would purchase or invest in what they could not judge. It also demonstrated the degree to which appearances could be deceiving, and indeed, it staged the specific capacity that gold has to signify anything: to become not merely the burnished surface in which any visage is reflected but the cipher for chimerical visions and an infinity of desires.

Translating Agricola was not an attempt, on the Hoovers' part, to induce the caution that Baines believed to be lacking or that *The Friend* was advocating. Nonetheless, *De Re Metallica* was a kind of theatrical set piece for the idea that the miner—insofar as he would become a capitalist—would depend on procedures of both verification and risk management. As such, the translation offered a kind of belated antidote. It sealed the distinction between mineworker (labor) and miner (capital) and elevated the latter figure to the status of the modern man in whom the residue of Renaissance polymathy would be given its economic raison d'être. It did so through the concept of *payability*. Payability is not merely the calculus of profitability, but an entire system of what Foucault terms "veridification," in which the assayable presence and distribution of gold in ores at particular depths and embedded in particular geological formations that make the gold more or less extractable, is rendered as a truth that then legitimates the organization of the social field in terms of the investment costs required to transform that geological "fact" into revenue. Veridification is the process that generates what Foucault termed "savoir." As Francesco Guala neatly summarizes Foucault's argument, the emergence of a new savoir determines that "an entity or domain becomes a legitimate object for a discourse that can be evaluated in terms of truth and falsity."[13] Economic geology, which would ultimately be instituted at the University of the Witwatersrand in the mid-twentieth century, was already a savoir by the time Hoover undertook his translations, and its emergence can be traced to Agricola. In South Africa, however, it acquired a new dimension, or intensification, which had to do not only with processes of financialization but also with the grounding of the concept of payability in the domain of waste, in which was sublimated the fantasy of value beyond labor, of a sublime excess.

Punctuation Marks: Phrases and Phases of Gold-Mindedness

Perhaps the most astonishing description of gold's depth and inaccessibility on the Witwatersrand comes in a public relations brochure issued by the Transvaal and Orange Free State Chamber of Mines in the 1960s: "Imagine a solid mass of rock tilted . . . like a fat, 1,200-page dictionary lying at an angle. The gold bearing reef would be thinner than a single page, and the amount of gold contained therein would hardly cover a couple of commas in the entire book. It is the miner's job to bring out that single page—but his job is made harder because the page has been twisted and torn by nature's forces, and pieces of it may have been thrust between other leaves of the book."[14]

In this remarkable word image of the earth-as-book, the comma is the figure that mediates, without resolving, the apparent contradiction between plenitude and paucity. For, if the commas were few and far between, the book was large. In fact, the narrative of the comma, which made the miner's labor seem so heroic (occluding that performed by the mineworker), was always accompanied by and counterposed with another tale about the density and richness of the ore deposits.

The fact that the gold-bearing ore of the Witwatersrand seemed plentiful, and, moreover, confined to a relatively small space, made it initially appear to be an easy source of fortune. In retrospect, the fantastical dreams and often maniacal pursuit of wealth in that territory could seem to have been given in or by nature. In a mere century and a half, the gold mines of South Africa generated more than 50 percent of all the gold ever mined on earth. Ever. This includes thousands of years of alluvial and underground mining, and the use of gold first in trade (in Mesopotamia and Anatolia) and then as coinage in empires as distant as Lydia, where Croesus is credited with inventing the first gold coin in about 550 BCE; to East Asia, where the gold Ying Yuan was in use from about the fifth century BCE onward; to South Asia, where it was circulating even before the Mauryan (322–187 BCE) kingdoms used it. It includes the even deeper history of gold's use in ritual objects, regalia, sacral offerings, and personal ornamentation. It includes the shimmering product of the great mines of the West African kingdoms plundered by competing European powers from the fifteenth century onward. And it includes that excavated from the mines of the Americas, and then stolen by the Spanish, of whom Herrera wrote, "no Divinity . . . ha[d] been so fatal to the Savages as gold, which they believed with certainty to be the Spaniards' Fetish."[15] Even in southern Africa, gold was being mined and traded as early as the twelfth century, and likely earlier. Archaeologists now recognize that the inland kingdom of Mapungubwe emerged as an imperial center thanks to wealth that arose from its command of the gold trade with the Swahili coast, which underwrote its trade along routes that extended not only up the eastern coast of Africa but also as far as China.[16] It was in fact the "discovery" of this southeast African gold complex that led to the legend, propagated by the archaeologist Karl Mauch, that the Biblical Queen of Sheba had built a temple on the model of Solomon's in Zimbabwe, and that she had overseen the local extraction of gold for that purpose. That myth incited the archaeological treasure hunt for King Solomon's mines so famously (and speedily) fictionalized by H. Rider Haggard in *King Solomon's Mines* (although Haggard narrated them as the repositories of diamonds).[17]

In any case, these vast accumulations, variously figured in the mythopoetic texts of each empire as the glittering attire and seat of power or the toxic allure of all that would render divinity impotent and incite men to murderousness, would be surpassed in South Africa's mines. But for nearly three decades, prospectors had limited success in finding the metal, and early mining efforts in the region were focused not on gold but on iron ore and copper, as well as coal. Nonetheless, the sons inherited the dreams of the fathers. With the first promising discoveries, the Transvaal government, or Volksraad, began experimenting with leasing strategies aimed at keeping profits in the country while encouraging the development of the industry—not because they wanted gold diggers but because they wanted gold and all that it could buy, including, of course, money in the form of credit. The discoveries were fantastic, indeed. In 1874, a nugget discovered in Lyndenburg, in the Transvaal, weighed 119 ounces.

If valued in today's prices (e.g., when the stock markets opened on September 1, 2023, gold was priced at $1,940.55 per ounce), it would have had a valuation of $230,925.45—far less than would have been fetched by the largest nugget ever discovered (found only five years earlier, in Ballarat, Australia), a mammoth 2,280-ounce piece with a worth of US$4,424,454 (as of September 1, 2023), but large enough to incite global delirium, mobilizing the fantasies that had found their periodic site of realization and then exhaustion in the rushes of Australia and the United States during the prior half century.[18]

Before the discovery of the Lyndenburg nugget, and anticipating the arrival of diggers seeking fortunes such as they had found in Australia and the United States, the Volksraad's strategy required farmers on whose land minerals were found to lease or sell them at a "fair price" to the state, a policy that was quickly followed by one that opened mining to companies that it both protected and regulated. Initially, the distribution of concessions provided the Volksraad with quick and easy revenues—which it desperately needed, given the recurrent threat of bankruptcy and its bloated currency, which ensured not only that the government had difficulty securing bank credit but also that local trade tended to take the form of barter.[19] The Volksraad, however, would not grant licenses for public works until there was evidence of payable gold on the property, lest unproductive speculation despoil agricultural land. Companies that first entered the field often lacked the capital to sustain the activities necessary to make such a determination and folded before they could demonstrate the extent of reserves on their provisionally licensed territory.[20] So, activity developed in fits and starts. When it first began to appear as a viable industry, the gold sector began to elicit stern opposition from the larger landholding and culturally conservative Boer farmers. Farming was not only the primary activity of the Transvaal economy but also the wealthier farmers exercised significant political influence over the government—and they would remain the major competitors for labor for the mining companies. No matter how much the two forms of capital (agricultural and mining) seemed to converge in the language of the field, they anchored radically distinct modes of being and understandings of the world. Moreover, their labor needs were both mutually exclusive and subject to competition in wages.

With the discovery of significant alluvial gold at Zoutpansberg and especially Blaauwbank in the 1870s, things began to change. Nonetheless, it was not until the 1880s, when several handsome finds near Kromdraai were made, that the "rush" for which South Africa would become famous began to take shape. It did not take long for the rush to take hold, but the first to be possessed by the phantasm were not prospectors in distant lands but rather smaller farmers nearby—and it was this specter of agriculturalists abandoning their crops in the hopes of a golden harvest that sowed such anxiety in the Volksraad. These anxieties were not new, of course. Agricola had commenced his treatise in defense of mining with a litany of the arguments that had, until then, attributed penury and depravity to the pursuit of metals and had noted that "the strongest argument of the detractors is that the fields are devastated by mining operations, for which reason formerly Italians were warned by law that no one should dig the earth for metals and so injure their very fertile fields, their vineyards, and their olive groves."[21] In rebuttal, he argued that agricultural land was rarely that which miners sought and claimed that the "gloomy valleys and sterile mountains" could be profitably exploited for mineral wealth, without touching the hills and plains on which the farmers might yet till the land.[22]

The irony of Agricola's name was to be vindicated in South Africa. Born Pawer or Bauer, he Latinized his name while studying in Leipzig, but it meant *farmer* either way. As with the classical precedents invoked by Agricola, the suspicion of mining's risks were more commonly held by statesmen, clergy, and big landowners, than by the small farmers who were often quite eager to turn their hand to prospecting, if only as a side activity. This was especially true in times of economic hardship—as when drought diminished or destroyed crops. In many parts of the Transvaal, the lack of markets and transport for produce, and the limitations on access to consumer goods imposed by barter were taking their toll, and gold mining promised one of few routes to both money and capital accumulation.

Thus, in 1880, Thomas Collingwood Kitto, a Cornish mining engineer who had arrived in South Africa by way of Australia and who had been contracted by the Transvaal government to advise on mineral matters, reported that "every person who holds a farm believes himself to be the possessor of great mineral wealth, and if a quartz reef of any kind crosses the property, he invariably pronounces it auriferous."[23] James Gray later summarized Kitto's assessment of the situation: "In a *word*, the resident population had become essentially *gold-minded*."[24] The phrase, gold-minded, evokes without containing the mania that had so recently possessed the consciousness of American and Australian settler-colonial societies. Evidence from other places where the narcosis of gold-mindedness had been associated with huge social upheavals led the Volksraad to attempt to professionalize its own mineral-rights granting operations and to contain the possibility that gold would leave in its wake the filth of which it was said, in ancient myth and psychoanalysis, to be the sign.

Once more, and as before, gold was associated with shit, and shit with social failure.

"Gold is the excrement of hell [Dreck der Hölle]," wrote Freud, in an essay on dreams in folklore.[25] Elsewhere, also in a commentary on folk belief, he noted, "Gold which the devil gives his paramours turns into excrement after his departure."[26] Gold conceals its nature as useless. This is its cunning: the fact that it receives the image or impress of that which is desired until the power that would otherwise secure its illusory receptivity and its imaginary value disappears. Often, Freud turned to folk, premodern or so-called primitive lore for insight into his more proximate interest, namely the pathologies of bourgeois European life. In this latter context, gold's excessive valorization was, for him, the inversion and displacement of a process wherein that which was once valued becomes reviled, thanks to cultural norms, only to return in another image so that it can be beloved once again.[27] The love of gold was the love of what had been morally prohibited—whether on the grounds of its incitement of greed and lust, or because it led people to spend their time in non-productive (mainly non-agricultural) activity. Moreover, the love of gold as such, and not merely as currency, was thus the love of that excess beyond its function as a medium of exchangeability.[28]

Two histories are invoked by this proposition, one having to do with the specific conditions under which gold, which Marx deemed to have been the first metal to be discovered as such, came to function as a privileged kind of currency and subsequently as the universal standard of value in international trade (although these are not the same things). Without reducing the structural analysis at the heart of Freud's reading to a mere symptom of economic history, Freud was writing at a time when an international gold standard of exchange was being sedimented. The second history evoked by Freud's discourse thus pertains to its role as a signifier in the economies of superfluity and of imperialism, more generally. And this is because, functionally, gold is largely useless.

The fact that South Africa's emergent economy would be, for some time, grounded in uselessness drew Hannah Arendt's perplexed and condemning attention. Before the discovery of gold, efforts to draw European emigrants to South Africa had met with relatively little success. According to Arendt, after the discovery of gold, neither speculators nor diggers needed much prodding, and Britain's stuttering imperial project found its last and necessary outlet. The scale and rapidity of the initial influx was phenomenal. In 1886, the year of the first strike on the Witwatersrand, 3,897 passengers boarded British ships destined for South Africa, landing at the ports of either Cape Town or Natal— far fewer than were destined for the United States (152,710) or even Canada (24,745). Within the decade, that number had increased dramatically, to 24,594, while emigration to the other English settler colonies others had decreased (with the United States receiving only 98,921 and Canada 15,267).[29] Anthony Trollope had foreseen the influx, which to him represented a desirable contribution to the moral and civilizational project of imperialism, even as he doubted the likely extent of the other gold reserves when he traveled throughout the country in 1877 (spurred by his observations of prospecting elsewhere than the Witwatersrand). Nonetheless, it was not the diggers who would profit from the rush, he said, but "the bankers and the wine-merchants and the grocers and the butchers and the inn-keepers who have waited upon them."[30] And he proceeded to describe the consciousness of the "gold-dreamer" as a kind of enchantment, a flight from every reality principle: "There is a charm and a power about gold which is so seductive and inebriating that judgment and calculation are ignored by its votaries. If there be gold in a country men will seek it though it has been sought there for years with disastrous effects. It creates a sanguine confidence which teaches the gold-dreamer to believe that he will succeed where hundreds have failed."[31]

Not surprisingly, Trollope's assessment was much kinder than Arendt's; she invoked Conrad to depict these immigrant prospectors as "reckless without hardihood, greedy without audacity and cruel without courage."[32] And this was mainly because Trollope saw them as the laudable instruments of a transformational drive interior and intrinsic to imperialism, for which he was unapologetically enthusiastic. Thus, while conceiving of South Africa as Britain's final frontier, he wrote that even if the goldfields had "hitherto created no wealth . . . [and] henceforth they should not be the source of fortune to the speculators, they will certainly serve to bring white inhabitants into the country."[33] Indeed, they did.

What caused these tens of thousands of white men and women, but mostly men, to leave for a region so remote from home? In *The Origins of Totalitarianism*, Arendt writes that "although the discoveries of gold mines and diamond fields in the seventies and eighties would have had little consequence for the imperial forces, it remains remarkable that the imperialists' claim to have found a permanent solution to the problem of superfluity was initially motivated by a rush for the most superfluous raw material on earth."[34] She adds that there was an "ironical resemblance to the superfluous money that financed the digging of gold and to the superfluous men who did the digging." These superfluous men were, in her estimation, not only the "adventurers, gamblers, criminals" and "elements outside the pale of normal sane society" that had characterized gold rushes in ancient times, but "very clearly the bi-product of this society, an inevitable residue of the capitalist system and even the representatives of an economy that relentlessly produced a superfluity of men and capital."[35]

Superfluous men, social byproducts. Thus, does Arendt offer her own narrative of the excremental dimension of capitalism's metabolism. It was this superfluity that projected itself, first as an inverted image and then as a demand to be realized, in the rendering of black workers as wastage. The diggers to which Arendt refers are, of course, still white. In her usage, the term refers to the first generation of prospecting claim-stakers and not those who would dig within the financialized and then industrialized mines once the claims had been bought up and consolidated and the role of mere digging had been assigned to mostly black men. Arendt does not trace this development; her project concerns the development of imperialism as seen from Europe, and not from its peripheral zones of dispossession and accumulation. But it is to those zones that one must turn to understand that this superfluity, which exceeded what Marx termed the lumpen proletariat and the reserve army of labor, was not an exception, nor was it evidence of any malfunction within the system; it was coemergent with the transition to international finance capital. And it was there that superfluity was divided, within and against itself, and divided again. It was divided into waste and glorious abundance. But waste was divided into human and material filth, remnant and excrescence, on one hand, and a source of renewed value and second boon, on the other. So, too, abundance was doubled and divided into the usable and the disposable, and once again, into satiety and a drive for conversion and expansion.

Back to the Future

For Paul Kruger (and the Boer powers that he represented), the Republic's second president, gold was not so much a sign or symbol of filth, as it was an omen: a force that he feared would dislodge and destroy the white separatist rural society that had only recently established itself far from the colonial port city of Cape Town, with its freed slaves and Malay Muslim servants, its creolizing mercantilism and (often violent, but sometimes desired) interracial promiscuity. A. P. Cartwright ventriloquized Kruger's pious anxiety as follows:

> Do not talk to me of gold, the element which brings more dissension, misfortune and unexpected plagues with its trail than benefits. . . . Pray and implore Him who has stood by us that He will continue to do so, for I tell you today that every ounce of gold taken from the bowels of our soil will yet have to be weighed up with rivers of tears, with the life-blood of thousands of our best in the defense of that soil, the lust of others yearning for it solely because it has the yellow metal in abundance.[36]

Having been forged in flight, on the backs of the Voortrekkers' insistent agrarianism and their resentment of abolition in the Cape Colony, the Transvaal government feared the arrival into its austerely antimodernist rural world, of the "Uitlanders" (foreigners) not only from the Cape Colony but from throughout the British empire and Europe more generally.

Nonetheless, in a manner that displays a nationalist pragmatism somewhat at odds with the moral conservatism it claimed to express, the Volksraad (government) would resist the influx by hiring experts and forming alliances with individuals from that same empire, strangers from those same strange lands. Personal friendships and contractual politics were a crucial element of statecraft as well as of economic influence. Opportunism did not always conform to the ethnonational and racial divisions that animated the legislative realm or that would be centered in the historiographies of later periods.[37] Thus, in 1885, only a year after the Transvaal recovered its sovereignty following the British Annexation in 1877, and even before the famous auriferous conglomerates of the Witwatersrand Main Reef series were discovered at Farm Langlaagte, Kruger's Volksraad appointed an assayer and chemist in the person of an Englishman named William E. Dawson. Dawson, who owned his own assaying company (W. E. Dawson and Co.) and thus stood to realize considerable profits from the contract, which originated from the application for recognition in this role. His assay results alerted the government to the potential riches to be found in the region. And it was his name that appeared as guarantor on many of the prospectuses that were advertised in the local newspapers, as stocks were floated and investors sought. He was the beguiling Uitlander face of the nascent industry and the symbol of its scientific verity. If he also bore the aura of Boer rectitude by virtue of his association with the Volksraad, it neither curtailed his entrepreneurial ambitions nor mitigated the fraudulent misrepresentations that took place in the back rooms of hotels, where "mine-agents were running around all day offering gold-mining prospects and shares to the travelers" and when "even a man taking his midday nap could on waking find such a mass of printed matter thrown in through the open window that he felt giddy."[38]

In any case, and despite the shameless dissimulation that the brokers practiced and that would culminate, in 1895, in the collapse of the international market in South African stocks (pejoratively referred to by the Europeans as the "Kaffir market"), Dawson's confidence in his results and what they portended can be judged by the fact that he also applied, in that same year of financial catastrophe, to supply electric lights to Potchefstroom. This modest city and trading center established by the Voortrekkers was to be transformed into a regional hub by the influx of prospectors on the Far West Rand when it opened. He died before he could realize the opportunity, or before losing his money, as so many others would in that fateful year, when resentful Uitlanders attempted their first coup against Kruger's Transvaal regime in the form of the Jameson Raid.[39]

If Dawson's combination of scientific and entrepreneurial energies was common at the time, there was a simultaneous proliferation of more amateur activity. In the same year that Dawson was recognized as official government assayer, the Volksraad also began offering free courses on the subject of minerology, taught in Dutch (the autonomization of the Dutch-Malay creole, Afrikaans, was yet to be accomplished) by a Gröningen-educated botanist, naturalist, and mineralogist named Jacob Wilhelm Fockens.[40] Amid the growing flurry of gold-dreaming activity, crushing equipment was being set up on farms where richer finds were anticipated, but until that point, large scale capitalist interest had been almost entirely absent. Thus, in 1875, the first company established to survey and develop mining on the Main Reef, the Nil Desperandum Co-Operative Quartz Company, advertised its prospectus with capital of only

£850 ($4750 US), in thirty-four shares of £25 ($140 US).[41] This was a tiny offering when compared with that of the more capacious (although still modest by international standards) and multimineral South African Republic Mining Company, which was floated in 1853 in the amount of £10,000 ($48,900 US) at two thousand shares of £5 ($24.40 US) each. The small scale of the first offerings reveals just how insignificant gold was as a part of the mineral industry only twelve years before the first find of the Main Reef.[42] It paled next to the joint stock companies formed to mine gold elsewhere in the country, such as that created by Edward Button, who had resigned his position as gold commissioner of the South African Republic to raise funds in England for his mine at Eesterling (on the Pietersberg Greenstone Belt, in what is now Limpopo). In 1872, with the assay results from alluvial quartz obtained on his farm, he raised £50,000 ($272,000 US) in £10 shares ($54.40 US) for his newly formed Trans-Vaal Gold Mining Company, Ltd. That stirred, though it did not yet rouse, the behemoth of speculative capital in the metropole, promising that outlet for expenditure that the empire craved and that capital required. When Thomas Baines encountered Button in 1873, he was returning from London to what was then Natal Colony with a "powerful 12 stamp battery, and suitable steam engine," as well as a "crushing apparatus on the pneumatic principle."[43] His ambitions were thus not merely speculative but rather were aimed at relatively large-scale extraction. He was an industrial man.

The initial discoveries at Eesterling led the Volksraad to revise the Gold Law and asserted state title and oversight of all mining rights and activities. Henceforth, it not only tolerated mining but also began actively encouraging it, offering rewards for the discovery of gold: £500 ($2770 US) for five hundred ounces of gold generated in the first twelve months; £750 ($4,160 US) for five hundred to one thousand ounces, and £1,000 ($5550 US) for production of more than one thousand ounces. Later, the Gold Law was amended so that £500 ($2770 US) were paid to anyone discovering a field on which three thousand licenses were issued in the first twelve months.[44] The Law would be frequently amended—often eliciting pique from mining capitalists, although it was later recognized by the Chamber of Mines leadership to be an extremely generous (for capital) legislative structure within which profits could be pursued and industry developed.

Eesterling would be in operation until the Second Anglo-Boer war broke out in 1899, but during that period, the center of investment shifted to the Witwatersrand, which would become the pivot of the spinning gold world within a decade. Initially, however, it was not in productive mining but rather in pure speculation that the pounds flowed. In 1890, fifteen years after the Nil Desperandum Co-Operative Quartz Company was established, the industry centered there could boast capital invested in the amount of twenty-two million pounds. By 1899, the number had grown to seventy-five million pounds and by 1914, at the commencement of World War I, it had grown to one hundred and twenty-five million pounds.[45] The prospect of such profits made a drug of gold, and its pursuit became an addiction.

The astonishing increase in investment and profits, as Charles van Onselen has so vividly shown, had its corollary in the transformation of scattered camps of prospectors and diggers into a thriving frontier and financial hub centered in Johannesburg, or, as it was known then, and as it is often still referred to by migrants and other black South Africans, Egoli. The city of gold. Just as Trollope had predicted. The population of Johannesburg alone grew from three thousand to more than one hundred thousand in the first decade after the strike at Langlaagte.[46] Is there any wonder that Kruger's agriculturally oriented Volksraad was frightened?

Its efforts to stave off the political influence of the newcomers (who were quickly becoming a numerical majority), through the insistence on a fourteen-year residency before naturalization and the franchise could be obtained, was at best a deferral of the inevitable. This would become a key source of discontent among Uitlanders, and, ultimately, an alibi for British imperial intervention—first in the Jameson Raid and then in the Anglo-Boer War (1899–1902). And all of this took place within a decade. The velocity of transformation was not, however, the same everywhere; and the product was less a new mode of being, than it was a radical heterogenization of the social field. This transformation was entirely inassimilable to the neat stages of the mode-of production narrative or to the later concept of a mixed mode, which was offered for a while (especially in 1970s South African historiography) as a solution to the analytic problem of accounting for an unstable and striated field across which individuals and groups of many languages, historical traditions, and political persuasions moved and were moved at different times.

In 1886, within a few months of gold's discovery on the Witswatersrand, the newspapers of South Africa, and especially those English-language papers in Cape Town and Port Elizabeth, began printing the prospectuses and offerings of the companies that were buying up stakes on the Witwatersrand. These papers had different headings, used different type-fonts, and arranged the announcements differently, but the advertisements were identical in other respects, having been issued by the companies themselves. What differentiated the newspapers was the material that surrounded the financial discourse of the mining companies and that carried the traces of local city life: the addresses of merchants and their services, items for sale, properties to rent or buy, amusements to be enjoyed and fashions to be worn. These smaller boxes of text and lithographic images abutted each other like so many buildings in an urban milieu—or so many stakes and plots on a cartographic plane. For example, in the *Port Elizabeth Telegraph*, the prospectus for the Paarl-Pretoria Goldmining and Exploration Company, which was announcing the Paarl syndicate's acquisition of a quarter of the Langlaagte property, appeared to the left of that of the Deepkloof Gold Mining Company. The latter boasted that its property abutted the already famous Langlaagte territory. Both companies legitimated their offerings with summaries of Dawson's assay reports. The paper also featured ads for Callard & Bowsers' Butter-Scotch confections; Little's Chemical Fluid and Powder Dip to treat sheep scab; Nanucci's cleaning and dying, including feather cleaning services (the boom in ostrich feathers, which had lasted for a decade starting in 1875, had left many wardrobes full); annuities from the Liverpool and London and Globe Insurance Company; Waters' quinine wine; the Port Elizabeth Foreign Bible Society; and the Clan Line of steamers.[47] The *Cape Times*, by contrast, featured numerous other gold prospectuses, and in the paper's left-hand column carried several "wanted ads," including one for female compositors ("six first-class hands" were sought). The *Times'* much larger, urbane audience could also find out about the "China crepes" and "the most fashionable Dress Material of the Season," as well as the "Prettiest Selections of Paris Trimmed Hats and Bonnets seen in Cape Town in a long time" from "Busy Bee" hatters and hosiers. Even "Zulu hats"—an early example of ethnic fashion—could be had, along with birthday cards, by those who were also invited to consider a vacation at the "summer resort" otherwise known as the Sea Point Hotel, operated by its proprietor W. C. Norman.[48] If one needed evidence that the Uitlanders were oriented toward Europe, and that their aesthetic and consumer tastes demanded its reproduction in South Africa, the advertisements in the newspapers would surely suffice.

The feather-wearing ladies with their French lace, and the quinine-sipping gentlemen with their waistcoats and kid gloves, came to reside in the vicinity of the rougher European diggers, on whom they depended but with whom they shared little except an interest in gold and an antipathy to the agrarian Boers' devotion to moral restraint and economic self-sufficiency. The Chamber of Mines would later describe this motley gathering of mainly white prospectors as "the people, transplanted from all parts of the world," whose supposedly "common interest" the Chamber claimed to represent.[49] Some years later, in 1924, Sol Plaatje would wryly describe White "Randites" in an idiom that evokes both the geological and the anthropological discourses within which South Africa has since been represented: as "an heterogeneous ethnological conglomeration."[50] They came from England and Cornwall, but also from parts of Eastern Europe, the United States, and Australia. At the Kimberley diamond fields, from which much of the early capital for the gold industry would come, prospectors had included a significant number of black diggers (albeit still a minority). In 1875, they accounted for 120 of 757 male and female claim owners. By 1883, however, all had been bought out except Reverend Gwayi Tyamzashe, who has gone down in history as the last black stakeholder on the diamond fields. "Thereafter," as V. L. Allen writes, "the role of Africans was purely as wage labour."[51] This early racialization of the mining industry at Kimberley determined the nature of the gold industry in the Transvaal to a considerable degree, both in conception and in method. One might even say that the gold industry perfected what had only been rehearsed in the diamond fields, while providing it with its retrospectively discovered purpose, namely, to finance an economy on which all other economies would be grounded by virtue of a global investment in gold's phantasmatic status as money's truth.

Detour: Shadowlands

It is necessary to pause, here, and consider the economic preconditions of these historical processes.

Henri Lefebvre has remarked, in a vein not far from Arendt's, that "from its very beginnings, the era of finance capitalism was characterized by the extreme abundance of unfixed capital on the move, seeking investments—or avoiding them in a series of *exoduses*, some unobtrusive, some turbulent." He assumes that this unfixed capital was moving in pursuit of "some safe haven."[52] In fact, there were a variety of different rationales for that movement, structurally and affectively. Moreover, these motives changed over time as the status of gold changed and as the international economy came increasingly under the sway of a gold standard. Marx writes, "gold or silver *as crystallisation of money* is, on the one hand, not only the product of the circulation process but actually its *sole stable product*."[53] In fact, this strangely stable liquidity is a retrospectively valorized quality, generated in the very process of expanded exchange. A reading of Marx on gold and money can help us understand this development. We note that the thought and forms of economic practice on which he brought his critique to bear were the same thought and forms of economic practice that were generating those superfluous men whom Arendt described trudging and sailing from the metropole to that space at the limits of empire where another much larger group of people would be treated as wastage. And all this unfolded because of gold's supposedly natural capacity to generate surplus, to materialize wealth, and to transform itself into anything.

It is no coincidence that Marx's theorization of the intimacy between gold's superfluity and its function as a form of appearance of money developed at the time of the great Californian and Australian gold rushes (beginning in 1848 and 1851, respectively), which were also spurs to exploration in southern Africa.[54] Certainly, there had been discoveries of gold before, but the great nineteenth-century rushes were distinctively marked by the international scope of their attractions and the intensity of the exploitation as well as by the rapidity with which individual diggings were bought up and transformed by capitalists, who did not so much instigate the initial prospecting as appropriate it. This pattern reached its apogee in South Africa under the "group system," which, unlike the modes of exploiting gold and silver in the Americas under Spanish and Portuguese imperial rule, was not primarily oriented toward the provisioning of state coffers but rather toward the increase of private wealth and capital. This was enabled, however, by the state, both the British imperial state and those states—especially Germany and France—whose financial regulatory regimes facilitated the money markets and capitalization of the industry.

At its most basic, Marx's concept of superfluity means uselessness: "the commodity which has the least utility as an object of consumption or instrument of production will best serve the needs of *exchange as such*."[55] Here, "uselessness" is less an attribute of an object than the outcome of a complex series of negations. Marx is not speaking of individual exchanges, but of exchange in general, in the abstract, although this abstraction emerges through and as a result of innumerable material and sensible processes. For exchange as such to appear, a historically emergent concept requires a form, and it was as such a "form of appearance" that gold figures in his analysis. To say so implies that gold is not only matter but also its own representation: body and shadow both.

This conception of an apparently material object serving as the appropriate expression of abstraction drew the frustrated ire of many early readers, not least George Bernard Shaw, who would not travel to South Africa until 1932, but who reviewed *Capital* just as news of the Witwatersrand discoveries was grabbing the headlines in Britain. In that early, unsympathetic account, Shaw complained that Marx had lost sight of the way in which people actually calculate value: "men are governed in production by the painfulness of their efforts, and in exchange by their desire for the wares they seek, rather than by calculations of the labour embodied in wares."[56] Nor was Shaw's response unusual. The belief that value is an expression of objects' desirability, calculated in terms of that which is willingly sacrificed to obtain them, was intrinsic to liberal theories of the time, which construed sociality in a contractual idiom. Georg Simmel crowns this tradition with his famous assertion that "objects are not difficult to acquire because they are valuable, but we call those objects valuable that resist our desire to possess them." For Simmel, this determination of value by desire was linked to a conception of social life oriented by sacrifice (a notion he shared with the Durkheimian school): "Sacrifice is not only the condition of specific values, but the condition of value as such; . . . it is not only the price to be paid for particular established values, but the price through which alone values can be established."[57] Privileged in Simmel's formulation was the psychic element of exchange, for in addition to the emotional investment or intellectual calculations made by sacrificing subjects, he was interested in the connections generated through sacrifice. That is to say, he was interested in the subjectivity of exchange only insofar as he was interested in the problem of the social. But, at least in *Capital* and the writings on political economy, Marx was not talking about what motivates subjects of exchange in any psychologistic or transhistorical sense. He was addressing the question of how a particular system of value encourages people to believe that their calculations of what they should receive as recompense for their labors (by virtue of pain, skill, and time) and what they should expend in pursuit of commodities (to satisfy needs or desires) are the expression of an equivalence between price and value, wage, and labor. The singular contribution of Marx's analysis is to show that this equivalence is an illusion, the extraction of surplus by capital being the source of that wealth whose form of expression becomes, at a certain moment, gold—and all that it can buy—when converted into coin and other representations of itself.

To say this is to open a space between gold in its material, sensible form and gold in its signifying function. Indeed, this division is a crucial element of all commodities and the reason for gold's particular function as the commodity *par excellence*, but it is also that which can be extracted and abstracted from commodities to enable their mutual substitution in a relation of illusory equivalence. Thus, "the price or money-form of commodities is, like their form of value generally, quite distinct from their palpable and real bodily form; it is therefore a purely ideal or notional form. Although invisible, the value of iron, linen and corn exists in these very articles: it is signified through their equality with gold, even though *this relation with gold exists only in their heads, so to speak.* The guardian of commodities must therefore lend them his tongue, or hang a ticket on them, in order to communicate their price to the outside world."[58]

In *Capital*, gold is this guardian, this signifying entity that lends its tongue to the commodity, whose value would otherwise lay secreted within. As a "mere commodity, gold is not money," but its destiny is to function as money nonetheless. Somewhat strangely, Marx says, this is because money is in itself already gold (or silver): "Gold and silver are not by nature money, but money consists by its nature of gold and silver."

A caveat has to be introduced. Gold and silver *do not always* function as money, and their capacity to do so conflicts with their capacity to function as commodity and to thus be consumed. Given that many different commodities have functioned as money in the course of human history, the privileged status of silver and gold are generally assumed to be a function of their natural attributes: divisibility, durability, portability, malleability, homogeneity, and luster. But these attributes become relevant only when a certain spatiotemporal scale of exchange arises, when the translocality and rate of exchange develops to a degree that such qualities become relevant. This is what Farouk Stemmet terms the social specification of gold's capacity to function as a measure of value. He rightly insists that the material qualities of precious metals are useful only when the forms of exchange require the attributes that they possess.[59]

Two developments condition the emergence of gold as a money commodity in this analysis. The first is the development and growth of trade among internally differentiated and mutually distinct societies across vast distances at relatively and increasingly high velocities. Such trade will require a substance that is homogeneous and divisible. The second development is the scarcity of the metal itself. In Stemmet's account, it is only when silver ores and placer gold deposits become relatively depleted, when they "begin to run out." that they acquire sufficient scarcity to be withdrawn from the realm of commodities for consumption. Silver never appears in such a form—that is, in placer form, although restrictions or monopolies on its use and access to ores affected its depletion quite as much as the exhaustion of placer deposits for gold. Even so, "running out" is a relative concept and should be understood in tandem with the costs of production rather than with the absolute disappearance of a metal. During the gold rushes of the sixteenth and seventeenth centuries, in West Africa and in the Americas, the world's gold and silver economies experienced a relatively sudden devaluation of both metals. As Stemmet notes, this is not simply because more such precious metal was circulating in the world, but because of the mode of its production, namely plunder: "a method far more productive than mining"—if, that is, productivity is understood from the point of view of capital.[60] From the perspective of the European plunderers, the mines of West Africa and the Americas, including both the technologically intensive silver mines, and the technologically simpler alluvial gold mines, appeared like so many placer deposits. After the near exhaustion of the mines of Potosí and the Americas, silver's value became linked to production costs, whereas the gold rushes of the nineteenth century, initially driven by surface mining, made gold seem to be available at relatively constant and indeed low productions costs. So, gold could appear to be a more ideal and certain currency—*insofar* as the idea of money was that it was a mere medium of exchange and not, first and foremost, a commodity.

Shaw had opened his review of *Capital* with the terse sequence of questions and answers with which he believed Marx had started his analysis: "what is money? Money is value materialised in gold. 'Gold, as gold, is exchange value itself.'" This was the translation to which Shaw had access, but it is not quite what Marx had written. The German original reads somewhat differently: "*Umgekehrt gilt das Goldmaterial nur als Wertwerköperung, Geld. Est is reel daher Tasuchwert.*" The Ben Fowkes translation renders this, more aptly, as "the material of gold ranks only as the materialization of value as money. It is therefore in reality exchange-value."[61] It is easy to understand how Shaw could have been confused by the tautological statement, "gold, as gold, is exchange value itself." But even if this is not quite what Marx had written, it is not easy to grasp how and why money is not reducible to gold, although gold is its historically natural form, or that gold is *both* commodity and money, even when money takes the form of gold.

This is where the question of superfluity enters. As they become rarer, precious metals become less available for consumption, or as Marx says, "their direct utility for consumption and production recedes while, because of their rarity, they better represent superfluity, the form in which wealth originates."[62] The oddity of this development is that, once it has occurred, its product seems to have been generated spontaneously. Moreover, this spontaneity is precisely the mark of the historical process, as opposed to a deliberative act. In other words, gold is not money by fiat, but by habit-forming practice. Only history generates the appearance of spontaneity; contractual deliberation is visible as artifice and often as artlessness. Nonetheless, spontaneity seems to be natural. If it had the quality of divine miracle, conjuration, or even accident, it could not be counted on in the future. Only repetition makes second nature. Only history can make gold appear to have been given by nature as that which is destined to become money and, thus, wealth.

From the outside, says Marx. *"From the outside, they* [silver and gold] *represent superfluity, the form in which wealth originates."*[63] Because gold represents superfluity does not mean, of course, that it was directly implicated in the creation of that social superfluity of which Arendt wrote and for which the British empire sought its outlet in southern Africa. Gold assumes its specific and ambivalent role in this theater of wealth precisely because it is also a specific kind of commodity, the commodity that represents all other commodities, the signifier of value that signifies all values, in short, the form of appearance of general equivalence—where it is finally cloaked in mystery. It is the linkage between superfluity and money per se that is at stake. The relationship between these two kinds of superfluity (of Arendt's men and Marx's money) depends on a complex mediation that links the epistemic valorization and aesthetic investment in gold with its specific functions in an international economy emerging at a particular moment. That moment is the moment of high imperialism, whence a truly world order would emerge. And that process also entailed the appropriation of a prior historical development:

> Gold functioning as a medium of circulation assumes a specific shape, it becomes a *coin*. . . .] Coins are pieces of gold whose shape and imprint signify that they contain weights of gold as indicated by the names of the money of account such as pound sterling, shilling, etc. Both the establishing of the mint-price and the technical work of mining devolve upon the State. Coined money assumed a *local* and *political character*, it uses different national languages and wears different national uniforms, just as does money of account. Coined money circulates therefore in the *internal* sphere of circulation of commodities, which is circumscribed by the boundaries of a given community and separated from the *universal* circulation of the world of commodities.[64]

There are, of course, numerous cases in which the technical work of mining does not devolve on the state, and the determination of mint price is not a mere matter of sovereign fiat. But the more important point is the discernment of a tendency within money, as distinct from coin, that breaks local boundaries and opens local worlds to the forces of the foreign, bringing into contact what was previously often in conflict. Unlike the more narrowly circumscribed coin, bullion—that is to say, gold before its minting, gold not yet inscribed with the mark of a particular sovereign—has the capacity to traverse national boundaries. The difference is that "between the denomination of the coin and the denomination of its metal weight. What appears as a difference of denomination in the latter case, appears as a difference of shape in the former. Gold coins can be thrown into the crucible and thus turned again into gold *sans phrase*, just as conversely gold bars have only to be sent to the mint to be transformed into coin."[65] The world-changing nature of this development could not but terrorize those who cleave to the narrow circumference of their familiar worlds—men like Kruger. Invoking Shakespeare's *Timon of Athens*, Marx gave voice to the sentiment of insular communities in the face of this bond-breaking capacity— such as the Boer Republic's hostility toward outsiders or Uitlanders: "'Thou visible God!/That solder'st close impossibilities,/And mak'st them kiss!'"[66]

The difference, as well as the relation between coin and money, or gold in its distinct phases as commodity and medium of exchange, is a temporal one, which Marx describes in the idiom of interruption. That is, circulation entails the movement of coin, but the money status of this coin, which Marx terms "ephemeral," arises only when circulation is interrupted.[67] Which begs the question: When is gold a commodity and when is it money? Marx's answer to his own question, which he posed as "*Wie, warum, wodurch Ware Geld ist?*" (How, why and through what the commodity is money?), may illuminate gold's status in the development of monetary relations, but it begins with an enigma. Having argued that gold's function as coin is spontaneous *because* it is historically produced, rather than contractually and situationally determined, Marx then argues that "this physical object, gold or silver in its crude state becomes, immediately upon its emergence from the bowels of the earth, the direct incarnation of all human labour." But, as he explains, this "magic of money," results from a "false semblance" created when "the universal equivalent became identified with the natural form of a particular commodity, and thus crystalized into a money-form."[68] At this point in *Capital*, having delineated the historical production of a "false resemblance," which then generates the sensation of a natural function for gold, namely to displace the relations between people onto the relations between things, Marx introduces the discussion of the fetish character of commodities. Marx also argues that the function of money "as a measure of value is the *necessary form of appearance* of the measure of value which is immanent in commodities, namely labour-time."[69]

The aim of *Capital* is, of course, to get behind or beyond the "false resemblance" and to expose the ostensible truth of "labour-time," whose dissimulation constitutes the basis of surplus value extraction in Marx's analysis. Under contemporary conditions of mass unemployment, wageless labor, and the return to piecework (as in South Africa's abandoned mines), the labor-theory of value now lacks persuasiveness (although that argument must wait until later in this book). But the prospectors and the financiers of South Africa were driven by that false semblance. The self-impoverishing diggers and the sometimes self-bankrupting investors did not pursue gold because they believed it constituted the appropriate and universal form of labor-time. They sought gold because it could function as a commodity, and thus it could be sold, but also because it could be speculated on. And it could be speculated on because it could be dissimulated in and by the very tokens of value that it ostensibly grounded. Money could be made not only because gold enjoyed a double destiny, as coin and as the body in which wealth could be incarnated, but also because of gold's function in the imagination.

Today, informal miners in the region of which I write generally refer to gold, even when it is embedded in the rock, as money, using one or another cognate of the word *imali* (X/Z). They use this term for the sand that is suspended in water during sluicing, for that which is being amalgamated with mercury, and for the glinting nugget of smelted metal at the end of their arduous manual processes. The term originally referred to valuables in general, or stores of value, but among the miners whom I know, this older signification has given way to one much closer to that which Marx describes under the name of money. Rarely, do they refer to gold (*igolidi*), whose derivation from English already bespeaks the foreignness of this economy, and their lexical choices reveal the potent remainder of the transformations that were affected by the gold industry more than a century ago. Indeed, there is a profound resemblance between the discourse of these polyglot migrants and that which emerges from Marx's texts. It is a question of the name—of the name of gold and of what gold names.

"The name of the thing is entirely external to its nature."[70] This statement appears in *Capital*. In the earlier *Contribution to a Critique of Political Economy*, Marx had written, "The names of coins become . . . detached from the substance of money and exist apart from it in the shape of worthless scraps of paper."[71] There had been long and vociferous debate wherever this substitution had taken place; nearly every state in which paper currency had substituted for metallic specie had seen riotous opposition, and often enough, it was perceived as a radical derealization of value, and a threat to the divinely sanctioned order of meaning. Goethe, writing shortly after Britain's establishment of a gold standard, but while most of Europe was still operating on the basis of bimetallism, gave this anxiety its lasting poetic (and antifiat) form in *Faust* (1832). There, the emperor, amazed, asks of the new paper currency, "And people value this the same as honest gold?" He is assured that "there is no way these bills can be recaptured;/they fled with lightning speed and are dispersed./

The money changers' shops are all wide open; there every note is honored and exchanged–/at discount, to be sure." But Mephistopheles, the advocate of paper, who lauds the "notes" as "handy," also speaks of "phantom money."[72] At the end of *Faust*, Part II, the holders of paper contracts are unable to convert them into gold. The phantom money's relation to gold has been a delusion conjured by the devil.

This is precisely the phantom nature of money that Marx would discern, not because it is a mere shadow of gold but because this penumbral attribute of gold is what permits it to function *as money*.

Among the most enigmatic and important distinctions made in Marx's efforts to analyze this function is that between representation and symbolization. Here, the task of reading him is made difficult by his constant acknowledgment of colloquial discourse, and his simultaneous insistence on a more precise terminology: "Money is not a symbol, just as the existence of a use-value in the form of a commodity is not a symbol."[73] So, what is the paper note that "stands for" a particular value measured in gold? Why is it not a symbol for Marx, as it was in the common sense of nineteenth-century bourgeois economists—and as it is for many still today? In this case, the term symbol denotes the specifically autonomized quality of the representation and is quite distinct from other kinds of signification. Marx's explanation implies that the materiality that grounds gold is itself imaginary: "The transformation of commodities into money of account in the mint, on paper or in words takes place whenever the aspect of exchange value becomes fixed in a particular type of wealth. The transformation needs the material of gold, *but only in imagination*. Not a single atom of real gold is used to estimate the value of a thousand bales of cotton in terms of a certain number ounces of gold and then to express this number is £,s,d., the names of account of the ounce."[74]

The material of gold is needed, but only in the imagination. Later, Marx provides this formulation with a narrative figuration, as follows: "gold has not sold its shadow, but uses its shadow as a means of purchase."[75] In the infinite regress of a commodity selling its shadow or rather not selling it to engage in purchase, Marx conveys the logic of a regime that drives relentlessly toward the monetization of everything, in a dizzying process of abstraction that is the condition of possibility of generalization. He concludes by asserting that the token of value is effective only when it "*represents gold* with regard to every commodity-owner"[76] *Every* commodity owner. Increasingly the tendency expressed by gold's monetization is toward universalization. Once again, however, and despite a certain automaticity that seems to inhere in the logic of money and that masquerades as a natural propensity of both gold and *homo economicus*, that tendency is a product of historical processes—things might have been otherwise. That tendency was realized in concrete forms in the age of empire that, in no small part, were enabled by the gold that came from southern Africa. Nor have recent developments in electronic money entirely displaced the special function that gold acquired a century ago by virtue of these developments. It remains in the shadows, as it were.

To reiterate: money (and not merely coin) does not originate in any primordial, presocial utility of something called real gold. Rather, from within a given tradition (and indeed from within numerous traditions), gold's value is projected backward where it comes to appear as its own ground. In attempting to explain this counterintuitive temporization, Marx proposes an analogy drawn from the realm of art history as well as from agriculture: "Painted grapes are no symbol of real grapes, but are imaginary grapes."[77] The allusion is apparently to Pliny's *Natural History*, which includes an account of a painting contest between Zeuxis and Parrhasius; Zeuxis paints grapes so realistic that the birds flock to the painting to feed on them (although he loses the competition to Parrhasis, who produces a painting so realistic that it fools even Zeuxis).[78] Marx writes, "a thing cannot be its own symbol." Images of grapes are not grapes, any more than the word *pipe*, say, is a pipe. He continues: "Even less is it possible for a light-weight sovereign to be the symbol of a standard-weight sovereign, just as the emaciated horse cannot be the symbol of a fat horse."[79] What follows is the apparently paradoxical assertion that "since gold thus becomes a symbol of itself but cannot serve as such a symbol it assumes a symbolic existence—quite separate from its own existence—in the shape of silver or copper counters in those spheres of circulation where it wears out most rapidly, namely where purchase and sales of minute amounts go on continuously."[80] In other words, copper and silver are at once substitutes and representations of gold's function, and this is achieved because of an external force that supports it without originating it. Despite clippings and the loss that results from wear and tear, copper and silver coins retain their value in nations with a stable and authoritative enough state to guarantee their value. These tokens "are, by their very nature, symbols of gold coin, not because they are made of silver or copper, not because they have value, but they are symbols in so far as they have no value. Relatively worthless things, such as *paper*, can function as symbols of gold coins."[81] Here, it is the externality or foreignness of the symbolizing medium that grants it the special eligibility to serve as symbol, in this case, copper or silver for gold. With characteristically playful syntax, catachresis, and inversions that reveal hidden asymmetries, Marx describes coinage's persistent circulation despite material debasement: gold "circulated not because it was worn, but it was worn to a symbol because it continued to circulate. Only in so far as in the process of circulation gold currency becomes a mere token of its own value can mere tokens of value be substituted for it."[82] The shadow falls away, only to rise again in the form of an image. Even gold can serve as the image of gold. In exchange, says Marx, "real gold . . . functions merely as *apparent gold*," and it is for this reason that "a token of itself can be substituted for it." The reality of "gold in circulation, is merely the reality of an electric spark."[83]

We may now understand the famous English rendition, and, from Marx's point of view, mistranslation of Mephistophele's formula in Goethe's *Faust*, Part II: "what you don't coin, that cannot be gold."[84] But how shall we understand this reference to the "spark" that courses through the field of exchange, igniting ever more desires for ever more commodities? Edouard Gourdon, whose text, *Reapers of the Night*, is quoted at the beginning of this chapter, had given his character words that resonate strongly with Marx's, and Walter Benjamin recognized their relevance for a study of gambling in his notes for the Arcades Project.[85] Something about the spark, its flashing errant immediacy, is linked to the speculator's desire to multiply his pleasures and to resist being limited in his satisfactions to only one commodity. He wants to want everything. This is why the gambler wants not just what money can buy but money itself. This in anticipation of risking money in the pursuit of obtaining even more. He is a strange kind of hoarder, always on the verge of sacrificing his present accumulation for another. His enjoyment consists of anticipating other enjoyments. In this sense, Benjamin's gambler incarnates the specific function of money *before* it becomes capital and is the antithesis of Weber's protestant capitalist who withholds his money not only from circulation but also from his own consumption by investing it in production.

The spark moves, but money, the gambler's object, is gold that is *not* in circulation. The gambler is, in this sense, a technician of rhythm and not merely a player of numbers. For the transformation between gold as commodity and gold as money is not a matter of the coin's two sides. It is rather a function of the alternations between stasis and circulation. Marx writes: "Gold becomes money, as distinct from coin, first by being withdrawn from circulation and hoarded, then by entering circulation as a non-means of circulation, finally however by breaking through the barriers of domestic circulation in order to function as universal equivalent in the world of commodities." It is here, when it ascends to the status of "universal equivalent," when it functions as the "material aspect of abstract wealth," not one commodity in particular but all commodities in general, that it "becomes *world money.*"[86] It is still not yet capital. It must become the object of investment, a second if only fictitious withholding, to be capital. We are not there yet, but we may conclude this detour and return to the ethnographic surface.

Dead Letters Office

A short distance from the squatter settlement in which Virgil-Umholi and Dante-Xolani were walking and talking about the vanished plenitude of the now-closed mine are a series of buildings, mostly in ruin now, which once housed the company's administrative offices. They include the relatively sturdy old drawing offices, which are presently used to house a nongovernmental organization devoted to community-based animal welfare, the personnel office, and several other structures, including houses that have entirely collapsed, and the remnants of a rail depot where the cars transporting ore arrived for unloading. The latter was once a grand building with vaulted ceilings and framed glass windows—all of the glass is now broken and laying in shards on the cement floor where grasses protrude from the cracks. The old tracks are still visible, as are the remnants of entry and exit signs above the tall doorframes, although every season sees more of the edifice vanish or fall to the earth. Not far away, posters announcing hours and pay distribution schedules, although faded, still adhered to the window of the personnel office, which, tucked away behind other buildings and sheltered by trees (some of which now grow in the midst of the abandoned rooms), was relatively well-preserved until a year ago. The name "Rand Mines Gold and Uranium In-House Safety Competitions" formed the heading of an unspoiled yellow sign that had somehow resisted the depredations of weather and theft. Beneath that title, on the left, were inscribed the names of the five still-operating companies that were under Rand Mines' control when the operations here finally came to a halt: Blyvooruitzicht, Durban Roodepoort Deep, East Rand Proprietary Mines, Harmony, and Rand Mines Milling and Mining. In the columns to the right of these names, empty spaces seemed to await entries for the accident rates of the previous three years, the current year, the percentage change, and the ranking among the five subsidiary companies.

The sign stopped me. Here in the ruins was a cipher for that group system that had emerged amid the rush to consolidate claims all those years ago in 1893, when Alfred Beit and Julius Wernher joined up with Hermann Eckstein (who would also serve as the first president of the Chamber of Mines), to form Rand Mines, offering investors shares that covered both surface and deep-level operations, while using the immediate profits of the shallow mines to subsidize deep-level drilling on the assumption that the long run would pay. The generational depth of the names (some very old, some more recent) spoke of the complex history of consolidation, merger, acquisition, and liquidation that had been inaugurated. The sign was large, the names of the mines neatly lettered on the yellow backdrop, which measured about two by three meters. But no one ever stopped to read it, as far as I could tell.

Was the sign a remnant of the past or of a radical amnesia unreachable from within contemporary discourse?

Virgil-Umholi and Dante-Xolani never spoke about the group system. But they frequently described the mines recalled from the worst era in their own memory, that of the evictions, as owned by "Germans." I did not initially understand this reference, and I wondered if I had misheard it. What Germans? Did these isiZulu- and isiNdebele-speaking men assimilate Afrikanerdom to a more generic ethnolinguistic category of the Germanic? Did they assimilate the Germans to the English, with whom they were often allied as Uitlanders in the days of Kruger (even though many Boers would ally with the Germans of German Southwest Africa in opposition to the British in World War I)? I asked for understanding: "Who were the Germans?" Neither Virgil-Umholi nor Dante-Xolani could or would say more than that it was a well-known fact that this mine was a German mine. "They owned it. It was a German mine. It was like that. Germans ran this mine." Did they speak German, I asked? "It was Afrikaans here, and English." And all the languages of southern Africa. I asked again, this time differently, "Where did the Germans come from?" Silence indicted my question.

The effects of the past may be transmitted below and beyond discursive or reflective knowledge, conveyed in secrets and silent gestures, encrypted in stories and borne along in the flow of associations. They occasionally arise in the form of a question, a shudder, or an uncanny sensation prompted by the scent of a particular fruit, a musical refrain, or the taste of cement in the moment that a storm breaks open. Psychoanalysis provides us with an idiom and an analysis of those reencounters with the past that emerge in the aftermath of repression (the uncanny), to shock and unsettle the subject who had otherwise thought herself free of these remnants. Some contemporary theorists have argued that the memory of that which one did not experience (i.e., narratives of experience that one inherits from one's forebears) may be adequately parsed with the concept of re-memory. But neither of these approaches captures the nature of the trace structure that expressed itself in the men's references to the Germans, whose apparently obvious place in the history of these ruins prohibited any further questions and testified to the depth of the second nature into which this history had been plunged for these men—by time, by repetition, and by all the forces that ensure that the signifier ultimately leaves its origin for dead.

To ask about a term's possible significations and associations is not to ask what it symbolizes or about what the speaker really meant to say. Nor is it to ask for evidence of a collective consciousness or unconsciousness.[87] The question might be better expressed as follows: What is being spoken in and through the discourse of men whose speech (like all speech) carries both more and less than they know? To ask this question is to treat it analogously to the way Lacan treated the story of the purloined letter. In Edgar Allen Poe's story, *The Purloined Letter*, as read by Lacan, the letter has its effects even without its contents ever being known. And this is because people respond to others responding to the fact of the letter (with alarm and secretive gestures that nonetheless must be made in public) and often by repeating those same gestures and ways of treating the letter. It is not merely a question of rumor, and thus of the mercurial transmission of a story that becomes distorted in the retelling and whose origin is lost to memory. Rather, the purloined letter acquires its force because of the sequence of specular scenarios, in which one person seeing and acting toward the missive (the signifier) in a particular manner (including fear at being discovered with such a letter) solicits a relay of comparable gestures—without having read its contents.

If the reference to Germans is the letter, in the analogy I have just constructed, then the source of the letter's effectivity in my own narrative lies in the fact that it shows us something about how the symbolic order operates in the specific context of the gold economy. It shows us how the form of speculation at the origin of the gold industry operated and, as we have seen, depended both on something being occluded and by others responding to the investments that they saw being made by the men who claimed to know something more than what was visible to everyone else. The transformation of that radical speculation into a secured investment in the industrial extraction of gold was a kind of reverse alchemy and an inversion of the specular economy typically associated with commodity desire, with technology being placed on the altar of display as the redemption of waste—as already stated.

In fact, Rand Mines was founded by the German-born financiers of the Wernher, Beit, and Eckstein group, who, with Rhodes's Consolidated Gold Fields, formed the most powerful of the deep-level groups in the early days of the Rand. Rand Mines would be on the verge of financial ruin after the stock collapse of 1895, perhaps because they had less access to the major German banks than their more recently arrived compatriots, Adolf Goerz and George Albu (from Mainz and Brandenburg, respectively). The company emerged victorious after the Anglo-Boer War, as a beneficiary of English imperialism even though Eckstein had been a close friend of Kruger's (Beit was Rhodes's ally). The triumph of the German-originating finance houses in the British empire was not necessarily predictable in 1895, for Kruger's relationships with the Kaiser and Germany, and concerns over the privileging of German over English companies in the tender of Transvaal government contracts, was one of the reasons adduced by Rhodes as grounds for the Jameson Raid.[88]

In this sense, perhaps, German finance, which was largely allied with British imperialism even when the English were in conflict with the Germans in South Africa, was a missive languishing in the dead letters office of the now-defunct mines. This unread but overheard letter, like that of the postman recalled by Virgil-Umholi, was still being sent. Moreover, just as Virgil-Umholi's speech about the postman had been invested in his person, and thus his personification of an entire structure, so too the talk about "the Germans" allowed the history of finance to become a narrative about individual owners. One can see how the story of capital becomes that of capitalists in this account—as it does in so much political economic analysis. Marx warned us against this kind of characterological reading of economic structures, even as he invested the specular scene in which "the Worker" (a figure irreducible to the myriad workers who would form a class) would finally confront Capital, through the figure of "the Capitalist."[89] Nonetheless, characterology is difficult to resist when faced with a history in which so few people dominated so much of the field of capital. In 1887, Cecil Rhodes and Chares Rudd formed Consolidated Gold Fields. Two years later, in 1889, Barney Barnato formed Johannesburg Consolidated Investment Company, at the same time that J. B. Robinson created Randfontein Estates Gold Mining Company. Julius Wernher and Alfred Beit created Rand Mines in 1893, just as George Farrar was establishing East Rand Proprietary Mines. Hermann Eckstein had started his own company in 1888, which would join with Wernher and Beit's undertaking soon thereafter, to form the Wernher, Beit, and Eckstein group. These men and their five companies were later to be joined by George Albu, who started General Mining and Finance Corporation (later to spawn Gencor, when combined with Union Corporation) and Adolf Goerz, of the eponymous A. Goerz Company. Consolidated Mines Selection Trust was to be founded last, in 1897, and would ultimately emerge, along with Consolidated Gold Fields, as one of the system's most powerful companies when, under the stewardship of Ernest Oppenheimer, it became the Anglo American Corporation in 1917.

Remarking the "distinctively international" and "concentrated" nature of the financial power at the origin of the South African gold industry, John Atkinsons Hobson counted thirteen men at the center of the industry. They controlled an astonishing 114 out of 124 mining houses on the Rand, typically through structures that involved financial houses functioning as "parent companies" to publicly traded subsidiary mining corporations, with which they shared administrative and accounting support, and whose labor and purchasing needs they distributed across their subsidiaries.[90] Each mining company was, however, floated as an individual company; control was exercised at the level of the boards of directors but mainly through the group members' control of majority shareholder status. The group or its members were also typically the titleholders of the land that was needed to mine. Having purchased it in the early days of stakes consolidation, when such land was cheap, the groups' owners then sold the land to their own subsidiary mining companies in return for shares in the company. According to Kubicek,

> ... all the mining and finance companies operating on the Rand, issued the lion's share of its author capital to vendors whose contribution to the company's assets in the form of mining claims and cash was invariably exaggerated. In other words the vendors obtained the vast bulk of the shares very cheaply while the regular shareholders, who put up much of the working capital, often had to pay a premium to obtain an interest in the company. Dividends calculated on the basis of a percentage of the par value of a share often appeared impressive. And for vendors, they were. For outside shareholders who had not got in on the ground floor and who often paid several times the par value for their shares, they were not.[91]

During the boom years, the financiers achieved fantastic profits in this form—without ever having to undertake actual mining.[92] And it was the delirious image of such profits, seen by others in the specular relay that lies at the heart of all jointstock markets—whether they are busting or booming— that spurred that gold-mindedness of which we have been speaking. In these theaters of fantastical moneymaking, the signatures of Randlords (many of whom would later be granted Baronets in England) were but masks. Their proper names are metonyms for the larger forces of capital burning across the Highveld.

Addressing the need to distinguish between capital and capitalists in the analysis of South African history, and to resist its tendency to make biographical detail the medium of heroic (mythic) individualism, Donald Denoon has noted how volatile and changeful the policies, practices, and apparent commitments of different capitalists were in South Africa in the early years: "The personal and political ambitions of the nominal controllers of capital were quite distinct from—and in certain cases opposed to—the needs of the capital they controlled." He then adds, wryly, that "it is very clear that capital in the Transvaal was a subtler and more imperious force than the capitalists: it has never yet lost a war."[93]

For the early speculators, who had little intention of waiting for returns on investment until the mines were in operation, gold stocks were merely a site at which money could find the means to realize the interest-bearing or money-generating capacity of money. A necessary moment of concretization in a nonteleological history that would ultimately take the form of currency speculation, investment in the mines for the men who rushed to the stock market was investment in the idea of gold *in the abstract*. This early speculation had then to become the engine of a real social abstraction, through wage labor and the creation of differentially territorialized regimes of governmentality. But once that had occurred, an inversion could take place.

Economic theorists had, from the time of the Panama Canal crisis, been trying to distinguish between speculative and other kinds of investment, and the public inquiry into the scam, effected an inversion. As Rudolf Hilferding put it: "Tempora Mutantir . . . In place of the ideal of speculation we now have speculation about an ideal condition of 'stable prices' and of the demise of speculation."[94] One problem replaced another, and the ostensible "certainty of cartel profit" acquired increasing public approval in the very moment that the South African group system emerged. Hilferding's description of the European scene could well have been applied to the South African gold mining industry: "Industrial profit incorporates commercial profit, is itself capitalized as promoter's profit, and becomes the booty of the trinity which has attained the highest form of capital as finance capital. For industrial capital is God the Father, who sent forth commercial and bank capital as God the Son, and money capital is the Holy Ghost. They are three persons united in one, in finance capital."[95]

In many ways, the South African gold industry followed the European pattern described by Hilferding—with cartelization and monopolization developing in ways that enhanced industrial power, with certain caveats. The processes by which this transformation occurred and the rationale by which it was authorized took a specific form in South Africa. The structure of argument, which is to say the form of grounding adduced from within geological reason, construed the earth as the origin of an economic necessity. In other words, it provided the tendency toward concentration that was inherent in capital with an explanation derived from nature, thus naturalizing capitalism. As a result, questions about representation gave way to those about geological nature—displacing onto an ever-receding horizon the question of why, if at all, one needs to mine gold in actuality (and at the expense of human life) for it to be available as a representation of itself.

Here, then, is the argument: As mentioned, the Chamber of Mines described the gold of the Witwatersrand as scarce: a mere "couple of commas" strewn across 1,200 pages. The metal is nonetheless quite evenly distributed, meaning that "the amount of gold per unit quantity of ore generally varies fairly smoothly in any given mine from high to low values," with the result that "if either the price of gold increases or working costs decrease, ore that was previously unpayable now becomes worth mining."[96] The gold occurs in thin reef leaders, some only a few inches thick; these are the pages of that book referred to by the Chamber of Mines. The main leader, uninterrupted, is about forty miles long and is nearly uniformly tipped at an angle of twenty-three degrees, from west to east.[97] Once the slanted nature of the reef was ascertained, the profitability of gold was linked to the possibility of consolidating the small claims made by individual diggers to create coherent units of land extending aboveground in the direction of the reef that dropped off below it. For that to happen, sufficient capital had to be expended to permit the consolidation of staked claims. This, in turn, meant that finance capital was necessary as the precondition for the establishment of the industrial "mining corporations," typically owned by the finance houses. Moreover, the more gold to be sought, and the longer the term in which it would be payable, the more necessary was a lateral consolidation of claims.

After the initial speculation on stakes (when money changed hands without any actual extraction taking place), most of the early investments and profits came from surface mining. Thus, in 1888, 97.9 percent of all dividends came from outcrop or shallow mines of less than one thousand feet in depth. Within a decade, by 1898, only 4.6 percent of dividends came from such operations.[98] This shift reflected transformations in the capital structure of the mines and not merely the deeper penetration of the earth. Charles van Onselen refers to 1888–1889 as the first of the joint stock booms, and it led in 1889, to the formalization of the Witwatersrand Chamber of Mines, a body already conceived in 1887, just one year after the first discovery on the Main Reef. It was initially composed of three mining houses, Corner House, Consolidated Gold Fields, and Robinson Group, who, together, offered to "validate" the prospectuses of the companies that were buying up the diggers' small claims for interested investors.[99] For, as much as the Volksraad had attempted to ensure the veracity of assay results, its own courses for laymen and publications by autodidacts and would-be experts (Fockens published a "manual for all who wish to learn about the minerals of the S. A. Republic") threatened to transform the drive for wish fulfillment into financial disaster for investors.

This was the scene of the industry's early, flagrant profiteering, when speculation was more akin to gambling than to investment, and when many unknowing investors were simply and "systematically defrauded."[100] The early financiers cultivated delirium, but the mirage they projected was not the same as the fever it suffered. Insider trading and market manipulation were common.[101] Most of the Randlords took their profits in the form of stock deals, mobilizing the public desire for gold that was already gripping large and small investors around the world. In the 1880s, outcrop mining brought relatively quick profits for relatively little effort, but this had already slowed by the turn of the decade, and investments were being solicited with little promise of long-term viability. The depth and dispersion of the ore was already an obstacle.[102] In London, brokers promoted stocks regardless of likely profits from production. Because the companies were listed in the Transvaal and were thus "freed from the necessity of giving a reckoning to shareholders," they often "failed to meet requirements to be dealt with on official exchanges in Europe."[103] The interests of small shareholders were in any case diluted and overwhelmed by the larger shareholders, including, for some companies, the large German banks. The decision making was thus in the hands of a few men, who, although they formed a limited number of groups, often sat on each other's boards, were friends (or enemies but collaborators), and shared interests even when their companies were in competition. Denoon sums up the situation as follows: "Buccaneering capitalists fully understood the appalling risks of capital invested in gold mining, and those on the spot chose to gamble with other people's money, and to take their own profits in the form of capital gains through 'insider trading' on the share market. Some mining capitalists did indeed invest large sums in long-term mining development, but even the most development-minded took care to manipulate the share market. They were not gamblers: they encouraged gambling, but loaded the dice."[104]

The names of these men are memorialized by street names in Johannesburg and throughout the country. They appear on many edifices throughout southern Africa (one of the main borders between South Africa and Zimbabwe is named Beitbridge) and they are inscribed on honorific monuments—some of which are now falling, or rather, being and have been felled (those to Rhodes). They were also more and other than themselves; the names of these technicians of necromancy are also metonyms for the larger process of which they became beneficiaries. And that process or *technē* has its aesthetics, which will be addressed in the next chapter.

CHAPTER 4

CYANIDE DREAMS AND THE REDEMPTION OF WASTE

Or, Snowballs in Hell

Judge Boshoff: *Yes, but now capitalism really develops and wasn't Britain powerful and because she was powerful she developed, she became an empire and then that is how capitalism, it is like a snowball, it just grows and grows?*
Biko: *Yes.*

—Steve Biko, "The Righteousness of Our Strength"

La Svengali . . . The fame of her was like a rolling snowball that had been rolling all over Europe for the last two years—wherever there was snow to be picked up in the shape of golden ducats. . . . The dream of it all came over you for a second or two—a revelation of some impossible golden age— priceless—never to be forgotten! How on earth did she do it?"

—George du Maurier, *Trilby*

We danced the dance of fools,
We celebrated the beginnings of every fashion.

—Mazisi Kunene, "The Age of Fantasy"

If you're thought of as a murderer, Dick, you canna say you're a failure. Murderers are the only popular heroes who are never forgotten. Every Englishman knows all about Dick Turpin and Eugene Aram, but not one in a million knows or cares who invented chloroform or matches. Every Johnny come lately on the Rand can tell you the story of the murder of Honey and whom they suspect, but ask 'em who discovered the main reef or the cyanide process.

—Douglas Blackburn, *Richard Hartley, Prospector*

World money, worldliness, and the cosmopolitanism of commodity capitalism were all recognized potentialities, if in displaced or unconscious form, by the leaders of the Boer Republic. These leaders often projected the responsibility for bearing these world historical forces onto the individual foreigners who, as Arendt suggested, were the byproduct as much as the agents of change. The primary status of gold in the international economy did not go uncontested, of course.[1] Bimetallists in the United States, for example, resisted its promotion as the medium for international trade and saw in its elevation an erosion of U.S. sovereignty born of Britain's efforts to reconsolidate its imperial hegemony through its South African adventures. The Coinage Act of 1873 had prohibited the minting of silver bullion into coins, but as late as 1892, this use was still being debated in Congress, where the gold standard appeared as a means to extend British imperial power through its control of U.S. debt:

> Until the passage of this law debtors could pay their bills in either gold or silver. By it contracts were changed so as to allow the creditor the right to demand gold so far as Congress had the power to so change. The change affected all contracts that were in existence at that time. Without stopping now to argue whether the act was passed by fraud or not, I do not hesitate to say that it was unjust to the debtor class of our country and to the Government as well. It was not dictated by any wise, judicious financial policy. It was confessedly the same policy that had been originated by England and followed by Germany, both creditor nations, whose financial policies are formulated by a class having fixed income and who are interested in increasing the purchase power of money.[2]

It was this sentiment that fueled the tide of national(ist) *ressentiment* incarnated with such charismatic authority by William Jennings Bryan.

After the gold rushes in the United States had abated, U.S. politicians like Bryan worried that the States would be marginalized by developments in that distant nation that, even in 1896, was producing 17 percent of the world's gold and was clearly capable of an even greater share (it would be generating

40 percent of global bullion by 1908).[3] In that year, the orator of U.S. populism addressed the Democratic National Convention with the siren song of silver in a speech referred to as "The Cross of Gold": "If they dare to come out in the open field and defend the gold standard as a good thing, we shall fight them to the uttermost, having behind us the producing masses of the nation and the world. Having behind us the commercial interests and the laboring interests and all the toiling masses, we shall answer their demands for a gold standard by saying to them, you shall not press down upon the brow of labor this crown of thorns. You shall not crucify mankind upon a cross of gold."[4]

A full-blown global gold standard would not be established for another two decades, after World War I, and before that could happen, a complex series of technological and social developments had to take place. This is how John Dos Passos narrates the events of that techno-industrial history, assessing them from the point of view of the conspiracy theorists at the heart of his first novel in the U.S.A. Trilogy: "But McArthur and Forrest, two Scotchmen in the Rand, had invented the cyanide process for extracting gold from ore, South Africa flooded the gold market; there was no need for a prophet of silver."[5]

In fact, there were three Scotsmen: John Stewart MacArthur, William Forrest, and Robert Forrest. None of them were in South Africa, although they transferred the rights for the use of their process in South Africa to the African Gold Recovery Company in 1891. Bryan had not mentioned the Rand or South Africa in his speech at all. His claim on the populist imagination referred to the accumulating influence of gold and the internationalism that it underwrote on the basis of discoveries in Australia and the Americas (and to a lesser extent, Russia), which were simultaneous with the decline in global silver production relative to gold since 1848 (from 16:1 to 4:1). By century's end, the abandonment by most European nations of silver as the basis of their currencies and its use in trade followed Britain's lead, which facilitated the integration of the international monetary order that was to ground Britain's late, if doomed, imperialist consolidation.[6]

But there had been a major hiccup, for, England's own gold stores were insufficient to underpin its currency; the pound sterling depended on gold, and Britain had a slender claim on supply, the Australian mining sector notwithstanding. This is why the newly discovered mines of South Africa presented such an irresistible object for British imperialism. The truth of Dos Passos's narrative, a truth for which his novels provide the voice but not the evidence, was still to come. The MacArthur–Forrest chemical technology did indeed constitute a lynchpin in the historical development of the Witwatersrand goldfields and of the financial transformations, as well as the sociopolitical developments, that would define the form of capital accumulation in that country. It was summoned, if also fortuitously discovered, at a point when the payability of the gold, that mass of commas in the earth-as-book, could no longer be exclusively determined by the repression of wages, even if black labor could be recruited and paid significantly less than what white minework-ers expected and received—a question that would remain permanently open, if repeatedly answered with coercive regulations and brutal enforcements.[7] The entire British financial industry depended on it, as the near collapse, in 1890, of the country's largest merchant bank, Baring Brothers, (formerly John and Francis Baring, and Co.) demonstrated.[8] But the cyanide process did more than provide a technological fix for a geological crisis. It provided more even than an economic rationale for socioeconomic and administrative practice. It provided a concept-metaphor and an aesthetics, which together transformed and intensified an entire system grounded in the idea of separation. It is to that transformation that we now turn. Let me set the scene.

Mise-en-scène

At times, such as certain winter afternoons, after the still-weak sun has burned the paraffin clouds away and the early morning frost has ceased filling the hori-zon with the faint mist of evaporation, the Highveld sky seems to take on the blue of a cyanide-poisoned lake. At such times, the world lays as if transparent and it is tempting, if one has been schooled in the British colonial curriculum, with its poetic vaults of heavenly blue, to contemplate questions of origins and cosmic significance. Such a person may be surprised to realize that a blue sky can be perceived by some as an anomaly, indeed, as the very index of a world transformed by mining. It is thus for the character Xuma, in Peter Abrahams's novel *Mine Boy*. Having recently arrived from his rural home in the Eastern Cape, Xuma is surprised by the color of the sky in the Highveld, a strange and alienating space that he knows only as the site of the gold mines. At the tran-sitional moment of the narrative, as he is seeking without finding a pedagogue to guide him into the labyrinth of strange and alienating labor, he finds only contrasts with what is familiar: "Xuma opened his eyes and looked at the sky. It was blue up there. And at home in the country it would be green now and there would be cattle on the hillside."[9]

Blue, in Xuma's fictional world and in the external world to which Abra-hams's 1946 novel refers, is the color of pass cards (the "stiff piece of paper," as Xuma refers to it[10]) and of service uniforms. Neither pass cards, the documents required of black subjects as a condition of movement under the segregationist system of racial surveillance, nor service uniforms were cyanide blue.[11] But they are not unrelated to this color. The history of that relationship has yet to be plumbed.[12] It is this history that I now want to explore to better under-stand not only the economics of superfluity in the development of the South

African gold industry as conceived by Marx and Arendt but also what Achille Mbembe terms the aesthetics of superfluity. Mbembe discerns this aesthetics in contemporary Johannesburg, in the glittering shopping malls-cum-theme parks for which the city became famous in the 1990s. I have found them at the city's origin. My point, ultimately, shall be that the aesthetics of superfluity not only contain a form of ambivalence that permits the conflation of structurally distinct positions and tendencies—in the manner that the term *blue* can contain and conceal the differences between cerulean and ultramarine or Prussian blue—but also, and perhaps ironically, open onto an aesthetics of separation. Cyanide (or, more properly, hydrocyanidation) is central to this phenomenon and was the secret core of many of the developments on the Witwatersrand.

The MacArthur–Forrest process and the variants of hydrocyanidation were an answer to the question of how to extract gold from pyritic rock. The gold of the Rand buried more than about 120 feet deep cannot be easily separated when compared with rock near the surface, where natural erosion and oxidization has loosened the metal from its bed in a quartz conglomerate. So, just as the large financial houses and mining groups had begun to buy up adjoining land to enable deep-level mining, some of them beginning to experiment with combinations of surface-level and deep-mining with an eye toward long-term profits, they hit a wall—a hard rock wall, as it were. Many speculators withdrew their monies or held off on investments—and those companies that did not have stable sources of capital were threatened with ruin. The result was a financial crisis that soon became a depression.[13] Efforts to manage the crisis with coercive pass laws aimed at securing cheap labor were insufficient to ameliorate what was, for the mining houses, an existential crisis. Thus, shortly after it was discovered that suspending gold in a cyanide solution would liberate up to 96 percent of the gold from the ore, including that extracted from the depths, gold fever took off again. MacArthur had imagined that the method would contribute mainly to the North American industries (he mentioned Sierra Nevada, the Rockies, and Nova Scotia), but in 1890, it was introduced to the Witwatersrand. And it was there that it ascended to the "front rank as chief agent of gold extraction."[14]

As with so many promises of gold, however, this one entailed a Faustian bargain. The process was toxic even when slaked lime or soda were added to mitigate the dangers. The runoff of the sluice, which produces those uncannily beautiful blue lakes and leaves its morbid traces in the sunburned slime damns so characteristic of the Witwatersrand, is full of poisonous materials, most notably cyanates and thyocyanates, although the aqueous solution breaks down when exposed to sunlight. The effects of these toxins are now widely recognized, and the histories of cyanide suicide pills, execution chambers, and genocidal applications, like Zyklon B, have made the chemical virtually synonymous with death.[15] But more common effects are carcinogenesis and neurological damage resulting from long-term low-level exposure. The toxic chemicals not only last for years but also are liable to leach into the groundwater, where they then seep back into the underground world, through the porous rock and channels carved by its ancient sea. It did not take long for problems with toxic seepage to arise after the technology's introduction. Testimony about cattle deaths was given at the meeting of the Second Chamber of the Volksraad in July 1895 and complained that regulations concerning cyanide required only the fencing of the dams and did not account for water.[16] An editorial in the *Johannesburg Times* on September 4, 1895, called for the mines to be compelled to "precipitate all cyanide out of the water they use before allowing it to escape into the creek."[17] Beyond economic concerns raised by the mining companies who otherwise came to depend on cyanidation, much of the opposition to the granting of licenses for the local manufacture of cyanide of potassium (when that issue arose, beginning in 1894) had concerned the fact that it would expose the residents of nearby urban areas to the toxic by-products and the risk of gaseous leakage.[18] Little was done to mitigate those risks early on, however.[19] By 1901, the Vaal River was considered to be so contaminated, thanks to cyanide runoff from the mines, that it could not be used for drinking water, even in the desperate wartime circumstances. Today, the lakes and dumps associated with cyanidation are typically encircled by barbed-wire fence with signs bearing skulls and crossbones. But, as had already been recognized in 1895, such signage implies the possibility of a containment that cannot be guaranteed and that is always at risk of being breached. These toxins constitute another remainder, one that persists by virtue of its dispersal. This is a waste beyond disposability.

In 1890s Transvaal, the new technology, which seemed to initially solve a technological problem, also opened onto another financial problem, for the process required expensive equipment and skilled labor, and this demanded more capital. It was the promise of profits coupled with the demand for fixed capital that ensured that cyanide would become a political problem. Indeed, it is not unreasonable to propose that it was gold cyanidation—as much as any other technology—that provided the motive for the consolidation of the political authority of the Chamber of Mines, for it was the ground of deep-level payability, *if* other costs could be kept low. It was cyanide that promised to solve the problem of dispersion, thereby transforming paucity into plenitude, while leading to the legislatively coerced transformation of labor *scarcity* into *abundance* by territorializing the difference between black (male) subjects and black labor. Cyanide renewed gold-mindedness, opening up a horizon of nearly limitless growth—a growth at once downward and upward, material and oneiric. As it did so, it reactivated verily mythic forces, as capitalism invariable does.[20] But it also provoked a shrewd real political strategism on the part of the mining corporations.

The Chamber of Mines, which had been ineffectual in resisting the Volksraad's granting of a dynamite monopoly, experienced one of its early political

successes in its opposition to similar efforts on the part of the African Gold
Recovery Company, which had acquired rights to the patents for the
MacArthur–Forrest patent and had proposed that the state grant it a monopoly
with fixed royalties. Lionel Phillips, the British-born financier who became
president of the Chamber of Mines in 1891, began an 1894 letter to Julius
Wernher, the founding partner in Wernher Eckstein and Co. and later partner with Alfred Beit, with one emphasized word: *cyanide*. He then noted that
"the Government contemplates taking over the MacArthur Forrest patents as
another State monopoly, giving MacArthur 5 percent and charging a uniform
7 to 7.5 percent royalty. I suppose I shall have to go to Pretoria next week and
try to persuade the President not to commit this new folly."[21] A month later, he
complained to Beit that "the Cyanide Monopoly . . . which I thought out of the
range of probabilities after the action we took, suddenly comes up again and it
is in a rather dangerous state." Relieved that people within the government were
opposed to the monopoly, he nonetheless bemoaned the fact that "Next year,
however, it will probably come up again. . . . The other side is spending lots of
money in bribes and we shall probably have to spend more next year than this
[year] to oppose it. Of course [in the] meanwhile, the High Court may declare
the patents invalid and thus put the matter to rest."[22]

Phillips was partly correct, but when the government issued a direct solicitation for response to a proposed monopoly in the newspapers in July, it
indicated royalties of 5.5 percent.[23] In response to the solicitation and in an
effort to galvanize the mining sector, an enraged Phillips channeled his concern through the industry's press organ, the *Johannesburg Times*, in a thinly
veiled editorial:

> On Monday we were all so happy in the belief that all danger of the Volksraad
> interfering with the Cyanide question was over, that we even felt some pity for
> the indefatigable Mr Webster [who led the monopoly's charge] and his prin-
> cipals. Now, Mr. L. Phillips tells us that an attempt will probably be made to
> induce the Volksraad to assent to the introduction of a clause into the Patent
> Law by which any three-year-old patent will be made unassailable for the
> period letters had originally been granted. [. . . If] the Volksraad definitely
> decides to over-ride the High Court and interfere with a sub-judice case, the
> Transvaal Republic will cease to rank as a civilized State.[24]

On August 10, the Chamber's executive committee reported that it had
received communications from 119 companies indicating opposition to the
monopoly.[25] Phillips's intervention made clear that the monopoly question
was not merely economic, and the editorial's invocation of the concept of a
"civilized State" summoned more than the indignation of local capital. It also
invoked an international gaze, a European judgment of the Transvaal Republic

within the hierarchized schema of state forms. The implications are clear: such a gaze threatened to banish the Republic from the league of civilized gentlemanly nations. In this context, the politicization of mining capital in opposition to the Volksraad would take place in solidarity with white labor as part of a temporary and tenuous alliance.

According to testimony given before the Select Committee on British South Africa into the origins of Uitlander grievances and the failed Jameson Raid of 1895, the mines had spent £30,000 pounds (or about $146,400 US dollars) in a single year (1893–1894) to have the patents rendered invalid.[26] As the August 3 *Times* editorial made clear, and as the Select Committee report reiterated, the bill that would have retroactively immunized the cyanide patents against challenge was deemed to be a key instance of juridical malfeasance and grounds for overthrowing the Kruger regime.[27] In fact, Charles Leonard, the founder of the Uitlander National Union Party, and chief agitator of the British move against Kruger's Transvaal, claimed that "large sums of money were spent in Pretoria in connection with both the cyanide matter and the attack on the companies just described [those of Rhodes and his allies]. I think I am right in saying that these grave abuses, and the risks that constantly threatened of a recurrence of such things, finally satisfied the capitalist class that they would have to join in the endeavour to get better government."[28] As it happens, the proposal to exempt the cyanide patent from legal challenge failed by one vote (12–11).[29] But the Chamber of Mines thought the tabling of the motion was an outrage, given that a case was already before the High Court to test the legitimacy of the patents.[30] The courts saved the financiers' day, largely on the grounds that the patents had been rendered invalid in England and Germany. In this context, it is possible to read Leonard's account as evidence that cyanide not only was a technology precipitating gold but also a signifier of potential abundance and equally potential loss, in whose name the alliance between white capital and white labor, both of which were multiethnic and foreign-born, could be formed, albeit within an ethnonationally circumscribed domain. That is to say, in this early moment in the long history of nested and overlapping triangulations, in which British and Boer and different African populations would variously arraign themselves or be arrayed in ethnonationally discreet or racially cohering entities, nationality— or at least the opposition between Uitlander and Boer—encompassed and subordinated racial difference.

Each success on cyanide's toxic terrain seems to have impelled the alliance forward.

In addition to the defeat of patents, the Chamber's other success on the cyanide front was centered in its opposition to protected government contracts and associated tariffs for the local production of cyanide. In 1895, E. Mawby, Silvain Oppenheimer, and E. Kaufmann each submitted draft contracts that would have granted them the exclusive privilege to produce cyanide of potassium and related compounds in the Transvaal. The *Manifesto* of 1895, in which English opponents to Kruger and the second Volksraad had complained vigorously about such concessions, had asserted that "no sooner does any commodity become absolutely essential to the community than some harpy endeavours to get a concession for its supply."[31] Cyanide had become that essential.

As far as I am aware, no one has taken seriously Charles Leonard's suggestion (oblique though it was) that the concern about the cyanide monopoly was a significant factor in motivating the deep-level mining companies' participation in the Jameson Raid. It has been convincingly argued, however, that the mining capitalists who joined and indeed underwrote the popular uprising had a heavy (if not exclusive) representation from the group of companies concerned with relatively capital-intensive deep-level (rather than surface) mining among their number. Thus, it is not unreasonable to imagine that the risk of a cyanide monopoly was a significant factor—albeit one of many, including taxation, the railways monopoly and press freedoms, the Kruger government's insistent subsidization of agribusiness, and, of course, the franchise.[32] One might presume that cyanide paled next to the existing dynamite monopoly, about which so much has been written. At the mass meeting of concerned Johannesburg residents held in August 1892, when the National Union was formed, the dynamite monopoly was adduced as the key example of Volksraad oppression of the Uitlanders. But that monopoly had been in existence for years before the Jameson Raid and had not spurred the capitalists to join in armed revolt. The successful challenge of the threat of a cyanide monopoly emboldened the deep-level mining companies, whereas the dynamite monopoly had only frustrated and infuriated them.

In 1892, many agitators expressed their contempt for the mining magnates and their press outlets for *not* supporting the popular movement. The newspaper reportage of the meeting, at which an estimated three thousand disgruntled Uitlanders gathered, depicted a spectacle of insurrectionary working-class enthusiasm and mercantile irritation, encouraged by the oratorically florid Leonard, who, with citations of Shakespeare and Daniel Defoe, addressed what they believed or wanted others to believe was the absence of capitalist support for their cause.

> It has been said we have not the capital of the Rand with us. Now, what is capital? Capital is the accumulation of property got by other people's labour. (Hear, hear.) By itself it is simply scrip or cash locked up in safes. It depends for its continued existence upon the labour of the thousands of people whom it collects around it. It is a thing without which the world of industry could not get on at all. (Hear, hear.) It is the part of thousands of people to work for it; but it is not its part to say to those who labour: "You shall be slaves."[33]

The merchants in the group may not have been swayed by Leonard's worker-ism, but the Select Committee that later inquired into the origins of the upris-ing was told that the agitators had accepted money from the mining companies, and especially those with strong footing in Rhodes's Cape Colony, mainly to underwrite the cost of arms: "We could not send the hat around in Johannes-burg for subscriptions to buy arms."[34] From within Leonard's and the Commit-tee's account, capital appears to have been belated to the question of political sovereignty. Initially content to remain at a distance from the state, if able to carve out a zone of immunity and impunity from its regulatory regime, it found itself converted (at least partly by cyanide) to a more interventionist role, ulti-mately subordinating the state to its own interests. In contemporary (2010s and 2020s) South African parlance, such an inversion of the ideologically norma-tive hierarchy of state and capital is referred to as *state capture*. But it was there at the beginning, in the place of origins, as it were.

Rhodes had initially been suspicious of the technological revolution prom-ised by cyanide. Indeed, when the early limits on the extraction of deep-level ores first made themselves felt, he determined that greater profits could be derived elsewhere and attempted to withdraw his company's investments in gold.[35] Alfred Beit, his most trusted confidant, persuaded him otherwise. Rhodes's support for the Jameson Raid proved that he had learned the lesson of cyanide's promise. His intervention transformed the endeavor, giving it at least financial viability—although the Raid's ignominious conclusion demonstrated that money did not always buy victory, even if the war that would follow in 1899 began the process by which the Uitlander investment would finally pay its returns. The Chairman of the Select Committee on British South Africa inves-tigating the uprising voiced the embarrassing fact that the workerist Union would have been incapable of pursuing its agenda in the state where it resided without external assistance from its erstwhile class foe. He summarized that "the capitalists joined it, and the thing was hastened by their action and their adhesion; but to say that this thing was the work of capitalists is absurd so far as Johannesburg is concerned."[36] The Select Committee seems to have accepted the narrative of mining capital's late entry into the struggle, when John Hays Hammond (the American in the group) and Phillips, among others, agreed to join Rhodes and underwrite the Raid: "It was further proved that it was not until 1895, that the active cooperation of the capitalists was secured."[37]

Nonetheless, it is clear that, between 1892 and 1895, the National Union Party had come to perceive the interests of mining capital as its own—at least in opposition to Kruger's regime. The references to the dynamite monopoly in the *Manifesto* and the many invocations of the threatened cyanide monopoly in Leonard's statement before the Select Committee make that evident. Con-trary to what Carl Schmitt might have us believe, politics is not reducible to the dyadic relation of friend and enemy.[38] Neither enmity nor solidarity is ever strictly dyadic. It requires a third, an external force and a force of exteriority, a gaze before which alliance is produced or hostility declared.

For South Africa, the locus of this external gaze would vacillate between Europe and the European settler colonies. The white English workers for a time threw in their lot with the capitalists, their erstwhile enemies, against the Boers, with whom the internationally minded anti-imperialists would throw in theirs. But they would later withdraw it in opposition to the recognition that they feared mining capital was about to confer on black labor, for whose interests the *Manifesto* also claimed to care. They would repeatedly strike against the opening of skilled labor categories to black mineworkers, insisting on their protected status and, in this respect, learning much from the Kruger government's strategies for protecting its own "poor whites." In their insistence on such protection, they too would inhabit the terms on which cyanide had conferred its sacralizing power: separation. It is bitterly ironic to realize that Leonard ended his rousing address to the nascent National Union Party with lines from Thomas Babington Macauley's *Lays of Ancient Rome*: "Lest they should learn in some dark hour how much the wretched dare."[39] He had no idea just how much wretchedness the cyanide process was about to unleash. Nor could he imagine that the soon-to-be immiserated population whom Fanon would name the wretched (*damné*) of the earth could and would also dare. The dark hour was still blue.[40] Cyanide blue.

Register of Expenses: Interim Audit

This hypothesis of the importance of cyanide may appear far-fetched until one realizes how great a percentage of production costs were accounted for by cyanide immediately following its introduction. To understand a total technē and not merely a technology, economic reductionism will not suffice as explanation. It is necessary to grasp its relationship to the broader valorization of waste and to apprehend the strange forms within which it acquired its potency, its fetish status. Nonetheless, one cannot ignore these driving economic elements, which encompassed both patents and production, as well as the organization of labor and the encrypted histories of dead labor embodied in the knowledge on which the industry's new *savoir* was based.

Almost immediately, cyanide became the third-largest expenditure, other than labor, on the Witwatersrand mines (only coal and explosives ranked higher).[41] The Chamber also received support in its treatment of cyanide as a border technology in the maintenance of racial difference, from the European manufacturers. The major German suppliers of cyanide, Stassfurter Chemische Fabrik (formerly Vorster and Grüneberg) protested by submitting to the Chamber of Mines a paper entitled "Is the Manufacture of Cyanide of Potassium

Rationally Possible in the Transvaal?" In making their case, the paper's authors, Harz and Beauhbock, sought to inflame what they rightly assumed to be the shared racism of the Chamber's representative members: "This process of manufacture direct from ammonia requires the utmost exactness in every detail, the greatest care as regards temperature, so that the process only can be carried out under the supervision of scientific chemists and intelligent white workmen; moreover requiring special and complicated machinery."[42]

In the same year that Stassfurter Chemische Fabrik issued its thinly veiled warning, 1,991 "natives" and 156 whites were employed in the cyanide works.[43] But black workers were excluded from skilled positions, and the likelihood of their having oversight of chemical fabrication was virtually nil. They were far more likely to suffer from direct exposure to the toxic chemicals when the crushed rock was submerged in the solution or to be injured by the ore transport equipment than to be erring with the calculation of temperatures.[44] The protective clothing given to them was mainly limited to rubber gloves.

One way to think about this episode of technohistory is demonstrated by the geologically minded historians of the Rand, who, regardless of their liberal or more materialist tendencies, their social or economic emphases, read the invention of the cyanide process as a straightforward technological solution to what would otherwise have been an economic blockage born of geological intransigence. Without a capacity to mine the depths with a high level of efficiency to make up for the costs of extraction and the low-grade quality of the ore, the Witwatersrand would have lost its payability: "Had these deposits been discovered a century ago, few, if any of them, would have been worth working, because miners did not then possess the necessary means for extracting the gold from its intractable matrix."[45] In a speculative history of what did not occur, it would cease to exist as a long-term source of wealth—even if, as was the case in the early days of the industry, much of the initial capital was cajoled out of investors with spurious promises, manipulated data, and little concern for the actual business of mining. Many analysts share this sense of the cyanide process's centrality to history even when they disagree on the status of the relationship between outcrop and deep-level mining in the individual histories of the mining groups, or in the overall development of monopolistic and monopsonistic tendencies that were nurtured by the Chamber and driven by the ostensible need to keep labor costs down even with technologies like cyanidation. The fact that gold prices were set through an international agreement and were thus independent of local production costs provided a structure and an alibi for cost-reducing measures in other domains. These same historians treat cyanide as a simple fix, which, having been implemented, recedes into the story of mining as a strictly technical matter and becoming second nature. Thenceforth, the costs are naturalized and the need for cheap labor taken as given. This retrospectively perceived givenness, a givenness that only five years earlier was absolutely unthinkable, is precisely the symptom rather than the cause of a transformation born of the valorization of gold and the development of the world economy under British imperial influence. We should not lose track of the structure that was effected as a result, for in addition to a relative intensification of production through technological means, the use of cyanide and global restrictions on gold valuations ensured the need to supplement this relative source of value with an absolute source of value, namely, cheaper and cheaper labor—labor that is paid less rather than organized differently. Here, the stamp was paid, in the ever-deepening reductions to the means of subsistence provided to the black workers whose lives would be consumed in the crucible of gold.

Much remains to be thought in this lengthy history, at once banal in its bureau-cratic rationalism and mythical in its heroic overcoming of seemingly impossible obstacles. For, the process not only permitted the excavation of the depths, the upturning of the world (remember Vilakazi), and the depositing of that which had been underneath on the surface of the earth. It also enabled, to an unprece-dented degree, the perception of waste as a source of value. As much as the tech-nological mastery of the process, it was this reconfiguration of value within the system of mass production that emerged from the MacArthur–Forrest invention.

The Secret of Success

The reported returns for 1895, the year of the Jameson Raid, now included reported gold yields from milled rock, concentrates, and tailings. On the com-bined register that forms part of the Chamber of Mines's *Annual Report*, under the headings of "From Concentrates" and "From Tailings," is a column indicat-ing the "process." This column includes the reference to MacArthur–Forrest, cyanide, and chlorination. The fact that there are references to both cyanide and the MacArthur–Forrest process is a token of the patents war that was soon to be settled against the Scots inventors (Dos Passos's forgetfulness of this loss notwithstanding). To a certain extent, the law was merely catching up with industrial fact, for almost immediately after the process had been validated as a commercially viable undertaking in South Africa, geochemists everywhere began experimenting with adjustments to their formula—and especially with the proportion of cyanide in the solution.[46] In addition, the Chamber began testing "direct cyanide" treatment of poor dry-crushed ore derived from upper-level mining. The authors of the initial study, A. F. Crosse and W. L. Hamilton, were enthusiastic about the results and called it the "secret of the success of the process."[47] For the foreseeable future, the tabulation of value in the registers pro-duced by the Chamber in its *Annual Reports* would include the amount of fine gold caught on plates by panning as well as that recovered along the line of finer and finer residue: tailings, sand, and slimes. The treatment of slimes (the finest residue of the grinding) had formerly been resistant to cyanide, because of its tendency to cake, which prevents the cyanide from coming into contact with the material. But in 1895, the Rand Central Ore Reduction Company developed a process that mitigated this problem, and it quickly became lucrative enough that the company could actually purchase old slimes from productive mining companies and generate profits.[48] Other companies undertook the process, at least with respect to newly generated slimes, and it was the output from this treatment that was inscribed in the Chamber of Mines's register. The ultimate question (albeit not the last on the page) of the register was noted in the column headed "Fine Gold *Saved* per ton by Cyanide." MacArthur–Forrest and the cyanide process were saviors. So much had been "carried away untreated" before their arrival. Now, it was being saved. Here was the real secret of the MacArthur–Forrest process: not merely a solution to the question of how to extract the plentiful but dispersed gold of the Rand from its hard-rock bed, and in so doing, to convert it into payability, but a new way of intervening in the process such that what was the waste of an initial extraction would become the source of a new and potentially fecund value when reprocessed.

"Lazarus, come forth."[49] This was more than the "magic and necromancy" with which Marx describes the aura of commodities in which the history of labor has been effaced.[50] This was a dream of resurrection—and in two senses. The first resurrection was of the industry, wallowing in depression after the second stock boom (1894–1895) had collapsed (the first had been in 1889). The second resurrection was of the wasted value that was otherwise imagined to lie in wait as an immanent potential of all the earth that had previously hosted gold—like Lazarus before the miracle, covered by (a) stone. The cyanide process heightened the aura that surrounded mining technology and made it worthy of being put on display, as it would be, at fancy dress balls and in corporation brochures. Industrial know-how now appeared as the completion and not merely as a supplement to manual labor.

But cyanide was costly. In 1895, combined expenditures for cyanide on the Witwatersrand were £165,526 ($809,422.14 U.S. dollars), whereas the amount spent on mercury for amalgamation during the same period was only £6,240 ($30,513.6 US dollars).[51] In 1895, the Chamber could not yet determine which method was better, based on the incomplete data at hand. But this did not alter the structure of its proposal, which was conceived in terms of recovery from what had previously been allowed to disappear. This was saving; this was salvation: to not waste waste. That was the goal, with gold as with men.[52]

The Stakes

What was at stake? To pose this question is to summon a double entendre, a second possible hearing, in which value and property converge. And more. "The stakes" is a phrase indicating that which can be risked and thus lost in the future and that which expresses the value to be derived at the end of a process (as the ends of means). Staking is also an assertion of property rights and a gesture of appropriation. Finally, it is a gesture that promises the transformation of an area into a depth. That which drives, which can be driven into the ground, produces the transection of the horizontal and the vertical, bringing together natural contingencies with historical structures. And of course, a stake is that with which one slays the vampiric undead. It is an instrument of final mortification. To ask, then, "what was at stake?" with cyanide will mean bearing all of these possible hearings in mind.

A week after the cyanide question was posed in the press, the *Johannesburg Times* reported the fantastic percentage of gains on the British stock exchange that could be attributed to the mines. In 1895, the capitalization of the 1,568 companies registered on the London exchange was valued at £81,646,921 ($399,253,443.69 U.S. dollars). This reflected an increase of three hundred companies, and £30,000,000 ($146,700,000 U.S. dollars) in the period January to June from 1893 to 1894. The rate of increase had also grown relative to that between 1893 and 1894. But the most fantastical figures were those reflecting the South African mining sector's contribution to the British market. Its relative share of the capitalization registered at Sommerset House had grown from £9,802,312 ($47,933,305.68 U.S. dollars) to £34,773,933 ($170,044,532.37 U.S. dollars), to account for a staggering 42 percent of the capitalization on the London Exchange.[53]

These fantastical numbers reflected the flight of unfixed capital that Arendt and Lefevre, in their different ways, saw as the driver of the European efflux to South Africa. That the capital that "traveled" was registered on the London Stock Exchange, in a country where many of its investors continued to live, makes clear how complex this so-called movement was. A share certificate for the United Langlaagte Mining Company from 1894 (circulating on eBay in 2020) provides a neat visualization of the deterritorialized nature of the gold economy (figure 4.1). The certificate, for the company that bears the name of this book's opening mise-en-scène, indicates that the buyer, Baron E. de Jacobs-Kantstein, an Austrian resident of Paris (at 21 Rue Laffitte), purchased twenty-five shares, which were registered on the London Exchange in June 1894 and validated under seal in Johannesburg on September 29 of that same year. On the verso, the certificate bears the seal of the Consul General of Austria in Paris, verifying the signature of the baron on March 6, 1897.

Distilled in the names of the locations where the transfer of shares took place is the material trace of a phantomatic movement, enabled by the extensions of credit, represented by and on paper, held in the hand but as the mere shadow of the capital or interest that it represented. Like the grapes of Marx's analogy, the paper represented the representation of gold as a percentage of the value of the company, not gold itself. It moved like dust but was not, in fact, even gold dust.

4.1 Share certificate for the United Langlaagte Mining Company, 1894.

Between 1889 and 1894, a number of developments in the global financial markets converged to make South Africa a favored outlet for that "plethora" of English money, to which the *Rhodes Banking Journal* referred when discussing what was about to emerge as the crisis of the Panama Canal Company. The editors of Rhodes's journal noted that "in every country in Europe, there is at present a decided 'run' after Government paper, established industrial concerns, etc. Many factors have combined to bring about this condition of financial affairs—it is, too, a condition which threatens to be aggravated rather than lessened in time. The saved capital in Europe has been increasing year to year, while paying safe investments have not at all kept pace with this annual increment. It must not be forgotten that the great railroad building age is now practically over, at least in Europe."[54]

The contributor to the U.S.-based journal, which would, a month later, observe a similar decline in the profits to be made in the U.S. rail industry,[55] notes that the "Panama Canal and the disastrous speculation in metal relieved the French of some of their surplus cash," thereby deferring the question of "rentes," which is to say interest rates, for these had been extremely low given the abundance of money. From the writer's point of view, the Panama Canal

Company had prematurely paid out interest on the capital to shareholders. He observed the likely need for legislative reform in French finance following the enactment of this "reprehensible policy," given that the interest had been paid long before the canal could have been completed. He noted, in passing, the difference between shareholders, who claim a percentage of the capital, and bondholders, who expect only interest at a predetermined rate. In 1889, the scandal of the Panama Canal was only beginning to be perceived. By 1893, that year in which the mine on which Virgil-Umholi and Dante-Xolani stood was founded and when the first arguments about the cyanide monopoly were making their way through the Volksraad, the scandal had broken wide open. Hundreds of thousands of French investors had been entirely swindled. Members of government had not only concealed their knowledge about the company's failures in the construction of the canal but also were exposed for having taken bribes to permit the issuance of stocks in the first place (in 1888). Many of the investors in this joint stock enterprise, including a remarkable fifteen thousand unmarried women of the eight hundred thousand buyers of shares and bonds, were individuals with little or no speculative experience. They invested on a very small scale (as in the £1 shares for the Langlaagte Mining Company in figure 4.1), having been sold the promise of an engineering masterpiece and economic gateway to ever-growing riches, albeit on the other side of the world. Such small investors—shopkeepers, merchants, wealthier tradespeople and professionals of the new bureaucratic classes, and women seeking the means to achieve financial autonomy—were becoming increasingly common in Europe and provided much of the initial capital necessary to underwrite the exploratory stages of industries that had acquired the allure not only of payability but also of money's magical massification. If, however, the enterprises proved efficient and if payability could be ascertained, the small stakes were generally bought out and consolidated by big capital—as happened in South Africa, with the Group System to be discussed in chapter 5. The point is that safety was not the immediate driver of money's movements; it initially travelled in the pursuit of rents, that most fetishistic dimension of the money commodity, and it did so initially in gravely dangerous forms, with the first triage or culling of risk taking place at the expense of the most modest investors.

When it finally entered the popular consciousness through the press, the Panama Canal Scandal inflamed fears in the money markets and chastened the major financial institutions, especially in France and Germany, which, growing more skeptical about overseas investments when the means to adjudicate the assets were limited, pulled back in their willingness to finance new operations. The threat of a cyanide monopoly was fuel on the fire. To calm the markets and keep credit flowing meant staving off the cyanide monopoly. But this effort required more than this if—across the vast distances in which the fantasy of future wealth enlarges—money was to be transmogrified into capital on the other side of the globe. It needed a technician of necromancy, a Svengali, to mesmerize the world of small investors and big bankers, British imperialists and Boer republicans . . . and German financiers if not French ones. Such a person was Alfred Beit.

Like any Svengali, Beit's greatest skill lay in his capacity to discern the tendency of a milieu and to use it to make people believe that his desire was their will. His desire was not his alone, of course. He was but one of the personifications of financialized mining capital in the moment of its emergence. He was its medium, its face, and even its style. As George du Maurier, the novelist who invented the character, well knew, Svengali is only one of the names of a figure in whom a particular structure of desire can both appear and disappear at the same time. Alfred Beit was also one such figure, and although apparently retiring as a person, he knew how to conjure an atmosphere to bedazzle and beguile those who wanted to become something other than what they had been—both in Europe and in South Africa. Some people were becoming "white Europeans" in a way that they had never been before (and certainly not in Europe), just as others would become "Black" and "Colored" South Africans in ways they had never been before. Let us then attend his séance.

Atmospherics: Banknotes and Gold

No sooner had Svengali appeared in the pages of Du Maurier's novel *Trilby*, first serialized in *Harper's* magazine, than it was on stage around the world, including in South Africa. Two weeks before the Jameson Raid, the *Johannesburg Times* approved the performances of Miss Marguerite Fish (Baby Benson, as she was known) in the role of Trilby and Charles Warren as Svengali, the hypnotic. "The craze for Trilby exists everywhere, and the performance at the Empire is crazy enough to satisfy the most exacting."[56] Were the theater-going crowds of Johannesburg seeking distraction to stave off anxiety? The same page of the *Times* featured ominous warnings about the softening of the Johannesburg stock market and lamented the "bears" that seemed to be making "the worst of every bad point, trying to paint the dark clouds darker, and their efforts have been attended with considerable success so far."[57] Future analysts would attribute the crash to several factors, including the aforementioned contraction of the French money market and the realization that the deep-level mining was going to be slow, expensive, and unpredictable, Phillips's sanguinity on the matter notwithstanding. Before that happened—and before Beit and Rhodes threw in their lot with Leonard, the National Union, and the Reform Committee to try to overthrow the Boer government of the Transvaal—Beit returned to Johannesburg to try to quell the tremulous markets and revivify the sense of excitement that had been ebbing in the early months of 1895.

Du Maurier's novel was published in 1894 but is set in the Paris of the 1850s, long before South African gold had even been rediscovered. "An atmosphere of banknotes and gold," is how du Maurier depicts Paris where Trilby, victim and protégé of the hypnotist, Svengali, had gone to perform.[58] Nonetheless, Johannesburg audiences must have recognized that aura and felt the rush of its transformative promise. Even so, the upper classes dreamed mainly of London.[59] And they surely recognized the window-shopping reveries that Trilby fans indulged when they stood "assembled in front of the windows of the Stereoscopic Company in Regent Street, gazing at presentments of Madame Svengali in all sizes and costumes."[60] As much as Trilby, Johannesburg's residents lived in a world in which wealth bought the capacity to become something other than what they had been, where masquerade was hypnotic. The newly wealthy built mansions "with conservatories, gardens, tennis courts and croquet lawns," although they had lived in brick houses in London. Homes in the style of Turkish palaces, Victorian manors, and Schloss-styled buildings named for German principalities sprung up on the ridges overlooking the city's center.[61] Their extravagance was eminently visible, for Johannesburg did not yet have avenues of oak and walnut trees, nor the sentinel conifers and canopies of jacaranda that began to be planted only in 1887, and then, only to line the roadway to the first cemetery and to shade the first park. As early as 1875, eucalyptus trees had been planted in South Africa for timber in construction and were soon used in the mines, but these were initially grown in the Horticultural Training Center and street tree planting in Johannesburg commenced only in 1904. The city center, emulating European post-Hausman cityscapes, was initially a spectacle of imitation, where almost everything, including both technology and greed, was on display.

Nothing gave form to the delirium of the moment, nor to the promiscuity of desire running through it (so typical of gold rushes), than the farewell fancy dress ball that Alfred Beit hosted at the newly opened Masonic Hall in June 1895, just before returning to his base in London from Johannesburg, where he had come to assuage the markets and push the case against the cyanide monopoly. There were many Masons among the financial elite—most notably Cecil Rhodes and George Richards—not a few of whom were central members of the Reform Committee that backed the Jameson Raid. A number were in attendance at the ball, including Richards (he came attired as a Black Watch Highlander—although the real Highlanders would not be sent to South Africa until 1899).

More wives and daughters of industrial captains attended the ball than captains themselves, a fact lamented by the *Johannesburg* columnist, A. L. Fom, who described the events with acerbically Wildean wit: "It is said that over 400 people went to enjoy themselves at the ball, and another 200 stayed home. There's an upper 'ten thousand' in Europe—or is it only in England!—and now, henceforth, it must be known that there's an upper six hundred in

Johannesburg. Certainly, everybody who had any real pretensions to being anybody were invited and right cordially did the vast majority respond."[62] The hall was decked out with flowers "requisitioned" from Cape Town, Port Elizabeth, and Durban, it being the middle of winter in Johannesburg. The "fashionable multitude" arrived before ten o'clock and stayed until the wee hours of the morning.

If, as Gertrude Stein once said, "fashion is the real thing in abstraction," then the fashionable of Johannesburg were the bearers of the new urban reality in its abstract form—and not least because the reality of the gold economy was itself abstract.[63] Many of the guests were attired, as one might expect, as objects of colonial desire. Among them were a "Coolie," a "Mon," a "Gypsy Queen," a "Polish Lady," a "Spanish Lady," a "Wild Irish Girl," an "Indian Hill-girl," a "Chinese Mandarin," a "Japanese Maid," and "two Turkish ladies [who] wore thin costumes with true Eastern languor [sic]." They were joined by the "Mephistopheles," whom Goethe had made the advocate of banknotes as opposed to gold (Gounod's version of *Faust* was playing at the local opera houses). As though to calm the excitement, or to incite fantasies of a repressed desire liberated, several pastoral figures were also among the guests: a "Negro Parson," a "Malay Priest," a "Trappist," and a "Friar in White." A "Maori Chief" was impersonated by Percy Tasman Morrisby, a mining engineer from Australia who served as the cyanide manager for the Witwatersrand Gold Mining Company.[64] Cecil Rhodes's brother, Captain Frank Rhodes (who had fought in the Sudan, at the Battle of Khartoum, and who would lead the Jameson Raid) was dressed as a "Turkish Pasha." Peter Marais (also a Mason) came as "Lobengula," the Matabele chief who had died in a battle with Rhodes's and Beit's British South Africa Company only a few months earlier. The victors, attired in the image of their conquests, danced with (or at least watched) Marie Antoinette, in a robe of "richest brocade, square cut bodice, paniers and train of soft shimmering white satin, brocaded with an exquisite design in yellow, kerchief of *Mouslin de soi*, edged with fine old Brussels lace, powdered hair dressed in the fashion of the period, with a yellow Marrabont mount, Louis XVI shoes, with old silver buckles, and diamond ornaments." Here was the costume as trophy and death-mask, "this mask of death which the white lights make stare."[65] And more. It was pure fetish.

"In fetishism, sex does away with the boundaries separating the organic world from the inorganic," wrote Walter Benjamin. "It is as much at home with what is dead as it is with living flesh."[66] In one of his notations on Marx, Benjamin remarked that the fetish character of commodities also attaches to the society that produces them, and in a statement that seems almost to have been written in response to Beit's ball, he wrote that the "image that it produces of itself in this way, and that it customarily labels as its culture, corresponds to the concept of phantasmagoria."[67] How better to describe this catwalk of industrial allegory? The women were divided in their emblematic charade between those who wore the imagery of nature, and thus gave the artifice its organic visage, and those whose costumes incarnated nature's mastery by technology. In the former category, women came dressed as seasons, as nights and summer days, as starlight and snow, as well as numerous varieties of flower—poppies, vivandier, and violets were mentioned in the press coverage.

Men came in the "ordinary costumes worn on such occasions," such as courtiers, military men, and cavaliers. In addition, there was an "Uncle Sam"; a generic "American"; a "Red, White, and Blue"; and, astonishingly, someone dressed as the "Attorney General of Alabama" (i.e., William C. Fitts, a Wilsonian-styled lawyer and future campaign manager for Franklin D. Roosevelt, had recently been elected to that role in the United States[68]). Americans, and especially American mining engineers, were enjoying favored status among the deep-level companies, as Mark Twain would note when he visited the next year.[69] And there was good reason for this, given that an American named Hennen Jennings had introduced the MacArthur–Forrest process to Rand Mines, and John Hays Hammond (Mason and coconspirator of the Raid) is credited with having persuaded Consolidated Gold Fields of the viability of deep extraction.[70]

If Hays Hammond's advocacy of the cyanide process was paired with his impatient advocacy of U.S. republicanism in South Africa, the traffic went both ways. In many respects, South Africa was incorporated into the U.S. minerals complex as a grand experimental site. Thus, in 1894, when A. Scheidel submitted his report on the cyanide process to the California State Mining Bureau, which had been a pioneer in its application, he thanked especially the inventor, John S. MacArthur, and, second to him, J. M. Buckland, the general manager of the South African Gold Recovery Company. His comparative study remarked that "it is the duty of the historian to date the cyanide process *as a commercial success* from 1890, when it was introduced as 'the MacArthur-Forrest process' on the Witwatersrand goldfields, in the South African Republic."[71] Before its deployment, it had merely been a metallurgical experiment (in New Zealand). Scheidel used the case of Langlaagte (that "origin" of the deep-levels industry) to exemplify the use of cement vats—a major advance for preventing leakage and thus poisoning of the earth.

TABLE 4.1

$2\,Au$	+	$4Kcy$	+	O	+	H_2O	=	$2\,AukCy_2$	+	$2\,KOH$
(gold)		(Cyanide of Potassium)		(Oxygen)		(water)		(Auro-potassic cyanide)		(Potassic hydrate)

Source: "Chemistry of the Cyanide Process," after A. Scheidel, *The Cyanide Process*.

Whenever Scheidel quoted one of his South African colleagues' estimates of costs associated with the treatment of ores with cyanide, two categories of labor were mentioned: white and native. This was nowhere else repeated—not in the United States, not in Australasia, nor in Mexico, Columbia, the Straits, Russia, or Borneo, from whence Scheidel drew his data. He quotes one South African manager stating that "one native, working about eight hours a day, can easily keep the works going, with an output of about two thousand ounces of gold monthly."[72] At Langlaagte, the men tending the cyanide works included "one manager, one assayer, two shift men, one mechanic, two native gangers, and the native crew." For comparison, Scheidel invoked the testimony of two other managers: "The Nigel Company employ two white men of twelve-hour shifts in the works, whose duty it is to 'make-up', pump in, and drain off solutions, and to attend to things generally, and one white overseer over the natives (about thirty in number), who attends to charging and discharging the vats (W. A. Radoe). The Crown Reef Company employ one white man per shift of eight hours and seventy native laborers, handling 500 tons of tailings (G. E. Webber, Jr.)."[73] Scheidel also shared estimates from the Rand Central Ore Reduction Company, also based in Johannesburg, indicating that, for every 80 cents required to process a ton of rock, about 3.8 cents (4.75 percent of total expenditures) went to native food and wages, compared with 9.2 cents (11.5 percent) for white labor, despite the significantly higher number of black workers.[74]

It was therefore appropriate, if unconsciously so, that Dr. Keenan arrived at the ball, attired, as Fom put it, as a "happy Study in White." A Mr. Schloesser brought added irony to Dr. Keenan's self-idealizing costume with "Innocence up to date." Both terms were generally used for women, but it is unclear whether or not the men were cross-dressed.[75] Even more remarkable was the number of people dressed as institutions, commodities, and even ideas. Among the women, the cyanide-pioneering "Rand Mines" (of the Wernher, Eckstein, Beit group) made a costume appearance, as did the "Rand Club," and a third edition of the *Star* newspaper. A Mr. R. M. Connelly suited up as "Liberty of the Press." One woman even dressed as a "Johannesburg tramway ticket"! The parade was a hybrid of fashion and industrial exhibition, a waltzing phantasmagoria in which any and every idea or object was available to be animated. Past and present, the living and the dead clasped each other's waists; the corporations sashayed, twirled, and fanned themselves to the accompaniment of the "large string band." Entertainments were rendered as moving billboard spectacles or, indeed, as advertisements of themselves. Thus, Miss Botha's dress depicted the " 'Johannesburg Handicap' with the 'finish' exquisitely painted thereon, and the winning sweep tickets well in evidence. A jockey's cap and jacket complete[d] this perfect costume, the fair wearer also sporting the colours of today's winter in prospective—Mr. Francis' Yarran." A Mrs. White dressed as a "Wedding Cake." Thus was fortune offset by the supposed certitude of the oath. For, if the

"Johannesburg Handicap" materialized the thrilling business of betting on horses (the outcome of which could be experienced within), the wedding cake was a sign of the lifelong pledge and, of course, the ritual of consumption that anticipates consummation.

Max Ernst's surrealist masterpiece, *Les Femmes 100 têtes* (1929), could barely surpass the hallucinatory forms that tittered in the hallways and leaned disappointedly against the walls of the Masonic Hall under the host's encouraging gaze. The images of objects—that is, the object-images that Ernst cut from the illustrated magazines and that appear in his 1929 "novel" as fetishistic recurrences of the archaic—were yet new in Beit's time.[76] The guests incarnated not merely the objects but also the spaces that they typically occupied; in their costumes, they defied every principle of scale—both miniaturizing and exaggerating these objects—and inhabited the dream of unobstructed progress and the aspiration for membership in upper-class society that Ernst was mocking with his fantastical collages. If there was mockery at the ball, however, it seems to have taken the form of (gentle and self-congratulatory) self-mockery: A "quaint fancy . . . must have led Mr. Lionel Phillips to go as 'A Fool,'" remarked Fom, adding that "it was really worth while for the average man and woman to have had a peep at the ball, just to have it to say in after-life that he once saw Mr. Phillips 'look like a fool'!" In retrospect, once the markets had crashed and the Jameson Raid had been defeated (events that would take place within the next six months), Phillips's gesture appears to have been more oracular than droll.

The costumes were professionally made, but some were deemed by the *Times* columnist to be excessively earnest, thus violating the terms of the event's tacit contract, namely, to play and to play seriously enough that the hypnotic spell of the game would go unbroken. Thus, with barely contained contempt, the columnist noted that "Mrs Matthews' zeal for the welfare of the Children's Home led to her wearing an original dress, representing her pet charity. On her head was a miniature of the proposed building, while on her dress was depicted childhood in all stages." Unpleasantry, if not prohibited, certainly appears to have been unwelcome if it could not be rendered as the medium of a surpassing wit. Certainly, charity was deemed a virtue, but at the party, within the shimmering space of desire's theater, its object and strictly ameliorative economy had no reason for appearing.

It thus seems inevitable that the pièce de resistance of the ball, the dress for which the entire event seems to have been staged was none other than the cyanide process itself. Structurally speaking, it occupied the place of the wedding dress in the fashion show—the last to be comported, and the symbolic terminus of desire. There is no list of arrivals at Beit's ball, so one cannot be sure that the cyanide dress actually performed this role in the order of events, but the relative loquacity of the description, and its placement near the end of Fom's lengthy column, accord it this role. It was the real vision in white. Only the journalist's own description can possibly convey the extravagance of the concoction, and I quote it in full:

> Mrs. Britton's dress was certainly one of the most remarkable in the room. It was intended to represent the cyanide process. The skirt was entirely composed of zinc shavings and produced a most brilliant effect, a smart bodice of the same being edged with bars of gold and pieces of cyanide. The heard piece was a most faithful representation of the tank vat, the figures of the large per cent of the actual extraction being painted in gold letters 99.9 per cent on the tank. On each shoulder were the cyanide boxes, joined to the tank by means of small tubes. The costume is *really a work of science*. (emphasis added)[77]

The imperially well-named Mrs. Britton's percentages were high (cyanide could claim only a 96 percent recovery, and that at best), and this was surely the point. The excess in her percentages gave form to the entire structure of the event's aesthetic economy, in which the extravagance was not only indulged but also was the very signifier of the event, its autonomized value. Beyond quantity even, this was a theater of surfeit.

All that appears to have been missing was the semblance of dams bearing the designation of "pregnant" or "barren," this being the idiom in which the separated sluices are identified as either gold-bearing or unpayable waste according to the new method, which since 1893 had been improving on MacArthur–Forrest's process. In this latest, most up-to-date (most fashionable?) process, ore that has been crushed and piled in heaps, is covered with cyanide solution and the drainage from this heap enters what is called a pregnant pond. From there, gold is recovered. From this, a final so-called barren solution is then distilled and recombined with new solution, before being applied again to the heap, to which more crushed ore or agglomerate has also been added. Effectively, this makes cyanide a kind of inseminator, a source of life. And more: it becomes a medium of perpetual reanimation. This is how Carl Maria Pielsticker described it: "In this manner my process becomes a continuous one, of dissolving the precious metals from the ore, preparing the solution *pregnant* with dissolved metals for electrolysis by separating continuously the suspended matter therefrom, precipitating continuously the dissolved metals by electrolysis, and *regenerating* continuously the solvent for further action on the undissolved precious metals still contained in the ore."[78] The terminology stuck. To this day, diagrams of the cyanide process still identify the ponds as pregnant or barren.

It is not clear where such ponds—pregnant and barren—would have appeared on Mrs. Britton's costume. But, in all likelihood, these terms would have crossed discretion's threshold and exposed the limit of anthropomorphosis and the threat of mortification in this allegorical play. They would have revealed the fact that this kind of fashion, fashion at its absurd limit, "is only another element enticing [sexuality] still more deeply into the realm of the inorganic."[79] The special status of women's bodies as the bearers of commodity desire, familiar to all analysts of fashion since the eighteenth century, seems to have been brought to a climax in the transformation of these female forms into symbols of technological mastery.

Reproductivity is not sexuality, any more than sexuality is a synonym for sexual relation, but the transposition of the organic idiom into the realm of mining, not merely as ornament but as interpretive frame, reveals something of the way in which technology could and did permit the (re)mythification of the world. As Georg Simmel noted, "The illusions in this sphere are reflected quite clearly in the terminology that is used in it, and in which a mode of thinking, proud of its . . . freedom from myth, discloses the direct opposite." Simmel added, "Natural events, as such, are not subject to the alternatives of freedom and coercion" but rather, "anthropomorphic misinterpretations . . . show that the mythological mode of thought is also at home within the natural scientific worldviews."[80] One may well ask where the line can be drawn that would divide Mr. Pielsticker's discourse, with its passing animism, and that of those contemporary zama zamas who say that the earth, once exhausted (but never barren), is recovering and regenerating gold? The mark of reason in the rationalism that denies its self-mythification is merely the self-consciousness of metaphor. The womb-vats (pregnant or barren, no less than the ventilation shafts described as "breathers" by mining engineers, reveal mining science's incapacity to secure the perimeter around magical thinking, which, according to the settler colonialists in this context, meant African unreason. But in this case, they (rather than their African laborers) were the magicians or fetishists, as Roy Campbell would later observe.[81] One of the accomplishments of this technology would be the transformation of people into things—albeit not without a remainder, for the reification of personhood works precisely by sustaining a residual ambivalence in which people are both things and more than things. This was not the first time, of course. Nor was it done in precisely the same way as had been the case under slavery. As Achille Mbembe writes, summarizing the outcome of this process, "For racism to acquire such power [as it acquired in Johannesburg], profit and delirium had to be so closely connected as to constantly trigger the vertiginous capacity of the native to be both a thing and a metonym of something else."[82] This is what makes of the cyanide dress the emblem of its day.

The bathos of the six-hundred-person upper class did not seem to tarnish the sense of the city's arrival. To the contrary, with the "lime-light" that "was thrown on the dancers at intervals," it conferred on its aspirant members an unimaginable luminosity.[83] After all, limelight was stage lighting, the technology that conferred that halo of visibility on the emerging celebrities of the popular entertainments. By the end of the evening, the columnist of "What The

Ball Was Like: From a Woman's Point of View" remarked, there had been "inconveniences and troubles, and worries and anxieties galore" but added that "we all enjoyed ourselves, and from the courteous host, who afforded *so much* pleasure to so many and, above all, right royally spent, and caused to be spent, so much rich gold coin in local circles, to the merest onlookers from the doorway, I think there are none of us ever likely to forget having been present at Mr. Beit's fancy dress ball." The glow, that is, was seen from without. The implied spectators who had not been invited, but who were not excluded from beholding the display, seemed worthy of remark. Twice the columnist mentions these onlookers—these eyes from and off the street. The first mention had been that in which the onlookers would recall Lionel Phillips as a fool. The second was the moment they would realize the gold coin that had been expended. Theirs was the function of the audience, granting recognition to the actors by admiring the artifice and the sheer improbability of it all. It is doubtful that any dreamer at the shop window of any arcade has ever beheld a more fantastic assemblage of valued goods—including perhaps those fictional gawkers of du Maurier's novel, peering at the photographs of La Svengali in her many costumes through the illuminated plate-glass window of a London shop. Or the shoppers of the Johannesburg development complexes like Melrose Arch and Montecasino, whom Mbembe describes as the consumers of fakery, beguiled by the simulacra of a lamented but never really possessed European cosmopolitanism.

It would be wrong, or at least inadequate, to imagine that what these nineteenth-century onlookers were being given to see, to admire, to desire, were the mere objects represented in the signage on dresses (e.g., the prices of tickets and winning sweep tickets) or the miniature headpieces of architectural plans or scientific drawings. The personae of imperially defeated cultures were signifiers of the social types from which the British empire had distilled an image (one that would be scientized by the nascent discipline of anthropology), and they were obvious examples of the erotic economy within which conquest operates. But, if the other more thing-like costumes were merely the advertisement for commodities, they would be no more interesting than the walking cans of soda and the human hotdogs that greet arrivals at Times Square today. No more (and no less) interesting than the spectacles of Lady Gaga or Katy Perry at a Met gala. Achille Mbembe is correct to call for an investigation of the aesthetics of superfluity—and Beit's ball provides what may be the perfect case study. But it is not merely superfluity that is at stake here.

The costumes demanded to be looked at, to be desired. But what, precisely, was one admiring in a woman dressed as a cyanide process, wearing a costume whose extravagance could be explained only by its being a "work of science"? The redemption of waste, the salvation of value, and the belief that these miracles were a matter of technology (the technology of separation, and separation as technology) were the secrets of success hidden in the limelight. But, as fetish, the technology demanded obeisance: capital investment and scrupulous calculating oversight. These costs had to be accommodated if profits were to be maintained in a context in which the price of gold was fixed by international agreement and could thus not express the expense of production. Cheap (black) labor was the sacrificial offering.

According to the well-known history of South Africa's mining industry, the representatives of already racialized capital constructed the oscillating labor migration system in answer to the so-called needs of the industry that were themselves created, one might say liberated, by the cyanide process—without which deep-level mining of low-grade ores would not have taken place. It is equally well-known that this system forced black male migrant laborers to move between the agrarian hinterlands and industrial centers, where they were housed en masse to keep wages down, thereby exempting mining companies from paying enough to cover what is typically described as the cost of the "reproduction" of labor. The separation between black and white labor was made essential to this process, insofar as the low wages, according to the liberal fantasy that wages were true representations of labor's value, could be given only for the most unskilled labor. White workers, many of whom came from strong traditions of unionism in Europe, and especially Cornwall, would not tolerate such paltry recompense. In this sense, the technology of separation required separatism. This is why—and with full recognition of the imaginative leap it requires—I think it is possible to comprehend that a woman dressed as a cyanide process, "standing on the stairs and listening to distant music, is a symbol" and an oracular emblem of Apartheid: its cunning Minerva.[84]

After the Dust Settled

Fom concluded the report on Beit's ball with a lament: "At an early hour this morning the great gathering dissolved, with somewhat of a regret that an end had come to such a delightful entertainment, from every point of view." But before then, a photographer of the name R. H. Davis had "photographed the guests, arranged in two groups, with magnesium flash-light exposures, which will form a most interesting *souvenir* of the occasion."[85] The guests had already inhabited that temporal consciousness of the modern, which imagines itself from the vantage point of the future, as having been in a time that will have passed. Future anteriority is the grammatical tense of this modern and modernist consciousness; anticipatory nostalgia is its affective register.

Nonetheless, Fom's claim of having entertained every point of view must give us pause—for his account has many blind spots. After the dust settled, and the guests returned to their homes to contemplate the future in which

they would recall this splendid spectacle of technological mastery, this orgias-
tic celebration of transformative possibility, there was surely an extraordinary
labor of cleaning to be performed. And no doubt, this arduous task—of gathering the china and washing it, of scrubbing the floors and the linens, of taking
the wilted flowers from their vases and clearing the ashes from the fireplaces,
of sweeping up the horse manure left in the wake of the carriages, and of dis-
posing of the cigar butts left by the gentlemen attired as their own trophies—
certainly fell to teams of domestic workers who, like the mineworkers, were
already divided by race.

Quite unexpectedly, while writing this chapter, an invitation to reconsider
this omitted point of view came to me from the pages of Mangaliso Buzani's
marvelous collection of poems, *A Naked Bone*. I was introduced to his work by
the *Daily Maverick* newspaper, which, in April 2020, under the editorship of
Ingrid de Kok, commenced publishing poetry about, or legible in relation to,
the COVID-19 pandemic, as it unfolded in South Africa. Struck by the evocative sensuality and acrid wit of the verses that appeared in the paper, I immediately ordered the volume of this young Xhosa writer. There, amid the love
poems and the lamentations for lost innocence, and the adoring recollection of
a grandmother's love of gardens (apparently inherited by the writer), is a poem
entitled "Revelation." Summoned from the past and into a new moment of danger, this poem delivered to me another vision of Beit's ball:

> I say to my aunts
> The choir of god was here
> wearing clothes of dust
>
> they look at each other
> and laugh.[86]

Buzani is not writing about Beit's ball, of course, nor about the gold mines, but
in some sense, he is writing because of Beit's ball and the gold mines. "The wind
came down the road whistling an ancient song. It was dragging along stones,
papers, huge boards decayed tree trunks, dust, and glass splinters that can make
you go blind forever."[87] The afterlife in which Buzani will appear, that afterlife
which will also become his past, is shaped there. But his deceptively simply
lyricism also allows for a metareflection on method, a metareflection that is
provoked by the very nature of poetry's self-conscious, self-reflecting intensification of language. In the reader, the resonances of a previously unheard and
even unthought reference can become the means for a resignification of a prior
text, and indeed, it is such a principle, reactivated in the encounter with Buzani's
poem, that informs this book's return to stories that are both familiar—and to a
certain extent already read—and yet still full of unsounded depths.

As for the servants sweeping the "real dust," we might note that, in Johannesburg, a year after Beit's ball, the census revealed that domestics were nearly equally divided between black, white, and colored workers, but the first group had the more menial and less remunerated jobs. White women from Europe and especially England sought work in Johannesburg partly because the wages there were higher (in England average wages for women between twenty and twenty-five years old, ranged from £15 to £18 ($73 to 88 U.S. dollars) per year, but they could earn between £50 and £60 ($245 to $294 U.S. dollars) in South Africa, although the cost of living was much higher and the risks were significant).[88] According to van Onselen, German women were preferred as cooks, and English, Irish, and Scottish women as housemaids, but they often supervised large numbers of black staff. When the wages for black miners were reduced in 1896, many of the young men who had been employed in that sector, or who would have sought employment there, also entered into domestic service.[89] Within a decade, in 1906, the South African Native Affairs Commission expressed its vexation that so many men had entered domestic service in pursuit of wages exceeding what they could earn in the mines or other industrial fields and argued that the encouragement of black women in service would "release large numbers of men and boys for employment in occupations more suited to them."[90] Charles van Onselen has written a pathbreaking study of the transformations in domestic service during this period, and it is not my intention nor is it within my capacities to extend that discussion. I merely pause here to consider what the ball's newspaper editorialists thought could go without saying. Who was actually employed to sweep the dust that would have accumulated in the corners of the great Masonic Lodge, brushed here and there by the hems of the fantastic dresses, is unclear—these details have vanished in the fissures of an archive in which the presence of African subjects occurs mainly in the moment that a law is transgressed, or legislation enacted, or a catastrophe reported.[91]

Archives are systems of normativity, structures of both legibility and effacement. But, as Carolyn Steedman has so evocatively shown, they are also full of dust, and this dust, which is the source of the archivist's fever and the element of her passion, can be thought. Writing of the great and often fevered French historian, Steedman says, "Michelet knew that the unconsidered dead were to be found in the Archives Nationales, and that the material presence of their dust, the atomistic remains of the toils and tribulations and of the growth and decay of the animal body, was literally what might carry them, through his inhalation and his writing of History, into a new life." She invokes Jacques Rancière's response to Michelet as well: "There is history because there is the past and a specific passion for the past. And there is history because there is absence."[92] If I invoke the dust that settled after Beit's ball, it is to bring forth the sense of a dispersed presence *and* absence, of a movement that is irreducible to an itinerary or a trajectory, which exceeds the questions of territoriality and deterritorialization that are otherwise so persuasively recounted in Mbembe's protean notion of the aesthetics of superfluity. Dust is one figure for this dispersion. And this is true in two senses.

On the Highveld, in winter, before Johannesburg's streets were paved and adorned with trees, its gardens planted, dust was everywhere. A contemporary commentator described it in 1897 as follows: "the streets and roads alternate between mud for the two wet months and dust in the rest of the year; and in the dry months not only the streets but the air is full of dust, for there is usually a wind blowing."[93] The dust was either ochre-colored or russet. It is still there, in areas where trees are scant, as in informal settlements where roads are still or once again (because of neglect or erosion) made only of packed dirt. Today, as then, people sweep the barren earth and sprinkle water on it to calm the clouds that stain the hems of dresses and conceal the color of shoes or feet. If this dust settles, it does so only temporarily, and thanks to fastidious but repeatedly doomed efforts at containment.

Dust is the bane of the domestic worker's (including the mother's and the grandmother's) life. It is also the name of that matter that invades the lungs of the underground mineworker. It is the earth in its infinitesimal smallness that threatens to bury him (and now her) from the inside, that which makes of the lung an archive of time spent underground, in the inverted world. A month or so after the ball, in the latter days of July and into August, Johannesburg entered its windy season. The dust clouds would have been vicious, given that there had been a terrible drought throughout the spring of 1895.

Theater makers (including the designers of Beit's ball, one assumes) know that, in the darkness, the presence of dust makes light itself visible. The magnesium flash that the photographer Davis used to illuminate his subjects would have reminded people of this fact, for dust makes the beam emanating from a bulb—or a flame, or the moon—acquire the appearance of near solidity. In a sense, dust renders the medium of visibility visible. It is thus an apt term with which to conclude, temporarily, this consideration of cyanide's aestheticization. To think of dust in this light, as it were, adhering to everything, penetrating every crevasse of the fissured world, is not merely to be captivated by sensuous detail. Such thought makes of dust a kind of antifigural figure that, rather than metaphorizing a single concept, such as dispersion, incites an aleatory reading practice that moves *between* levels of analysis, making use of both association and metonymy while recognizing the inherent openness and historical contingency of the readings to which such thought gives itself.[94] Reflecting on this form of reading, which recognizes dust in its empirical facticity and, simultaneously, recognizes its constant escape from figural fixity, enables us to take some distance from the imagery and the imaginary of dust as that which accumulates and functions as the index of stillness and irrevocable pastness, an imagery that informs many fantasies of the historical archive. For history is not settled. It escapes and returns, recomposes itself. and becomes newly visible—and often newly abrasive—by virtue of shifts in both the atmosphere and the manner of representing (figuring) it in different moments. This is why it is important to return to these early moments of Johannesburg's gold industry *from the vantage point* not only of those who recorded (or silently observed) the events as they occurred but also as they are recalled and felt in the futures to which they open.

CHAPTER 5

"WE'RE GROUND UNDERFOOT"

Movements Without Mobility

Think, thy slave man revolts, and by thy virtue
Set them into confounding odds, that beasts
May have the world in empire!

—Shakespeare, *Timon of Athens*

Go and we'll follow you
woman who protested passes;
confronted by protests
the white man quailed,
and kept his pistol holstered.

—Nontsizi Mgqwetho, "Go and We'll Follow You"

"Too much dust." A young zama zama mutters these words as he coughs in one of the tunnels of the mines that Wernher, Beit, and Eckstein built. Still young, in his early thirties, his body is nonetheless visibly marked by his repeated sojourns into the deep: "Going there, underground, it's not easy like outside. . . . You may walk, hard, sometimes you may walk like a cow, using your knees and your hands. Sometimes you use your stomach, just pulling like someone who's swimming whereby you're on the rocks and then they scratch you. Always, if you're going to see, some of my scratches. My body is scratched, somewhere, everywhere."

He has become other than he was. Animal similes provide a language for this passage into alterity, which occurs with every descent. It is an idiom that people use to describe the lives of underground miners, both when they oppose it, and when they practice it. Since the very earliest days of mining, people have described the descent underground as that which transforms people into animals that burrow and scurry—especially rats or rock dassies. For some, the metamorphosis is a dehumanization they will not endure, for others, it is a humiliation they must transcend. It is the latter for this zama zama miner.

When he returns to the surface, he returns to himself, except that he is scarred. He wants me to see his marks of suffering, but decorum prevents him from lifting up his shirt, or rolling up his pants legs. I ask him if he uses anything to protect himself, any clothing or coverings to limit his exposure to the rocks and the dust. His speech hurries in response, but it also dilates.

> We do not cover anything. We work for ourselves. We are not employed. We're risking. We just need life. Just, to get something to eat. We do not cover anything. We only breath the air which is inside. Some places, they do not have air. If you reach some places, who doesn't have air, you may hear your ears, just get like they're closing, you feel yourself breathing hardly, and then, if you know, we call it *mpilo-moya athina* (no oxygen), it's *mpilo-moya*. The air is . . . gets finished. So, you have to get out from that place. Fast, before you get affected. You may breathe hard, gasping [he gestures to show me what it sounds like] and then, if you know the situation, run away from the place. And that is very, very dangerous. It sometimes affects [you]. You come out, maybe . . . If you get out, you can get sick. Get affected with TB, or something called hard coughing.

He has chosen to speak in English, although his native tongue is Chitonga, and his capacity in this foreign language (English) is a point of pride for him, one that he earnestly desires for his daughter, whose teachers he judges based on their pronunciation of English. Nonetheless, when it comes to the point where he has to name the absence of oxygenated air (which words he knows very well), when he gets to the very kernel of his traumatic narrative, he reverts to his own tongue. In a profound sense, this experience constitutes the limits of translatability, the point where communication ceases. Death touches him in this story. And not incidentally, the place where death waits in this narrative is preceded by the sensation of not being able to hear. Then, there, both foreign language and his own language fail. As it must in death. Approaching that point in his story, he must simulate the event of breathlessness. His entire body becomes onomatopoeic.

More than many of the zama zamas I know, this young man often describes such moments. Perhaps it is because on his second trip down, he got lost. Trying with more than a little bravado to prove his strength and capacity to the other members of the team that he had just joined (a group of fifteen to twenty), he rushed ahead. He did not notice when they had turned into another tunnel. But when he realized, he tried to track back, only to get confused, more lost in the labyrinth. Knowing that he would perish if he tried to follow without knowing the terrain, he sat down and waited, hoping that someone would come upon him. For two days he was underground, waiting for the batteries of his head-lamp to die, waiting to die himself.

> Where I came from? Where am I going?
> I started using the wrong paths, then I . . . was underground for two days, directionless. I can't know which way can take me outside. It was Friday, Saturday, Sunday . . . and then my torch—eish—it was like. . . . to switch off. I didn't have batteries any more. My torch was just showing me closely. I can't see far. I can't walk, because even if I can walk, where am I going to go? And then I decided to sit on the same place. And then the other guys, when they came Sunday, going to work, they found me.
> "Hey, what are you doing here?"
> "Hey guys, I am directionless, I do not have, I don't know the path going outside."
> And then that guys helped me. I told them, "I'm very hungry, guys. I'm two days, no food. I'm directionless, I can't walk. I can't talk to anybody. So, guys, if you can help."

The men gave him food and drink, and brought him to the surface. In retrospect, I have sometimes wondered if his companions were not actually teaching him a lesson. Did they perhaps abandon him knowingly, turning away in order that he contemplate his fate and his need for them? Typically, men underground do not abandon their mates and will risk death to rescue them and even to retrieve their corpses. Every tour underground on which I have been (and not only in South Africa[1]), there has come a moment when the guide pretends that the lights have failed, thereby attempting to instill in his followers a sense of their extreme vulnerability but also their dependency on him. Such brutal pedagogy may have its benefits in a world of absolute danger. It produces an intense mutual dependency, one in which hierarchy shifts but never disappears, just as it produces the possibility of mutual support in which care for the other subordinates every tendency to exclusive or competitive self-interest.

After being rescued, this zama zama told himself, "No more. I don't [want] to go back there. I told myself, I won't go back there. This is my last time. I was almost dead there." When he describes these moments, his speech is both a description of the terror that afflicts the underground miner who works in the absence of ventilation or other safety measures, and a rationale for submitting to it. "I was almost dead there. Then, as time goes on, some people encourages you. As I said, sometimes, there's money." Neither is there always money, nor is there always death. But the one is linked to the other, through chance but also necessity. Need drives him. He is, like Rukeyser's hard-rock miner, Mearl Blankenship, unable to escape the dream, which is also often a nightmare: "I am asleep in the dream I always see:/the tunnel choked/the dark wall coughing dust."[2]

The young zama zama's nickname, whether he conferred it on himself or was granted it by others in childhood, is not uncommon in this area, and it translates as "behold (him)" or "look! (on him)." It connotes renown, and I will therefore refer to him has Mwanga, meaning "Light"—that which enables visibility. Mwanga's desire for renown has recurred in our conversations over the years, but it is that which he feels he lacks. He says that when he greets other men, who are more successful than him, they will ask, "why is he greeting us?" He anticipates them pointing at him, laughing, mocking. Because he is not a "somebody," he is a "nobody." Because he "has nothing," he feels he lacks the right to address them. That he says this while laughing in droll self-deprecation does not take the sting from his sense of inadequacy and the disappointment that accompanies it. Two years after our conversation, he lost an eye in a mining accident. But at this meeting, his handsome face is open, his eyes sparkling. He knows he is beautiful, and this makes his invisibility all the more painful to him.

This concept of being nothing in the eyes of others, and sometimes in his own perception, is linked to Mwanga's lack of documents. A year later, after having survived being shot by thieves in an attempted robbery, Mwanga told me that he would have to return to the underground after his leg healed because he had no other recognized skills: "I don't even have a CV to say this is who I am. Nothing. Even if I had a CV with my name on it, when I'm looking for a job, and they asked me what job do you know, I would say . . . nothing." He has no passport. He is like millions of migrants in South Africa, a person without documents. In the distant past, when mineworkers initially traveled along the same routes that he had traveled to these mines at the behest of recruiters or subcontracted agents for the Witwatersrand Native Labour Association (WNLA), registration was required and passes signified both the possibility and the restriction of movement. Today, for those who lack documents, these passes represent (which does not of course mean they enable) mobility, the possibility of recognition, and an escape from illegalized status. In the period in between the WNLA's recruiting and today, the vernacular category of the "pass" has mutated and expanded to encompass not only work permits and travel passes but all manner of identity documents that can be demanded by the state or by private employers as the basis of a claim to rights—whether of residence, access to government services (especially healthcare and education), opportunities to work, or mere exemption from deportation.

One of Mwanga's fellow zama zamas and a cousin of his, described his situation in ways that reveal the specific linkage of documentation with liberty. Like his cousin, he had entered the country illegally, attempting to cross the border more than once before finally making his way to the ruined mines. He too had followed the routes of his forebears, following roads that had been first plied by his relations, following therefore not merely routes but roots.

> I am not working permanently on a job which would give me a salary at the end of the month. Absolutely no, I never applied for the job, because they need a passport, the permit, or ID. So, for those documents, I don't have even a single one. In Zimbabwe there's no work. That's what I can say. . . .] I'd like . . . to go back to my country.
>
> Actually, I am stuck, currently. I'm stuck, because that's not the life which I wished (for) before. You know, living in a country where you are not free, especially in terms of those documents, which they need in the road—I didn't know it would be that difficult to me, like that. So, I have to go back there and complete my studies and if it can happen, come back again, with all my documents, which can make me free.

It is interesting to hear this young man, whom I shall call Benefit and who was about twenty-three years old at the time, with no memory of Apartheid but considerable experience of police oppression in Zimbabwe, speak about documents as that which can be asked of him "in the road." He means at roadblocks, but his speech summons the long history in which being other than a white man—and sometimes other than a white woman—in South Africa meant vulnerability to the demand to adduce documents whenever in public, and especially on the road (not only at roadblocks), when traveling from one place to another. Passes did not merely identify people as black or colored, in South African parlance, they pinned them to a place, circumscribed the possible destinations to which they might travel, and (often) specified the hours at which they could make the journey. The application of these limitations to women varied over time, and their generalization to include women occasioned widespread resistance, as shall be discussed.

When Benefit first "jumped" the border at the bridge that crosses the Limpopo River, having come from a rural area in Zimbabwe's north, on the Zambezi River, he was caught by the police and jailed with his traveling mates for two days. He tells me that after he was released from prison, he and his comrades found their *malaicha* (N, smuggler) waiting for them when they emerged from the police station. On their second attempt, loaded into a van and traveling under cover of dark, they succeeded in getting into South Africa, but upon arrival, they were set upon by hijackers who, he says, attempted to rape the women in the group. Their collectively assembled cash, totaling 200 rand (about US$20 at the time), apparently sufficed to ransom the women, and they all escaped. "It was worth it," he says.

Such freedom as might be enabled by documents does not, of course, constitute exemption from persecution by thieves, police, unscrupulous security forces (public or private) or *tsotsis* (thugs). It is a very specific form of freedom that comes with the documents that Benefit so longs to obtain—that is, the freedom to enter the licit economy. It is also the freedom of a specific form of visibility. In the ideal scenario described by Benefit, an individual with papers does not need to hide and is not presumed to be hiding anything. He need not fear a gaze that will find the lack of papers to be a lack of claim on presence or proof of a crime: the crime of not having such papers. It is the freedom to look at and be looked at with the confidence of legitimacy. This is why almost all official papers certifying one's status are valorized by so many people in this world: they are wrapped in plastic, laminated, hidden under beds, or even framed. In particular, documents attesting to education and, even more, those documents issued by highly ranked institutions are prized, and the threatened loss of such recognition as is coded in these certificates can prompt revolt (see chapter 11).

Benefit's poignant speech expresses the ideology of the administrative state, which has inscribed its logic deep into his innermost being. Like his cousin, Mwanga, Benefit will respond when hailed by the state's authorities, with that mysterious spontaneity described by Althusser in his analysis of the policeman's address to a passerby.[3] The "strangeness" or mystery in Althusser's analysis concerned the degree to which an individual would feel called and would thus turn to the source of that hailing even in the absence of being named. He or she would respond to the open-ended solicitation, "Hey, you." Response thus constituted an avowal of power more than an expression of subjectivity. The implications of this response are profound, for insofar as the police are imagined (as they are in dominant discourse) as the preservers of law, the subject's response is something like a confession. In the "special" example of being called by a police officer, Althusser's ideologically interpellated subject is always prepared to be called, which is to say accused and found guilty of a concealed crime, including one that he or she does not know they committed or which they commit by virtue of a mere presence in an area deemed off-limits. Benefit, however, dreams of an illusory world in which he will be recognized as a bearer of rights, and not merely as a violator of the law, and hence rationale for the police to appear from what Walter Benjamin described as its "formless" cloud. He dreams of an appearance in which he will appear to be both proof of a crime and of a state's failure to ensure that it does not occur. As Benjamin writes, "the 'law' of the police really marks the point at which the state, whether from impotence or because of the immanent connections within any legal system, can no longer guarantee through the legal system the empirical ends that it desires at any price to attain. Therefore, the police intervene 'for security reasons' in countless cases where no clear legal situation exists, when they are not merely, without the slightest relation to legal ends, accompanying the citizen as a brutal encumbrance through a life regulated by ordinances, or simply supervising him."[4]

Like his cousin, but with less pathos, Benefit wants to be visible, but not as the cipher for a hidden or secret sin. Rather, he longs to be a transparent image of himself. In other words, he wants to inhabit a world of perfect representation. This fantasy of a just representation and representational justice is, of course, the ideology of the liberal administrative state and, in this respect, it conforms to Althusser's analysis, narrativized in the story of the police officer's arresting gesture. When referring to his "little theoretical theater" as an artificial sequence, Althusser tells his readers that the narrative is merely a pedagogical device, one that risks betraying the structural nature of the phenomenon: in fact, "the existence of ideology and the hailing or interpellation of subjects are one and the same thing." But in the footnote accompanying this text, he acknowledges that the police officer's hailing is a "quite 'special' form . . . which concerns the hailing of 'suspects.'" It is the escape from this status of the suspect, that is from the "special status" that he is condemned to by lack of documentation—not only in fact but also in his psychic life—that Benefit desires.[5] Or, I should say, desired.

A few years after this conversation, Benefit was able to obtain a passport and even to complete some education. He photographed the results of each exam and sent them to me over WhatsApp, proudly displaying the certifications of his accomplishment. But he still lacked work permits and thus remained unfree to seek full salaried employment. And he remained vulnerable to the demands made by police "in the road." His life was a Kafkasque scenario. Every set of papers enabled but also demanded another set, and he was repeatedly stranded in bureaucratic limbo, denied entry for lack of what he did not know he was supposed to have. What Josef K, the protagonist of *The Trial* says, might equally well be spoken by Benefit or any other undocumented migrant: "it is in the nature of this judicial system that one is condemned not only in innocence but in ignorance."[6] Walter Benjamin's parsing of *The Trial* is relevant here: "the written law is contained in lawbooks, but these are secret." Unlike in Kafka's novel, however, the secrecy of this law is not a function of it being mythic. It is a function of that Letters Patent by which a radically foreign law (Dutch and then British) takes the place of myth, usurping and displacing local mythologies, and in the process, to quote Benjamin again, "exerts its rule all the more boundlessly."[7] The mark of this mythification of law is its passage into a domain—a state above and beyond territoriality—where it becomes not only irresistible but also that for which an alternative cannot be thought. Here, pass, password, and passport are gold, the really real representations of transportability: the signs that traverse all boundaries and dissolve differences to enable the momentary experience of a weightlessness that perhaps only digital capital truly incarnates.

I was never quite sure whether Benefit's remark, "it was worth it," referred to the difficult journey or to the paying of the ransom to spare the women from rape. As I would learn in a later conversation, the story was more complex than that—and he had played a crucial role in protecting one of the women from the police at the station where they had been held. His assumption of this protective role had earned him some repayment from one of the women, who advocated on his behalf and helped him find transport after he had been swindled by another malaicha. Everything for the undocumented person is economized in this world, and for those coded as men, the function of woman is often that of a bridge or an obstacle in the narration of the economizing movement across borders.[8] Exclusion from this economy is not merely vulnerability to persecution by the bureaucracy but also exposure to other forms of violence—often performed by those who are charged with upholding the law. Thus, for example, a young woman who crossed the border on foot, and who eked out her living selling sweets and cigarettes to the zama zamas, described her journey as a relentless labor to evade abduction and rape:

> The first time I came through the bush, I didn't have enough papers. . . .] It was very hard, because in the bush there are tsotsis. They can rape you, and take everything from you. . . .] I came with friends. There were about 120, [at] that time. From Beitbridge, we came with a truck, and they dropped us in the bush. From that time, we cross and we made the groups, so that, if you we cross the river, the soldiers, if they catch the first group, the second group can pass while they take the others in the camp. Yes, some of the people, they got caught with the soldiers. Because, at the last time, we were about twenty—which means the rest were taken by the soldiers. And, after the soldiers, there was game. There was animals, you see. So we just separated. Some, they go the other [one] way. The others go the other way. So, twenty of us, we came through, and we passed, and we stayed in the other bush for, just like, the whole night.

The vast majority of the women who attempted this harrowing journey were not merely turned back but were captured, violated, and scattered. Their lack of documents made them visible to the state's agents—as a kind of prey (the proximity between the soldiers and the game is significant in this narrative, and not just because the terrain *is* indeed full of predatory wildlife). It also gave those same agents cover, providing them with what we might call "an illicit license" or impunity. Because those who lack papers also lack the right to have rights (at least practically speaking, although the South African constitution still criminalizes the violence directed at them), the crimes of those who abuse them are rendered virtually invisible.[9] Like many of the women I know who work as rock crushers or as vendors to the zama zamas, the young woman telling me this story is a devout Christian and member of one of numerous Zionist churches.[10] She exercises a severe moral judgement with respect to her daughters, who remain in Zimbabwe out of fear about what might happen to them in this place. She knows that they are doubly jeopardized by being women and foreigners.

The perpetrator can count on the migrants to keep their secret because the migrant, fearing deportation, will generally not reveal it. There are, of course, brave women who bring charges, report their violators and loudly declaim their victimization, thereby refusing it. But far more women are imprisoned in secrecy. In this context, it becomes possible to speak about the predicament of the undocumented as a specific form of visible invisibility, which, borrowing from Foucault, we may understand not as a condition of individuals but as an entire structure of the gaze oriented by suspicion. In this form of visible invisibility a person constantly gives him- or herself to be seen and fears or experiences his or her unrecognizability in the bureaucratized world as both a failure to escape suspicion and a vulnerability to the force that is exercised in its absence. It is at once a global phenomenon and an outgrowth of the history of industrial mining and the administrative forms developed by the Chamber of Mines in South Africa and its labor-recruiting arms. This history is anything but linear, and it cannot be fully grasped as dialectical. There are inversions and involutions, folds and regressions, along with the pulsing vacillation between the restriction and territorialization of identity, on one hand, and deterritorialization or delocalization of alliance and generalization on the other. To understand how what was once the icon of unfreedom (the pass) has come to be an object of ardent aspiration, and how the organization of labor came to be instituted as a system of visibilities accompanying the aestheticizing technē of separation, we need to return to the early era of the industry's development.

My purpose in this chapter and the next is twofold. The first, as outlined previously, is to understand this history as a series of contingencies that, considered in retrospect, no longer have the status of necessity. In the pursuit of that end, I explore how the technological principle of separation became the rationale (grounds) and paradigm for social processes of segregation and separatism via the pass system. My second aim, introduced here but to be realized mainly in chapter 6, is to understand how, at the time, this non-necessity was being articulated in critical discourse and practice by those who were being negatively affected. This entails a consideration of both the "literal" production of radical poetry addressed to the pass system and that kind of poiēsis described by Marx, as a radical thought of alternative futures. It also includes an account of the embodied practices by which political spaces were at least momentarily reconfigured by pass protests. These protests, undertaken by women in the name of sexual difference, contain not only a critique of their present but also an interrogation of the linkage between legal formalism and the universalism on which British and then more properly South African governmentality worked. This interrogation was accompanied by a form of appearance in the public domain that sought to counter the visible invisibility in which black subjects were otherwise confined. Although pass protests were a recurrent but transient, and even a passing phenomenon, that political practice has retained its relevance in South Africa throughout the Apartheid era and since as well as around the world. Thus, in this chapter, I offer an account of the groundwork done in the anticipation of a future freedom, in the very moment that the terms to be apotheosized in Apartheid were being consolidated.

It is admittedly more common to discuss opposition to this development, especially as it was aided and abetted by mining capital, as a story of labor movements and strikes. By focusing on the history of passes, including the context of their development and the gendered protests against them, however, I explore the philosophical and practical political groundwork and not merely the oppositional economic practice undertaken in the early days of the nation's formation—when a nation and state were being reconciled in the service of transnational capital. To this end, it is necessary to retrace an apparently well-known story. Once again, I return to this history with a slightly different lens. This one is clouded by dust. But some phenomena show "through a glass darkly." Let us then go back to the point at which the previous chapter left off— to the dusty roads of Johannesburg where the Randlords and the Uitlanders were forging their provisional peace with the Boers of Kruger's Transvaal, on the road to the worlding wars over gold. There, we encounter the early traces of that system—a totalizing technosocial infrastructure—that would both link and separate the colonized populations of the territorializing state grounded in the cyanide revolution.

On the Road Again

On December 15, 1896, after the failure of the Jameson Raid had been followed by the improbable but temporary conciliation between the Boers and Uitlanders in a process that would ultimately lead to the convergence of white (that is to say racial and not only national) interests, Paul Kruger presided over a celebration of national independence, starting things off at the monument in Krugersdorp, the town named after him. With incredulity, international observers had noted Kruger's "generosity" following the clemency granted to the raiders ("after the cashing of the little checks left behind them when they bade their gaolers adieu in Pretoria," as Griffith sardonically remarks[11]). The party, largely paid for by the Rand capitalists, included theatrical and musical events, paid for by Barney Barnato (partner with Rhodes in DeBeers and founder of the New Primrose Mining Company in Johannesburg). Trains for the festival-goers were provided between Johannesburg and Pretoria and fares were paid for by J. B. Robinson (founder of Randfontein Estates Mining Company). Alfred Beit underwrote service from Kimberley and Capetown for three continuous days. And Solomon (Solly) Joel contributed comparable fares for the white public from Port Elizabeth and Natal. Joel was the brother-in-law of Barnato and head of Barnato Brothers, among whose properties was the Langlaagte Estate. The celebration was, as Griffith put it, "a luxuriant magnificence worthy of a city of millionaires."[12] Nothing like the concluding ball at the Rand Club, he says, "for brilliancy and splendor, [had ever] been seen in South Africa before."[13] Given the exorbitance of Beit's recent fancy-dress ball, with its spectacle of technofashion culminating in a cyanide dress, this is saying something.

The underwriters of the party appear to have been enthusiastic about using the infrastructure developed for the mines as platforms for the celebration. This infrastructure, by which capitalism's development in South Africa was enabled, was not merely a web of connection. It was also an infrastructure of separation. The distance between Pretoria and Johannesburg, one the seat of Afrikaaner political authority and the other the locus of Uitlander capital, was not only symbolically vast; it was physically significant at forty-nine miles—as Gwayi Tyamzashe had learned, so viscerally, when he first arrived on the Rand in 1884. Only six weeks before the fête of European reconciliation, the Lovedale-based *Christian Express* had run an obituary for the famous Reverend, expressing sympathy for his "sorrowing relatives."[14] When Tyamzashe, that last black stakeholder to own shares of a mine, traveled from Kimberley to Zoutpansberg at the beginning of the gold rush, anticipating the itinerary of capital but traveling in the name of the Word, he had been arrested at Johannesburg on the grounds that he did not have a pass permitting his travel on the Witwatersrand.[15] An early pass law had been effected in the Dutch territories in 1834, ostensibly to protect newly Boer farmers from the "incursion of hostile natives."[16] The first pass law of the Transvaal had been put in place in 1866, and it forbade black men to leave their designated territories without a document granting permission from an employer, magistrate, missionary, field cornet, or principal chief. Along with the Free State, where pass laws were introduced in 1867, following the discovery of diamonds, these early passes were initially intended to prevent men from leaving their agricultural employers in favor of the mines—although that would change profoundly as the mining capitalists assumed more influence over legislation in the Transvaal, and passes began to serve an antithetical purpose, namely to force men to the mines.[17] Tyamzashe had traveled there with his wife and three children, with a caravan of two ox wagons, several milk cows, and two horses. The journey, according to his biographer and the compiler of the *African Yearly Register*, "would fill a volume."[18] Unfortunately, we have only a few pages of that possible narrative, but they include reference to Tyamzashe's matriculation at Lovedale College in Greek, Latin, and Hebrew, and his ordination as the first black (Methodist) minister to be so recognized in 1873 or 1874.[19]

Tyamzashe's remarkable accomplishments included not only the mastery of Biblical languages, as well as English and Dutch (in addition to his native isiXhosa and, likely, several other African languages), but also a considerable editorial and essayistic career.[20] He nonetheless advocated for the use of English as a language in which the rhetorical resources of writers from Francis Bacon to William Wordsworth could be appropriated in the interest of an emancipatory universalism.[21] It was not roads but language and Christian revelation that Tyamzashe believed would link the worlds of the Cape and the northeastern Transvaal. His cosmopolitical affinities, which might have elicited parochial suspicion had they been manifested in an Englishman, were apparently invisible to the Boer authorities who greeted Tyamzashe at Johannesburg. As Mweli Skota reports, he was not only arrested but also "handcuffed behind his back and hurried off to Pretoria in front of four fiery horses of the 'Zarps' (Zuid Afrikaanse Republiek Poliese)."[22] What dreams and revelations came to the Reverend on his long, no doubt exhausting and humiliating walk, on those infamously dusty roads? "And power was given unto them over the fourth part of the earth, to kill with sword, and with hunger, and with death, and with the beasts of the earth."[23] No theologian of Tyamzashe's erudition and exegetical skill would not have been impressed by the awful and mistranslating resemblance between these four mounted policemen of the ZARP and the apocalyptic horsemen "whom the Lord hath sent to walk to and fro through the earth."[24] It was surely for this reason that Skota described them as "fiery." Given that he had been an eye-witness to the catastrophically destructive cattle killing inspired by the young prophetess Nongqawuse in 1856–1857, his father having been a councillor at Sandile's court, it is entirely plausible that these same horsemen came to resemble for Tyamzashe the allegorical monsters of Ezekiel's prophecy: "sword, famine, wild beasts, and plague."[25] Indeed, by the time of his journey, these were not so much visions of the future as figurations of the recent past.

There was, however, no Biblical script for Tyamzashe's rescue. It was his wife who followed him to Pretoria and demanded an interview with President Paul Kruger, whereupon, in Skota's account, "he was not only released, but given a *free pass* to his destination." (We can wonder if "free pass" meant there were no fees or if the phrase connoted a more general concept of liberty; often, as Benefit's story made clear, these two phenomena were related.) Who was this formidable woman who could demand and receive a meeting with the president of a republic, persuade him of her husband's rights, and secure his passage into a promised land of possible conversion—even though every other law of the land denied him recognition? That woman was Rachel MacKriel, the child of a Scottish colonel and a colored woman. She bore and raised seven or eight children with George, including the composer Benjamin Tyamzashe and the labor organizer Henry David Tyamzashe, before returning to her family in Mafikeng (then Mafeking) when her husband died.[26]

The consecrated, officially recognized relationship between the son of a Xhosa noble and the daughter of European colonel transgressed every written and unwritten law of separatism on which the Boer project was otherwise grounded. Perhaps for this reason, in its very exceptionality, it resisted subjection to a more general law, and to the violence that subtends that same law in its generality. This other force—of exceptionalism—would be the lure of many in the emerging black intelligentsia and the dubious consolation of white liberals who could avow the rights of blacks as exceptional (white-resembling) individuals but not categorically as human beings like themselves—and certainly not as those who could signify the universal (that which is generalizable without exceptions). Nonetheless, and by virtue of his very exceptionality, Gwayi Tyamzashe stands as an exemplary figure in many ways, for his is a life story in whose fantastic achievements and poignant losses is sketched the general structure of what would evolve over the next decades as a series of dialectical relationships: of loss and removal or revocation of right, on one hand, and the emergence of a discourse of universal right, on the other; of particularizing racialization or ethnicization in one instance, and racial generalization on another; of regression and the aspiration for progress; of immobilization and movement.

The history of the mineral industry's role in these processes is typically imagined as a story of the management and transformation of sexual difference, but it is often told as a story about men—both individual white men of the ruling classes and black men as a lumpen category of potential labor power. Between them were white male workers, who often acted as mediators but who were also defenders and advocates of racial separation through the color bar. Nonetheless, women also played a crucial role in this process, both as agents of resistance to the changes being effected and as figures of transformation, representing a passage through whom the new world was to be born. That passage is what concerns me here.

We can anticipate the journey to be made by returning to the present for a moment and attending to the words of the zama zama Mwanga's common-law wife, whom I will call Slindile, meaning "We're waiting." In 2017, she described to me her situation as an undocumented woman living in a compound with her husband, where other women also resided although some of them were unmarried and lived alone. All of the residents of this compound were tenants deemed to be illegal, but they had erected shacks with the permission from and on the condition of paying rent to the landholder, a long-time resident of the township. They tapped into the unstable local electrical grid without a license, but they had no running water or toilet. Slindile, who, like her husband, was from northern Zimbabwe, explained that "even if you go looking for domestic work, sometimes, they ask you for ID or a passport. You don't have a passport. You're just a regular person. You came from the bush, you're a nobody." Without papers, she was reduced to irregular piecework. Mwanga once sardonically joked that she went to wash other people's clothes so that she could buy her own. Later, she got employment cooking for a local food vendor, but she arrived one morning to find that he had closed up shop and left her, owing two months' pay. Both she and Mwanga were enraged by this violation of trust and obligation, but they resigned themselves to it on the grounds that they could not ask the police to enforce their rights.

Like her husband, Slindile felt the absence of documents to be the mark of nullity and the denial of a right to enter the licit economy. She was not ashamed of the absence of documents, but it did make her vulnerable to shaming whenever she encountered an authority figure. An acutely intelligent and handsome woman, with a wry sense of humor and a street entrepreneur's calculating savvy, she was constantly finding ways to survive and had a seemingly inexhaustible capacity to persevere amid adversity. She exuded strength if not confidence. But she was also concerned about the vulnerability that being alone entailed for other women, and she indicated that even she was afraid to go out after dark. Being an undocumented woman and a foreigner meant, for her, the threat of being raped. She would not, she said, be able to call on the police for help in the event of an assault for fear of the possibility that the police would uncover her status. If this occurred, she expected deportation, perhaps violation, and even death: "If the police came today, to chase us from here—in this country, we know that we are foreigners. The way things are, what we would do, if they came for me and said, 'Leave' . . . there's nowhere that I can go. If they want to kill, let them kill. Because I have no money, I have nothing, I'm just an ordinary person. The only thing I could do is to leave this place, and go live in the bush."

Without documents, she is also a nobody, she says, and such a person has no rights to presence or even to life. Being without documents is an exposure to death, as surely as her husband's sojourn underground is an exposure to death. Shimmering in Slindile's speech, moreover, is her claim that, if confronted by the police, she would have to flee to the bush. The meaning of this phrase, spoken in a tone of searing rage by a woman who is more characteristically composed, is not a return to the village but madness, and may entail prostitution; in both cases, it is a displacement not only from a specific territory but from oneself. Other speakers of her language, namely Chitonga, were shocked to hear these words and recoiled visibly to hear this dignified woman anticipate her becoming animal-like.[27] Like the young woman who could not describe her traveling companions' possible abduction by the military without mentioning the threat of rape or becoming prey to wild animals, Slindile's story evokes a radical exteriority to the bureaucratized world, a space beyond the state, beyond the political, beyond humanity. For the bush, in this sense, is a space beyond the threshold not only of recognition but also of all recognizability. I am not claiming, of course, that the state is the source of right and that, once legislated, equality is actual, or that the state exercises its monopoly on violence in a manner that provides its citizens with real and consistent security. Rather, I am pointing to the phantomatic force it exercises in the imagination of those who are cast beyond its pale, and who feel its absence as lack or loss—even when, ironically, state agents often exercise the violence that is experienced by the undocumented as a dispersed and omnipresent rather than monopolized force whose controlling structures they wish to access. For them, these state agents are acting against the ideal of the (liberal) state. These agents are also becoming like animals in the spaces in which the undocumented live, move, and seek the conditions of habitability (an issue to which I return later in this book). The depth and spontaneity of this sentiment in Slindile's discourse is evidence of the effectivity if not the success of the "system of the pass." We can interpret her remarks as a silhouette or a negative image of the politics of recognition that were operationalized in that internally striated system. The history of its fabrication—including its laws, its commissions of inquiries and their reports, and the elaborate apparatuses of registration, surveillance, and policing, many developed by the Chamber of Mines—demands some accounting.

The Chamber-Made World

When the Chamber of Mines (now the Minerals Council of South Africa) published its roseate institutional autobiography, *In the Common Interest*, in 1967, it referred to its founders as "enterprising men" acting "in their personal capacities rather than the company representatives."[28] Despite such reverence, the Chamber described its first few years as ones of almost immediate dissipation: "the Chamber became moribund and might have disappeared from the scene had not a number of far-sighted mining men reconstituted it as the Witwatersrand Chamber of Mines in 1889." In the frenzy of a gold rush, two years is a sufficiently long period to encompass bursts of institutional growth, stagnation, and morbidity. And also regeneration. Lazarus once more.

The Chamber was registered as an Employer's Organization in 1887.[29] Its purpose, succinctly presented but expansively conceived in the original Articles of Association, was "to promote and protect the mining interests and industries of the South African Public."[30] Later this would include a commitment to assist them "technically, financially or otherwise." In construing its members as having *common* interests, it worked both to mitigate competition over labor and thus wages among its constituent members and to lobby the government and other legislative bodies "to promote or oppose any proposed legislative measures affecting the mining industry."[31] Essentially, it took over what Phillips and others had done on a personal basis, although its members continued to use their contacts to act individually and sometimes in competition with each other. Personal proximity to power, as much as institutional representation and class solidarity, gave the Chamber its force, if not its official mode of operation.

Under the terms of its mature constitution, it represented members in industrial disputes, and arbitrated complaints brought against them by labor as well as extra-industry interests (such as agricultural land-owners) (2.c, j).[32] It considered patents and monopolies that could affect them, and, as we have seen, opposed their being granted (2.d), ostensibly ensuring the equal access of all mining entities to new technologies, while keeping costs low. The Chamber's remit nonetheless exceeded extractive operations. Within a few years, it could acquire, sell, hold, mortgage, and dispose of property, and it could borrow and raise funds for the Chamber as well as invest the proceeds of member subscriptions in excess of operating costs (2.f, g, h). It could subsidize associations or institutions, and it could provide managerial services to other institutions in the industry and charge for the service (2.i, k). In the long run, it would undertake research, fund technological development, and provide training and education for employees and scholarships for students pursuing the study of earth sciences. It would cultivate cultural programs, establish museums, and promote the ideology of ethnic or cultural difference while operationalizing racial hierarchy. It would devise policies for security, policing, and surveillance of its members' properties, and it would establish provident funds, pension plans, and medical services for its employees. It was, in short, the governing body of a shadow state within the state, performing the functions of biopolitical governmentality that were, in many regards, far in advance and far more intensively administered than was the case beyond the perimeter of the mines. At the same time, the decisions taken by these individuals, in the interests of capital, were increasingly determining the policies and legislative agendas of the state, if not always the implementation of those policies, which remained dependent on municipal governments and their agencies well into the second decade after the nation was formally rendered a union in 1910.

The Chamber's latter-day use of the concept "common" performed that ruse we now recognize as the mark of capitalist ideology—generalizing the position of a limited but collective interest and thereby effacing the experiences, needs, desires, and interests of those whose exploitation it demanded. It was originally a subscription-based entity, and representation was directly linked to the fees paid by members.[33] Eligibility for membership required being listed on a European or the Johannesburg Stock Exchange, but after a breakaway of some members led to the reconstitution as the Chamber of Mines of South Africa the following year, the requirement for listing on the stock exchange was dropped.[34] This latter decision permitted the consolidation of private ownership of companies, as individuals or groups could buy back stock and take companies off the exchange without losing their status in the Chamber and hence their influence over government and Chamber policies.[35]

In 1897, the Chamber's annual report addressed a new pass law and described its own interventions to secure the incorporation of numerous areas under the new law's jurisdiction and a move toward the homogenization of territorial logics. In 1890, it had begged the government to intervene to enforce pass laws, on the grounds that it could not do so itself, and it was especially vexed by the so-called molestation of recruits on route to the mines.[36] By 1895, it had persuaded the Volksraad to enact a pass law specifically designed for mining districts (another regulation applied more generally) that required bearers to wear a metal arm band inscribed with a number (this was later replaced with the requirement for a document only) and that limited Africans' access to urban areas. The purpose of the broadened jurisdiction for the pass laws in 1897, it said, was to mitigate "desertion" by recruits. According to Alan Jeeves, the felt need for the "pass law for the Rand followed directly from the industry's inability to restrain competition for labour among its own members," and the "promise of greater government action to control labour and recruiting practices enabled the groups to initiate their plans to reduce wages and to establish a cooperative recruiting system."[37] The Chamber's monopsony—derived from a state intervention, itself a response to a composite corporate request to mitigate problems generated by the companies' competition—had spawned the aggressive tactics of touts or labor recruiters. It emerged from a procedure that was generated by a committee modeled on a government structure. The regress of resemblances and transgressions between the private and the political gave to the Chamber the appearance of a cave on whose walls are projected the images that function to imprison all who look upon them. The illusion is expressed in the previously cited institutional autobiography *In the Common Interest*. And it consisted of the belief that there was a separation between state and capital.

Etymology did not fate the Chamber to this ambivalent predicament, where private and public become indistinguishable, with the former being dissimulated as the latter. Nonetheless, a certain element of this simulacrum of the Chamber's tendency can be discerned in etymology. Chamber is one of those terms whose significations encompass its own opposites. It can refer to either a private or enclosed space and a site of representative deliberations. It extends from the privy to the privileged room in the house—the former for intimate ablutions, and the latter for receiving the public. It can refer to the space of secreted or "in camera" discussions or, those of a deliberative, judicial, or legislative assembly. It can connote the bedroom or, by contrast, the place where public funds are received or the large venue where commercial activity is conducted. In mining, it may refer to the place in which ore is found or a charge is placed. In photography, of course, the chamber is the camera as well as the particular space in which an image is projected, in inverted form. It is on the basis of the photographic analogy that the young Marx formulated his concept of ideological critique as a task of representational inversion, of standing the upside-down world back on its feet.[38] In the case of the Chamber of Mines, the apparent vacillation between and fusion of these functions and dimensions of the private and the political is especially notable. It is the very (capitalist) space in which these two domains converge as the mirror images of each other. This is why it is so well described by Luce Irigaray, who, in her masterful reading of Plato's allegory of the cave, writes, "What cunning and utterly convincing necromancers these are who sacrifice (even themselves) to the greatness of their specters and thereby rob, rape, and rig the perspicacity of their public, blinding it with their exhibitions."[39] We will return to Irigaray. But for now, we can note simply that, by 1897, the Chamber was effectuating government logics and not merely corporate or managerial regulations. Its coherence was interrupted, and then only briefly, by the Anglo-Boer War.

In the meantime, 1897, marking the first decade of its existence, was a year of triumph for the Chamber, and the annual report disclosed the extent of the power that the groups could achieve when acting in concert. Now representing 121 companies, the Chamber had managed to effect a reduction in Native wages by 20–25 percent. Faced with insurrection in the face of these reductions, the Chamber redoubled its efforts, and successfully lobbied for an increase in fines, raising them from ten shillings or one week's imprisonment for a first offense, and twenty shillings or two weeks' incarceration "with hard labour and lashes," and further punishment at the court's description for every offense thereafter, to £3 and £5 (US$14.70-24.50), with the accompanying imprisonment.[40] Later, as pass protests became a dominant form of political insurrection, the radical newspaper, *Abantu-Batho* would assert that "all the work that should have been done by our wage labourers [is] now done by prisoners who are imprisoned for nothing but passes."[41] This prospect had been anticipated in the Cape Colony already in 1889, when the possibility of uniform pass legislation was brought under discussion in parliament. An editorial in the *South African Outlook* had decried the proposal on the grounds that it would constitute a "non-moral" "manufacture of crime and criminals." It worried about the fine that would be levied against accidental trespassers and noted that the law effectively made it "a crime for a Native to live in the land where he was born."[42] But in the Transvaal, this possibility became an actuality.

Whether because of the severity of the punishments for absenteeism, the desperation for cash of the labor-sending communities, or the promise of the lucre and the experience of new freedoms away from elder men at home, the supply of black labor had become so plentiful within the year that the newly renamed Chamber met again to "consider the question of the reduction of native wages." The result was a further 30 percent reduction and a decision to "take the necessary steps to enforce such reduction."[43] Thus, both labor surfeit and labor shortage were an alibi for wage repression. Francis Wilson has calculated that between 1910 and 1969, profit margins for the mines varied from 17 to 23 percent, while expenditures on wages for black workers declined from 16.4 to 8.8 percent of mine costs.[44] But the pattern of increasingly diverging ratios, which is to say, relative surplus value extraction, was set long before Union in 1910.

When war broke out in late 1899, ostensibly to secure the civil rights and especially the franchise for Uitlanders (which prospect and demand had been held in abeyance since the failed Jameson Raid), but largely over an effort to control the growing revenues and potential of the goldfields, the Chamber suspended activities after having made provisions for additional police enforcement to protect the workings during what it assumed would be reduced operations. At the war's onset, the mines came under direct control of the government, which appointed a board to assist in oversight of reduced operations.[45] Despite or because of the war, they were being incorporated into an increasingly disciplined and integrated apparatus of governance. In May, they adopted a uniform time, based on the Thirtieth Meridian, to correct for the "different time being kept by the mines, in the town, and by the Government offices."[46] Clockwork, we might say, was the idiom and not merely the object of the change, which aimed to synchronize the operations of industry and government. Later, it would be said that time had been lost. Time being money, the deficit was calculated in pounds, shillings, and cents. Immediately at the war's end, however, the drive to achieve rational governance was enmeshed with a technocratic approach to labor management, supplemented by increased mechanization. A new, higher 10 percent tax on profits (it had previously been 5 percent), effectuated in the early days of Reconstruction in an effort to both pay off the war debt and repair national infrastructure, was adduced as one reason for the need to reduce labor costs again. Yet another reason, the Chamber claimed, was that whites had taken on jobs formerly carried out by black workers, when there had been a rush to restart operations following the end of military hostilities. The new shortage of black labor was attributed to competitive wages in other areas of the reconstruction economy and abundant harvests in rural areas. Together, these pressures had led to increased investments in mechanization, of which the Chamber was exceedingly proud: "Nowhere in the world, in metalliferous mines with a thickness of deposit similar to the Rand, are labour-saving devices employed to the same extent," asserted the Chamber in 1902.[47] In addition to cyanide, processes of drilling, dewatering, ventilation, and transport were also mechanized.

This technological advancement of the mines was attributed by the Chamber to managerial genius, in the manner of seized opportunity: "The shortage of labour has also a tendency to train the inventive and organizing faculty of the Captains of Industry." However, the experiment with white labor in unskilled positions was deemed to have been "*unsatisfactory*," according to the Chamber, "as the white men have been unsettled, are fearful of reduction in their pay, and have agitated."[48] It conceded that the black worker, insofar as he could be deemed "a mere muscular machine," was "the equal of the white man," whose "brain and industrial training are the white's only superiority."[49] Let us note in passing, as it were (to return later), the Chamber's consciousness of a resemblance rather than absolute difference between white and black workers as the basis of its policy of separation.

To maintain low operating costs and to avoid the reduction of white standards of living, as is well known, the Chamber adopted a policy of race-based employment categories—a development that would mark forever the future history of South African industry: "no other conclusion can be drawn than that, under existing conditions on these fields, the continuance and expansion of the mines, and the prosperity, contentment and existence of the white population depend, in a large measure on an adequate supplementary supply of cheap labour through the medium of coloured races."[50] The war did not merely permit the resumption of an older racial hierarchy. It seemed to unleash a vindictive and contradictory relation to black labor, one riven by the simultaneous aspiration to incite the desire for cash wages and the anxiety that wealth already accumulated was undermining that very prospect. By this accounting, even a modest accumulation of capital, or at least assets, by black workers (and the chiefs in whose territory they resided when not on the mines and to whom they paid their tribute) was inimical to the Chamber's self-contradicting fantasy of patriarchal industrial modernity. It was premised on the relative exclusion of women from waged labor and should thereby ensure men's dependency on it. But this was not happening. Or so the Chamber feared. Instead, they said, black male workers had come to enjoy an "abnormal prosperity," enabling them to "invest in" multiple wives, whose labor, in turn, "release[d] native men from the necessity of ever laboring again." The problem, from the Chamber's self-contradictory point of view, was mineworkers' failure to develop an "acquisitive faculty." They were, that is, not developing a consciousness of their own lack. In these early days, it was said, black workers did not expend enough on consumables or even display values. The problem was said to persist in 1904, when the Chamber sent a communication on the matter to the Commission on Native Labor: "The volume of native labour in circulation is regulated by the wants of the labourers. If by earning higher wages they can supply their wants in less time, their period of service will be proportionately less. By increasing their personal wants they will in due course extend their period of service. This is, however, a gradual process. Meanwhile the reactionary effect of high wages should not be overlooked."[51] Black workers were thus stranded between the Scylla and Charybis of insufficient desire and desire in excess—they were not eager enough for commodity consumption to want more wages and thus to work more, but they were ostensibly too desirous of the comforts that could be provided by wives and juniors laboring for them. They were not becoming good workers, but they were, perhaps, becoming proto-capitalists.

When Anthony Trollope had visited the diamond fields, he had prophesied that "as the love of making money, and as tribal reverence for the Chieftains dies out, the [black] men will learn to remain more constantly at their work" because they will have "learned the loveliness of 10s a week paid regularly into [their] hand every Saturday night."[52] In some places, tributary labor for the chiefs was actually diverted to the mines; and many young men wanted to claim as their own wages what previously had been paid into the pockets of their leaders, who (in the name of traditional authority) were subordinating the new economy to a feudality that had been artificially propped up by indirect rule. In 1902, as the war came to an end and it became clear that, with some significant exceptions, Boers and Englishmen would resolve their differences through opposition to black workers, Plaatje published an editorial on equal rights, with an epigram from *Song of Solomon* ("I am BLACK but comely") that claimed, in an implicit address to British readers, contra the Boers, "We have not demonstrated our fealty to the throne for the sake of £.s.d." By 1924, however, he could say with regret that "to the mind of the Native of today, the first and last qualities of the effective leader should be 'a well-dressed man with a lot of money.'"[53] Or, in the poetic rendering of Mbuyiseni Oswald Mtshali, "He pays cash/that's why/he's called Mister."[54]

Within the remarkably short period of a generation, monetization associated with the minerals economy and especially the gold industry in the Transvaal had effected many of the changes that Trollope foresaw and that Plaatje lamented. As late as the 1930s, Isaac Schapera claimed that money had become indispensable without becoming in itself desirable, but the combination of coercion and what Rosa Luxemburg had called "gentle compulsion" had worked its magic. In addition to its role as the medium for settling debts related to taxes, polls, and pass fees, cash was the only means to pay for imported goods, and in particular, those ordered from mail-order shops: clothing, appliances, or objects for household décor, and even postage stamps.[55]

"Chairs, tables, bedsteads, saddles, crockery and linen; . . .] trousers for men (compelled by government laws against nudity), overcoats, ornaments like brass bangles," and new tastes, not only for coffee and sugar but also alcoholic spirits. Such were the accouterments and pleasures of modernity that Florence Nolwandle Jabavu, a student of Lovedale College and staunch advocate of Christian child welfare, described as the effects of "Westernism" in her essay "Bantu Home Life" (1928).[56] These accouterments and pleasures had been brought by missionaries and conveyed in the aura of the goods with which people of power and wealth adorned themselves and their homes. Nonetheless, they moved at different velocities and with differential intensities, soliciting more and less enthusiasm, more and less resistance in different sites, across

On the road to the Goldfields

5.1 Postcard, "On the road to the Goldfields," 1905.

generations, between men and women, in and between families.[57] The changes that Florence Jabavu noted had been normalized by the early 1800s in some places, and especially in the Cape, but they were still revolutionary in other places well into the 1900s. The territories being integrated by the Chamber into a single government field even before the Union would undertake the full harmonization of laws, can be described in Ernst Bloch's terms as a "synchronous non-synchronicity" or a "simultaneity of non-simultaneities."[58] But everywhere, they entailed a new urbanism. Because "these new needs and tastes could no longer be provided by the meager earnings of rural life," she wrote, young people "continuously drift[ed] to their supposed Eldorado."

A postcard from 1905 shows men at a train station, waiting for transport to the mines (figure 5.1). They're dressed in dandyish style, hats jauntily askew. They're fashionable men. In the face of contrary evidence (of which the postcard is but a token), what remains perplexing is how the Chamber could simultaneously discount black participation in consumer culture (the ostensible lure for entry into wage labor) and, at the same time, do everything in its power to inhibit a capacity to do so. The remedies it proposed to overcome this supposedly insufficient acquisitiveness included applying "more legal and moral pressure to a greater number of natives in British Possessions, and for longer periods"; and enhanced recruitments. To use a local idiom, the mines ate people and exhibited a gluttony that seemed in the immediate postwar years, to be insatiable.[59] The specter of a refusal to be consumed, and not only of a refusal to consume, was always already on the horizon. By the end of the war, it was being leavened by influences from revolutionary, communist, and anarchist movements from around the world, and African uplift movements from the United States, all of which were being channeled through vernacular black newspapers, brought by missionaries, and students returning from study abroad, few though they were. Hence, the post-war government conceded to the Chamber of Mines' pleas that an exterior force was needed, a foreignness that would not be assimilable to the emerging universalism among black subjects who took the British claims to liberty seriously and expected to eventually be included in the franchise along with the Uitlanders. Thus, between 1904 and 1908, and despite opposition to the idea from some sectors within the mining community and even more in other sectors, the country undertook an enormous experiment in labor substitution, recruiting workers from China on three-year long contracts (the last concluding in 1910).[60]

Perilous Journeys: Between the Devil and the Deep Blue Sea

The first ship to arrive carrying the newly indentured Chinese workers was the *Tweeddale*, which docked at Natal on June 19, 1904. The last would arrive on November 26, 1906, the year of the Bambatha uprising against the poll tax. At that point 63,296 Chinese subjects, almost all men, had been landed in South Africa.[61] It might have taken three days to travel from the coast to Johannesburg by train, depending on the schedules, but news of the ship's departure had arrived via Reuters telegraph from Hong Kong on the same day. The *Mafeking Mail and Protectorate Guardian* printed a column on May 25, 1904, headed by the following title: "Reuter wiring from Hongkong this morning says the steamer "Tweedale" [*sic*] sailed at daylight to-day for Durban with 1,055 Coolies for the Rand Mines. The men are jubilant at their brilliant prospects. They are accompanied by surgeons Hall and Wright."[62] Rumors of jubilation turned out to have been exaggerated, however. Within a year, the Duke of Marlborough would lambaste Lord Coleridge in the British House of Lords and refer to the experiment as a "disaster" created by the Chamber of Mines, as desertion, work stoppages, and strikes had become common and the Chinese laborers, having been recruited for their ostensible docility, proved themselves to have a powerful sense of their own rights.[63] In Marlborough's opinion, the Chinese worker had been reduced to "the kind of human pump which is to suck out from the bowels of the earth the natural wealth of the soil in the speediest possible time":

> The first step was the formation of the Witwatersrand Native Labour Association, the Chamber of Mines under an alias, and the first act of that association was to stamp out all independent contracting of Kaffir labour. It placed all

recruiting of Kaffir labour in the hands of the trust; it prevented Kaffirs from choosing the mine at which they would work—they must accept the alternative of working in what was perhaps the deadliest mine in the Transvaal, or of refusing to have their labour accepted at all. Then there was the fearful mortality in the mines, enough of itself to deter black labour, a mortality which was remediable because it has, in fact, very largely been remedied. We next had the lowering of Kaffir wages by 50 per cent. Were these things not enough of themselves to deter Kaffirs from seeking freely and spontaneously the labour that was offered to them? I do not hesitate, my Lords, to say that the combination of these circumstances produced what was the desired effect—namely, an *artificial scarcity* of black labour, and that *artificial scarcity* had to be proved before a case for the importation of the Chinaman could be accepted.[64]

Such Liberal sentiment was, in turn, being caricatured by conservatives, who found the professed outrage over Chinese indenture to be little more than a fig leaf hiding the aspiration to power: "An appeal to the hatred of Englishmen to slavery, or anything that may plausibly be described as slavery, is a card which is always safe to play."[65] The real issue, wrote Edward Dicey in the pages of *The Nineteenth Century and After,* lay elsewhere: "Anybody who knew anything of South Africa was aware that the labour difficulty is due mainly to the persistent refusal of the British working men in South Africa, to use Mr. Karrie Davis's phrase, 'to work alongside a black at the same job.' I quite admit that this refusal is not consistent with the 'man and a brother' doctrine, and hardly increases one's respect for the Liberal theory as to the 'dignity of labour.'" Black workers, he said, "are excellent workmen, especially underground, but they are lazy by nature and can only be induced to give good work for good wages by some form of compulsion, and any form of compulsion the Home Government declines to permit." In its naked racism, the debate of the House of Lords makes difficult reading. But it contains little that was not being spoken or written in the white public sphere at the time. And its defense of not-so-gentle compulsion won the day, although the importation of Chinese labor would cease.

On the same page of the Mafeking newspaper on which the story of the *Tweeddale* appeared, two other stories testified to the global web of information and connectivity in which the migrants from across southern Africa were also making their journeys. The first concerned the arrival in Natal of the Scottish American Zionist preacher, Alexander Dowie, and the other had to do with the question of women's suffrage. With respect to the former, the editors of the Mafikeng paper expressed much suspicion: "Salvation through a phonograph is the last novelty introduced by the sensation mongers of religion, the Zion City is to be introduced to the people of Durban through the medium of a Cinematagraph [sic] and Dowie the Elijah is to convey 'the Word' to them through a photograph. We are gradually getting nearer to the pray-by-turning-a-wheel condition."[66] With respect to the second issue, the paper expressed no opinion. It merely announced the week's debating topic for the Mafeking Literary and Debating Society, namely: "Women should be granted the franchise." The copresence of these two forces—of cinema and of women's suffrage—testify to the arrival of new forces and media of desire, which were soon to be conjoined. And it is not incidental that South Africa's first feature film, *De Voortrekkers* (1916) would parallel *Birth of a Nation* (1915), building itself around the specter of a Back peril retrojected as the object of historical surpassing, with the Battle of Blood River/Tugela River at its center.

What would be integrated into the audiovisual narrative of the film as a national and white nationalist or supremacist phenomenon is visible as a dispersed set of merely juxtaposed elements on the Mafeking paper's page. For, alongside the announcements of the debate about suffrage, the report of the *Tweeddale*'s departure, and the denunciation of cinematic sermonizing, there appeared a critical response to Roderick Jones's incendiary article on "The Black Peril in South Africa," which had been published in the same edition of *The Nineteenth Century and After* and directly followed Dicey's denunciation of Liberal piety. Jones's essay expressed concern about demographic disparity between white and black population growth rates and their consequences for white rule, and thanks to his status as director of Reuters, his opinion traveled with exceptional force.[67]

We can take this page of the Mafikeng newspaper as a metonym as well as a metaphorical snapshot of the forces traversing the social field—as they were perceived from a particular locus of authority. This is not a function of mere coincidence or serendipity (although serendipity is certainly present in every archival "discovery"). Rather, it is a matter of the web of translocal connections that were being both produced and enabled in papers like this one. The article by Roderick Jones had arrived on its pages as an object of editorial commentary after having traveled almost as rapidly as news of the *Tweeddale*, but it had already been reiterated and augmented in newspapers and parliamentary debates across the empire. In 1904, the "Black Peril" had been adduced as the grounds for the importation of Chinese labor, with a claim that "Native indolence" explained the shortage of labor on the Rand.[68] In a screed against black internationalism, Jones worried that South Africans would learn from African Americas and "strive after something beyond that to which they had been born."[69] It was the diminishing gap between black and white South Africans that set the stage for the crisis that he anticipated. The Cape Colony permitted natives who owned property of a certain value to vote, and even to run for office, and because cash wages earned on the mines promised an expanding voter base, he foresaw a time of black majoritarian rule.[70] John Tengo Jabavu had already run for office, although he had not succeeded, and Jones saw his bid as the opening of an oceanic wave. It was to be thwarted for another ninety years, however, in no small part because of the sentiments that Jones himself was articulating and disseminating in his capacity as the director of Reuters.

Views from the Other Side of the Speculated World

Among the heirs to J. T. Jabavu's political aspirations and indeed to the influence of African American emancipation, was his son, D. D. (Davidson) Jabavu. We find in his reported discourse both an insightful rebuttal to Jones and the advocates of white supremacism as well as an analysis of the impossible structure of desire into which black men were being shunted by the Chamber of Mines, a structure that would return in the period of high Apartheid and oppositional "ungovernability" in the form of an accusation: of self-destructive expenditure.

In April 1923, the pages of *Abantu-Batho* featured the translation of an article by W. Gumede, a report by the Chief Native Commissioner to Peter Nielson entitled "Summer School e-Cabhane: An Address by Jabavu." Gumede's article is remarkable for its hybrid form and translational labor, the traces of which are strewn throughout the text in parenthetical remarks that offer glossings of specific idioms. That such glossing was deemed necessary indicates something about the linguistic and educational diversity of the paper's readers as well, perhaps, as about the editor-translator's belief that either Gumede or Jabavu (or both) used excessively arcane metaphors. Although the tenor of Gumede's editorializing is one of disagreement, the article appearing after a rift had opened between the editors of *Abantu-Batho* and Jabavu's own paper *Imvo Zabantsundu*, it is worth considering Jabavu's reported speech in some depth, not for its evidentiary status as representative of widespread belief (this is unknowable) but because of the questions it makes possible.

The article opens with a frame narrative in which we are told that "the man [Jabavu] often came to the great gathering of teachers at Cabhane." Having opened with a narrative about prior encounters, the author turns away from his tempting biographical digression to say, "I will not bite the head, or hold on to the tail and have the heart," to which a parenthetical gloss is added: "I will not worry about side issues but will deal with the cardinal matter." Rather, he says, he will "get to it" and "let the blood (the information) gush out so that the thirsty ones may drink if they want to do so."[71] Only those desiring the information will seek it, but the rhetorically masterful speaker denies that his presentation is itself an attempt to persuade anyone. This is a classical rhetorical gesture, familiar to every student of Shakespeare and especially *Julius Caesar*—of whom Jabavu, educated in English literature at the University of London, was one.[72] According to Gumede, Jabavu frequently "would throw out little words like that," the diminutive adjective indicating his scorn. But he adds that, on this occasion, the orator was doing something different. He was using a parable to determine whether his audience had understood him or not: "he told us to see if we had understood his words, by way of telling us and explaining to us."[73] And he was soliciting his audiences into a comparative gesture—that is, to learn to conceive a future that they had been told (by the likes of Jones) was not available to them.

Jabavu's parables reference two sets of events: one in the Cape and one in the United States. In both cases, a black person resides near a white person who despises him. Both black people are the recipients of relentless "nastiness," including not only epithets but abuse and beatings. In both cases, the black man refrains from responding in violent kind (the translator notes that the original phrase, "throwing cold water on himself," means to keep one's temper). But over time, both are able to produce a surplus of goods—in the first case, a garden of cabbages and tomatoes "and other things that are liked by the whites," and in the second case, chickens and pigs sought after by a hungry white girl "who had run out of food." After the whites had learned that the blacks could indeed produce in excess and in this manner could come to possess something that the whites desired and for which they could pay, their attitudes changed. Jabavu, as reported by Gumede, says they earned the "respect" of the white people. Jabavu's moral is this: "If you cultivate the soil and get much food you will become the respected on earth, because, as you know, the teeth do not rest?" The gloss tells readers that this means "all people must eat" (451).

In the structure of this relayed story, respect accrues to the one who is able to produce in excess, but only because that excess has been converted into the object of an exchange, mediated by money. After relaying these stories, Gumede reported, "He [Jabavu] said that the trouble was that we had none of the things which the whites had not" and the translator adds the following clarification: "we had none of the things they required" (452). The author then follows a series of syllogisms and analogies by which the parable might be rendered more legible, thus becoming the basis of a rational comparison: a pauper who brews beer is addressed as "sir" for the day in which "the beer lasts," and white merchants purchasing goods from black producers address their orders to "Mr" but are insultingly blunt when black consumers come to ask for food, withholding all honorifics from those who, in turn, must now address the white seller as chief (Nkosi). Jabavu is then reported to have asked, "How can we expect white people to respect us if we have nothing to attract them to us?" And he concludes that he does not "counsel (ineffectual) struggle," and "there is no other way" (452).

Quite apart from the question of possible redaction, this text articulates a structure of desire that I have often encountered in the archive and that is all too palpable in Roderick Jones's article on "The Black Peril in South Africa," which ends as follows: "The blacks, under the influence of civilization, are becoming year by year a more formidable element, and, if unrestrained, must inevitably undermine the very foundations of white supremacy. Self-preservation is the first law of nature. It is not necessary to be a prophet or the son of a prophet to foresee that that law will yet compel the white man in South Africa to adopt measures against the native at which to-day nine people out of ten would raise their hands in pious horror."[74]

Prophet or no prophet, Jones could not resist the temptation to a Biblical figure, warning that "the white man is nursing a snake in his bosom."[75] In this gesture, he inadvertently discloses another dimension of white supremacy, for the serpent at the bosom is a figure of desire, of seduction, and of an impending fall. It is here, in what we can term, following Freud, his own parapraxis—that the truth of his discourse exposes itself.[76] Not alterity but too much proximity and not difference but a possible identification is what horrifies Jones. This is what Jabavu's parable teaches his readers and us to see.

In the dialectic of recognition derived from the paradigm of the lord/master and bondsman, and in the psychoanalytic tradition derived from it, the master confers recognition on his inferior and hopes to be inserted in the place of the (divine) Other, the absolute bearer of knowledge and authority. But this omniscience and omnipotence is always at risk. If the master requires the bondsman to seek him out in this capacity—as one who confers recognition on his inferior and who appears to bear the truth about him—then he too is lacking, is in need of an Other.[77] The illusion that the earthly master is the Other (and not simply an other) and the locus of absolute power comes crashing down as soon as this double dependency is realized (and this is what the transferential relationship is supposed to induce for those who take up psychoanalysis). The task of racist ideology is to cover over this absence, this lack in whiteness-as-mastery. Now, the therapeutic institution is not at stake for ethnography, but there is something to be learned by the speculative analogy between them. For, when Jabavu (or his editorially hallucinated double) says that the problem of white disregard for black people is a function of their lacking what whites lack, he is opening an analysis as profound as that which Fanon produced in the aftermath of his critical encounter with Octave Mannoni's psychoanalysis.

Initially, the white characters in these parables seem to treat black people as though they are radically different and beyond any reciprocity. Moreover, this difference seems linked, in Jabavu's account, to their belief that they lack what the whites have. As such, it would be a mere case of presumptive inferiority. But Jabavu does not say this. He says rather that the blacks lack what the whites lack. That is to say, the white denigration of the black men, as narrated, rests on the *resemblance* not the difference between the white and black figures. It is not that the whites have more (although they surely do at this moment in time) but that they both lack the means for self-sufficiency. Like the bondsmen, the masters are incomplete and incapable of self-satisfaction. Instead of alterity, then, the blacks appear to them as mirrors of what they lack. This is why the whites of the story hate them. Jabavu goes on to remark that when blacks have what whites do not have, they become not only worthy of recognition but are granted honorifics. Whites then make their monetary obeisance, submitting themselves and their requests to be satisfied at the risk of rejection. They do so in ressentiment.

One could read this whole scene through recourse to some transhistorical theory of desire rooted in *"the* subject's" constitutive lack—except that it is not enough for the black subjects in this story to have what the whites lack; they must agree to *sell* it. They do not give it. And only insofar as they do so, does recognition operate. We must, as Fanon says in his argument with Freud and Mannoni, "put this dream *in its time.*"[78] Fanon writes these words after recounting the dreams of seven young Malagassy patients, whom Mannoni had analyzed in terms of an inferiority complex, which he believed originated before colonization, although he thought such a complex was revivified in that context. Not incidentally, it is after reflecting on the societal or structural racism of South Africa, where, he said in 1952, "2,530,300 Whites cudgel and impound 13 million Blacks," thanks to the pass system, that Fanon makes the case for a reading of the historical contingency of the dream images that haunt Mannoni's young patients.[79] A similar tactic is necessary if we are to read Jabavu's story as a conscious expression of a transformed unconsciousness that is inflected by the contingencies of *its* moment. If we read Jabavu's story in such a manner, we begin to understand that money has become the only vehicle through which whites, or rather, white capital, wants to access alterity.

The structure of desire is not one in which blacks are radically other than whites (although whiteness is positioned as Other to blackness from its own vantage point) but rather, one in which only money, in the form of capital, can secure a difference that is constantly threatening to disappear. It is possible that today in South Africa, in the era of Black Economic Empowerment, national capital formation, and the rise of an uber-rich black elite for whom equality means equal access to inequality, marks the final demise of the racial dimension of this system. It is possible. But the lesson we will yet learn from the women pass protestors is that appearances can be deceiving. And what counts as racial emancipation is not evenly distributed; black men's emancipation is not yet or always the same as black women's emancipation. We must now consider their teachings.

CHAPTER 6

DOWN, IN AFRICA

Women Surpassing Protest

Go and we'll follow you
woman who protested passes;
confronted by protests
the white man quailed,
and kept his pistol holstered.

—Nontsizi Mgqwetho, "Go and We'll Follow You"

T he task outlined in the previous chapter can now be approached: to provide a partial account of the protests against the partiality of the entire system of separation and separatism grounded in the so-called needs of the gold economy, secured as it was by the chemical technologies of cyanidation and the alchemical dreams of turning waste into profit. Although the regime of Apartheid had yet to be formalized and might appear to constitute the absolutization of such separatism, the women whom we will encounter in the following pages repeatedly reveal the limits of every effort to think economy and politics, racialization or ethnicization, in ungendered and universalist terms.

The doubled comparativism that compelled D. D. Jabavu, discussed in the previous chapter, to read between the anticipatory ressentiment of the white supremacists in the United States and the Cape, and that furnished Roderick Jones (author of the incendiary article on "The Black Peril in South Africa") with his bad example, required an explanation. For his part, Jones recognized in the rise of Ethiopian churches and especially Dowie's Zionist church a new internationalism that was bearing with it the demand for universal rights and especially for education. The first of these churches, he noted, was Reverend Mangena Maake Mokone's breakaway Wesleyan church, which he termed part of a "cult." The word cult signified two forces: the first was its refusal to submit to official orthodoxy and the second was the intensity of its claim upon the minds of its adherents.

What enabled these sectarian churches to acquire their power? In her account of the Christian Zionism among the Barolong boo Ratshidi of South Africa, Jean Comaroff pays particular attention to the sensuous intensity cultivated by these churches and to the affective consolations afforded by their healing practices to alienated and newly proletarianizing people.[1] One has a sense that Jones recognized these tendencies and was repelled by them. He also notes the sense of empowerment that came when Mokone's church was recognized by the American Methodist Episcopal (AME) church in the United States in 1896. But he neglected to mention the reason for the Wesleyan church's turn to the AME or the 1896 conference in Pretoria where the decision was taken to send Reverend Dwane to the United States in pursuit of the Americans' formal benediction.

The conference had aimed to unite several independent churches and thereby to recover a divinely ordained originary unity. It had been urged and enabled by a young woman named Charlotte Maxeke, who was also Reverend Mokone's niece.[2] She was born in 1871 or 1874 to Anna Manci and John Kgope Mannya, who had himself grown up in the village of Ramokgopa near the town of Zoutpansberg at the time when Gwayi Tyamzashe was proselytizing there.[3] But Maxeke's father had not converted at Tyamzashe's behest; he had gone to Kimberley to buy arms to fight the Boers, and while there, he had come under the sway of Christian pacifism. In Kimberley, near the diamond fields, Charlotte acquired a desire for education, for experience of the world, and for a freedom tempered by modesty. In Johannesburg, at Evaton near the goldfields, she became a teacher, the founder of schools, and the advocate of black women's leadership.

Maxeke went to the United States in 1894 to attend Wilberforce University, where she studied under W. E. B. Du Bois and it was there that she converted to the AME. In 1901, she became the first black South African woman to obtain a college degree.[4] She would later found the Bantu Women's League while working with her husband (also a student at Wilberforce) as a teacher, missionary, probation officer, and social worker. Du Bois later praised Maxeke, writing that he and his wife "were interested in Charlotte Manye because of her clear mind, her fund of subtle humor, and the straightforward honesty of her character." He added, with sympathy: "She was having difficulties with language and the new environment, but she did her work with a slow, quiet determination that augured well for her future. . . . I regard Mrs. Maxeke as a pioneer in one of

the greatest of human causes, working under extraordinarily difficult circumstances to lead a people, in the face of prejudice, not only against her race, but
against her sex."[5]

Maxeke's appetite for U.S. education had been whetted even before she had
traveled to England as part of the Jubilee Choir's tour in 1891. The choir had been
renamed in homage to Orpheus Myron McAdoo's Virginia Jubilee singers after
he performed with the first nonminstrel troupe of black U.S. musicians to visit
South Africa.[6] That encounter had inspired Maxeke and opened one of many
portals to the outside world through which Ethiopianism entered. Jones may
have referred to it as a cult, but he took his analysis of this development from
the man whose run for office had so horrified him, namely John Tengu Jabavu,
D. D. Jabavu's father. A moderate Kholwa intellectual, John Tengu Jabavu had
called Ethiopianism a "social movement" in the Lovedale-based newspaper that
he edited, *Imvo Zabantsunda*.[7] It is one of the earliest uses of this term in the
sense that it now circulates, as an assemblage beyond class and irreducible to
the formal structures of civil society. Jones acknowledged the ethos of respectability and self-discipline within the movement, much influenced by Booker T.
Washington, but for him, the religious element of Ethiopianism could not be
contained by rendering it as a kind of latter-day Protestantism à la Max Weber.
To the contrary, it threatened to extend the political developments in the Cape,
namely the assumption of civil rights and electoral participation, beyond that
territorial jurisdiction. It was this deterritorializing threat, this spreading force
of universalist ambition across linguistic and local political boundaries, also
apparent in the black press, that he said ought to unite the English and Boer
subjects of South Africa in their whiteness against the emerging subjectivity of
blackness that the migrant labor system of the mines was producing, despite its
efforts to stoke interethnic or tribal rivalry: "only by presenting a solid front to
the oncoming hordes of superficially civilized blacks can they escape complete
annihilation."[8] For this same reason, he advocated for the importation of Chinese labor, not only as a supplement to the productive engine in the mines but
also as the basis of a new racialized nationalism. The legislation of that white
solidarity would fall to the Union government.

Retrospect

Solomon Tshekisho Plaatje would analyze the developments of these years with
typically sharp eloquence:

> In the beginning the popular cry was "tax the Native and thus force him to
> come to work"; the next slogan was "we should increase his wants and teach
> him the dignity of labour." Now the Ministry of Labour only wants to teach

him the indignities thereof; for when he wants to work to satisfy his increased wants he is told that work is the monopoly of another race, and a colour bar should be used to force him back to his native environments. But when he flees from the colour bar to those environments he finds himself between horns of the same dilemma—the Natives' Land Act, which prohibits his stay there. In fact when a Native shuns Scylla he falls into Charybdis and hardly knows where he is.[9]

Plaatje wrote these words following the passage of the draconian Natives Land Act in 1913, which extended and generalized, as well as reconciled the exclusions that the mining and the agrarian capitalists (and their political representatives) had already developed in the respective domains. The Natives Land Act relegated black subjects in South Africa to a miniscule 7.3 percent of the total arable land, and granted to the white population, accounting for less than 20 percent of the nation's residents, 80 percent.

Before 1913, most of the pass laws were municipal affairs, enforced or not depending on the predilections of local officials. A Native Commission had been struck in 1905, as the Chinese importation scheme began to show its weaknesses and had recommended segregation as a solution to urban problems. Between 1905 and 1920, a culturalist argument had emerged to justify the exclusion of black South Africans from urban areas, and thus to deny them rights to tenure and property ownership. This would be articulated by Colonel C. F. Stallard, who would ultimately chair the Transvaal Local Government Commission, and declare that urban modernity, being the product of Western civilizational processes, should be the exclusive domain of white people (designated Europeans at the time), except insofar as black people were there to serve them. The Native Urban Areas Act that would finally be passed in 1924 was substantially more restrictive and more oppressive than many of the draft bills that had been submitted over the previous two years, when President Smuts was in power. Among the most important elements to have been eliminated were proposed relaxations of the pass laws. As T. R. H Davenport describes it, Colonel Stallard "triumphed" with a law that gave urban local authorities enormous power to separate the races and effect a "cordon sanitaire," while also giving the minister of Native Affairs the power to make these authorities enact the federal law.[10] Bloemfontein and Johannesburg, the seats of power in the former Boer Republics, the former the center of agricultural capital, and the latter the site of mining capital, were the first to implement the act's provisions. Although it did not require black property owners who held title outside of the newly designated locations to dispose of it, "non-exempted Africans in an urban area—that is, men who were not voters in the Cape, landowners, chiefs, headmen, clergy, teachers of court interpreters—could be compelled to move out of the area if accommodation in the location was available."[11] In other words, exemption from passes, which Charlotte Maxeke would later insist constituted its own form of pass, became all the more important in this moment.

One of the consequences of the new rationalization of government powers was that town councils became entrusted with the task of registering black workers' service contracts, "with the aid of a somewhat strengthened pass machinery."[12] Black and so-called colored South Africans had to present themselves upon arriving in urban areas and had to demonstrate their means of livelihood, provide documents of prior employment, and show records of habitation. In this manner, the new law generalized what had been the practice at Bloemfontein for more than a decade, while merging what one might call the "best worst practices" of segregation and bringing the pass laws developed by the Orange Free State municipalities and the labor contract practices of the Witwatersrand Native Labor Association (WNLA) together into one tight web of repression.

Julia Wells describes the motives for the Orange Free State initiatives as follows: "Topping the list of white complaints about the servant problem was the desire to prevent workers from changing jobs, to compel servants to sleep in the employer's premises and to 'keep servants much more reserved.' In other words, whites wanted limited job mobility for servants, longer work hours and no complaints about working conditions."[13] To enable this, a labor bureau was set up to match potential employers with employees, with the latter having no choice in the assignment. It also used fingerprinting—to which development black activists strenuously resisted: "To black women this smacked of enslavement."[14] A "slavery badge," is how Mrs. A. Serrero and Mrs. C. Mallelo described it in a 1917 resolution on the later Native Women Pass Law.[15] The pages of *Abantu-Batho* are full of the comparison: "This pass is a chain whereby you are tied up in such a way that you have no saying anywhere"; "the Pass system . . . causes a person to be a slave"[16]. Following the Native Urban Areas Act promoted by Stallard, the same newspaper published an editorial asserting that "we are slaves who ARE NOT BEING FED AND CLOTHED BY THE MASTERS AS WERE THE SLAVES OF TWO HUNDERED YEARS AGO. We are slaves who are not being sold and bought at the market places but who will be forced to enslave themselves because we shall have no land to live on. That *this is a worse form of slavery* no sane man can deny."[17]

The *regressions* of the Native Urban Areas Act of 1924 were not merely the outcome of white supremacism's relentless forward march but also were a defensive response to women's resistance. This resistance was based in a critique of the formal universalism underpinning South Africa's increasingly restrictive law of spatialized racial order. Women's pass protests ran alongside strikes and other kinds of worker protests, but they were grounded in the question of sexual difference rather than the demand for better wages and reduced surplus value extraction. Their protests showed how the regime of invisible visibility was transformed under the new pass laws—in the new age of cinema and mass communication, we note—to entail a violent specularity directed at them. Because they refused the lie of equivalence while creating a new form of appearance in the political domain, they command our attention.

They Were Not Chamber Maids

In 1913, Bloemfontein was the locus of both the most ardent support for the most restrictive version of segregation and for the emerging women's protest movement, both because it was the seat of a relatively large and stable population of African women, not all of whom were domestic servants, and because it had been a destination for war refugees. As Wells explains, the problem of refugees in Bloemfontein following the Anglo-Boer war was especially piquant, and although whites had generally seen their legal rights enhanced in the period immediately following the cessation of hostilities, areas with high concentrations of refugees also became the locus of what would later become "poor whitism." Among other things, the thousands of refugees and their servants despoiled the agricultural lands of the smallholders. Many of these people advocated for the exclusion of black people from trades, and other possible sources of competition. On this basis, blacks in Bloemfontein were required to obtain "work-on-own-behalf" permits if they did not work for whites, and in 1908, new vagrancy laws were enacted. Poverty resulting from the depression and drought in 1908 led to terrible rates of death among children. As the situation worsened, so did the penalties for nonpayment of rents, fines, and taxes.[18]

What initially incited the women's protests was their uniform inclusion under the laws—a development that had two specific consequences. First, the wives of educated men and others who could obtain exemptions under the existing law (if only because their white employers vouched for them) lost their right to their husband's exemptions. In this case, more prosperous or highly ranked women became subject to the same protocols as poor unmarried women in domestic service or otherwise living alone. Second, the women seeking both passes and exemptions became subject to mandatory medical inspections. On these doubled grounds, women of all class positions rose in opposition. The medical inspections were especially resented because they extended a mortification previously borne only by men to women, and required all women and not merely those seeking employment to expose themselves to a sexualizing gaze as a result. It was not only that the pass laws introduced a new vulnerability to predatory inspectors. Once the law applying to women was passed, women with and without passes became uniformly "to-be-looked-at."[19]

In March, 1912, the women of the Orange Free State had written a petition, signed by more than five thousand, arguing that the subjection of women to pass laws "renders them liable to interference by policemen at any time" and "has a barbarous tendency of ignoring the consequences of marriage in respect of natives." It also "lowers the dignity of women and throws to pieces every element of respect to which they are entitled."[20] The women took their petition to Cape Town and presented it to the minster of Native Affairs, Henry Burton. Although apparently sympathetic, he was also weak and merely urged municipal authorities in the Free State to refrain from enforcing their laws until a new legislative order could be instituted. Shortly thereafter, a committee was struck to inquire into "Assaults on Women," the report of which was referred to in "The Commission of Inquiry into the Pass Laws of 1920." The 1920 Commission was also moved by the women's protests, and in its conclusions, it asserted that "there should be no indiscriminate stopping of natives by the police for the production of the Registration Certificate per se as the harassing and constant interference with the freedom of movement of law abiding natives is without any doubt the most serious grievance which the natives have against the pass laws and is one of the principal causes of the recent agitation against the existing systems."[21]

Burton may have been sympathetic, but some of the men in the African Political Organization (APO), formed to represent the interests of colored Africans at the turn of the century and led by Dr. Abdul Abdurahman, were miffed that the women had not obtained their permission before seeking an audience with government. Women had been excluded from the early meetings of the South African Native Congress, and when Charlotte Maxeke had attended the annual meeting in Queenstown in October 1902, her request to become a member was tabled and effectively rejected.[22] Plaatje later excoriated the men who kept her from membership, comparing her "adventurous missionary life among the heathens of the Zoutpansberg" to their demonstration of "manliness by leisurely enjoying the sea breezes of the coast."[23] And so, in 1912, when the South African National Native Congress was formed (heir to the South African Native Congress and the predecessor of the African National Congress), having arisen in the aftermath of the failure of the Native delegations to extract rights before the achievement of Union, she was again present and became its first female delegate. From there she advocated "passive resistance."

The early protests were theaters of contained outrage. Wrapped in rags, the passes were carried by silent women, led by leaders who bore the "Union Jack as an emblem of freedom and liberty" with "young women and girls carrying sticks, whips and sjamboks." Their theatrics were partly an attempt to secure support from the English officeholders and partly a display of ensorcellment by the politics of recognition. Such tactics were common at the time, part of an effort to force the bearers of colonial power to actualize their discourses of universalism, by which all would be treated equally under the law.

The protests were in no other way typical. Older women carrying broomsticks enforced the silence, so that, "for want of a biercoach and two black horses, it might have resembled a funeral procession."[24] Emerging here, perhaps for the first time, was the form of a funerary protest that would become integral to the anti-Apartheid struggle. The women did not merely plant their passes at the pass law office, however. They burned them. One of the women protesting was quoted as saying, "we are determined to go to Edenburg (meaning to gaol), and to reduce the pass law into ashes, as we did the 'dirty papers.'"[25] To reduce the pass law and not merely the dirty papers, which is to say the individual passes, to ashes, would be not only to destroy it but also to destroy the very memory of it, to render every form of it inaccessible even as a trace. For ashes are that from which a form cannot be retrieved.

Equally important, the protests were generating a new mode of appearing and thus a new kind of political space. As Hannah Arendt notes, "the *polis* . . . is not the city state in its physical location; it is in the organization of the people as it arises out of acting and speaking together, and its true space lies between people living together for this purpose, no matter where they happen to be."[26] Arendt is correct to note that such a space does not always exist, and we can understand the pass laws as an effort to inhibit the entry of black and colored individuals into the space of the political, as people who "are together in the manner of speech and action."[27] Insofar as the pass laws were also working, in their accumulating and extending force, to remove people who had already entered this new national space, as in the Cape or through exemptions, the South African case provides a dramatic instance (and warning) that the political space is always vulnerable to disappearance.

With their funerary theater and much-remarked silence, the women protesters asserted, in their bodily self-presence, that political space is not limited to that which creates the conditions for rational discourse, as Arendt and others have sometimes implied. Its transience does not have to entail its disappearance (even if this is always a risk), for these otherwise apparently ephemeral events entered into the consciousness of other women, took up residence in their memories, became the subject of poetic witnessing and celebration, and nourished the long, slowly emerging "mass strike" that would eventually topple Apartheid, even though it emerged before that system was formalized.[28] The radicalism of the women's gestures is all the more profound when one recalls that it was being enacted in a context in which, under the new laws, the demand made of women was, precisely, visibility. In this sense, the protesters were attempting to transform the space of "to-be-looked-at-ness" into one of real political appearance.

The writer of the article for *Abantu-Batho* reporting this event did not yet grasp this transformative force (which would always be vulnerable to usurpation for violent ends), but he was struck by the corporeal potency of their acts. He took pains to contrast the disciplined "gentle manner" of the protesters with the reputed riotousness of English suffragettes and took pride in their relatively "ladylike" conduct.[29] From this perspective, in the protests spurred by the inclusion of women under laws previously directly toward men only, it could appear that women were militating against universality and the notion of equal treatment under the law. Julia Wells, for example, argues that these insurrectionaries harbored a "powerful conservative force" and that "racial oppression was tackled while traditional gender-defined roles were reinforced."[30]

But appearances can be deceiving. Certainly, respectability was a concern for the protesters. Maxeke, herself a social worker, later wrote about the "demoralizing effect" of life in Johannesburg on young women, who, she said, often ran out of funds before securing employment, and thus became dependent on prostitution. As solution, Maxeke proposed "industrial training schools for Natives, better housing and accommodation, and a closer police supervision over those landlords who let the rooms in question."[31] The latter proposal belied the coerced participation of these "free women" in the sex trade. Maxeke believed that urban landlords not only permitted young women to obtain their rents from illicit activities, and especially prostitution, but also leveraged the women's debt to necessitate it. Nonetheless, it was precisely the nonrecognition of that desire for respectability that initially incited the women to protest. Men were subject to physical inspection at the mines, but the possibility that "foreign doctors [would] publicly examine native women" was unconscionable to the women. Nor did the issue go away. In December, 1917, *Abantu-Batho* reported extended discussions on the topic by the Native Congress and clergy. It argued that the Women's Pass Law differed little from the employment registration required of men but conceded that the matter of medical examination marked a difference and stated, bluntly, "it's quite plainly unfair."[32]

This "passing remark" about the unfairness of the examination assumes that a uniform application of law to those who are differently situated, differently viewed, and subject to different forms of both exclusion and fetishization, has different effects. There is no such thing as equality under the pass law if the people subject to it are not equal. It was on these grounds that Maxeke would also reject the move to grant white women suffrage. Although she had met Emmeline Pankhurst while touring with her choir in 1891, and although she seems to have admired the suffrage movement in England, she, along with Ethel Wauchope and Esther Nciyiya, opposed the granting of suffrage to South Africa's white women on the grounds that the women so enfranchised "would consist chiefly of the class adversely disposed to Native aspirations and would therefore seriously jeopardise Bantu interests."[33]

Before she and her husband Marshall split from *Abantu-Batho* to pursue a more "moderate" or "third" path, the paper published a gushing review of Charlotte Maxeke's "stirring" speech to the National League of Bantu Women (Transvaal Province), which she had founded. It reported the cheers drawn from her listeners, members of the Bantu Women's League, when she claimed that, "It is impossible for a Bondman to preach freedom and liberate another bondman. How can men liberate women from the pass laws when they themselves are subjected to them? Let our men free themselves." She was speaking in light of the fact that, in the previous year, more than forty thousand people had been arrested and prosecuted on charges of pass law violations. And, she concluded by stating, in Latin, "'Dux femina facto.' Women must therefore wake up for theirs is the leadership."[34] Especially notable in Maxeke's speech is her comparison of the various registrations, certificates, and passes, and her inclusion of the exemption certificate in the category of pass (which statement apparently earned her the audience's "loud applause"). The pass laws would become more stringent and the prosecution rates higher in the subsequent years, so that by the time of the Native Areas Act's passage in 1937, the number of annual arrests had risen to one hundred and twenty thousand, and it would continue rising thereafter until the end of 1960s, when nearly seven hundred thousand people a year were being detained and prosecuted on these grounds.[35]

Maxeke's gestures have sometimes been read as the mere expression of Christian moralism coupled with racial nationalism. In fact, Maxeke's discourse makes two extremely significant analytical gestures. And they are related. The first rests on the claim that any exemption to the law secured by the authority that might otherwise enforce that law must be included in the category of its evidentiary presentation and actualization. Exemptions from pass laws, on the basis of education and professional status, or by virtue of an employer's special consideration, merely reinstate the identity between nativeness or Africanity and ignorance or baseness. Maxeke insists that special considerations (exceptions) were the means by which hierarchical, nonreciprocating relations between colonial authority and black Africans were secured on the basis of identification rather than recognition.[36] Maxeke discerned that the law traverses the entire social field as a uniformly operating principle, no matter how it is dissimulated under different names but, *for this very reason*, it is an instrument of inequality. For the women to whom it was applied were always already differently positioned than men in the sex and gender systems of both precolonial and colonial societies. Second is the claim that only women can liberate women, with men's incapacity to free themselves betraying a lack of knowledge about how liberty might be obtained.

At the time, what the women protesters were attempting to demonstrate was that they were subject to both a general and an exceptional form of the pass law. This fact put them in a distinct position, one from which they might emerge as uniquely representative of "the oppressed." Just as the Worker, the most oppressed and excluded part under capitalism is the one who, for Marx, was destined to represent the common interests of the entire social field, Woman becomes, in Charlotte Maxeke's discourse, the specific agent of a general emancipation. I use the form, Woman, to indicate that this is a figure, just as "the Worker" and "the Capitalist" are figures and personifications of structural interests in Marx's writings. Maxeke was calling for individual women to act, of course, but she was doing so in the name of a representative function that resides in the abstraction, Woman, or gendered subalternity, in whose name women may be interpellated.

How can we reconcile this with the fact, much documented and discussed among feminist historians of the pass protests, that so many of its advocates were champions of chastity, maternity, respectability, and domestic responsibility, often denouncing women whom they deemed to be sexually lax and morally weak?[37] The fact that some of these women, such as Maxeke's friend, the radical poet Nontsizi Mgqwetho, as well as her sister among others, did not marry even as they lamented shotgun weddings, divorce, and sexual promiscuity among women, should make clear that the defense of traditional marriage did not mean that everyone was destined for the hearth of a heteronormative household. Their discourse needs to be understood otherwise, partly because immorality was a code word for subjection to white depravity, given that most of the clients of black prostitutes in urban areas were white men and that sexual services were a primary means of accessing and paying for employment passes, also authorized by white men.[38] Women could also be subject to body searches even if they did have passes, and these searches, typically performed by members of the black constabulary, also elicited outrage from women and indignation from their husbands and other male kinfolk.[39]

Rather, what Maxeke and the protesters make visible is the lie of legal formalism and the function of difference. More specifically, the difference represented by the term Woman is linked to the kind of gaze to which those so-named are subject. Given the circumstances, modesty was for many women one of the few idioms in which a woman could claim sovereignty. This possibility was circumscribed, of course. It did not entail a full power of self-determination nor was it modeled on the masculine sovereign in whom divinity is supposedly mirrored. Rather, modesty was a concept and a discourse that permitted them a right of refusal—perhaps the bedrock of all real political sovereignty. The value of modesty did not come only from the Christian mission tradition, although it surely acquired additional strength as a result. It was shaped by older patriarchal histories that reserved the prerogative of access to women for mothers (or mothers-in-law) or those charged with policing women's chastity, and later, their husbands—in part by the colonial histories within which women had come to expect modesty and desire privacy, and in part by the pseudo-medical gaze to which they were subject, which approached women's bodies as the object and medium of its own violent consolidation. Indeed, the concept of modesty functioned precisely because it signified and was rooted in these many traditions—all of which share a presumption of heteronormative reproductivity.

Significantly, by 1917, when protests that had been temporarily suspended during the war years resumed, opposition to the inclusion of women under the new pass system in Orange Free State (it had not yet been extended to the Rand at the time) was most approved by those with interests in the mines. With an eye toward the possible spread of the Free State protests to the Witwatersrand, many in the mining sector expressed sympathy and agreement with the women. And no wonder. For, the growing threat of labor disruption held particular risks for them. If passes had originally seemed like a method of compelling men's movement while keeping women in the peripheral areas and thereby ensuring the agrarian production that would permit the suppression of wages, its purpose from 1913 onward, from the perspective of the Randlords, was to force men to the mines and to force them to return from closed compounds to agrarian areas at contracts' end. Hence, the specter of a male workers' strike in support of the women had initially led the minister of finance to support the women's position.[40] Indeed, many in the mining sector felt that women's demands could be indulged if it permitted the retention of the pass laws for black and colored male workers. To this extent, the women's insurrection could appear to be a mere passage en route to the tightening of limitations for men, but that is to make the failed struggle responsible for the oppression against which it asserts itself. For their part, the women paid dearly. They were arrested, often beaten, imprisoned, deprived of shoes in the coldest months of winter, made to eat rotted food, and forced to do hard labor imitating that of their male mining counterparts: breaking rock. They grew gaunt and gray. And after it all, following an apparent respite in the form of a revised bill exempting women, the worlding world of black and colored South Africans closed again with the passage of Native Urban Areas Act of 1923. "A worse form of slavery," indeed. And it would get worse.

Yet, the analogy is also a gesture of differentiation. And the additional burden of reproduction should not be confused with a simple reduction of women to the maternal function. Indeed, as Hortense Spillers teaches us, this function must be understood in its fullest sense not in terms of the enfleshed body that gives birth (the role to which women were reduced in chattel slavery, having no right in their children), but as the role or structural position of one who confers siblingship on children, a function that was being denied to black women.[41] For, the pass system, when coupled with the growth of domestic service and the restrictions on black residence in urban areas under Stallardism, discouraged black women from mothering, at least in a generationally limited sense (the role was often transferred to grandmothers). And it did so while attempting to foreclose the emergence of work-based solidarities among members of different ethnolinguistic traditions. Indeed, the disavowal of this sibling-enabling capacity was the core of segregation, which, above all, wanted to inhibit the emergence of a black political community cast in the idiom of fraternity. The issues that emerge from this consideration—about the way in which political community is coded in patriarchal societies as fraternity and about the differences between societies in which the majority of black subjects are descendants of slaves and those in which this is not the case (the difference, that is, between the Americas and Africa)—requires more than a parenthetical remark, and I will return to this issue in subsequent chapters. What segregationist South Africa shared with the history of the post-enslaving society in the United States, from which both white nationalists and black activists drew inspiration, was the deployment of sexual difference in the service of racialization—as the poet, Nontsizi Mgqwetho well knew. Let us listen to her, now.

Passages: Ariadne in Plato's Cave

"Parliament's on the hunt/for laws that will oppress us."[42] These words (or rather, the isiXhosa words of which these are the translation) appeared in a poem entitled "Unity, Black Workers" (*Imanyano! Basebenzi Abantsunda*) published in 1924 in the multilingual newspaper *Umteteli Wa Bantu*, edited by Charlotte Maxeke's husband Marshall. It was created and funded by the Chamber of Mines in 1920 as an alternative to *Abantu-Batho* and other workerist or communist organs, and it was intended to both encourage a middle path between labor and mine management oriented by an ostensible future (if asymptotically deferred) conciliation between black and white South Africans. At the same time, the paper was funded to reveal to the powers that be what was on the minds of workers. It entered a diverse and energetically edited media sphere. As Natasha Erlank has noted, the black press of the time was edited by a small group of largely mission-educated intellectuals of varying political commitments, some of whom had also been educated in Britain or the United States, who "shaped their content using articles and content culled from other newspapers, journals, magazines, and just about anything considered wordy enough."[43] They cut and culled, ventriloquized, borrowed, and quoted from each other and did so across vast distances knitted together by telegraphy. Their pages hosted political news and events from around the world; criticisms of legislation and coverage of parliamentary debates, news of conferences, strikes, and trade union activism; Biblical exegesis and religious sermons; poetry, literary analyses, and theater reviews; births and deaths announcements; advertisements; editorial commentary, debates, columns addressed to women; and literacy lessons for children. They were multilingual and if, in their pages, English represented and enabled a certain appearance of cosmopolitan universality, it did not assume the status of a lingua franca. The space of these papers, both visually and linguistically, was one of both discontinuity and comparison, disjunction and juxtaposition.

The use of vernaculars (isiXhosa, isiZulu, Sesotho, Setswana) permitted a heterogeneous readership to engage their content, and at times, to hide their radical sentiment from official view. These languages were not merely the media for translated English text, and vice versa; they were used for distinct journalism, voicing ideas and positions, as well as poetic forms, that did not always enter English or Dutch/Afrikaans at all. That such translocal and often global discourse was read in a context in which most people remained illiterate discloses the nature of a society I have already described, following Ernst Bloch, as "synchronous nonsynchronicity." Accordingly, they worked to address and represent the interests of those who could read as well as those who had to rely on others both to hear and to overhear. Many of these outlets published verse, and *Umteteli*, in particular, published a great deal by Maxeke's friend, Mgqwetho. Often her poems addressed specific events and timely issues, including factionalism within the black political community and, of course, the pass protests. The first poem of hers in the record, cited in the chapter epigraph, is an ostensibly autobiographical work that nonetheless repeats the refrain, "Go and we'll follow you," which is variously addressed to *Umteteli* and Charlotte Maxeke: "Go and we'll follow you,/woman who protested passes; confronted by protests/the white man quailed/and kept his pistol holstered."[44]

Although her verses feature a number of narratorial personae, male and female, hers was an uncompromising voice, perhaps best described in her own poem, "Listen, Compatriots" (*Pulapulani! Makowetu*) as follows: "Mercy Nontsizi! African moss,/you strip poetry bare to the bone/and the nation's mountains swivel/as you sway from side to side."[45] Beginning in 1920, she wrote and published a remarkable series of occasional poems, delivered at the end of each year, that repeat the following melancholy stanzas:

> The year has passed and left us,
> > all signs point to its passage:
> > the trials of ushering the new year in
> > are with us

> The year has passed and with it
> > News of people on earth,
> > Their conduct, their cruelties,
> > All recorded.[46]

The same lines appear in the 1923 poem titled "A Long Lying-In, Then the Python Uncoils and Leaves" (*Yacombuluka! Inamba u 1923 ebisoloko ifukamele ukunduluka*). In the years between the publication of these two poems, the pass protests had reached their temporary apogee and been thwarted by the new Urban Areas Act. In this context, she wrote,

> Why are the houses of Africa burning?
> Poll tax, Pass, and Special Permit.
> Where can we live? Up in the clouds.
>
> Laws outnumber those of Moses.[47]

Mgqwetho writes of Johannesburg as a city of "booze and thugs," where people "shack-up" and criminals run riot, where tradition is lost and education is a farce, and where police brutality and legal oppression are the foundations of everyday life. She is as contemptuous of the African intellectuals educated in America and alienated from their own tradition (with the exception of Charlotte Maxeke) as she is of the whites, the cops, and the fork-tongued missionaries, as she calls them. She writes from "Crown Mines," but she never writes about the mines per se. Only in her eulogy, "Mother's Death" (*Umpanga ka Mama*), does she invoke them, and this in a "quoted prayer" attributed to her mother: "'Lord,' she implored,/'shield our land/from the threat of fire,/of the mines/and of flood/of tempest and lightning,/of locusts,/of whirlwind,/of hunger and plague.'"[48] In a Biblical idiom that Tyamzashe would have recognized, the mines are coded in a litany of divine curses. They are catastrophes and punishments, but also events in which the absolute power of the absolutely foreign comes to bear on the living. They are death itself. This is not so much because of the so-called accidental deaths they cause as because of the forms of behavior and the social disintegration that they provoke.

To understand Mgqwetho's analysis of this mortifying power of the imperial foreign, as well as her apparently contradictory embrace of it, we would need to read her entire oeuvre, a task assisted by the handsome anthology of her work assembled by Jeff Opland. That is not possible here, but it will help to consider Mgqwetho's praise poem, "*Yeha! Watshona! Afrika! Elundini!*" (translated by Jeff Opland and Pamela Maseko as "Alas! Africa, you fade into the horizon") to get some sense of what a deeper reading could enable.

"Alas! Africa" is a study in righteous invective, notable not only for its homage to the protesters and a sneering repudiation of police violence but also for how it reappropriates the events and renders them in agrarian idiom, thereby recoding protests not in the image of industrial action or incendiary rage but agrarian fecundity. As with all praise poems, "Alas! Africa" opens with an address to the people whose deeds are to be chronicled: "Here are the leaders of the nation who bleated in Johannesburg and the cops trotted down the mountain!" Mgqwetho then lists the participants from highest to lowest ranking, starting with the mayor (Mr. C. S. Mabaso) and moving toward those who were arrested or killed, including J. Mookoane, whose name is followed by the designation "supreme sacrifice" (the descriptions, and the term "pass" are in English, although the rest of the poem is in isiXhosa). The poem then continues: "Here then are the heroes who reaped the seed from the sacks of passes planted at the Pass Office! Today let them wear the skin robes worn by chiefs."[49] The sack of passes is planted at the threshold of the state bureaucracy in the sense of a seeding for the future. It is that which will grow, that which can be harvested. Thus, after the opening preamble, the poet describes the senior men "who scooped the old corn of the pass from the pit/and the council broke out in a sweat." The young protesters are likened to elephant calves, whose "trunks plucked wealth from passes, striving so Africa would taste freedom."[50] The corn, which is not just any food but the staple of the region and the metonym of food in general, is nourishment for people and the entire creaturely world. The elephants being figures of political power, this sustenance is to be grasped in its potential for the symbolic order where people are not, in fact, reduced to bare life.[51] Perhaps the other of bread (with which, say Christians, humans cannot live alone), corn is the name of all that exceeds need, without ever being superfluous. And the coding of protesters as elephants is another idiom for describing that form of appearance that Arendt termed political.

Mgqwetho followed this poem with another, dedicated to the "child" who "departed this life in the course of the Pass protest." It is an homage to the young man, whose "bravery shaped the seraphim," and to Jesus, whose love "amazes the sinner here on earth." But this second poem of the sequence ends ambiguously, with a question addressed to "Jehovah, God of our fathers," namely: "why screen your face/from Africa? Mercy!" As if to remind the Almighty of what He has overlooked, and what she herself observes, she asserts: "There they all are in prison,/even her children./Remember what you must do/about our country. Peace!"

The intertextual references that thread Mgqwetho's poem and her seeming rebuke to the God she otherwise acknowledges, calls for a reading of the text she invokes, namely 2 Kings, in which Moses constantly speaks to God but is deprived of any direct *en face* relation with the deity. As Jeff Opland tells us, speculating on her authorship of a letter to the Williamstown newspaper, *Imbo Zabantsunda*, on October 14, 1897, she was likely the author of a critical review of a new translation of the Bible, which she condemned for its "flat style" and inappropriate use of unfamiliar terms.[52] She knew her Bible as both a document of revealed truth and a literary work—even if she often denounced its use by white missionaries as a tool of oppression: "heed its word and heaven's lost."[53]

Essentially, Mgqwetho's poem puts Africa in the place of Moses, the recipient of the Law and the representative of the chosen people, he who leads his people out of slavery. The Zionism that she expresses would be taken up in a number of the African churches of the region, and not only those that sprouted from the formal Zionist movement and especially the Christian Catholic Apostolic Church in Zion (C.C.A.C.Z.) established by Dowie (the missionary reviled for his cinematograph in the Mafeking paper).[54] If Mgqwetho's reading of protesters as being like sheep risks implying weakness, it is redeemed by the reference to the young man, Mookoane, whose death is termed a "supreme sacrifice," and who is thereby allied with Jesus through the trope of the lamb. In this case, Zion is in Africa.

But, as the poem's interrogative plea reminds its readers, Moses is also he who remains in exile, who does not make it into the promised land, the one whom God addresses but to whom he remains hidden. When Mgqwetho asks, "Why screen your face from Africa?" she both identifies Africa with Moses as the rightful beneficiary of divine grace and inserts herself into the place of Miriam, who, along with Aaron, questions God's exclusive conversation with Moses. In the Biblical narrative and the exegesis devoted to it, Miriam is also known as a prophet in her own right, although she paid a relatively high price for impertinently daring to question God's preference for Moses. Mgqwetho had considerable familiarity with this experience. Like Miriam, she was a vessel in whom a speaking that came from afar was taking place; the praise poet is close to a medium, a sybil, or a prophet in this sense—and can speak a critical truth to power.[55] Like Miriam, she bridled at her exclusion from the inner circle, self-consciously referring to herself as the "Woman Poet" (*imbongikazi*) to mark her marginalization in relation to S. E. K. Mqhayi, who referred to himself and was referred to by the literati as the "Poet of the Whole Nation." Her public performances were delivered in spaces typically reserved for men, but they were renowned throughout Johannesburg, where it was said, her "poetry could be heard at a distance, so that [people] perceived [their] deliverance was at hand."[56] She sang praises at City Deep Hall, at Congress Concerts and political rallies, leaving her audiences "with their hand to their cheeks, crying out loud."[57]

If Mgqwetho's poem recodes or resignifies the pass protests in a local idiom, this vernacular appropriation is nonetheless not a gesture of nativization. This use of vernacular is the form of entry into a transnational community, woven from the intertextual fabric of innumerable events and voicings, many of which came from afar but were also incorporated into local practice, where they became part of second nature. Corn itself is an import, brought to southern Africa from the Americas by colonial merchants around 1500—it arrived in what would become South Africa only in 1655. Its domestication in economies dominated by gathering and bovine husbandry is part of the story by which cattle came to signify both wealth and continuity with the past. The corn referenced by Mgqwetho is thus both foreign and at the same time the substance of local agriculture. By the form of cultivation and consumption, and in its imbrication with other forms of life, it had become the sign of Africanity by the nineteenth century.

Mgqwetho may or may not have consciously thought of it this way. The alterities that resonate in her poems are not limited to overt local references; her verse draws on the oral traditions of the otherwise exclusively male *imbongi* or praise poet, and incorporates the preacherly traditions of the female prayer circles or *manyano* (whom she defends against male clerics' criticisms), but it is peppered with English and Afrikaans and deploys the stanzaic structure and rhyme schemes that were otherwise alien to local genres of orature.[58] Foreign references are also intertextualized in this poem. It is useful to distinguish between the citationality that is intended by the author and the intertextuality that exceeds authorial intention and traverses the discursive field by virtue of both prior uses, resonances and associations, as well as future readings. After the fact, it is often difficult to distinguish among them. We cannot know what Mgqwetho thought she was doing; we can only read her poem and open ourselves to its potential significations.

"Alas! Africa" culminates with a reference to Benoni, a town on the East Rand established in 1881, just before the gold rush commenced. The Biblical reference of that town's name is a character in Genesis, whose first name, Benoni, means "son of my pain." Nontsizi's own name (possibly self-conferred) meant "Mother of Sorrows," and she may have found a mirroring relation between her name and that of the town, as well as echoes of her fate as a neglected writer and that of the doomed young Mookoane.[59] But Genesis also tells the story of how the moniker, Benoni, was ultimately replaced by Benjamin, which has been interpreted by exegetes to mean "Son of the South." Such references had great appeal to southern African Christians. Mgqwetho repeatedly alludes to this spatialization of grace in poems that address and refer to God "below in Africa," as in the memorialization of Mookoane, which ends by invoking the mounted police officer with which "Alas! Africa" opens: "They spur their horses to trample us,/ we're ringed by dangers./Oh! Lord God below, down in Africa."

In choosing to end "Alas! Africa" with the reference to Benoni, Mgqwetho not only completes the cartographic gesture that began in Johannesburg and sweeps along the route to the mines of the East Rand but also arrives at the story of a woman's death in childbirth—the pain of Benoni—that, like her own labor, is effaced by the act of renomination. When she writes "Mercy, slashers of ropes that bind Benoni," she also summons the ghost of the newly named Benjamin, who, in Genesis, is threatened with enslavement. This is key. For the threat of enslavement is precisely what she and the other protesters discerned in the new pass laws, as we have seen. This does not mean that they did not grasp the specific violence performed in the nexus of wage labor and pass-mediated migration in the Chamber-made world. The term slavery functioned as a figure and temporizing mechanism even in the midst of that form of hybridized industrial capitalism practiced on the gold mines. Cast into the future in the discourse of the protesters, rather than in the past as it was for American Pan-Africanists,

it was akin to those prophetic figures from Revelation in Christian messianism invoked by Mgqwetho in her eulogy to her mother, where the mines are
included among the omens of death.

Printed poetry was not the only vehicle for this kind of critical pedagogy,
however. Nor were newspapers the only vehicle for its dissemination. Poets like
Mgqwetho performed their works before large audiences. Moreover, the peri-
patetic oral sermonizing of both missionaries and political organizers transmitted news and reports of oratorical artistry, even as they enacted their own.
And those who traveled the country constituted something like an animated
medium through which messages from afar traveled, and through which the
possibility of a translocal imagination was cultivated. Nonetheless, both the
itineraries and the discourses of these traveling salespeople of deterritorialized
solidarity often clashed. In the previously cited poem, "Unity, Black Workers,"
Mgqwetho lampooned those American-influenced educators who were moving across the country, claiming the mantle of leader. She was especially severe
with the Cape-based political elite, including Dr. Rubusana:

> Dr. Rubusana, roadside diviner,
> Wails in a mountain cave
> He says our nation's progress
> Must be driven by our own leaders.
>
> So says the doctor, Rubusana,
> He snarled and the monkeys scattered.
> Press on and speak out in your travels![60]

A line follows that recurs throughout Mgqwetho's verse: "Oh I blundered in
going to whites!" (*Awu! Nakhubeka ndibke aemlungwini*).

In "Unity, Black Workers," one gets the impression of a veritable academic
touring industry. Few are assailed with more corrosive contempt than D. D.
Jabavu, son of the politician whom Jones had held up as harbinger and husband
of the noted Christian moralist, Florence Nowandle Jabavu.[61]

> Welcome, Professor D. D. Jabavu,
> B.A. with an antelope's guile
> You've earned a mark of distinction;
> Your speech in East London delighted me.
>
> You criss-crossed the country delivering talks
> On the way we Africans live;
> You took long voyages over the oceans,
> Kite with a home on the moors.

We're oppressed! We develop! Mercy!
All the time our minds develop.
So says Professor D. D. Jabavu
Beckoning those who took to the hills.[62]

We already know what D. D. Jabavu said on this tour to elicit the dubious report of delight.

Postscript: The Woman Still on Show

One of the lessons we may glean from the women's pass protests and the verse of their greatest female poet is that appearances are deceiving and that inheritances from elsewhere are the space within which insurrection must take place. Another concerns the need to interrogate the history of emancipation and the struggle against segregationism and Apartheid as one riven by gender and sexual difference; every effort at universalism is contaminated when not grounded in a thorough transformation of consciousness, and decolonization always brings with it the lure of merely accessing the power that was previously held by the dominant. What Maxeke and Mgqwetho perceived a hundred years ago remains, in many ways, true today. Alongside the media spectacles of fast cars and glittering gold chains, shopping malls and ersatz culture, as described by Achille Mbembe, there is something else. In 2019, some years into our shared project of making a documentary film about the lives of zama zamas, Benefit told me that he had quit mining. He explained that he had come to understand what had not initially been visible to him, namely that some of the informal miners whom he was meeting underground or on the road were not there of their own free will—despite the rhetoric of self-willing autonomy with which these illegalized itinerants of the underground speak. They had been press-ganged by tsotsis and gangsters who had, he said, virtually "enslaved" them. The gangsters of whom Benefit spoke were from his own language world. And they enjoyed impunity because the zamas zamas were undocumented and dared not expose their predicament. Benefit said that he would have expected it from whites, but not from his own people. Then he mentioned, almost in passing, that the men were held in place underground not by chains, per se, but by the threat of rape ("they wanted to make us their wives"). This put them in the place of Woman, as understood by the undocumented women.

It is in this sense that the Chamber-made world is a cave in the manner given that Platonic figure by Luce Irigaray, where sexuated people and not merely the men dissimulated as gender-neutral *hoi anthrōpoi*, are chained, where they are beholden to illusions projected on the wall.[63] In this state, they are discouraged (by nationalist discourse, by corporate public relations, and by educational institutions that now avow what Bantu education enforced, namely the instrumentalization of thought) from considering both the historical complexities and the epistemic ground of the identity structures that, operating on the basis of sexual difference as well as race, hold this world in place.

"The show is also a pass-time," writes Irigaray.[64] By this, she means it unfolds in time as a series of repetitions, in a space that is a speculum, a reflecting surface on which reproductions proliferate but are always inadequate: "A margin outside inscription which like a star both guides and at the same time strikes to the ground, frames and freezes all forms of replicas, all possible relation between the forms of replicas. Limning and limiting the show, the dialogue, the language outside time or place in its extrapolation of light. Or else stealthily opening it up into an abyss of blinding whiteness."[65] This sentiment was not unfamiliar to Mgqwetho, who lamented the loss of tradition even as she reveled in the role of *imbongikazi*, female poet, which had no known precedent in the region. What she despised was mimicry, which she saw in people like Rubusana and Jabavu. Postcolonial critical theory has a long tradition of writing against mimicry. But we have seen, in a reading of Jabavu's text on which Mgqwetho's own poetry reflected, and from the history whence both writers emerged, that he understood how the boundary around whiteness was secured economically—as class—only in the face of a fear that it would pass over into its other. The pass system functioned as that boundary, and survives today in the technē of the document. As Kafka well knew, the cavernous prison, we might even call it the Chamber-made prison, is made of papers. From its golden interior, letters are still being sent.

PART II

THE DEEP

CHAPTER 7

FIGURE, GROUND, AND SINKHOLE

I went down to the bottoms of the mountains; the earth with her bars was about me forever.

—Jonah 2:6

I thought it was the sea
Dragging me to the surface,
And away from you . . .
. . .
And I heard myself fill the space
Falling away beneath my feet with screaming
As I tried to find my way across all eternity
Back to you.

—Michael Cawood Green, "Falling (Hettie's Love Song)"

Mja bona bophelo ke bja ge ba boa dirapeng
Tše rapaltšang baepi maleng a lefase.

[Their lives start when they return from the graveyards which make the diggers lie in the belly of the earth.]

—Moses Bopape and Stephen Ratlabala, "Diepegauta" [The Gold-Diggers]

Survivance is a sense of survival that is neither life nor death pure and simple . . . but a groundless ground from which are detached, identified and opposed what we think we can identify under the name of death or dying.

—Jacques Derrida, *The Beast and the Sovereign*

M emory, punctuated by forgetting, is broken, fissured, and frayed; it has gaps. These gaps may be plumbed, or they may be crossed over. From the other side, they may be examined and mined, as it were, again. The metaphors of the mine, of the possessive mine, and of mining cannot be assuaged or put to ground; they must be tarried with. Let us then leap forward from the gold mining industry's consolidation in segregation via the early pass system to its maturation as Apartheid, and from the world of Langlaagte to that of Carletonville—the modernist dream town incorporated on the eve of formal Apartheid. Let us, as it were, go west—and down, along the arc of the Witwatersrand, tacking back on the map and the surface of the earth, beneath Johannesburg. This gesture, which can take a cartographic form, is also a movement (forward?) in time. Making it, we arrive at a question, or series of questions concerning the status of narrative in the historical consciousness of the constantly emerging present. My aim in this first chapter of part 2 is to show how the particular history of gold mining on the Far West Rand offers general lessons for conceiving of and doing historical and philosophical anthropology—because it is a scene in which the boundary between the living and the dead, the below- and the aboveground, the accident and violence, and the past and the future constantly dissolve. The entire history of the effort to draw boundaries—between territories, between racialized communities, and between concepts—and of the processes that brought them and that may still bring them to crisis can be seen here. I began part 1 by asking "What has gold done to people and what has it made them do?" Without abandoning those questions, part 2 is oriented by the following additional concerns: In what forms does that history of which I have said so much, which nonetheless exceeds this inevitably partial account, persist and subsist in the unfolding present? How do we consider the future of a past, and the past of a future still to come? What are its traces? What are its effects? What follows is not a hauntology, but it is an exploration of traces, the first and perhaps most obvious of which is the mine dump—that material concretion in which all the forces of extractivist abstraction are manifested and, at the same time, occluded.

Time Was: Tailing Histories

The tailings dump to which I have repeatedly alluded is not merely the trace of mining. It is also the figure of the mine and the extruded index of its wasteful economy. It is the crypt of value, and the figure of encryption. This is why so many descriptions of the landscape around Johannesburg, by both residents and visitors, commence with the observation of these artificial flat-topped hills. I too have made recourse to this figural gesture. And often enough, when orienting myself on my first drive from Oliver Tambo airport after arriving in South Africa and adjusting my northern hemispheric inner compass, I have measured my travel by the mine dumps that mark the route and distance between the airport and the city center, and beyond. Over the years, I have memorized them—the older ones next to particular intersections or flyovers on the highway stubbled by grasses or sprouting trees, the more recent ones in the distance still bearing a chalky lime-tainted appearance. They have been my directional *aides memoires*. They are disappearing now, being reclaimed for residual gold, thanks to even more efficient extraction methods than those inaugurated with the cyanide process. But their uncanny geometries and their looming enormity remain even in their absence—in photographs and artists' renditions of this scene and of its transformation by reclamation. In fact, one of the most characteristic tropes of recent landscape art in South Africa is addressed to this *disappearance* of the mine dumps.

A perusal of newspapers from the 1970s reveals that the process of reclamation has been around for some time. A column wryly titled "Down in the Dumps Over Sand," from the *Rand Daily Mail* in early 1980, asked its suburban readers, "Have you noticed recently that you cannot seem to lay your hands (or wheelbarrows) on mind dump sand?" And it answered with a folksy explanation that linked the disappearance of the dumps to the rising prices of gold, while making these fluctuating prices the very index of time—the time of waste's valorization.

> Time was if you wanted to lay a brick path or driveway and needed the dump sand as a base, you just motored a few kilometers out of town and there it was waiting for you. Skyscrapers of the yellow stuff. Help yourself.
>
> In the old days you had to go early in the year, otherwise the August and September winds would blow the sand down Commissioner Street into your eyes. Then the mines started grassing over their dumps.
>
> And when the price of gold started to climb, Anglo American with its Ergo "gold from dust" recovery company, began making the mine dumps smaller. Now you are hard pressed to find any dump which is not surrounded by a two

metre fence and a locked gate. Any bets that by the turn of the century there won't be any mine dumps surrounding Johannesburg? Sad but true—this city of gold is undergoing a face change.[1]

The affect of the story vacillates from lamentation for a disappearing horizon (and a past synonymous with certitude about white control over the industry and urban space) to anxiety over the ascendant power of highly capitalized recovery operations to claim what white middle-class subjects had presumed was theirs to expropriate. The white suburban idyll in which the dumps are a kind of nature to be harvested for domestic gardening is made to work here as a screen, immunizing the suburb-dweller from any sense of complicity as the beneficiaries of industrial capital—whether as the subject bypassed by an emergent and more heterogeneous economy in which manufacturing, information technology, and services were already dwarfing gold as a source of gross domestic product, as was the case in the 1970s, or as the perceptual center of a nostalgic and hallucinatory suburban pastoralism.

Time was.

The sign of value takes the form of a silhouette, a displaced outline: namely, securitization, the fencing and bordering of the dump. If the gate was, for Virgil-Umholi, the image of a passage and an opening, the fence is a border and an enclosure. It is also part of the theatricality of the dump; it asserts not merely value but the presumptive desire for its illegitimate appropriation. Here is that other signification of mine, the possessive and proprietary claim of the mine owner, the owner as one who says, in English (and in the etymologically grounded rhymes of many Germanic languages, including Afrikaans), "mine." More generally, the recurrent discourse of disappearance amid gold's repeating recrudescence as a source of value is the mark of a repeated encounter with the finitude of gold reserves and the idea that waste is value *in potentia*. In this sense, the tailings dump is the stage on which are played the mutant forms of revival to which gold (and even a phantasmatic version of the gold standard) has been repeatedly summoned over the past century. This is why a certain rhythm characterizes the growth and diminution of the dumps, one that corresponds to, or resonates with, the fluctuations in gold's commodity price in the international market, and South Africa's status in the international risk-assessment economy. (Not incidentally, "to resonate" is yet another signification of the phrase zama zama.)

The pathos of this theater assumes a quality of terror or melancholy depending on the position from which the drama is observed. But in all cases, it is a scene of phantasmatic projections and intense attachments. In invoking the notion of the phantasmatic, I imply that which is both phenomenal and imaginary, somatic and ideational: a threshold phenomenon where the dream of borders and bordering runs aground. For this reason, the theater of the mine dump is not just a reading of the vast, material formations that testify to the histories of deep-level mining, cyanidation, and extractivist industry. It is also intended to stage the problem of ethnographic representation in general, of positing concepts and discerning differentiations in the thought, discourse, and practice of others—in full recognition of the contested status they have in worlds where they are put to use or called into question. The status of the accident, of the event, of all the figures of exception (from the catastrophe to divine grace and ancestral beneficence) depends on positing a ground against which it might be differentiated, of drawing a line in the sand as it were. But there is not one line, nor one place from which to perceive these differences. The ground underfoot, if I may borrow a cue from Mgqwetho's poem, shifts.

Around the deep-level mines that mark the outer periphery of the Witwatersrand crescent, the dumps are especially large and numerous, and they can be seen on the horizon from a distance of several dozen kilometers. Near Carletonville, the town closest to many of the country's deepest mines, they seem almost to constitute a fortifying perimeter. It is not too far-fetched to imagine that someone from another time or unfamiliar with this area's history might, at first glance, mistake them for memorial pyramids in whose hidden recesses the royalty of an imperial culture is secretly interred. When I first visited Carletonville in the mid-1990s, I was dumbfounded by these great monuments to extractivism. Early on in my apprenticeship to that community's history, I interviewed a former prison warden and member of the local government from the days when it was dominated by the conservative National Party. He was eager to show me around the area, and on an initial tour, he took me out onto one of the large inactive dumps. It was a brilliant day, and the light that reflected off the blanched surface was blinding. Stung by both the light and the dust, my eyes shed defensive tears. My tour guide, who had welcomed me with apparent hopes that I would sympathize with the plight of the now-displaced white minority, merely squinted as he described the size and toxic contents of the dumps, including their relatively high uranium content, with an odd mix of macabre exaggeration and nonchalance. As we walked, he told me that these dumps were not merely mounds of toxicity but perfect places to dispose of unwanted things and even evidence of crimes. If anyone were to be buried in one of these dumps, they would almost certainly never be found, he said.

The Hole in the Story

It was not, however, the mine dumps that took me to Carletonville. I had grown up near dumps, not far from what was at the time the world's largest lead and zinc mine, a combination of open-pit and underground shafts, which, like the mines of South Africa, were surrounded by mountains or disinterred rock.

Rather, what called my attention to this place was the story of a sinkhole, a mythified occurrence whose recounting seemed to be spontaneously provoked by the very mention of the town's name. When driving along the highway leading from Johannesburg on an early visit to the country in the late 1990s, friends had pointed out the road sign leading to Carletonville. From disparate backgrounds and racial positions, they repeated the stories of Carletonville's sinkholes in tones of recollected horror. Others whom I met at that time recounted similar stories whenever I mentioned the town, named for a Canadian mining engineer, (Guy) Carleton Jones, who, having been trained in Montreal, went to South Africa as a surveyor for Consolidated Gold Fields in 1914. He later served—when it became New Consolidated Goldfields—as an engineer and then as resident director of the board (more about Jones in chapter 9).[2] All of these stories converged on the disaster that occurred on the evening of August 3, 1964, when the house of the Oosthuizens, an Afrikaner family sharing the name of the early Langlaagte farm's first owners, had disappeared into an enormous hole shortly after they had returned from vacation. In the stories then recounted to me, it was said that they and their domestic servant had vanished in a cloud of flame and red dust, and had been buried alive in the hole's unreachable depths.

There was something awful and compelling about that story's uncanny figuration of a predicament at once unbelievable and somehow representative of a terror that has been mythified time and time again in the theological-political literature that inscribes this existential threat, of being buried alive, in one or another idiom of hell; or in the secular literature that renders it as a gothic nightmare at the very heart of a godless unconscious. Then too, there was an oddity to the fact that this disappearance of a house into the earth and the story of those buried alive seemed both so similar to and so different from the stories of miners lost underground in more common accidents. A morphological rhyme often tempts one to analogy. I wondered if the story of the sinkhole was a condensed and displaced image of what happens in industrial mines all the time, a kind of waking dreamwork. This dreamwork would transpose the experience of the more likely sufferer—a black mineworker—so that it could be assumed by a white working-class figure, the kind whose paltry privileges had been so urgently defended by Stallardism and then protected by legislation aimed at staving off poor whitism. If such a transposition was indeed occurring, it could be read as a gesture of both identification and disidentification. But why did this story hold such allure, these many years after the fact? I would learn that the story had not simply perdured, but that it had reemerged with an additional potency around the time of the democractic transition, and as it did so, the signification of the sinkhole was generalized. It now referred to the loss of value in the era of democratization, which was also the era of actuarialization and of neoliberalism, more generally. A sinkhole became that from which investment could not be recalled, a kind of antiproductive scene, where the fetish-like capacities of capital to grow, fertilized only by itself, were said to be annihilated.

In the meantime, the story's ubiquity and the coherence and recurrence of its elements among people of a certain generation (i.e., those who had been alive or knew those who had been alive in South Africa in the 1960s) incited my curiosity. Adults who had grown up in other South African mining towns recalled their childhood fears that they would be sent to live in Carletonville, which they imagined as a place reserved for badly behaved boys and girls or those whose parents hated them, for why else, reasoned these now-adult children, would grown-ups subject their sons and daughters to this unspeakable danger. Some of these same adults recalled a sentimental folksong called "*Kom Haal My Pappie*" [Come find me Daddy] by the Afrikaans duo, Die Briels, believing it to be about a boy lost in a Carletonville sinkhole—even though the referent of that song was nowhere near the collapse at the nearby Blyvoor property, where the sinkhole of 1964 occurred. The song's writers, Frans and Sannie Briel, often took their subject matter from newspaper stories of disasters, but as it happens, they had found inspiration for "*Kom Haal My Pappie*" in a much earlier incident.[3] In the time of recall, the resignification of the song ensured that it became what it had not originally been: a song about Blyvooruitzicht, the name of one of Carletonville's mines and its village compound, and the beginning of Apartheid's end.

In the ballad's refrain, a little boy calls out for his father to come find him as he looks for his mother and his sister, while praying to Jesus that his daddy will rescue him from the dank earth. Was the pathos accompanying this recollected sense of violated innocence a symptom or at least a sign of a desire for the possibility that there might have been such innocence in Apartheid's industrial heartland? And did the Blyvoor story's resurrection express a desire to claim such innocence in some domains of white South Africa at a time when the Truth and Reconciliation Commission (TRC) was asking people to come to terms with the depth of political violence enacted against members of that other underground—that is, the anti-Apartheid movements, led by the African National Congress (ANC) and *uMkhonto weSizwe*, the Communist Party, Black Consciousness, and church-based liberation movements? It is certainly notable that the stories of the Blyvoor disaster resurfaced in the 1990s, in new histories of Carletonville such as those by Elize van Eeden. Her revisiting of the original media accounts were published not only in scholarly journals but in the local newspaper, the *Carletonville Herald*. Not incidentally, this publication was established shortly after a series of sinkhole events in 1963 as part of an effort to keep local residents apprised of subsidence hazards—in the face of perceived corporate intransigence and dissimulation about the possible relationship between mining and subsidence activity.[4] Then, in 1996,

Michael Cawood Green published *Sinking: A Verse Novella*, built around the narratives of the disaster. One of the purposes of his work was to interrogate the status of the eventfulness ascribed to the 1964 sinkhole. Two questions hover above his text: When is a disaster an event, and for whom? When is an accident not natural?

In part 1, I spoke of the event in psychoanalytic terms as a certain punctuality and as a singularity: the incomprehensible singularity that demands an explanation and that may be experienced as that which comes "too soon," and in relation to which the subject feels belated. In part 2, I am interested in the event in its political significance, which is to say within a narrative project that attempts to generalize from the subjective to the social and from the particular to the general, leaping across the aporetic space between the empirical and the transcendental. Recognizing this space as aporetic also means asking, on what grounds, what groundless ground, does one make the leap? The virtue of Green's text is that it poses this question from within the narratives that have assumed the generalizability of the sinkhole disaster that claimed the Oosthuizen house. I want now to follow his reading, or more properly, his rereading of the myth in pursuit of history.

Not in Time

The generic category of "verse novella" does not fully capture the formal range of Green's self-consciously postmodern volume, which includes, in addition to the verse narrative, an epigraphic archive constructed out of fragments of modernist poetry, newspaper headlines, and reported witness testimonials from the 1964 disaster as well as a series of appendices signed by pseudonymous authorial personae. In the latter, various literary and theoretical references are invoked as partial explanation of the sinkhole's renewed topicality—often in an acerbic tone of parodied academicism—even as the author flirts with the autobiographical genre and the anxiety of influence vis-à-vis John (J. M.) Coetzee, South Africa's preeminent novelist of the time. In one appendix titled "Autolyscuthony and the Black Hole," signed by Green's alias, "Alan Murray Charles," *Sinking* is described as "a poem concerned with the erasure of apartheid . . . set in the middle of the dominance of grand apartheid because it is interested in exploring the failure of apartheid to achieve being at all."[5] The fictive critic continues, "Apartheid can only be transcended if it never existed. Granting it existence traps us forever in 'anti-s' and 'posts' to the degree that we must always be defined by it. No transition is free from the place it began." Before turning from the idiom of the sinkhole to that of the black hole, in which disappearance is so rapid that one cannot get hold of an image even to analyze it, this same phantom critic writes that the Blyvoor incident was *not* an event, "in either the narratological or historiographical" sense because it did not precipitate any transformation in state: the "sinkhole disaster does not qualify as a story: it signifies the collapse of a sequence, the implosion of a development—in short, an end."[6] It lacked an afterward. At the time of his writing, and perhaps, too, in the time of my own writing, the possibility of a future not determined in its content and the forms of subjective identification solicited by Apartheid. and the colonial processes that preceded it, remains open.

Green's text marks the apogee of a certain correspondence between the resurgence of the sinkhole story and the end of Apartheid, 1996 being the year of the first hearings of the TRC (although the commission had been established in law in 1995). The book also partook of that convergence and of the sense that it was in the mining communities of the Witwatersrand where an event might have taken place that did *not* in fact occur earlier—namely, the termination of formal Apartheid. This is because 1964 was not merely the year of the sinkhole disaster. It was also the year of the Rivonia Trial, in which ten members of the ANC, including not only Nelson Mandela but also Walter Sisulu, Govan Mbeki, Rusty Bernstein, Ahmed Kathrada, Dennis Goldberg, James Kantor, Andrew Mlangeni, Raymond Mhlaba, and Elias Motsoaledi, stood trial on charges of treason for their avowal of armed opposition against the Apartheid regime. All those who stood trial were sentenced to life imprisonment (two others, Arthur Goldreich and Harold Wolpe, had been arrested but escaped).[7] And thus, it appeared, at the time, and in Green's retrospective glance, that the Apartheid regime had been stabilized rather than shaken by the end of that fateful year.

In Green's account, one failed event, that of the sinkhole, provided another, a political transformation if not a revolution that did not (yet) occur, with the figure or form of appearance *and disappearance*. One of the reasons for the revolution's (or even simply transformation's) nonoccurrence was that, at that time, the South African economy was grounded on and in (gold) mining. Mandela's speech from the dock indicated the ANC's intention to nationalize the mines as well as the banks and other monopoly industries—albeit under the terms of an African nationalism based in private property.[8] But the Blyvoor sinkhole incident of August 1964 did not lead to major changes in local mining practice, and this fact—which, in Green's account, makes of the sinkhole a nonevent—is attributable to the way in which the hole was explained away as a mere accident and a *natural* disaster. In this sense, both proto-events were circumscribed and obstructed in their politico-historical eventfulness by gestures that aimed to protect the mining industry's investments. One might say that the sinkhole disaster threatened to reveal the negligence of mining capital only to be buried in the discourse of nature, just as the entire argument for racialized migrant labor had been buried in the discourse of nature by means of the cyanide process.

Rough Roads and Slippery Slopes:
The Syntagma of Mytho-History

Soon after the Oosthuizen house was sucked into the earth, three other houses fell into the pit, although their residents managed to escape. This was neither the first nor the last such incident. A few years earlier, on December 12, 1962, a screening, sorting and crushing plant at the mine, along with twenty-nine mineworkers, had collapsed into oblivion. The men all drowned when a flood of waters rushed into the sudden new depression where the plant had stood. Their awful demise had been presaged in 1959, when houses built for the mine management of Western Deep Levels (also called Western Deeps), which had been erected on Aster Street in Carletonville, began to crack to such an extent that "daylight could be seen through the walls."[9] Within a year or so, they had been demolished, and the ground had sunk by about four feet. In 1970, the local recreation club's tennis court plummeted, along with one of the game's spectators, into the hell of water and stone. Today, the landscape is pocked with myriad holes and depressions, testaments to the ongoing reality of sinkholes in the region. Repeatedly over the decades since 1960, and hastening during more recent years of the new millennium, several areas of the larger municipality within which Carletonville is located have been designated as official disaster areas.

In light of this continuous history of seemingly predictable occurrences, it is worth noting that in August 1964, local newspapers reported that some of those who survived the catastrophes had dreamed of the events before their occurrence, which was why they were able to save themselves. But those same survivors also reported having heard from those now among the dead, that they, too, had dreamed of the catastrophe. "Murmurs from the earth of this land, from the caves and craters,/from the bowl of darkness."[10] The dream image had not saved them, however. It had not helped them to recognize the sounds of impending disaster when they arrived, like some unbidden guests bearing death. Perhaps they imagined that they were merely "hearing things." Those who escaped the collapse of their houses were able to do so because they interpreted the sound of earth falling as a warning, a sign prophesying an event rather than a mere symptom of an underlying problem. A deafening swoosh or roar, some of the survivors had likened it to the sound of "wagonwheels on a rough road" (*wawiele op 'n ruwe pad*). It had been a long time since any wagons had rumbled across this landscape (though donkey-pulled carts are still occasionally seen). In *Sinking*, this phrase is cited in a poem entitled "From Structure to Event: Willie Britz." The poem is preceded by an epigraph from Jacques Derrida's "The Parergon" and recounts, in poetic form, the reported speech of Willie Britz, a neighbor and witness of the events at Blyvoor.[11] Green, this time under the pseudonym, Donnée Phelps, quotes this description of a misrecognized, mythologically coded seismic sign as an example of "historico-mythology." He translates *ruwe* as rough rather than dirt, but he remarks that "what could be taken as a rather forced association of the coming disaster with an image straight from the heart of Afrikaner historico-mythology turns out to be a detail produced from the horse's mouth, as it were."[12] Here, he is underlining the degree to which the events of the time were subject to such clichés by those who, turning to the past, could not grasp what was demanded by the future. Green notes that the citation on which his poem is based comes from the *Carletonville Herald*, but he does not tell his readers that the paper had only come into being in 1963, after the first crushing plant disaster and a series of smaller sinkholes, which Elize van Eeden was resurrecting at about the same time that Green was writing his verse narrative. But in the 1960s most people got their news elsewhere. In August, 1964, the *Rand Daily Mail* quoted Willie Britz as saying he could not sleep on the night of the disaster and had been awakened by "a noise which sounded like a horse-drawn trolley passing."[13] In the difference between a wagon and a trolley, the one spoken in Afrikaans, the other in English, or which term Britz used in speaking to different journalists, is the whole history that pits Afrikanerdom and antimodernism against English colonialism and industrial modernism. Most likely, Britz switched between languages and shifted his idiom according to his interlocutor, although Afrikaans was almost certainly his first language.

The national papers that reported the sinkhole of August 1964 had been writing, for several months, about the problem of sinkholes and subsidences. Since the crushing plant disaster, which was relatively unstoried in the national press (a paucity not separable from the fact that its victims were mainly black workers), they had been publishing investigative reports on the matter. In February, 1963, for example, a decision to build a new hospital was reconsidered out of fear that it could be undermined by a sinkhole.[14] In March, the *Rand Daily Mail* shared with its readers that geologists were on the verge of discovering the cause of sinkholes. The reporter conveyed to his audience that he had taken a flight and seen three large holes and several small ones, including one that had opened the day before, and measuring two hundred feet by three hundred feet across. Geologists, he said, distinguish between sinkholes and subsidences. But the cause was said to be "subsurface erosion of a thick dolomite limestone layer" generated by a "disturbance of natural drainage conditions." In consequence of the holes that had recently emerged, he added, fifteen houses and a church had had to be demolished, while another fourteen had been damaged.

The effort to pretend that the mines were not the immediate cause of the proliferation of sinkholes continued. In May, a special ad hoc committee was established by the national government to investigate the causes, with equal representation from industry and government. The mine representatives argued that subsidences were natural phenomena, and therefore that the mining companies were not culpable for the damages caused by them. At stake was the cost of a new rail line, which had had to be rerouted around the area, out of fear that it too would vanish into the earth.[15] Then, in September, as the first buds began to open in the company gardens at the entry to Carletonville, roadways began to crack wide open, with crevasses of two feet in width extending several hundred feet along the roads, leading to more investigations by the Geological Survey Division of the Department of Mines.[16]

Quite remarkably, these proliferating depressions, crevasses, and holes, demanding the elimination of houses and churches, the cordoning of territory, the relocation of hospitals, and the rerouting of railways, did not inhibit the development of the mines nor substantially limit their profitability. This was partly because many of the mines were on ridges of thicker strata of more stable rock overlaying the porous dolomite than the residential areas, which were generally located on a flat plane. It was also partly because of the ways in which the cost of demolishing and building substitute homes was covered. In a gesture reminiscent of the foundation of the Chamber of Mines, the area's mines voluntarily joined together to create the Far West Rand Dolomitic Water Association. Its purpose was to distribute the costs of settling "claims arising from damage or loss which is directly attributable, as the proximate physical cause, to the implementation of the policy of dewatering."[17] But this proximate physical cause was then blamed on political policy. In 1965, blaming the government for prohibiting the return of water pumped out of the mine back into the now vacant compartments, the management of Western Deep Levels, asserted that the risk of subsidence for the mine was "remote." Yet, in 1962, the crushing plant had fallen, and it took 175,000 tons of waste rock, dumped back into the hole, to stabilize the situation.[18]

In November 1962, the West Driefontein Company published its annual report in the *Rand Daily Mail*, as per custom, and announced that the company had been able to "increase dividends," which it called an "outstanding achievement in view of the fact that in December, 1962, it lost is main sorting and crushing plant in a sinkhole, whereupon it had to suspend milling operations for a period of sixteen days and thereafter make arrangements for some of its ore to be milled at neighbouring mines."[19] No mention of the lost black workers dampened the company's enthusiasm. Only real estate values had suffered.[20] In the same report, it was noted that the profits of the Carletonville Estates Limited (a real estate entity) was down 13 percent for the year, which the report explained with reference to "two reasons: in the first place, the ground movement problem in the area required a considerable amount of drilling and other work, and secondly, it was considered prudent to write down the value of stands presently deemed unsaleable in the light of technical investigations so far made." It continued, "In view of possible calls on the cash resources of the company, it was decided to pass the dividend." What gave the company cause for optimism was the belief being generated by the Geological Survey and the ad hoc committee that it would "be possible to delimit large areas in which ground movement is unlikely to occur."[21]

In other words, the accident as a future possibility could be territorialized, circumscribed, and therefore avoided. Not prevented, but avoided, and the cost of such avoidance could be actuarialized. The mining companies' position, that limestone, prevalent in the dolomitic ridges of the area, dissolves in water and that this causes subsidences, made water the cause of the problem, which was then said to be naturally occurring. In fact, it was in large part the dewatering of the mines to enable safe working below the water table that was creating the vacuums that then fell under the weight of the no-longer-supportable earth, and which, newly vacant, received the torrents of those ancient underground rivers and lakes when a rock wall broke: "Like limestone, dolomite dissolves in water,/So holes./Eaten out by water./And now filled by water."[22] Hundreds of millions of gallons were being pumped out of the earth every day, transported by pipes away from the shafts and often allowed to drain into unlined dams, where their acids leached into the earth. This is now widely recognized as the mechanism underlying the sinkholes of the West Rand, and so it is perhaps unsettling to encounter in the moment of these occurrences the strange strategy of self-defense deployed by the mines.[23] For, in their attempt at a representational inversion—of blaming water rather than dewatering—they revealed the fact that dewatering actually exacerbated the very problem that the mines were attempting to obviate—namely, the intrusion of water into the holes beneath the earth. The problem of absence, of vacuity, was displaced into that of presence and even excess. Green writes: "Still, it is a happy prospect indeed/For those of us who live to extract a living/Out of that which supports us,/Whose dependence is/Poised/Between the impenetrable/And the need to penetrate."[24]

We've (Not) Heard This One Before

The resemblance between the problem and the remedy, and the fact that the remedy was itself a source of the problem implies the structure of the pharmakon, in which that which is remedy is also poison.[25] I can think of few examples that better manifest this uncanny nonlogic of the pharmakon than that which appeared in the newspaper in October 1963, as the sinkholes were proliferating along the roadways that passed by Carletonville. An "enormous 700 foot-wide cave" was collapsing into a sinkhole. The *Rand Daily Mail*, announced that "Geologists Race Against Time to Study Cave," while reporting that "the cave structure has weakened over the years due to the drop in the water table caused by mine pumping. It soon will be filled with slime to prevent collapse." Until this point, the cave had been a veritable cornucopia of exotic phenomena and a site of natural historical curiosity. Apparently, one could observe within it the "evolution of spiders and cave moths" and see "blind white shrimp."[26]

The story, which appeared only on page nine and was more science reporting than news, is significant for two reasons. First, what has been denied with respect to the sinkhole damages afflicting human beings is conceded in regard to the cave. Water removal is the cause. Second, the description disclosed the difficulty of drawing the line between the cave and the sinkhole. Or rather, one is led to question the conceptual stability of this difference, as one imagines the cave collapsing into the interior of another cave, of being destroyed by being absorbed into an industrially produced replica. Here, then, was the precise rendition and reiteration of the entire problematic of the cave as an allegorical theater of representation bequeathed by Plato, in which the problem of knowing the difference between the image and the real is the very task of philosophy. In the story of the cave on the Witwatersrand, the real vanishes into its simulacrum, which is no less effectual. Just as the heads of those chained men in Plato's allegory are directed to the shadows on the wall, with the puppet masters observing from behind (from whom Plato wishes to save us), and just as those enchained men are led to believe that those images *are* reality, so the mining corporations and their scientific and technical agents insisted on the separate identities of the sinkhole and the cave. Yet, in their race against time and thus the inevitability of the sinkhole, the geologists conceded that, in this uncanny space, where a mimetic force binds nature and industry in a resemblance that can only be seen from outside its ideology machine, the techno-industrially generated hole could destroy, by undermining, the ground on whose surface the cave assumed its figural identity. "From in it too a *secret system of caves and conduits*/That in places (and this we did not know)/Is all that supports a surface/Seemingly secure enough/For the weight of our efforts . . . for us dolomite contained no geology lesson."[27] So wrote Green, ventriloquizing the position of capital and indexing its delusions with that parenthetical remark "and this we did not know."

The cave, which is typically thought of as a spatial absence or recess, has a figural presence when set against a ground that either constitutes its stabilizing outside (in this sense ground is a frame, like the mouth of the earth) or that will destroy it by withdrawing. In my rendition of the newspaper account, which serves as a parable drawn from the reportage of a historical phenomenon, the problems of representation, of ethnographic imagination, and of philosophical reason as the process of demarcating the boundaries between concepts are all operative. The fact that the cave was to be stabilized by reinserting what had been removed elsewhere—the slimes—and whose removal was linked to the sinkhole, only intensifies and underlines the whole structure. But parables are sometimes difficult to read. And they are sometimes offered to the initiated only to conceal something from others: "Speak I to them in parables: because they seeing see not; and hearing they hear not, neither do they understand."[28]

Soon after I commenced field research in Carletonville, the man who had walked me across the surface of the slimes dam invited me to join him and some friends for a tour of the existing sinkholes in Carletonville. We drove out around the landscape, beyond and behind the mines, and, in their four-by-four, arrived at one of the largest depressions in the earth. This hole, however, is the residue of an ancient meteor hit. Nonetheless, for the men, it was one of the large category of holes that included sinkholes, subsidences, and other earthly indentations. This concatenation of holes was possible because it was understood by them to be a natural (if divinely ordained) artifact rather than an effect of industrial activity.

Down into the hole we drove. Although the descent was dramatic and not a little unsettling, the "hole" was hardly more remarkable than any steeply sided valley the size of a few football fields, or perhaps a shopping mall parking lot. A few spindly trees were trying to grow horizontally from its walls. But this otherwise common valley was mediated in our conversations by the palimpsest of stories organized around the horrifying image of a family and its sudden disappearance, its being buried alive. For every gesture asserting the naturalness of the hole, another arose asserting the mystery of that event. One afternoon, interviewing an older couple who had lived near the Oosthuizens, I was shown a grainy eight-millimeter film of the house in its final moment of collapse, taken by the family patriarch. Flickering in the curtained darkness of their small bungalow's living room, the film continued to elicit hushed awe, from them and from me, as the broken houses slid from the precipice into the gaping hole. The film testified to the disaster's final moments, but it also testified to the sense, then, that something of significance was happening and that they would want to remember it in the future. For them, of course, this collapse and the deaths of their neighbors constituted an event in the fullest sense of the word; it demanded and resisted explanation. They turned to God and spoke of fate, they repeatedly revisited the specter in their dreams, and neither could they let it go nor would it leave them alone. Many conversations began with "if only . . ." and were followed by the imagination of another time: of a delayed return, of a warning, of anything that would have prevented the house from going down on that night, when that family, so recently returned from vacation, was in that home. So, it is not a matter of choosing, absolutely, between the event and the nonevent, but of grasping what ideological work has to occur for the personal tragedy to assume the dimension and the function of a national allegory.

The newspapers at the time likened the earth to Jonah's whale. "Sinkhole Swallows Family," read the headline of the *Rand Daily Mail*. Its subheadings added three additional elements to the story: "Rumble, Flashes, and Flame," "Houses Vanish in Crater," "Women Weep in Night of Horror." These are the elements of almost every version of the story I have heard, and they correspond to three distinct narrative principles, namely the phenomenological or sensory experience of the disaster by the survivors; the object of that experience; and the affective aftermath.

> A House and its occupants—a family of five—disappeared in a sinkhole at Blyvooruitzicht at 2 A.M. today.
>
> A neighbour said that there was a loud rumbling, flashes and flames as the house vanished down a 100-ft. hole.
>
> Mr Johannes Oosthuizen, his wife Hettie and their their [sic] three children Dalene, 12, Johannes, 7, and Ria, 5, were in the house in 29th Avenue, Blyvooruitzicht, when the subsidence occurred. They are presumed dead.
>
> Their house was one of three which disappeared. The others—one of which was empty—were wrecked.
>
> "Mr. J.L. Britz, a neighbour, told the "Rand Daily Mail" this morning that he was unable to sleep last night. At 2 A.M. he heard a noise which sounded like a horse-drawn trolley passing.
>
> "I jumped out of bed and ran to the window," he said. "I saw Mr. Oosthuizen's house lights coming on. Just then I saw the roof buckling.
>
> "It broke in half. There were flashes and flames. Then the house was gone."
>
> "Mr. Britz and his family rushed out. They immediately started evacuating their home. Other families in the immediate vicinity followed. Many of them ran into the street in their night clothes."

In the reports that followed, it was revealed that the Oosthuizen family had been on vacation at the seaside to celebrate their daughter's recovery from jaundice. Mr. Oosthuizen was to have returned to work the next day. Each segment of the *Rand Daily Mail*'s coverage added both a new dimension and a counterpoint to the previous one. Matching Mr. Britz's story, for example, is that of their neighbor, Mr. Boet Kriel, who was awakened by his wife, Alla. She asked him "Is it raining?" Apparently, she had heard "something like thunder."

The crowds that gathered initially were witness to the collapse, which far from being punctual, stretched through the hours and days to come:

> The remains of two houses, half of each having disappeared, are balanced precariously on the edge of the sinkhole. They are expected to fall in at any moment.
>
> I went to within five yards of the edge of the crater, but was unable to see the bottom, states a "Rand Daily Mail" reporter. All around were cracks in the earth.
>
> Weeping women were among a vast crowd held back by mine officials and policemen. Barbed wire fences and rope barriers had been hurriedly erected around the perimeter. The atmosphere was tense and one of speechless horror.

The evacuated people are unable to return to their homes for clothing or furniture.

At the time of going to press, two more houses were slowly sinking in the ground. Hundreds of people stood watching as the walls collapsed and disappeared in to the ground.

Tim Rossi, the *Rand Daily Mail* journalist who flew out over the hole in an army plane, described it as "red scar," remarking the "fresh red earth," and a "hole smashed into the middle of a block of red-brick mine houses, gaped open to the sky. The sides," he said, "were sheer, cutting through the middle of two houses." The perfectness of the circle astonished Rossi, as did the fact that "No rubble, brickwork, or corrugated iron roofing of the vanished houses was visible. Every remnant of the tiny houses was buried under piles of clean, red earth."

Rossi writes from above and afar, in a manner that leads him to speak of the distant houses as tiny. His perspective collapses into the object. But perhaps the most enigmatic element of his account of this aerial view of the hole, whose enormity cannot be seen from the surface of the earth where it occurs, is his note that "the figures of two Africans were bent over small mounds of earth in a street leading to the stricken houses." The detail is an inexplicable punctum in this otherwise single-minded text. Something—but what?—pushes through it, and asks to be read. Who were these people, visible as "figures" and racially codable, but notable only because they were "bent over small mounds of earth." Presented in this manner by Rossi, it is as if they are tending to graves for those whose bodies will not be found. But, of course, they are not. There are no graves in the street, only piles of soil that might be used for the gardens of the white residents. The black figures disappear in the story. They disappear like the other figure, the "domestic worker," who was also said to have been in the house at the time of the collapse, but whose name and other details are not to be found in the *Rand Daily Mail*.

That woman was nonetheless recalled by the contemporary inhabitants of Khutsong, the township whose residents were to service the town of Carleton-ville, at the time of my first visits in the late 1990s. They were pleased to narrate to me a story in which the young woman who worked in the Oosthuizen house-hold had been absent from the house that evening, visiting her boyfriend. As improbable as it might seem, given that returning employers would surely have expected the house to be ready for them, she survived, they said, and disap-peared into the night of the story—like a ghost, and thus free from the constric-tions of the passbooks and all that would follow in that town. I asked who she was, what was her name, what language she spoke, to whom she had returned, to which part of the country she had fled. No one knew. They had only this figure of a woman who had escaped a tragic fate by virtue of love.

This was the pure counterpart to the narrative of August 3, 1964—and we will return to it next. But the narrative of August 3 was oriented by the sense of tragedy that comes from having arrived too soon and thus having been exposed to the danger of the sinkhole (had they come back a day later from their vacation, they would have survived). This arrival extended of course to their deaths, premature for all. As already discussed, such is the nature of traumatic events, as Freud and Lacan show us; they often involve a sense of being touched by that which reaches us from the future, too soon, and which does not admit of historicization, of being put behind.

For days after the initial reports, newspapers proliferated stories that thickened their details, filling in the picture not only of a family but also of a community with modest means. In this winter landscape, mention of people in the streets with only their pajamas, relying on others for coats and blankets, make visible the thinness of the privilege that was enjoyed by the white working-class members of this world. The responsibility for providing food, clothing, and accommodation for the evacuated was initially allotted to government, although family and church members took on the task. A member of the Executive Committee of the Mineworker's Union, which at that time did not represent black workers, told an inquisitive reporter that "funds were available from the union for relief of this sort and that people merely had to apply." Beyond the seeming indifference to the possible desperation of the evicted residents, and the presumption that the onus for accessing aid lay with the victims, the phrase "of this sort," indicated familiarity with disaster, and even its expectation.

One of the nearly ritual gestures of response was the convening of an investigative inquiry. In this case, the investigation was undertaken under the direction of the Geological Survey of the Department of Mines, and while its director, Dr. O. R. Van Eeden, demurred that the preparation of a report would take time because "so much work remained to be done," he promised that people in those areas "subject to subsidence" would be forewarned if these were "found to be dangerous." There was either a set of knowledge and a mechanism for discerning and predicting sinkholes, or the Geological Survey was dissimulating. Given the reports of real estate companies writing down losses but planning ahead on the assumption that the delimitation of danger zones was possible, the former seems more likely. This is to be expected for, as we have seen, "such occurrences are by no means uncommon." These words, which one might have expected to read in the *Rand Daily Mail* in August 1964, nonetheless come from an earlier story about a sinkhole into which a family house fell. That incident took place in 1907, near a colliery on the East Rand, in Springs, where the house and family of a Mr. Tibbott were similarly sucked into a vast sinkhole. (The area also hosted gold mines, and gold deposits on the East Rand were often found beneath coal.) Tibbott's wife and three of his four children were rescued from that disaster, although one of the girls was wounded by a falling piano. Their son, Robert, was never found, and it is his voice that is summoned in Die Briels's *"Kom Haal My Pappie."* What strikes the reader now, in addition to the extravagant loquacity of the reportage, is the early recurrence of the same tropes and figures.

First of all, there is a sense of rumbling and the sound of subterranean movement:

> For some days past the local inhabitants state strange rumblings have been heard resembling distant thunder, and late on Wednesday night the whole neighbourhood began to vibrate with what one man describes as a "subterranean [*sic*] rattling. . . . After midnight the rumbling became more and more pronounced, and the inmates of the houses in the vicinity of the Great Eastern became so alarmed that they got out of bed and came out on their verandahs, where they shivered and huddled together, their position being rendered worse by their incapacity to do anything. It seemed useless to run for safety as no one knew where the catastrophe, which the terrifying noise indicated was approaching nearer and nearer at every moment, was going to happen.

The catastrophe is rendered here as that which can be sensed without being amenable to deferral. It gives off signs but not meanings. And a terrifying passivity envelopes the potential victims, who, knowing that something is coming, cannot quite be sure "where" it will arrive and when. They nonetheless fear that they will be in that place where an accident occurs:

> Mr. Tibbott, who occupied one of the ill-fated houses, with his wife and four children, the other being occupied by Mr. and Mrs. Lewis and their daughter, was of the opinion that the noise was nearer the colliery, and, thinking that something had happened there, he rushed over to see what it was.

THE COLLAPSE

> He had only got about twenty yards away when a terrific crash came, and on looking behind, he saw that the house which he had just quitted a few moments previously had disappeared and that there was a yawning hole in the earth. The horrible truth soon dawned upon him, and he realized that a subsidence had taken place and that his wife and family and neighbours were plunged into the depths of the fearful abyss at his feet.[29]

A more dramatic narration could not have been expected from a novelistic rendition of a myth. Like Orpheus, Mr. Tibbott turned back only to have his beloved family snatched from him. Unlike Orpheus, he was able to bring several family members back to the surface. His son, and the future of his patronym, according to a certain law of patriliny, did not survive. But, of course, it is the son's very death that permits the father's name to survive in this story. In this, as in so many other cases, a death serves as the crypt in which one is buried in order to be remembered. The story, in other words, is that crypt, that space of interment in which a certain living on and living after becomes possible.[30]

Will It Hold Water?

Much of the narrative of the 1907 event is devoted to the heroism of the rescue by the mine manager and other members of Mr. Tibbott's surviving family. But the *Rand Daily Mail* article concludes by noting that, in the aftermath of this disaster and those many other occurrences of what was then referred to as land slippage, several of the local residents were calling for a Commission of Inquiry into "the whole matter of the safety of the districts bordering on the mine workings." As they did again in 1964, but on the other end of the Reef. In fact, the residents of the West Rand had been so frustrated by the lack of information coming from the mines and by the contradictory or evasive nature of the information that they did receive in Carletonville that they established the local newspaper, the *Carletonville Herald*, in late 1963 with the hope of more timely and more objective accounting.

Four years later, the West Driefontein Mine, another mine in this complex, located on the ridge adjacent to the Blyvoor property and similarly situated beneath what is referred to as the Oberholzer Compartment, was flooded, trapping four thousand miners underground. But this time, there was very little equivocation about the causes. And this geological certitude is related to the fact that all of the miners survived following what was at the time deemed an unprecedented feat of engineering and managerial heroism. A. P. Cartwright memorialized the struggle to save the mine and its workers in an account that is part hagiography and part paean to technology. Here is the "simplified geology" that he deemed necessary to understand for the purposes of grasping the enormity of the accomplishment achieved by the rescue:

After describing the "vast bank of dolomite that extends from almost immediately below the surface to a depth of 2,000 to 4,000 feet," Cartwright continued:

> Through countless thousands of years, this slightly porous formation has acted
> as a vast receptable for the natural water of the district—seepage of rain and
> underground springs. This water, working ceaselessly to erode the dolomite

through the centuries, has carved itself reservoirs, some big, some small. In these it lies peacefully until it is rudely disturbed by the collapse of a dolomite layer that forms a wall for the bottom of its particular reservoir. Then it either flows into another cavern at a lower level or occasionally finds a fissure that takes it down.[31]

The earth, in Cartwright's rhetoric, resembles a great ocean in which a Leviathan waits—to be "rudely disturbed." The weight of that myth is perhaps as heavy as the water that courses through this world. In any case, the process of downward collection leads to the development of increasingly large reservoirs. Cartwright went to great lengths to point out that geologists do not consider this series of linked reservoirs to constitute an underground river or ocean, as many people believe, but rather a series of springs continuously feeds the compartments. These springs, he noted, are referred to as "eyes" by farmers.

More important, all of the deepest mines of the area at that time— Blyvooruitzicht, West Driefontein, and Western Deep Levels—were under the large Oberholzer Compartment characterized by proliferating fissures, making the mines particularly vulnerable to flooding, if water was not removed. They are colloquially referred to as "wet" mines, and as I have experienced, their tunnels are often muddy, the ceilings damp and dripping, and the passages slippery under the foot. To ensure the safety of the miners, no less than seven million gallons of water were pumped out of the mine each day between 1962 and 1964, the time of the sinkholes that destroyed the crushing plant, the recreation club, and the Oosthuizen house. After this, the West Driefontein Mine obtained pumps permitting the evacuation of sixty-two million gallons a day, and a storage system produced by installing "doors" to the pumping shafts was installed that enabled the mine to keep one thousand million gallons of water out of the lower levels (up to level sixteen).[32]

In 1963, West Driefontein began expanding, and opened a shaft that crossed a large fault line referred to as "Big Boy" into another compartment of water, referred to as Bank Compartment, about sixty miles in length and holding an estimated one hundred thousand million gallons of water. At 9:15 A.M., on Saturday October 26, 1968, a fissure opened in this ocean-size reservoir, perhaps as a result of seismic activity linked to the mine or a natural tremor, which then began to pour its torrent into the mine where the four thousand workers were engaged. The result, wrote Cartwright, "as far as the men and the mine were concerned, could scarcely have been worse had a drill tapped the bottom of the Mediterranean."[33] Those Christian men would have recognized Noah's sublime terror: "And the waters prevailed exceedingly upon the earth."[34] Later, they and Green would recall Jonah's lament: "The waters compassed me about, even to the soul; The depth closed round about."[35]

Big Boy, an oxymoron, seems an odd moniker for a force of such incomparable intensity. When I toured the Blyvooruitzicht mine with a safety crew as part of their accident preparation training, my guide told me that the pressure behind the rock of wall where we stood was equivalent to "two Hoover Dams." Cartwright wrote his account of the drama that followed the first breach of the fissure and culminated only on November 18, after the last two mineworkers had been brought to the surface and the leak sealed in a fevered fortnight, at which point the mine was declared saved. His narrative was based on intensive interviews with all the players—from engineers and managers, to the stranded "pump boys," Alberto Noife and Luiz Sandela, and the "boss boy," Vascoe, who volunteered to go down and retrieve his compatriots by tying a rope around their waists and pulling them into a cage so that they could be brought to the surface. Their photographs appear at the end of *West Driefontein—Ordeal by Water*, with snippets of their first-hand reports. Bookending the hall of heroes are the Technical Director of Gold Fields, Mr. R. R. M. Cousens, at the front, and Vascoe, whose last name appears only as the initial "C" in the citation he received for his bravery, alongside "Mr. Theron," who is credited with rescuing the men at Level 13 3/4.

Buried Alive

Cartwright's account is riveting—and tropologically predictable. The enormity of the threat is matched in its narrative by the ingenuity of the men battling that Leviathan so "rudely disturbed." The title makes clear that the entire episode is to be grasped in the idiom of a trial, a proving of mettle and merit. The judgement is to be read in the survival of the men and the mine. What rises above this ideological function is Cartwright's effort to convey the psycho-affective experience of the men underground, faced with the sensation of an ocean descending on them and of being buried alive. Again and again, he notes the raging noise and deafening power of the water. He writes of the "shattering noise," and "the roar of the torrent rushing down the shaft" that had "risen to a crescendo." The men underground had had some sonic fore-warnings: "it was reported that . . . the ground . . . had 'bumped' in the night." A stoper remarked that the "stope was 'talking' and bumping," although he did not understand their significance or anticipate the disaster.[36] When the water entered, it was initially misrecognized as a modest inflow, but as the water rose, and it became apparent that the men at the "dead-end level which had no outlet" would be trapped and possibly drowned, concern increased. The telephones linking the surface and the depths failed. Jack Cuthbertson, the mine overseer, recalled his worry for the men he described only as "two Bantu." They were stranded in their pump chamber above Level 14, and were cut off from the others and access to the elevator cage by the new river that had formed in the tunnels. Some of the shaft foremen went in pursuit of possibly missing men, and one of them discovered one of his miners, "a Frenchman named Louis La Butte," still working away. He "and his men had no idea that anything was amiss" for the simple reason that "the drilling machines had drowned all other sounds."[37]

Once again, Cartwright's language reveals the strangely redoubling nature of the problem. The noise of the machines intended to stave off the disaster had drowned out the sound of the catastrophe, which bore the risk of drowning. This predicament, of one noise canceling another while oddly amplifying its effect, is consonant with the history of hearing and its loss in industrial mines—and continues into the present. The phenomenon of industrial hearing loss had long been conceded, but it was only in 1951, when the Chamber of Mines authorized reimbursement to "mine officials" (white) of up to £30 for hearing aids necessitated by deafness due to long service in the stamps.[38] Twenty years after the flooding described by Cartwright, and soon after its establishment as a nonracial union, South Africa's National Union of Mine Workers (NUM) published a small, plainspoken book, *A Thousand Ways to Die: The Struggle for Safety in the Gold Mines* (1986). The guide was written mainly to assist recruitment for the NUM. One of its most poignant observations regards the paradox of "noise deafness" and ear protection. The use of ear coverings or plugs to protect hearing not only simulates but also produces in a temporary fashion the very deafness that the measure is intended to avoid, thus depriving miners of the sensitivity that they require to stay alive. With ear coverings, miners cannot hear "moving rock" and other warning signals. And most refuse to wear them, precisely because it obstructs their other sense, sometimes referred to as their miners' sixth sense, which attunes them to the earth's soundings. In the typical listing of activities undertaken under Chamber auspices, the *Report* of 1968, which included Muller's Afrikaans address, noted that "audiometric equipment" had been installed at the hospital in Wenele "to enable accurate assessment of hearing impairment." The cost for medical aid borne by the Chamber for the white employees was estimated at 1,108,359 rand (the ZAR:USD conversion rate was about 1.4:1 at the time) for the year, but individual employers were responsible for medical aid to black workers.[39] Hence, they are not accounted in the *Report*.

Cheaper than silencers, which would be applied to the machines rather than the men, earplugs and coverings were the mining companies' favored ameliorative technology. Ultimately, their failure to listen to those who were going deaf and those whose deafness led to accidents would finally incite an increasingly voluble response, one that gave NUM a central place in the history of South Africa's anti-Apartheid movement. The predicament is captured in Vilakazi's great poem "Ezinkomponi," which begins with an ekphrasis addressed to that which will not hear him, the deafening sound that makes his own voice inaudible:

> Roar! and roar! machines of the mines,
> Roar from dawn till darkness falls;
> Roar, machines, continue deaf
> To the black men groaning as they labour.[40]

The opening line, "Roar, without rest, machines of the mines," is an invitation to sounding. It recurs with the rhythmic repetition of a stamp machine throughout the poem, driving to the prophetic conclusion, the moment when the white mine owners will have to listen to the men whom they tried to reduce to mere boys:

> Growl more softly, you machines!
> Because the white men are as stone,
> Can you, of iron, not be gentler?
> Hush your roaring in the mines
> And hear what we would say to you.[41]

One way to understand the disaster of the sinkholes and the flood, as they were narrated in the heroic national mythology of the Apartheid era, is as a refusal to listen within a structure of "overhearing." That overhearing included both a suspicion (and an over-reading) of the speech of black subjects and a passing by of this speech. That is to say, such speech was muted, or subalternized. This doesn't mean that the "two Bantu" did not speak or were not recorded as speaking, but rather that they were not heard to say what they were attempting to articulate. Let us listen a little more closely.

As Cartwright recounts, the initial realization of the flood's extent led to the withdrawal of almost all the workers, who made the treacherous journey out in water up to their knees and thus (although Cartwright does not mention it) pouring into their boots, those famous gum-boots of the South African miner. Those boots had already been iconicized in the gum-boot dance (Z, *isicathulo*) spectacles that formed one of the elaborate "cultural" entertainments of the mines—typically staged for non-mine-worker audiences. But while ignoring the drag and struggle of these water-filled boots, Cartwright was impressed that, despite fear, the workers marched in disciplined fashion, without panic. From one shaft alone, 1,500 "Bantu mineworkers and 20 odd white miners" made the orderly trek out. The nominal distinction between miner and mineworker, as already mentioned, was one of the idiomatic codes of racial difference and rank in South Africa's mines, with miner reserved for higher-level and better paid employees, mineworker for less skilled wage and contract labor. In Cartwright's and management's estimation, it was this rank and hierarchy that enabled the escape, for "thanks to the shift bosses, led by Bruce Bailey," no stragglers were lost or left behind to follow doomed tunnels. "By 5:30 [about eight hours after the breach] all the men had reached the surface—all that is except the two unfortunate Bantu pump men marooned in their 'cave' at 13 3/4 Level."[42] Describing their plight, with only their headlamps for illumination and a "solid sheet of water . . . roaring between, down the shaft outside the pump chamber where they were cowering," Cartwright notes that "there cannot have been two more unhappy, frightened men in the world that day than these two Shangaans." When they were finally reached, they stood naked, having stripped off their clothes in anticipation of having to swim. Rescued by Theron and Vascoe, and treated for shock and cold, Cartwright quotes them saying, "Bass, we thought we were dead."[43]

The progression of the narrative, nominally and syntactically, presents these men in terms of their place and function (pump men at the "dead-end" of the mine), their racial identity (Bantu or black), their ethnicity (Shangaan from Mozambique). Finally, when speaking, Alberto Noife gives voice to the entire social architecture of the mine, in the deictically marked gesture by which Noife recognizes his white superior as his boss and then describes that awful sensation not only of being about to die, in his words, but of actually being dead: "We thought we were dead."

In a cave, in a mine, underground, where earth and ocean have merged in the space that we can only call "the Deep," the logic of the Apartheid economy persists to the point at which an absolute transgression occurs: the living are both alive and dead. This is perhaps the most poignant expression of necropolitical destitution imaginable, for it bespeaks not the sense of being left to die but of being dead alive. The men's relieved joy is to be able to speak this predicament as an occurrence in the past. They are in this sense able to historicize their trauma. Partly this is done in a manner that implies an error of judgment; "we thought," says the miner, implicitly indicating that the worst fears had turned out to have been unwarranted. Partly, too, this historicization is accomplished by allowing the expression, "we thought we were dead" to recede into the status of an idiom or metaphor in which it does not mean that the speaker was really dead, or even that he truly thought himself dead, but only that he was almost dead, and even *as though* dead. At the eye of the underground storm, then, in the moment of greatest terror, when the cave within the shaft is a refuge against a catastrophe in which the sky beneath the earth is flooded—when, that is, all directionality and conceptual distinction is undone—there, one is *as though dead*. And this being *as though dead* is what the stranded miners experienced when fearing they were being buried alive.

The last entry of Cartwright's book is quoted testimony from these two rescued men, offered after the fact, followed by that of their savior:

We are the men who were rescued from the pump chamber on 13 3/4 Level, No. 4 Shaft. We are both Shangaans from Portuguese territory. Our kraal is near Masinga. We really did not know what was happening on that day when all the water came down the shaft except that there was a big noise. At first we had the telephone and we tried to get the boss boys at the bottom of the shaft but there was no one there. Then we rang the banksman and he said to stay where we were till the cage came to get us. But no cage came. Then the lights went out. Then the telephone was no good and still the water was coming down. When the lights were gone we used one of the lights on our hats and kept the other one for later. We were very frightened. It was cold and we thought we were going to die. Much time went by and no one came for us. We climbed up on the sets and sat there. When the cage came we saw no lights and could hear nothing until suddenly the boss boy came with a rope and they pulled us into the cage. We were very frightened when we had to go through the water. But we were very very happy when we got to the top. We felt bad afterwards and we were sneezing but soon we were well again . . . Alberto has sent a letter to the chief and to his wife telling them about it.[44]

I quote this narrative fragment in full to draw out a few elements absent in Cartwright's text and to recall, once again, the importance and tropology of the letter in this world that, still in 1964, was organized on the principles of coerced migrancy, and still, in 1964, suffused with the yearning for communication between home and this unhomely world of the mine compound. Only one of the men writes a letter; it is not so much an intimate gesture as a representative one. The other man does not write but he speaks. And his speech is also representative insofar as it is articulated in the first person plural: "*We* are the pump men." The final element of Alberto Noife's testimony is to describe his colleague's epistle, which does not merely communicate news but also sutures them to a social world organized on principles that are at once continuous with preindustrial political life (under the name of chieftainship) and transformed by colonialism (also under the name of chieftainship). Recall, here, that the chiefs of the Portuguese territories were often bribed by labor recruiters and were often recipients of remittances. Alberto seeks recognition from his chief, as well as contact with and consolation for his wife (in whose eyes, his dramatic survival will perhaps increase his renown).

More than this epistolary history and the tracery of the migrant system encrypted in the story of survival, is the poignant assertion of dignity and status: "We are the men." Not pump boys. If Alberto Noife nonetheless refers to the boss boy who saved him and his coworker, this claim to manly status is a direct refusal of the infantilization that defined the racialized labor hierarchies of the mine. To be sure, Noife accedes to the logic of ethnicity (and thus to the logic of Apartheid governmentality), but ethnicity is quickly supplanted in his discourse and by means of affectionate identification, by a more local affiliation, namely a kraal in Masinga. Speaking thus, Noife reveals the extent to which these men inhabited a multiply fissured world, at once deeply attached to a specific place *and* experienced in the forms of travel and temporary uprootedness that formed the basis of migrant cosmopolitanism. Worldly travelers, they had not left behind their attachment to home, although this home had only recently become coded as "the rural" (as will be discussed in chapter 8).

For his part, Vascoe described responding to the request for assistance from Mr. Cuthbertson, when asked if he would help rescue the two Bantu. "I had not been afraid, but I must admit," he said afterward, "that when I saw the amount of water, and the noise it was making I was afraid, but felt something must be done to save the pump boys." Once again, it is the noise that haunts his memory as that which incited in him the most profound fear. Most of the other witnesses and interviewees whose testimony appear in *West Driefontein—Ordeal by Water* describe the days that followed this rescue, when the second act of salvage was undertaken and enormous plugs inserted into the fissures to stop the flood and enable the dewatering that would once again open the shafts, fill the earth with air, and, as Mr. Buley, the mine's general manager would later say, submit nature to technological know-how: "No feat in the history of the mining endeavour can surpass the work and the devotion of the men of West Driefontein, who successfully subdued the forces of Nature in the twenty-six days, October 26 to November 20, 1968."[45]

Without Mourning

Under such circumstances, when, in his opinion, "that mine may well give thanks to God," Cartwright was surprised that very few people attended the thanksgiving service held in the mine's recreation club following the determination that it had been secured. "For reasons that I cannot explain, the people of Carletonville weren't there," he wrote.[46] Is it possible that the (white) townsfolk felt too much had been wagered on their behalf? Perhaps they were simply exhausted by wondering, day after day, if the men who were descending into the deeps would come back out alive. Perhaps they were tired of waiting and worrying. Perhaps, too, they recalled the sinkhole disasters of only a few years before, when the mines had claimed that there was an ambiguous relationship between dewatering and underground compartment collapse. Was their absence a critical repudiation of the mining companies' dissimulation? Perhaps they did not feel so personally affected as when their neighbors vanished and their households seemed at risk. After all, the vast majority of those men who survived the ordeal and who had been threatened with death, were black men, unknown by name even to he who wrote so sympathetically of their plight. The absent townspeople referenced by Cartwright were white. Between them was that distance enforced by pass laws and territorial practice, the distance of disidentification.

In Apartheid's logic, of course, it was these black men's function to undertake the arduous labor of the mines and to suffer the physical consequences of doing so. To wit: the Chamber of Mines's *Annual Report* for this same year, echoing and defending against the issues that had arisen in Stallard's time, responded to what it called "extravagant" criticism for increasing black employment and "allegedly advancing the Bantu to the detriment of the job-security, safety and health of the White employees." Not to worry, retorted President Muller, who placated members and assured shareholders, "We are strongly opposed to any step that would undermine the security or the safety and health of the White or any other class of worker on the Mines." He added, "In the public and other sectors of our economy the status of and material well-being of the White worker is being advanced and strengthened by the allocation to Bantu of tasks of a routine nature formerly done by White men."[47]

The *Report* of 1968 was significant for reasons beyond its declaration of support for the National Party agenda of preventing downward class mobility for whites. It also introduced an entirely unprecedented element into the format of the president's, Dr. T. F. Muller's, address, namely an alternation between English and Afrikaans. In his response to this address, Mr. A. Louw remarked the fact as follows: "Mr. President, members will have noted that a portion of your address today was delivered in Afrikaans and I believe it is fitting that you should have done so, not only because it is the home language of the majority of our mine employees, but also because you are the first member of the Federale Mynbou Group to have held the position of President of the Chamber."[48] Indeed, the first Afrikaner-owned mining company had only come into being in 1963, part of the nationalist project by which Apartheid governance was to be coupled with Afrikaner control over major capitalist enterprises.[49] In this manner, cultural nationalism was linked with ethnonational capital formation.

That the majority of the mine employees did not claim Afrikaans as a first language is obvious: they spoke Sesotho, isiXhosa, Sepedi, isiNdebele, isiZulu, Chitonga, Setswana, Shona, Shangaan, and Tshivenda among other languages. Louw had the white workers in mind. Eight years later, the implementation of the Bantu Education Act's requirement that Afrikaans become the medium for all instruction throughout South Africa's state-funded schools would lead to the insurrections of 1976, most visibly in Soweto, and thereafter among the residents of Khutsong township, near Carletonville. But in this moment, looking back on that noisy terror of West Driefontein, neither Muller nor Louw could hear the rumbling on the horizon—a rumbling that would *not* sound like wagon wheels on a rough road, but, perhaps (remembering the descriptions of riots from chapter 1) like fire on the Highveld. That rumbling would betoken the transformation of the political underground and the beginning of the end of formal Apartheid.

If, in this gesture, I speak of hearing by way of analogy to identify an intuition and anticipation of historical forces, thereby implying as well a kind of deafness or impairment of the critical analytical faculty in the present, it is because the phenomenon of hearing in the mine partakes of a more general problem of representation, one that the mine incarnates, and which reaches its apogee in the phenomenon of the mine accident: the incapacity to delimit the figure in relation to the ground. But the problem of hearing, and of being heard, is also the problem of subalternity—the subaltern being that subject who cannot be heard to say what she intends to say, and thus to access power, except in death.[50] It is clear that the Shangaan men were not heard, in their time. They continued to be rendered as boys in the discourse on the flood, which, despite Cartwright's admiring mythification, did not achieve the status of an eventful transformation.

Muller, who spoke in Afrikaans about the West Driefontein "flooding" devoted only two sentences to the story, and these privileged the technological rescue rather than the dangers endured or the risks betokened: " 'n Merkwaardige prestasie gedurende die jaar was die geslaagde stuiting van die Vloedwater wat die West Driefonteinmyn in Oktober en November bedreig het. Die redding van die myn is, sonder lewensverlies, ten spyte van 'n totaal onverwagte instroming van sowat 85 miljoen gelling water per dag, moontlik gemaak deur die moed, die uithouvermoë en die vakkundigheid van al die betrokkenes" (A remarkable achievement during the year was the successful staunching of the floodwaters that infiltrated the West Driefontein mine in October and November. The rescue of the mine was, without loss of life, and despite a totally unexpected influx of about 85 million gallons of water per day, made possible by the courage, endurance and expertise of all those involved).[51] Although the residents had failed to attend the memorial events, they would later recall the rescue as a high point of the mines' achievements. In the late 1990s, this story of heroic rescue was among the first reported to me by older white residents who had worked in or been associated with the industry at the time of the ordeal. Soon into our interviews, they would ask, "Did you know . . .?"

What did I know?

The flood at West Driefontein remained an exception in the narratological imagination of the area, an event distinct in kind and outcome from the sinkholes afflicting residences aboveground. It shared with the story of cyanide a fascination with a technological mediation of an ostensibly natural problem, cast in a humanist idiom through the tropes of invention, ingenuity, and, above all, courage. It entirely obscured the political economic drivers in the story—which introduced the crisis in the pursuit of gold and which would not have existed in its absence. No such narrative legitimation offered itself in the case of sinkholes, which, as I noted, could be avoided at best. If, as in the case of the cave, sinkholes could be stabilized by injecting slimes, this would always be a gesture a posteriori. Mythification of the more dramatic holes certainly occurred, but it was myth of a premodern or Old Testamentary sort. It could be mobilized to service the value of the patriarchal family, but not of the self-possessed and possessing individual of the bourgeois era. Indeed, as Green noted, the story of Blyvoor was a myth of myth: a narrative of nontransformation pretending to the status of event. The story of the flood at West Driefontein was its counterpoint, the effort to restitute a belief in technologically mediated heroism in a space where accidents were as much the effect of technology as the occasion for its exercise.

For a long time, the Chamber of Mines attempted to blame the increasing rate of sinkhole occurrence in the West Rand on improper land use: the excessive watering of lawns, broken and ill-tended sewer pipes, and unpredictable natural events such as flooding by rain waters—anything but the dewatering of the mines. Such explanations were often repeated to me and derided by critics and township residents, whose homes were cracked, their floors slanted. Often pointing to the scarred and asymmetrical surfaces of their dwellings, they adduced these qualities as proof of the mines' dissimulations and as the basis of hoped-for compensation. For them, the sinkhole was, above all, a problem of property value—rather than a mortal threat. Indeed, the number of deaths resulting from sinkholes is miniscule compared with those that have occurred in other mine accidents. According to official corporate statistics, between 1911 and 1994 (shortly before my conversations on these issues), sixty-nine thousand (mostly black) miners had been killed and more than a million injured in South African mines. This number does not include those who died or were severely impaired by illness caused by conditions in the mine: the victims of phthisis, silicosis, tuberculosis, and other lung diseases. Still, the sound of wagon wheels on a dirt road and the image of patriarchal families suspended in midair, plummeting downward, transfixed the people of Carletonville and deafened them to the warning signs of what was about to occur. The mythic status of the (non)event was sealed some years later, when lightning struck and entirely destroyed the commemorative plaque that had been established in memory of the Oosthuizens. It had been affixed to an enormous boulder near the site of the disaster, and read: "*God het hulle self ter aarde bestel*" ("For their sakes, God has appointed them the earth").[52] The words *ter aarde bestel* are spoken at many Afrikaner funerals as the body is interred.[53] In this case, the formula implies that God actually buried the family, short-circuiting the ritual process in a terrifying, time-compressing immediacy. That the rock, symbol of Christian community and endurance, should have been destroyed in such dramatic fashion after this signifying gesture—by an act of nature that is also stereotypically rendered as a sign of divine wrath in Christian iconology—led to a further sense of unsettlement. Some people felt that the boulder had been received by God as a gesture of presumptuous human certitude, or perhaps as a substitution for what had been severed, hence as a kind of fetish. For, if God had indeed buried the Oosthuizens, there would be no need for human labors to commend the deceased into His care. Accordingly, the plaque's destruction was received as a sign of rebuke and a restitution of divine mystery. A more modest replacement memorial was eventually erected but without a boulder. Eventually, all the houses were demolished. The only evidence of the disaster now visible is a depression on the surface of the earth. And the stories.

Buried, Dead and Alive

The stories of sinkholes, in which people, houses, pets, and the accouterments of everyday life are buried, invariably start in medias res. Most stories of mine accidents narrate the terrible interruption of life as an inexplicable occurrence, not as the telos of any internal life process but rather as a tear in the ontological fabric of the universe. The suddenness of an errant rock, a misfiring stick of dynamite, a collapsing piece of earth, or the gush of water from behind a suddenly failing rock wall: these elements are central in the narratives of sudden and premature death. But in each of these stories, as they have come to me over the decades, there is a moment of hesitation when the teller of the tale seems to wonder if the deceased knew what was happening in the moment before they died. The narrators seem terrified by the prospect that the person dying was actually conscious of becoming dead, that it was not merely dying but death that they experienced.

Jacques Derrida has described the literary artifact as a "living-dead machine," a dense corpse/corpus of traces that is resuscitated in each act of reading. What he terms the "survivance" of the book, or literary tale, is "neither life nor death pure and simple." It is neither additive nor subtractive from life—though this life is to be distinguished from living beings; "it is something other than life death, but a groundless ground from which are detached, identified, and opposed what we think we can identify under the name of death or dying so-called."[54] The literary artifact shares something with the proper name in this form of survivance, and is, says Derrida, actually "twice a proper name."[55] Just as the name has an existence and a capacity to survive the one who it names, and indeed to travel independently of that one, so the work of literary fiction, which bears a title in the mode of a proper name, has this enduring quality. It is not incidental, for my purposes, that Derrida's theorization of this phenomenon, of survivance, is oriented at least partly by his reading of Robinson Crusoe, whose fear of being "buried alive" is read as a real fear, and moreover a fear that has been realized by the fact that Robinson Crusoe, the character, is encrypted in *Robinson Crusoe*, the novel, where he "lives" the eternal life of the literary creation. Derrida finds in this storied fear, at once justified and superfluous insofar as burial of this metaphorical sort is a form of survivance, an analogy or a narrativization of a general structure, if not precisely a logic, of mourning. In both cases, the possibility of living on depends on being exposed to and, indeed, incorporated by others. He would have us learn from the literary example a principle for ethical life, one that not only recognizes the difficulty of ever drawing the line between the living and the dead but also permits and even encourages a recognition of our dependency on others, whom we may otherwise fear will consume us, if we are to not perish completely.

There is perhaps a dangerous proximity between the language of being buried alive, as Crusoe uses that phrase to describe his fear of being eaten by cannibals or merely annihilated by time and the elements on his island, and that referred to by the miners who face this predicament in a seemingly more "literal" fashion—beyond metaphor. Crusoe, it might be said, treats his ship as a mine: a container from which he can extract the remnants of his bourgeois existence and that remains as a figure of possible return to that surface (that heaven), where life will no longer be vulnerable to consumption by labor. In this manner, the underground is both split and displaced: the threat of death onto the cannibal, and the dream of survival onto the storehouse of things that is Crusoe's wrecked ship.[56] Crusoe becomes the locus of a bourgeois fantasy of a laborless life. There is an additionally dangerous proximity between the mortal threat faced by miners and Derrida's use of the phrase as a general and generalizing means to describe the encryption performed by the proper name and every act of mourning. But in the South African literature devoted to the mines, the metaphoric nature of this living dying is plumbed in ways that share Derrida's sense of the conceptual and directional confusion. Consider, for example, these lines from Vilakazi's *Ezinkomponi*:

> And all our world is upside down;
> At dawn we're roused to stand in lines . . .
> Have you seen buried men survive
> Walking and seeing and staying alive?[57]

And recall those by Moses Bopape and Stephen Ratlabala, which appeared as epigram to this chapter:

> Mja bona bophelo ke bja ge ba boa dirapeng
> Tše rapaltšang baepi maleng a lefase.

> [Their lives start when they return from the graveyards which make the diggers lie in the belly of the earth.][58]

At least two dimensions of Derrida's reading offer some guidance for think-ing about the storying of accidents—in the mine and as a result of mining, in and as a result of sinkholes. And these become most available, conceptually, when one considers the affinity between the stories of the men buried alive and of the domestic worker who may have escaped the tragedy of the sinkhole that took the Oosthuizen house. She may or may not have survived in actuality (and who cannot hope that she did?), but she most assuredly survives in the narratives still told today in the nearby township. This does not mean that the fantasy of survival suffices as compensation for actual deaths, but it does help us understand the force of story, of narration, and of the intense desire of the young zama zamas to be known, to have their names spoken by others.[59]

The stories I have recounted make it clear that, structurally but also sub-stantively speaking, it is difficult to draw a line between the literary story and that told by those who have little relationship to the institution of literature and who rarely read what is generally called literary fiction. This only intensifies the question, a question asked by insurance agents, lawyers, and forensic investiga-tors alike, about whether the seemingly too-familiar tropology of such stories should make one distrust them. Should they dismiss them as if they were "only stories," as if their narrators had merely been "telling stories"—as happened, for example, in the TRC? But if one does not dismiss stories, the resemblances between them start to seem both meaningful and uncanny. The mystery that surrounds them also opens a space of suspicion and potentially critical ques-tioning, which may, if prepared and directed, also assume a transformative capacity. The questions commence: How can this be happening? And how can it be happening again? They may be enabled (prepared for by critical intuition, by reason and imagination) to continue: If it is happening again, can it really be an accident? And if it is not an accident, how shall one explain this recurrence? Can one prevent and not merely avoid accidents? Is there something more to be done than rehearse for disaster?

By the turn of the millennium, as sinkholes continued to propagate through-out the Witwatersrand, the residents of Khutsong township had no illusions that they were accidental phenomena. They blamed them on the mines, and the destructive dewatering of the underground. One report has claimed that more than 90 percent of the territory in Khutsong township is "unfit for human habita-tion," because of its subterranean dolomitic foundation and the risk of sinkholes associated with dewatering.[60] But, in residents' analyses, it was not the sinkholes so much as the distribution of proximity to the sinkholes and of the exposure of particular people to their earth-shaking effects that provided the evidence for this claim.[61] Or rather, the structured and relative exposure to sinkholes is for many the proof that the sinkhole is that which can be appropriated—despite its character as a negation of the earth, of surface, of that which can be rendered as property and alienated. Something like debt (to be discussed later), it is a new mechanism for managing the still largely racialized divide between classes, one that is inscribed within the economy that works by submitting nature to its rule. It is thus an extension, transformation, and development of that machine of economic division.

For many Afrikaners in the region, the destruction of the rock and its plaque by lightening was proof of a transcendental force operating in the world, one that would resist any effort at containment or placatory obeisance, let alone managerial circumscription. Even those who would not avow such a reading acknowledged a sense of something mysterious. Nor were they alone in this respect. One of the most elderly of Khutsong's residents, a black man who had first sought employment in the mines at Randfontein in 1938, starting as a "tea boy" before moving to Crown Mines in 1941 and then transferring to Blyvooruitzicht as a cook in the mine hospital in 1945, described to me a fantastical network of secret highways beneath the sinkholes. For him, the sinkholes were shallow spaces beneath which were mines and routes that extend all the way from Carletonville to Bultfontein. "Some white people cross through the hole to Bultfontein," he said in a hushed voice. In addition, he described the sinkholes as repositories of fragile treasures and precious domestic objects: "In a sinkhole there are things like glasses and some other things like plates but if you take one from the sink holes, things like the glasses they break the minute they come across light or the sun." That which is buried must remain concealed, he seemed to be saying. Did this apply to gold?

The disinterment of that which God had interred was akin to the violation of a secret, which, as Derrida reminds us, can be told but not revealed.[62] Revelation destroys the secret, just as the sun, signifier of omnipotence, shatters or corrodes the object overexposed to sunlight in the old man's narrative and in the manifold mythologies that deploy the figure of the sun to allegorize absolute power and the dangers of proximity to it. The old man emphasized this point when he said that "the underground things that we do not know who created them, we believe it is God's nature." This phrase is ambiguous; is it the nature of God to inter things in the earth, or is nature, figured as the earth, that which belongs to God? If the former, God is a keeper of secrets; if the latter, He is the origin and owner of property. Both of these possibilities are inscribed in Christian theological and exegetical traditions, to some form of which the old man adhered.

There are two renowned Bultfonteins in South Africa (as well as a suburb in Johannesburg, and perhaps others elsewhere). One is a small town, which, depending on the surface route, lies about 275 kilometers from Carletonville, on the way to the city of Bloemfontein. Formed in 1873, it is known (if at all) for its enormous grain silo and its old prison cell (one of the oldest in the region, dating to the turn of the twentieth century). If this Bultfontein was the referent of the story, then perhaps it was testimony to the extravagant mobility of whites, their immunity to pass laws and all the other encumbrances that inhibited the mobility of black subjects. But there was also a diamond mine called Bultfontein in Kimberley, and it was there that the nesosilicate (i.e., Bultfonteinite) was discovered in 1903 or 1904. It has since been found in many places in the world, where it is associated with Kimberlite pipes.[63] Bultfonteinite is a pink or colorless crystal. It looks like a composite of minute needles of glass or some forms of asbestos. Was this the crystal that the elder had imagined as being like "glasses"? Or, was he implicitly narrating the direct link between the financial capital of Kimberley's diamond economy and the gold mines of the Far West Rand? Had the geological object metamorphosed in his imagination, sliding along the chain of association, word becoming image across languages and idioms, to become conflated with the china of a white household, fallen into oblivion?[64] Or were the associations and homonymies just accidental?

Alas, I did not know anything about Bultfonteinite when the old man told me his story, which my marvelous associate, the artist Songezile Madikida, was enabling and translating. And when I finally learned about it, it was too late to return to ask him whether this too had been in mind. I had only the video recordings of our interview, the now posthumous image of his smooth face, the sound and cadence of his voice, rushing enthusiastically and then slowing as the afternoon grew long. But the operations of the unconscious are not directly available to reflection. What sounded forth in this elder's discourse exceeded what he intended to say—as all speech exceeds the intended message sent by all speakers, being that which comes from the past and which resonates in the tenebrous field of language. Its meaning moves along pathways unconfined by reason, sometimes splitting and doubling, sometimes leaping from object to object by virtue of a vaguely perceived resemblance or a remembered utterance from another context.

Regardless of its intended significations, this simple dream image condensed the entire order of this Chamber-made world as one in which value is secreted in the earth and extracted at risk of its breakage, loss, or dissipation. Just as the long history of gold's fetishization has been accompanied by a fear of dissimulation, alloying, contamination, and clipping, so too the old man's imaginal description was a cipher recapitulating the problem of value's representation and expressing the anxiety about exposure and falsification that accompanies it. In many ways, his narrative seemed to offer itself as allegory. And if it can be read as an allegory of the gold industry's representational regime (at least as understood in the popular economic imagination), it is because, as in Plato's allegory of the cave, the sun is behind everything—if, that is, we concede that this sun that stands behind everything is itself a dissimulating representation. "Inside that cave, burns a fire in 'the image of' a sun," writes Luce Irigaray. And it is casting shadows, shadows that are coded within the ideological apparatus as "the real thing."[65] If the old man's account can indeed function as an allegory, it is because, in that same cave, a puppet master in the form of financial capitalism emerging from gold-based world money, rules because (almost) everyone believes that gold is the true representation of true value. Within this "specular cave," as Irigaray calls the epistemic system subtending that economy and the society erected on its ground, everything depends on the belief that real value can be differentiated from its mere simulation, nature from artifact, truth from falsity. Her demythologized cave is the space of illusion, where people are captured by the victors' history. In this history, gold is allied with phallic power and is one of the forms or, as she says, "mirages" of wealth. It is also an aspirant to the role of transcendental signifier—that impossible signifier at the end of signification, a formless figure of the absolute.[66]

Within this regime, truth is always a limit point of allegory, the place at which metaphor, including the metaphor of the cave and of the landscape, comes to die. It, the "it" of verity's discourse, simply is. This is why the sinkhole of the old man's story was the point of *demetaphorization* as much as metaphorization (in figure and allegory). With the haunting references to the beautiful glass that would shatter if exposed to the light, he pointed to an order of invisible powers with violent effects. This is perhaps best grasped if one considers the counternarrative of the plate as the prop of Apartheid racialization. Consider, for example, the text of an exchange with one of the area's elder women, a woman whom I will call Promise, who was born in East Driefontein in 1922 and who moved to Khutsong in 1969.

Madikida had nudged Promise gently about her sense that things had improved since Mandela's release, given that the township remained exclusively black, although black residents now accounted for some portion of the householders in the formerly white town of Carletonville. He had conceded that upward mobility for some blacks had not meant that the truly destitute spaces of the black townships had in any way been transformed. And, the humiliation of the plate that she was not allowed to eat from remained in her mind as an index of a specifically painful exclusion.

> There is nothing worse than what they did during meal time. You worked for this person, cooked for them, but when they dish up they would tell you to go fetch your plate outside—the same plate that is used for the dog! You were expected to eat from the same plate that a dog eats from, you see? Should they ever find you eating from the plates that they use, you would be fired immediately. You poured your energy making them comfortable, the very food that they eat was prepared with your own hands, then they remember that you may have poisonous blood when it comes to dishing up the food that you cooked. What kind of a person does that to another? I don't have poisonous blood, I am created by God. You see the animals? They are also created by God. He could have created people only but he created animals as well. He wanted animals to be part of nature so that we could use them. Using them does not

mean they are not important, they are but they are there to help us. If you had to sit on a chair, you needed to make sure that you do not sit on chair that the *baas* [boss] used. Those were some of the things that were bad in the olden days, but we survived.

In many ways, this example is commonplace. Many people who worked as domestic servants in the Apartheid era, and many who continue to do so now, could and would reproduce some version of this account, although perhaps without the vernacular Christian humanism as an addendum. And one might explore this text for its expression of such humanism to ask what it implies about the ethico-cosmological orientation that characterized a certain generation of Khutsong's residents. We will return to Promise's story in subsequent chapters, but for now I want only to observe the social and signifying function of "plates" in this elder woman's discourse, for it helps to explain how and why this ambiguous figure, coupled with glasses in the old man's description of the sinkhole's secreted treasures, could become so redolent of meaning for him but also so evocative of taboo. What else could activate the magicality of a buried piece of china if not the memory of having been forbidden it and having been given instead supposedly unbreakable enameled mugs (which nonetheless chipped) and tin plates like those on which a dog might eat—as the corollary of blackness?

Promise was articulate about the violences of Apartheid, its causes and its perpetrators, as well as the forms and costs of resistance. But the rest of the old man's narrative, which emerged in a conversation that sprawled across hours, expressed the sense of taboo, of being forbidden to look on that which held him and this world in place. He was hesitant to describe the differences that structured his existence and that of the patients he tended to in the mine hospitals as a function of the racial organization of the industry. Thus, for example, he described how the black patients who had been admitted for tuberculosis, infectious diseases like chicken pox, or accidents, were given pap, corn-based porridges, or steamed bread, but no protein for breakfast or fresh vegetables with their meals. In contrast, he seemed still to relish the feasts that his white wards had enjoyed: eggs for breakfast, roast chicken or steak for lunch, tea and scones in the afternoon, fresh fruit, and vegetables with every meal. And relish is a key term here, for it is vernacularized in the local languages to mean any full meal—and not merely a tasty side dish. To relish, to have relish, is to eat to the point of satiety. Nonetheless, he was also quick to explain these differences as functions of the different illnesses for which the black and white patients were being treated, and he did not wish to state, at least in my presence, that these different meals were expressions of structural inequality.

It was at times like this that Madikida's presence was so important; for he spoke in solidarity and intimate shared knowledge of the injuries suffered during Apartheid, and often it was easier or at least more possible for black people to reveal their accumulated griefs, humiliations, and rages to him than to me, even if I was present. Thus, the old man's reticence was legible as a combination of deferential hospitality to me and evidence of the long shadow of Apartheid's colonizing traces. In some sense, he still resided in the allegorical cave into which he had been born and where he had lived most of his long life. At the same time, and for the same reason, the sinkhole was an insufficiently profound figure for him. It literally lacked depth, and it failed to evoke the ontological questions that concerned him. He mentioned the sinkhole only to make it open onto something larger, to leave it behind.

Confirming Green's hypothesis, the old man's account effectively displaced the sinkholes into the realm of the incidental where they became mere surface phenomena, and his narrative of the catastrophes of 1964 was both blunt and brief: "They started in Blyvoor and one house sank and a family sank to death. The house that sank was in Blyvoor number 2 shaft; it sank and everything was tried to rescue those people but in vain. They even called specialists from Germany and England." He could not quite recall the date, thinking perhaps it was 1959, but in any case, he said that such events also "happened in Merafong and also in Carletonville town but the houses just cracked and not really sank." It was only then that he invoked divine creation as a framework for receiving the geological narrative: "You know the area of Carletonville has tunnels underground which were created by God." Note that these are not the shafts and passageways of the mines but that which lies beneath them. If, however, in this man's narrative, origins were unfathomable, then creation was surveyable. And that which was surveyable was also narratable as a political history: "So, what happens is that the mines use water from these tunnels and later the tunnels lose strength, and when they lose [water], they become weak. Do you know a place called Bank station, they surveyed that place and declared it a danger zone, there are water tunnels underneath *so people and the farms there were moved*" (see chapter 14).

With these last words, we can discern that movement was a political signifier for the man as much as a geological occurrence—and this reading was symptomatic of the moment of our conversation, as well as of the history that arose but did not result from the sinkholes: the history of social and political movements oriented against Apartheid and against government failure in general. Not by virtue of geology but by virtue of the state's intervention (or failures to intervene) were people, submerged in intransitivity, who now had become the subjects and objects of an action. But that does not mean that movement as a concept is reducible to such political immediacies or even that the old man was thinking of insurrection more than he was contemplating a desired pastoral care for vulnerable populations on the part of the state.

Movement—of the earth, away from the earth, upon the earth and beneath the earth, above all into the earth: this dense node of significations also moved within and across the mythology of the sinkhole, contracting as it does around the tenuous and relentlessly dissolving boundary between the mine and the grave. And of course, that unstable line also divides the accident from violence. For most of the residents of Khutsong, however, exposure to the so-called accident of the sinkhole is not mysterious. Nor is it a matter of nature. It is one of the names of the violence of Apartheid, the social technē of separatism, born of gold and the cyanide process. Apartheid is also one of the names of racial inequality that continues to live on after its formal ending. Thus, an August 2016 report in the *Carletonville Herald* described a recent sinkhole disaster with reference to the anniversary of the Blyvoor disaster. It begins: "On 3 August 1964, a historic sinkhole caused the tragic deaths of the Oosthuizen family." One notes the mannered gesture of a small-town newspaper, which asserts the "historic" nature of the 1964 sinkhole. How far it is from the unadorned narrative of the old man who had lived through the period of its occurrence. The *Herald* story continues: "Fifty-two years later, virtually to the day, a huge sinkhole next to important infrastructure has caused thousands of Merafong residents to end up without water. It is situated just three kilometers from the site in Blyvooruitzicht where the house and its occupants disappeared, never to be seen again."[67] In the more recent case, the sinkhole opened up near two major water reservoirs and was associated with a recently constructed water pipeline, leakage from which had been reported previously. The result of the newly forming sinkhole was the interruption of water supplies to forty thousand residences in two main extensions of the Khutsong township. The story, accompanied by a photograph of the collapsed pipeline, ended with the observation that prior efforts by local councilors, including documentation of leakage and sinking, had failed to elicit action from the municipal officials: "Despite their complaints, no action was taken for several days. In the past, environmentalists have warned that the area in which the reservoir and some of the Extension 5 houses have been built is particularly prone to ground stability problems and, therefore, very dangerous."[68]

It is now time to consider the infrastructural and spatial politics of the towns and townships that were built to service these deepest of the world's gold mines, to understand how and why exposure to accident, rather than its technical amelioration, can be a technique of governmentality. This is partly because the idea of a natural accident works to obstruct the capacity of an event to be mobilized for transformative purposes—as Green's verse narrative tells us. In addition, the recognition of a structure of exposure is one of the forms by which it may be made available for deactivation, as we shall see, even as we confront the fact that the regime of the spectacle—whether figured as projections in a cave or incarnated as a fancy dress ball illuminated by limelight—will not finally be overcome by acts of exposure and the labors of demetaphorization.

CHAPTER 8

THE SKY'S THE LIMIT

Visions and Divisions of the World

We are in the epoch of simultaneity: we are in the epoch of juxtaposition, the epoch of the near and far, of the side-by-side, of the dispersed.

—Michel Foucault, "Utopias and Heterotopias"

How did we get here? I asked this question at the opening of this book, in the face of a tragedy in the ruins of the West Rand's gold mines. I ask it again, here, in the shadow of mythic narratives about sinkholes in that same region. Now, the question opens to include the towns and townships themselves. How did they get here? And how did those who were lured or attracted to the area come to inhabit this partitioned world, with its projections and shadows, its dreams of technocratic modernism and carceral rurality?

"I was transported from the village . . . on a donkey cart and it was so strange to me because there were buses and cars but I was on a donkey cart on a tarred road, I even remember it was in the afternoon, very misty and very dark, full of smoke and so forth. I was taken to my parent's house here in Khutsong. It was a two roomed house." Thus begins a narrative of arrival as well as return to the largest township of the municipality now called Merafong, by a respected church leader whom I shall call the Reverend. Merafong's name means "place of mining" in Setswana and Khutsong translates as "place of rest." The latter name implies a kind of bedroom community, a retirement village (if not a cemetery), or a vacation setting for those whose working day is over, although the township's reputation is that of a seething cauldron of conflict and its imagery in national media is that of insurrection and abandonment, anger and ennui. At the time of this arrival in the 1960s and even in the moment of our conversation four decades later, there were relatively few commercial establishments in the black township, which was still in many ways defined by its status as "outside." It was outside of Carletonville, outside of Oberholzer, off the main road, and a relatively long way from the mines and, when they functioned, the train stations. It was, in some senses, far from the ideals of urbanity, certainly far from the money. More of a sinkhole than a mine.

In the midst of the most contentious and violent antigovernment protests in more than three decades, the Reverend was narrating his arrival in the township four decades earlier. At the time of our conversation, the schools were closed and the traffic lights and street lamps had gone dark after being sabotaged. Many of the local government councilors' houses had been set alight and razed by protestors. The municipal representatives had either fled or drove gingerly through the unpoliced neighborhoods with private security guards. But roadways were often blocked by the smoke of tires. It was 2006, and the area was beset by outrage after the national government had decided to redistrict the municipality and place it under the jurisdiction of Northwest Province rather than Gauteng (see chapter 14). Northwest Province was associated in the minds of most of the people in Khutsong with the rustic and the rude. It was the place, imagined one elderly woman, where people "eat wild vegetables every day without meat, with *niks* (nothing)." The redistricting was felt by many to constitute an eviction not only from an administrative domain where the nation's political and economic capitals were located but from the very idea and aesthetic ideal of modernity as it had coemerged with the gold industry. The Reverend had been living there with the mine dumps crouching on the horizon for exactly forty years. Much had changed. And much remained the same. We conducted our recorded conversations in a shuttered house operated by a local HIV/AIDS hospice program.[1]

The Reverend had been born in the township and sent as a small child to a distant farming area by his parents until he was summoned to return to elementary school in 1967 or 1968 (he couldn't be sure). Having spent his earliest formative years elsewhere, he initially experienced his return as an encounter with the new. Perhaps because he had traversed such vastly distinct lifeworlds, each of which was identified with an epoch and a mode of production, the Reverend considered himself to be an elder, although at the time of our meeting, he was only about forty-seven years old. He had penetrating eyes and spoke in a powerful bass baritone that made the air resonate, and it was not difficult to imagine him rousing his congregation with that voice. But when he recalled his childhood, he grew pensive. He remembered the throat-burning smoke hanging above the horizon as itself a sign of Khutsong: "In the evenings the whole place would be smoky from the chimneys of the houses in the area because people were using coal stoves in that time," especially in winter. The acridity of the coal smoke had been a shock after the slow-burning dung fires of the farm that he had come to know as home.

It may be recalled that Xuma, the young migrant-turned-mineworker in Peter Abrahams's novel, *Mine Boy*, had been amazed by the blueness of the Highveld sky above the mines and recalled that of his native Transkei as having been green with floral humidity by contrast. The sky is not a mere ether or pro-scenium in these accounts. It is a dense medium and register of both place and changed location—changed life conditions, in fact—in many descriptions of the Highveld, although it operates differently in various traditions. The settler colonial narratives of this landscape are dominated by this sky, whose oppres-sive enormity is captured by Michael Cawood Green in *Sinking* when he writes of "*more sky than you have ever seen*."[2] Similarly, describing her drive across the Free State to towns not far from Carletonville and Khutsong, the writer, Antjie Krog, conveys her sense of a seemingly "intentional vast emptiness" where "everything human feels accidental and threadbare—a residue to be simply scraped off one morning from the majestic monotony. Nothing ornamental is tolerated. Nothing that cannot endure so much sky."[3]

For Krog and for Green, this Highveld sky is defined by its expansiveness and unfathomability. Theirs is a post-Romantic rendition, but it is still redolent of Enlightenment conceptions of the sublime. From either side of the English/Afrikaans divide, they write of an encounter with what exceeds intellection in verily Kantian terms. Kant wrote of the sublime as having two dimensions—mathematical and dynamic—and of provoking two conflicting sentiments. On one hand, he asserted, the confrontation with nature in its enormity leads to a crisis caused by the imagination's incapacity to encompass "nature's power." On the other, the reasoning subject can step back and think (rather than know) the infinity that neither sense perception nor imagination can grasp. Oscillating between these two incompatible perspectives, the solace of reason is constantly threatened by what Kant termed a state of agitation.[4] And reason, which is opposed to, rather than supplemented by, the imagination in this scenario, must therefore labor to find comfort in its capacities. Its arduously acquired mastery is, in this (Enlightenment) conception of the intellect, fragile and self-defensive. For Green and Krog, it often falters beneath the Highveld sky.

But psychic life is not identical to the activities of the intellect. Thus, Krog asks, "What effect does a landscape like this have on a psyche?" Her answer is that it produces not only fear and anxiety but also distrust and the self-protective consciousness that informed Apartheid and white resistance to democracy, if such democracy would entail, as it inevitably had to, black majority rule. In Krog's reading, the white supremacist unconscious reels beneath the huge and indifferent sky, which has become the surface on which is traced the anxiety-producing quantity that writers like Roderick Jones had described as "the black peril."[5] At the same time, Krog observes that, like other white middle-class subjects who have anticipated their displacement by processes of democratization in South Africa and elsewhere, people like Jones were and often are quick to abandon reason in what Siegfried Kracauer once termed a "short-circuiting" messianism, the forms of which are not limited to religion but encompass various political utopianisms, including separatist nationalism.[6] For these short-circuiting people, the horizon promises an eventfulness beyond ordinary time, and a radical renewal premised on the effacement of prior history.

For the Reverend, however, the horizon was not infinite—as would be typical of both Romanticism and the related forms of utopianism to which I shall turn in the following chapter—but the dense meeting point of earth and sky. It gathered its significance as a domain in which different ways of being could be perceived and registered. The differences between coal and dung smoke (frequently remarked by elders who shared their memories of earlier times) and the relative heaviness and visibility of the pall constantly return in his stories of childhood—just as the specter of the red cloud repeatedly haunted the stories of the sinkhole disasters and those of a domestic worker's possible escape at dusk discussed in chapter 7. This is surely because the Reverend did not see that sky through a glass pane, with its aesthetically enframing boundary. He did not see it through the windshield of an automobile. He arrived on a donkey cart, amid the speeding cars and buses on smoothly tarred roads in 1967 or 1968, a few years after the Blyvoor sinkhole disaster and just before the ordeal at West Driefontein. He breathed those "plague clouds," as Ruskin referred to the coal-fired sky of England's Industrial Revolution, along with the musk and dusted hair of a draught animal—not as an invisible, life-giving medium but as evidence of something toxically foreign and *unevenly* urbanizing.[7] In this sense, his story is a sensory archive of that "synchronous nonsynchronicity" that Ernst Bloch had theorized[8]; it encompasses (at least) two modes of production and (at least) two temporalities nested within the overarching order of modernity: one subordinating the other without eliminating it, feeding off and invading it, but also preserving its forms of life and consciousness.

And yet, this division of life into antithetical modes of production is itself a mark of modernity. The Reverend, like so many others, left a village—*ekhaya*—and at some point the village and agrarian world became synonymous with the rural and, in many cases, with the peasantry.[9] From that perspective, the redistricting that would recode Carletonville and Khutsong as parts of the ostensibly rural Northwest Province, could feel like a negation of the previous decades and of the desires for urbanity that had germinated therein. Yet, the simple metonymy that makes animal dung the sign of rurality and coal the emblem of industrial life is just that: simple. Too simple. For those who came to the area in the 1960s and earlier, this entry into a new code was often preceded and accompanied by more ambiguous forms of life than can be fully captured by the concept of the rural—ones with elements of pastoralism, statism on a small scale, agrarian feudality, petty trading, and artisanal production for markets as well as occasional wage work, tenancy, and landlordism.[10] And this same heterogeneity persisted in the townships. This is why even those who arrived later—in the 1970s—often describe the township as an ambiguous zone through which they entered into a new conceptual system and not merely a new geophysical and geopolitical space. Although this new opposition between rurality as peasantry, and urbanity as Euro-originating industrial life had been described and valorized by Colonel C. F. Stallard (the chair of the Transvaal Local Government Commission) several decades previously, the discursive and administrative techniques of its actualization were not fully realized until after 1950, with the Population Registration Act and the Group Areas Act. Until Apartheid finally collapsed, that system made of the township a space of permanent impermanence, expressed in the vulnerability of township residents to state inspection and forced removal, the incapacity to freely purchase and transfer land, the prohibition on the accumulation of capital, the paucity of markets and manufacturing activity, the underdevelopment of infrastructure, and the requirement to seek permission for every move and even limits on the presence of adult children in their parents' homes, among many other factors.

The townships of the West Rand were far more separated and, as a result, were cut off to a greater degree from the surfeit of industrial life than were the older townships that had grown up in proximity to the settler colonial metropoles. The "surplus" people of these new domains were ensconced in the field as subjects of lack. In this sense, the townships of the West Rand were more like cul-de-sacs or folds, zones of the detour and spaces of involution defined by their simultaneous exteriority to both the mine compounds and the white towns established by the mines. Through the techniques of modern urban planning, the mines became the ideological agent of "tribal" kraal- or preservation in the heart of industrial life. And this meant that they were also the coinventors of rurality. For rurality makes no sense as a concept if it is not arrayed in some relation to its other; In this sense it is not identical to agrarian and village-based life.[11] Rurality is a structurally determined conceptual category rather than a substantively infilled one, and it must be separated from both the pastoralist readings and the mode-of-production narratives concerned with the peasant-proletarian distinction within which the rural has been conceived. Indeed, there is an affinity between the assumptions about African rural life in settler colonial pastoralism and structural Marxism, as we shall see. But the mines were less concerned with maintaining a precapitalist society than they were concerned to sustain what they perceived to be indigenous cultures of proto-statism. For they saw in African tradition not societies against the state but precisely the anticipatory valorization of its hierarchical drive.

The mines advocated for tribalism and rurality primarily because they associated these terms with systems of patriarchal hierarchy and obedience that were useful for financialized industrial capital. In turn, the segregationist and then the Apartheid state attempted to ensure that this rurality, despite being central to extractive modernity, was spatialized and localized on its perimeter, in the reserves and then in Bantustans—where that hierarchical cultural logic would supposedly reproduce its "tribal" workforce at its own expense. As Mahmood Mamdani has argued, while focusing on state and thus political discourse rather than capitalist practice, the cultivation of authoritarian tendencies in the field of "culture," coded as ethnicity, was a pillar of colonial governance throughout Africa—in more or less centralized forms.[12] If it was coded as traditional and thus as prior to the colonial state form, this artificial rurality, overseen by appointed chiefs, was nonetheless assumed to be necessary in its persistence, rather than an object to be swept away by modernizing reforms. This utilization or instrumentalization of so-called tradition (or rather, one part of an invented tradition) was simultaneous with the developments by which "scientific township" planning was endeavoring to override and overwrite the black and mixed suburban developments that had otherwise grown up on the perimeters and in the interstices of major metropolitan centers like Johannesburg and Pretoria, Durban, Port Elizabeth, and Cape Town during the early post–World War II years, and even earlier.[13] In those areas, the scientific township had to be disentangled from the already existing and more complexly imbricated communities like Alexandra or Sophiatown. On the newly opening areas of the Rand, however, they could be created anew.

Two Modes and Three Worlds:
The Rural, the Urban, and the Township

When the Reverend's donkey cart brought him to the periphery of Carletonville, it was "up and coming" and already referred to in the national press as the "hub of the Golden West," even though it had been granted independent municipal status only ten years previously. Already, it was advertised as a "modern" center of sophistication and opportunity, despite the sinkholes, which were at that time being prematurely spoken of as a thing of the past. Already, some of its residents could recall having spent decades or, as they fathomed it, an entire generation in the vicinity. In the Reverend's unfurling narrative, which would join other accounts as part of the frayed text of this community's history, his arrival into the spectacularized future through this image and idyll of the new mining town was not only mirrored but also distorted by an imagination of another future that glinted on the horizon but never arrived (at least not yet). In that image, the promise of utopian modernity opened itself to the Reverend and people like him. He could see himself there. And yet he was not there, and it was not here. The longer he lived in the anticipation of this utopian ideal, the more it seemed to be deferred, thwarted, or withdrawn. Captured in this strange space of imagination, the Reverend and other immigrants found themselves in the odd predicament of leaving the village only to enter rurality—*in the township*. Or at least, their stories can be understood as an arrival into the conceptual binarism that pits the rural in opposition to the urban, even if only to demand a shuttling between them.

In this chapter, I consider this strange fact: that towns and townships around the gold mines were part of the apparatus for producing both peri-urbanity or suburbanity *and* rurality rather than being the mere way station en route to full and teleologically overdetermined urbanization or the exit from its perils. And I argue that this was a by-product of a failed utopianism, which aspired to make and remake, to world and unworld the lives of both white and black subjects who lived in proximity to the mines without necessarily living or working on the mine compounds. To do so means reapproaching and questioning the axioms of the canonical literature on the socioeconomic transformations wrought by the migrant labor system on the mines and especially the gold industry. That literature, the product of a scrupulous critical investigation of the gold industry's political economy, written from within as well as against Apartheid logics, has focused mainly on the industry's specifically recruited labor forces and its strategic maintenance of the oscillating migrant system as a mechanism to ensure "lower wages, less leave and absenteeism, better control, less risk of the men getting silicosis, and greater output in jobs involving hard physical work."[14] In this literature, the regular, time-limited movement between labor-sending areas and the mine compounds is correlated with a figure, the "peasant-proletarian" mentioned in chapter 1, who, until the 1970s at least, was thought to shuttle between spaces defined by distinct modes of production. These are the "men of two worlds" described by Philip Mayer.[15] And, according to T. Dunbar Moodie, these men "[bore] in their very 'souls' (in Foucault's sense) the scars of the articulation of two modes of production whose economic bases are mutually incompatible."[16]

The rendering of oscillating labor migration as a movement between mutually exclusive and not merely distinct economic modalities is commonplace in the literature on South Africa. But Mayer adds an interesting qualification to this putative duality when he hesitates and wonders (writing of the Xhosa in East London) whether "perhaps one should say 'three worlds' [rather than two worlds], for if the country home is one world, [the Apartheid city] itself comprises two others—the White town where the Xhosa works and the non-White town where he lives *meanwhile*."[17] The notion of the township as a third space and territory of the meanwhile might also be grasped in Bloch's idiom of synchronous nonsynchronicity, but the more quotidian idiom of the third space intimates a consciousness at once suspended and waiting. It implies a sense that life is going on elsewhere, in another place and another form. Meanwhile. Or meantime. The word signifies time's splitting and parallel unfolding. It is the organizing principle of modern novelistic narrative and of totalizing social scientific discourse. It is also the principle of Apartheid's ideology—that is, of separate development. And it is the temporal locus of an anticipatory and often frustrated consciousness driven by a desire for full recognition within the terms of a supposed universality that is both foreign in origin and limited in actuality.

The goldfields may have been the generic name of the region where gold is found (through a distended metaphor), and the proper name of a corporation (when written in upper case), but it is also the secret expression of the gold industry's desire for a permanently rural workforce. Through recourse to the notion of the meanwhile, the Chamber of Mines articulated the goals of the migratory system as a strategy for maintaining the imagined rural consciousness of its workers—even when they were working in the rationalizing order of the mine, that order of the "in a file" men mentioned in the *lifela* sung by Sotho migrants and described so movingly in Abrahams's novel. This anti-urban strategy, founded in a theory of local political conservatism, was threatened less by the rationalizing forces of the mining industry than by the urbanizing tendencies in the manufacturing sector, which, following World War II, had become increasingly significant in the South African economy as both a source of gross domestic product and a space of new desires, social forms, and political aspirations. Thus, in 1952, C. S. McLean, then president of the Chamber of Mines, observed that much of the competition for mine labor was coming from employment that had "the *added attraction* of an urban existence." And he conceded that "the detribalized Native of the towns does not offer himself for underground employment."[18] It was to compete with this more attractive (and often better paid) employment in the centers of manufacture that the Chamber agreed to increase wages in 1953.[19]

Oddly enough, if the advocates of Apartheid and their critics, the structural Marxists, would later converge in their identification of precapitalism with subsistence farming and pastoralist activities, in the early 1950s, it was precisely the absence of an agrarian tradition and sensibility that seemed to be such a problem for the South African state. A report from the Commission for the Socio-Economic Development of the Bantu Areas in 1954 stated that "the Bantu of today regard it as natural procedure to spend the greater part of their working lives outside of the Reserves in European Employ." Although it referred to this normality as a "new tradition," implying a vanishing world of self-sustenance, it also stated that the "male Bantu *has never been* an arable or livestock farmer in the Western meaning of the word and because of this historical development of this country he has never been obliged to become a farmer." No doubt there is some truth in this statement, if the emphasis is on "in the Western meaning of the word," but the effacement of local herding and cultivating practices in a discourse that can only recognize its mirror image is here a mere alibi for colonial and therefore racial capitalism.[20] Claiming that this same "Native" "preferred" to be an employee of whites, the report also asserted that the "Native" was, in the absence of agricultural traditions, "incapable of self-sufficiency."[21] In this manner, black South Africans became the surface onto which the contradictory projections of African rurality as *both* failed agrarianism *and* an incapacity for urbanity converged in the feared image of a potential dependent on the state.

A stark sketch of the oppositional structure within which those differences were enacted might be phrased as follows: The white towns around the mines were oneiric theaters of impossible self-sufficiency. The black townships were spaces of containment, operating through simultaneous processes of exclusion and encirclement in what we can describe, following Foucault, as "heterotopias" that "represented, contested, and inverted" the logics of the mining corporations' company towns.[22] Indeed, the townships functioned as doubled heterotopias wherein the dominant society attempted to place or circumscribe both its crises and the deviations to its norms and self-representations. The perimeters of these destituted heterotopias were secured by forms of "negative space," namely emptied landscapes or blank spots of private and state property traversed by few and thus surveillable roads, which were then policed through roadblocks and pass inspections (techniques that would be brutally mimicked during the anti-Apartheid boycotts) as well as more diffuse regimes of terror. As Foucault writes, "Heterotopias always presuppose a system of opening and closing that both isolates them and makes them penetrable."[23]

The history of Apartheid social engineering and of forced removals in the interest of white privilege is, of course, well known—at least in the abstract if not always in particular, heartbreaking detail. But the towns and townships of the Rand were also increasingly secured by notions derived from the mode-of-production narrative, which provided the illusory conceptual unities on which the other divisions, boundaries, and enclosures were erected and enforced. Together, these practical and social-technological perimeters enframed the utopian urban planning initiatives of the mining corporations— functioning like the gilt frame of Kant's aesthetic analogy (or the frame of a windshield that is its distant, technologized heir). Moreover, these seemingly external demarcations not only set off the internal imagery of those corporate ideals but also enabled their appearance of wholeness. In many ways, the dialectic between the utopian and the heterotopian was brought to its apogee in Carletonville/Khutsong, a dyad that has been incorporated without being integrated, in the municipality of Merafong that was formally invented by the gold mines in the image of American suburbia. Yet, the social construction of a self-consciously South African town in the image of a self-universalizing postwar (American) elsewhere was also, in some sense, an image or mytheme of the *nearly* sovereign power (but everything hangs on this *nearly*) of the mining corporations and the notion that gold can make *almost* anything happen. To evade corporate mythology subtending this industrial and segregationist creationism and to escape some of the more ossified and economistic axioms of the critical tradition that first assailed it, we must reopen this analytic and historiographic horizon not with the stories told by the mining corporations about the creation of these towns or the structural analysis that bypassed the lived experience summoned and hemmed in by corporate rule, but with the accounts of the more desultory goings and comings preceding the big bang of the company town's formal origin.

Before Division

Consider, for example, the narrative of a man whom I shall call Funani, who was eighty-three at the time of our interviews in 2008. He was fourteen when he and his family moved to the area in 1939, not long after Gold Fields had determined to buy up the land of the Far West Rand where the mines of Blyvooruitzicht (est. 1937), West Driefontein (1945), and New Doornfontein (1947) would underwrite the designation of the area as the "Golden West." The family first settled in nearby Louispan, which Funani described as "an old farming settlement whereby people relied on farming and ploughing the land." For many who arrived in those years, taking up residence meant clearing land to make room for a dwelling, and given the presence of the huge rocks and boulders that are strewn over these rolling plains, this often entailed burning the rocks to make them more amenable to cracking, splitting, and breaking. Heated for a prolonged period and then cracked open, the boulders can be reduced to rocks small enough to either be removed by hand or incorporated into architectural structures, often in stone and mud conglomerates. But not all rocks can be so easily removed, and the surfaces on which people had to sleep in these new homes were infamously hard and uneven. For this reason, one of the areas of what would become Khutsong is still called *Theka lea thunya* (or the "hip is sore").[24]

Funani knew of people who had erected homes in this fashion, and I spoke to one woman who recalled her family laboring for days to accomplish this task. But that had not been Funani's parents' experience. They arrived not to scenes of labor but to ones of death. Like the pattern of the agricultural season in this part of the world, where preparation of the fields often commences with a burning of the grasses (rather than stones), the origin of his story is one of desiccation, followed by a clearing and then growth. "There were a few houses around but there were few people because most of them had died," Funani said. Despite the deaths that emptied the houses, the population grew because people kept moving into the area, and they arrived at a rate exceeding the deaths. These new immigrants were not mineworkers, but cattle herders, farmers, drivers, and petty traders. In Funani's narrative, the majority of the black newcomers who were not actually residents of the still few mine compounds lived as tenant herders and sharecroppers. The Reverend told a similar story: "At that time we had a white person owning the land so we sort of hired . . . an area that he [the white farmer] would demarcate for us to graze our cattle and we were not allowed to graze beyond that area." Many other elders recapitulated this account, or one similar to it.

Later, it would be said that these communities of tenants and sharecroppers would become breeding grounds for crime, after the tenants first became brokers or petty landlords themselves. Indeed, these allegations were adduced as rationale when the township was formally established in 1957–1958 by the Peri-Urban Health Board. Mike Makgalamele, one of Khutsong's mayors and a man who was resident in the area in the 1960s, told Buti Kulwane, who was conducting research on civic governance in the district, that "a farm labour tenant would ask the farm property owner to allow a few of his homeless friends to move in and most farmers later decided to charge them rental for staying on their property. This encouraged people to move in and communities would develop within a short period."[25] As time went on, especially on the farms that abutted the railways, the tenants' subtenants formed a host of recognizable communities where beer brewing and the sale of commoditized sex attracted truck drivers and where those who had left their mine contracts or who were evading pass laws found refuge. But that was later. At the time of Funani's arrival, places like Diloring, near the Welverdiend station where the truck drivers would congregate, or Tsantsabane, near Oberholzer station where the domestic servants for the white farmers would reside, did not yet exist.

Across the decades, a doubled migration would take place—to the mines, yes, but also to the worlds around the mines, the latter increasingly motivated by a belief that money would flow or at least trickle outward from the scene of extraction, despite the fact that the mineworkers were supposedly taking their wages back home. Migration to the mines is perhaps the most thoroughly documented and analyzed element of modern South African history. But it was not only the shaft sinkers and winch operators but the cattle herders, beer brewers, and farm tenants who first brought their value-producing labor to the world around and beyond the mines of the Far West Rand, and they did so in a stereotypically feudal form. For example, it had been Funani's job to graze his grandparents' stock just as it was the Reverend's task to tend the cattle and to milk the animals in the later afternoon—all on the land owned by white farmers. "Since the owner of the land was a white man, we would share with him our produce. Out of three bags we would give him one," Funani explained. In the late 1930s, and during the era of segregation but before the Group Areas Act of 1950, the idea of whiteness as a virtually divine, rather than legally grounded, right to property in land, explained this surrender, which Funani described as verily automatic. The word "since" betrays the ideological structure: "*Since* the owner was a white man we would share with him our produce." Neither blunt force nor the promise of lucre nor religion fully explains this surrender. Indeed, spontaneity and automaticity are the symptoms of ideology, testimony to the unconscious nature of domination. They are evidence that more than force was at play even if, at the time, the ideological apparatuses were diffuse and unevenly solicitous of black subjects. None of the earliest residents with whom I spoke at that time had had more than a few years of schooling, and many women had none. Of the apparatuses to which they did have exposure, other than the prison, the churches and mission-educational institutions were among the most powerful, and it is not incidental that the elders I interviewed and who narrated the payment of rent in kind as an unquestioned right of the landlord, expressed a passionate attachment to their Christian faith.[26]

Nonetheless, if the situation relayed by Funani resembles feudalism as understood in a Marxian tradition, in which religion rather than economy constitutes the invisible and determining force (the final instance) by which one group of people is compelled to surrender its surplus to another, it was additionally distinguished in this (pre-Apartheid) moment of South African history by being grounded in a discourse of divinely sanctioned whiteness as right to property.[27] Moreover, this form of feudality persisted in the increasingly industrial context. Certainly, the situation on the farms had all the hallmarks of the personalism that otherwise accompanies the feudalism of pre-industrial European life, but in the newly emerging communities on the West Rand, which was developed relatively late in the gold industry's history, we are speaking of a racialized *feudality without feudalism*. For, in the vicinity of these new mines, as opposed to the more predominantly agricultural areas, the rest of the social order was dominated by financialized and industrial capitalist principles and these farms (e.g., unlike the agribusiness of the Free State, KwaZulu Natal, or parts of the Western Cape) were in other respects relatively marginal to the national economy. By contrast, in the townships, there would eventually emerge something that I shall later describe and theorize as *capitalism without capital*. It is important to note the persistence of forms of feudality across the generations and under profoundly changing circumstances (but always marked by gendered and generational hierarchy)—far from the major scenes of capitalized cultivation and cattle grazing. Inscribed over and above, on the very surface of this persistence, the Apartheid regime nonetheless marked a departure from the segregationism of the earlier order.

A Divided Discourse

It may now seem obvious that Apartheid did not merely displace or supplant segregationism, but the nature of the transformation has long been a subject of debate. In the 1970s, materialist and structural Marxist scholars led by Frederick Johnstone, Martin Legassick, Stanley Trapido, and Harold Wolpe rejected the notion that Apartheid could be understood as a merely ideologically transformed segregation—that is, a *more racist* society. They were concerned with the fact that South African society was indeed more violent and more overtly coercive and that rights had been retracted rather than expanded for the majority of the nation's subjects under Apartheid than in previous eras. But this was not, for them, a question of degree or quantity. Legassick insisted that the economy of the postwar Apartheid era was altered by the development of secondary industry and the importation from the mines into the manufacturing sector of segregation in the service of repressed labor costs.[28] Wolpe, working with Ernesto Laclau's distinction between mode of production and economic system, amended Legassick's argument by noting that South Africa's economic system depended on several modes of production, including both the sharecropping or labor-tenant system on the white farms and what he referred to as the redistributive economy of the reserves (what anthropologists would generally refer to as a moral or a gift economy). In 1972, Wolpe could insist that secondary industry was far more important in the functioning of the entire order than labor tenancy, while also observing that the increasing coerciveness and violence of the Apartheid state was underwritten not by the supplementary order of something called precapitalism, as had been assumed until then, but by the fact that the redistributive economy was "rapidly disintegrating." Indeed, he referred to the wholesale "destruction of the pre-capitalist societies."[29] And he claimed that this destitution of the reserves on which black subjects had been confined was a result of the legislative machinery of the Native Lands Act, the Group Areas Act, the Population Registration Act, and myriad local ordinances. This legislation had ensured the continued and even increased movement to the mines and other low-paying jobs for the simple reason that cash had become necessary but could not be generated in the villages, which were no longer generating surplus sufficient to "reproduce" the social world and thus the laboring populations of the margins. Legassick conceded the point, but added an addendum to Wolpe's correction, asserting that the matter of Apartheid's transformation was not reducible to a question of cheap labor but rather had to also account for its rationalization and the qualitative effects of this process. This transformation entailed a deskilling of labor in relation to increased mechanization in the secondary industries—and all the psychosocial corollaries that accompany the transformation of people into the enfleshed prostheses of technology (although this is my language and not his). And so the debate continued, variously inflected by Althusserianism and Laclau's post-Gramscian perspectives, with Nicos Poulantzas's notion of blocs and factional conflict leavening the mix.

Although some people in the mining industry had already asserted in 1961 (at a major industrial conference) that the notion of cheap labor was an "illusion," it would be some time before the axioms of cheap labor could be questioned by critical social theorists, as they would be by Jonathan Crush. He has noted, for example, the enormous costs to the mining corporations and their shareholders of migrant labor and not only its cost-saving elements, including the recurrent drainage of skill from the mines and the limitation that migrancy put on the mines' capacities to regulate labor or to override the seasonal considerations of potential migrants whose involvement in agrarian activities (where these existed, however curtailed) shaped their willingness to leave home.[30] Why, asked Crush, would the mines pursue the strategy of oscillating labor migration if it was *not* actually cost-efficient? Such factors, in addition to the changing conditions in labor-sending countries as they achieved independence, and growing labor militancy throughout the region, ultimately contributed to the stabilization of the mineworker populations, including their move into the more permanent residential communities around the mines. This does not mean, however, that such stabilization was the *origin* of the communities that arose there. And stabilization was not equivalent to urbanization either, with the former being a term of duration rather than psychosocial orientation, affect, or even aesthetic predilection. But neither was urban consciousness completely dictated by, or perfectly correlated with, wage-earning.[31]

Across these debates, the figure of the peasant-proletarian provided the mode-of-production narrative with its characterological form of appearance. But then, other debates arose as to the nature of that character and the subjectivity inherent in its structurally overdetermined position. Was this figure split or doubled? Did he inhabit two worlds, or was he inhabited by them in the agony of contradiction—such as that incarnated and apotheosized in the madman, whom Jean and John Comaroff read as the human hieroglyph of the incompatibility sublated in the hyphen of the term peasant-proletarian?[32] Did the attachment to agrarian life, which supposedly continued to define the peasantry, mitigate the proletarianization of the migrant mineworkers (and was peasantry even the appropriate category)? Was this oscillation between so-called rural and urban worlds a means for seeding rural areas with worker consciousness and political opposition to Apartheid? Or did migrants leverage the wages, wealth, networks, and authority acquired in the mines to enhance and even entrench their relative positions and forms of practice at home?[33] Or yet again, did they merely bring the debts accumulated in the mines to the countryside? The question of biculturalism versus alternating habitus has been repeatedly phrased in the local idioms as follows: Were the migrants using *mmereko* (or *bereko* or *pangela*, depending on the language), which names the logic of alienated, wage-based labor *for whites*, to sustain *tiro* or *ukwakha*, the supposedly nonalienated logic of self-fashioning and social fabrication of African lifeworlds?[34]

Dunbar Moodie claims that, until the 1970s, migrant miners "appropriated" elements of the mine compounds' institutional organization to buttress what they valued most: "patriarchal proprietorship over a rural homestead."[35] And he concedes that this implied a resistance to proletarianization. He does not emphasize that, to the extent that this was true, it also ensured that wage labor on the mines would exacerbate gendered hierarchies on the reserves. William Beinart nonetheless demonstrated that it was entirely possible for rural subjects to retain a commitment to their homes and even to pastoralist lifeforms while also advocating for worker rights, better wages in the industrial sector, and even the overthrow of Apartheid. Proletarianization was not, he claimed, isomorphic with urbanization or politicization.[36] Philip Mayer insisted that all waged workers were at least partially proletarianized. But Lucy Mair claimed that the advocates of proletarian class consciousness on the mines tended, through the 1960s at least, to be members of the educated elite, who made schooling and achievement rather than place of origin the basis for association. She described them as "bourgeois." And with a certain suspicion, she claimed that these oxymoronically named "bourgeois workers" (not unrelated to the labor aristocracy of the future) were appointing themselves to the role of raising consciousness among their less-schooled coworkers. In other words, she accused them of vanguardism. Other mineworkers, she said—here agreeing with both the Chamber of Mines and Dunbar Moodie—were more likely to feel affinity for their "homeboys," and this fact was entirely usable by the architects of Apartheid, who coded such local attachment first as tribalism and then as ethnicity.[37]

It was not only the anthropologists who were reading the phenomenon of oscillating labor migration as a culturally mediated one, and neither did the question of culture remain at the generic level of the rural versus the urban. As William Eksteen of Gold Fields told the Myburgh Commission in 1996, the mines operated on the basis of their own pseudo-anthropology and a typology of supposed ethnolinguistic affinity for particular job categories: Sothos were deemed most adept as shaft-sinkers, Zulus and Swazis as drillers, Xhosas as smelters, and Shangaans as mechanics.[38] But if one needed any more proof of the spuriousness of this cultural mapping of aptitude, one had only to compare Eksteen's list with that of J. A. Gemmill. Speaking on behalf of the Native

Recruiting Corporation and the Witwatersrand Native Labour Association, in 1961, Gemmill had nominated the Shangaans as "boss-boys," and the Swazis and Pondos as machine-operators, although he also shared the notion that the Sothos were ideal shaft-sinkers.[39] Perhaps the most interesting thing about the juxtaposition of the texts of these two moments (1961 and 1996) is the fact that Gemmill was already claiming that these ethnic or cultural stereotypes were being replaced by more scientific forms of aptitude testing in 1961, whereas they still animated Eksteen's discourse in 1996. In other words, the displacement of cultural stereotype by supposedly rational aptitude testing was another event that did not happen, if we may borrow or extrapolate Green's analysis.

The loquacious and sometimes truculent debates about the peasant-proletarian and the mixed mode of production were sometimes detached from more empirically oriented social historical accounts, and even the observant reports of the recruitment organizations' management. They were, as David Bunn pithily summarizes them, organized by a spectral opposition between surface and depth. For advocates on either side, the transcendental signified was not to be found or felt in the overwhelming and changeful canopy of the sky but rather in the doubled deeps of the mines. The structural Marxists read these depths as loci of both gold and economy's truth, and indeed the truth of a world in which economy was the deep and determining force of social life. Eventually, the metaphors that sutured truth to depth to gold begat more metaphors, and slowly, they turned in on themselves or lost explanatory persuasiveness. The structural Marxists, Bunn writes, "had in mind a revolutionary new understanding of the surface relations of production being articulated with depth explanation in a manner that would cure the illness associated with shallow liberal explanations." And the consequence of this relentless effort to explain everything in terms of that deep structural source of value, including not only gold but also the mode of its production, which, as we saw in part 1, was naturalized through reference to ore grade rather than the phenomenon of world money. In any case, the result was a certain blindness to the complex forms of life in urban centers, which Bunn says were portrayed as "a kind of integument, beneath which an irreducible body of truth lies hidden."[40]

The object of the dialectical materialists' objection was the liberal concept of the frontier, and with it the presumption of opposing and, in some sense, equivalent forces engaging on the political horizon, neither contaminating nor transforming the other. Bunn's recollection of these debates, which he likens to a recalled nightmare, is impelled by a concern to redress what he claims is the missing theorization of contemporary (in the new millennium) metropolitan life, especially in Johannesburg, and the artistic inventions that emerged over the decades in the aleatory movements of city dwellers who inhabited its labyrinths without thought about what lay beneath, or at least without believing that their lives were wholly determined by that underground.[41] It would appear that Bunn wants also to think of the South African metropole as something other than the margin to which so many scholars of the world system and underdevelopment had relegated other African cities. As V. Y. Mudimbe paraphrases Samir Amin, marginality in Africa often "designates the intermediate space between the so-called African tradition and the projected modernity of colonialism," where (now quoting Amin) "vestiges of the past especially the survival of structures that are still living realities (tribal ties, for example), often continue to hide the new structures (ties based on class, or on groups defined by their position in the capitalist system)."[42] In Mudimbe's account, and that of many critical theorists, the marginal and intermediary space was conceived within the theses of underdevelopment arising from colonialism, for which South Africa was "the most extreme manifestation."[43]

It may well be important, as Bunn claims, to redeem African cities, including Johannesburg, from the despair-inducing binarism that Mudimbe so rightly repudiates. It may also be necessary to resignify the township as a space of desire and pleasure and not merely of poverty, as Jacob Dlamini urges.[44] But the other of the compound-village dyad is not only the magnetic capital city, with its glittering skyline and secretive alleyways, its illuminated public space and its shadowy recesses of clandestinity and liberatory transgression. It is not only the vibrant world of the large townships on the metropolitan periphery. It is also the small towns and townships that arose around the mines, the peri-urban and suburban worlds that both doubled and transcended, mimicked and condemned the compounds as impossible fortress-like institutions of (inevitably failed) totalization, even as their full urbanity was foreclosed. This other of the compound-village dyad is also a conceptuality beyond binarism. This is why it is necessary to rethink everything around the mines from the ground up, in flight from that binarism: to think as far as possible about everything that seems, from on high, to constitute their periphery while also enabling the world of the compound to operate as an apparently enclosed site of exceptionality.

Spears and Ploughshares

Even though the Chamber of Mines understood its workers to be "rural," "traditional," or "tribal" people temporarily removed to the mines, the experience of the mine is more often than not read by both apologists and critics of Chamber policy as a locus of the proletarianization that is otherwise coded as urban. Yet, at least until the 1980s, the compounds were deformed simulacra of urban worlds. As Charles van Onselen has already told us, the mines were originally part of a prison industrial complex, and the mine compound is no more a city than is the prison.[45] To be sure, there was money there, and there was a residential density and corporeal proximity that is often associated with cities. In the period before the 1980s, many practices were also in place that transgressed the local norms of pastoralist and ethnically African masculinity. For example, circumcised and uncircumcised men were forced to be in each other's naked presence during public medical examinations and ablutions on the compounds, a situation that would not have been tolerated in areas where initiation defines age-sets and circumcision is the *sine qua non* of adult masculinity (although this practice is ethnically distributed). Many mineworkers recoiled against the transgression of generational authority implied by these physical exposures. Similarly, same-sex relations between senior and junior mineworkers, which were widely practiced (more so in some groups and sites than in others) and sometimes encouraged by wives when their husbands were at the mines, were not so welcome at home. But even the brewing of corn beer was encouraged on the compounds if this facilitated attachment to so-called rural lifeways and a relinquishment of the desire for more permanent settlement in town and cities. And, of course, ritually salient aesthetic practices, such as dancing and stick fighting, even when transformed into spectacular exhibitions of cultural kitsch for white tourists, were also intended to nourish that attachment. These feared and lamented transgressions of village norms do not legitimate the inverse notion that the compounds were scenes of urbanity. Nor do they add up to a description of those norms. They merely leave us with a question about what, precisely, was encoded in the term *tribalism* as it was being avowed by the mining corporations. For insofar as it named a putative commitment on the part of black South Africans to both local (ethnic and place-based rather than racial) attachment and gendered hierarchy, it was the projected ideal on which Apartheid utopianism depended.

In its official discourse, the Chamber of Mines considered and desired its employees to be "tribal" Africans and seemed to believe moreover that the residents of the country's peripheries did not wish to leave behind their customs that, in its analyses, were characterized by two primary values: gendered hierarchy and "obedience to authority." These were the pillars of the "redistributive economy" that both the mines and structural Marxists assumed to be the essence of Bantu precapitalist life—depending on the idiom being used in any given moment. It was "the urbanization of natives employed in Commerce and Industry, a process which relieved them suddenly of all tribal restraint," that threatened the redistributive moral economy and thus the entire system of separate development.[46] This opinion appeared in the report issued following the first major strike by black mineworkers in 1946, as the Chamber considered for the first time (and rejected) the possibility of substituting a permanent residential workforce for the migrant system.[47] Later, in the 1970s, in response to high local unemployment rates in the now-established townships, the Chamber experimented briefly with recruiting in those locations. It even opened offices in the townships, but despite strong interest and uptake among residents in the

Witwatersrand, Rand Mines, the leading experimenter (which had interests in East Rand Propriety Mine as well as Blyvoor), soon abandoned the project, having found the township recruits to be less skilled and less likely to stay in their jobs than those from neighboring countries.[48] The foreign labor, coming from more agrarian contexts, but especially Lesotho, Malawi, and Mozambique, as well as the Rhodesias, represented for the Chamber that combination of intergenerationally transmitted technical skill and adherence to hierarchy (gendered and gerontocratic) that it nominated as "tribal." By then, this combination was deeply under threat in the townships as well as in the reservations in South Africa. As we have seen, the structural Marxists had seen this very destruction as the grounding condition for the radicalization of coercive power under Apartheid. Perhaps both of these perspectives are correct insofar as that which enabled Apartheid ultimately ensured its collapse inward (as though that ground was always already a sinkhole). In any case, they converged with the Chamber on this point: that the core of a "tribal" agrarian society was its redistributive morality. It was the phantom of a vanishing virtue, the ideal whose existence and whose destruction were produced simultaneously in the crucible of modernity, as the gold industry moved toward its inevitable apotheosis. At the time, the Chamber voiced the phantasmatic ideal thus: "[The Native's] generosity is very natural as he is unaware of it himself. He who has, shares readily with him who has not, and considers it his right to receive under similar circumstances. The aged and infirm become the liability of the family and tribe and have a form of security which has been lost in the passage of time to more advanced forms of civilization."[49]

Here, as ideological alibi for migrant labor, and suffused with the essentializing habits of a still-colonial anthropology, was the idea and the ideal of a society of the gift in the pure sense of the term. And like the societies described by Marcel Mauss in his classic text, *Essai sur le don* (Essay on the Gift), this society of the gift was one of severest law and lawfulness, of hierarchy and obedience.[50] According to Mauss's theory, the gift was the medium of this lawfulness, and bore a force capable of superintending the law. It was this hierarchical order of lawfulness on which the Apartheid state hoped to feed—in opposition to the equality espoused by labor organizers. Ironically, this hierarchical principle, inseparable form patriarchy, may be the most persistent survivor of the Apartheid system, the perduring crypt of its antidemocratic axioms.

Across the archive of its meticulous self-documentation, there is a recurrent and revelatory slippage in the Chamber's discourse, from the idiom of the political—which refers to black African subjects under the heading of the tribe (with its associated valorization of the chiefly authority that colonialism had so carefully cultivated)—to that of economy, in the form of the gift or its synonymous terms *generosity* and *sharing*. If generosity is the idiom that expresses the ideology of the gift, rather than its animating principle (which is less pacifist, as Mauss argues), sharing is the idiom of a depoliticized communalism: a communalism without equality, and beyond communism. As noted previously, South Africa's mineral industry was self-consciously concerned with mitigating communism among miners, and it competed with the Soviets in both gold production and in claims to worker productivity.

Against the backdrop of the Cold War, as independence movements across Africa began to realize their ambitions, and competition between the superpowers took the form of proxy wars and reciprocal assassinations throughout the continent, South Africa's gold industry engaged in propaganda wars of its own. In 1959, it staked a new kind of claim by staging a drilling competition with the Soviets. The workers at West Vaal mine (in what is now Northwest Province) beat their rivals by drilling 922 feet in thirty days compared with the Soviets' 868 feet—apparently establishing South Africa's supremacy in an industry that it dominated but that was increasingly subject to competition. British Pathé's promotional film was, among other things, an assertion of the success of the oscillating labor system and of the racially hierarchized labor force now enforced by the Population Registration Act and the Group Areas Act. The sententious voiceover in the promotional film about the triumph pronounced that "this sort of rivalry is a lot better than the Cold War."[51] But of course, it was part of that war, a war not only of geopolitical forms but also of economic logics. Moreover, some of the engineering know-how, and especially the capacity to drill shafts at speed, had been developed by the South African Corps of Engineers, colloquially known as the Springbok Sappers, during World War II. Reciprocally, the engineering know-how of South African miners also contributed to the military work of tunnel construction, and to the survival of rock falls and other events familiar from deep underground mining.[52] Military and economic function enabled each other—and served political ends long after the hot wars had ended. Thus, a monstrous parallelism structured the competition, in which the workers of the Soviet system (called "Russians" in the film) faced off against the so-called colored men of the South African scene, where they nonetheless worked under the theatrically avuncular supervision of their white bosses.[53] In other words, racial segregation, structured and intensified as Apartheid, was intended not merely to separate workers within South Africa on racial grounds but also to obviate the emergence of internationalist solidarities between black mineworkers at home and other mine laborers elsewhere.

Beyond the overt opposition to communism, we may recognize in the slippage characterizing the Chamber's discourse the pure expression of capitalism, insofar as it makes of the economy the determining instance, the basic, or as Bunn reminds us, the deep structure animating the social and cultural surface. The moment of this reduction, when everything can appear to be determined by the economy, and when this appearance assumes force in the world, becoming indeed its operative truth, is the moment when capitalism becomes truly fetishistic, says Étienne Balibar. In that moment, capitalism takes into itself the magicality that previously authorized the master by virtue of a claim to God-given right.[54] So, it is not incidental that it was as a corrective to the failures of industrial society in the aftermath of World War I that Mauss turned to what he saw as the transcultural and extrahistorical institution of the gift in aboriginal societies—those he believed to be uncontaminated by modernist secularity—in search of a force that could command mutuality rather than mutual hostility, communalism but not communism, in modern techno-industrial societies. He recognized the failure of voluntary charity and sought in the idea of the Maori "hau" a compulsive force that would not require overt violence for its enforcement. Of course, this aspiration presumed a certain homogeneity and thus totalization of the social order. But, in South Africa, as understood by the structural Marxists, this fantasy had been relinquished precisely because the redistributive function was divided into two racialized modalities: first, the unconscious logic of the gift in the so-called tribal societies now forcibly confined to the margins; and, second, the bureaucratized welfare state for the whites. One order internalized the redistributive function at the level of the unconscious, and the other externalized it in the juridically regulated, institutionally bureaucratized realm. In this sense, South Africa was a paragon of juridical modernity, perfectly enacting the Hegelian model of the difference between supposedly ahistorical society (Africa) and Euro-modern society, as that between unconscious submissiveness to an unwritten law, on one hand, and freely chosen accession to its text, on the other.[55] Even so, the Marxists' concern was less with redistribution than with the extraction of surplus value from those surplus laborers who, according to the Chamber of Mines, were almost always in such short supply—even when there was excessive unemployment.

Like a nightmare, writes Bunn. To him, these arguments weighed on the brains of those who would escape the legacies of both Apartheid and the analysis that sought to expose its secret logic. These arguments often became entangled in the conceptual axioms that were shared across the doubled discourses of modernism, rooted as it was in binary opposition and the dream that precapitalist societies in South Africa contained a difference useful for capitalism. How to escape this knot, this endlessly entangling web in which the analysis of Apartheid's project, and Apartheid itself, constantly threatened to overwhelm its critique? That question would preoccupy the gold-made world for many decades, and we must now consider that effort, as well as the continual tightening of the mesh in which shuttling migrants made their way. To do so requires that we reconsider the utopian projects that seemed to demand this fabrication.

CHAPTER 9

UTOPIA ON THE HIGHVELD

This is where landscape comes to die.

—Ingrid de Kok, "Into the Sun"

Past your tall central city's influence, outside its body: traffic, penumbral crowds, are centers removed and strong, fighting for good reason.

—Muriel Rukeyser, "The Road"

"All paradises, all utopias," claimed Toni Morrison, after having written her masterful novel, *Paradise*, "are designed by who is not there, by the people who are not allowed in."[1] We might amend this statement, to say that they are built by those excluded people, even when not designed by them. Such a sentiment would surely resonate for any student of the gold mining towns on the Far West Rand. Certainly, it did for me when I interviewed people about the early days of Carletonville and Khutsong.

From behind the roll-down door of our Khutsong refuge, the question of oscillating migration between the mines and other spaces was itself a horizon, or at least a backdrop for other histories that would unfold in the long days of recollection. Those days were punctuated by meals of pap and stewed or curried lamb (catered by a cook from the township); trips to the grocery stores to buy cooking oil, net-bags of citrus, and bottles of Coke or Fanta; and drives along the unpaved and largely unsign-posted roads of Khutsong to pick up or deliver one or another storyteller. The stories that unfolded were also about migrations, sometimes passing through the mines, but this was surprisingly rare. Many of the people who spoke to me had never been to the mines or their compounds, and their accounts of how and why they moved to the area did not conform to the explanatory frameworks neatly laid out on the rural-to-urban axis. Among the elders, but also among the more impov-erished new immigrants, tenancy was a frequently mentioned moment of the recounted journeys. Moreover, the poorest of the squatter communities that I would visit resembled those described by the elders who had arrived before Apartheid. They were scattered shacks of tin, cardboard, and castoff wood erected on white farms, with no running water, electricity, or flush toilets. They were occupied mainly by people who had migrated illegally, many of whom were women living by means of prostitution. These women lived with the permission of the white landowners, paying rent more for protection than services. Quite clearly, then, the financialized industrial capitalism of the mines did not displace the old tenant system on the farms surrounding them. If it is true, as Harold Wolpe claimed, that this tenant system was less significant than reserve-area redistributive economies for the operations of Apartheid, its survival beyond those spaces begs some reflection. Petty landlordism may, in fact, be one of the most persistent ghosts weighing on the post-Apartheid township—and one of the institutions through which feudality persists beyond feudalism. Throughout the early Apartheid era, the social sphere was an assemblage of different economic logics and different modes for enforcing racial hierarchy. But until the era of active forced relocations (some ten years after the formal commencement of Apartheid), when black and colored sub-jects had no choice as to their residential placement and re-emplacement, new immigrants had many reasons for moving to the area around Carletonville. It was not merely as a solution to the blockages or deprivations of life in the hinterlands that they found their way to the region. They were not all seeking to retain proprietorship over their homesteads in "rural" areas, and they were not all dreaming of the bright lights.

For example, it was not poverty or insufficient surplus at home that brought Funani's grandfather to nearby Vereenigeng and that led him to take up tenant farming. Rather, according to his grandson, he had been driven by the envy and covetousness of the white farmers in Free State, where his family had gone from KwaZulu via Lesotho: "My grandfather's herds increased in numbers and that unfortunately was great cause of jealousy among the white farmers. They did not like to see a black man with so many cattle, so they chased us out of the Free State. We left the Free State and came to settle in Vereeniging." His grandfather had not merely bridled, however, at the acquisitiveness and envy of white set-tlers. Initially, he had asked white ranchers to help him reclaim his cattle from a Sotho chief who had appropriated the herds for his own kraal when the grand-father had endeavored to take up residence in Lesotho. The white farmers, initially reluctant, had been persuaded to join in the liberating raid, perhaps out of a sense of adventure, perhaps out of vindictiveness, and perhaps for more nefarious reasons, but they had not made the grandfather welcome once he had reclaimed his bovine property.

We can presume that a man with two wives and twenty-one children, as was the case with Funani's grandfather, was a man of plenty in the eyes of his peers. This despite the fact that, as Funani describes it, their households were without furnishings and included two simple mud-floored dwellings. His mother, the junior wife, certainly was not the beneficiary of her husband's wealth in cattle. She cooked for these many children on an open fire with only two dishes in which to serve the meal and waited until everyone had eaten before taking her share. Rather, the patriarch's wealth consisted of his wife and children because they were for him a source of labor. In Vereeniging, whence his children found their way to Khutsong, he perhaps recognized a rhyme between the appropri-ative drive of the white farmers and his own demands for the produce of the structurally weakest dependents. In any case, there was no longer an alter-native. And he stayed. He lived to the age of ninety-three, having been born before the second Anglo-Boer War.

The mines in Funani's and the Reverend's stories, and in many more like them, are not always the destination of migratory journeys, but they are often grounds for moving. They are elements on a horizon and markets for pro-duce, scenes of disaster, and sources of wealth. Funani, who had originally been assigned by his father to perform agricultural labor, was later given the task of selling produce—peaches and mielies—to the mineworkers at Blyvooruitzicht when it was established. Gradually, the young man expanded his trade and began buying fruit from towns as far afield as Rustenburg (about 100 kilometers away): "I stocked apples and pears, came back and sold them as well. It was a good business then because the miners would buy all my stock." He, too, "used a donkey cart to fetch [his] stock," and like the Reverend, he traveled the roads to his wholesalers alongside a growing stream of British, French, German, Italian, and American-made automobiles. They incited in him a desire for mobility—including movement among strangers. Proudly, he asserted that he sold to *all* of the miners: "Xhosas, Sothos, and the Tswanas. *Everybody* was buying my stock." That was before the opening of the "Hitler War." Hitler was the proper name of the enemy in his discourse. Hitler rather than Germany named a menace elsewhere. Germany or at least Germans were, by contrast, part of the local scene (recall chapter 3)—and this sometimes meant that Nazism was also part of this scene.

Meanwhile: Another Origin Story

Shortly after I first arrived in Carletonville, I was given a four-paged text titled "A Short History of Carletonville by a Geological Survey Carried Out by a Young German Geologist Rudolf Krahmann Who Immigrated to South African in February 1930." The text appeared under the signature of one J. P. Botha, but in truth, it was plagiarized and abridged from A. P. Cartwright's 1967 institutional history of Gold Fields, *Gold Paved the Way*.[2] Carefully penned in minute and impeccable script, it had been produced for the edification of a group of German and Belgian exchange students who had visited the town as guests of the Lions' Club in 1993–1994. Written in the moment of the Reverend's arrival, to describe the moment of Funani's arrival, the text represented the dominant if not official Apartheid-era record of the town's creation—which it rendered as an expression of the gold industry's fantastically potent will. Unlike the previous stories of township dwellers, this one makes no mention of the farms of the area. Rather, it extends the narrative of techno-scientific invention, heroic perseverance, and corporate sagacity that defines almost all of the industry's discourse.

In both Botha's and Cartwright's account, Krahmann occupies the role of a lesser secular prophet. According to their texts, he recognized that the gold deposits of the West Rand were to be found exclusively in the shale beneath the dolomite and that the shale was magnetically detectable. It could therefore be precisely locatable with a magnetometer even before drilling assay boreholes. The son of a professor of geology in Berlin, Krahmann had trained at the Technischë Hochschule in Charlottenburg, and then worked as his father's assistant in Economic Geology at the University of Berlin before coming to South Africa—a year before Britain abandoned the gold standard. Lacking the funds to undertake the kind of systematic research needed to prove his case. Krahmann sought out a consulting geologist for Gold Fields, Hans Merensky, who had similarly studied at Charlottenburg, but had been born on a Berlin Missionary Society station in Botshabelo (near Middleburg, in what is now Mpumalanga). Merensky had urged the young Krahmann to persist with his experiments in secret—anticipating the value of a technology that could enable investors to buy up the land where the magnetic surveys promised gold, assuming they had sufficient financial resources. But when it came time to capitalize on the discovery, Merensky was otherwise preoccupied with his diamond interests in Namaqualand and Namibia (then German Southwest Africa), where his capital was invested in less liquid assets.[3] Still enthusiastic, he introduced Krahmann to another geologist, Leopold Reinecke, also the son of a German missionary. And he, in turn, sent Krahmann to Carleton Jones at Gold Fields.[4] Their actual connection is traced in the cartographic toponyms of intersecting streets on the maps of Carletonville. As the well-rehearsed story goes, Carleton Jones foresaw the economic advantages of the technology and persuaded Gold Fields to invest heavily by buying up the stakes that would ultimately reveal the ores at Venterpost, Blyvooruitzicht, Libanon, West Driefontein, and Doornfontein mines, making him a pivotal figure in one of the world's most lucrative gold prospects.[5] He would go on to serve as chief executive officer of the Gold Fields holding company created in 1932 to manage the new properties under the name of "West Witwatersrand Areas, Ltd." before becoming chair of the board of the Chamber of Mines, an office he occupied twice, in 1942 and 1946.[6]

Botha's jubilant historical summary makes no mention of Krahmann's Nazism,[7] although Cartwright acknowledged the fact. Instead, it concludes punctually with the following:

> Britain abandoned the gold standard on the 21st of September 1931. The South African Government decided not to follow [the] British example, in the mistaken belief that [the] South African economy was strong enough to stand on its own feet. The results of this policy were disastrous. The Government clung [sic] to the gold standard as long as it could. It was announced on 28th December 1932 that the South African pound be allowed to find its own level. The announcement set off the biggest boom in gold shares that Johannesburg had ever known. By a stroke of the pen the ore reserves of the old mines had been doubled and their lives extended by twenty years. To conclude, streets in Carletonville were named after prominent and professional people mentioned in this summary, as well as metals and minerals. To my opinion, this in short is the summary of the history of Carletonville. → From a Geological point of view.

The last phrase, "From a Geological point of view," appears in handprint (rather than cursive) at the side of the page (an arrow guides the reader's eye) and appears to be a belated addition for which room had not been left at the bottom of the page. Also in neat square print is the name, Martin Botha, and the title, "Mayor Carletonville, 1993–1994."

In 1931, the Chamber of Mines had published a slender volume, *The Gold Standard*, and its narrative lays down the paths for J. P. Botha's summary history. The Chamber acknowledged that it had initially opposed the abandonment of the gold standard out of a fear of inflation.[8] If adherence to the gold standard was to be borne by primary producers, it claimed, it would require "a scaling down by industries and public authorities of all expenditures upon stores, wages and administration; a cheapening of interest rates; effective reduction in the cost of living; and lowering of taxation."[9] The Chamber's fears, it then admitted, had been "unfounded." The real problem was the need to support the agricultural sector, then in a "parlous condition," by somehow overcoming, on an international scale, the low commodity prices that were at that time being subsidized by the South African state. Abandoning the gold standard was anticipated to increase the premium on gold, and thus the tax revenues available to the public purse, thereby buttressing the otherwise suffering agrarian sector. Indeed, this is what happened, at least for white farmers, although as the previous stories suggest, these farmers did not cease hosting sharecropping tenants who paid in produce—a contribution unmeasured in the taxation figures of the Chamber.

As William Beinart states, wool producers—South African sheep farmers, including the white farmers and their black and colored farmhands—had been among the agriculturalists most profoundly affected by the depression. The farm owners had responded to the drop in wool prices by increasing flock size in unprecedented ways. The result was environmental devastation, severe drought, and the death of fifteen million sheep.[10] On top of this, the price of maize declined by 50 percent between 1929 to 1933, thus undermining that vast sector of the economy devoted to its cultivation.[11] J. P. Botha had claimed that the gold reserves had doubled. In fact, it was the price of gold that doubled following the demise of the gold standard, and this meant both more employment and more tax revenues for the state. White employment in the mines more than doubled, from 22,654 to 43,183 between 1931 and 1939, when the war began to compete for bodies, absorbing considerable populations of the unemployed from agricultural areas. In this same period, the number of black mineworkers on the Witwatersrand and Extension mines grew from 210,238 to 321,400—a massive increase although proportionally smaller than that among white miners.[12] A new taxation policy saw the contribution of the gold industry to the now-growing public purse rise from a mere 6 percent to 33 percent of its total revenue.

As Beinart explains, the major beneficiaries of the state-led projects were white farmers rather than white miners, although this newly supported constituency would ultimately turn away from the relatively bipartisan government of then–prime minister J. B. M. (Barry) Hertzog, who had orchestrated their rescue on the model of the American New Deal. They increasingly, although not uniformly, embraced the ethnonationalism of D. F. Malan's purified National Party, many of whose members avowed the Nazism that Krahmann had espoused.[13] It is one of the recurring paradoxes of history that it was the wealthier urban-based communities of Afrikaans speakers in the Cape and Pretoria who mobilized white supremacism among the poorer more agricultural sectors of the population, not least by pointing to the putative risks of cultural contamination that were being attributed to the gold-mining communities whence the new dividend was arising. They incited this defensive white supremacism partly through recourse to the emerging anthropologically derivative discourse of *Nasionalisme as Lewensbeskouing* (total outlook on life) that was being doubly disseminated in German universities (through Spengle-rian *Lebensphilosophie*) and at Stellenbosch, where the so-called architect of Apartheid, Hendrik Verwoerd, taught psychology and sociology.[14] Ultimately, although it was the Fusion Party that orchestrated the white farm-saving economic redistributions, it would be the National Party that benefited from the gold industry's success, even though it would take another fifteen years before an Afrikaners-owned mining company would come into being and, as we saw in chapter 7, twenty years before chair of the Chamber's board would address its members in Afrikaans.

Nonetheless, the affective consequences of the victory, still resonant and traceable in J. P. Botha's story sixty years later, are to be seen in the sentiment—differently expressed by both the most exalted beneficiaries and the most exploited workers—that the gold industry was the generous heart of this heartless world,[15] the source of its wealth and of a socializable dividend. It was to preserve this dividend for whites that so much of Apartheid's legis-lation was enacted. These affective consequences could also be seen in that automatic surrender of agricultural surplus to the white farmers, whose confidence in their right to demand produce from their black tenants was consolidated only by the new discourses of cultural nationalism. Access to money, as Jabavu's story showed us, was increasingly the only mechanism for separating what was otherwise defined by intense propinquity on the farms. The more such proximity, it seems, the more vehemently the landlords exer-cised their extractive powers.

After the calamitous expenditures of life and surplus in World War II, the establishment of the Bretton Woods system aimed to restabilize the world economy by combining the otherwise antithetical-seeming elements of a clas-sical gold standard with floating currencies. To do so, the capitalist nations represented at Bretton Woods agreed to "an adjustable peg system of fixed parities that could be changed only in the event of a fundamental disequilib-rium."[16] Gold prices once again rose. But by then, the industry's sense that it had secured the nation by contributing the lion's share of the state's revenue had emboldened it to assume an ever-expanding sense of its own power (not for nothing did Gold Fields take a lion as its logo). It was from this perspective that West Witwatersrand Areas Ltd., under the leadership of Carleton Jones, started fabricating the new towns and townships of the West Rand, naming them into being in a mode of what can surely be called corporate dictatorship. Or at least that is how the mines represented their accomplishments in the news media, including the newspapers that were essentially their propaganda organs. In a dictatorship, the power of speech moves from the realm of idea into that of actuality through enunciation, such that what is said is brought into being. This is why the political system most consonant with utopianism has as its visual analog the urban planner's map.

On the Map

J. P. Botha's brief history was given to me in a neat file folder on the front of which is a striking graphic representation of the Carletonville City Hall building (which would become the municipal library at some point), including its coat of arms—an improbably medieval figure, in which a shield featuring waves (emblem of water) and bushels of wheat (agriculture) is flanked by two standing bucks. Above the shield, an armed figure is hurling an arrow. Below, a banner reads *Ex Dubio Proveniat Spes* (from doubt hope arises). A ponderous motto for a relatively small town, it also refers to the farm first converted into urban real estate: *Twyfelvlakte*," meaning the Plains of Doubt. In fact, Twyfelvlakte was only one of the sites destined for the influx of people who would eventually be encompassed by the administrative authority of Carletonville. But the official narrative privileged that farm or its name: as a place of both origin and invention, the point from which its fantastical growth sprung.

The town's officially recorded historical growth is visible on the map in the numbered extensions that radiate out from the main southwest–northeast axis. Even before it had been granted municipal status, Carletonville had three extensions.[17] Each number marks a new addition, accreted to the first neighborhood. At the northernmost horizon is the train line and the area known as Oberholzer, which is populated with Afrikaans names. To the train line's south is a neighborhood of feminized streets: Adda, Beatrix, and Juliana (royal Dutch names). The center of town is a cartographical-geological fantasia, with streets named for all that can be mined (or, in the case of pewter, alloyed): Agate, Amethyst, Amosite, Anthracite, Bornite, Braunite, Calcite, Carbon, Chrome, Cinnabar, Cobalt, Diamond, Dolomite, Emerald, Flint, Fluorspar, Galena, Granite, Graphite, Gypsum, Halite, Iolite, Iridium, Jade, Kaolin, Lignite, Limonite, Mercury, Mica, Monazite, Moonstone, Nickel, Nitre, Onyx, Opal, Osmium, Palladium, Pewter, Platinum, Pyrite, Quartz, Radium, Ruby, Sunstone, Talc, Topaz, Tungsten, Uralite, Uranium, Vanadium, Zeolite, Zinc, and Zircon. A veritable alphabet of minerality (only W and X are missing). And, of course, there is a Gold Street. Toward the route that leads to Johannesburg, where the actual intersection was, until recently, adorned with a floral welcome, the streets offered their botanical supplement to the inorganic litany, with succulent Aloe and Arum, hardy Geranium, perennial Dahlia, more delicate Zinnia, Lantana, and Aster, with Gardenia promising fragrance.

On the then-outermost periphery of the town's southwest, a different order of naming can be read. Here, the street names both designate a route and divide it internally, pointing away from themselves to absent places, the kinds of places where the earth is a surface on which to graze rather than to penetrate. Umtata, Amanzimtoti, Umkomaas, Umlaas, Umgeni, Usuthu, Limpopo, and

Pongola: these are place-names of another southern Africa. Many designate the towns that became trading posts in the previous century, which fact then ensured that they would become the entrepots of the mines' labor-sending regions. Yet, this neat neighborhood was not originally created for black residents, many of whom originally lived, as we have seen, on the surrounding farms before they were assigned to remote Bantustans or incorporated into the heterogeneous black-dominant townships of nearby Kokosi and those farther afield, near Potchefstroom. Nor was this neighborhood created to welcome the black subjects who would be assigned to the township of Khutsong where they were supposed to reside in neighborhoods identified with ethnic or tribal identity when it was formally created to serve Carletonville. No. The African-named streets of Carletonville were rather like the figures of vanquished cultures transformed into costumes at Beit's fancy dress ball. They were markers of appropriation rather than identification.

The name most identified with the town, (Guy) Carleton Jones, adorns an arching drive that joins Reinecke Street (named for the geologist who introduced Krahmann to Jones) at the southernmost part of the town's perimeter road, and links it to Annan Road, its central artery. Annan was the name of the deputy director of Gold Fields when Jones persuaded the company to buy up land in this area. It is for this reason that his name denotes the street that orients the town and commands its mobilities; he is there as a trace of that corporate oversight that substituted, in the early days, for state-based governmentality. Indeed, all these names are crypts of that history. Moreover, they are crypts that the owners appointed to themselves in a mimetic usurpation of that divine prerogative invoked on the Oosthuizens' memorial plaque. Truly, they appointed themselves the earth.

Not long before the Bretton Woods agreement was announced, Carleton Jones addressed his company's shareholders and announced that the plan to establish Carletonville on farm Twyfelvlakte had been put into action. He informed them that the town would bear his name. Already six hundred stands had been laid out, with plans for future extensions already in the works.[18] Carleton Jones enthusiastically asserted that "the township is being laid out on modern town-planning lines, and comprises, apart from the usual centre for local and Government administration sites for residential, business and flat purposes, with special provision for children's playparks and areas in the business centre for car-parking."[19] A hotel and a cinema were also in the offing. By township he meant town—the reservation of the term *township* for a black residential area for service workers had not yet been settled. Speaking of the white town(ship), then, Jones added that, "light, water, and sewerage are being installed by the company" and noted that they were being implemented in a manner that entailed "a big advance on the usual methods." The company was also "macadamizing" the roads and planting trees. Four hundred trees had been planted in the first year, thus initiating the greenbelt that still circles the town, with the tallest of these trees being those that line the road to the cemetery on the eastern perimeter.

Carletonville's growth was avid. Even before the approval of the township by the company administrator, 148 houses had been constructed and 52 occupied. Within a year, advertisements began to appear in major newspapers featuring bold typeface and line drawings of a pretty bungalow, to which a cobbled path led (the romantic counterpart to the macadamized roads). In the neatly framed image of the early ads (figure 9.1), a couple is seen from behind, surveying the house. The white man, feet confidently astride, is wearing a suit cut to Humphrey Bogart's style and smoking a pipe. He is accompanied by a svelte woman whom the format leads us to believe is his wife, in a fashionable knee-length skirt. Radiating above the house and the numbered text are lines of sunlight, and a map showing the town wedged between the railway line and the main highway to Johannesburg. It is a dream image of suburban domesticity, focalized in stereotypically romantic fashion; we look over the shoulder of the proxy bearer of a desiring gaze. But it is romanticism in an American mode, imported into the Highveld—along with the American engineers who played such a significant role in the Witwatersrand mining industry—as a signifier of modernity unmoored.

The name of Carletonville appears five times in the ad. The area is described as being owned by West Witwatersrand Areas, Ltd., forty-six miles from Johannesburg on the Randfontein-Potchefstroom line and "conveniently situated" less than half a mile from the Oberholzer Station. Although near the three operating mines at the time, Blyvoouitzicht, West Driefontein, and Doornfontein mines, it is said to be "beautifully situated on a rich fertile plain." The bucolic allure is redolent of suburban pastoralism, but it is embedded within a discourse of right—white right. And this right is in turn embedded within the framework of familial reproduction and thus oriented toward a future horizon—an abstract horizon moving toward infinity but anchored in biopolitical value. Carletonville, the reader is told, is the "kind of healthful home your children have a right to."

By the time of this ad's appearance in 1947, two hundred homes had been built, and a sports stadium had been planned. Interested parties who responded to the address could cut out the coupon and send off for a brochure before applying for a quarter acre stand at a starting price of £305 ($1,230.00 US).[20] As with all mining towns, this one attracted and demanded other kinds of corporate activity. Driefontein Brick and Potteries Co., Ltd. quickly saw the new town as a potential market as well as a solution to what it had imagined to be the problem of insufficient housing for whites, and thus became a major investor.[21] Mining companies were not interested only in the gold either. Nigel Gold Mining and Estate Company, for example, announced in

9.1 Advertisement for the real estate by the South African and General Investment Trust, 1947.

1947 that it was taking out a 21 percent stake in a new "Carletonville Property Investments, Pty," a joint company of the South African and General Investment and Trust Company, Ltd. (SAGIT) and the West Witwatersrand Areas, Ltd. Its representative explained to shareholders, "your Directors are satisfied that ultimately the investment will be a remunerative one, but at the outset there will be a period of building up on the low side, Carletonville Township is being planned on the most modern lines and, as the mines in that area are brought to the production stage or their production increased, the development of the Township should be assured."[22] This fungibility of the categories of real estate and mining property had been realized on the Witwatersrand at an early stage in two ways: (1) in the purchase of land that preceded and anticipated the drilling of shafts to access leased subterranean mineral deposits, which remained the title of the state; and (2) in the appropriation of surfaces for construction, including for housing and other rentable structures. This double coding and purposing of land had the effect of tripling the sources of rent. It could now be charged on minerals, on money (for the investors who had contributed to the capital of the companies obtained rent in the form of dividends), and on land as real estate. The latter is not merely an added source of rents, however. It is also a new horizon of future value. In the long term, as mines exhaust the payable content of their reserves, the surfaces can be reconverted again into residential or commercial real estate, making of the mine a strange kind of alchemist—one that generates money in gold through several metabolic processes (what Katharina Pistor would call codings of capital[23]) while seemingly disinterring value from the earth. No wonder then, that the town's early maturation was marked by the opening of banks. By April 1948, Standard Bank had opened two branches in town—one next to the recreation club and another in the newly erected West Wits hotel. This was in addition to the branches it already operated on the mine compounds at West Driefontein and Doornfontein.[24]

The town planning, in all its phases and extensions, fell under the purview of the Pretoria-based Peri-Urban Health Board, which regularly held meetings to hear the schemes that Carleton Jones was proposing for development.[25] In some cases, the mines were both the originators and the consumers of the town's development. Thus, for example, West Driefontein mines owned 171 stands as of June 30, 1949.[26] Much of the town's real estate was intended for management rather than labor, which would continue to reside in racially segregated barracks on the compounds. By November 1949, the company reported that "the reticulation" connecting houses to sewerage was continuing and that 344 stands had been sold, while another 239 had been made available. A golf course and bowling green had been established. More than six hundred thousand trees had been planted in an area covering one thousand acres. The growth was being attributed not only to Carleton Jones's foresight but also to the fact of currency devaluation.[27]

Carleton Jones died quite suddenly in late 1948 at the age of fifty-nine. Reflecting on his passing, the new company director had stated that "since the close of the year the prospects of the gold mining industry have been transformed as a result of the increase in the gold price brought about by the simultaneous devaluation of British and South African currencies on September 1949."[28] But he cautioned that "against the rise of approximately 44 per cent in the revenue from gold must be set the increases in costs arising in consequence of devaluation." In a manner that had assumed the reiterative quality of a ritual, the company reported its concern over rising wage rates and employee benefits. But it acknowledged the outcome of a Commission of Inquiry that had found "the position of the workers on gold mines in comparison with workers in other industries had deteriorated in terms of basic wages and earnings as compared with the position existing in 1938."[29] This was another way of addressing the seeming "attraction" of jobs in the manufacturing sector, and the lure of the urban against which the mines were competing. Claiming that previous conditions would have seen wage increases result in the closure of mines, the currency devaluation had permitted an upward, and enhanced, employment. What the Chamber now worried about was the possibility that wage rates in other sectors would continue to rise, thus robbing the mining industry of the claims on workers that it had orchestrated through the decades of its sector-specific monopsony: "If wages and salaries are allowed to rise to any degree outside the industry, extra costs will again be passed on to the industry and the benefit from devaluation will be dissipated."[30] The devaluation would permit an increase in working costs of between 10 and 15 percent, if a general wage suppression could be effected. This, then, was one of those limits—those boundary moments that made the corporations dependent on the state or at least on extrasectoral agreements. In and of itself, the mining industry could not effectuate the suppression, even if it could claim to have saved the nation through its contribution of tax revenues, which were not inhibiting the payout of dividends, as we have seen.

The new Chamber president paid tribute to Carleton Jones's final speech as Chamber president, when he had contended that there was "a serious unbalance between the monetary price of gold and the price of commodities in general which will require adjustment sooner or later." He then expressed his confidence that "such readjustment will take the form of a rise in the price of gold" but also that this was "unlikely" to "be brought about by full agreement in respect of a simultaneous general revision of the gold price in an international sense." Instead, he had anticipated that "the weak exchange position of most countries outside the United States makes it likely that an increase in the gold price will, as after World War I, arise out of successive separate devaluations."[31]

Indeed, this was the case. As the Chamber president stated, "Following devaluation of the British pound on September 18, 1949, the currencies of over 40 other countries have also been devalued against gold and the dollar, in most cases to the same degree. The position is that the dollar which has been held constant in terms of gold is more or less surrounded by currencies which have been heavily devalued in terms of gold and so depreciated in terms of dollars."[32] Or as Gertrude Stein had already said in 1946, with that characteristically sardonic wit and deceptively simple abstraction that marks all of her prose: "The dollar the United States dollar is a very lonesome dollar, it's all alone, it's riding wide and handsome but it's riding all alone."[33] In addition to being horrified by the future of work in mass production facilities, her characters were tormented by the fact that U.S. wealth was as much resented as desired by others. This would remain the case throughout the coming decade, during which the United States would continue to amass a relative share of the world's gold reserves while using the extension of foreign-dollar aid to secure its global influence in opposition to the Soviets, who were nonetheless producing more and more gold (recall the propaganda film discussed in chapter 8).

The Transvaal Chamber of Mines believed that the U.S. opposition to an increase of the gold price in the post–World War II era was largely based on its fear that this would enhance the Soviet economy (given Soviet gold production), and it worked to secure the U.S. dollar as a proxy for gold. By the end of the decade, as global recessionary forces accumulated, the Chamber observed that "dollar holdings can continue to function as monetary reserves so long as special conditions such as those which have obtained in the world during the post-war years ensure a universal acceptability of the dollar. But a structural change in the United States' economy, towards which the current recession may be pointed, could very well accentuate the inferiority of the dollar as a medium of settlement compared with gold." The Chamber undertook a thought experiment, in which "foreign central banks were to turn their dollar balances into gold," in which case "the pressure on the dollar might become sufficient cause for Americans to reconsider their objections to an increase in the price of gold."[34] That would happen, but the United States, under Nixon, would not abandon the modified gold standard that had been reestablished after Bretton Woods until 1971, when China as much as the USSR was emerging as a potential economic competitor. In the meantime, it seemed, no country other than the United States stood to benefit more from the increase of gold prices associated with currency floating than South Africa (see chapter 10).

The experience of previous floatings had permitted Carleton Jones to anticipate the devaluation long before it occurred, which happened in piecemeal fashion. He had gained his reputation because of his skill at "mining the pay sheets," by which was meant he had reduced operating costs. His success at Sub Nigel generated the profits that allowed Gold Fields to expand not only west along the Reef but also globally), but at the time of his death, and despite his prophetic capacities, he was no longer needed for Carletonville to continue to grow. Nor did the company intend to continue expending its resources in that function of socializing the dividend that normally accrues to the state. As it sold off its property and realized that the revenues were not actually keeping up with the costs of servicing them, it sought to transfer the administration to the local government, and eventually, the municipality would become another rent payer of the company for the services it had laid down. Anticipating this cost, and the growth that would be necessary to generate that tax-paying capacity, West Wits announced, in 1950, construction of a primary dual-medium school, serving more than three hundred white children, two commercial garages, three churches, and several shops. Afforestation continued at a rate of three hundred thousand trees per year. Newspapers in Johannesburg, Rustenburg, and Potchefstroom registered these developments as supply stores started advertising in their pages (figure 9.2). Soon Grosvenor

9.2a and 9.2b Newspaper advertisements for Carletonville real estate by the South African and General Investment Trust, 1954.

REMEMBER: The fabulous Blyvooruitzicht, West Driefontein and Doornfontein Mines are served by Carletonville and its extensions.

To "SAGIT"
P.O. Box 155, *Johannesburg.*
Please send me further particulars about Carletonville Ext. No. 3.

Name ....

Address ....

....

All services are waiting to assure your comfort in ideal surroundings for your own home
PLUS
a sound investment for your future.
Erven prices from £325.
On easy terms to fit your budget.

EASILY ACCESSIBLE

Contact "SAGIT"

The South African & General Investment & Trust Company, Limited, Sagit House, 30, Loveday Street, corner Fox Street, JOHANNESBURG.
P.O. Box 155.   Telephone 34-1761

CARLETONVILLE

c/o S. Perkins, Ingot House. Telephone Carletonville 97
P.O. Box 55.

9.2b (*Continued*)

luxury car mechanics had opened a shop in Carletonville. Produce shops and restaurants were established, along with a pharmacy, a bottle store, a butcher, and an animal kennel. The rapid growth led the new West Wits chair to antic- ipate that Carletonville would become a "large and important residential and industrial centre."[35] The activities of managing this proliferating operation were complex enough that, in 1952, West Wits as it was colloquially known, created a wholly owned subsidiary to take over the interests of Carletonville and deal with them exclusively.[36] A bilingual, English-Afrikaans high school was established in 1952, and shortly thereafter, the Chamber of Mines made a £10,000 ($27,900 US) donation toward the creation of a technical college in town, encouraging white workers and their families to imagine Carletonville as a destiny, and not merely a stop-over on the typically transient itinerary of mine managerial employees.[37] This confident sense of progress finds itself reflected in the changing aesthetic of the advertisements seeking buyers for real estate. By 1954, these had been dramatically modernized and now featured a jazzier typeface and the slogan, "A garden suburb set in the growing centre of Golden West Rand." Stands in Extension 3, already under construction, were being offered at £325 ($913 US).

It was at the time that the white residents began to flock to the area and take up residence in its pretty bungalows, creating new jobs (though not always paying jobs) for domestic laborers and gardeners, that Funani first left Khutsong, if temporarily. He had been selling his produce to the mineworkers until life in the area was interrupted by the "Hitler War." He recalled this period once again as a changed sky. In the war, blackouts had been mandated, and this had meant a new darkness even in the white parts of town. It was this darkness above all that had frightened Funani, at least in his memory of boyhood. And while the war's end had brought relief, he lamented that the black soldiers he knew had received little in compensation: "it was not a white man's war because there were others who were soldiers and who joined, like the Maseko boys. It's just a pity that the only thing they received for participating in the war were black painted bicycles," he lamented.

In 1947, after turning a good profit on grain from a newly enlarged postwar market, Funani persuaded his father, who had until this time claimed all of his earnings, to let him keep some and move out from under his father's roof. He traveled to Sophiatown, then a bustling center of black urban culture where his brothers lived, and got a job at a brewery in Johannesburg before becoming a "packing boy" for a wholesaler, earning a little more than £2 ($8 US) per week. He still brought remittances home to his parents, as did his brothers. Later, he obtained a driver's license and got a job driving buses, ferrying people from townships to the city center or the stations where they boarded their commuting trains. According to Funani, when the Carlton Center (which, despite the rhyme, was not named for Carleton Jones and was in fact modeled on the Seneca Tower in Buffalo) was erected in Johannesburg, he took work in construction, again with his brothers. The Carlton Center, which was the tallest building in southern Africa when it was erected, represented South Africa's claim on architectural modernity; however, ground for the building was not broken until the late 1960s (it was the scene of an attempted bombing during the riots of 1976[38]). In the meantime, Funani had returned to the municipality that was by then called Carletonville: "When I came back this time around the situation had changed completely from the time I had left. Now there was a number of mines that had developed like Western Deep Levels which was at its beginning, Stillfontein, and Doornfontein. I came back and I started from where I had left by selling my fresh produce. I was back to selling oranges and apples to the miners but this time I was fetching the stock in Johannesburg."

Funani's narratological practice identified every development with a particular individual. Thus, what Carleton Jones and his shareholders had measured in stands sold, trees planted, services reticulated, and commercial space opened, was calibrated by Funani as a sequence of singularities, each of which bore a proper name:

> The first building was in **oudorp** (old town), a pharmacy which belonged to Dr. Kroonman. This is the building next to the filling station, you can see it when you make a turn there. Another white man came along and built a wholesale shop in Oberholzer. . . . The building of a Post Office came much later. When they built a Post Office it was a small one on the other side of town, next to the bus station. . . . Yes, the town was growing because in Oberholzer a white man by the name of Wax came along and built a wholesale next to the bus station. After the Post Office another establishment was erected and it was Pholana Fish & Chips, on the way to Blyvoor mine. Then came along another white man and built a liquor store. The name of the liquor store was Bolton and that's when things started to get exciting. By this time the town started to feel the rush.

Not a map, then, nor even a litany, but Funani's history was a spatiotemporal discourse woven together as a text of personal identities and proper names. His history was also a list of economic activities. There is something like a ver-nacular sociology of economic history here, entwined with a recollection that resists the demand for generalization. It is possible to describe such narrative as a chronicle, given that it is organized mainly by sequence and given the fact that "events" in this narrative are not associated with a profound change of life con-ditions. But the narrative is also infused by a sense of arrival in a new time, the time of the rush, of speed, and of acceleration. The utopian time of the modern, as grasped from the interstices of its machinic, rationalizing, and totalizing ideology. And in the counterpoint between the official narrative and Funani's personalized history, in the two orders of naming—the monumental naming of the map and the orientational naming of the chronicle—we can discern the traces of the dialectic between utopianism and heterotopianism. On the other side, or rather on the underside of that dialectic was the dystopia of black life in townships like Khutsong, which, unlike Soweto, would not become full towns or cities, but would retain their relations of dependency to the formal towns invented to satisfy white desire.

To the Limit: Utopia on the Highveld

In Thomas More's *Utopia*, gold is the sign of "infamy," unvalued on that island of extreme utilitarianism for the very reason that it is valued in the context of world money: namely, its scarcity and uselessness.[39] More's Utopians use it mainly to mark their slaves, and it is they who must bear the heavy burden of jewelry and crowns. History repeats itself—if only analogically speaking. In the gold industries anchored on the West Rand, the laborers bore the weight when gold's price was lowest, and it was the corporations and their investors, like the ruling classes whom More referred to as "gentlemen . . . and goldsmiths," who profited when the South African rand was again devalued and gold priced upward.[40] This is why More refers to them as usurers.

In Louis Marin's intellectual historical account, utopia, as a concept and a proper name associated with a particular but fictive location, emerged in European discourse when the concept of the horizon was losing its status as an actual boundary (between earth and sky) and becoming, instead, the signifier of the infinite. In aesthetic terms, the latter is the special accomplishment of Romanticism and can be traced to the eighteenth century, when the expansive vista—oceanic or mountainous—became linked with the thought of the sublime. The tension between these different conceptions is, as discussed at the beginning of chapter 8, traced in the differential narratives of the horizon that orient the accounts of travel on the Highveld—and that are sublated (and debased) in the image of the middle-class couple beholding their suburban dreamhome. In the European Enlightenment tradition, says Marin, the concept of the frontier was externalized (by what he calls "an expanding thrust") to become both the limit between two states and the point of their meeting.[41] As a result, the term, *frontier*, subsumed the semantic content of "the horizon" while the horizon came to express a universalist ambition, one that Marin says was brought to its apogee in a certain U.S. aspiration to be at home anywhere in the world. It was this at-home-anywhere sensibility that permitted the modularization and transfer of the suburban ideal to Carletonville. But modularity was also valorized in the more spectacular and specularizing theater of architectural exception.

During the twentieth century, this architectural ambition to become universal could be accessed as a sensory intuition by looking from on high over a city laid out in space as something to be "appropriated through the gaze."[42] Such acts of looking, typically from the viewing deck of a skyscraper, were exceptional, of course, but for this very reason, they acquired exemplary and even iconic status. Indeed, it was in the pursuit of such iconicity—the iconicity of a universalizing modernity—that the Carlton Center was built in Johannesburg.[43] Now, Marin's conception of the utopianism that is figured in the skyscraper entails both the spectacle of power as materially centered and the predicament of being subject to it—depending on whether the tower is viewed from the earth or the earth is viewed from the tower. It is a double figure of mastery and of being mastered, of oversight and submission to the gaze.

With their bucolic depictions of neatly fenced bungalows overseen by white couples in U.S. fashion, the advertisements for real estate in the early days of

Carletonville's development, suggest that Marin's analysis of the U.S. form of utopianism is specifically and not only generically relevant for the history of Carletonville. But this is less because of its skyscrapers, of which there were none, than because the town combined in itself the aspiration of the sky-scraper, inverted as the mine shaft, and that other U.S. fantasy, *undescribed* by Marin: its low-lying pastoral suburban counterpart. Both of these mythic iconicities were manifest in Carletonville, and for this very reason, the town's history, including the range and multiplicity of its residents' economic activ-ities and forms of being, permits one to see that the externalization of the limit described by Marin took forms that were not always shaped by a strict opposition between difference and homogeneity. They were not shaped any more by this opposition than they were exhausted by that between the rural and the urban, traditional and the modern, *mmereko/bereka/pangela* and *tiro/ukwakha*. It did not always entail the ideal mediation of two terms, namely abstract homogenized space on one side, and centered power commanding the plane of nondifferentiation on the other. Indeed, the utopian drive in South Africa was never limited to the matter of a single territory's frontiers, even if these frontiers are understood as doubled to include the frontier that limits the utopia and those that it traces.[44] Under Apartheid, which extended, transformed, and made absolute the logic of segregation, utopianism came to imply the multiplication of enclosed, boundable, and social spaces—the perimeters of which could be secured so that the mode of governmentality operating within them could be differentiated. The relative intensities of polic-ing in some areas and the abandonment of others, the intrusion into domestic space and the withdrawal of support or protection in others, and the demand for uniform education in some contexts and the neglect in others were all enabled by the differentiation rather than the homogenization of the national territory as governed space. In this sense, Carletonville was not merely a social plane on which the forces of globality worked themselves out; it was the scene of their anticipation and experimental development. This is because it was an economy that depended on and actually created zones of incommensurable but usable (by capitalism) difference: zones of life and of relation to power, forms of authority and vulnerability, forms of production and consumption— all that has been inadequately captured by the concept of a mixed mode of production, and all that has too often been assumed to have become uniform in the service of administrative rationality.

Avant la letter of the millennium's end, and *après les lettres* we have been reading throughout this text, Carletonville and subsequently Carletonville/ Khutsong was a living experiment in the simultaneous enactment of utopia-nism and its undoing. After the so-called end of history had been pronounced following the fall of the Soviet Union, Marin noted that the end of the millen-nium, which he said, "never ceases to end," was taking the form of a "universal mode of high-tech democratic hyperliberalism."[45] He further observed that its so-called universalization was coincident with the proliferation of new border-ings, new nationalisms, and new islandings—everything that utopianism had promised to transcend. But this event had already happened in South Africa, as Jean and John Comaroff have argued.[46] Far from the ideal of absolute homog-enization, modern planning in South Africa enabled not merely the opening of territories and the smoothing of flows, but their organized interruption and blockage. The consequence of this was a spatiotemporally differentiated world. For some, travel was mandatory but onerous and constantly interrupted, and distance was thereby dilated in time. For others, it was the medium of freedom and the experience of mobility as well as connectivity. Such differences are precisely denied by utopianism. And yet, I would argue, Carletonville was a utopian formation. In what sense is this contradiction to be understood?

As already stated, no architectural structure in Carletonville simulates that towering edifice, from which, according to Marin (and scholars like Michel de Certeau and Roland Barthes), the spectator is permitted the illusion of mastery over the limitless but ordered space of a designed and homogenized world. Carletonville is squat and sprawling. It lays prostrate, hugging the horizon as tightly as a scab. Except from a low-flying plane or helicopter, a bird's-eye view is sensorily unavailable except perhaps through acts of imagination and the representational inflation of the mine headgear through analogy with the Eiffel Tower. Like the Eiffel Tower, the headgear appears as a protuberant geometry of steel, in which the structure is transparent. In more modern mine architec-ture, those structures are largely enclosed and concealed, but the fact remains that the headgear points downward. Height is here depth, and the shafts that descend four kilometers into the earth mock even the most audacious build-ings aboveground. It cannot be understood without reference to the obverse of utopianism's limitlessness, namely the dream of a completely secured interior. This was accomplished in a set of nested and contracting social forms—race, ethnicity, family—each of which acquired its territory in the context of South African Apartheid—and nowhere more so than in the towns invented to serve the gold mines. Marin is surely correct that the displacement of utopianism into politics is a product of imagination embedded in specific acts. He terms this the "fiction-practice" of utopianism.[47] And yet, the moment of the displace-ment into politics arises precisely in the act of giving the structure its image—in this case the map—even if that very process entails a submission to the limits that utopianism would leave behind.

When a town is built, virtually ex nihilo as part of an extractive project, the map, including the map of claims and stakes, and that of streets and roads, is precisely the form in which utopianism moves from the fantasy of limit-less self-universalization into the bounded image of territory. We might read this space and place as the domain in which the territorialization—the coding of difference as a blockage, containment, or interruption of flows, connections, and relations, in the idiom of Deleuze and Guattari[48]—reaches its apogee *by virtue of the reduction of difference to its image and to place-bound form. To identity.* It is as though the recognition that utopia is not only a dream of limit-lessness but also a limited dream, achievable only as bordering and bounding, found its perfect form of enunciation in Apartheid and one of its purest mate-rial instantiations in Carletonville and Khutsong. If that is true, it is because the utopianism of that regime commenced with the understanding, not unrelated to the entire history of gold's production and valorization (dependent, as we have seen, on cyanidation), that *there is no purity that is not a product of sep-aration.* It is the antithesis of the original and the originary. In the ideology of Carletonville, as in so many other places, however, utopianism took the form of a belief that such a separation could be a structuring principle at the origin of a new society, and not merely a belated historical effort at restoration or as a negation of historical mixing. It is a town whose creation, development, and transformation is within the memory of its oldest inhabitants. And thus, it gives us a particularly advantageous point from which to grasp the relation between social engineering and town planning as an artifact of the globalized gold industry and of the gold industry in the service of a worlding economy—one whose image was often something called "American." In J. P. Botha's brief history, we saw a world conceived as an assemblage of properly named individ-uals and minerals, with an outlying perimeter of signifiers whose referents were elsewhere, in an African history transformed through trade into the ground of migrant labor. This set of proper names stands in for, and occludes, the absent periphery, the blank, or (in art historical terms) the negative space of a map and the domain that lays beyond the perimeter of the page. And that space, which is beyond the frame, as it were, is nonetheless the condition of possibility of that interiority that Carletonville was fabricating. But its history *cannot* be narrated from a geological perspective. It requires a different focalization.

CHAPTER 10

GOOD AS GOLD

Standards and Margins of Value

These roads will take you into your own country.
Seasons and maps coming where this road comes
into a landscape mirrored in these men.

—Muriel Rukeyser, "The Book of the Dead"

Viral carriers
loaded and lonely,
the trucks speed
from city to big city
and home again
for a week or two
past the truck-stop
where the waiting women
turn to dusty mealie sheaves
in the midday sun,
ashes to ashes.

—Ingrid de Kok, "Truck Stop"

Danger ahead. Within two decades of its emergence from the hallu-cinatory image of semi-urban separation, the idylls of high Apart-heid on the Highveld proved to be less utopian than chimerical. But even nightmares operate in images derived from the metamorphoses of language. In them, words become material signs, at once dense and opaque, alluring and terrifying. Confronted by these oneiric images, one can only follow where they lead. Only later, in waking and in retrospect, can one ask, "What do they mean?"

The roads leading to Carletonville, and to many mining areas in South Africa, are signposted with warnings about abnormally wide vehicles, rough surfaces, concealed exits, crossing livestock, relatively high rates of accidents, and, in recent years, the elevated risks of being hijacked. Beyond the remon-strations about local dangers, signs announce speed limits and measure the distance to petrol stations, named urban locations, and touristic game reserves. The signs announcing distance puncture and punctuate the time-space of driving, and they ask the motorist to calculate the rate by which space will be converted into duration. Others orient the driver.

When I first began making regular trips by car from Johannesburg to the mining towns of the West Rand, I was perplexed that the spelling of Carleton-ville varied from sign to sign. Sometimes, within less than a mile and even within sight of each other, two signs with distinct spellings were visible: Car-letonville and Carltonville. No doubt, some of these signs had been painted in error, and the person who had installed them either did not recognize or did not care about the difference. After all, when read aloud, they sound the same. Yet, a more general question can be derived from this otherwise trivial fact of divergent spellings, spellings that, in another time, might have appeared to be evidence of a not-yet standardized orthography. What does it mean when a dream-town has no single signifier in the realm of proper names? Is the dream less real or effectual for lack of such standardized representation? And what can it mean to speak of a standardized proper name in any case? These questions might seem contrived in relation to a roadside misspelling, if it were not for the additional fact that, near these conflicting designations of the still meta-morphosing town, were other signs bearing the names of the mines that also changed continuously as one after the other property was bought by another entity, then sold, or broken up, consolidated, or submerged in financialized shell companies. The repeated changes in the names of mines and locations could, on occasion, induce a vertiginous and even uncanny sense of directionlessness. Sometimes, when expecting to pass a sign pointing to a place familiar from memory but finding an unfamiliar name instead, I wondered whether I was not lost on these roads. The landscape I thought I had known had begun to dissolve or metamorphose—like the tremulous images projected on a cave wall.

Those displacements and transformations in the chain of signs and signifi-ers lying next to the road can also be read, by way of analogy, as a transposition of the question posed by the Carletonville/Carltonville signage. In this context, we might ask: What is the relationship between these signifiers and the objects and sites that they otherwise seem to designate? And: What happens when the signifiers previously thought to refer unambiguously to an empirical referent—one often assumed to be transparently and universally available—become unmoored from that referent? What happens when faith in the possibility of transcendental signification is lost or, indeed, repudiated? This question has been asked in every moment when a regime of value and authority that previously seemed self-evident has been displaced, and it has been asked with special intensity in every moment that the status of gold as a privileged form of appearance of value, as world money, has been disputed. But the question of gold is never only a question of economy, and the economy is never only a question of money. Moreover, changing conceptions of the appropriate forms for representing value are often registered in domains that initially seem far from economic life and indeed may sometimes claim autonomy from them.

In capitalist contexts, or at least within the bourgeois fantasies of capitalist contexts, there are two privileged loci of autonomy: the household and the aesthetic. With respect to the household, historians of the nineteenth and twentieth century have remarked the unevenly changing status of middle-class women who obtained waged or salaried employment outside of the house in a manner that depended on the professionalization of caregiving and domestic labor. And they have noted the combined effects of commodified and socially redistributed reproductivity on concepts of family and on the sex-gender system more broadly. In the process, they have shown that the so-called autonomy of the household, whether construed as a structurally prior condition of possibility or an interior zone of the market economy, has entailed the subordination and occlusion of some female-gendered labor, and increasingly, the racialization of domesticity.

With respect to aesthetics, the gradual and spasmotic displacement of gold as the primary form of appearance of reserve value in international monetary relations has been associated with the end of representationalism and the advent of Euro-American modernism, which is said to have occurred first in the plastic and literary arts, in concert with transformations in science, mathematics, and philosophy, somewhere between the mid-nineteenth century and the turn of the twentieth century. The process is then said to have been generalized across the subsequent decades and disseminated by mass media and economic globalization, until it reached its apotheosis in postmodernism—the aesthetic of neoliberalism.

The question of how changes in the economic domain and in the order of sexed and gendered relations relate to more general theories of value and representation will occupy us later in this chapter. Suffice it to say that the unmooring of (some) women from the function of reproductivity and of gold from the function of signifying real value are simultaneous phenomena. To grasp the nature of that transformation (which, in its fullness, far exceeds the ambit of this book), we must try to understand the effects, the reverberations, and the traces of what is generally registered as a world-historical event, namely the collapse of the Bretton Woods system and the gold regime of international monetary relation, on the lives of men and women in the place of gold's primary production. Far, that is, from the sparkling metropolitan centers of global finance with its markets for high-end commodity art. It is less in the domain in which art claims its autonomy than in the order of sexed and gendered life that the unsettling effects of gold's displacement were registered in South Africa.

A truncated version of history might run as follows: In 1971, what had been the residual form of the international gold standard was officially displaced following the U.S. government's severance of the dollar from gold. In the aftermath of that event, gold prices on the commodities market rose dramatically, the value of South African national currency fluctuated wildly, prices of basic goods and imported commodities rose with inflation, and indebtedness grew. Widespread labor strikes challenged both the mining and manufacturing sectors, which ultimately developed into recurrent general strikes aimed at the overthrow of Apartheid. The Apartheid state's efforts to maintain white rule through racial separation by intensifying the enforcement of pass laws and forced relocation to the Bantustans—not to mention a reign of terror that included detention without charge, torture, disappearance, assassination, and imprisonment of political opponents—became increasingly ineffectual. The rise (and repression) of black and nonracial trade unionism, student dissidence, and the Black Consciousness movement (led by Steve Biko) along with varieties of Christian radicalism led to an international call for divestment and boycotts. Following the spectacularization of state violence against students and youth in Soweto in 1976, the underground itself began to move, traveling, along other axes, from Soweto to Khutsong and neighboring towns (and, through different networks, to other cities around the nation) as the network of exiled militants and their allies spread out across the region to lay a cloak of outrage and insurrectionary hope over the labor-sending territories. In every way, the ideological ground of Apartheid was being destabilized, its core values displaced. Neither the value of gold nor the virtue of whiteness, with the associated anxieties about a need to protect white femininity, could sustain a claim to universality in this context.

Nonetheless, the consequences of gold's displacement and replacement in the world economy turn out to have been rather more ambiguous than this neat historiographical miniature may suggest. Not all of these consequences can be grasped in the schema of racialized would-be totalitarianism's demise. Nor can they be assimilated to the grand narratives of modernism's emergence based on the discernment of homologies between language, economy, and aesthetics, and the simultaneous if partial abandonment of transcendentalism. The account that follows is accordingly complex and necessarily convoluted, if also abbreviated, and for this reason, it may be helpful to describe its contours in advance. The decline of gold as a privileged reserve in international monetary policy and the destabilization of its value led not merely to the upward revaluation of gold but, indirectly, it informed a new drive to "stabilize" the black mineworker population. In the service of this goal, the gold industry, leading and contradicting the state in many respects, raised wages and encouraged an attenuated reproduction of the domesticated and privatized middle-class life that had prevailed in the self-representation of white South Africa during segregation and under Apartheid. The central institution in the project of stabilization was not the township, which was beyond the mining industry's authority and under pressure from the Apartheid state, which was in fact attempting to prevent the stabilization of black populations in urban areas. Rather, it was the (initially small-scale) development of familial residential complexes called, in vernacular idiom, *skomplaas*-es. These were, strictly speaking, internal to neither the compounds nor the townships, and they were used both to enable the more skilled and more highly paid black mineworkers to reside with their spouses and children and to facilitate temporary liaisons between mineworkers and their wives or sexual partners. The discourse of stabilization nonetheless exceeded what was possible, given the financial means of the workers and the antipathy of the state. Moreover, it depended on an excluded and differently structured economy—one that operated as both an external perimeter and a secret interior. We will now consider that strange limit-space, that space of and at the margin.

Rest Areas: Signs of the Times

No U-turns. Nonetheless, a certain return is necessary—a return to the question with which I began: How did we get here? They, I, we? At each moment, the question is renewed. Let us then go back to those roads where the first inklings of a problem in the representational order of the gold-made world appeared.

In addition to all the painted names and distances, there were and are other markings, other kinds of signage at the roadside for those who know how to look, and then to see and read. An umbrella, for example, and a few chairs occupied by women, fanning themselves in the heat or braiding each other's hair during the summer months, an empty car or truck nearby. The women squint against the clouds of dust when, before the summer rains, cars pull in or accelerate away, gravel and sand thrown skyward like the puffs of red earth above the sinkholes. In winter, the same women might be warming their hands over a fire in an oil can, dust-laden sweaters and jackets wrapped tightly around their hips and woolen caps pulled down against the chill. Sometimes, a woman emerges from the bushes nearby. Sometimes, her back is seen, followed by the figure of a man. For these women, the time of the road is not that of speed or an unwanted slowness but of waiting, in boredom, in trepidation, in anxiety, in needfulness. Sometimes, a young man is sitting among such women, selling bags of citrus or hubcaps scavenged from car crashes or stolen from the vehicles stopped nearby. Such little gatherings, seemingly distant from any residential community, and invariably not more than a few miles from a mine, are roadside brothels. They are scattered along most of the arteries to the mines. Fridays and month-ends are busy times for these brothels. Afternoons most of all. On those days, men often arrive in groups.

"These roads will take you into your own country. . . . mirrored in these men."[1]

Informal brothels of the sort just described are in one sense roadside stopping places. Often, they are simply referred to as "Truck Stops." From the perspective of the men who visit them, they are spaces of detour, leisure, and expenditure—enabled by the slender margins of disposable income that can be earned in the mining sector (whether underground or in auxiliary services) or through gambling and petty crime (men of means do not generally patronize Truck Stops). What is shocking for many, including many of the women who arrive into this economy for the first time, is their exposedness. Unsheltered, unprotected, at the edge of wildness even when located at the periphery of old farms, the roadside brothel can appear as an extreme limit to the social organization that the Apartheid state, and all capitalist economies, otherwise propagate, depend on, and even assume. In economies of this sort, the sexual domain is both invested and cordoned off through moral discourses and legislative codes, and sex is the signifier of the unalienable, of that which should not be sold but rather preserved for romantic and conjugal relations, unless displaced into the realms of advertising, fashion, and the culture industries (and not only as pornography).[2] It is in this context that we can listen again to what Slindile, the migrant woman we met in chapter 5, said when speaking of what she might have to do in flight from the police, should they demand a bribe. When she said she would be driven to the bush, she implied not only an abandonment to wildness but also sex work at a Truck Stop.

In most Euro-American contexts, and those where the bourgeois ideals of nucleated family life and household autonomy reign, a series of homologies operate by which the nonalienated and the domestic sphere are aligned and sequestered spatially and temporally, such that the household is the place of precommodified life. This space is also one of prepolitical kinship, which is to say of conditioned unconditionality. Within its confines, family is the limit of obligation and the rationale for women's and, as we have already seen, children's unremunerated labor. It is well-known that such an enclosed and interiorized domestic sphere was largely denied to black subjects in the gold-mining world, where oscillating migration and the hostel system separated male mineworkers from their families for extended periods of time, just as it is well known that the female domestic laborers who were resident in their employers' households were separated from their families. It is also well known that the same-sex hostel system was accompanied by both contractual same-sex relations among senior and junior male workers in the mines and compounds, and commercial sex work by both women and men on the perimeters of the mine compounds. A loquacious discourse has analyzed the twin effects of this dimension of the mining economy on South Africa's HIV/AIDS epidemic. Less well recounted is the strange inversion that was produced in the spatial and libidinous economy within which indebted women moved and resided near the mines.

Consider, for example, the phenomenon of the *skomplaas* on the mines' margins. *Skomplaas* was the informal term used by black residents to designate the residential quarters for married mineworkers when and where this was permitted, and they were typically established at the outskirts of mine compounds and sometimes on farms nearby.[3] At various points, mines agreed to provide substitutional accommodation pay to employees who did not wish to reside in hostels if they were married; this was (and still is) referred to as "living out." On some occasions, they were provided with rations and access to the residences rather than cash payments. And sometimes, retired employees could be kept on in this kind of demonetized economy if they had good relations with members of management and performed other nonremunerated services (gardening, domestic work). This was the case with the nurse we met in chapter 8, the man who had described the terrible beauty of the treasures to be found in sinkholes, and who lamented the dietary apartheid of the hospital, the same man who had imagined an underground network of roads uninterrupted by either mine shafts or pass inspectors. He had been given quarters near Blyvoor by the matron of the hospital where he had worked. She had encouraged him to return with his wife, as unofficial employees, after his job came to an end. That was in 1954. He and his wife had accepted the offer and remained in that *skomplaas* until 1984 (he was in his nineties when I met him). Like much in his memory, there was a halcyon glow about the *skomplaas* of that time, and he recalled his receipt of rations in the image of a gift, for which he felt immense gratitude. When I met him in Khutsong, he was proud to show me a home of meticulously curated working-class domesticity, with family photographs on the walls, and doilies on the heavy wooden coffee table. Layer upon layer of protection— from plastic covers on the sofa to locks, bars, and bolts on the door—testified to the value of these things. He was surrounded by his children, who shared in his pride and offered hospitality with unstinting generosity.

This narrative of the *skomplaas* as an enabling outside to the compound and a site of proper domesticity and domestic propriety, as well as the scene of commodity accumulation, is not generalizable, however. It is an ideal image and often is contradicted in actuality. For many women, it was also a site of subordination and containment in a manner that deprived them of money or that demanded that they manage insufficient resources and, often enough, barter dependency for subsistence. As a term, the word *skomplaas* has also migrated. It has accumulated ambiguous significations as the zones for "living out" have expanded and, like almost everything else, has become increasingly informalized. In particular circumstances, the word acquires an aspect of the proper name. Indeed, the word *Skomplaas* is visible even in the ruins of the desiccated mine described at the opening of this book. Painted on the crumbling wall of the old complex, half-graffiti, half place-name, it is not only a designation but also the very signature of ruin and the point at which the proper name and its defacement converge. In that specific location, (the) *skomplaas* is a squatter community, and the painted sign, *Skomplaas* is not simply a translation of "the quarters" but rather the name of a particular destination, a grouping of several dozen households with a self-organized local governance committee, and an address known by the police and other state authorities. In 2019, it received water from the municipality, but otherwise lacked all services—including sewerage, electricity, and waste removal. Nonetheless, while it still resembled a self-governing community, permission to visit and ask questions had to be obtained through its representatives. The largely unemployed residents spoke of the place not as *a* skomplaas but as *Skomplaas*—as though it were Carletonville, or perhaps Carltonville. (In 2024, it had been overrun by gangsters, zama zamas and refugees from the national government's siege against informal miners.)

In these ruins, and in other such places where a literal signage bears a ressentiment barely concealed as cynical wit, the nascent and residual significations of the word are revealingly materialized. For *skomplaas* implies both sex and excess. *Skommel*, in Dutch, refers to a kind of rocking motion and is associated with sex and especially male masturbation. The derivative, *skom*, also evokes scum and froth, what is spent and what is wasted—all that is neither productive nor reproductive. The term *skommel* has entered vernacular idiom through Afrikaans and has been lexicalized across most of the local languages in South Africa, including the urban creole, Tsotsi-taal, where it dominates the formal meaning that would otherwise denote shaking and shuffling (of cards as well as bodies). As is so often the case, gambling and sex occupy adjacent fields and many metaphors work in both discursive domains.[4] And perhaps for this reason, polite conversations about such places were sometimes referred to in proper Afrikaans not as *skomplaas*-es but *schoonplaas*-es, meaning clean or empty spaces.[5]

What then does it mean to describe the married quarters of a mine as a *skomplaas*? What does it tell us about the relationship between sex and the political economy in the gold sector? What does it indicate about the instrumentalizable function of women in that sexual economy? And what does this tell us about the status of those Truck Stop brothels that line the highways linking the mine and the *skomplaas* with the farm and the market? For the *skomplaas*, as an exterior domain and a marker of the compound's boundary, is haunted by that other periphery or limit which is experienced as a mere stopping point on the roads that link otherwise enclosed and privatized realms. As in the realm of stocks, this limit indicates a threshold beyond which payment will not be made.

The Truck Stop brothel is an institution of great ubiquity and strange invisibility. The lack of discussion about it compared with the phenomenon of hostel same-sex relations, so widely analyzed in the scholarly literature on gold mining, is notable. If, however, the *skomplaas* was not a township but rather a form of exception and an alternative to fully urban life, and if the Truck Stop brothel was its antithesis and alibi, the narratives of sex workers reveal the porosity and instability of the boundary between them. This porosity does not derive from either categorical distinctions or category mistakes related to a differentiation between actual prostitution and something called "transactional sex." And it does not lend itself to a sociological comparison between the transactional sex aimed at acquiring subsistence goods, said to be more prevalent in informal settlements, and that seeking luxury or consumption goods, ostensibly more common in townships.[6] Such distinctions are part of an entirely different (epidemiological) discourse, even when they concede the mutual contamination of these categories. My purpose is different. It is not an effort to understand sexuality or population logics but rather to grasp the discourse of economy as sexed and gendered.

In the accounts of the women relayed and analyzed in this chapter, the entire and accelerating project of stabilization in the post–Bretton Woods era, which included a concerted effort to overcome the so-called demasculinization that accompanied migrancy and single-sex hostels, is grounded in the reencompassment and instrumentalization of women. It took place within what Glen Elder refers to as the "procreational geography" of Apartheid.[7] The effort, which bypassed any interrogation of patriarchy, was not the exclusive purview of the industry; it also suffused the critiques of migrant labor that oriented opposition to Apartheid on the grounds that it destroyed traditional familial logics and the normative forms of male subjectivity grounded therein. Thus, the psychologist N. Chabani Mangyani invoked both Albert Camus and Frantz Fanon to write of the "dilemma of discontinuities" and the "contradictions" between desire and its satisfaction that "ultimately killed" the migrant. He identified migrant labor with a specifically sexual deprivation: "the secret anguish which must befriend these men at night—subduing a raging sexuality from within and having to make fun of a lively erotic imagination."[8] Manganyi, who founded the Department of Psychology at the University of the Transkei and later taught at the University of the Witwatersrand, regularly served as an expert witness in trials of political dissidents, adducing the destruction of the traditional family as an extenuating or mitigating circumstance in an effort to prevent the application of capital punishment in sentencing. Disbanding what Manganyi called the "institutionalized wifeless existence" of migrancy was one of the tasks of emancipation and the precondition of that humanism in whose name he questioned both Apartheid and Black Consciousness.[9] He believed that the sign of such emancipation would be a redemption of the image of the mineworker, which he associated with "a patchwork identity" concretized in the stereotype of a "motley patchwork of colour."[10] Discerning in the dress of the mineworker what Jean Comaroff and John Comaroff also described as the articulation of otherwise "mute experience . . . in a fortuitous clutch of images," Manganyi contrasted the image of the identity document with a fuller expression of subjectivity.[11] This other, more adequate image would come from outside, emerging from a relation of mutual intersubjective recognition. Manganyi had in mind that mirror image in which a subject finds the (misrecognized) figure of their wholeness. Instead, he claimed, the "migrant worker, as father, is limited . . . from being an adequate custodian of what is valuable in the history and culture of African peoples by parading a paltry image for identification purposes."[12] The *skomplaas* was not conceived as a general solution to this problem, of course, and it was offered only to the upper echelons of the workforce. Even so, as we shall see, the redemption of the male migrant mineworker's burden and indeed of his image would depend on the transformation of and increasing investment in Woman (this figured multiplicity) as the locus of display value, although this would occur differently for black and for white women.

This does not mean that life in the *skomplaas* was an unrelenting source of alienation for women who resided there, or that they did not often want to live with their husbands or that their husbands and lovers did not want to live with them. It does not mean that they were always unsatisfied and that they were deprived of tenderness or joyfulness, hope or contentment. But insofar as the *skomplaas* and the Truck Stop brothel arose as elements in a system organized around racial separation and the disavowal of black urbanism, the accounts of these women expose a violent subterranean logic within Apartheid, namely that it depended on women's partial reduction to the function of male satisfaction. This is somewhat different from the more common story of women's reduction to reproductive functionality—and this difference is imperative to grasp if the history of globalization is not to be confused with one of the Euro-American bourgeoisie's and then middle class's universalization. The tragedy of the women we shall meet in the following pages is that their experiences of such instrumentalization did not end with Apartheid, that the Truck Stop brothel and the *skomplaas* did not disappear with the fuller development of the townships. What follows is a story *of* margins—margins of exchange and profit margins, but also margins of spaces and social norms in the changing moral geography of the gold-mining communities at the heart of the (cyanidic) Apartheid state. What follows is also a story *from* the margins, one that implicitly demands a reconsideration of the supposed truths of the political economy and the critical theory of modernism in the era after Bretton Woods. In the service of that analytic purpose, it is first necessary to understand what precipitated and what followed upon the U.S. closure of the "gold window," as its was called until 1971. For that closure was felt especially powerfully in South Africa, although the famed television broadcast of Nixon's announcement never reached the Highveld, there being no television in South Africa at that time.

Detour: Turn Right

There were warning signs before 1971, and until the moment when Richard Nixon addressed television audiences on August 15, speculators were arguing the point. Thus, on August 11, the *Rand Daily Mail's* correspondent reported from the London stock exchange that the "gold fever continued in the world's bullion markets" and added that "gold speculators are convinced that the final showdown between gold and paper currency [was] at hand, with the dollar at last exposed to attack."[13] They lost the bet. U.S. administrations had been considering such a move at least since 1964, and it had been under direct and continuous consideration since 1968.[14] Many critics have posited a relationship—whether understood as homology, reflection, cause, or effect—between the abandonment of the Bretton Woods regime (often conflated with the older gold standard) and the abandonment of all universal standards, from the moral to the aesthetic, and from the ethical to the political. This sense of ontological dislocation and epochal unmooring has persisted. Thus, for example, in a debatable reading of Walter Benjamin's fragment, "Capitalism as Religion," Giorgio Agamben writes that "from that moment on, the inscription that we still read on many banknotes (for example, on the pound sterling and the rupiah, but not the euro),—'I promise to pay the bearer the sum of . . .', countersigned by the governor of the central bank—had definitely lost its meaning."[15] He does not mention the South African rand, but he might have, for it too bore this promise.

Agamben continues:

> That there might be a resemblance between language and money, that (according to the Goethean adage) "*verba valent sicut nummi*," is a legacy of common sense. If, however, we attempt to take the relation implicit in the adage seriously, it reveals itself to be something more than an analogy. Just as money refers to things by establishing them as commodities, by making them commercial, so language refers to things by making them sayable and communicable. And just

as what for centuries enabled money to perform its function as the universal equivalent of all commodities was its relation with gold, so what guarantees the communicative capacity of language is the intention to signify, its actual reference to the thing. The denotative nexus with things, actually present in the mind of every speaking being, is what in language corresponds to the gold standard of money. . . . If this signifying nexus collapses, language literally says nothing (*"nihil dicit"*). The signified—the reference to reality—guarantees the communicative function of language, just as the reference to gold secures money's capacity to be exchanged.[16]

Agamben's linkage of a crisis in the monetary system with an analogous crisis in language was both belated and based on a theory of reference that had been in question at least since Saussure (it is already intimated in Goethe's *Faust*). In the world of economics, John Maynard Keynes had already questioned the anxiety about gold's displacement in 1930, invoking Saint Paul's condemnation of *"aura sacri fames"* (the accursed greed for gold): "The long age of Commodity Money has at last passed finally away before the age of Representative Money. Gold has ceased to be a coin, a hoard, a tangible claim of wealth, of which the value cannot slip away so long as the hand of the individual clutches the material stuff."[17]

Even Joseph Gold, the serendipitously named historian of the International Monetary Fund (IMF), found it appropriate to quote Gertrude Stein's 1936 suspicion of fiat currency, noting that goldbug anxiety was distilled in the feigned jejunity of her question: "Is money money or isn't money money?" Gold invoked Stein (whose essays on money were anthologized in the year of Nixon's declaration) not with respect to the difference between metallic and paper currency but in reference to the new and "unique legal concept" of Special Drawing Rights (SDRs), which had been created in 1969 to substitute for an "equivalent weight of gold valued at the par value of the US dollar price of gold."[18] Stein was for Gold the spokesperson of an outmoded goldbug ideology. She was referring to the New Deal and deficit financing during the depression—and her fiscally conservative conclusions were presumed to be sufficiently attractive to a broad audience to be published in the *Saturday Evening Post*.[19] But Gold believed her question, posed in the space between the end of the gold standard and the institution of its revived simulacrum at Bretton Woods, was newly relevant after the latter agreement fell apart.

In fact, there had been a two-tier system for valuing gold for years before the Nixon government had declared what was at the time a still temporary policy. Under this two-tier system, the monetary value of gold, which functioned in the realm of sovereign debt management and interstate financial relations, was distinct from the commodity value of gold. The latter fluctuated according to market valuations that depended both on the costs of production and on the capacity of the markets for jewelry and industrial application to absorb that gold which was not otherwise destined for state and IMF coffers. The monetary value of gold, as discussed in previous chapters, was fiat money but it was not originary. It wasn't even very old. Keynes actually referred to gold's status as the "sole standard" as a "parvenu" of the global economy, which, until British imperialism had been consolidated on the back of the empire's possession of most of the world's gold production, more often permitted other media to function alongside it (from silver to shells).[20] Its disjuncture from production costs and market demand had for some time been a source of concern for gold-producing corporations and states, and especially the Chamber of Mines of South Africa. However, it was not fiat in the classical sense of sovereign dictation.

In the Bretton Woods era, the monetary value of gold could fluctuate by agreement of the participating nations, albeit at the margins and in limited ways, but local currency values could and were in fact supposed to be adjusted in relation to gold in the event of a "fundamental disequilibrium," the definition of which was never substantively determined.[21] The Chamber, like the United States and the IMF, felt that many member nations were not doing much to rein in their economies, and it advocated austerity enforced by limited access to credit and thus debt. In the 1960s, the United States both bought and sold gold at the rate established in 1944—$35 per ounce. As Joanne Gowa explains, the "system could not function unless one country remained out of the foreign-exchange markets, passive with respect to the level of its exchange rate."[22] This made the U.S. dollar effectively the measure of measures, the form of appearance, to use Marx's idiom, of the general equivalent. An adjustable peg system was then linked to a system that permitted member states to draw credit if they went into deficit—and if the other voting states in the IMF agreed to their request. In this system, even with the dollar and SDRs as proxies for gold, the precious metal functioned as the "ultimate reserve asset," for which reason, international liquidity in an ever-expanding global economy depended on an ever-enlarging set of reserves. Until August 15, 1971, that meant access to newly mined gold.[23]

In essence, then, global capitalism in the Bretton Woods era was directly dependent on gold production in the world's two main centers of gold mining: South Africa and the Soviet Union. The latter, however, could not be counted upon as a source of precious metals by the U.S.-aligned states during the Cold War (the full significance of the propaganda film discussed in chapter 8 acquires its significance in this context). Kennedy's and Johnson's administrations had been increasingly concerned with the coupling of gold and the dollar because the United States was running deficits on two fronts: at home, where social programs aimed at the support of the civil rights transformation had ballooned; and abroad, because foreign aid had become a significant factor in U.S. foreign policy and a mechanism ensuring dependency if not alliance. Above all, the dollar had been stretched or the capacity to convert them (gold and the U.S. dollar) challenged, because the wars in Southeast Asia had become so expensive. Ironically, Nixon's speech announcing his new economic policy was titled "The Challenge of Peace." The wars whose end he predicted were the cold wars of Europe rather than the white-hot fires of Vietnam, Cambodia, and Laos. He also promised job creation, a stable currency (rather than wild devaluation), a temporary wage and prices freeze, and a modest 1 percent import tax. The cost, however, was not to be covered by income, capital gains, or property taxes; to the contrary, Nixon announced a personal income tax credit. The gap generated by the resulting shortfall, which was corollary for such credit, was to be covered by a 10 percent reduction in foreign aid and reduced troops in Europe.[24] U.S. capital exports would nonetheless continue, permitting U.S. capital to invest elsewhere, outsourcing production to low-cost facilities enabled by currency differentials. In fact, private capital had exceeded military expenditures abroad already at the time of the first gold crisis in 1960.[25]

In a profound sense, and half a century before it became a slogan for a new populism sometimes called Trumpism, Nixon's agenda was that of "America First," by which was meant the U.S. domestic economy first. But it was enabled by U.S. capital's internationalization. Nixon radicalized what was the de facto basis of the Bretton Woods system, which was structured to privilege U.S. interests by granting to the United States a disproportionate 30 percent and then 20 percent voting power.[26] In this context, the United States could and did effectively support Apartheid in South Africa, despite popular opposition in some quarters, because that meant access to gold at a low, relatively stable price (the Anti-Apartheid Act was passed in the United States only in 1986[27]). In addition to international opprobrium, what accelerated U.S. withdrawal of such support was the growing doubt of other nations that no matter how much gold it had purchased from South Africa, there was not enough in U.S. coffers to enable conversion. As economic historians recount, the reticence to raise taxes in the United States and the growing, rather than diminishing, expenditures abroad—thanks to both U.S. consumerism and U.S. military involvement in Southeast Asia—led to problems in the balance of payments that incited fear and suspicion among many nations that the United States would not be able to service its debt. Fear that nations holding U.S. dollars would demand their conversion into gold, which the United States had promised to do under the terms of the Bretton Woods agreement, had justified the two-tier system among other strategies (such as capital controls and the creation of SDRs) in 1968. By 1971, much of the world had lost faith in the United States, and the United States had lost faith in the faith of others. Thus, Nixon called his nation back to the church of competition. The economy was war by other means: "We can be certain of this: As the threat of war recedes, the challenge of peaceful competition in the world will greatly increase. We welcome competition, because America is at her greatest when she is called on to compete."[28]

What was in question in 1971 was not gold's status as the true ground of real value, and thus of economic referentiality, but the U.S. dollar's capacity to function as proxy for that fantasized function. The problem was U.S. debt as well as U.S. accumulation of other nations' debt, which was encouraged in the effort to get everyone to "buy American" and to desire, as in the advertisements for Carletonville, an American way of life (either by soft power or at the end of a gun). Increasingly, accumulation was taking place in the realm of debt. Debt had become what Rosa Luxemburg had termed a "zone" or "territory" (*Gebiet*) of accumulation. This development has only intensified since. And this is why the floating of the dollar assumed the role of signifying an epochal transformation through the social sphere, and not only a change in the monetary order.

Nonetheless, as these reports on volatility in the 1970s gold markets suggest, it was always clear that the end of the Bretton Woods regime would be particularly significant for the gold-producing countries, and especially South Africa. On the one hand, its cheap gold was no longer needed by the United States. On the other hand, it was now much freer to sell more of its gold at the commodity price to a global market that the Chamber had cultivated. And the price leaped heavenward. If *oikos*, from which Greek term we derive the word "economy," originally referred to the management of the household, then we may expect, and will indeed see, that the effects of these distant machinations of the monetary policymakers would be written in the innermost domains of the intimate sphere in South Africa. That inscription was mediated in and through the dream machine of the mass media, which operates the mythology linking gold, the idea of truth, and sexuality, in narrative mode.

End detour.

Silver Linings?

Nixon was criticized for announcing his administration's new policy during the primetime television broadcast of *Bonanza*, a series revolving around the life of a wealthy family whose ranch was near the location of the famous silver mines of Nevada, discovered in 1859. The "Comstock Lode" on which the mines were built had been called a "bonanza."[29] *Bonanza*, with its memory of silver and its patriarchal and fraternal framework, became the space and the scene of an address to the nation-as-family. The rest, as they say, is American history—in which domestic economic politics drive electoral cycles. But elsewhere, there were many unexpected outcomes to the supplementation of gold by SDRs and the floating of the U.S. dollar. Among these perhaps unexpected effects was the growth in wages for black workers in South Africa's gold mines. But this outcome was neither immediate nor automatic. Initially, the Chamber of Mines responded to the end of Bretton Woods, about which it had complained bitterly for many years, by noting that the rising price of gold was due partly to South Africa's withholding of its gold from the market (for its own reserves) and to U.S. wars in Southeast Asia as well as to "political uncertainty in Europe and the Middle and Far East."[30] But mainly, the Chamber claimed, the rise in prices was due to the growth in the jewelry market, which it was pleased to have spurred. It noted that these rising prices would ensure that mines that had previously been destined to close could be reopened, their lives extended— even as the Chamber remained uncertain about the future role of gold in the international monetary order. A whole new domain of payability had been opened, and with it, abandoned veins of low-grade ores began to glitter again, as they had with the introduction of hydrocyanidation. An industrial afterlife now appeared where the horizon had seemed closed. This afterlife would be opened and closed and opened again in the relentless and unresolving dialectic between production costs and profits, one dependent on the scale and intensity of operations as well as the desperation of the unemployed. In the meantime, it was not to the enhancement of black wages or changed living circumstances that the industry initially imagined devoting its growing profits. Rather, militant agitation and strikes, and the violence that accompanied them, played the crucial role in ensuring that some portion of the enlarged revenues from gold sales would be—slowly and unevenly and always inadequately—transferred to workers. As Ernst Bloch wrote: "The ruling classes capitulate only falsely, abstractly, and undialectically."[31]

Between 1970 and 1977, as the price of gold climbed from $40.95 per ounce to $144.15 per ounce (it would hit $737.50 in 1980 before declining to $411.50 a decade after the Nixon declaration), the proportion of mine expenditures on black wages grew from 13.4 percent to 25.5 percent.[32] The strikes, in which the black laboring population asserted the economic interests as well as the aspirations of the mainly male labor force, and a persistent deficit of skilled labor in the mines, led to a reconsideration of the axioms on which the oscillating migratory system had been based. It was against the state and in ironic parallel—but not in concert—with the interest of black labor that a number of mining corporations began to argue against the hostel system and for more permanent settlements for black laborers. In the analysis of Jonathan Crush and Wilmot James, the demand for a more skilled, more stable, and more productive labor force was the corollary of the rise in wages. But the central powers of the Chamber of Mines were divided on the virtue of settling the migratory population, just as they had been divided about importing Chinese labor seventy-five years previously. The Anglo Gold Corporation, led by Harry Oppenheimer, avowed the idea of settled black labor in the vicinity of the mines, as well as marital and familial accommodations for at least the more skilled workers, even as it acknowledged the likely dependency of South African mines on migrant labor from outside of the country. Because not all migrating workers returned to their place of work, or not to the same mine, Anglo's management wanted to keep those in whom it had invested training closer—in long-term employment—and thus in settlements nearby. But Gold Fields (then British-owned) disagreed and asserted its preference for foreign labor. The Chamber, which had once been the face of monopoly and monopsony, and the locus of apparent, if occasionally faltering capitalist unanimity, was riven.[33] This did not mean that Anglo Gold was aggressively establishing residential facilities for its workers—its professions of intent notwithstanding. Even in 1985, a miniscule percentage (less than 2 percent of Anglo's 170,000 workers) were living in married quarters—in the *skomplaases.*

The early Apartheid government had prohibited more than 3 percent of the black mine workforce from living on the mine property—and Anglo Gold was not able to match even this exclusionary threshold. Nonetheless, the 1970s saw the gold-mining companies increasingly at odds with the South African state, insofar as the latter was working more and more fervently to expel black subjects from the national territory, partly by stripping the subjects of the Transkei and Ciskei, major labor-sending areas, of their citizenship (the so-called autonomy of the Bantustans precluded dual membership). Anglo Gold led the effort, and in a five-year period more than tripled its rental units for married black workers, from 876 to 2,653.[34] Many of these were established in the black counterpart to Carletonville, Wedela, a community whose "model" status and "modern housing" nonetheless lacked the utopian excitement and capital investments of the white town that was by then a few decades old.[35] G. Langton, speaking on Anglo's behalf, noted that, upon the first phases' completion, the "standard of housing, the layout of the village and the amenities provided are exceptionally good and compare favourably with other such schemes elsewhere in the word." He added, "Western Deep Levels [the mine near Wedela and Carletonville] can be proud of the fact that it is involved in such a development, and will ultimately reap benefits flowing from a more motivated supervisory group of black employees enjoying a much-improved quality of life." Nonetheless, in 1984, less than 1 percent of the black mineworker population was residing in family accommodations, although some 40 percent professed a desire to do so.[36]

Wedela's creation, intended for a newly emergent black supervisory class, neither absorbed much of the workforce nor impeded the growth of Khutsong, which remained the destination for the multitudinous population, which, although not exclusively or even mainly composed of mineworkers, lived in the shadow of the mines. The more that wages rose, the more that homeownership and proximity to work became bound together as vehicles and signifiers of class formation. Eventually, after 1986, when the state would be compelled to revoke its remaining pass laws, mainly because of the collapse of so-called "influx control," black workers who had evidence of employment and access to state-approved housing, could officially settle or resettle near their places of employment in the mines and those who had been deprived of citizenship during the era of the Bantustans were able to rejoin the possible national community through their work on or near those mines. This was not merely a concession to the demands of militants; it was, as Crush and James assert, a means to interrupt the growing power of the National Union of Mineworkers, which had, throughout the 1980s, used the hostels as sites for organizing.

In polite local parlance, Wedela was referred to as a "township," rather than a *skomplaas* but it was neither, and perhaps Anglo's nomination of it as a village was more accurate.[37] In any case, the public sphere of Khutsong township was relatively unaffected by these laborious rearrangements, aimed as they were at obviating racial solidarity as much as "stabilizing" the population, and, for this reason, it could and did become one of the sites at which political militancy could develop. Many excellent histories of mineworkers' militancy, the struggle against the hostel system, and the pursuit of family housing exist. But across that literature, the question of the *skomplaas*, an idiom that nonetheless rarely appears in the sociological or radical materialist accounts, has been that of the male mineworker's capacity or right to live in residence with his family and thus to act as the head of a unified household. In this sense, the end of Bretton Woods was not, in South Africa, the destabilization of the signifying chain that links all of the transcendental signifiers—the signifiers of the real, true, and universal "things" to which Agamben's mourned dream-language would refer—but the beginning of its reformulation, restoration, and generalization beyond whiteness. The discourse of workforce stabilization signifies this fact. What then about that other sign of the times, the one that I suggested could be read at the roadside en route to the mines, the one that worked to secure the perimeter of *both* the compound and the *skomplaas*, by granting to the reproductive economy its sense of incommensurability? That place of woman, waiting. Of course, *that* woman is a sign (i.e., Woman) only for others. For the stereotypical (figure of the) mineworker with his little boon and newfound, if limited, purchasing power, that woman appears as the "feast day," in a Bataillean sense: she is the occasion of his expenditure and momentary escape from the otherwise unceasing weekday. In and on the Truck Stop prostitute does he expend what he has left over from the wages accumulated by his labor, that not extracted as surplus value. And it is through this expenditure that he is able to secure his masculinity, to ground it again.

The norming and normativizing power of prostitution, which is not at all undermined by its prohibition in Christian moralism, lies in the fact that it marks an outside, a limit and a counterpoint to the ideal of nucleated, reproductively oriented familial life. This is why, even during the early years of the twentieth century, mining companies anticipated and budgeted for women's corn-brewing activity on or near the mine compounds—for they knew that such beer-drinking, even if merely coded as a cultural tradition, was also a scene of prostitution. And as Charles van Onselen has so clearly documented, the early history of Johannesburg as a city produced for and by the gold indus- try is incomprehensible without accounting for the central role of prostitution in its development. For prostitution provided the means by which immigrant white men and migrant black laborers could be both sustained in heterosex- uality and kept working, for their expenditures had to be paid for with wages and these had to be replaced by those earned in more work. Nonetheless, the Truck Stop brothel, if the term *brothel* can be stretched in this manner, is of a different time, and its clients include not only mineworkers but also all those who move on these roads—the day laborers, the truck drivers and taxi operators, the petty merchants of roadside stalls, the construction and service workers, the gangsters.

Alternate Route

The Truck Stop brothel is located, literally, at the roadside. But the term is redolent with implication, and the metaphor of the highway lends itself to life-historical narrations that lift off from this banal fact of location. Thus, the narratives recounted by the women who work there are also typically lain down in a manner that makes prostitution a kind of destiny on the journey defined by a series of wrong turns, with the contingent encounter with a predatory male often anchored on a precisely measured map. In the life-histories I have conducted with sex workers, place-names are almost always the signifiers of an event in an increasingly irreversible trajectory toward absolute dependency on the money or the material goods that come from this kind of activity. The women them- selves refer to that activity in the cliché of global moralism: as selling their bod- ies. But in more complicated if not unexpected ways, it is also imbricated with desires for ideal forms of family life and—this is crucial—in the remembered violation of gender norms by other members of the extended family. As odd as it may seem, for many women, prostitution is the expression of a desire and belief in normative reproductivity and for family values. For family as value.

Thus, for example, a woman I shall call Akhona, born in 1970 in Ficksburg in the Free State, tells the story of her early life, where she was one of two daughters. Her father worked on the West Rand mines, and when her mother died in 1978, she was sent to live with her maternal grandmother. The elder woman died shortly thereafter in 1980. When it became clear that the two girls could not look after themselves, their maternal uncle took them in.

> Our uncle had other children as well but he made us clean the house and if they felt we did not clean well they would not give us food for the night. We would sleep with hunger and the other children would eat even though they did not

clean at all. We could see that he did not treat us as his children. And we were taken by another family member also. We were just living but life was still not good at all. We were girls but they expected us to look after the cattle and livestock.

Akhona's sister left the household to obtain a job, initially hoping that she could support her younger sister to continue with her schooling, but as Akhona says, she had no time for homework, tending cattle as she was, and so "lost interest" in school. Their father remained on the mines, but sent no remittances to them. It was at this point that Akhona met a young man who offered to help her tend the cattle—in exchange for her sexual favors. In fact, the young man was also a family relation. Akhona recounted her predicament, which afflicted her like a sudden illness, with a modesty that one might not expect from a woman who has worked as a Truck Stop prostitute for more than two decades, "I was pregnant with the favors that I used to do with this family boy." In her memory, Akhona's crisis is twofold: she is asked to perform the tasks of a boy, and these make her vulnerable to predation. Her rescuer, a kinsman, offers to preserve her femininity but only if she enacts it as submission to him. Becoming a woman was thus for her a monstrously excessive confinement within the "family," but one subject to the laws of the market economy. This confusion, for which the word *incest* is entirely inadequate as a descriptor, inaugurated the journey to prostitution.

One might say that Akhona was overexposed to family members or that there were insufficient limits to the intimacy that it granted. But saying so merely reveals an old structuralist principle, namely that the girl's sexual autonomy demands that the family, far from being the space of unrestricted intimacy and proximity, or unconditional reciprocity, requires internal differentiations, laws, and zones of exclusion. In places where the household is a shack, a few square meters encased in zinc siding or cardboard and plywood sutured together with chicken wire (places typical of informal settlements but far from the ideal villages of Wedela), such exclusion is often impossible. This fact has often been palpable to me when, in shack settlements, I have conversed with women or men about matters of an intimate nature—whether these be about sexual activity and domestic violence, marital transgressions, fears of witchcraft, financial worry, or HIV status. Often, when we have broached such a topic, it has been suggested that we go outside—for privacy. Precisely that which is inside is available to be overheard or spied upon. Only in the moil of other people, drowned by the noise of other conversations and the throng of other bodies, could women in these situations feel secure in speaking about what they did not otherwise wish their closest kin and household members to know. The walls of the township shack were for them almost demonically attentive—as though they themselves were ears. The public, however, was indifferent to them, and this fact—which was a source of such wounding to many men, who, as discussed previously, desired recognition when they walked through the world—made it a space of liberating anonymity for women, at least in the daylight. Nighttime was different. Then the world turned inside out, and what had been liberating became threatening, and conversely, what had been a source of exposure became, instead, a source of relative security.

Akhona believed that if fate had not robbed her of her mother, if her father had sent remittances home as he had promised to do, if she had been permitted to go to school and live as other girls lived or at least wanted to live, she would have become a woman, in the sense of entering reproductive life, only by leaving the family household behind. Her access to being a woman, in this sense, would have been parallel to men's access to adult masculine subjectivity in the Hegelian program: an entry into the public domain. But unlike that male's movement from the household into the public, Akhona did not imagine she would become a rights-bearing citizen and member of the polis. She simply hoped to be someone to whom others would be obliged to speak truthfully.[38] This is the quotidian idiom in which a woman imagines what is available to her as the shadow of that Enlightenment ideal, formulated by Kant in "What Is Enlightenment" as the "public use of Reason."[39] Its reduction to the hope, if not the expectation, that others would not deceive her is not necessarily evidence of that ideal's failure, but it may reveal its limits; in some circumstances, it can be the spark of a possible publicness available to be kindled for political purposes. Such a spark was occasionally ignited during the anti-Apartheid struggle, which was thoroughly dependent on Enlightenment conceptions of citizenship but unable (still and yet) to overcome the translational aporias that were built into the colonial educational system or to escape the burdens of its patriarchal-fraternal bias. These are issues to which I shall return in subsequent chapters. But here, now, let us simply observe that, for Akhona, in a seeming contradiction of the normative telos to which young girls and women are expected to submit, leaving the house meant exposure to the family in the name of an economized protection. That is to say, outside of the household, kinship and sexual relation were for Akhona neither separated from, nor immune to, economy. They merged with it. But in the "public domain," Akhona's family exercised an even more profound effect on her than it had in the household—where she was treated like a casual laborer or an indentured servant. And this was because, in public, she could not publicly refuse the family. In public, she was asked to perform normativity in anticipation of a public judgment (or rather a prejudgment) that remained beholden to the otherwise antiquated or inappropriate belief that a girl could not become pregnant except through her betrayal of the norms of femininity and family.

In the end, there was no place for a visibly pregnant teenager, just twelve at the time, in a small town, or at least a small neighborhood. So, Akhona went to

Johannesburg, to be cared for by two aunts, one of whom was in domestic service in Vanderbijl Park, about seventy kilometers from Carletonville. This latter aunt hosted Akhona until she gave birth, but her employers did not want a child in the servants' quarters, and so Akhona once again moved to reside with the other aunt, this time to another suburb, closer to Johannesburg. Akhona was soon thereafter introduced to prostitution. One evening, she was taken to the outskirts of a mine compound where her aunt claimed to be selling handmade clothing. And there, while waiting, she was introduced to other women who told her that they were working. When she asked what this meant, she was told that she would "see." It did not in fact mean that she would make money, as her aunt had told her, at least not in any way that gave her access to cash. Instead, she met a man who acknowledged her child (in the sense that he did not reject her for having a child) and asked her to come back the following week. When she did return, he had disappeared, but a friend of his, whom she had previously met, was there waiting.

This other man, the friend, quickly inserted himself into the role of paramour, buying her food, and even giving her a radio, which fact she noted carefully in our interview many years later. He asked her to take up residence with him. For a while, it seemed to Akhona that she had been lucky.

> When I arrived at the place I found this guy waiting for me and the baby. He asked me if I would stay with him with the baby and by that time the baby was three months old, but I agreed. I then started to live with this man and he was from [X] in the Eastern Cape. I used to go and visit my family in the township while I was staying with him and it was just nice. This guy told me that he liked me and does not have a wife at home either. He asked me to marry him and I agreed because I felt that I owed him love back; he stayed with me and my baby and showed me love. His mother came to fetch us and we went to his home in [X], I realized that he really did not have a wife at home.

The man worked on the mines, and although he was not in a supervisory role, in every sense, he was doing what the mining corporations, or at least Anglo Gold, hoped he would be doing—establishing a stable family home so that he could retain employment, while also planning on returning to his natal home when he aged out of work. Buoyed by the prospect of security and a normative family life, Akhona moved to his village in the Eastern Cape and took on the task of building a house for him and their little family. But money soon stopped coming, and Akhona was increasingly desperate. She took up beer-selling. When her father died, and she needed cash to pay for his funeral, she traveled to Johannesburg to ask her common-law husband for money, only to find that he had lost his job and that there were only 300 rand in his bank account. Angry that he had spent his entire accumulated earnings while she scrounged to build his home, she left him. Soon thereafter she was working as a prostitute near another mine on the far West Rand. She was earning 20 rand per sexual encounter (at the time the rand to dollar rate was about 2:1).

Although she sought and found temporarily stable relationships with men, Akhona was never far from prostitution after that and eventually ended up near Carletonville at a Truck Stop brothel, turning tricks in the bushes. Often, she says, men refused to pay her. As HIV/AIDS swept the country, and she learned that condoms could protect her, she found herself increasingly vulnerable to violence when she requested that men use them: "When you ask for your money, the man will tell you that he will stab you, and there we did not use any condom but just toilet paper. . . . We used the toilet paper to wipe ourselves after we had sex and throw it away, but all the dirt and diseases remained with us." This last phrase, in which Akhona lamented her having become the repository not only of semen but dirt and disease was among the bitterest moments in her narrative. It was accompanied by relative equanimity in the face of her own HIV-positive status, partly because in the years before our meeting, she had been recruited as a peer educator for an HIV/AIDS education program in the mining area. It had provided a modest but steady income, access to testing, medical information and antiretroviral medications, and a community of support.

One might expect, given the foregoing account that Akhona considered this relation with an Eastern Cape mineworker, failed though it was, to constitute an outside and alternative to her life as a sex worker. For a while, they had lived in the image of a domestic couple, building a home and planning a family, with the husband as breadwinner on the mines, sending remittances to his wife who had taken up residence with his relations. Yet, she was emphatic that, even before he stopped sending money, even when they were cohabiting near his place of work, the relationship was one of prostitution:

> I can say the first man that I slept with in prostitution is the guy from [X] because he never told me that he loved me but he just showed me his car and house and insisted that he wanted to stay with me. I told him that I had a baby who was still breastfeeding and he told me it did not matter as long as I slept with him alone. It was painful when I was sleeping with him because I used to think about how bad was what I was doing, sleeping with a man that was not the father of the baby but I had no choice as I depended on him for life.

Akhona vacillated in describing his sentiment, but in the end, she seems to have believed that the man had not loved her. This was, however, secondary, to the graver accusation of duplicity and domination through indebtedness. He had shown her neither his love nor his wealth, but its mere simulacrum, for he had merely advertised his power, and she thought it unlikely that he was the owner of the car or the shack. Moreover, she had stayed with him out of a sense of obligation: "I felt that I owed him love back" and that she "depended on him for life." Akhona continued to come back to this issue of debt, repeatedly stating that "I had to pay him back for looking after me and my baby. I thought it would be a sin to refuse to marry him after all he had done for us."

Akhona was not disappointed that she was not in a freely chosen companionate marriage uncontaminated by market forces. What made the relationship one of prostitution was that he had not given her the money he promised. What made the relationship one of prostitution was that his performance of wealth had been duplicitous. To put the matter slightly differently, what destined her to sex work rather than marriage was that the man failed to live up to his contractual commitments. He was not true to his word. By contrast, Akhona could and did speak of the young relation who had impregnated her when she was just a girl tending cattle, as her first boyfriend: "I can say my first boyfriend is the father of my child even though we were just playing to have sex." The young man had given what he had promised and had not concealed his motive. Prostitution for Akhona was thus not so much the exchange of sexual favors for monetary or material reward (that was normal and appropriate), as it was mendacity in the intimate domain. Real family was truth.

I have lingered with Akhona's tale, as I will with that of Sisipho, whose narrative follows, because it exhibits, with special and revelatory force, the patterns that I have heard and seen articulated by other women across the years. Other women's experiences before entering prostitution differ and their analyses also vary. But if one woman's story is not completely generalizable, that does not mean it is without general significance. Immanently, Akhona's narrative discloses a truth about the sexing and sexualizing of market logics in the space of industrial capitalism. Although no woman, and certainly not the prostitute, is granted the capacity to signify the universal in patriarchal discourse, sex work indeed represents the system of exploitation within capitalism. The (sex) worker is the one who is not paid properly, whose pay is a kind of theft. The (sex) worker is also one who works out of obligation and a sense of indebtedness—if only to the future. So, Akhona experienced the theft of surplus value not merely as the theft of her labor but of her body itself.[40] To be autonomous, or at least free from prostitution, would be to have the real value of her labor represented. And this value would be preserved in and as her body.

As with all manual labor, (sex) workers are dissipated, and as a result, their capacity for more labor and self-reproduction withers away. When Akhona narrates her experience of being diagnosed with HIV/AIDS in the early 1990s, she discloses the way in which she endures this dissipation not only as depletion but as disease. This diseased-ness is both like and different from that suffered in other kinds of manual labor (even the terrible dissipations of silicosis or miner's lung) for the simple reason that it is a function of the prostitute's body having become a merely mechanical thing, a pure instrument, rather than the human user of an instrument. If what the manual worker generally suffers in the course of laboring is loss of that vitality that permits him to act as the handmaid of technology, the sex worker on the edge of the mines is mortified precisely to the extent that she is reduced to her bodiliness; her body becomes thing. Recall Benjamin's reading of fetishism as that form of sexual relation in which the boundary between the organic and inorganic dissolves.[41] Hortense Spiller's analysis permits us to understand this development as a specific condition of racialized femininity.[42] More than a ribald allusion allows us to understand the prostitute who works at the margin of a *skomplaas*, or between the *skomplaas* and the township, as a manual laborer. For even if it is supposed to serve as the space for preserving black family existence, the discourse of the *skomplaas* effectively makes the woman the instrument of the mineworker's (self-)satisfaction. Far from the limelight and the magnificent spectacle of waltzing cyanide vats, the sexual fetishism that could attire itself in "richest brocade" and "shimmering white satin" becomes for some women a horrible reduction to mechanical acts beneath the eternally unthinking headgear of a mine.[43]

Pattern, not Rhythm

It seems important to witness the actual circumstances in which this reduction occurs, lest the temptation and the longing to discover a woman's agency in her experience of marginalization lead one to bypass the wretchedness that it entails. The bushes near Truck Stops are invariably soiled. In them, the earth itself is dirtied. Clumps of tissue paper and plastic bags, beer bottles, tattered clothes and the occasional remnant of broken jewelry—a watch strap, a single earring—lie about. In some places, the grasses are flattened; in some, a branch has been bent or a blanket hung to afford something like privacy.

Among the sex workers with whom I have spoken, there are both repeated kinds of experience and recurrent tropes in which they arrived at such places. Almost invariably, the stories commence with a pregnancy, which is often the result of a betrayed expectation from someone who was otherwise supposed to protect the girl-woman or at least to observe a prohibition on sexual relations with her. In this sense, although not all of these first pregnancies are incestuous in the narrow sense—notwithstanding the fact that many are—they are almost all born of a transgressed prohibition that should have rendered the girl-woman off-limits. Typically, the girl-woman was young, barely entering sexual maturity, when she became pregnant, often with no prior knowledge of its possibility. Nonetheless, in many conservative accounts (from church sermons to gossip), the explanation of prostitution redoubles the woman's condition. Taken, she is often said to have given herself too easily. Too young to have known what was about to befall her, she is said to have acted or appeared older than her years. Having been lured by the promise of a radio, a car, or a cellphone, she is forced to sell sex to acquire commodities, which of course includes food, although these are coded as the objects of excessive commodity desires—of wanting things beyond her means.

One of Akhona's coworkers at the HIV/AIDS program had similarly become pregnant as a child. She was a little older than Akhona, having delivered her son in the "year of 1976 when there were some riots in the country," she said. I shall call her Sisipho. The birth occurred shortly after she had been sent from her grandmother's home in Queenstown to Port Elizabeth, where her parents resided. She was in Standard Five, about twelve years old at the time. Her conservative Xhosa parents had demanded payment for the "damage [the man] made to me as a girl," but they had not insisted that the man marry her. In another time, the money would have been *lobolo*, and she would have entered his household: but in the 1970s, however, Sisipho's parents had simply taken the money and then demanded she end her studies, it being too shameful and practically impossible to be both a student and a mother. Sisipho's parents separated in the aftermath of this payment, and her father died in a car accident shortly thereafter, in 1980, after which time she shuttled between her paternal grandmother's home and her mother's. After the older woman died in 1981, Sisipho says, she lived for some years with her child at the home of her stepmother and a stepsister. The stepmother was suspicious that her husband was having sexual relations with the stepsister and eventually, elders were asked to intervene. As a result, the stepsister was married off and sent elsewhere, and Sisipho was left alone. The elders, believing her child to be ill-cared for, removed her boy from her supervision. She, by then in her late teens, was left to fend for herself. With neither education, nor any marketable skills, there were few options. Friends introduced her to the Truck Stop, where, she says, she initially earned 50 rand a night. Once again, incest or a transgression of the laws of the family precipitates a new exposure; Sisipho was not herself the victim of incest, but she suffered its consequences.

In her account of what happened next, Sisipho's narrative elongates and accumulates detail. It becomes dense with place-names, distances traveled, and locations in kinship networks, each farther from home than the other. She describes a journey to Johannesburg, arriving at night in a crowded, artificially illuminated world, where throngs of people obscure every sign with which she might have oriented herself.

> We arrived in Johannesburg in the middle of the night and we were not familiar with the place at all. We passed a place that had many people as we were looking for the famous Park Station. We asked another security guard where Park Station was and he told it is the place that we passed with many people in it.

So, we went back to Park Station and sat on chairs for the night until the next morning. As we were sitting on the chairs, we were approached by two guys who were drunk and you could see that they were coming from the night clubs for the whole night.

More than twenty years later, Sisipho could still recall that the men bought her and her friend meat pies and that she had joked to her friend that the pastries were only "bread and horse meat"—and that people in Johannesburg considered that a good meal. In fact, she could recall almost every address, the amount of money promised and delivered by every man she met, the taxi fares from place to place on the meandering journey that took her from small town to small town and township on the Rand. At each stop on this recollected journey, she met a man with whom she took up an apparently domestic relation. In each of these relations, a moment came when the man, her source of money, lost his job. After each of these occasions, she moved on, sometimes finding temporary shelter with an older woman, only to be trafficked by the woman when she did not bring money in. Some of the relationships were more congenial than others, some entailed severe physical abuse—beatings that left her unconscious or requiring stitches. She drank heavily. But she also "fell in love" with one of the men, who installed her in a shack on a farm near the mines where he worked in Stilfontein. He paid the rent although, in the early stages of their cohabitation, she worked on the dairy farm where the shack was located and received payment in milk.

As already discussed (chapter 8), such payment in kind was common on farms, where a persistent feudality keeps many women in near bondage to this day. But in a little theater of normative family life, he asked her to stop even this unwaged work and gave her an allowance. Thus, when he lost his job at the mine, she no longer had access to the milk, which she had previously sold for cash. Beer brewing became a temporary source of income, but eventually, it was not enough. Sisipho returned to her natal home briefly but could no longer relate to the world of her parents and finally felt that she had no option but to go back to the Truck Stop where, now older, scarred, and ravaged by sexually transmitted disease, she earned 20 rand a night.

Whatever its limits, it was on the farm that Sisipho felt, for a brief period, to have been loved and to have had relative plenty. It had all started when her lover rescued her from a beating by his coworker, who was at the time Sisipho's sometimes "boyfriend." This new savior had given Sisipho money to go to the hospital for stitches, but she had used it to purchase "a plate, two glasses and a pot." Perhaps he was moved by sympathy for this neediness; perhaps, he saw it as an opening. Later, he bought her other things. He was the one through whom she got access to the market, to the world of desire, and to its satisfaction. She recalled with great fondness the "day he told me that we must go town to buy groceries and other stuff that I needed and we did. He bought all those things and he was also paying my rent, an amount of R150 a month in this farm." What thrilled her most was that these things and this satisfaction did not require her to work. After that, Sisipho "stopped working and stayed with him full time."

The weak glow of recalled happiness that emanated from Sisipho's otherwise blunt narrative was perhaps little more than the dim reflection of that middle-class dream depicted in the real estate advertisements for Carletonville discussed in chapter 9. Indeed, Sisipho's story not only gains in tragic effect by contrast with that advertisement and the expectations and aspirations it encoded, but is spitefully mocked by it. This is because Sisipho was not only unable to access that dream image but also because she wanted to. It possessed her; the spirits of a few glasses, a plate, a pot, and a well-stocked fridge haunted her as surely as any ghosts. And there is more than a distant affinity between her dream of a modest place setting, conjured by lack, and the enchanting image of blue glass beneath the earth that animated the old man and one-time mine hospital chef's narrative about sinkholes (chapter 7). Sisipho's unadorned wish lends to his reverie an additional and mythic beauty, which, in its turn, casts her modest aspirations in the harsh and demetaphorizing shadow of need.

Unlike Akhona, who wanted only a correspondence between the promise and the act, Sisipho wanted a life without labor. Yet, she, like Akhona, did not think that the economization of intimacy was in any way antithetical to "love," a word she used frequently. To the contrary, the most joyful love of her life, the only intimacy she recalled without revulsion, was one in which the exchange took place as promised. There was perfect equivalence. Sisipho described her lover as a kind and generous presence, who worried over her physical safety and wanted to ensure her comfort. If we can believe Sisipho's account of her lover's deeds, we can conclude that he too wanted her to leave work behind, but whatever motive informed this request, it had generated a profound dependency and an incapacity to survive his lost employment. He had become the sole medium of relation between their domestic world and the world of the market. Not only his money but also he, himself, had become this medium, and he thus partook of the power that accrues to every medium that opens without limit to the universe of commodities. It is no exaggeration to say that he had become her golden boy. In the little circle of their affection, he became even more than this: he became the origin of her money. And thus, as soon as his money disappeared, the relationship ended. Without ceremony and without hesitation.

Good as Gold

Bearing in mind the aesthetic implications of the gesture, we might say that Sisipho was a realist. She didn't expect more than she was likely to receive, and she was not sentimental about the need to sever a relationship when it no longer provided the means to survive. Or at least this sentiment did not dissuade her from the practical decisions that she believed were necessary under the circumstances. Realism in this sense (and in art historical discourse) is not a matter of inner feeling but of appearances. It is an attitude and an aesthetic of apparent correspondence. When there was money, both the men and women in Sisipho's life granted the other the status of perfect complement and means of becoming for others what they lacked and wanted to be. But in both cases (Akhona's and Sisipho's), the men are for the women the source of value—whether it takes the form of cash, commodities, or care. I am shifting idioms now, by introducing a concept of value that traverses the monetized and nonmonetized economy. *Imali*, often translated as money, is in fact broader: in all of the language of this region, it refers to all forms of appearance of value. In the gold-mining world, focalized from the point of view of the Truck Stop brothel, it is indissociable from gold and appropriated by and for masculinity, to which its return is figured as a destiny. Only masculinity can spend it without dissipating itself. But these men are, for the women, also its source—being the ones with relative capacities to earn cash. A different economy operates in other domains, where, for example, domestic labor for whites or middle-class blacks provides women with access to wages. Of course, being a wage-earner does not make one the origin of money, except for others of lesser means.

Often domestic laborers are among the most stridently moralizing critics of sex work. But they are not alone, and the exclusion of sex work from the more general and representative category of labor is widespread in much critical and scholarly literature. In the long history of analyzing labor in South Africa, the gold mineworker has served as the iconic representative of "the worker," and in this respect, even the union-based anti-Apartheid movement is burdened by its complicity with the system that could and did conceive of women as the necessary supplement through whom men could become those who "made money." They were, in this sense, the most instrumentalizable of human beings. It is here that the alliance between gold and the phallus described by Jean-Joseph Goux becomes visible. An axis linking masculinity and true value traverses the whole social field in the gold industry. In other words, heteronormativity and patriarchy grant to masculinity the appearance of what is valued and the basis for both accessing and signifying universality. This is why the women can and do leave as soon as there is no money—not because the women did or did not like or love the men, but because their intimacy was determined by the equivalence between men and money.

People almost never say as much, of course. The logic of this system is mediated, sometimes repressed, displaced or concealed, and disseminated through aesthetic and religious forms and codes. Even Keynes's argument against the return of the gold standard, and what he believed was the conservatism accompanying it, was inscribed in an allegorical mode—as Goux notes. Initially "stationed in heaven with his consort silver, as Sun and Moon," the metal descended

to the earth through autocracy and then to constitutional monarchy—a signifier
of power in each era, but increasingly dissipated through time, wrote Keynes.[44]
He mocked the fact that gold had been cloaked in a "garment of respectability
as densely respectable as was ever met with, even in the realms of sex or religion."[45] Goux, writing in the moment of Bretton Woods' collapse, observed
the "echo, virtually a precise mirror image, in psychoanalytic discourse" of the
"economist's metaphor." And he insisted that this is "more than [an] accidental
or contingent resemblance." Rather, it is

> the existence of a signifier intended to define all effects produced by the signi-
> fied and to prevent arbitrary, floating, slipping signs of the linguistic chain from
> losing their convertibility in the game of substitutions, from being loosed from
> the fixed points that anchor them in a primordial soil—this existence globally
> indicated by an axis linking phallus and father (whence "sex" and "religion")—
> fulfills within the specific spheres of the signifier and the subjective position a
> symbolic function that is homologous to the function, in economic exchange,
> of fiduciary currency, of standard and reserves of gold, which provide a *social
> guarantee* of value and limit runaway inflation.[46]

The "figurative standard," as Goux called it, corresponded with the Bretton
Woods order, but in 1973, as international currency speculation began to accelerate, he claimed that such a logic was becoming anachronistic.

In lieu of gold, Goux used the metaphor of soil for an inconvertible truth-
value. We cannot help but notice that every time the economist and the theorist
refer to the desire for a still point in the symbolic world, when they seek refuge from the centuries of moralizing metaphors with which money has been
represented, they speak not only, and sometimes not at all, of gold but of a
material grounding in the earth. So, it is interesting to note that for Keynes
the soil was the metaphor for the reserve bank cache, and the return to the soil
was an image of hoarding: "The little household gods, who dwelt in purses and
stockings and tin boxes, have been swallowed by a single golden image in each
country, which lives underground and is not seen. Gold is out of sight—gone
back again into the soil."[47] These metaphors share a sense that the real and the
true exceeds sense perception and this is why the imagination works by analogy with sense perception. If the bearer of the standard (gold or the phallus) is
not visible, it can only exercise its effects if people believe in it. This is why the
gold standard and its derivatives, and the forms of international monetary relations that it enables are, above all, matters of faith. What kind of faith is this?
It is faith born of debt, of a radical indebtedness. This is why Walter Benjamin
referred to capitalism as a religion.

Benjamin did not understand the relation between religion and capitalism in
the manner that Max Weber did.[48] It was not for him the outgrowth of a specific

Protestant doctrine and its severance of worldly and unworldly concerns based on the notion of divine inaccessibility. Rather, he considered it to be a cultic religion. This cultic religion was, in his analysis, the first in the world's history (although he had only Europe in mind) to offer "guilt, not atonement." Its relentlessness was thus coupled with a sense of inescapability: "Capitalism is the celebration of a cult *sans rêve et sans merci* [without dream or mercy]. There are no 'weekdays.' There is no day that is not a feast day, in the terrible sense that all its sacred pomp is unfolded before us; each day commands the utter fealty of each worshiper." In this sense, Benjamin would have treated the little spectacles of expenditure that Bataille analogized to archaic festivals as having been surpassed by capitalism and incorporated into its inner core as entertainments. Whether or not one believes that the exultation and dissipation of post-work visits to brewers and brothels are fully within or partially escape the capitalist order—a question made much more complex in a colonial situation in which noncapitalist forms of production are used in their difference—Benjamin's conclusion is powerfully relevant for South Africa and the order of debt more generally. He adds, "the cult makes guilt pervasive."[49]

In German, the word for guilt is the same as that for debt: *Schuld*. Afrikaans echoes this root and extends its etymological tree in the term *skuld*. In both languages, and one might say, in both traditions of national capital formation, capitalism works by disseminating guilt, which is also, and at the same time, debt. In this enigmatic and incomplete fragment, Benjamin emphasizes that capitalism has no higher purpose than itself, no "transcendental ideal," and in this respect, it resembles what he terms *heathen religions*.[50] Within such forms of cultic religion, nonbelievers are members of the community regardless of their inner commitments and secret beliefs. With or without real belief, with or without a job, they are inside capitalism. Not that it has no outside but that this outside is within, or at least is usable (in the sense that the agrarian bantustans could, for a while, be transformed into the scene for reproducing industrial labor in the migrant system).

Many scholars have written at length about how poll and hut taxes, evictions, and economically coerced migration "converted" people to colonial capitalism.[51] But conversion through such "originary accumulation" is not an event, and it must be reproduced in every generation as a subjective orientation in all individuals—who are not "born" as capitalists and do not inherit the orientation of being for capitalism.[52] In the 1970s, everything from home and car ownership to consumer commodities available on layaway and installment plans became a vehicle for inducting people into debt. But black prostitutes bore debt and represented the state of indebtedness in especially acute ways, and this is because black women not in domestic service or marriage had relatively limited means to access cash directly as wages before the post-Apartheid era of social grants. Payment in kind defined their worlds. They had to convert milk, or sand, or their sexually embodied time into money. Recall that what first drove the young women described in this chapter into prostitution (or into unwanted relations that they thought to be the mere counterfeit of love) was their being in debt. This debt exceeded the question of owing money. Rather, the debt that afflicted these women was correlated with their identity as women. They felt they owed the men something, and the men wanted them to be obligated in that way.

Benjamin treated the prostitute primarily as a figure in whom the specific dimension of early twentieth-century industrial capitalism could be discerned: "In the form taken by prostitution in the big cities, the woman appears not only as commodity but, in a precise sense, as mass-produced article. This is indicated by the masking of individual expression in favor of a professional appearance, such as makeup provides."[53] It is not merely that she is treated like a mass-produced article, but "insofar as this represents the utmost extension attainable by the sphere of the commodity, the prostitute may be considered from early on, a precursor of commodity capitalism."[54] The revolutionary potential that he sought in this figure (not to be confused with the women who work in this way) consisted in its severance of sexuality from reproductivity. Neither are the women with whom I have spoken akin to street-walkers of the metropoles, nor are they like fashion mannequins. Prostitution was in no way severed from reproductivity for them—only men experienced prostitution this way; they were not entailed by the pregnancies they induced. Nonetheless, Benjamin's intuition that prostitution reveals something about the organization and value structures of capitalism is relevant. But that truth becomes available only when one reads the particular figure and function of prostitution at a time of epistemic and political dislocation (i.e., the end of the gold standard, and the movement to stabilize the black male workforce as part of an effort to reground values) in relation to the other figures through whom these processes were also registered. On the most destitute peripheries of mining towns and in the Truck Stop brothels beside the roadways linking them, fashion plays a relatively insignificant role. The women's sexual services are the commodity on sale; there is little need to dissimulate that role in the commodities with which the women adorn themselves. But in the upper echelons of popular culture, that built on gold's shifting ground, one discerns the integuments that bind the roadside brothel to the shopping mall—just as one could discern the arcade in the underground, as I attempted to argue in chapter 1. In concluding this chapter, I want to now turn to that sphere, for it is there that we can see the relationship between gold's demonetization and the problematization of value across the entire social field. It is there that we see how the price was paid as the effort to contain these forces led to a reinvestment of masculinity, the proliferation of debt, and, simultaneously, the opening of liberatory possibilities whose endgame was not yet visible.

After the One, the Many—and One, Once More

Another consequences of demonetization (beyond the raising of wages for black mineworkers, and the concomitant availability of money for expenditure on entertainment and prostitution) was that, in the 1970s, the major destiny of South African gold shifted from the realm of the true reserve to that of the decorative object, from the national bank to the body of a woman. This is reflected in the iconography of cultic capitalism in South Africa that, in the 1960s, had been the tinselly image of a suited couple standing at the gate of a Carletonville bungalow. It ceded to the glamorous image of a white woman wearing J. Friedman's prize-winning necklace, choker, and bracelet "in 18 carat gold" and "set with 13 diamonds" (figure 10.1). That image appeared inside the cover of the 1972 *Annual Report* of the Chamber of Mines, completely fusing the figure of woman with the mannequin (as Benjamin said was revealed in prostitution). Given the caption, the reader may be forgiven for wondering whether it is the necklace or the woman who serves as "prize" for the design. The previous year's report had featured a less alluring woman taking notes while leaning on a stack of gold bars (figure 10.2). Both she and the gold are overseen by a white-coated inspector in the image, which is captioned "Refined gold bars in the vaults of the South African Reserve Bank in Pretoria." The difference between the two images provides as neat a depiction of the transformed status of gold and the displaced locus of value as any two images possibly could. And the woman is key to both.

The displacement of gold from store of wealth to fashion, from savings to expenditure, and from referent to signifier, might summon the art historical theories that have tracked the shift from modernism to postmodernism and then linked them to gold's displacement as a transcendental signifier. And much modernist theory discerns a homology, and sometimes a relationship of direct dependency, between the changing status of gold in the economic domain and the emergence of modernist and then postmodernist aesthetics in Euro-U.S. contexts.[55] Somewhat different developments took place in South Africa (for reasons that lie beyond the scope of this book), but if, in the realm of high culture in the Global North, there was a displacement of illusionism and representationalism in general, there was also a set of counterdevelopments in popular culture everywhere. These often entailed efforts to restore some kind of naturalism—even if only the fragmented forms described by Fredric Jameson—and this typically included efforts to secure or reestablish normative forms of nucleated family life. Given that television was not established in South Africa until 1976, and given that literary texts were not widely read, it was in the domains of cinema (and radio) that the aesthetic mediation of economic transformations mainly took place.[56] For this reason, I close this chapter with a brief

10.1 Frontispeice of the Chamber of Mines *Annual Report*, 1972.

consideration of two landmark films that entered South African consciousness in the moment of gold's transformation. For in them, we see how the desire for a restabilized social world in the color-coded image of bourgeois domesticity was disseminated: not through the kitchen table romance of love and marriage, but through the dream of piracy and prostitution as the absolute limit of economy. In that same moment as black male workers' wages were about to rise, Blaxploitation film and the image of black leisure and heterosexually contained

10.2 Frontispiece of the Chamber of Mines *Annual Report*, 1971.

power, signified in the image of fashionable women in need of rescue, was recoded as an advertisement for racial segregation.

In May 1971, three months before Nixon's announcement, but well into the era of SDRs, the Hollywood film *A Man Called Sledge* made its way to South Africa to play in cinemas, or as they were called in South Africa, bioscopes. It received an extraordinary review by Peter Wilhelm in the pages of the *Rand Daily Mail*. Calling it "emotionally derivative and atrocious," Wilhelm nonetheless lauded it as "near to being the finest Western of the year—a strange, violent tragedy with the moods and orchestrated movements of a troubled dream." The review was addressed to an audience that had come to think of the West Rand as the analog of the Wild West and, according to that tropology, as a terrain on which the values of violent individualism and speculative adventurism played out. We already encountered this tropology in the official historiography of the Chamber of Mines, where it was also infused with the added dimension of scientific virtue. In *A Man Called Sledge*, official discourse and popular imagination converge and are distilled in the tagline, "Gold was their aim."

For Wilhelm, this "nearly best" Western was significant because it was also an inversion of the genre and its moral cosmology: "Perhaps the Western, grown cripplingly conscious of its stereotypes, can survive only in films such as this: films in which the very characters once righteously gunned down by Gary Cooper, recognizable by their eroded excuses for faces and their pig-like wants edgily dominate the screen and insist against all possible odds on being the heroes."[57] Wilhelm attributed to the film's writer and director, Vic Morrow, the revelation of what might be termed an ecologically oriented postcolonial unconscious *avant la lettre*: "At times, the dark theme emerges clearly: that American society itself, and by implication all societies that face across the Atlantic and see what they will become tomorrow, are themselves based on rape and subjugation." But, writing in a late-Enlightenment prose suffused by the rhetoric of darkness and light, he could only grasp this rape and subjugation as a metaphor: "The despoliation of the wilderness is the despoliation of man." The indigenous peoples and inhabitants of those vanquished lands vanish in this blank space of the frontier.

The South African censors deleted the sexually explicit material as well as the rape scene of the film, while declaring it unfit for anyone under the age of eighteen. Like much narrative cinema, the violation or feared violation of a woman orients the narrative and incites competition in the form of vengeance among men. Beyond this inaugural and structuring principle, the film's convoluted plot is composed of a series of episodes that are linked by association and metonymy. There is little by way of metaphoric logic to suture these elements of the syntagmatic chain together or to subsume the metonymic signifiers in a single story. The film starts with the hero's visit to his prostitute-girlfriend—the first of the collapsed binaries in the sex-gender system. From there, murder and the desire for vengeance leads the plot, only to be diverted when Sledge (played by James Garner) learns of a shipment of gold that he decides to waylay when the entourage bearing it stops, as it always does, at a prison. Gathering his old gang, he liberates the prisoners of the jail not out of commitment to their liberty but to foment a riot that will deter the police. Through a series of subterfuges, Sledge and his men obtain the gold, kill the cops, and get away, but not without succumbing to their own greed. When deceit and counterfeiting confuse the political order and economy of the gang, with Sledge claiming more than his share, his former allies kidnap his girlfriend, Ria (played by

Laura Antonelli). For her devotion to Sledge, a devotion that belies her status as a prostitute, Ria pays the ultimate price, but not before the gold is once again hidden and not before Sledge has killed everyone, including the only person who could know where the cache is concealed. Ria's final assertion, that they didn't need gold to be happy (in other words, love is beyond economy and can't be confused with prostitution), has the appearance of a moral lesson but any concept of happiness is entirely annihilated by her death. In victory, Sledge has lost everything—although this destitution can be lamented only at the cost of assigning the woman, or at least her affection and fidelity to a romantic value beyond all economy, to the status of his property.

Wilhelm was not impressed with Antonelli's acting but he did not blame her for not being able to kindle a heteronormative fire in the film's otherwise bleak milieu: "the dimness of her performance seems inevitable in a film of this sort where the tenderest emotions are between men huddling together in bars or gun battles." It is not incidental that the most pungent idiom available to describe this milieu was, for Wilhelm, that of "blackness." He thus concludes with reference to an "encroachment of blackness, a gradual thickening of the air as disaster comes" and "a movement from physical to spiritual coldness." Blackness is not always a racial code, but the extent to which this idiom was indeed implicated in the racial logics of Apartheid depends on the degree to which blackness and massness, as signifiers of spiritual desolation, were counterposed to those of a sovereign (white) masculinity. The value of such sovereign masculinism was not only fetishized in the Western, whether in its heroic or antiheroic form. It also subtended the ostensibly black culturalist cinema that would be produced by and for the Apartheid state—often with the gold mines as backdrop. The first and exemplary instance of such cinema can be found in the film *Joe Bullet*, which was made just as *A Man Called Sledge*" was arriving in South Africa, although it would not be released until 1973, when, after a brief run in Soweto, it was banned in its entirety.

From a film historical perspective, *Joe Bullet* is better remembered for having been banned than seen. Influenced by Blaxploitation cinema and especially *Shaft*, it features a black hero (Bullet, played by Ken Gampu) who is part outcast, part detective, part protection agent, part savior. The lyrics of the theme song introduce him as the "man who fights evil" and "the man who money can't buy." From the start then, he is beyond economy: the logical inverse of the prostitute. And this extends so far that he refuses the entreaties of the female protagonist and takes no sexual reward for saving her. As the film opens, a soccer team is being brutalized in anticipation of a cup game on which a local gangster (Rocky, played by Joe Lopez) has bet heavily. First, the club trainer is killed, then the star players are kidnapped as part of a plan to fix the match. Joe Bullet, the taciturn hero, is brought in to both save the team and coach it to success. He is a martial artist and a marksman with a mysterious past, a stoic demeanor, and the aura of incorruptibility. Part way through the film, he becomes the love object for a woman (played by the singer, Abigail Kubeka) who is both the daughter of the club president and the lover of another man, and who will also be kidnapped by Rocky. Her name, Beauty, is her identity, and the deliriously extended party scene in which she appears, singing and eyeing the hero, establishes her as the one object whom all the male characters desire—one way or another.

As in *Sledge*, the kidnapped woman is the medium and terrain of the fraternal conflict. And as in *Sledge*, she is sidelined in the process. Bullet and Rocky end up fighting to the death on the decrepit headgear of a defunct mine—the actual mine that served as location for the film was near the mine described at the beginning of this book. Despite its aesthetic and technical tawdriness, the film is remarkable for the absolute absence of whiteness and its silence about the social-historical situation of Apartheid in which it was made. This does not mean that the film does not refer to its milieu, and Beauty, the beautiful singer and actress, is a kind of hinge figure that permits the diegesis to point outward, toward the world, through the literality of her name, which refers to both the character and the actress. In the opening sequence, however, this reference is at once oblique and ambivalent. At a practice session in a Soweto stadium (which would become famous for political rallies within the decade), one of the characters remarks that the team needs to pass more: "It seems to me that they ought to play more like a team. They are inclined to be all individuals." The critical reader may wish to discern a solicitation of collectivist sentiment, and given the casting of the film, one might, in retrospect, initially imagine that this utterance is the opening salvo in a work of guerilla cinema. The underworld is awash in guns, and even bulldozers are used as weapons. A little later, we hear the gangster refer to the possibility of killing those who will not be bribed and noting that it would be "simple." Later, he will demand the murder of the club president. Again, the audience member whose disposition leads her to receive the film in the spirit of insurrection may read this as incitement to insurgency, the word *president* permitting recall of the assassination of Hendrik Verwoerd in 1966 and suggesting the possibility of its repetition.[58] But the initial gestures turn out to be lures more than invitations. And just as counterinsurgency often works by soliciting the very insurgency that it will then use to justify its counteraction, so *Joe Bullet* was intended not to instill a collectivist fantasy nor to induce thought of assassination and the overthrow of a regime, but rather to make Apartheid the scene of a totally naturalized separateness. This is the function of the all-black world in the film. *Joe Bullet* was in this sense oriented toward the colonization of the unconscious—albeit one that could not guarantee its own itinerary in the minds of its audience members, for which reason, perhaps, it had to be banned.

Written and produced by Tonie van der Merwe, a filmmaker who helped create the Apartheid cinema for black audiences, the purpose of which was to mitigate political agitation, *Joe Bullet* was an unusual error of judgment on his part. But its banning did little to blunt the producer's access to further resources or slow his output. He made some four hundred films for black audiences during the Apartheid era. Nonetheless, biographical criticism does not suffice as a basis for grasping the film's complicity with Apartheid, nor its representative status—a status that was only seemingly contradicted by the fact that almost no one in South Africa saw the film.[59]

Let us then consider that in *Joe Bullet* everything that has enabled and enforced the mineral economy throughout its long history is ambivalent and available for use by either "good" or "bad" characters—from the armaments to the technology and even the space of the mines. According to the narratological structure so well analyzed by Teresa de Lauretis, the goodness of the hero is demonstrated when he rescues his girlfriend (the enabling obstacle) from the rapacious gangster.[60] This heroism is further intensified but also homo-socialized when Joe Bullet liberates the kidnapped players. He sends them to win the game fairly while he pursues the deranged criminal mastermind, a one-time zoologist with a specialty in herpetology. Ludicrous and artless, the film lurches from one poorly integrated scene to another. Shuttled from one close-up to another, with little or poor match-cut editing, the viewer often struggles to understand the film's "big picture."[61] It is the simulated terror of the fight high above the ruined quarters of the mine, with bits and pieces of untended machinery offering themselves as weapons to hand (the gangster's ready-made), that finally locates the film in the political space of 1971 and grants it the status of cipher for the time and omen of the future. For, the gold mine of this film is dead, already, in 1971. And this morbid state, at a time when the price of gold is about to soar, is the uncannily premature emblem in a future allegory of the industry. The decrepit mine's headgear is the death's head of allegory. It is as though the world that will temporarily be inflated by gold sales in the aftermath of the U.S. decoupling of gold and the dollar is reduced to its destiny and thus already a corpse.

That such mines can be called dead bespeaks the transposition of the organic and the inorganic that industrial capitalism always entails and that Benjamin thought was both predicted and captured in the figure of the prostitute. Here it designates a symbolic order that is both obsolete and unredeemed. No afterlife has yet emerged. Whiteness has been displaced, but a politicized black or nonracial collectivism has not yet taken root—or at least it has not become effectual. If the film retains the old moral codes of the Western, in which a masculinist individualism is aligned with natural law, it is no longer grounded in any particular content. And it does not pretend to be descendent, like gold, of a divine origin. Neither transcendent nor immanent, it is an eminently base substitute for that abandoned divinity. The gangster wants money (not gold), escape (not freedom), and sexual satisfaction dissimulated as recognition by the woman he has captured and whom he threatens to rape. As he announces his plan to flee the country for a destination where he'll be free and rich, with "a beautiful girl to keep me company," Rocky's speech transforms Beauty's name into a mere adjective, a signifier detached from the singularity with whom the word had been linked only moments before. In this respect, and despite the awful primitivism that emphasizes Rocky's physical repulsiveness, he is a perfectly modern character in a perfectly modernist mode. Even his affinity for snakes, which might have implied duplicity in a Christian allegorical form, is here a contingent instrumentality born of his scientific training.[62] The mamba's poison is the weapon of Rocky's power/knowledge. The snake is no more and no less organic than the gun, which is no more nor less inorganic than the phallus that "goes off" automatically. Thus, natural law gives way to second nature, as gold is abandoned for money and revolution is surrendered to individual heroism—all on the basis of the woman's simultaneous fetishization and exclusion. This is a black heroism in the image of the white heroism of the old Western, now anachronistic, and of its successor, the revenge film. Such heroism is anchored not in moral law but in the law that binds heroism to gangsterism through the economization of justice. In this world, payback is everything. And the restoration of justice is reduced to a game on which wagers can still be cast, but fairly. The joy of the audience stands in lieu of the satisfaction of the tribunal. Such was Apartheid cinema on the eve of the world-transforming development of gold's displacement as the vehicle of international monetary relation, thus marking the beginning of the real conflict between an increasingly coercive state and increasingly militant opposition.

If I linger on these simultaneous but otherwise unsynchronized films, it is to draw out the ways in which the crisis of value for which the U.S. severance of the dollar provided the globally circulating signifier was linked, in various narrative forms, to other crises of values, including those that organized the sex-gender system and, by extension, the racialized and increasingly ethnicized order in South Africa. The narration of this crisis is of course not the crisis itself. And I am not positing one (the symbolic) as prior to or causally related to the other (the sociopolitical and material), any more than I am reading it as a mere reflection. I am attempting to trace the convergences, the homologies, and the discontinuities in a history that was understood from the dominant position as a loss of grounding and from the still-emergent position as a task of grounding or regrounding a different order. The labor of "stabilization" can be read, in this context, as an effort to appropriate an emergent and oppositional possibility and to annul it in the form of a mere alternative—which, in South Africa, is inseparable from the very idea of separate development.[63] That story remains now to be told. In part, as intimated, it is the story of the political underground in its movement between townships. But just as the *skomplaas* and the Truck Stop persist as both actual places and signifiers of the limit that the sex-gender system continues to rely on, so too do the logics analyzed in both the narratives of individual women and the cinema from which they were banished, except as instigating objects, persist in the new normality whose historicization remains for the future.

CHAPTER 11

―――

CATALYTIC CONVERSIONS

Becoming Organized

The free market system and the efficient functioning of the labour market (as well as the market for consumer goods and services) in such a system depend on free responsible and rational decision-making by economic subjects. For this a certain basic level of literacy (also called functional literacy) is an absolute prerequisite. Literacy of this kind means that a person's ability to read, write, speak, listen, calculate, bargain and spend must be such that he is able to handle normal, everyday transactions and situations with ease.

—Riekert Commission, *Commission of Inquiry Into Legislation Affecting the Utilisation of Manpower*

Go nineteen seventy-six
We need you no more
. . .
You were not revolutionary
Enough
We do not boast about you
Year of fire, year of ash.

—Oupa Thando Mthimkulu, "Nineteen Seventy-Six"

I t's 2008. A group of school-age boys greets me as I pull up in front of the decaying cement wall on an unpaved road in Khutsong. Behind it, the yard, with its garden of red soil, is neatly swept. Lace curtains hang in the windows of the cinder-block house. I open the trunk of the car to remove the groceries bought at the local OK Bazaar. This is how most of the interviews in what I have come to call the Khutsong oral history project end—with food. The children in the street hope for an orange or a piece of fruit when I arrive: a "piece of fresh," as they say. The boys swagger, pull up a t-shirt, stick out a tongue, laugh, and tease. And then they commence, in unison, to "toyi-toyi," and ask me if I know "the dance." Yes, I say. Do they, I ask, know what it means to "toyi-toyi"? "Struggle. It's how you Struggle." They run away, laughter trailing. Songezile Madikida, my research associate also chuckles, but somewhat sarcastically, and tells me that they don't know what "The Struggle" was. They are post-Apartheid kids.

Something had happened. The event that did not occur in 1964 had come to pass. Its coming to pass was marked in the ghost dances of national holidays and in the ritual speech about "The Struggle" that accompanied them. And if, as Michael Cawood Green reminds us, the "post" in the term "post-Apartheid" marks the persistence and even the haunting of the present by that prior regime, the hyphen also marks a problematic historical relation: of an afterward that is not entirely after what came before. Reading the surface of this formula, the hyphen can be analogized with another hinge—this one between the student movement and the labor movement, which together form the core of, but do not exhaust, "The Struggle."

The boys' dance took place on the eve of National Youth Day, instituted to recall the events of the Soweto uprising in 1976. It was the loping, marching, and lunging, strangely energizing dance in which the memories of generations and the concept of generation itself seem encoded as pure gesture. As Fredric Jameson says, "generationality" is a specific experience of the present," but one that arises in the movement between subjective and collective experience.[1] The ritualization of 1976 seeks, in the name of the nation, to renew a past sensation of the present as one of ecstatic collective being recovered from its effacement and the blockage of black collectivity. This ecstasy of the present, of presence, is not unrelated to the "magic" of nationalism that can "turn chance into destiny," as Benedict Anderson writes.[2] Perhaps all nationalism feeds on this power of generation, while also containing it in the conservationist discourse of inheritance, but it seems to do so with special force in South Africa through the twinned legends of 1976 and the work of the Youth Leagues of the African National Congress (ANC) and the Communist Parties. Many of the nation's leaders have come through those leagues, and many have established their political credibility in the name of a youthful critique of their own party's older generation. The Struggle is also the name of a contradiction, in which two different representational ambitions are in tension. One of these is that staged in the films with which chapter 10 concluded; it is the heroic individual as the bearer of ethico-political and historical purpose. The other is that of the collective emerging from within an otherwise heterogeneous social field that is organized on the principle and through the aesthetic of separation—a principle that, as we have seen, is at once technological and ideological.

What happened? To begin to answer that question—for it cannot be answered in any final sense (the elections of 2024 being evidence of this fact)—means recognizing the tensions and relations between the two distinct axes of oppositional politics in South Africa, namely (racialized) generation and class. These axes were incarnated as, and represented by, youths and especially students, on one hand, and organized labor on the other. It has often been said that the Soweto uprisings of 1976 inspired a transformation of the political practice of opposition across South Africa. It is also often claimed that the formation of the National Union of Mineworkers in 1982 marked the transformation of labor into a political force that was to be central in the overthrow of Apartheid. The relationship between them is then assumed to be one of sequential development and mutual encouragement. But historical actuality is more complicated and in fact, there were often tensions between student activists and mineworkers. Moreover, as we shall see, strike activity on the gold mines preceded the Soweto uprisings. Nonetheless, or perhaps for this very reason, conflicts between youth and labor unfolded with particular intensity and consequence around the gold mines of the Witwatersrand. They are forgotten in the ghost dance of the boys, and in the constant recourse to an abstract category of The Struggle, increasingly imagined as the property and expression of a "Struggle Generation." In what follows, I explore the relationship between student protest and labor activism, both by investigating their respective trajectories and contradictions in communities around the goldfields, and by exploring the structural opposition between mental and manual labor that traversed both the gold industry and the governmental logic of Apartheid. For, it was in the shared confrontation with this opposition, more than through organizational collaboration, that youth and labor attempted to lay the groundwork for emancipation. That confrontation took place in the earnest pursuit of something that would be called "talking politics."

Raising Standards, Emerging Unions

As we learned in the previous chapter, when the gold standard was abandoned and prices of the precious metal rose in the early 1970s, a new window opened: not the gold window, as it had been called in the United States, but one of new expectations—for racial justice premised on the universalisms for which the general value form substituted, and for profits, for which that same value form provided its invisibility cloak. The rising price of gold seemed to promise a solution to problems on all sides of the social and ideological divide, but mainly for the established powers. But the inflation caused by the oil crisis made the state all the more dependent on gold revenues, raising the stakes of labor disruptions, and the power to be had in threatening them. Even at the beginning of the following decade, when gold was trading at $465.50, down from $614 in 1980, Joseph Lelyveld could write that the gold boom could still appear for the Apartheid regime like a mechanism for resisting international boycotts and embargoes and therefore ensuring its survival.[3] But starting almost as soon as the dollar was untethered from the precious metal, the rising price of gold also represented the possibility of higher wages and thus of an escape from poverty for at least some of those immiserated by Apartheid.

The promise of labor's new power was, however, first realized in other places, most notably in Durban, which was also the port through which so much of South Africa's imports entered. The decade commenced with successful strikes by workers against the Public Utility Transport Company (PUTCO) in Durban (1972), which, after protracted stoppages, arrests, and violence by the state, finally led to wage increases of between 22 and 48 percent for black workers.[4] Durban was not only a locus of strikes, however. It became the time-space of a dreamed total social transformation, later named the "Durban Moment" by Tony Morphet.[5] There, the student movement that had seen the black South African Students Organization (SASO) emerge from its multiracial roots in the National Union of South African Students (NUSAS), was radicalized by Steve Biko and the Black Consciousness movement. NUSAS also included an increasingly radicalized white intellectual class, much of it under the influence of Richard (Rick) Turner. Before and even after both men were assassinated by South African security forces (Turner in 1977, Biko in 1978, although both were also banned in 1973), the groups that formed around them undertook research on the newly established international poverty datum line, organized around wage issues, and set up new publications, including the *Black Review*, started by Biko, and the worker newspaper, *Isisebenzi* (The Worker, Z),[6] under the editorship of Halton Cheadle.

The relationship between education and labor radicalism was, in this moment and its movements, one of mutual supplementarity. It was also circumscribed by a certain instrumentality and economism. Radical students were both theoretically and practically concerned with matters of labor, and labor organizing was tied to educational projects of more and less formal kinds. But they were also afflicted by the hierarchy between mental and manual labor that structured the entire economy, and especially the gold industry, which, since the late 1950s, had been exempt from other labor legislation prohibiting job reservations and which used the putative intellectual deficiencies of ruralized and tribalized racial groups to sustain its restriction of supervisory authority to white employees. In this respect, *Isisebenzi* was an exceptional but also symptomatic intervention. It was emphatically workerist, but its vanguardism was a combination of literary critical close reading in the service of ideology critique and a didacticism born of doubt about workers' self-knowledge. The first issue opened with a citation of a typical employer (a cement manufacturer) defending his low wages on the grounds that he was never short of job applicants. "Let us look at this statement," intones the editor, who proceeds to diagram its meaning on the model of the "Working Day Chapter" of Marx's *Capital* by pointing out its errors and misprisions. Beneath that opening lesson is the magazine's mission statement: "In this magazine we shall endeavor to bring to the workers what we feel they should know." A concluding section is headed, "Let us talk," and continues to consider what "we as black workers" can do, given that strikes are illegal.[7]

Talking was crucial. Not only was talk crucial for what got said (or indeed for what was not said or mistranslated) but also for the experience of talking, of being heard to talk, and of being deemed a person capable of speech, especially eloquent speech. It was, in a classically Arendtian sense, the kernel of politicization. No doubt this is why virtually every history of radical politics of this time is punctuated by the figure of the orator and has as its recurrent mise-en-scene the theater of a public address: a rally, a funeral, or a demonstrative strike.[8]

Banned or under suspicion, organizations like SASO recruited by word of mouth and clandestine pamphlets. By 1971, it had a membership of more than six thousand students. When they called a strike in 1972 following Onkopotse Abram Tiro's convocation address indicting the white supremacist regime and especially its educational policies, he and 1,146 striking students (at the University of Fort Hare) were expelled. After the boycott-cum-strike led by Tiro, students were attacked, detained, arrested, tortured, disappeared, and killed. Tiro was himself assassinated by parcel bomb while in exile in Botswana. Yet, as V. L. Allen describes, these strikes and repression were their own source of learning and that experience led many, although certainly not all students, to join the banned ANC or the South African Communist Party or to join the union movement.[9] Perhaps even more than had been the case in the early decades of the century, the protests and labor actions became a pedagogical scene and a counter public sphere in the 1970s.

Inevitably, the strikes of this period were concentrated in urban areas. Although commencing as demands for improved wages, strikes in the transportation sector assailed the entire system that had spatialized racial difference and made blackness an experience of distance and travel, of time spent away from home and *en route*. This issue was also raised in the student uprisings at Soweto, to the extent that the Commission of Inquiry into those events (to be discussed) made special note of it as a source of political discontent; commission members were even taken on tours of the public transport into Johannesburg so that they could grasp something of the average black commuter's daily experiences—experiences that were otherwise structurally occluded for whites. Beginning in 1972, strikes by dockworkers and stevedores assailed the import economy that was the corollary and flip side of the export-based minerals economy.[10] In 1973, in Durban, black physicians walked out over wages and against the inequalities of the racially distributed health services.[11] Stoppages by municipal workers in Durban also included garbage collectors and grave diggers, crippling the city's capacity to get rid of its waste and using the unburied corpses to signify the deathliness that had otherwise been inscribed in poverty-level wages made even more paltry by rising consumer prices and avid inflation. Textile workers, cleaners, tea packers, metal workers, milk delivery services, tile workers, newspaper office workers, and nearly every element of South Africa's industrialized and bureaucratized society were affected. In the first three months of 1973, 160 strikes involving 61,410 black workers had taken place. In 118 of these strikes, the workers had obtained increased wages, sometimes more than 40 percent, although in the case of PUTCO, the increases were passed on to consumers, driving further protests and boycotts.[12] Lessons were being learned.

It would be wrong, however, to read this period as one of smooth expansion and the linear growth of union membership and self-conscious power or the direct access to representation. In some cases, unions were actually formed in the process of striking, as was the case with the PUTCO workers, who formed the Transport and Allied Workers Union in the midst of their action.[13] In 1970, only seventy thousand black workers were members of trade unions, and even in 1983, a year after the establishment of the National Union of Mineworkers (NUM), that number had gown to only three hundred thousand, representing only about 8 percent of the black labor force.[14] Overall, the tempo and temporality of the strikes' movement across the country was one of acceleration and intensification, followed by pauses and apparent blockages. Strikes were often prompted by ambitions for improved wages and benefits, but they were also sometimes motivated by the simple need to claw back what was being retracted. The textile workers in Benoni, for example, struck because their working day had been *extended* to twelve hours; their strike was an attempt to return to an earlier status quo, and the extension of hours may well have been a cynical effort to divert potential strike activity into this function of restoration. This does not mean that the strikes were the result of, or identical to, the activities of unions. What is remarkable is how widespread and apparently synchronous they were despite the fact that black trade unionism had been so thoroughly suppressed, and its organs disbanded. In 1968, the Trade Union Council of South Africa (TUCSA) had terminated its long-lived African Affairs Section in response to state mandate, and then severed relations with five affiliate organizations of black workers the following year.[15]

A great deal of coordinating, mobilizing, and organizational activity had therefore to take place in other venues. Some in Natal, such as Turner's Institute of Industrial Education (IIE), offered night classes and created multilingual workbooks on technical subjects as well as conceptual matters. Turner wanted to instill a "theoretical orientation" in workers as an antidote to the skills-oriented vocational projects of so much worker-focused education, but that ambition would remain unfulfilled.[16] In offering a posthumous appreciation of Turner's work, Tony Morphet notes that this effort—a project of epistemic reorientation and not just skills development—failed in part because of Turner's banning but mainly because of the slowness of the process. This process did not appeal to those more concerned with developing a "union leadership base on the shop floor," or, per the Black Consciousness journal, *Black Review*, the cultivation of well-informed community leaders. And this sense of urgency, sometimes collapsing into a fantasy of immediacy and often into fury over deferral, persisted across the decades.[17] And so, too, would the substitution of certificate-bearing leadership for a well-educated population; the dream of the commandment often displaced the cultivation of reciprocal communication.

Some of the IIE's initiatives, such as the *Labour Bulletin*, continue to operate into the present, although they are perhaps read more avidly by university radicals than mineworkers. But in general, other initiatives had to provide the locus for a new kind of education—as preparation for social change and self-representation—one that was knowingly foreclosed by the entire apparatus of Bantu education. In this space, it was sometimes the church, the institution of the spirit, that provided the means for advocating on behalf of the body, lending its notion of the transcendental as a means to think the possibility of reclaiming that (divinely given capacity for) surplus that capitalist industry was otherwise expropriating as mere profit.[18] Such activities were undertaken from within the Anglican Church, in particular, and in 1971, it established a formal Urban Training Project (UTP), which offered skills-oriented education on matters ranging from secretarial work to labor legislation. The latter became, effectively, if clandestinely, preparation for unionization.[19]

It may be said that the union was a compromised instrument for politicization and that such an instrument is typically complicit with the gendered dynamics of the dominant society. Certainly, this was true in South Africa, where the limitation of early union activity to the question of wages and grievances deferred or diverted discussion of broader social issues, beyond race. Kally Forrest has referred to this concern with wages and grievances as the basis and expression of the working class interests in the union movement, and she notes how this differentiated its concerns from those of both the Communist Party, which lacked a large-scale popular base, and the ANC, which although a mass movement, was more concerned with political questions, and particularly the overthrow of the Apartheid state on the model of anticolonial nationalism elsewhere, than with the overthrow of the class system itself.[20] But they shared many axioms about gender norms and shared an ideal figure of the Worker as male.

Many women in the union movement have described, in poignant detail, the difficulty of educating male colleagues about the specific needs and additional burdens befalling women, from domestic labor and caregiving, to fending off sexual harassment at home and in their workplaces. Female organizers were often greeted with "mockery" by the men when confronted with these issues. But women too needed to be persuaded of their own interests. And this was both practically and conceptually difficult. For women, organizing meant finding time at the end of the day, and escaping the surveillance of husbands or male relations, who often felt that a claim to gender equity, even within the framework of labor, was "disrespectful" of their natural or culturally inherited prerogative. Refilwe Ndzuta, a one-time labor organizer and later member of parliament for the ANC in the first post-Apartheid government of Gauteng, described what she would explain to her comrades, whose wives they could not imagine as unionists, as follows:

> When women knock off at work they would come to the offices and would talk over about these issues. They would be nervous and be in a hurry because they have to get home as soon as possible, they have to go and look after their husbands and things like that. At that time the following things were common: when a woman wakes up in the morning, she has to take care of the kids, she has to clean them and prepare them for school; she has to do the same for the husband as well, she will be the last to get ready. When the husbands arrives home, he has his *Sowetan* [newspaper] and reads the newspaper and wait for the woman to get back, at times he would not even make fire so that the poor woman must find the fire ready for her to cook. The poor woman will first make fire, prepare supper and prepares for the following morning. We used to call this triple oppression because a woman at that time, of course even now, was oppressed because her gender, of her colour and at work because she was not properly recognised, even if she is doing the same job as a man she would be paid less compared to her male counterpart. We used to make a joke and say then there's the fourth oppression, after all of this, the man is waiting for you he wants sex. You are too tired, he does not understand that you are tired.[21]

When the depiction of this exhausting daily routine failed to persuade, Ndzuta would invoke the men's proprietary concern for their wives and daughters. And sometimes, this would help. But it should not go without saying that people like Akhona and Sisipho, described in chapter 10, could find no place in this new field of representation even within a gender-broadened conception of labor. But given the reduction of blackness to labor power, with the male worker signifying the general category of labor, the ground of political organization remained heavily masculinist. Nonetheless, the strikes in Durban made clear that labor-based activity and unions could indeed combat legislatively empowered corporations.

And yet these waves of action, strikes, and demonstrative protests as well as the engagement of workers through night classes and informal tuition did not initially find their echo in the gold industry. The first years of the decade saw relatively little strike activity compared with what was occurring in other sectors and places, despite the fact that wages there were lower than in most sectors other than agriculture. Across even the most worker-sympathetic literature on mining, the migrant mining population was depicted as being what the Chamber had sought to make it through its cultivation of "tribalism" and its corporeal training methods.[22] It was described as "docile." But in September 1973, two conflicts at the Anglo American–owned Western Deep Levels mine near Carletonville marked the opening of a new epoch in which so-called compound revolts erupted at one after another gold mine.[23] In the course of a few days, eleven mineworkers were killed by police, another by unknown forces, and dozens injured. Commentators read the deaths as the mark of an unprecedented escalation in state violence against strikers on the mines, although there had been bloody repression before.[24] Outrage over the events spread to universities, where students took up the cause and offered themselves as prosthetic mouthpieces for the subalternized mineworkers. Their task was to insist that the conflict was indeed a labor conflict and not a mere eruption of so-called tribalism or faction-fighting. That is to say, their self-understood purpose, as scholar-activists, was to certify the truth of the mineworkers' claims. It was not easy, for the dispute at Western Deep Levels was not merely a matter of wages; it was born of the systemic division and distribution of mental and manual labor, that very division of which the students were beneficiaries and that, in the long run, the union bureaucrats would valorize.

It Goes Without Saying: The Miseducation of an Industry

According to the *Rand Daily Mail*, "Trouble had been simmering on and off at the Western Deeps mine since the beginning of the year," although most later analyses represented the events of September 11 as relatively spontaneous.[25] A first outburst had occurred a month previously, when thirty-six machine operators who had gone on strike for higher wages had supposedly terminated their contracts when their efforts failed and then they had been repatriated.[26] Despite the termination of these contracts, the strike a week later was represented as being continuous with the first one in the *Rand Daily Mail*, which subtitled one of its columns, "One week from dissent to death." What had precipitated the escalation? A day later, the paper reported on the dissatisfaction over relative increases and wage restructuring for some categories of labor: winch drivers, loader drivers, and loco drivers. But, as Allen recounts, it would take an interview with James Motlatsi (the first president of NUM) some years later to explain what, at the time, remained hidden from view in the mainstream media: a problematic translation in which was conveyed the denigration of workers' intellectual capacities.

In Allen's rendition of Motlatsi's discussion of the negotiations, machine operators went on strike following the implementation of a new job performance evaluation system, which had rewarded higher-ranked job categories relative to the other workers. A mediation session was then called. The first of two meetings was apparently uneventful, but the second was marred by a catastrophic rendering of the rationale for the wage disparity into Fanakalo, the pseudo-creole invented for the purposes of managerial control and worker safety in the multilingual underground. The assistant mine manager, through an interpreter, explained the new evaluative process, based on what was termed Anglo American's "Swazi system," as follows: "the rest did not receive as big a wage increase as the team leaders because *they had no brains*."[27]

It is always difficult to know what is heard in translation, and this is complicated by the fact that Fanakalo is characterized by an extreme paucity of words and verb forms. For this reason, it is both overly direct and semiotically polyvalent. Mineworkers were dissuaded not only from using their natal tongues underground but also from using English, even when they spoke it fluently. Fanakalo was thus a language of confinement, justified as a lingua franca but implicated in the maintenance of racial distinction and hierarchy. It was the medium of remote control. As one former miner explained,

> the use of Fanakalo . . . was a deliberate attempt to . . . ensure that as blacks we were inferior. I realised, because at that stage I was able to express myself fluently in English at that time already, but I could tell you that that was strongly discouraged, but if you could be seen to be talking a white man's language you would actually be ridiculed, that you consider yourself clever and better than anyone else. That's the kind of experiences that we went through at the time. So you had to express yourself in Fanakalo if you had to communicate across ethnic or racial lines.[28]

Whether or not Motlatsi's retranslation and explanation of the labor-management impasse can capture the full complexity of the situation at Western Deeps, the mineworkers, upon hearing whatever they heard, walked out. More than eight thousand workers refused to go down the shaft on the night shift—a number that reveals just how enormous the mine was at the time. When the mineworkers were confronted by the company's own disciplinary agents, namely *indunas*, scuffles broke out. The police, called in by the company, fired tear gas and live bullets at the crowds, prefiguring similar events in the coming years, including those at Soweto in 1976 and Marikana in 2012 (among many other protests and strikes). Nonetheless, only strikers were charged with public violence before being released on bail, although none went to trial.

A formal day of mourning in Carletonville and the creation of a fund for the victims was accompanied by protests at universities around the country, in which students demanded that Harry Oppenheimer (son of Ernest Oppenheimer, founder of the Anglo American Corporation), then chancellor of the University of Cape Town as well as chair of the board of Anglo American, resign his academic post. (He did not, and he remained in that office until 1999.) The students also called for a formal commission of inquiry, a report on compensation to the families, and the creation of black trade unions.[29] For its part, the management at Western Deeps, represented by its chair, John W. Shilling, admitted that "we may have made a mistake in our wage structuring. . . . Maybe in the African mind, we have done them an injustice." He then added that the mine would reconsider its "whole approach to communications and human relations."[30] In shifting from wage structures to communications and human relations, Shilling betrayed the fantasy of a transparent communication in which the will of the company would have become the understanding of the mineworkers, which would have in turn led to their acquiescence. And it reverberates in every effort to equate information dissemination with the transformation of consciousness—an error that afflicted not only the mining industry and the Apartheid state but also both the student protests and the union movements.

In his speech at the annual meetings of the Chamber of Mines in June 1974, B. E. Hersov repeated the claim, describing the "tragic events which have recently occurred in several of our Black hostels," and implored his audience (fellow board members) about the "urgent need for improved communications between Whites and Blacks." He also reiterated the depiction of the situation by the Chamber's president, R. A. Plumbridge, as "ironic," because the demand for higher wages was coinciding with rising pay rates. The rest he blamed on "tribal clashes unconnected with matters of pay," but even these, he said, should be minimized by efforts to ensure "better understanding."[31] To say that Hersov misread the situation is an understatement—he also misrepresented it. But to say that he misread the role of reading in the task of transformation is to render him as the industry's true figurehead and mouthpiece.

Although the rendering of the rationale for the wage decision into Fanakalo was surely a source of outrage, the translation was not simply an erroneous representation of policy. It disclosed a truth of the system, which might have been as easily represented in the terms that Marx used to describe the despotic nature of the supervisory classes in what were, at the time of his writing, relatively new joint stock companies. In such conditions, he argued, the delegation of control functions is a means to intensify that control while giving it the illusory appearance of a personal relationship.[32] Such was the system of the *induna* and the so-called boss-boys, authorized through recourse to a notion of cultural custom and inscribed within the bounds of ethno-linguistic identity. The problem of translation was internal to the system that mobilized the distinction between mental and manual labor in a new context and that attempted to extend the already failing effort to commensurate people with their value-generating capacity while also extracting more from them than they were paid for. These events were taking place almost exactly two years into the shadow of gold's floating. And on that day of death on the compounds of Western Deeps, gold traded at $102.75 (more than twice the price it had been selling at when the gold window closed). It was down slightly but would recover more than $30 over the next year. Perhaps only the Chamber and the companies' boards of directors thought the mineworkers did not know that there was money to be had.

The Mental, the Manual, and the Mean

The Swazi system was Anglo American's regime for grading labor and thus wage eligibility status according to skills required and tasks performed, and it grew out of the simultaneous "need" to rationalize and contain labor costs and, at the same time, to recognize the transformations in black mine labor as more workers began to acquire technical skills and settle near the mines in the anticipation of longer-term employment and "stabilization" (as previously discussed). The system first emerged from the conflict between mining corporations as they confronted the growing demand to reconsider their dependency on migrant labor. In the 1940s, there had been ten surface grades and eight grades for underground labor, most of which was deemed to be unskilled. Almost all black workers underground were concentrated in the lowest paying "band," as it is called in the literature.

In the 1960s, Anglo had experimented with a new system that divided workers into three broad bands (unskilled, semiskilled, and skilled), which it then supplemented with new aptitude tests that promised to calibrate the likely fit between worker capacity and job requirements. I rely here on Allen's sprawling but precise historical summary: This new system had sixteen points, which could be differentially combined, but its putative virtue lay in its generalizability across all races, given that it was ostensibly based on the assessment of technical potential rather than fixed and essentialized cultural traits. Anglo American applied this system first in its coal mines in Swaziland and then uniformly across all mines (hence its designation as the Swazi system) in an effort to subordinate the heterogeneity of its personnel to an abstract enumeration, thus diverting the potential for justice in Marx's concept of human species-be-ing by generating an entity called "human resources." Not surprisingly, when Anglo American applied this system to white workers without prior approval of their union (the Mine Workers Union or MWU), the Swazi system was rejected precisely because it threatened to undermine white privilege. It was also rejected by the management of other mining houses, notably Gold Fields, for related reasons.

Gold Fields responded by adopting an even more elaborate aptitude system, this one assessing rational decision-making capacities and supervisory func-tions in ways that permitted cross-sectoral and cross-professional analogizing. Designed by a Scottish economist named Patterson, the system ranked all jobs according to their "decision-making content" and purported to be "racially neutral" (a concession to the growing criticism of the obviously racialized dis-tribution of poverty wages in the United Kingdom and around the world). Ever since black workers had been caricatured as "mere muscular machines" by the Transvaal Chamber of Mines in 1902,[33] they had been excluded from these functions and were, in effect, preassigned to the space of the manual— not so much the embodied as the merely fleshly, as Hortense Spillers has said in another context.[34] Quite simply, as Allen explains, "the scheme took over a racially determined occupational structure that excluded all black mine-workers, except team leaders, from all decision making and defined them as unskilled. About 90 percent of all black mineworkers, in consequence, were in band A, which paid the lowest rates while the remaining 10 percent, namely the team leaders, *indunas*, and clerks, were distributed fairly equally among the four grades in band B."[35] In this context, we may understand that the translator working for Anglo American's assistant mine manager was confusing the Swazi system with the Patterson system, which was only nascent at the time. But this very confusion reveals the proximity between the two.

In any case, when the mineworkers at Western Deeps were told they had no brains and that this was the reason for being denied wage increases com-parable to those being given the team leaders and especially the drivers, who, from another perspective, performed less labor than those they ordered about, they were responding to what seemed to be a renewal of history in the guise of bureaucratic scientism and modernization. One of the most insidious dimen-sions of this ancient division between mental and manual labor is its presump-tion that the bodies of the mineworkers were not themselves trained into the role of technology's muscular accompaniment. This is Althusser's lesson, which he offers in a meditation on Pascal. In his well-known account, ideology is said to be inscribed as acts in bodily practices, and these in rituals, which account for the "material existence of an ideological apparatus, even if it is just a small part of that apparatus: a small mass in a small church, a funeral, a minor match at a sport club, a school day or a day of classes at university, a meeting or rally of a political party, or of the Rationalist Union, or whatever one likes." On this model, should we not consider the processes of so-called acclimatization, by which underground miners were readied for their work beneath the surface following medical examinations, a kind of ideological interpellation, one more absorbing than the church mass, the funeral, or the rally of a political party? Should we not grasp this as a primary means of instilling the so-called "docility" that management otherwise misrepresented as a function of attachment to tribal homelands and the respect for gerontocratic authority (a misrepresentation to which many mineworkers themselves often adhered)? If Pascal's scandal consisted of saying, "Kneel down, move your lips in prayer, and you will believe," then surely the climbing and stepping and stretching of the lungs could also be seen as inducing belief. But here, belief is simply belief in the capacity to endure, misnamed docility.[36]

All this took place in the inverted, devilish church. In deep gold mines, this acclimating pedagogy included a five-day process in a location described by mineworkers as the "House of Satan," namely a room kept at 34 degrees Celsius (93.2 degrees Fahrenheit) and subject to an artificial wind of one hundred feet per minute.[37] There, individuals had to "trot" up and down stairs, commencing with 1,560 pounds per minute on day one and 2,120 pounds per minute by day four. This process took about four to five hours of nonstop work per day. So awful was it that mineworkers were reported to avoid lengthy vacations or sickness leaves because they would have to undergo the acclimatization again after more than six weeks away (during which time they lost an estimated 90 percent of the physical capacities cultivated through this method). People who could not endure the process, who had low oxygen intake rates, or who had low heat tolerance, were assigned to surface jobs (some of them higher ranked, although they were sometimes menial tasks like sweeping and cleaning). All of this added to the impression that the new system repaid those who could do least. The mute critique of this education, which could take the form of avoidance through an ironically observant work schedule, was of course not imagined as anything other than lethargy. But such issues did not appear in the newspapers, and the commonsense identification of education's purpose with mental labor persisted.

Conjunctions, Mediations, and Catalytic Converters

The pages of the *Rand Daily Mail* devoted to an explanation of the wage dispute at Western Deeps, where it was merely stated that management had felt an increase was not justified, also featured stories about student "placard protests" in support of the mineworkers and Anglo American's refusal of an open inquiry. Next to these was a story about the establishment of school libraries and their integration with classroom learning, a concept that was being promoted by A. L. Kotzee, the Transvaal director of education. In Potchefstroom, just fifty kilometers from the mine, he told his audience of visiting regional delegates that school libraries could enable holistic learning rather than the fragmentary instruction led by teachers in discipline-specific class. It could also foment "interdisciplinary relationships cutting across subject boundaries," and although it might not be usable by everyone, he said, the library had the potential to enhance self-directed study at a level determined by each learner's capacities and needs. Here was a pedagogical utopianism that has been little updated in the discourse of the most elite private universities even today, although it was, in that place and time, the discourse of the Apartheid state, and its promise was limited to white schools. Beneath these stories was another regularly featured item of the *Rand Daily Mail*, namely a "School Quiz" asking student readers to recall stories from previous issues of the paper. It included reference to a letter bombing in Lusaka, an attack on press freedom, Muhammad Ali's recent "revenge victory," and assorted local news—but not the mine deaths.

There is no immediately discernible relationship between the newspaper stories about the wage demands and the murder of striking mineworkers, on one hand, and Kotzee's discourse about the educational promise of libraries, on the other. They are mere adjacencies, fortuitously, or perhaps (depending on the editorial board's aims and the layout artists' spatial calculus) intentionally linked because of the intermediating story and imagery of student protests. On one side, a discourse about the virtues of education and its individuating, character-building potential; on the other, a story about outrage at the deprivations rationalized through recourse to a racially categorical division between mental and manual labor, and the exclusion of black mineworkers from the former. But as we saw in earlier readings of print media, one can read the seemingly "random" juxtapositions of the newspaper discourse for the tracery of a structure that generates these many phenomena and the relations among them.

Despite the strike at Western Deeps, and despite a growing number of labor-based actions across the gold industry, it would not be until 1982 that NUM was recognized and enabled to operate on the gold mines near Carletonville. In the space between, a space at once conceptual, cartographic, and temporal, something else was needed to "catalyze" the transformation. In most labor histories, this catalyzing force is deemed to have been the student movement of 1976. Thus, for example, Allen titles a chapter of *The History of Black Mineworkers in South Africa*, "Soweto: The Catalyst for Liberation, 1976–1982." He was not wrong, but only insofar as a catalyst is understood as that exteriority, that foreignness which works on and with the existing materials, converting them from merely constituent elements into a potentially changed state of being. How were the Soweto uprisings catalytic? How did they realize, or open this potential for something more, liberating it from its interment in profits made possible by the assignment of black subjects to the function of manual labor? This surplus, this possibility of being and making beyond what can be used, is not limited to capitalism and is not reducible to the matter of excess or waste; it is the ground for possible transformation, and thus liberation. It is present in every society in which people care for the infant and the indigent, or even the pet. It is present in every society that makes offerings to its divinities; that sacrifices its wealth in combat; that produces poetry, chants, and dances; that decorates itself and its milieu.[38] All of these phenomena result from a capacity to make more than what is needed for subsistence. Capitalism does not do away with these capacities, but it does colonize that surplus, transforming it into surplus value (as profit) through wages and thereby making its privatization possible. And it confines what might have been a liberatory surplus to the function of enabling capitalism's own growth.[39] It also generally differentiates and legitimates enjoyment of that surplus as an intellectual function, to be cultivated as an aesthetic capacity, while also condemning the expenditures of the poor as excessive, destructive, or wasteful. This is one reason why any alliance between students and workers has to overcome a partitioning of the epistemic domain.

History has shown how very difficult that task is, and its intractability is registered every time worker ignorance and superstition are adduced as explanation for passivity or workers' voting against their own interests, and in every condemnation of intellectual practice as an obstacle to radicalism in the material domain. It is also why something like a religious fervor often seems to suffuse oppositional politics, for religion is another institutional domain for colonizing the intuition and the capacity for something more and other, something beyond bare life. Typically (and this is one of Marx's insights), such an intuition arises at a threshold moment in the contradictory movements of different forces in a divided social field. Often, this occurs when people sense that something is about to be lost. Such was the case in the movement of protest along the arc of the Witwatersrand: from the gold mines to Soweto and back, and from the compound to the township and back. And back again.

So, then, what happened to make the black students in Soweto rise up in pursuit of that more that was being denied them, and which denial was the condition of possibility of the gold industry? As analyzed in the *Commission of Inquiry Into the Riots at Soweto and Elsewhere*, the instigating factor in the protests was not (only) the Bantu Education Act of 1953 so much as the revocation of exemptions from the requirement for instruction and examination in Afrikaans. Initially, the lack of qualified Afrikaans-speaking instructors permitted schools, through their boards, to request exemption from the requirement that classes and exams be conducted in Afrikaans. In 1975, black schools in the racially segregated system were restructured and the years of possible tuition were reduced from thirteen to twelve years, with primary schools now limited to the first four standards. Standard V was moved up to be included in secondary schools, and Standard VI vanished.[40] And then, in 1976, compulsory education was introduced.[41] The result was both an upward reassignment of younger learners to the more senior schools and a sudden expansion in the numbers of students subject to examination in Afrikaans in state-funded institutions. Standardized natal languages remained the medium for nonexamination subjects, even though Afrikaans had been encouraged in nonacademic activities for some years. Quite apart from the ideological value of Afrikaans as a language of white supremacy (although English could also play this role), there was a problem of capacity. Although the number of students required to perform in Afrikaans expanded astronomically (sometimes multiplying fourfold), there were not sufficient numbers of Afrikaans-speaking teachers to serve these students. At the same time, the Department of Education began to increasingly decline the recommendations for exemption from local school boards.

The generalization of Afrikaans through the withdrawal of exemptions was thus the means for condemning black students not only to mandatory instruction in the master's language but also to instruction without instructors. And the impasse brought to a crisis what had been known all along, namely that the Bantu education system was training for servitude and for exclusion from the public sphere of reason that the dominant society had claimed for itself. Hendrik Verwoed's (Apartheid ideologue, former Prime Minister and author of the Bantu Education Act) response to the ANC's protest against the initial Bantu Education Act in 1953 had made this all too clear: "When I have control of native education, I will reform it so that natives will be taught from childhood to realize that equality with Europeans is not for them. People who believe in equality are not desirable teachers for Natives. There is no place for him (the Black child) in European society above the level of certain forms of labour. . . . What is the use of teaching a Bantu child mathematics when it cannot use it in practice?"[42] Nonetheless, it was not until the simultaneous restructuring of black schools and the enforcement (through the withdrawal of exemptions) of the mandate that the ground was finally ready for revolt. Although the student uprisings in Soweto were said to have catalyzed the radicalization of mineworker unionization, they were themselves catalyzed by the labor movement, which in turn had been leavened by student radicalism in Durban.

The restructuring of schools partly explains why so many of the protestors in Soweto were so young relative to the students who had gone to the barricades in Europe and the United States in 1968; upper-primary students of the old system were the ones most immediately subject to this newly intensified double bind, which only the ideologues in the Department of Education seem to have wanted. Surveys of school boards, directors, and circuit inspectors, which were disclosed in the Commission of Inquiry, show that the vast majority did not advocate single-medium instruction in Afrikaans, and most, except in the

Cape Province, wanted an official policy of bilingualism. Bilingualism was, of course, the name of an internally reconciled white rule in education. The flip side of the falsely universalizing drive, however, was the discovery among learners in relatively elite institutions of a sympathy, perhaps an identitification, with those who were so affected. Private English-medium schools not dependent on state funds were not immediately subject to the changes, and students attending such schools might well have clung to their benefits. Some did, but others rallied to the cause. In the process, they discovered a sense of generation as the basis of political subjectivity and self-representation.

Consider, for example, the testimony of one Mofokeng, who attended the English-medium Naledi High School, where much of the organizational activity in preparation for the protests took place. He describes his and his age-mates' decision to join the protestors in solidarity as a willed relinquishment of an "elite" privilege. One of the signs of that privilege was "debate," the kind of activity that permits people to rehearse for their participation in the public sphere of reason. That debate also became the means of his learning:

> The people who started the movement towards '76 were the junior secondary schools . . . according to our understanding that is where the system of the time wanted to impose Afrikaans. And somehow, when we were debating, interacting amongst ourselves . . . because in the debating society you form a kind of community or elite within the school itself. Now when we were interacting, exchanging views and said, gentlemen, we are not target for Afrikaans. We are senior students . . . we were not using Afrikaans. Naledi High was not targeted by the Department of Education to use Afrikaans. That is why, even Jimmy Kruger of the time said, "Naledi High and other high schools are interfering in matters that were not actually affecting them. Because this Afrikaans was not imposed on them." Actually, that was the mobilisation on our side. We said, exactly, that's why we are intervening, because that is going to destroy the academic careers of the people or studies, etc.[43]

Many former students describe these debating clubs in similar terms: "There were also debating societies within the schools. Those were also important in preparing us really for understanding the environment where we lived in to say, 'yes, we have a government in this country that does not provide equal services, for example, to all the South Africans.'"[44] These debating societies were, says Welile Wilson Chief Twala, a one-time activist and later senior member of the Department of Health, "all anti-authority. Actually . . . because it had to start from anti-authority. Anti-authority had to be the teachers, the principals and so on because they were the ones who were carrying the Apartheid mantra on their heads. Once you started to talk about something then they would say, 'now you are talking political.' And then we would be interested in what is this 'talking political.'"[45] Prohibition as incitement; Foucault has taught us to recognize this dynamic.

Jabulani Mayaba, a former labor organizer on the mines, adds the important observation that the incited speech entered into a twofold learning process, divided between and shared by the speakers and those who overheard the conversation. He urged the interviewer of the Wits Oral History Project to "interview some people who didn't participate, who were not interested in politics who used to listen to some of us talking politics. [He refers here to a local athlete.] At some stage when we partied he said some interesting things which I never thought people observed. He talked about things which he observed during those days. He had no interest in politics but we were there talking politics and for some reason we didn't comprehend that we were teaching them about politics."[46]

What was such teaching? It was not only a matter of informational content, or of conveying the truth of an analysis. One imagines that these other youths who heard their colleagues "talking politics" listened because they found in that discourse something recognizable from their own experience, but also because they heard something new in the manner of speaking. Having overheard this speaking and this speech, at once familiar and foreign, they found themselves addressed in a way that they had not expected and discovered in themselves a possibility as yet unperceived. Such descriptions of "talking political" and the excitement that accompanied it captures the frisson that also often characterized conversations during the redemarcation protests in Khutsong (to be discussed more fully in subsequent chapters). There, the young men who were also "talking political" exuded a shimmering sense of confidence. When they spoke, an impatient but radiant quality characterized their speaking, which accelerated and was amplified by their sense of righteousness. It was mainly a masculine enthusiasm—young women rarely spoke this way, except in the context of the Women's League, and they were not so young, or so uniformly confident. But among the young men, the excitement accompanied a desire that was equally capable of becoming art or violence. It did not matter that this speech was often formulaic, and even that it had the quality of slogans. Indeed, at times, this very ritual formulaicness seemed to be the source of its energy. It permitted these youth to be swept up by their own speech as though they were listening to someone else or being compelled by a force coming from elsewhere.[47]

Of course, in Carletonville and Khutsong, Soweto *was* elsewhere. This is also why talking about Soweto could be its own source of power, and that power could accumulate the further one was from the events, if one could claim to have been there. As Walter Benjamin remarked, "The storyteller [is] someone who has come from afar."[48] Sometimes the spatial remoteness was redoubled by a generational and occupational distance, and it structured the nonidentity between student and mineworker, which, then as now, recapitu-lated the asymmetrical distribution of the mental and the manual. Thus, Zolani Ngwane, a young boy at the time, describes how, in late 1976, stories of the Soweto uprisings moved along the pathways of both institutionalized media and through the personal narratives of migrants who bore with them accounts of the uprisings. The male migrants from Cancele (Eastern Cape) who had worked on mines in Carletonville told stories of their own heroic acts, but, con-trary to representations of the protestors as members of a democratic vanguard or vulnerable children under attack by the state, these older men were often suspicious of insurrectionary youth. At least with their village comrades, the elders were more likely to describe rescuing bystanders from stone-throwing or knife-wielding young men than cheering on self-appointed representative youth in the pursuit of liberation. Indeed, their narratives, says Ngwane, were part of a different "struggle" over the "imagined form of the household," which was also being invoked in the discourses about stabilization on the mines—and that discourse, as we have seen, was aimed at reinforcing precisely this patriar-chal and gerontocratic hierarchy that the students were increasingly concerned to overthrow.

Youth were not outside of this system, even if they were, as Twala says, anti-authority, and the desire for change sometimes devolved into the desire to merely appropriate power. Such is the lure in every revolution that does not address both capitalist exploitation and the preexisting systems that it has absorbed and made newly useful. Such is the lure of every revolution that does not conceive of its project as changing consciousness and reorienting desire as well as redistributing wealth. And it is therefore not surprising that women migrants who had been in Soweto recounted matters rather differently than did their male counterparts, whether elder men of the mines or school-going youths. Often, they "painted a picture of a wild landscape where danger lurked everywhere."[49] The punctuation of the *Report of the Commission of Inquiry Into the Riots at Soweto and Elsewhere*, with uncommented-on reportage of women's rapes, some of which were perpetrated as acts of vengeance in conflicts among "factions" in the folds and shadows of the "unrest-ful" streets, is the trace of their otherwise muted experience, the narration of which is marginal to the main text of the inquiry.

Ngwane attends to this violent asymmetry with scrupulousness and adds that the claims to firsthand knowledge were improbable for people working in Carletonville, describing it as being located "an impossible distance away" from Soweto. Impossible is perhaps too strong a word, for people commuted between these locations on a weekly and sometimes even a daily basis. Soweto was a destination for recreation and a storied world of urbane possibility. It was full of movie theaters and stores selling Florsheim shoes and Defy appli-ances, its shebeens were full of music and conversations that attracted people from across the Rand. We might therefore temper Ngwane's sense of distance while conceding the exaggeration of proximity as well as the power acquired in distance traveled. Certainly, the uprisings in Soweto did not initially have any counterpart in Carletonville or Khutsong. The township did not have any high schools at the time. Nonetheless, within a few weeks, the discontent of Soweto's youth did find its way along the reef, and some of the largest mass protests in the country took place on the road between Carletonville and Khutsong, including one in which more than six thousand people blocked the transport routes and made of their bodies a living barricade.[50] That blockade, which occurred on August 4, appears to have been spurred by the Greyhound bus company's decision to terminate transportation into the township in light of protests, and thus it entailed both a repetition of protests in Durban as well as Soweto and the migration of "revolt" from the compound to the township. But the first signs of discontent had appeared on July 20, when students apparently carried placards inscribed with "Black Power" slogans. The Commission of Inquiry found that these students had also attacked the Bantu Administration (BAAB) vehicles. Almost in passing, it noted that, on the first day, "school attendance was poor."[51] On the second day of protest, however, stones were thrown at Hlangabeya, Phororong, Tsitisboga, and Kamhohelo schools in Khutsong. As in Soweto, schools and transportation were primary targets. As in Soweto, liquor stores were also attacked, mainly because owners were local councilors and BAAB representatives who had obtained licenses by virtue of their work with the Apartheid government. As in Soweto, weaponry consisted mainly of stones and fire. In this sense, the protests in Khutsong (and the other mining towns of the Witwatersrand) appeared to resemble those of Soweto. Generalization worked by mimesis.

But Soweto was not self-same, was not its own origin. In addition to having its own margins and zones of exclusion, it was internally fissured by forces from afar. People came and went. They talked about other parts and struggles of the decolonizing world and about art and politics and relatives in other towns. Newspaper and magazine advertisements extolled products made in faraway places. There was music from the United States, England, Ghana, and Nigeria. There were churches linked to global movements stretching from Ethiopia to Brazil. And there was literature to be read. In Soweto, students and others could imagine life beyond the determining structures of the law that confined them. One might say that it had its own elsewhere within, if by *elsewhere* we mean not only the identifiably foreign (whether that be the migrant or the commodities displayed in shop windows and purveyed in newspaper advertising or real estate brochures) but also the principle of something more, something beyond the figures of the foreign that constantly seek to domesticate it. Such an elsewhere, which I referred to earlier as the principle of surplus liberated from the value form, exceeds the matter of geographic distance and

ethnic difference. It connotes justice beyond legality, reparation beyond restitution, surplus beyond surplus value, the transcendental beyond metaphysics.
It is the inflammatory force, the passional other dimension of revolutionary
fervor, which is sometimes imagined as mere affect and often confused with
the jouissance that culminates in a revolutionary outburst or accompanies the
enactment of its vengeance.

Not a Textbook History: Rereading

The official death toll for the period of June 16, 1976 to February 28, 1977, was
575. After Soweto, where 258 people were killed, and Western Province, where
a great deal of the conflict took place between students and so-called migrants,
most of the deaths took place in the gold-mining regions of the Witwatersrand,
where 46 people died.[52] The uprising, which we would now term a *social movement*, had moved, as we have seen. This movement was understood by later
historians to have catalyzed the development of black mineworker unionization. Yet the sites of protests in the Witwatersrand were in the townships and
not on the compounds, and indeed, mineworkers did not initially appear to
identify with the students, whose anti-authoritarianism they often rejected.
The Commission *Report* repeatedly details open fights between hostel-based
migrant workers and students, in terms familiar from the Chamber of Mines'
earlier descriptions of migrant workers as fundamentally cathected to their
natal villages and politically apathetic: "The hostel residents are mainly contract labourers residing in the urban areas, generally in hostels, without their
families; their sojourn is temporary and extends only over the period of their
contracts. As a result they are not interested in strikes and in the local grievances of the other inhabitants, their interests lying with their homes in the
rural areas or in the homelands."[53] We may question this interpretation. Nonetheless, in other places, too, workers resented the demands by the students
to stay away because it meant lost wages, and some walked to work when the
transport system was brought to a halt by boycotts, risking assault or opprobrium in the process.[54] So, without rejecting the notion that a transformation
occurred, we have yet to understand if, how, or to what extent the Soweto
uprisings precipitated a change in oppositional organization and practice in
and for the mines, as is so often claimed. We can rephrase this question as
follows: How did Soweto become a trope in the story of radicalization on the
mines? What was learned in this troping, and what learning was troped (and
thus contained) as "The Struggle"?

   If I phrase these questions this way, as a matter of tropology and not, say,
paradigmatic enactment or reproduction, or even simply development, it is
because the effort to achieve political representation does not proceed as a

linear progression in which an already existing coherent and self-knowing bearer of interest finds a form of appearance and, being recognized as such, is thereby empowered. To be sure, that is the fantasy of much unionist discourse, which orients its education toward the goal of "worker control." But it is not easy to enter into representation in circumstances in which the perception and sensation of social bonds and interest in collectivity (not yet class) have been systematically obstructed. Indeed, this blockage, this being "cut off" from others, was only the starting point for a possible class consciousness in Marx's account of the peasant proprietors in *The Eighteenth Brumaire*, as Gayatri Spivak has taught us to recognize.[55] To overcome this division, including that between the so-called intellectual classes and the laboring classes, requires an understanding of the broadest dimensions—if not the totality—of social factors and forces that otherwise inhibit a coming together in common. From the perspective of the South African state, of course, Bantu education was intended to limit the intellectual trajectories of black learners and to thereby forge a fissured collective-in-service, but one lacking consciousness of itself as an agent of history. In contrast, generational hierarchies, gendered asymmetries, and linguistic and regional divides stood in the way of transforming race-based exclusion into anything like a class for itself—and thus a political subject.

It is in light of this fact that Vincent Joseph Gaobakwe Matthews, one-time ANC activist and codefendant with Nelson Mandela at the treason trial of 1956, later turned businessman and Inkatha Freedom Party member, claimed that the Marx who wrote *The Eighteenth Brumaire* was actually not "obsessed" with class (and certainly did not invent the idea of class).[56] Class was merely the ultimate instance of collective identity-in-difference, if we may borrow Spivak's phraseology from a reading of their shared text. Matthews made this argument in a remarkable interview in which he pays tribute to the intellectual generosity and theoretical rigor of early South African communists, but especially Oliver Reginald Kaizana (OR) Tambo, president of the ANC from 1967 to 1991, and Moses Kotane, secretary general of the SACP from 1939 to 1978). The interview was made for the previously mentioned oral history project and concerned with the legacy of union formation and labor organizing in the fight against Apartheid, and interviewees included members of the ANC, the SACP, and the Pan African Congress (PAC) and came from a diversity of industrial unions. Some had been active in the national or regional branches of the national umbrella organization, the Council of South African Trade Unions (COSATU), and its forerunner, the Federation of South African Trade Unions (FOSATU), which formed during the strikes in Durban.

In the period of black unions' banning and in the immediate aftermath of their unbanning, union organizing meant, first and foremost, education about the need and possibility of unionizing. This entailed persuading workers of the existence of a heretofore latent or secreted right within themselves, one that they might otherwise not realize was their own. In this sense, it was a project of recognition that created the desire for a right and then posited that right as anterior, because of people's positions as workers. But this was only the beginning of a process that demanded alliances between otherwise remote sectors of the economy, and among individuals who were systematically forbidden to gather in groups. This is why, at least for leftists, organizing was also a matter of learning to read for commonalities in difference (whether professional, ethnic or local) and staving off the belief that middle-classness could substitute for and satisfy the desire for the common with the in-betweenness and the consumer-based mimesis of the capitalist classes. In 2009, Matthews could say that the ANC had become overly concerned with protecting the interests of the rising middle class and that it had lost sight of the need for communism to supplement the national liberation project and to remain its unremitting critic. What had been useful at one point (overcoming the Apartheid efforts to forestall the emergence of a black middle class and to prevent black capital accumulation) had become an end in itself, and this becoming an ends-of-means was also associated for him with a new anti-intellectualism and a turn away from reading.

Matthews's political trajectory has been much discussed, and he has been accused of political fickleness (and even traitorousness), especially by ANC partisans.[57] His remarks, however, which are irreducible to his person, bid one to take note of a generally unaccounted dimension of the June student uprisings, most of which point back to 1973 or 1974 as their germinal moment. In many of those accounts, former students recall that encounters with the images and ideas that would radicalize them—the news of the Frente de Libertação de Moçambique (Liberation Front of Mozambique or FRELIMO) and its efforts to oust the Portuguese in Mozambique, the events in Angola, or the speeches of Martin Luther King, Malcom X, and the Black Panthers in the United States— all came through reading. "Reading about Martin Luther King in particular," claimed a student named Khala, "because he had a particular influence also . . . not so much [in terms of] politics, but forming ideas as well as identifying with a leader that could articulate the aspirations of his people so eloquently. It was just the in-thing to get to read those books." Twala also described himself as "always reading," "reading everything" (even James Hadley Jones, he joked) and in his recollection, it was this reading that made him receptive to the pamphlets first brought to him by a cousin.[58] Television was nonexistent. But this absence does not explain the depths to which reading was thrilling for him. For it threw him toward others, from whom he received literature, and it threw him toward other others with whom he would share these texts and his excitement. These became the subject of that political talk whose suppression the teachers had attempted to ensure. The schools and their debating teams were thus not merely the locus of schooling or ideological subjectivation, although they were that, too. They were places where the learning and rehearsal of what we can still call, by way of shorthand, modern political subjectivity took place.

Rehearsals do not always make a good performance. In Matthews's estimation, the purpose of the Communist Party—which would ultimately be realized in the elimination of all classes, and thus the working class—had metamorphosed within the tripartite alliance into the defense of the middle class, and this transposition was masked by disingenuous party-political jargon. Talking political became "superficial verbal adherence to progressive ideas." In such cases, there is language, but it cannot serve the purposes of articulating the necessarily self-effacing leadership that, for Matthews, is the only form appropriate to working-class representation:

> Now of course there's a danger in that which we begin to see. There is a danger of the communists' responsibility to the working class being diluted in the national and a loss of, which is very important, of the independence of the party of the working class. Now when we say independent we don't mean it in a vulgar sort of way ... it's not in a vulgar way but it's in a way which protects the interests of the workers in the interest of the furtherance and progressiveness of humanity where at times the party has to be, not only critical of the national movement but even fight against wrong tendencies which occurred in a national movement. Now if the party is not strong enough intellectually and otherwise, it doesn't play that role. Now we seem to have lost that guiding role.[59]

Matthews adds that, in the absence of "unselfish" leadership, one is "left with language." What he describes in this phrase is language as remainder, detritus, the corpse of communication. A selfish monological language. The kind spoken by populist demagogues.

Matthews's invocation of *The Eighteenth Brumaire* in a discussion of the ANC leadership and especially its Youth League proposes an analogy between the new ideologues and Louis Napoleon, the petty despot who promises to represent the multitudes who have not otherwise been able to generate the conditions of self-representation, who have not learned to produce commonality on the basis of reading the social field in its full heterogeneity. It is interesting in this context to attend the description of an even less sympathetic critic of the ANC from within the union movement. Jabulani Mayaba, the COSATU operative cited earlier, recalled the rallies that had been such central events in the anti-Apartheid movement as sites of distraction more than mobilization. "It seemed at the time," he said, "that the people who were in the ANC camp or UDF [United Democratic Front] were not really concerned about reading politics. Politics to them was attending rallies, listening to so and so speaking." By contrast, he said, "We used to go house to house in East Rand talking about politics."[60] For Mabaya, reading politics and talking politics were one and the same, and they were the antithesis of that ecstatic being together of large rallies and demonstrative strikes, the mark of which was thralldom to a single orator and the sensation of pure identity. The labor of producing collectivity through persuasion could not be bypassed. This is why, after the rallies, he and his fellow union members "would have to start from scratch."[61]

Some of that slow work took the form of reading poetry to mineworkers and discussing it with them. The point of such reading was to both present and represent mineworkers' accounts of their experience in a way that was recognizable and compelling and to dislodge them from the sense of the normal that made such experience seem necessary: "Sometimes you've got challenges but because people who came before you, they had these challenges, so when you come, you think this is a way of life, that things must be like this."[62] This is radical pedagogy: putting that which has become normal into question. And if there is anything that points to the incompleteness of this project it is this expression, in the midst of strikes and riots, of a desire for things to return to normal. That aspiration is indeed common, and it is perhaps the common sense of those who are most afflicted during times of unrest

In his recounting of this antinormative poetic pedagogy to the Wits oral historian, Mayaba described a particular poem whose author he could not recall. It is an especially charged moment in the interview, quite unlike the rest of the recorded conversation. As transcribed, his description of this process is interrupted by an actual eruption of the poetry in a recitation of Vilakazi's *Ezinkomponi* (On the Mine Compounds).[63] One senses in the transcript a kind of giving way to the poem, as though to a powerful spirit. It had remained in Mayaba's mind, above all the others, for decades. We have encountered that poem as both a work of literature and a reference in the critical literature on migrancy. Mayaba's invocation testifies to the reach and sway of that text in its oral transmission, where it became a medium and incitement to "talking political" despite or perhaps because the author's name had vanished into the memory of a collective project.

The first book that Mayaba recalls reading that "had anything to do with things political," was Ngũgĩ Wa Thiong'o's *River Between*. Reading it, he had "realised that these books . . . are like a quiet deep water because when you sit down, when you read it for the second/third time and you get somebody who can help you analyse the book, you realise that it was something more than the river between."[64] In this case, something more figured into the topographical idiom as depth, which referred not only to the history of colonialism but also to the understanding of its effects. Mayaba's later reading was heavily influenced by Malcolm X, and he found the latter's disquisition on the difference between the house and the field slaves to be an apt paradigm for thinking about the changed relationship between the ANC and the workers who, he thought, could be represented only by the unions, the kinds of unions that recite poetry and go house to house, the kinds that were not just agitating but also educating: "Our comrades got into power, it raises the question of the relationship between the master and the slave, it became clear, as it is now people just don't want to read it, you cannot be a master and have an interest at heart for slaves." Mayaba also believed that this paradigm explained the problem of education in South Africa: "Now when you are a house nigger you get crumbs from Master so you're able to go to school, but the child of a field nigger will never get an opportunity to go to school. So when you read that book [*River Between*], that's what you pick up, that those who are in Christianity they are afforded the crumbs from the Master and their children are able to go to school and those who reject Christianity their children will always—." His interviewer finished the sentence, saying their children will always be "slaves of slaves."[65]

This imagination of the place of colonial Christianity, which links it to both learning and slaving, marks a point of departure between Mayaba's and Matthews's discourses, with the former conceiving precolonial society as having been entirely subordinated by Christianity, and the latter seeing Christianity as having been encompassed by that prior but heterogeneous tradition. Matthews speaks appreciatively about what he understood to be the strength of *ubuntu* in Kotane's thought, namely its ethic of being with and listening to others of different traditions and commitments. His examples extend even to the Zulu chief Shaka's prohibition on killing the white missionaries who arrived, as prophesied by Ntsikana, with their book and "buckles" without holes, namely coins, which is to say money (in the 1820s). For Matthews, *ubuntu*, if taken seriously and not fetishized in a nostalgia for the prior or imagined as an essence of Africanity, is on the side of reading. It is likened to reading precisely insofar as it enables and encourages the encounter with others, and the discovery in that process of a common interest or purpose in being together.

Now, this common interest or purpose is not yet common identity. Indeed, the mark of his nonidentitarianism comes in Matthews's praise of Kotane's commitment to and enactment of *ubuntu*. This commitment permitted him, as an atheist, to share a political project with his more devoutly Christian and Jewish contemporaries, including Tambo who, he notes, carried with him a recording of the Messiah by the London Philharmonic, conducted by Sir Malcolm Sergeant. *Ubuntu*, intones Matthews, "was the common thread, it's deeper than Christianity, the whole outlook of African[s], if you call *Ubuntu*, that is the concept of humanity which Africans have got *and we shouldn't perhaps say Africans* but particularly in this part of the world there's something about their attitude to humanity."[66] To the extent it operated, such a concept would prevent the kind of ideological tests that the "vulgar" Marxists, as Matthews called them, wanted to impose. It would also prevent every kind of exclusionary gesture based in identity. Others have noted, sometimes suspiciously, that Kotane himself assumed a representative function, in many ways becoming the personal proxy of the Communist Party in and for the ANC, even before the creation of the Tripartite Alliance in the democratic era. His willingness to play that role, which Matthews praises but others, like Chris Hani (head of the South African Communist Party and key figure of the ANC's armed resistance), criticized, enabled but perhaps also confused the party's autonomy in relation to the project of national liberation.[67]

It would be too easy to say that the difference between these modalities of representation was made visible in or by the tension between the students and the mineworkers and, by extension, between a racialized generation and something called the "working class." To begin with, these two categories are themselves internally heterogeneous. The students at Naledi High School had a practical awareness of this, which, for a while, enabled them to pursue the work of persuasion and the eventful act of becoming a collective. This was a new kind of event—unlike the sinkholes, as Green has argued. But the temptation to short-circuit the work it required and promised—which, as Matthews suggests, is also a work of reading—often proved irresistible. One of the tropes by which this task of reading and fabricating a collective subject was short-circuited was that of the *baptism by fire*. In that term, the awful power of fire, which, as we have seen, continually erupts in the place where communication fails, was invoked in a description of education by analogy with the forge, as tempering by experience. It thus partakes of the whole constellation of terms, figures, metaphors, and tropes grounded, as it were, in mining as well as in the mythology of Christian sacrifice. And as one might expect, given this cluster of significations, the baptism by fire was more like a hardening than a transformation of consciousness.

Forging Relations?

The *Report of the Commission of Inquiry Into the Riots at Soweto and Elsewhere* invokes the notion of trial by fire in its account of one the commissions' few interviews with a student: Tebello (sometimes spelled Tebelo) Motapanyane, titling this section of the report "The riot as a baptism by fire." In its summary, Motapanyane is referred to as both an ANC member and a "scholar," the latter term marking him as a high school student, although he was about 21 years of age at the time:[68]

> This youth leader also said that the youth had gained invaluable experience of combat in the riots. It had provided "fertile ground" for the armed struggle and for other forms of positive action against the racist regime. In reply to a further question, he stated that the youth now listened to what their leaders said. If the leaders assigned a task to them, they carried it out without hesitation. The hesitancy found among people who were afraid of arrest of similar action no longer existed. The people have become more involved. It was the experience of the struggle at home that had removed this fear; fear of

the police, fear of the Government. They were becoming progressively more involved in the struggle against racism, social injustice, and exploitation.[69]

Tebello Motapanyane appears many times in the Commission report, especially in regard to the burning of a police vehicle following a dispute over getting medical care for a student. One witness explained that Motapanyane only set the car (a Volkswagen) alight after a policeman had refused to speak to him, saying "*Ek nie praat met Kaffirjies nie*" (I don't talk to little kaffirs; this latter term being an extremely pejorative one).[70] In the first place, Tebello did not accept the image of himself that was solidified in the abuse. It was a hallucinatory figure to which he refused to conform—and how could he conform to an image of pure negativity? But it was his being told that he would not be spoken to, and told as much in the language that the youth were refusing, that was like a match on waiting fuel. It was indeed that other strike, that catalyst, that marked the place where language exploded. The burning was nonetheless its own form of communication, one announcing the failure of communication: the very apotheosis of language.

In the epic poem by H.M.L Lentsoane, titled "Laboraro le lesoleso," the episode with the Volkswagen is recounted, not only as a source of transformation in the growing rage of the neighborhood, but also as the locus of overwhelming sensation, and the experience of being surveyed. It is poignant testimony to the confusion of signs that was taking place.

> A Volkswagen squatted nakedly in the fire,
> then a Ford went to lie on its side,
> a Bedford was burned to ashes.
> The owners were visibly upset,
> weeping while gazing at the charred bones.
> The sky was adorned with thick black smoke,
> tufts of tail exploded with Air-That-Made-One-Sneeze,
> people were left crying helplessly.
> A small iron bird tilted to and fro in the sky,
> it hovered but never sat down,
> it kept vigil controlling the day's riots,
> it made us inhale a thick wind,
> it left us with a bitter tase,
> a deadly smoke.[71]

Shortly after giving his testimony, Motapanyane, who had been secretary general of the South African Students' Movement (the high school partner of SASO) and chair of the Soweto Action Committee, fled to England. In late 1977, he was interviewed by *New African* and asked about the apparent tension between student activists and migrant laborers as well as parents. This was his answer: "There was no disunity—the migrant workers were misinformed. They are not educated and are people who can be easily influenced, and the police were clearly involved in this. The government just told them that if they stayed away from work they would never get work again and would be taken back into rural areas." He continued, "Some talks took place between the students and the migrant workers and as a result during the second stay-away from work in September last year they also struck. They understood that their struggle and our struggle is the same. There is now also increasing co-operation and under-standing between the parents and the students."[72]

Much of the interview was taken up with possible sources of division in SASM, including Black Consciousness. Motapanyane "did not see black con-sciousness as an end; black consciousness was there as something to sensi-tise the people, but it could not liberate. It was simply an attitude of mind." Emancipation required something else. In another, more extended interview, he explained why the students, who had initially been brought together through "discussion groups," "no longer believe[d] in talking and talking." He continued, "The very act of struggle will teach the youth new advanced methods of raising the struggle to a new level."[73] And this meant joining the then-banned ANC, the local party with most robust international infrastructure. According to Motapa-nyane, "There is no reason for us to make ourselves martyrs making a lot of noise and getting ourselves killed by Vorster. The best is to go underground and organise the struggle in a most disciplined and a most professional way."[74]

Go underground. And indeed, the movement went underground and going underground, burrowing in the darkness beneath the law, beyond the law, to claim legitimacy for the anti-Apartheid cause, meant organizing the labor that went underground. And this is precisely where the double specter of hierarchy and authoritarianism arose. It arose as a mimesis between the corporate fan-tasy of a pared-down instructional language that could affect a perfect hierarchy, and a workerist fantasy of homologous hierarchies, with shop stewards receiv-ing training and assuming the function of representation. It arose, too, between many political undergrounds—both anti-Apartheid and white supremacist—and the military system on which they were modeled and of which they partook, organized as they were around clear lines of command and shared vocabularies of rank, order, and authority. We will discuss those undergrounds in the follow-ing chapters, but we can already discern this double specter in Motapanyane's rendition of the relationship between students and migrant workers as one of commanded unity. Indeed, his description of the resolution of generational antag-onism implies a nearly magical communication and a process of transformation that seems oddly devoid of persuasion. The migrant workers are declared misin-formed, and the students, it seems, had only to expose this fact to change antag-onism into alliance. Motapanyane apparently never doubted that his own speech and analysis could command the mineworkers to recognize the student move-ment as its representative and its proxy.[75] His imagination of what was learned in the trial by fire was obedience to the party leadership: "If the leaders assigned a task to them, they carried it out without hesitation. The hesitancy found among people who were afraid of arrest of similar action no longer existed."[76]

Motapanyane clearly overestimated the purity and depth of the transformation as well as the potency of the student argument with older workers. More than four decades later, the same arguments are being adduced—about the ignorance and unschooled nature of mineworkers from the national periphery and about their concomitant vulnerability to unscrupulous creditors, manipulative union bosses, and deceptive labor brokers. One is left to make sense of the many seeming contradictions in this vacillating history of the effort to enter into representation and to form common causes—against Apartheid and predatory capitalism—among students and workers. Talking was the source of an excitement and a politicization associated with a practice of reading by which conversation could open to others—their struggles and ideas—and to alterity more generally. It grew out of debates and was cultivated in discussion groups. And this excited and exciting conversation was offered as antidote to an experience of alienation associated with being forced to speak in a foreign language—not just any foreign language, but that in which black subjects were being consigned to the manual and the menial (Afrikaans) or that in which mineworkers were receiving instructions (Fanakalo). The bearers of power would not speak to the youths or workers and yet, they sometimes said as much, announcing their refusal in such a way as to assert the duality of language (that it communicates messages as well as a desire to communicate) while nonetheless conveying a refusal to communicate (the opposite of what Walter Benjamin imagined as the redemptive essence of language).[77] When communication failed, there was fire. That was true in 1973 and 1976, just as it was true in 1987 and again in 2005. And then again in 2012. In each of these moments, a remarked failure of communication led people to bemoan "just talking," In each of these moments, "talking and talking," as Motapanyane said, was intolerable. An eloquent loquacity could seduce, but it could also appear to be a deferral or an obstruction of social transformation. By contrast, slogans, jargon, and the verbal adherence to doctrine could be precipitously deadly.

Again and again, the stories of labor organizing in the mines depart from the simple story of catalysis or from the mutual excitement of student and workplace insurrection. This difference between narrative tropes hangs on the perception and the cultivated actuality of a nonurban, presumptively rural workforce—one we have come to think of as "tribalized" rather than tribal, ruralized rather than agrarian, even in the most intensively industrial sectors of the industry. The stigmata of the rural as the condition of the unschooled intruded at the point at which the student movement and the mineworkers seemed otherwise aligned in opposition to the Apartheid government. And this is why the first movement from Soweto to what is now Merafong was not to the mines but to the township. If township residents responded to their brethren's calls to solidarity, it would take another force to bring the mineworkers into a

more fully politicized oppositional movement. As already noted, many mineworkers were antipathetic to the youth-based insurrection, and students, as
we have also seen, were often skeptical of mineworkers' intellectual capacities.
The catalysis, if that is the appropriate metaphor, that precipitated labor-based
organizing around the gold mines would come from elsewhere. Or at least, the
local events would need to be mediated by other forces. In the end, the township youth would be the ones most neglected by the post-Apartheid alliance of
the unions and the parties. But that outcome was not yet determined in 1976.

More Mediations?

Only two weeks before the uprisings in Soweto, the International Monetary
Fund had commenced regular gold auctions, and it was this fact, rather than
the uprisings, that was blamed for the fall in prices and thus revenues by the
Chamber of Mines.[78] In its annual report, it nonetheless referred to the "disturbances" as a source of lost investor confidence.[79] A year later, it reported:
"Fortunately, the urgent need to make full use of the country's manpower potential coincides with the widespread acceptance embracing all political groupings
in South Africa that job reservation based on racial discrimination is no longer
defensible or practical."[80] This resolution would be reiterated in the report of
the Wiehahn Commission of Inquiry into Labour Legislation (1979), which
recommended the termination of the exemptions from the Black Labour Legislation Act that, since 1956, had been enjoyed by the gold and coal mines. These
exemptions had been based on the claim that black mineworkers were intel-
lectually incapable of and therefore should be excluded from better remunerated categories of supervisory responsibility. To "refute the contention . . . that
Blacks are not sufficiently sophisticated to accept responsibility for safety or to
acquire the necessary competence," a contention made specifically in relation
to the deep gold mines, the Weihahn Commission asserted, "reference need
be made only to the concessions allowing team leaders more responsibility."
Then there was the example of the "successful assumption by Blacks of miners'
responsibilities in Zambia." The Commission did concede, however, that those
of a "rural and tribal background" might lack the relevant capacities, but it laid
the blame on the industry: it had "not recruited better equipped Blacks, . . .
failed to stabilize individual workers, and has neglected their training."[81]

It is not surprising that the report had virtually nothing to say about the systematic production of tribality through pass systems and homeland policies, which
were the conditions of possibility of the oscillating migratory system. Nonetheless, the Wiehahn Commission recommended the elimination of work reservations and encouraged the industry to develop "a more satisfactory future basis for
the recognition of trade unions than that of the closed-shop agreements."[82] The

latter had been virtually identical with the reservation system by which white miners were promised never to be under the supervision of any black person. In response, the government issued a white paper with an ambiguous declaration of support, but it deferred the task: "The Government accepts that adaptations are needed in the Mining Industry, as other industries, in the light of the economic development and growth of the Republic of South Africa and the accompanying structural changes in the economy and changes in employment patterns and in the supply and demand conditions in the labour market. The Government is, therefore, in principle in favour of adjusting the definition of 'scheduled person' to a non-differentiating definition of 'competent person' *at an appropriate time and in a suitable manner.*" While scrapping the Black Labour Relations Regulation Act of 1953, it nonetheless demurred, "no legislative amendment will be made before alternative safeguarding measures have been affected [*sic*]."[83]

But strikes became more regular. Workers began to resist the explanation of their "compound revolts" as "tribal conflict." In 1982, for example, seventy thousand mineworkers on the East Rand walked out in protest over low wage increases at Gold Fields's and Gencor's mines. Not only was the low rate of increase (which was nonetheless 12.5 percent that year) resented but so too was the relative low rate of pay for those unschooled workers in the lowest "bands." Anglo, which gave the highest pay rise, offered its surface workers a 19 percent increase, but underground workers received only 15.4 percent, thereby exacerbating the already existing hierarchy of remuneration.[84] The Chamber of Mines had encouraged a relatively toothless Black Mine Workers Union (BMWU) and was said to have written its constitution, but that union failed to enroll many workers. And so, following the mass strikes on the East Rand, where the oldest and least profitable mines were located at the time, and in the same year that the Weihahn Report was published in full, the NUM was finally established, obtaining the right to recruit members on the properties of mines, with the consent of their owners. As is well known, Cyril Ramaphosa, a young lawyer at the time, was its first secretary, and James Motlatsi was its first president. Beyond improved wages, it aimed to address workplace safety, but the issue that was most politically significant was the "stabilization" of the workforce, which meant the gradual and still incomplete elimination of the migrant labor system, and, as we have seen, the reencompassment of women and the entrenchment in peri-urban spaces of that patriarchal and gerontocratic authority that had previously been written under the name of the *tribal*. The union would increasingly offer training programs to employees and bursaries for their children, and it would, in due time, become a party to power and the school of both scandal and political ascent.

One of the reasons for NUM's membership's early rapid growth, says Jonathan Crush, was its apparently democratic process: "The NUM's rapid emergence as the dominant black union on the mines owed much to the tactical skills of its organizers, the leadership's responsiveness to grassroots' concerns, and the democratic structures which were quickly put in place."[85] It is therefore notable that its initial recruitment strategies made use of the existing hierarchies to produce its majorities, which were in fact majorities of minorities. Union-organizing activity was permitted and recognized by individual companies, rather than by the Chamber of Mines. Moreover, the recognition of the union depended on rates of participation within job grades. According to Crush, NUM recruited first in the grades with the smallest number of workers, so that it could quickly claim recognition for that grade. This effectively meant that it organized first with supervisory and skilled workers—precisely those whose higher pay had been the object of striker resentment at Western Deeps and elsewhere. Working from within the ranked structure of the industry, then, the NUM's democratizing project was not initially and perhaps never aimed at overcoming hierarchy but rather attempted to subvert that hierarchy for the purpose of obtaining what it increasingly referred to as "worker control."[86] It also made use of other organizational structures within which mineworkers had affiliations, including, if rarely, political parties.[87]

For a variety of reasons, including its very willingness to permit unionization on its mines, the rate of unionization was highest at Anglo American mines, which drew its labor supply largely from Lesotho and the Transkei. But even as the NUM extended its base, its rate of membership was highest in the higher-skilled segments of the workforce. In 1986, for example, 78.5 percent of its membership were in grades two to four of an eight-grade system. The bottom four categories, including the vast majority of the labor force, accounted for only 15.5 percent.[88] In 1989, still early in the development of the NUM, Crush wrote sympathetically of the union's capacity to respond to the interests of its mass base of mainly unskilled workers, adding that "as long as this situation persists the union may be prevented from falling under the control of a bureaucratized 'labour aristocracy' which uses it to service the needs of a more skilled, higher paying, co-opted segment of the labour force."[89] In retrospect, that early pattern may have foretold the opposite tendency, which was inscribed as an inner lining and permanent risk of the drive for "empowerment," precisely because it did not include the difficult project of educating people to move out of the division between the mental and the manual. Ultimately, the displacement of the NUM in the gold and platinum mines by the emergent Association of Mineworkers and Construction Union following the massacres at Marikana in 2012 (see chapter 16) may be linked to this early domination by the skilled workers and by the idea of mental labor's supremacy, which the union absorbed into itself and which continues to haunt the goldfields and the worlds built on its unstable ground. Soweto would become increasingly important in the consciousness of Khutsong's youth, but this was as much because of the misrecognition of the status that the student movement had in the consciousness of mineworkers at that time, as it was a reflection of the fact that the youth, as urban aspirants, would continue to imagine mineworkers as unlettered people still bound to village worlds.

CHAPTER 12

GO UNDERGROUND

Or, When Was Youth?

*Therefore all things whatsoever ye would that men should do to you,
do ye even so to them: for this is the law and the prophets.*

—Matthew 7:12

If you wrong us shall we not revenge?

—Shakespeare, *Merchant of Venice*

R eturning, again and again, first to the past and then to the future,
I keep writing about specters, crypts, and ghosts. Perhaps that
is because this book is written from a shifting present. Perhaps
it is because the Apartheid Thing won't let go. The phenomena, the logic, the
violence of Apartheid keeps returning, even where it is most vociferously repudiated. As Walter Benjamin writes, "Mourning is the temperament in which
feeling revivifies by means of masks the emptied world in order to have an
enigmatic satisfaction gazing upon it."[1] This is why so many of the rituals that
commemorate Apartheid's ostensible overcoming are mourning plays: they contemplate something that is supposedly behind, but in doing so, keep it in mind.
The ritual remembrances of June 16, 1976, with which the previous chapter

commenced, are such mourning plays. But so, too, are the struggles that arose in the aftermath of the National Union of Mineworkers' (NUM) emergence.

One might have expected that the union's formation would have opened onto a horizon of gradual improvement and that its gains in wages, housing accommodations, safety issues, and death benefits would change the conditions of many mineworkers for the better. In the popular imagination in the gold-mining region, the NUM plays a crucial role in the grand narrative of progress toward the goal of Apartheid's dismantling. In addition to heroism, the story has elements of both mourning and tragedy. In distinguishing between mourning and tragedy, I am once again invoking Benjamin, who has argued that the mourning play is a form emerging in and appropriate to times of disjunction. Benjamin called this time *baroque*—a term that can be extrapolated to historical epochs other than seventeenth-century Europe. Indeed, many scholars have referred to the legislative machinery of Apartheid as "baroque," in more or less precise, art historical terms. And perhaps the "baroque practices" that Achille Mbembe identifies as typically postcolonial are, in South Africa, additionally inflected by this history, by which they are haunted and which they cannot help but reiterate. Nonetheless, Benjamin's definition implies more than the ambiguity and fluidity that Mbembe singles out as the postcolonial baroque's definitive attribute, and more than the groundless involution that is implied by art historical usages.[2] For Benjamin, the baroque lacks an eschaton and a scenario in which all humans are brought together in their singularities. This is, says Peter Fenves, in an especially astute commentary, more than a matter of lacking "access to grace." The baroque is a space in which neither detail nor singularity has any place. One thing can easily stand for another, everything and everyone is one of a kind, and randomness reigns. This is true of death as well. In the baroque, the indiscernibility of death is what takes "refuge in mourning." Fenves adds that the mourner in this milieu "mourns less for the dead than for the indiscernibility of death or—but this 'or' is more expansive than exclusive—the absence of the messianic, the inaccessibility of justice."[3] But of course, this universal substitutability was unevenly distributed; under Apartheid, it applied to black subjects above and before all others.

Mourning over the inaccessibility of justice is not a lamentation and is not a dirge. Its tonality may well be frenzied. The allegorical theaters of which Benjamin writes were often ludic and terrifying processions characterized by an arbitrariness in which the sovereign could appear simultaneously as tyrant and martyr. Mourning plays of the seventeenth century were frequently devoted to the story of the prince, whose purpose was to both prevent a state of exception and to rule by merciless decision in the event of a catastrophe. Benjamin claims that it emerged as the despotic aspect of the Renaissance and as a manifestation of its "ideal of stabilization . . . unfold[ing] in all its aspects."[4] That ideal was central to the theological-political mode of thought in the baroque epoch, which was marked by an "over-strained transcendental impulse," and which first elaborated a theory of a state of emergency.[5]

I am not proposing direct parallels between seventeenth-century Europe (although that is the origin of the influx of the first Huguenot populations on the Cape) and the Apartheid state. But there is something of a baroque aesthetic, which is, as Benjamin notes, defined by a continuity between the drama and the historical real, in the period following the NUM's formation. This is not merely because it was the period of intensifying and increasingly repressive states of emergency enacted by the Apartheid government but because, in the townships and on the mine compounds, conflicts unfolded in the context of supposed "stabilization" and in the mode of mourning plays whose purpose was to "fortify the virtue of [their] audience."[6] This statement can only make sense if one realizes that such virtue was considered to be adherence to the rule and even more, the ruler, of one or another faction. The brutal theaters of despotism that arose in the gold-mining regions in the 1980s and 1990s were both valorizations of sovereignty and expressions of a desire for a rule of law that could not be realized and that constantly devolved into commandment and its policing. Consequently, we may say that these same theaters staged the rule of the one but not of singularity, for they were either hampered by the legacy of ethnic and racial categorization, by which everyone is only one of a type, or they were constrained by a workerism that could not yet imagine the purpose of communism as the elimination of all classes, including the working class, and thus all categorical hierarchy based in the distinction between mental and manual labor (as discussed in chapter 11).

Yet just as the mourning play in Europe was the aesthetic form appropriate to a time of transition, one that would give way to rationalism and a belief in the rule of law in the seventeenth century, so too the period of the 1980s and 1990s was one of transition in South Africa—if not to a rule of law then to its ideal and even its fetishization.[7] The problem with confronting the youth and the labor movements in the townships of the Rand, and especially Khutsong, in the 1980s wasn't, however, quite what Benjamin took from Wittenberg—the notion of a new but empty world—but it was not yet a newly ordered world.[8] As Benjamin has taught us, the establishing of a new order entails violence precisely to the extent that it is conceived on the model of law, in the mode of a new constitutional order that must make a break from what precedes it and generalize its principle as exclusive and originary. Nowhere is that more visible than in the way in which the police function was exercised in the conflicts of the era—by the South African police, to be sure, but also by every formation that took upon itself the rule of policing The Struggle. Efforts to reform the South African Police (SAP) leading up to, and after 1994, however necessary and ultimately compromised, were insufficient to address this more diffuse police function, which spilled well beyond the thin blue line.[9] If, in the immediate post-Apartheid era, the Truth and Reconciliation Commission was devised as an institution that resembled without being a court of law, it was partly in recognition that law and justice are not the same thing. But as the next chapters reveal, those who came before the Commission often cleaved to the belief that they are the same, that law is justice, and that force is necessary for its enactment. It is their testimony at the TRC of the late 1990s that is so haunted by the ghosts of the 1980s. As for tragedy, that genre of inevitably failed heroism in which the effort to achieve singularity devolves into the muteness of the one who is unlike all the others and thus without any basis for representation or communication, also haunts this story.[10] Amid it all, there is farce.

Underground Again

When Tebello Motapanyane concluded his interview in 1977 by saying that the only way forward was to "Go Underground," he meant entering the world of the banned and the secreted, the clandestine and the outlawed. This is indeed how it was described by the historian of the African National Congress (ANC) underground, Raymond Suttner. He called it "an invisible area, a zone outside the vision of society in general," and "the space where dangerous, heroic acts occur," and one that was also "open for abuse."[11] When the NUM emerged, other struggles moved further underground. Unions, including both the white Mine Workers Union (MWU) and the mainly black NUM, concealed and protected activities that targeted state institutions and that were aimed at more radical social change as well as those that opposed them. In those places, which, like the dolomitic caverns beneath the surface, were concentrated in the gold-mining areas, conflict was both spectacular and often secreted. It was associated with terror, and it was experienced as tyranny. It had its martyrs and its heroes, its despots and its militias. It was also often economized in an inverted order where the golden rule (do unto others as you would have done unto you) devolved into mere vengeance. But such vengeance was also the mask within which the bearer of the law, whether gangs, political parties, or the police, was the one that could attribute guilt to the other.

Let us then consider the accounts of those who were present to these conflicts. The first among these is the man who was at the time mayor of Carletonville. I have described him in this chapter as a tragic figure, but this is not because he presents, in the mode of Hamlet or Aeschylus's Prometheus, the figure of one who has left behind the "ethos of the ethnos" and risen above all others, albeit at the expense of muteness. It is rather because his desire to be the perfect representative failed, and for reasons of his extreme adherence to the party whose decision the local population disavowed, he became *as one of a number*. In this way, he also became a virtual nobody. Because the party was deemed not to have listened to the people, no one listened to him anymore. So much was this the case that when he was appointed by President Jacob Zuma as finance minister, the unanimous refrain of the press was, "Who is Des van Rooyen?"

I interviewed the then-mayor of Merafong, David Douglas "Des" van Rooyen, in August 2008, against the backdrop of the redemarcation protests. His coming-of-age occurred within the historical arc outlined in chapter 11. I had spoken to Des many times before this formal interview. On this occasion, we were conversing in his office. It was shortly after his house had been razed, and he was no longer living in Khutsong. Two muscular bodyguards accompanied him to the door, inspected our gear (Songezile was recording as I asked questions), and sat in the waiting room, which we entered after having been formally greeted by the older Afrikaner secretary who had sat at that same desk for years and who had previously served the National Party-dominated local government. The hallways of City Hall, which was no longer the building that had graced the folder on which I had received the map of Carletonville, were stone, but the offices and stairways were padded with thin and fraying carpeting. It had the appearance of pressed ash-colored hair. The office was lined with heavy wood-paneled shelves neatly lined with binders of documents, but it seemed cavernous because of the sparseness of its furnishings. The mayor, a diminutive man, bald and with an almost cherubic face, was dressed in an impeccable black safari suit, with a black and white striped t-shirt. During our lengthy interview, he sat with military uprightness behind an enormous desk, rarely moving his hands and only occasionally pausing to sip from a glass of water. Behind him, looking down from high on the wall was a huge portrait of the then-sitting president Thabo Mbeki. It was not a painted portrait, but a hooked-rug rendition of his face, with his stubbly beard disappearing into brown and black acrylic threads.

Listening to this recording again in 2022, I was struck by the temerity of my own questions, and by the fulsomeness and forthrightness with which the mayor responded. It was morning and as the day wore on, different birds could be heard in the background: wood pigeons first and then Highveld songbirds. But what had struck me then struck me again, fourteen years later. It was the unrelenting story of learning: of wanting to learn and of learning to want, and above all, of learning the ways of violence. It was also the story of fidelity to the party and of the desire for power, in and through the party.

In the interview, van Rooyen recounted that he was born in 1968 in Mokokskraal and that he spent his first years on a farm near Ventersdorp, in the North West Province, about eighty-five kilometers from where we sat. A flat treeless plain of red soil and fields of grain, it is infamous as the home of the white supremacist and white separatist movement of the Afrikaner Weerstandsbeweging, or Afrikaner Resistance Movement (AWB). Today, it is also the site of an enormous and controversial statue of J.B. Marks, a member of the early Communist Party of South Africa and head of the short-lived Black African Mineworkers Union, who led its failed strike in 1946.

David was van Rooyen's Christian name, and Douglas was a name given after an uncle. Des was a nickname, but the only moniker he ever used. He traced his parentage to a mixed-race marriage between a Tswana woman named Festina and a man named Isaac, whose genealogy included, in its distant past, one Oom Japie. The mayor described Oom Japie as a "typical coloured" who used the surname of his farm employer van Rooyen. Later, when the mayor was appointed as Zuma's finance minister, a position he held for a mere four days, a former schoolmate would describe how the mayor was once beaten by a teacher for not having a Tswana name.[12]

Often commencing his explanations with the phrase, "I must indicate that . . ." the mayor told me that he had started his schooling in Ratsehai, just fifteen kilometers from Ventersdorp. After his first two years of study, he and his family moved. "My mother got officially married to my father, and we relocated to Khutsong." They had secured a three-room house with some extended relations, and he was enrolled in Phororong elementary school for grade three. The transition had been difficult, and he had not been able to pass his standard, "because I was still a bit in the dark, coming from the farm areas and landing into the township of Khutsong." Nonetheless, in retrospect, he was "grateful" that he had had to repeat standard one. This was a "wake-up call for me," he said, and not only that, for, having been given the opportunity to repeat, the young van Rooyen, who was one of six children, was "graded as one of the best performers." For his success, he was awarded "some textbooks" in the subjects on which he excelled, namely agriculture, mathematics, and English. Because of their "financial constraints" and because his failure had ensured that he and his younger sister were in the same class, however, the parents had had to decide which of the children would continue on with schooling. His belated success had made the decision. "Fortunately," he said, because of his good performance, he was chosen from among the two siblings, and it was he rather than she who was sent off to board at Bethel High School in 1984. Fortunately for him, of course. His sister's fortune was not as good.

The mayor's father had worked in a drycleaner in Carletonville and then for a painter. He had then become a taxi owner. His mother was a domestic worker until she became a "full-time housewife," looking after the family. When I asked him what he recalled about Khutsong, what had made him feel "in the dark," he remarked on the crowdedness of his classrooms. "This aspect of having to be in one class with many people. In Ratsehai, we were in small groups only." The whole village of his early youth had had a population of about one hundred. The move to Khutsong was "a bit scary," he recalled, and he had been bullied. "In those days if you came from a farming area, you were known as a *moho* or a *barrie*, someone who can't maneuver, or survive the daily routines of the township. One was a bit the center of attraction. Everyone wanted to test these 'travelers.'"

He developed "tactics to survive," and in a miniature act of guerilla warfare, he had used the classroom instruments to fashion weapons. "I was well known for using a pen to fight back whenever I was provoked. So, I used to stab most of my classmates with a pen. And I was notorious for that. As a result, most of the people wouldn't even dare to provoke me . . . not even the big boys. . . . I also enjoyed this temporary recognition as one of the best pen-stabbers, I mean, in a class."

I asked the mayor what happened to transform him from a classroom tough into a politically oriented activist. Did 1976 play a role? His response took me by surprise:

> I think, it all started in Ratsehai . . . a farming area, Coetzee farm, where my family was located and working, it's a farm that is annex [*sic*] with the farm, next to that of Eugene Terre'Blanche, one of the most notorious leaders of the AWB. So, the brutality that was unleashed by Eugene Terre'Blanche, using our own people to do it against ourselves. It was one area that made me to start questioning the disparities of our society. Because I remember at some stage, at an early age of 7, I was a victim of this brutality. I went to participate in a tomato farm—child labor—with the sole intention, during school holidays, of provid-ing for my family, my grandparents. On the way back, carrying these toma-toes as a form of payment—tomatoes as a form of payment—I met Eugene Terre'Blanche with his security team. They were driving into Ventersdorp . . . [he speculates on Terre'Blanche's security operations in service of residences and businesses]. They stopped. I tried to hide, but their search lights were very powerful. And they stopped there, and they kicked me and all of a sudden, all of my tomatoes were turned into nothing. They smashed those tomatoes. From that day, that's when I really started questioning the disparities of our time, and also mainly the treatment of our people by white farmers.

One has to listen past the party line, the ideological clichés, to hear the tragedy. A bag of tomatoes—but also a day's labor and a proud sense of the capacity to help his family. All gone.

That was in 1975. As in so many other narratives previously considered, the force of a residual feudality enveloped the future mayor's life and set the scene for this emblematic experience in the theater of Apartheid's petty cruelty. As for 1976, he had not been aware of the protests, or the more than six thou-sand people blocking the highway and stoning the Greyhound buses in Khut-song. "During that year of 1976. Obviously, the Soweto upheavals were at its height. I know that while I was in school there were some small incidents that were reported in Khutsong, of students trying to set light to a bar. But that was it." For him, the turning point had come in 1983, when a school assembly had been visited by members of the Western Transvaal Local Authorities. They informed the students about an incident at a camp where some senior learners had been taken. Apparently, some of the youths had "tried to talk politics" at the camp (they were resisting, he said, being brainwashed and recruited into the police force (as Black Jacks). Some had later been "apprehended and tortured." He had visited some of them upon their return, and, he claims, asked if they would be interested in starting a local branch of the Congress of South African Students (COSAS). Only one of the three was sufficiently unscathed to agree, but by then, it was 1984, and Des was to begin his more advanced studies at boarding school. As it happens, "in 1984, in Potchefstroom and Ikaheng, there was agitation already afoot to establish a branch of COSAS. So, I availed myself."

What did "establishing a branch" entail? For the mayor, who was not only young but notably petite, the assignment was recruiting new members. "Just signing membership forms and attending meetings to discuss issues that were pertinent at that boarding school and in education more broadly. As a result of the perfection of this assignment of recruiting, the ranks of COSAS were swelled mainly by people of my age." The threat, he says, was perceived mainly by the school management, and "they did their best to discourage me." To lure him away from these activities, he says he was offered a bursary to study abroad. The principal was rumored by learners to be the Central Intelligence Agency (CIA) or possibly with the South African Special Branches. Whomever they worked for, they sent recruiters to Khutsong to persuade his mother that he should accept this bursary. She had not been supportive of her son and "could not imagine challenging the Apartheid system. In fact, she cried," asking him why, as a child of a poor family, he could not accept this invitation to better himself. "But I was categorically clear, that it was not about me but about this system." The young van Rooyen was suspicious of the so-called opportunity. How could they make such offers to every potential opponent of Apartheid? "This is not a sustainable intervention. COSAS was calling for a total transformation of the whole system." A fellow student apparently took the bait, for which reason his membership in COSAS was terminated. But the mayor doubted that his classmate ever got to the United States, and he believed that the entire episode had been an attempt to "prepare infiltrators."

Then came the second of the three great trials that would precipitate his metamorphosis. In 1985, complaints about food at the school ("we were made to eat tripe that was not clean") led to a boycott. The campaign was widely supported "except some few matriculants, thinking that we were aiming to strop their education—which was not the case. These matriculants were ladies . . . who were resisting [the boycott]." The mayor's discourse began to accelerate as he described the scene. The students of COSAS "decided to have a meeting about it. It was a very interesting meeting. We had to agree that we had to act against these individuals and the best way of doing so was to cane them." He smiled as he said this. "They must understand that we mean business." Cane trees grew around the school, and weapons were thus at hand. "We then had to say, you'll have to excuse us . . . , the girls, because this action will need men only." He was now smiling broadly, whether awkwardly in my presence or in satisfaction I could not tell. "It is only us boys and men who will be able to handle this action. It was very interesting." Yet, the practicalities of the discipline soon revealed themselves, because the boys did not know where the girls who had refused the boycott slept. And it was the female members of COSAS who pointed this out, insisting that, if the boys were going to mete out this punishment, the girls would have to give the instructions on where to find the intransigents, and point the finger, as it were. The boys demurred.

The future mayor woke early that next morning, full of excitement, at "half past 3." He was, as he said, "in the forefront." But the effort "sparked chaos." The police were called, parents were called, and in the evening, the following day, all of the disciplinarians were arrested. At the police station, says the mayor, they were assaulted and then told the details of the deaths they would face if they didn't cooperate. The COSAS students were defended by the anti-Apartheid lawyer Krish Naidoo. For twenty-five days, they were held without bail before being released, and the charges were dismissed. It was near exam time. Having been exiled from the dormitory, the students had to prepare at home and travel to the exam site daily. Van Rooyen spent his days studying in the Khutsong municipal library, which would later be razed along with his house during protests against his government (chapter 14). But the young learner who had repeated standard one passed these exams and dreamt of medical school.

Between the self-defense of the pen-stabbing and the meting out of punishment against girls accused of violating the boycott, something had happened. What had enlarged the boy's sense of self and immunized him against the bullies was now abstracted by the sense of a cause and by the consciousness of other children as audience members. Self-regard melded with the ecstasy of the group, and for a brief time, before the arrest, the young radical experienced that potency that accrues to the one who, in the act of enforcing the collective's dictates, takes into himself the destructive force of law. But as in all mourning plays, tyrannical potency vacillated with ignominy.

In 1986, as the new school year commenced, van Rooyen thought he could continue his studies, but the school would not have him. When he and his classmates tried nonetheless to return and occupy the dorm, the police were called again, and the youths were charged with trespassing. Although they were granted bail, his parents feared his return, for his cousin had been killed earlier, and they worried that a similar fate would await him. So, they did not fetch him from the prison and let him spend weeks in the jail at Coligny police station, a dank and filthy place where the aspiring revolutionary was harried by fleas and lice. Worst of all, the station was next to a railway, and in the night, the sound of the train, which passed by the jail on tracks only a few meters away, made him believe that he would be smashed. In his sleep and his solitude, he battled his fear and nourished his determination. That was in February 1986. By then, the "township was boiling." And so, upon return, the future mayor joined with the newly established Khutsong Youth Congress (KYC). According to van Rooyen, "We were copying what was happening in other townships."

A few months earlier, in June 1985, the young radical had also been recruited as a courier of "banned literature" by the ANC Youth League. Precisely because he was a young learner who looked even younger than he was, he was able to move around, stuffing materials into his school bag and riding the buses from office to office. "I didn't even know what these books were but I knew I was transporting banned literature." Some of the books were also "meant to be distributed, to feed the schools," he said. When I asked which books he had borne, he recalled the name Ngũgĩ Wa Thiong'o (as had Mayaba, described in chapter 11), though he did not say whether it had been the *River Between* or some other book, and I am not aware of Ngũgĩ having been banned in South Africa. But he also carried the worker journal, *UmSebenzi*, and literature "about armed struggle." And those items were most certainly banned.

The journey away had indeed been a source of learning. Enrolled in 1986 at Khutsong's Badirile Secondary School, which had been built in the decade since the Soweto uprisings, van Rooyen bragged, "Guess what, in a week's time, I was at the forefront of the students' struggles, again." I asked him how that had happened, and how quickly. It was "not that difficult for me to emerge in that situation." He had acquired a great sense of theatricality, and he knew that struggle was in the air and that every authority was available as a target (see Chief Twala's remarks in chapter 11). Calling on his classmates to support students who had been arrested elsewhere, he led a delegation to the principal's office asking for a statement of solidarity.

> I remember it was a Thursday. It was my first week at that school. The principal was not prepared to listen to us and he dismissed us. He told us to leave the premises. We weren't even allowed to give feedback to our constituents. And what happened is that, in the afterschool, my cousin was given a notice that he must call my parents and bring me to the principal's office. Only me, only one of four, was taken to the office. He told my parents that I am dangerous and I am unwanted at that school.

The principal demanded an apology. The young student refused. The parents implored their son. But in addition to the tactical skills he had learned in the face of bullies, and the endurance he had learned in prison, the young van Rooyen had acquired a language in which to talk politics in a manner that identified his humiliation with his fellow students' unrealized interests. This was the inverted form of chiefly power, as Pierre Clastres describes it, but now in the idiom of a generational class.[13] Their desire was becoming one with his will. "Why must I apologize, because the reality of the matter is that we were here to present as delegated by other students?" he had demanded of the teacher. "We were not here to force you to maybe fight. What is wrong in that?" When he did "report back" to his "constituents," speaking now from a present in which he was an elected and accountable authority rather than a student claiming the empty floor for a not-yet-articulated desire, they determined that it was not van Rooyen but the principal who needed to be expelled.

In the story, as he narrated it, a sense of collectivity congealed in the act of accusation and expulsion. As in the case of the girls who were to be disciplined for violating the boycott, power concentrated itself in the moment that guilt was attributed. The task for the mayor was to make this fact appear to be the outcome of argument, a logical conclusion to a legitimate process even though there had been no formal charge, no evidence adduced, no trial or explication of judgment other than what the young man had told his classmates. To the extent that his word was believed, his speech gained in authority.

Among the students there had been fear of the principal and rumors that he "used muti." His power was so unfathomable to them, recalls the mayor, that it required the explanation of magical substance. To this notion, the young revolutionary capitulated only in explanation. For he agreed that the principal's power was unfounded and indefensible. In answer to what he deemed to be their superstitious fear, van Rooyen reportedly said, "muti doesn't work here, here we are in the revolution." For a moment, the revolution was a rationalist undertaking—as it often is in Marxist discourse—although most scholars in South Africa insist that popular protest movements are rarely devoid of some magicality.[14] But its rationalism was not reasonable, and it was infused with a passional intensity that would overflow it. Nonetheless, it was not easy to get the principal down from the podium, explained the mayor, especially because the more senior learners were having none of the action. So, he "took a stone, just a small stone . . . and threw it on the roof of the classroom. That caused many others to throw stones on the roof, and the old man had to take cover."[15]

Somehow the whole history of both youthful insurrection (stone-throwing from the barricades, in the street) and accusatory mass violence (the stoning of the morally condemned) coursed through him in that moment. Its force demanded mimesis and summoned its own massification. It also provided him with his opening. For, as the stones fell clattering, the future mayor was able to address the student body with his newly empowered voice. He says he explained to the other learners that he had been forced to apologize for nothing and that the principal was not supporting the cause. He (van Rooyen) had indeed apologized, but only for having brought inconvenience to his parents, not for what the teacher had thought was his impertinence, nor for mobilizing the students whom he claimed to merely ventriloquize. The teacher had extracted from him a false or at least an inauthentic speech. They had all been maligned in the process, they had all been deprived of the capacity to speak politically (to "talk politics" in the sense described in chapter 11). And for this reason, the principal was "escorted out of the office, as learners held bricks."

Once again, the police were called. Expulsions followed. And something was learned. "Now, that pushed us to focus on advancing our cause outside of the schoolyard," said the mayor. And, as a result of that advance, he said, the youth congress emerged as a "very strong" force.

The One of the Many

All of this is the mayor's narrative, and it can be treated as such. I am not in a position to verify it, nor to dispute it. It tracks with the official records of events and scholarly histories of the era. Some of the people I spoke to at the time of our interview cast doubt on the claims to youthful leadership that the mayor had made. Others affirmed his accounts and expressed dismay that he, who had been a struggle comrade, had become the mayor who presided over the most despised legislative decision in the history of the municipality, namely the transfer of Khutsong and Carletonville outside of Gauteng's provincial jurisdiction. By the time I met him, he was persona non grata in the township. And yet, he did not resign or abandon his post. His party loyalty was tragically pure.

The Truth and Reconciliation Commission heard a great deal about the conflicts that unfolded in Khutsong and Carletonville after 1984. But van Rooyen is not mentioned in its many volumes of published hearings that I can discern, including the list of names that appeared as witnesses and whose testimony did not become the basis of public hearings. The only reference to him appears indirectly, in the mention of his mother, Festina, who was reported to have been tortured by the police at the Welverdiend police station, near Oberholzer when they were searching for her "political activist son."[16] The mayor did not mention this when I interviewed him. He said only "some of us were arrested," and spoke of his own capture and transport to the Oberholzer jail in the "boot of a Ford Sierra." He described his arrest as the result of police paranoia, claiming that the police had had a distorted impression of the extent to which the youth were armed at that time. Later, he would admit to "handling" and "distributing" small arms.[17] But that was after 1988. Other accounts of the school boycotts and of the attacks on teachers and businesses, and then the descent into terror, make no mention of his leadership of the protests at

Badirile Secondary School. And in the only account of the burning of a teach-er's property in 1986 that appears in the TRC report, he goes unmentioned, although a United Democratic Front (UDF) supporter named Ephraim Jonas Israel Motsumi is said to have been shot and injured by the police as a result of the arson.[18] But this does not mean that he was not active or indeed instigating "actions." Nor does it prove that he was present—or absent.

If van Rooyen's discourse commenced—and I had asked him to commence—with his own story of coming into political consciousness, he was not exclu-sively concerned with his own deeds. Importantly, he distinguished the struggle as it unfolded in Soweto, where there were senior leaders guiding and assist-ing the youth movement, with that in Khutsong. "In Khutsong it was led by young people, of our age group." These youths were forced to negotiate what the mayor described as the emergence of a "serious challenge in 1985 in this area," with only the paradigms of the past in a zone that had been encircled and abandoned by the state. At that time, the township saw the hardening of ideo-logical differences between the two competing schools of radical thought: Black Consciousness (also identified with the Azanian Students Movement) and the Freedom Charterists. Adherents of the Freedom Charter and by extension of the still-banned ANC but also the Communist Party, some of whom were also members of the UDF, were, at the time, generally members of the KYC, but so too were some members of Black Consciousness. Nonetheless, their leaderships were elsewhere—the Black Consciousness group in Bekkersdaal and the ANC in Potchefstroom.

In the following years, the mayor acknowledged, all sides lost control of the fight. The line between politics and vengeance dissolved. The idea of study still beckoned, but after his father died in 1988, the mayor took a job at the Deelkraal gold mine to help the family. He was so appalled by the wages paid then—800 rand per month (about $333 US), he said—that he promised himself to quit. Others had not managed to escape the blacklists that, by 1987, according to at least one witness at the TRC, circulated in Carletonville's gold mines and ensured that activist youth of Khutsong remained unemployed.[19] But then, he says, his unit was exposed, and he was informed, while still on shift under-ground, that he needed to flee. Without even waiting for his too-small pay packet, he left after shift's end. And things got worse.

The Final Report of the TRC states that "from 1989–91, there were at least seventeen extra-judicial executions in Khutsong. . . . The victims were all mem-bers of the Khutsong Youth Congress (KYC)." It adds that the KYC had "split into two factions—the 'Zim-Zims' and the 'Gaddaffis' [sic], both active UDF/ ANC supporters. The Commission received over sixty statements relating to this particular period in Khutsong's history." They are harrowing testimonies. They include stories about stabbing, beatings, necklacings, and the branding by police of activists using domestic implements like forks. There were bombings, shootings, torture with electric shock, stonings, and arson of houses and cars. Included are tales of rape and sexual mutilation, death by pick-axe or panga, and even in one case the cutting off of ears, which the wounded were made to eat.[20] Many were recounted to me in person and in graphic detail; many I only read in that great archive of suffering that is the TRC's voluminous report. Anyone who attended the hearings, or read the transcripts of the TRC knows the range and depth of this unspeakably cruel violence. In the case of Mera-fong, this sense is only exacerbated when one opens the historical frame of inquiry, to include the years before and after that brief window covered by the Commission. Indeed, everything about the TRC's analysis is shaped by its periodization—determined in its content and in its possibility by what is within or beyond the frame.

My tabulation of all of the incidents reported to the TRC and published, from the decade between 1983 and 1993, the period of the NUM's entrenchment and the beginning of so-called stabilization, reveals 149 deaths and serious injuries in the conflict between the police and the various youth gangs who emerged along with the ideological rifts in the anti-Apartheid movement. This does not include those that occurred in conflicts not involving the police or that were not gang-related. Other sources indicate that, by the early 1990s, the town-ship was engulfed in a general state of conflict often referred to as the "Reef Township War." From January 1990 until December 1992, between 3,166 and 4,815 people were dying annually in South Africa in violence associated with anti-Apartheid protests, counterinsurgency, and related activities. Several more thousands were injured, although death rates were higher than reported injury rates. The West Rand was relatively quiet compared with the neighboring East Rand (also a gold-mining region) and more distant parts of KwaZulu Natal. Nonetheless, more than seventy-seven violent incidents (including "massacres" in which more than four people were killed) occurred during protests each year on the West Rand, and by far the majority of those committed in 1990 occurred in Oberholzer, the district at the edge of Carletonville, in Merafong.[21] Violence directed at black policemen in the area accounted for 13 percent of police deaths in the entire country during that period.[22]

Much well-intentioned literature on the early part of this period and these conflicts construes the problem in terms of ideological conflicts among the divided factions of the KYC, and their efforts to assert authority during the period of boycotts when the ANC was not yet fully established in the township and contempt for the government's appointed councils had produced a vac-uum of authority. Thus conceived, the problem becomes a version of what Apartheid's ideologues referred to as an ancient habit of "black on black" vio-lence, and blackness is its explanation. We will want to open this assumption to a more scrupulous interrogation. And that means both examining the peri-odicity of the violence and reading the descriptions by township residents who

recall it. What such a double gesture shows is that the police played a crucial role in the violence—not only as agents and objects of violence but also
as the spectral force of a terrible mimesis that gripped and continues to grip
the township in spectacles of accusation and purgation that I refer to as the
mourning plays of Apartheid. Before trying to grasp the logic or the alogic of
these political-theological spectacles, with their tyrants and martyrs, and above
all, their ghosts, it is necessary to count and to take account of the dead, the
wounded, and the disappeared. As one does so, patterns emerge.

First, the players: The amaZimZim, or ZimZims, were a group of enforcers
originally identified with the Black Consciousness–oriented Azanian Students
movement but often thought of by township residents only in terms of the group's
opposition to the competing enforcers or gangsters who went by the name of
Gadaffi. As the TRC claims, some ZimZim had been members of the ANC
or the UDF, just as the Gadaffis had. But the latter took their name from the
man named Gadaffi who was said to have come from Soweto in 1989. The
TRC reports also recognize a third group, the amaShenge, who are thought to
have been older mineworkers who became vigilantes in the context of spiraling
bloodshed. Also in the mix were the long-lived Basotho gangs of the area called
the Marashea or amaRussia or the Russians. And then there were the South
African Police (SAP), the South African Defense Forces (SADF), the Bureau of
State Security (BOSS), the municipal police, and the private security companies
of the mining corporations.

Then, the incidents or events that constituted these dramas: During the first
three years of the decade from 1983 to 1993, every incident of injury, torture,
and death validated by the TRC was committed by the police, with one incident
involving the police and the SADF. But something began to change in 1986.
In that year, violence escalated precipitously. There were thirty-two cases, and
two of them involved ZimZims, one in collusion with the police. Two saw the
SADF joined with the police in committing violence. Yet, only after 1986 were
significant numbers of deaths or injuries reported to have been perpetrated by
the ZimZims and, later still, the Gadaffis. If the record is remotely representative (although the instances and rates of violence were likely much higher),
we are left with the question of what happened. For, if this period of conflict
expresses, as the TRC made clear, a contamination of dispute by vengeance
and even a degeneration into urban and peri-urban warfare, the violence did
not precisely originate in that conflict and cannot be understood, simply, as
its gradual outcome. It is concentrated, it acquires a tempo, and even a style or
styles, in the fight among gangs, but unless one includes the police in the story,
the violence cannot be explained. Is this another moment of catalysis? Or does
the apparent transformation conceal or encrypt another set of relations?

In asking this latter question, I do not mean to follow the route of those who
insist on the prehistory of so-called intergroup violence on the mines before

the advent of unionization, and on that basis, to project it outward. That argument tends to treat the wage disputes that were discussed in previous chapters in terms of the ethnicization of the job categories that were resented along with the differential pay increases on the mines, especially after 1973. Thus, for example, J. K. McNamara notes how the ethnicization of the graded workforce intersected with changing immigration policies made the foreign-born workers, and especially Sotho from Lesotho and Mozambiquan migrants, proportionally numerous in the upper grades, intensifying after 1963. In this context, "militant union actions on mines, inspired in part by wider political tensions and events in South Africa" saw an intensification of violence to the extent that "of the 330 mineworkers who lost their lives in inter-group clashes since 1974, fully one-third (118) died during 1986 alone." Immediately after making this observation, McNamara invokes the "war of words" about accountability for the violence and notes that the union accused mine management of "fomenting violence through the use of paid mercenaries (the so-called Russians),"[23] while management accused the union of targeting and assassinating black supervisors in the process of enforcing boycotts and strikes. He adds that evidence is (or was, at the time of his writing in 1988) scant. But he assumes the general structure of catalysis that was put in question in chapter 11.

What seems to have characterized the Marashea or Russian gangs is that, at any given time, some of their membership were mineworkers.[24] Almost invariably under the concentrated authority of one or another "unemployed" chief, the economy of the Marashea was both deeply imbricated in the life of the gold mines and was quite beyond its wage-earning segment. They operated on its periphery as a site of recreation, where the sale of alcohol, *dagga*, gambling, and prostitution occurred, thanks to the money earned on the mines—increasing, as we have seen, since the 1970s. As Gary Kynoch acknowledges and Motlatsi Thabang has emphasized, the central pillar of the economy, the mechanism for recruiting members, and the lure that they used to attract "customers" to their illicit activities was primarily their "control over women," whom they prostituted.[25] We have already seen how the periphery of the mine compound world was secured by the fact of women, whose forced absence in the lives of the male migrants, also ensured their conversion—in a violent revalorization—into the desired source of restituted patriarchal wholeness. In the informal settlements dominated by the Marashea, women from Lesotho also had to pay protection money or goods in kind, which they obtained from working on the farms where the informal settlements were located.

Dependent as they were on the mineworkers' wages, the Marashea were eager to see stability on the mines and, it appears, could be coopted by mine management to oppose strikes, boycotts, and anything else that might interrupt the flow of cash that came from gold's extraction. This didn't just mean mercenary activity. Because some Basotho mineworkers had senior supervisory positions in the mines, and controlled shafts, they also could be persuaded to inform on organizers and to threaten potential recruits. These same well-placed mine employees could ensure that Marashea members could hide or reside on mine property and access food and liquor there.[26] They also obtained ore and undertook their own processing, selling the hand-smelted gold into the black market—as still happens today.[27]

Several investigative reports and commissions of inquiry into violence on the mines in the late 1980s and early 1990s found that the conflicts there were often exacerbated when the Marashea entered the fray, always in support of other Basotho mineworkers, many of whom happened to be in the higher pay grades, although the mineworkers were themselves not all members or clients of the gangs by any means. They were deeply threatened by the introduction of the union in the 1980s, not only because of strikes and boycotts but also because they used the *induna* system and the mine-endorsed systems of cultural patronage that the unions intended to eliminate. When unionists boycotted concession stores owned by Marasheas at the Harmony Mine in 1990, overt conflict arose and more than twenty people were killed. Both the union and the Marashea claimed that the other side had started the conflict. This had happened before, as reported in the Goldstone Commission. According to Kynoch, there were occasions when Marashea sided with the union, and mineworkers could be members of both groups. But certainly James Motlatsi, the NUM president, blamed them for colluding with mine security and the police in opposition to the union during its early efforts at consolidation. And he referred to 1986 as the exemplary moment and locus of transformation. Jeff Guy and Motlatsi Thabane shared this perception: "In our view, the NUM and the ANC were working to overthrow the whole system that had bred the different forms of deprivation which had driven Marashea to their activities, with all the attendant contradictions. It seemed to us that, if this were understood by Marashea, their attitude towards the ANC and the NUM, and their relationship with these organisations, would have been different."[28]

It is a persuasive reading, as is the argument against a culturalist defense of the Marashea on the grounds that they were merely pursuing their self-interest, as Kynoch contends. And Thabane's recognition of the instrumentalization of women in the wars among these many factions commends itself. But the limitation of a history of the Marashea to a dyadic conflict on the other side of which is the ANC and the NUM, does not grasp the complexity of the situation in the 1980s in Khutsong and Carletonville. It does not address the very formation of the political that subtended that fractured and proliferating set of antagonisms, which were organized on the basis of a certain understanding of language and its limits, on one hand, and by the treatment of black women as media of masculine communications, on the other. Nor does it account, as it must, for the specific force of the police as a representation and representative institution of violence whose deployment of force constantly and consistently inflames the situation. We will want to understand why.

Once More Into the Breach

If 1986 saw a quantitative increase in violence, in the township as on the mines, it also saw a qualitative transformation. Off the mines, five events in the TRC sample involved torture, and there were two disappearances. In six cases, for the first time, people were not only beaten but also shot. In the following three years (from the beginning of 1987 to the end of 1990), there were sixty-eight events of death, arson, and assault in the township. Ten were said to be the work of ANC-aligned forces, eleven by the Gadaffis, but fully thirty-seven occurred at the hands of police (five of these in collusion with ZimZims) and eight by ZimZims. The rest were undertaken by "known perpetrators" and "vigilantes" or were coded as part of a generic "left conflict." There were more gun-related incidents (thirty-two, all but four of which were perpetrated by police). But there were also stabbings, burnings (necklacings), hackings, and arson. Before 1986, none of the abuse that is recorded by the TRC led to death. After 1986, death was not uncommon. Forty of the incidents of torture, burnings, and beatings between 1986 and the end of 1990 culminated in death. That deadliness would continue in the following three years, as new actors also entered the field, including the amaShenge. Before 1986, all the victims had been school-age or young adults (ages seventeen to twenty-one) and male. After 1990, the ages ranged from eight (a child shot by a motorist angry at the boycott) to eighty-five (a woman beaten to death by police at a night vigil for her son). Women were often assaulted. So, with some hesitation given the incompleteness of the records, we may conclude that 1986 saw a massive escalation in the use of force as well as a generalization of violence that involved more use of arms and that was also more lethal.

If, in an act of labored forensic dispassion, I momentarily reduce this horror to its quantities, it is because enumeration in the abstract reveals the abstraction of violence and the massification of death that resulted from it. Nor do these numbers exhaust the carnage; they are only the aboveground extrusions of a much broader and deeper phenomenon (the mine dump is the analogon of the iceberg). This is because the TRC was concerned, in its legislated mandate, only with crime or violence that could be deemed to be politically motivated and for which witnesses and corroboration were available. Determining such motivation was a precondition of anyone being granted amnesty for deeds committed during The Struggle and only injuries deemed to be "human rights violations" were heard about. The strictures for presenting evidence were severe; for example, on one occasion, when a man from Khutsong brought his sister to speak in his stead, because he could not bear to testify about his mother's and his brother's murder, he was denied this possibility on the grounds that she had not previously submitted her own statement. With her at his side, he struggled through the procedure.

It would be wrong to simply say that the escalation and generalization of violence constituted its becoming indiscriminate—and the TRC classified only one of the 149 incidents previously mentioned as "random." It occurred in and as discrimination, and often it announced itself as a judgment. When carried out by the youth groups, this judgment—against those alleged to be collaborators, informers, boycott breakers, thieves, and embezzlers—was produced in shadow tribunals, typically in the absence of the accused. The punishments that it meted out on the basis of such judgments were often spectacular, but not always; their initial audiences were their victims and themselves, and rumor often sufficed to bear the news to others. Bodies were left, charred and disfigured, and often had to be searched for. When carried out by the police, this judgment, which was also produced in the absence of the accused and before the encounter, was similarly oriented toward the assertion and confirmation of the victim's guilt—in this case as transgressors of the Apartheid regime and its racial policies of separation. The police acts were also judgments against any transgression of the state's exclusive rights to violence, and especially to that lawmaking violence that the police claimed merely to preserve.

I first heard of the Gadaffis and the ZimZims in conversation with the Reverend (see chapter 8) who had spoken of his return to Khutsong on a donkey cart. He was the first one in Khutsong to speak to me of a relationship between 1976 and 1986, and the first to link the then-present (2008) unrest—in opposition to redemarcation—to that legacy. The destruction of government buildings and infrastructure of 2006–2008 was, he said, the only way to communicate with the municipality's leadership under Mayor van Rooyen:

> The only language that the leaders listen [to] is when things are demolished; people take out anger on properties because they are not given enough space to debate their issues, they are just told of what is supposed to happen—like this demarcation issue. It has a long history and when people said "no, stop," [when] we submitted our views on the redemarcation and the politicians did not listen, the only language that they understand is when they see fire and smoke. That is when they see now that the people are serious. People will not mind even burning their own houses if it comes to a push and demonstrates their dissatisfaction or anger to whoever is in authority. I am not advocating that this happen but as I have seen these two eras, the 76 and 86, the same thing happened.

He continued: "Now the very same person who is now the citizen of this very township Khutsong, he was the one in the forefront in 1986 burning houses, so that is perhaps how the politicians needs to be communicated to: through burning, vandalizing and so forth. So now, that is what I have come to learn from the political sphere, people do not want to listen and to reason."

I am not confirming the Reverend's accusation about personal culpability, but the mayor acknowledged that the effort to enforce boycotts in 1986 had seen houses burned. He had mentioned the case of Maki Skosana, who was burned alive in Soweto before television cameras in 1985 by anti-Apartheid activists who believed her to have been an informant. The Reverend also mentioned her case. By then, the TRC had hosted lengthy hearings on it. Both men said that such events had happened in Khutsong—as did others.

In 1976, the Reverend had been in standard three, and because ("amazingly," he said) there was no television, he and his age-mates knew nothing about the events in Soweto. But his elders did. He remembered that at break time, looking out of the window, "we saw a beer hall burning." Children from the neighboring Sotho school came running toward his own Phororong, and then "parents were running looking for their children, as on that tarred road there was a truck which was burning by then. This young boy from the neighboring school came to our school, he threw a petrol bomb into our principal's office and fortunately the only thing that burnt there was the curtains, as the offices were very small. From there we just saw the township in tear gas and in disorder. . . . It went on for about a week I think up until some were arrested, some killed, up until 86 when the uprising came again."

The uprising came again. It was like a ghost, a revenant. Like the spooks of Spooktown where the Reverend's uncle lived and that he visited on Sundays, despite the fact that he had to walk past the neighborhoods of differently ethnicized boys and despite the fact that they would beat him bloody every week. It was like a ghost insofar as death returned with it.

By 1986, the Reverend was himself a teacher, in the same school that he had studied in as a child. During the boycotts, he was forced to idle in a school being shunned by learners. This had been a source of boredom and frustration. But what he recalled most vividly was the murder of two policemen who had been stabbed and their skulls crushed by a local boy the Reverend had known and who lived in his neighborhood. He blamed the "Comrades." He blamed them for the deaths of the policemen but especially for the transformation of his friend, a tall slender boy from whom he would never have expected such mercilessness. The Comrades had a power, it seemed, to make people do what they would not otherwise do and the most frightening part of it was that, having experienced this previously unimaginable capacity, the newly enabled perpetrators often found that they enjoyed it and could do it again. They could do it again even on the bodies of the ones they had attacked. In the case of the policemen described by the Reverend, the executions had been followed by the frenzied pulverizing of the corpses. Such cases were not exceptional. This is one of the meanings of a state of emergency. Not only is there a suspension of law but, in the space of its withdrawal, a metamorphosis occurs that is more than either a regression or a recovery from repression, although it has elements of both—more too than a discharge of rage. There was something mysteriously awful about it, and this mystery, this inexplicability, and this inarticulability remain and perhaps are all that truly remain of the deed.

The violence directed against the police (and presumed informers') bodies bears some resemblance to that which is otherwise normatively (even if illegally) directed against people accused of witchcraft in this part of the world.[29] And it has even been argued that some of the widespread and widely reported necklacings of this period were not actually political if extrajudicial executions but witch burnings, including the burning of politically suspect witch-finders *as* witches. Ineke Van Kessel has suggested that youths (mostly male) who undertook such killings were also taking for themselves the authority that had previously been vested in traditional witch finders, and that they were thus part of the broader rejection of seniority as the basis of authority that we read of in the previous chapter.[30]

We may yet ask after the logic or alogic that traversed these otherwise porous fields of violence. Why did the political killings mimic the witch-burnings in their fury, even when lacking an overt referent to witches? Possibly, this is because, for the killers, they had come to appear to be sources of profound menace and even death. As James Siegel has so convincingly argued, a force which is thought to bear the menace of death but that is otherwise unrecognizable or unlocatable as such (which might turn out to be lodged in your neighbor, for example) is often the object of an especially violent effort at expulsion—the kind that entails mutilating corpses. Siegel has described the recurrent eruption of witchcraft accusations in modern bureaucratic states and links them to the dissolution of other regimes for conferring identity and recognition, and to the overwhelming nature of the fear that grips people when the old regime of power and recognition having lost its effectiveness, a new one has not yet been established to explain chaotic circumstances or otherwise terrifying events and changes. His example is Indonesia after the fall of the Suharto regime.[31] The end of Apartheid could in some ways be said to be analogous. And let us not forget that this end (of Apartheid) followed on the end of the gold standard, and the profound destabilization of the economy built thereon—a destabilization for which the entire project of worker "stabilization" was mainly a reaction formation, and a deeply ambivalent one at that. In this context, the growth of mineworker power, which would be expressed in union activity, was simultaneously an example and a threat to some township youth, whose own claims on political relevance and representative capacity did not immediately find their echo or their mirror in the discourse of the unions, and which were sometimes openly repudiated by the mineworkers themselves. The radical uncertainty of the era, unleashed by intensifying police violence and unassuaged by functional counter-structures surely infused the conflicts of the time with additional threat, and summoned a violent intensity that exceeded any combat function.

If a belief in "muti" or magic persisted despite the *comtsotsis'* (leftist gangsters) professed rationalism, as van Rooyen lamented, this does not mean that the gangsters thought the authorities and especially the police and their agents were witches. But it does suggest that something like witchcraft accusation was at play. And this in two senses. First, the victims were stand-ins or substitutes for a general threat; they were not (for their killers) individuals so much as representatives of whole systems of terror. And this is why the killings proliferated—their multiplication is evidence of the failure to eliminate the menace. As Siegel shows, the named figure cannot finally assuage the threat, which will persist until the system is undone—or people get tired of the killing, or a truly repressive counterforce intrudes. Second, the gang violence of this space—around the mines—could be coded as ethnic or cultural only with great difficulty, despite the fact that the mining corporations had mobilized some Marashea of the Basotho on these grounds. White supremacists spoke of a generic "black on black" violence in recognition of this fact. But to the extent that the gang violence expressed a combination of gendered, generational and territorial claims on power, and to the extent that it was directed against authorities who were thought to understand the world in exclusively ethnic (tribal or cultural) terms, it symptomized the waning of Apartheid ideological authority. It also symptomatized the not-so-ghostly (future) remainder of its secret drive: namely a mania for separation, and a rage against the crossing of identity's borders.

This was not how the Reverend saw things, however. The trauma associated with what for him remained the incomprehensibility of the violence had stained his consciousness in a manner that leaked into almost everything that he said about this period. Part of the mysteriousness of this brutality was that it was enacted in the name of, and ostensibly as mere means to, a political end. It could therefore seem excessive in the calculus of means and ends, and that excess threatened the very category of the political (at least within a liberal paradigm). As the NUM and other black dominated trade unions gained power, they also laid claim to the political sphere and its discourses, as well as its territories of practice. In a place like Merafong, that meant that the townships, where the NUM was not the dominant presence, were up for grabs. And this is perhaps why, there, the struggle against the Apartheid state was stained by so much conflict—and so much blood.

In the Reverend's recollection, the conflicts among the *comtsotsis* were "just a continuation of the struggle . . . at higher levels." In his memory, 1986 was the apogee of township conflict, although he acknowledged that the conflicts had persisted into the 1990s. In the process of escalation, the newly unbanned trade unions had played a mobilizing role, because their reach was translocal. What made the events of Khutsong so hard to manage was this sense that they were part of a broad pattern and, at the same time, that there was no outside. But this permitted them to combat the most powerful local forces. The Reverend explained: "If COSATU [Council of South African Trade Unions] was organizing something the whole country would support that, if businesses were boycotted around here, people went to Johannesburg, Randfontein and other places to buy their groceries because the businesses in Carletonville were in a comfort zone; they did not support the black majority."

Consumer boycotts were also organized by the union on mine properties. In those cases, boycotts referred to action taking place in the hostels and not in the shafts, even when their aims were the enhancement of worker's situations. Thus, for example, in 1985, a boycott was held in an effort to obtain "toe-caps" for safety, and management coverage for overalls and jackets for black miners as well as whites (not then the practice). According to the South African Labor Board, it was also a protest against "the fact that prices of goods were constantly changing; they were taxed on items which were exempted; rotten food was sold; they were subject to body searches and abuse by the shopowners." The union wanted bars and liquor outlets to "transform from profit making enterprises into a recreational facility under workers' control."[32] Everyone, even those not in the union, was said to have observed the boycott, according to the NUM's president. The deprivation of company store owners' earnings provoked an effort to find the organizers and, in this vindictive project, mine security and the police colluded, possibly with the participation of supervisory workers. Reflecting on the lessons learned, Motlatsi promised that, in any subsequent boycott, there would be monitoring of the "situation" and that workers would ensure that the shop stewards did not accept any bribes or visit the prohibited shops except for meetings (but what kind of meetings take place in a liquor store?). Such a surveillance mechanism implied that bribery had been or would be offered and accepted. Here was the spectral threat that would float above both the mine and the township and that would become the object of its relentless and yet repeatedly failing efforts at control. Here, too, was the phenomenon that would occasion the transformation of the revolt into a modality of policing, succumbing to a mimesis of the enemy in the very effort at purgation.

The Reverend described the severity of boycotts and the policing of them in painful detail and in a manner that exposed the fact that the boycotts in the townships, as opposed to on the compounds, were often experienced most acutely by women, on whom fell the responsibility of managing the household, buying food, washing clothes, and performing all those tasks that depend on staple consumables:

If you were found to be having groceries with you, they would demand a receipt and it would be indicated which shop you bought your groceries. Actually, there was an incident that happened to a lady that went to buy groceries in a shop and they happened to see that she bought around Carletonville. She had cooking oil and washing powder, they opened the cooking oil and poured it on her from head down, and they also took the washing powder poured it in her mouth and that was terrible. She was not the only victim, many people who were victims of the boycotts, the tsotsi elements called amaZimZim took and confiscated the groceries of the victims and gave it to their parents to eat at home. The situation wanted to calm down but because of such elements that took advantage of the situation, it was terrible.

It was Songezile who finally asked, "What calmed the situation?" Quite remarkably, the Reverend responded, "I think what calmed the situation is the disappearance of the people at the forefront." He mused: "You know, the funny thing is that whenever the leader of the gangs vanished the whole group just vanished. There was this short young guy and he was so popular; when he was taken out of the picture, the whole thing subsided."

Everything seems to be a question of the leader, of the authority of the one and the force of commandment, of terror and of the presence, carnal but also spectral, of power. Power is here demonstrated in the obedience that it compels, but also in the mimesis and thus multiplication and extension of its principle—namely, the rule of the one, the phallogocentric law. This is why there is no logical contradiction between the state's and mining corporations' drive to stabilization and the apparent proliferation of *comtsotsi* (leftist gangs) violence, even when there is conflict between them. This is also why, when the leader disappears, the threat seems momentarily to vanish, trailing the shadow of death with it, and leaving behind only the mourning of the victims. The absence of the leader, rather than the establishment of leadership structures was the cause of the hiatus, in the Reverend's estimation. But it did not quite explain everything. He spoke of the gangs as "mushrooming" out of the struggle, even if they only "pretended" to be carrying out its mission. For him, however, it was the ZimZim who ruled the night and used the evening hours to prey on people returning from work, "taking their belongings and groceries." Theft and the enforcement of the boycotts took the same form and, for their victims, were experienced as almost the same thing. This is what made the Gadaffis seem necessary. They had been created to counteract the ZimZim, but "both wanted to have an upper hand in the township."

The Reverend's narrative proceeded by adducing one and then the other force, each seeming to climb up and over the other. It turns out that the disappearance of the leader also needed an explanation. Enter the Basotho gangs known as the Marashea. When they became targets of the Gadaffis, who robbed them during the weekend revelries, they fought back. With the ferocity that had been caricatured and cultivated by the cultural stereotypy on which the Chamber of Mines had organized its labor force, and with the weaponry that had been coded as traditional (namely, sjamboks, knobkerries, and spears), they outdid or at least challenged the amaZimZim and the Gadaffis with blunt instruments as well as with the phantasmatic force of the image in which they resided and which they did little to dispel. Perhaps this is one of the reasons why some members of the Gadaffi gang sought the assistance of the *sangomas* in Natal, as reported in the Mvudle case at the TRC. Van Rooyen may have advocated a rationalist revolution, but, confronted by the mythical powers of the Basotho groups, the political gangsters wanted every source of power they could obtain, and that included bullet-immunizing and other apotropaic medicines.[33] Said the Reverend: "The Basothos would really leave you half-dead when they beat you because they carried sticks and sjamboks with them, but they are the ones that neutralized the situation of the two other groups."

I cite the Reverend's narrative in such detail because it both resembles and inverts the (once) more well-known account of these conflicts by Allistair Sparks, former editor of the *Rand Daily Mail*, an influential critic of Apartheid, well-known liberal, and author of several significant works, including *The Mind of South Africa* (1990). Contrary to the Reverend's account, in which the Gadaffis emerge in opposition to the ZimZim, Sparks read the activities of the Gadaffis as a case of thuggery hijacking the anti-Apartheid cause and as the motive force for the emergence of the ZimZims. In 1990, he interviewed two Gadaffai members who explained that "we would meet after school and decide what to target. . . It was mostly the police, who are enemies of the people, and others who sided with the police. Then we would take action." Appalled by the avowal of violence by the young men who meted it out, Sparks claimed that "township gangs may have thought they were fighting apartheid, but the only thing they furthered was violence against blacks by blacks—by taking part in the bloodshed and thereby giving rise to vigilante groups to oppose them." He quoted a local businessman who considered the gangs to merely be *tsotsis* (thugs): "Vehicles and business premises were set on fire, students were intimidated, young girls were raped, people who called for discipline were necklaced, and the police could do nothing to help because the gang drove them out of the township."[34] The Gadaffis did not only pursue police informants, by Sparks's account (and those of everyone I spoke to). They also disciplined those who had failed to deliver on their promises. A local town councilor who raised money for a daycare center that never materialized was determined by the group to have been guilty of betrayal, and his shop was burned to the ground.

The tribunals of the ostensibly leftist gangs or *comtsotsis*, were said by Michael Cross, whom Sparks cites, to have been enabled by the detention and removal of party leadership from public life under one or another decree and the declaration of states of emergency.[35] Cross, a scholar of education policy and history, has since seen the *comtsotsis* as one form of youth gangs in a black subculture that ran parallel to the highly orchestrated, formally supported and officially validated youth organizations of Afrikaner nationalists.[36] Internally, the black youth groups cohered as do many youth formations, along class and territorial lines. Cross typologizes them as "(1) 'lumpen' and unemployed youth delinquent and semi-delinquent subcultures; (2) middle-class cultural rebellion and reformist movements; and (3) working-class students and youth resistance culture, activism and political militancy."[37] Suspicious of the degree to which a class analysis could finally encompass the full complexity of the South African scene, where race inflected everything, Cross also describes the constraints affecting black youth cultures in the 1950s and 1960s before the *comtsotsi*'s emergence, emphasizing the breakdown of family life and its structures of authority, overcrowding because of immigration and housing shortages, and mass unemployment. The uprisings of 1976, he says, permitted the dissolution of boundaries between students and street youth, but it was the shift from total repression to low-intensity counterinsurgency that included "total war at the grass-roots level" coupled with WHAM (winning hearts and minds) soft tactics that marked the transition that I have described. He attributes the rise in violence after 1985 to a series of factors that culminated in a mirroring of the total war with a "total resistance."[38] Among the characteristics of this period, he observes, were "(1) unprecedented state repression; (2) a leadership and organizational crisis in the youth resistance movement; (3) increasing marginalization of youth following the disruption of organizational structures; (4) the resurgence of the street gang subculture; (5) the emergence of middle-class subcultures; and (6) greater polarization in youth politics."[39] At least in retrospect, Cross claims that the crisis of leadership was only possible because of a total crisis in the situation of the youth, as vigilante groups arose in the vacuum and exacerbated the problem of leadership.

For Sparks, it was the leadership question that assumed the most potent explanatory power. The eviscerations of party leadership and political institutional organs that occurred after 1976 and again in 1986 as a result of state repression was so determinant because, for Sparks, as for many, the ANC was the only party capable of organizing life in the township. And we may recall here Tebello Motapanyane's claims of a similar sort, along with his call for a "most disciplined" and "professional" resistance. In the absence of the party's alternative codes and its mechanisms for ensuring adherence, gangs claimed to be the enforcers of the just law that the future order would inscribe into the ashes of the burnt world and at the foundation of its new realm. Sparks also believes that it was in response to the reign of terror by the Gadaffis that the ZimZims "arose to counter them." They had been called into existence, in his analysis, after 1989, when Carletonville's town council had decided to rededicate itself to white supremacy by placing "whites only" signs in the public parks and other public venues.[40] The NUM had called for a consumer boycott against white businesses and the Gadaffis, according to Sparks, took on the self-appointed role of enforcing it. "Once an official ANC presence was established in the township," he argues, "the gangs could no longer claim affiliation with the movement. Both the Gadhaffis and the ZimZims are now believed to have disbanded."[41] That was in 1990.

Certainly, the intensified brutality of 1990 was a watershed, its official count of sixty-eight incidents followed in 1991 by "only" twenty. But there was more bloodshed to come. Moreover, Sparks published his assessment in January of 1990, before the most intense period of violence since 1986 would occur. The ZimZims had been active since 1986, and the Gadaffis only since 1989, albeit on an apparently modest scale or at least at a relatively invisible level—if the TRC's investigations are an adequate index. Yet, there is a pattern, as Cross has also argued: violence among the factions coincided with the most brutal periods of police repression. "In the armed struggle," observes Frantz Fanon, "there is what we could call the point of no return. It is almost always attributable to the sweeping repression which encompasses every sector of the colonized population."[42] This is why it is important to take cognizance of what the TRC made visible, namely the extent of the violence that was perpetrated by the police. Once again, this is not an exhaustive summation. Much, perhaps most, of the brutality went unreported, not least because contact with the police, even if it meant reporting a crime against one's home or family, could be perceived as informing and might be punished by the tribunals of the gangs, who forbade it as complicity with the Apartheid regime. Yet, the police beatings, torture, disappearances, and even arson, account for more than 62 percent of the cases reported at the TRC. And of the fifty-six shootings, forty-three were committed by police. Again, this is limited to the violence deemed political; other violence implicating the police goes untallied in its report. Nonetheless, this quantitative sample was registered and echoed by people who lived through the period and who gave testimony at the Human Rights Hearings of the TRC. W. S. Goliath, whose brother was shot to death in January 1986, at the beginning of this fateful year, said simply, "there was a lot of fighting in the township. The police was fighting the youth. It was terrible. Everyday there were fights." He had begged his brother to withdraw from politics after his friend had been shot to death, and he himself had no interest in The Struggle, but ten years later, he recalled: "There is only one reason. At the time you could not form certain groups. The police wanted to break down the ANC. It was just fighting. The group was fighting the police as well."[43] When W. S. Goliath's brother, Moozie, had been shot, he was apparently in the process of planning to bomb the police station in retaliation for the police assassination of his dearest friend. By this point, the conflict had assumed the quality of a vendetta, and its severe economy enveloped everything.

A Report of the Independent Board of Inquiry complained, in 1991, that police in Carletonville seemed to be obstructing their investigations into violence and harassment of ANC officials in town. At the time, there was an open investigation, under the authority of a special task force appointed by then–prime minister F. W. de Klerk, into police involvement in the local violence. Eleven policemen had been suspended in nearby Welverdiend. When the investigation opened in Carletonville, police arrested ten people involved, including a board researcher and the local ANC chair, and their bail conditions stipulated that they remain at least five hundred meters from the police station, making their participation in the inquiry effectively impossible.[44] The board also reflected on what it perceived to be the increasing militancy of the Conservative Party, the high point of which was a motion that all members of the ruling National Party (under de Klerk) should be tried for treason on the basis of their plans for a multiracial government.[45] In April 1994, the AWB would undertake a spate of pipe bombings on the West and East Rand to try to upend elections or at least dissuade people's participation. At least twenty-one people died, and forty-six were injured in the process.[46]

Myths of Violence and Mythic Violence

By the time of my conversations with the Reverend and the mayor, the stories of the conflicts between the Gadaffis, the ZimZims, the amaShenge, and the Marashea had already become legends, even myths. It is by virtue of their becoming myth that the mythic nature of their violence can be grasped. I use this phrase in the sense that Walter Benjamin used it to refer to a kind of violence that seeks to establish law and that works by positing guilt. "One of the most contested theses in Benjamin's 'Critique of Violence,'" writes Astrid Deuber-Mankowsky, in a singularly incisive reading of that text,

> is his claim that the mythic manifestation of violence he describes refers back to a problematic of legal violence [*Rechtsgewalt*]—more precisely to a problematic of the violence that establishes law [*rechtsetzende Gewalt*]: in analogy with mythical violence, the establishment of legal violence has a twofold function: on the one hand, violence serves as a means for establishing law, but, on the other hand, this violent establishment serves as a manifestation of the power of law and in turn legitimates that power by maintaining violence in an institutionalized, law-preserving form. This has the consequence that law-maintaining violence, no less than mythic violence, becomes a manifestation of itself.

Deuber-Mankowsky's reading helps us to understand Benjamin's suspicion of that kind of violence that, in its very effort to become law, departs from justice because its aim is to establish guilt (G, *schuld* or A, *skuld*; see chapter 10), and because it cannot terminate this drive to find guilt. Now, this understanding of law assumes particular relevance in a capitalist context, as Benjamin understood it, insofar as capitalism, which, we recall, Benjamin called a cultic religion, similarly assumes and distributes guilt as a general but also racially concentrated form of being.

Especially relevant for our consideration here is Benjamin's distinction, drawn from Sorel, between the violence of the proletarian strike and that of the state that is brought to crisis in and by the general strike. At the time of his writing in Germany, unions had the right to strike and thus had a right to exercise force, which was nonetheless understood by the state and by capital to be a refusal of violence, a withdrawal of labor ("a nonaction, which a strike really is, cannot be described as violence."[47]) In a limited sense, which would be avowed by left and right alike, such a strike could be called nonviolent. But in those instances when labor demonstrated a willingness to use this method beyond the situation in which it could be read as withholding labor from a particular employer, the full and conditional nature of this action as violence becomes visible:

> The moment of violence, however, is necessarily introduced, in the form of extortion, into such an omission, if it takes place in the context of a conscious readiness to resume the suspended action under certain circumstances that either have nothing whatever to do with this action or only superficially modify it. Understood in this way, the right to strike constitutes in the view of labor, which is opposed to that of the state, the right to use force in attaining certain ends. The antithesis between the two conceptions emerges in all its bitterness in the face of a revolutionary general strike.[48]

The state's typical response to general strikes—and South Africa is exemplary in this period—is violence. But South Africa, exemplary in one sense was also atypical in another (or rather typical of colonial societies organized on the basis of a racially differential distribution of the right to strike). The delayed accession to the right to strike by black mineworkers in South Africa coincided with the union's willingness to engage in actions, like boycotts, that departed from the narrow understanding of a proletarian strike, and that approached, through its insertion into a nationwide umbrella, COSATU, the general strike.

In 1987, Cyril Ramaphosa, by then a skilled negotiator for the NUM, described the early years of the union in terms that Benjamin's analysis illuminates: the union "had been 'trying to make fundamental change in a system using structures and instruments that were designed to perpetuate the system.' For the first three years of the union, they had organised around issues like safety, wages and working-class unity. Since late 1984, however, shaft stewards had urged the union to embark on more general resistance to white control both at the point of production and in the migrant hostels."[49] The NUM's development of a "two-pronged" strategy, ostensibly at the behest of the most empowered elements of the union, was addressed to both wage and workplace matters as well as general social conditions in the society. Wildcat strikes in early 1986 were read by management in some mines as evidence that the discontent of the townships was "spilling over" into the mines, which otherwise should have remained apart from the broader society. According to T. Dunbar Moodie: "What the 'subversives' are about [said the personnel manager at Vaal Reefs], is a process of instilling public fear into people. To make a show of a murder, to ensure that an explosion takes place in a place that should have been guarded by the police."[50] Spillage is an idiom erected at the perimeter and as the border guard of what might otherwise by conceived as a generalization of the right to use violence as means to a political end. This disavowal of the notion of a general strike implied that the townships were the origin of disorder—and this argument partook of the belief that they were bereft of leadership. It is also why, later that year, during a three-week long strike called by the NUM, the police collaborated with the private security of the Gold Fields mine at Carletonville and, according to Moodie, brutally beat the union's leaders, James Motlatsi and Elijah Barayi. The NUM leadership was feared as the source of opposition, of a "most disciplined" and "professional sort" as Motapanyane had said. It was also treated by management as a follower, however, for the general strike was not proper to it. Mine historians confirm this perception when they argue that the conflict on the mine compounds occurred mainly in shafts and hostels where union control was not fully established.[51]

The strike was for Benjamin a particularly revelatory example: "For if violence were, as first appears, merely the means to secure directly whatever happens to be sought, it could fulfill its end as predatory violence. It would be entirely unsuitable as a basis for, or a modification to, relatively stable conditions. The strike shows, however, that it can be so, that it is able to found and modify legal conditions."[52] Benjamin then argues that the establishment of law in those contexts where it is absent or in doubt, when exercised through the violence exercised over life and death, reveals law's foundation:

> For the function of violence in lawmaking is twofold, in the sense that lawmaking pursues as its end, with violence as the means, what is to be established as law, but at the moment of instatement does not dismiss violence; rather, at this very moment of lawmaking, it specifically establishes as law not an end unalloyed by violence but one necessarily and intimately bound to it, under the title of power. Lawmaking is powermaking, assumption of power, and to that extent an immediate manifestation of violence. Justice is the principle of all divine endmaking, power the principle of all mythic lawmaking.[53]

As is well known, Benjamin supplemented this claim with a recognition that so-called law-preserving violence is combined "in a kind of spectral mixture" in the police. He was referring to the particular German institution of a security police force dedicated to public order, but it is this principle, and this spectrality, that makes me claim that the *comtsotsis* were partaking of police violence *both* in the sense that such violence incited their spiraling activities and because they absorbed the logical contradictions that inhered in that institution into themselves.[54] This is also why the enactments of extrajudicial, and nonjust, punishment can be thought of as mourning plays in a baroque theater of not-quite-postcolonial South Africa.

Let us emphasize the historical contingency in Benjamin's argument. The particular pursuit of law and its misrecognition as justice takes place within a capitalist system. His turn to a notion of the messianic, explains Deuber-Mankowsky, was intended to counter the total absorption of religious sentiment by capitalism, and the idea of justice by law: "The concept of the messianic . . . constitutes the unapproachable, inaccessible, and unrepresentable counter-pole to the mythic, performative manifestation of violence."[55] And she rightly asserts that such mythic violence is associated with the "the making-guilty of mere life."[56] In South Africa, of course, mere life was precisely what Apartheid aimed to save Afrikaners from. And township gangsterism was a refusal of this same guilt, ironically and even unjustly expressed through violence that aimed to transfer (or attempted to transfer) the inexpiable guilt onto those who refused the power and thus the sovereign innocence of the *comtsotsis*.

Now, a primary aim of all the parties seeking to dominate Khutsong after 1976 and again in 1986 was to establish the guilt of those who were either violating the boycotts or disputing the authority of one or another group to undertake such policing. Ironically, and even tragically, this brought the gangs into a parallel relation with, and even mirroring of, the police, who, my evidence suggests, were inciting rather than repressing the violence in the townships. The collaboration between the ZimZims and the police is only one aspect of this mirroring, which entailed a complete absorption of the police function into the being of all the organizations that otherwise opposed them. Moreover, white underground forces responded to the boycotts of 1986 and the elections of 1989 with their own efforts to incite terror and to take on police functions that they did not believe were being adequately performed. Now, the specific quality of the white terror groups, especially the AWB and its breakaway *Die Orde van die Dood* (Order of Death), of which more will be said in chapter 13, is that they were seeking not to establish guilt as an attribute of the individual soul—and hence in conformity with a Protestant vision of the solitary and alienated subject always subject to the law of predestination—but rather to confirm it as an inheritance and as the core of black racial identity. This is why their violence, even more than that of the state police, had an element of the arbitrary and an indifference toward the victims. The commonsense of Apartheid is that randomness was a feature of black violence. In my estimation, it is, to the contrary, the essence of white supremacist and all racist violence in this sense: its object is always "any" racially marked person.

Perhaps we must recognize that this too is part of the dialectical drive in this space, an additional force enabling and encouraging the mimetic assumption of the police function. This is not to validate such gestures; it is only to understand that in the face of a radical abstraction, an arbitrary violence and a threatened negation, one—and only one—of the forms by which the claim to singularity can make itself appear is behind the mask of the sovereign and in the form of petty tyranny. I take this to be the lesson of R. R. R. Dhlomo, a writer of the midcentury, whose story about the misdirection of black radicalism on the mines in his time both prefigures and casts a critical shadow on a what would occur in Khutsong as the ghosts of 1922—when white mineworkers had threatened a general strike rather than submit to black supervision—returned.[57] Dhlomo was not concerned with white anxieties, however. He was concerned with what happens when, unprepared for or uneducated in the habits of radical democracy, the discourse of leadership is dissimulated as representativeness and leads to despotism. A contemporary of Benjamin's but certainly not a fellow intellectual traveler, Dhlomo provides us with the closing drama in this chapter of the mourning play and may well have written its first text. Its mise-en-scène is familiar by now: the multiply tunneled tailings dump of a gold mine.

Dhlomo's story "Murder on the Mine Dumps" opens at the end of a shift on a gold-mine compound (Dhlomo had himself worked on the mines), where a group of men are awaiting their manager's departure for the day.[58] When he goes, they join a "leader," a man named Sipepo, out on a tailings dump. Sipepo tells the men, much as my tour guide (described in chapter 7) had told me, that the dump "is our hiding place" and is "full of small holes," in which to seek cover "when we were in trouble with the police." The police, he says, would not dare to pursue them there and he tells his followers that "we can stay here for many months even without passes." The men can also hide their contraband in the holes, Sipepo says. And they can do so by right. This is because the dumps are their own product: "Remember, men, that the dump was piled here by our blood." And he adds, "Keep that in your minds so that on the great day you will know that you are fighting for your rights as all civilised men."[59]

The story is focalized by the character Sipepo, although the unnamed narrator seems at times to collapse into him. It is from his perspective that we perceive the men's fear ("Fear did not allow them to speak"), but it is from the narrator that we hear of Sipepo and his colleagues learning "from some foolish meetings" in which Sipepo "had been impressed by the idea that they should rise as one man and make the white people feel the pinch, too, as they felt it." It is this narrator (who may or may not ventriloquize Dhlomo's own skepticism about trade unionism) who concludes that, after the meetings, "they now hated white people." Sipepo has been recognized as a leader by the other men because he attended political meetings and "knew what was meant by 'exploitation' and 'revolutions.'" He is described as being enormously impressed by the words "passive resistance," "down with tools," and "to hell with our exploiters—the capitalists."[60] Sipepo is imagined for readers as a person who inhabits the actual historical world, and he has heard of, perhaps participated in, the pass protests that were discussed in part 1. Throughout Dhlomo's oeuvre, passes and the pass system function as narrative drivers, both in the lives of his fictive characters, and in the extradiegetic world to which they refer. Throughout that same oeuvre, the violence of the pass system (which we know constitutes the medium of the police) inaugurates or sets in motion a different kind of violence—the kind that refers only to itself. This violence is not without its mediations, but it operates in the space between two monopolies—that of the state and that of the elders in traditional patriarchal society.

In "Murder on the Mine Dumps," one of the miners is alleged to have informed on Sipepo and disclosed the group's hiding place on the dumps. As a result, Sipepo has been threatened with being fired, and he tells the others that the Induna knows about the "evil talks about burning passes" on the compound.[61] He, Sipepo, uses a Zulu phrase in which listening and looking are conjoined and says, "open your ears" to mean "look," and then tells the men to focus on a distant spot on the dump. He then urges another man, named July, to go to that spot. As the narrator tells the reader that this same July has revealed the insurrectionary plans of the workers, Sipepo directs the workers to look upon July as he begins to sink into the slimes. The rest of the story sutures together the reader and the frightened men in an anxious anticipation of the execution that we, the readers, know must come. Sipepo asks if the men see July, and they respond affirmatively to his call with a horrified, "Look at him! Look at him!" For his part, July does not understand why, if they can see him, the others do not attempt to rescue him. He assumes a fraternal bond born of his racialized (black) class position. In fact, July has been identified in the narrative focalized by Sipepo as Msutu (ethnically Basotho), and the other men are identified as Zulu speakers. In this way, Dhlomo discloses the limits of racial and class solidarity in a colonial system (not yet formalized as Apartheid) that has invested ethnicity as a strategy of divisive rule. Sipepo's use of this structure as an opportunity to consolidate personalized power marks Dhlomo's story as a cautionary tale—which may explain why, at the time, it appeared to some liberals to have indicted both unionism and pan-Africanism as a political failure.

July calls out in desperation, not knowing that his betrayal of Sipepo (if it has indeed been perpetrated—and no proof is offered to validate the accusation) has been found out and that, now, he must he exposed to the limit and at the limit. His death will be a spectacle of Sipepo's power and a threat of future violence, a demand for both fidelity and a promise to not reveal the secrets of the group. The brutality of the story is terminated with a Kafkaesque gesture, as Sipepo denounces the one "who told all our secrets to the white people" as a dog.[62]

Within Sipepo's world, the one who has betrayed secrets will go unmourned. This is the essence of this extreme violence, enacted on the cyanided slimes dam, for it not only effects the death of the outcast but also severs him from his ancestral community and from the narrative commemoration that follows on a known death in proper funerary ritual. In this case, Dhlomo offers his story as commemoration for a fictive character and a kind of proxy for the multitudinous and heteronymous silences that will follow on the real deaths meted out in this fashion, against real informants, or, and equally important, against those who are rumored to be informants. "Murder on the Mine Dumps" is suffused with the awful pathos of an attempt to obtain power through a mimesis that is itself a form of being captured—immersed, submerged, and buried, as it were, under the weight of a new world order. It is also a precise literary rendition of that mythic violence that Benjamin describes as "bloody power over mere life for its own sake."[63] And it is as literature that it can make the death of an individual appear instructive in a way that requires no actual death. Here, a new (or old) dimension of mourning can be considered—that to which Freud contrasted melancholia and that he conceived as a process of relinquishing rather than revivifying the dead, but only by bringing the mourned lost object into representation. The TRC attempted to do something analogous, and it did so by erecting a stage on which the presentation of the violence of the past could become, in its narration, an instructive occasion. The lesson it sought was, I believe, partly aimed at the distinction between law and justice. But it also restaged the blockage and the contradictions whose false solution took the forms we have seen, including that which distinguished racism from political motive in the case of white supremacist and police state violence and that which made political motive and personal responsibility mutually exclusive, in the case of the *comtsotsis* of Carletonville and Khutsong. It is now time to enter the shadowed underground of that double séance.

CHAPTER 13

ZOMBIES SING PATA PATA

The Impossible Subject of Political Violence

*Violence has been the single most determining factor in
South African political history.*

—*Truth and Reconciliation Commission of South Africa Report*

*And at this stained place words
are scraped from resinous tongues
wrung like washing, hung on lines
of courtroom and confessional,
transposed into the dialect of record.*

—Ingrid de Kok, "Parts of Speech"

How and by what means can violence be ended? At least two responses have been posed to this recurrent question. One urges the sublation of violence in representational forms, the other advocates a cancelling counter-violence. In what follows I consider these two possible tendencies as they unfolded around the gold mines of the West Rand.

An LP sits on my desk, wrapped in heavy plastic. It's an album from 1979 called *Egoli*, by The Zombies. "Soweto" is the fourth track on side one. "Egoli" is the fourth track on side two. The performers are unnamed on the album, which has no liner notes. But the producer was David Thekwane, a jazz saxophonist, and the engineer was the grammy-winning John Lindemann. Under vibrant fuchsia letters, in an art deco font, the cover image of *Egoli* has that gold tint of photographs from the 1970s—the Kodachrome look. But it gains some of its coloration from the enormous mine dump that looms in the lower left quadrant of the image, and from which perspective the vista of Johannesburg is seen, a commuter train cutting across the horizon in the midground beneath a hazy blue sky and against the darker blue silhouette of Egoli's cityscape, of Johannesburg. Judging from the color of the soil and the absence of foliage, the image was probably made in June or July. As for the music, the sound and style slide song to song. Metal and electric guitars are supported by a Hammond B organ on some tracks. *Kwela* is the dominant genre, but it is leavened by American funk and jazz.

Kwela became the internationally recognized "sound of South Africa" in the 1950s and 1960s, until it was overshadowed by the more organized male choral music called *mbaqanga*—so beloved by Paul Simon. His support lubricated its journey into recognizability as world music. Kwela's rhythms are joyously danceable, and this joyfulness is hard to resist when listening. One of the most covered songs in this genre is "pata pata," its most well-known rendition being that by Miriam Makeba. The music's popularity in shebeens during the 1950s and 1960s is widely documented. It is the kind of music that might keep the ghosts and thus death away. Then, it was youthful music.

In 2016, I overheard, through a video recording, some informal mineworkers recall pata pata as a nearly magical peacemaking song. Their conversation began with one of the zama zamas extolling the virtues of his favorite musician, Alick Macheso: "Once upon a time, there was a music professor, Alick Macheso, the maestro, who made the blind to see, the deaf to hear and to see the vibrations of his troubled soul. Show them the way, in the name of my . . . "

As it happens, these words, spoken with a combination of reverence and prophetic intensity, were taken, nearly verbatim, from Alick Macheso's Facebook page, which was posted on February 4, 2013, more than three years before their recitation in this recording.[1] Here is the "dialogue," that followed it, now among four men:

> If we're talking about dancing, he's number one. Number one, straight.
> Macheso?
> In Zimbabwe, or Africa?
> Africa.
> If it comes to dancing, really! He's the number one, all on his own.
> When it comes to the keyboard, it's the Pata Pata.
> Pata Pata . . . by, by . . . what's-his-name?
> It's by all of them. They all sang Pata Pata.
> Even B told us that, when the gangs were clashing, they'd be brought together by
>   Pata Pata.

The forms of the pata pata dance, derided (or valorized) by its contemporary white onlookers as a spectacle of erotic flirtation, is said to derive from the policing gesture of the pat downs, to which so many black South Africans were subject under Apartheid pass laws. And the name of the genre, *kwela*, meaning "climb-up" or "get on," was a phrase that was shouted during roundups; it was also spoken or sung "as encouragement" to pata pata dancers.[2] Improbable as this origin story may sound, it was neither the first nor will it be the last time that police-state gestures made their way into musical forms, sensuously and satirically incorporated and resignified as sites of pleasure. Nor does this playful aesthetic appropriation in any way blunt the mockery that accompanied it, even if it requires musicologists to excavate this dimension of the genre's sonic underground. Today, some zama zamas refer to police paddy wagons as *gumba gumba* vans. *Gumba* is a kind of jive, and *gumba gumba* is the name of a song recorded by Black Mambazo in 1963, but it now envelopes a metamorphosing array of party music genres. In 1977, Mafika Gwala published a poem called "Gumba, Gumba, Gumba." It is a lacerating indictment of the social wreckage over which Apartheid was presiding. It starts with the lines, "Been watching this jive/For too long./That's struggle." After a litany of violence and inverted social categories, it concludes, "You heard struggle./Knowing words don't kill/ But a gun does./That's struggle/For no more jive/Evening's eight/Ain't never late. Black is struggle."[3]

Among zama zamas today, the vans of smugglers (*malaicha*) who ferry illegalized migrants across the Zimbabwe borders are also sometimes referred to as *gumba gumba* vans. Thus, playing across the rhyme of the paddywagon/ party wagon, the zama zamas resignify the police as smugglers—both of people, whom they forcibly deport, and of gold and cash, which they take as coerced bribes from the zama zamas in payment for the temporary suspension of the law and that law-preserving violence that would otherwise lead to such deportation.

However nostalgic Alick Macheso's fans might have been in 2016, not many could have imagined dance as a medium for moderating, even temporarily, the gang conflicts of the Rand in the 1980s. By 1984, when twenty-year old Brenda Fassie first emerged on the music scene with a song called "Weekend Special," sung from the perspective of a woman who is only visited by her lover on weekends, that pacifist vision seemed absent. As Njabulo Ndebele has described with such sensitivity, Fassie was part of township life in South Africa throughout that time, entering people's homes and worlds through the radio in a "continuous performance" that accompanied without "charting" the sociopolitical scene. Ndebele cites the documentary history, *Mandela, Thambo and the African National Congress*, to evoke the situation in the summer of 1984, when he and his contemporaries were listening to "Weekend Special": "Stay-at-homes, roving demonstrations, challenging the police patrolling the township, and attacks on the businesses, houses, and persons of Africans charged with collaborating in the new Community Council system. Local grievances became the vehicle for protest against the Apartheid system as a whole, spreading from township to township through a population thoroughly mobilized by student participation in school boycotts and broader involvement in the anti-constitution campaigns."[4]

Fassie would famously live out her passions in public: lesbian and heterosexual love affairs, drug addiction, and AIDS. Her political passions were no less significant. In 1990, as the Apartheid era began to close down, with white supremacist terror answering insurrectionary anti-Apartheid violence, she released an album called *Black President*. It was not only, if at all, a prophesy of the future installation of Nelson Mandela, but rather a narration of his arrest in 1963. Its music is supported by African drums, and a male choir backs her with generous harmonies. Perhaps the most confrontational song on the album, and the one that seems most directly addressed to her own moment, is titled "Shoot Them Before They Grow." Its opening flute line recalls, without reproducing the signature sound of the American Western, Morricone's theme song for *The Good, the Bad and the Ugly* (1966). The lyrics imply that fantasies of white heroism and antagonism between liberalism and conservatism are partly to blame for the trajectory of conflict that did not so much culminate in the Soweto uprisings as converge and diverge there.

> Two white men fighting one another
> They're fighting for a black man
> The other one says the black man must be free
> The other one says the black man must be in handcuffs
> Who's gonna win now?
> 'Cause they both have power
> Who's gonna save the black man?
> 'Cause he ain't got no power
> 16-year-old kids protesting they want freedom
> Black children crying saying give us better education
> Good white man say give them good education
> The bad white man say shoot them before they grow[5]

The refrain simply repeats the last clause: "shoot them before they grow." Fassie's insistent repetition of the scandalously unthinkable but also already enacted principle forms the bookend of the period that opens with the passing of kwela and the gentler pata pata, which was punctuated by the doubled emergence of a student movement and a labor movement. As we learned in chapters 11 and 12, that doubled emergence, often referred to in the language of the former catalyzing the latter, was perhaps more dialectical than the word catalysis implies, and certainly less spontaneously transformative.

"Shoot Them Before They Grow":
White Zombies and the Arc of History

Fassie's refrain might well have been the motto of one of the most extreme paramilitary organizations, the Order of Death, an underground branch of the Afrikaner Weerstandsbeweging (AWB) or Afrikaner Resistance Movement whose members felt that the call from Eugene Terre'Blanche to oppose (by any and all means necessary) black majority rule could not be answered except by absolute violence. It was especially active in the gold-mining region centered in Carletonville, the mother organization having been founded in Ventersorp (Mayor van Rooyen's hometown). And its members grew increasingly convinced, during the period of boycotts, and then in the lead-up to the elections of 1994, that they were at risk of subordination and forced integration by a black-led government that even Terre'Blanche may have underestimated. Much of that otherwise rumored and feared organization's activities came into discussion during the Truth and Reconciliation Commission (TRC) and was revealed to be both less organized and less ideologically coherent than its popular image suggested. But its tempo and its temporality were well integrated with and related to that of the conflict in Khutsong.

One of the applicants for amnesty during the TRC's hearings, Cornelius Lottering, testified that he had joined the AWB in 1986. He was a supporter of the Conservative Party but preferred the more radical Herstigte Nasionale Party (HNP). There was no HNP in Carletonville, however, and Lottering was a friend of the Conservative Party's Carletonville candidate, Ari Paulus, who was also the head of the white Mine Worker's Union. On the towns of the Rand where the Order operated, cells of two or three people were operating more or less independently but receiving instructions from senior leadership through handlers. Their purpose was to both wreak havoc and undertake high-level assassinations of all who were supportive of a multiracial government. As Lottering described it, the purpose was to "initiate an underground movement which would execute political elimination with the objective of enforcing a Volkstaat."[6] The Order's aims included eliminating even National Party members, and Lottering himself drew up a plan to infiltrate meetings of Adrian Vlok, an extremely conservative member of the Apartheid regime and the architect of some of its most brutal repression, including torture, disappearance, and assassination, during his tenure as deputy minister of law and order (following his tenure as deputy minister of defense). The Order of Death was somewhere on the right of Vlok; this was a quite extraordinary position, although it paralleled other fascist groups around the world.

Lottering was coapplicant for amnesty, with Gert De Bruin and James Wheeler. Wheeler, a former worker at various mines in Carletonville, had done military service between 1986 and 1988, and in 1989, he joined the AWB after meeting De Bruin. In his testimony before the Commission, Wheeler described discussions held in the AWB as well as in meetings of the (white) Mine Worker's Union (not to be confused with the National Union of Mineworkers or NUM), where events like the Church Street and Magoos Bar bombings of 1983 and 1986, and other acts of sabotage by the African National Congress's (ANC) *uMkhonto weSizwe* (MK) units were the subject: "Within the Mine Workers Union, I heard that there was an ability among the white workers country-wide to cripple the country overnight by breaking up strategic services. The motivation for this possible action was found within the undemocratic actions of Mr F W de Klerk and his government, which were keeping white voters in the dark regarding their idea to hand over the country to an ANC/SACP government without protecting the interests of the whites."[7]

At stake in the amnesty hearing, as it was for everyone, was the determination of motive. If the purpose of his criminal activities had been political, Lottering would be granted amnesty. The means for making that claim depended on excluding two possibilities. On one hand, there could be no self-interest, no personal gain motivating the deed. In cases such as Lottering's, in which a robbery had been committed, the commissioners expressed doubt about the primary purpose of his crimes, including the murder, the robbery, and a later escape from prison. On the other hand, it was incumbent on the applicant to demonstrate that the motive was not merely racism. Racism itself was not deemed a political motive. And this is because it did not permit a differentiation among the ideological commitments and party political affiliations of people of the same racial category. The demand that racism and political motive be distinguished was invariably more acutely pursued in cases involving white supremacist actors, and here, as in so many other instances, the cases from Carletonville and Khutsong are painfully exemplary. As it happens, Lottering was denied amnesty for the killing of Mr. Makgalamele, a local taxi driver he had murdered on August 29, 1989. It was determined that he had undertaken the act not on orders from his superiors, nor in the cause of the party, but as a preliminary gesture to assuage his own and the leadership's doubts about his capacity to perform the deed or others of that sort (he was repeatedly described as a formerly "gentle" person, who had been radicalized by the Order). To explain this, he told the Commissioners that he had chosen a "Black taxi driver who transported white persons in his taxi. I basically chose him in order to protest against integration."[8] Lottering claimed to feel neither pleasure nor anger in relation to the shooting; it was the mere fulfillment of his purpose as an aspirant agent of the Order. He also undertook armed robbery and later set two bombs. The Commission's denial of amnesty to Lottering for the murder, but the granting of it for the robbery and escape rested on its determination that an act intended only to demonstrate one's qualities and thus eligibility for membership in the party was not in itself political. These were trials of admission, tests of valor, which reflected only on the individual. They could not be a means to a political end, but instead were confined to mere means: the disclosure of potential and the revelation of the perpetrator's fortitude. Lottering was granted amnesty for the robbery and the escape because these had been commanded by his superiors.

Some of the most revelatory testimony of the Lottering case came in an exchange between the commissioners and one of his witnesses, namely Barend Strijdom. Strijdom had been a member of the AWB whose purpose, he said, was to "correct the situation," and "establish a Volkstaat." He stated that he was a friend of Dawie de Beer, the leader of the Order of Death, and an acquaintance of Hennie de Binnemen, the organization's liaison chief and the person through whom the various cells were stitched together. When asked about the AWB's policy, Strijdom launched into an impromptu history of the Anglo-Boer war: "I will try and put it very briefly—after the Anglo Boer War we as the Boer people lost our freedom after 26,000 women and children were killed in a brutal way by the English. After that there was a peace treaty." Commissioner Steenkamp intervened, abruptly, in an effort to divert the Afrikaner nationalist apology: "I beg your pardon, the question was do you know what the policy was?" When pressed further whether there was an open order to kill black people, Strijdom hedged only slightly: "Let me answer it in this way—I attended many, many AWB meetings where there were calls made to act, to make war." What was war in this context? Andre Stephanus Kriel, a former AWB Brigadier who also testified at Lottering's hearing and who expressed contrition about his role in the bloodshed, put the matter bluntly: "I must indicate that the Commanders of that time saw the ANC as a complete enemy, it was the order of the day within the AWB that the ANC was regarded as an enemy and we all had consensus with one another that the ANC members should be killed. We had no doubts about that, that was what the AWB was about, there was an enemy, the enemy had to be eliminated."[9] His was a perfectly Schmittian understanding of the enemy, as the other in a dyadic struggle for political existence.[10]

Strijdom knew of the existence of the Order but was in prison during the period of its most intensive operations. Nonetheless, he conceded that "in a national context we had a special patriotic feeling which was closely interwoven, politics, religion was all closely interwoven and from this very specific situation it happens that one identifies a lot of enemies, in other words people who weren't with us were against us, that was the basic point of view." Makgalamele had been one such enemy of the Volk, along with the so-called traitors of the National Party, Strijdom affirmed. The exchange with the Commissioners grew brittle and was complicated because the victim had apparently been an advocate of the Bantustan policy and black autonomy. When Strijdom seemed to refer to the murdered taxi driver as a "nobody," Commissioner Gcabashe pressed him, asking if Makgalamele had been named an enemy of the Volk because he was a nobody or because he was black. More precisely, she asked, "So any black person was therefore perceived as an enemy of the Volk because he was a nobody?" When Strijdom insisted that the AWB's purpose was the promotion of the Boervolk cause and that it was not "purely" on a "racial basis, although it was that too (it also had strong religious elements), Gcabashe posed the question that would occupy much of the subsequent discussion: "Can you distinguish for me a racially supremacist motivation in a killing like this as opposed to a political motivation in a killing such as this?" Strijdom said he could tell from the name that the victim was not a member of the community of the Volk: "From the way his name and surname is pronounced it's clear to me that this person is not a Boer and cannot be one."[11]

The white supremacist AWB had supported the black Bophuthatswana chief Lucas Mangope and saw him as a defender of separate development. It had been a contention of AWB members, including Lottering, that there was no animus toward black people in general, only an insistence on their nonintegration with whites. Thus, the black champions of separatist government, such as Mantazima in the Transkei and Mangope in Bophuthatswana, could be allies. When it was pointed out by Advocate Bosman, also a commissioner, that the murdered Makgalamele had also been a supporter of Mangope, the conversation moved to the matter of what, other than "pure racism," could have explained the assassination. Bosman asked Strijdom to concede that Makgalamele was killed because "nobody knew really who and what he was." A nobody was then the person whom nobody knew. This is what blackness was for the AWB: a condition of unknowability. Any one black person could stand in for any other in the mass. It was this kind of randomness that led some members of the Azanian People's Liberation Army to pursue random "reprisals" against whites.[12]

Why had the AWB split, and what motivated the creation of this faction that took upon itself the role of killing, borrowing for its name the phrase generally used to describe the proper sequence of a burial rite? In the genitive formula of its name, the question of whether Death was its origin or its mission was in suspense. It would bring death, and it was death, and its members felt commanded to enact death, all in the interest of the life of the purified community. Kriel stated that Terre'Blanche made increasingly confused statements and that his failure to retain a position defined by his initial commandment to "destroy all the blacks"[13] had incited the creation of more radical paramilitary units. He and Aquillo had formed their own breakaway group, which was sometimes referred to as the Aquillos in the manner of the other gangs on the Rand. Although he was not a member of the Order of Death, Kriel affirmed Lottering's description of a cell structure, which he claimed the AWB "subtly encouraged" because they knew that its members would carry out extreme acts in isolation. The cell structure marked a significant difference with the gangs—from the ANC-affiliated groups to the Marashea—for, it was marked by a culture of relative solitude amid the network. Nonetheless, it produced spectacular violence. According to Kriel, the purpose of the bombings being carried out by the AWB was simply to draw attention to their "freedom struggle." They were not intended as methods of killing but rather as communicative acts that would sow confusion. But for both the bombings and the assassinations, members were chosen not on the basis of their ideological commitments alone but "according to the criteria of persons who would carry out instructions almost immediately."[14]

Commissioner Moloi asked Kriel, "What was the ANC to you, was it any black person, even your gardener? If he was black, your helper in the house, if she was black, was that part of the ANC—automatically? Simply because of being black?" And Kriel answered, "yes." In his mind, the fact that the AWB included whites in its list of enemies exempted it from the charge of racism. In his analysis, racism would have had to express and enact a categorical separation that immunized whites against violence. We might say that the ghosts of separation past (technological, ideological and sociological) weighed on his brain with all the dead generations of white supremacists. He did not grasp that the categorical targeting of a population defined as unknowable but rendered identifiable was racist. And the Commission rejected this argument. At the same time and in the very process of refusing Kriel's and the AWB's terms, the TRC narrowed the concept of the political, at least insofar as it would be eligible for amnesty, to a form of obedience and the submission of personal interest to the pursuit of the party's or the political organization's objectives. In this way, it did not escape but rather entrenched the double bind of political subjectivity that is the inheritance of the Enlightenment, according to which right moral action is willing submission to the law. Where, however, Enlightenment moral philosophy defined the good subject as the one who willingly submits to the law, another logic—at once more archaic and recursively emergent—operated across the multiplicity of gangs, self-defense units, and paramilitary groups in South Africa, and indeed within the party structures themselves. This logic demanded obedience not only to the rule of law but also to the ruler of the group. That same double bind, we will remember, had haunted Motapanyane's discourse. What the struggle had taught the youth, he said, was to follow the orders of the party leadership, immediately and without hesitation. As is so often the case when considering South African history, the local scene appears in retrospect to have prefigured what is now occurring throughout the authoritarian world.

Before his testimony concluded, Kriel was asked if the splinter groups of the AWB were still in operation after 1994. He claimed that the Aquillos had been disbanded and the Order of Death suspended. He said, however, that the Wen Kommando—which took its name from the first trek of Piet Retief, when the Boers had fled the Cape rather than relinquish slavery—persisted.

I was not present at this hearing. I read its transcripts after the event. But not too long before the Amnesty Hearings where Lottering, Strijdom, and Kriel were telling their stories about the AWB's and the Order's murderous rampage, and as they were failing to make the case for a political cause above or beyond "pure racism," I was walking across the mine dumps of Carletonville, accompanied by the former warden of the jails whose tortures were being enumerated in the Victims Hearings. It was the last time I would speak to him. I remember the day perfectly and have already described it (see chapter 7). The sun was high, and the sky was clear. It was winter but not cold. We were soon to depart. From his pocket, the man pulled a business card and showed it to me, not letting go. I had expected it to be his own card, but it was not. It was the personal "business" card of the Grand Wizard of the Ku Klux Klan. Speechless for a moment, conscious of the need to remain noncommittal on that emptied plane that the card's owner had described to me as a place where bodies might be hidden, I finally said that I didn't know the Klan was in South Africa. "Everywhere," he said. And he added, "I met him personally, you know." He put the card back in his breast pocket. And we left. The TRC hearings were happening elsewhere.

Crime and Crisis: The Language of Violence

Not far from where we stood, surveying the landscape where violence might have occurred, Nelson Mandela had delivered the anniversary oration of the ANC. On January 8, 1996, not quite two years after South Africa's first democratic election and on the eve of the TRC's opening, he had addressed a crowd of more than ten thousand people and spoke of a "struggle which intensifies with each passing day, to define the agenda of the democratic order." He was speaking in the soccer stadium of Khutsong about the struggle to end violent crime. The division between political and nonpolitical crime was strained in Mandela's speech, as he called on audience members to "ensure that the people themselves take up the struggle for an end to violence and the creation of a climate conducive to free political activity."[15] He was articulating the new state's claim to legitimacy as well as its right to a monopoly on violence. At the same time, he was eschewing any political claims that might be made on behalf of crime—not only by other political groups but also by the victims of Apartheid who might otherwise imagine vengeance as an adequate substitute for justice, and by those individuals who, frustrated by the limited opportunities to assert their new rights, might attempt to demonstrate their will-to-power in and through violence.

To a certain extent, Mandela's call for an end to violence as the condition of possibility for political activity implied an absolute antithesis between violence (violent crime) and political processes, and it indexed a nearly Habermasian conception of the political as a space of transparent communicative relations among all people. With its capacious multilingualism and recognition of eleven official languages, South Africa's new constitution materialized that conception in an explicit form. To make such a statement, however, Mandela also had to construe "political violence" as an exception, indeed as *the* exception on which the new social order would be based. Such exceptionalism also provided the axiomatic ground for the TRC, which indemnified the new state against civil liability for the violence committed by its precursor, and it offered amnesty to individuals if they could demonstrate that their offenses were committed "with political objectives and . . . in the course of the conflicts of the past."[16] As I noted previously, although the TRC and its members recognized the effects of "structural violence" in the generally high rates of nonpolitical crime through-out South African society, it nonetheless offered amnesty only for those deeds intentionally and proportionately perpetrated in terms of the fight for and against Apartheid.

As we have seen, the TRC labored to distinguish random violence structured by racism from targeted and specific violence with racialized goals. If we recall the argument from chapter 12, in which the baroque was considered to be an aesthetic arising in times of disjuncture, in which randomness reigned and a horrible substitutability afflicted the victims of the Order of Death, we can understand that the TRC was, in some ways, trying to bring this epoch to an end. It was trying to restrain the frenzied terror of high Apartheid—and all that proliferated in its shadows, not least the reign of gangsters pretending to be princes. It aimed to exclude randomness and to assert the establishment of a new regime in which the space of the political could be localized, with crime as its perimeter and redemption as its inner purpose. This redemption, more than the forgiveness that outsiders emphasized in their critique of the Commission's supposed Christian bias, constituted the messianic essence of the TRC.

In this process, the TRC posited two extreme cases of "criminality" within the law as the limit on either end of what could be encompassed within the political. The first was composed of the "clearly criminal deeds" committed by "bad apples" in the security forces. Although recognizing their criminality, the TRC granted amnesty to such perpetrators if their acts had been condoned or had gone unpunished over a long period of time, and hence, they could be said to reflect the policy of the state's security apparatus. The second was represented by the case of "*kitskonstabels*" (instant constables), who were recruited into the police force following minimal training as part of a contramobilization force. As black men, they were accused of using the power of their offices and the force of their quickly acquired arms to harass and terrorize politically active (dissident) community members. The TRC chose to "view these acts within their political context" and generally granted amnesty "*unless acts committed were clearly aberrations.*" The examples of aberration cited by the TRC report include "shooting the owner of a shebeen, or *raping someone in circumstances which indicated that it was a random crime*."[17]

The first instance appears to be a straightforward crime of economic self-interest, and one that would have been useless to the counterinsurgency. It is, however, the second that draws our attention, suggesting as it does that rape might be enacted in a random manner but also that it might on occasion constitute a political act. In its demand for full confessions, the TRC institutionalized (and theatricalized) a deeply ironic concept of individuated political accountability. Those acts that expressed a will-to-political subjectivity would be amnestied only if they could be explained as politically overdetermined and hence identified as acts that actually reflected the limit of the personal as the basis for political agency. Meanwhile, those illicit acts that had been carried out in a context that was saturated with political violence, but that lacked political purpose, remained criminal and unavailable for amnesty. As such, these latter acts came to represent a doubled failure, particularly in normatively masculine subjects: the failure to be political (or to channel disaffection into political struggles) and the failure of the Apartheid regime to equally recognize all people as full political subjects. Here, as admissions of accountability came to entail the surrender of any notion that individual acts could be a legitimate mode of achieving social justice, the political emerged as a category denoting the limit of the personal. If, in this sense, the TRC was a grand mourning play, in Walter Benjamin's sense, it also aspired to be the curtain call of that genre. It wanted to banish random violence to the domain of the criminal, even as it wanted to relegate political violence to the historical past.

Yet, in a milieu increasingly saturated with legal discourse, where televisual dramas of law and order and promises of political enfranchisement reinforce but also distort each other, the distinction between political responsibility and individual indemnity, on the one hand, and personal culpability understood as guilt or innocence, on the other, was sometimes lost. Its effacement can be seen in the petitions for amnesty in which perpetrators believed they were being given an opportunity to proclaim their innocence, rather than to admit their guilt as the means to freedom. It can, perhaps, also be seen in the forms of violence that seem to have proliferated in the wake of the TRC: sexual and domestic violence, incestuous rape, assaults on elderly people, and the transformation of economic crime into personalized and not infrequently sexually violent crime (very little of it taking place across racial lines). Elsewhere, I have considered some of these cases in detail and have noted the strained efforts of commissioners to determine, across the abyss of time and translational breakdowns, what happened in the conflict between the long-lived gangs of the gold-mining region, the student organizations that moved into the area post-1976, and the youth leagues of the political parties.[18] In reading the transcripts of hearings on these events, I have been struck by how often testimony faltered at the point when those confessing to violence were asked to explain why they took up arms and how rigorously the TRC commissioners attempted to maintain the boundary between language and violence. The argument that sexual violence can function as political violence, by virtue of its communicative role in the vindictive and terroristic competitions between groups of men, is an especially vexing problem and has generated considerable commentary in the literature about the TRC. As far as I am aware, however, this literature has not grasped such phenomena within the broader context of the social transformations that were taking place and that formed the ground of this violence, much of it at the behest of the gold industry, and the minerals complex more broadly—namely, the whole project of "stabilization," couched in the discourse of a return to a mythic patriarchal and indeed phallogocentric order (in which value and social power were oriented around a single phallic signifier and orchestrated to secure men's authority and women's domestication). Without such a history, one is left, as were the TRC commissioners listening to the stories of Khutsong's conflicts, with the enigma of how to differentiate the pseudo-military histories of gangsterism from those of political conflict. Just as the compound and the township were maintained through the border institution of the *skomplaas*, so too did the borderline between these orders of violence depend on the false opposition between the intimate or domestic spheres and the public realm, with sexual violence as the broken hinge between them.

Random Ghosts of the Secret, the Unspeakable, and the Spectacular

When considering cases of rape and sexual violence that were granted political status in the TRC, two distinct sets of phenomena can be observed (although the dispassion needed for such categorization is difficult to maintain in their face). In one of these cases, such violence is intended to terrorize the victim and to persuade her to abandon her political activities. Such violence was often secreted, undertaken in remote and concealed spaces, and it worked partly by mobilizing the victim's shame. In the other, violence was public and spectacular and was addressed less to the woman than to the man or men who claimed rights to her, or whose affective bonds would be injured by witnessing the victim's suffering. (There is no evidence of which I am aware of the kind of politicization seen in other warzones, where, for example, forced impregnation is part of a demographic violence, in addition to its terroristic functions. And this is not surprising given the legacies of Apartheid's prohibition on cross-racial relation.)

Violence against women was not exclusively a symptom of the conflict between gangsterism and the ANC, nor was it a mark of the increased tensions that had defined the last panicked years of the Apartheid state. It had been an irreducible part of the economy of both white and black masculinity, and it had been especially central to the world of the gangs, as these had emerged in the gold-mining towns around Johannesburg. Keith Breckenridge has called "the capacity for violence" the "heart of masculinity for both groups of men" (black and white) on the mines.[19] For most writers, sexualized violence against women, and the aesthetics of violence that sustained it, is linked to Apartheid, if only to the extent that the system of racialized natural resource–based capital that was cultivated reinforced the normed traditions of gendered hierarchy that were put to use by the Chamber of Mines and the mining companies, as we have seen. Thus, for example, Clive Glaser suggests that the only domain in which otherwise emasculated black male subjects could maintain a sense of the "ascendant" was in the hyperbolically masculine spaces of the gangs.[20] Without attributing a causal force to the Apartheid system, Catherine Campbell links it to sexual violence in a traditionalist account when she asserts that "the ability of men to control women . . . and the use of violence to ensure this control, is one area where the power of working class men has not been threatened by a racial capitalist society."[21] Glaser's analysis, however, goes further in not only comprehending the prevalence of sexual violence in terms of Apartheid but also in suggesting that sexual violence actually constituted one of the definitive practices of (urban) gangsterism: "Although many urban youth gangs mugged and robbed ordinary residents, probably the majority were not engaged consistently in serious property-related crime. Rather, the *most common manifestations of gang violence involved sexual coercion and inter-gang feuding.*"[22]

What does it mean to suggest that sexual "coercion" constituted a central activity of the gangs and the "most common" form of its violence? Glaser and Gary Kynoch read the centrality of such violence in economic and utilitarian terms. To quote Kynoch, "the control of women has been crucial to the economic survival of the gangs."[23] We have already discussed his argument that women were used as lures to seduce miners into spending their money in establishments run by the Marashea and that they were also deemed to enhance men's power through their praise singing. But they were also always eligible to become "spoils of war" or "trophies," and Kynoch quotes a gang member describing the ideals of masculinity as the capacity "to kill, commit robberies, and kidnap women."[24] In 2014, when gangsterism in Khutsong once again entered the headlines in stories about sexual violence, the same logic operated. This time, in frustration with police inaction, township residents murdered several members of the newly dominant Casanova gang after a series of rapes— in spectacular rites of popular justice that included burning the men alive.[25] Such is the brutal economism of popular justice: one spectacle of cruelty for another, but in a manner that seeks an end to violence by outdoing it.

Nor is this economism confined to the domain of vigilantism. For, invariably, it seems, arguments about violence against women devolve into these economistic explanations. Although it seems to me an unassailable claim that women in patriarchal contexts are the objects of a fierce extractive process, such explanations do not ultimately explain violence, and certainly not the forms of violence that are in evidence in the gang wars of Khutsong or the other towns and townships of the area. Those forms are differentiated in complex but also coherent ways, and this differentiation suggests that they aspire to communication, but they do so in a manner that can conceive of communication only as an instrumental operation, and thus they are a violent form of connection, a connection without real and responsible relation. Now this rendering of woman as medium in a violent relay is precisely her subjection to the function of means. Benjamin's critique of violence as means is insufficient to grasp this dimension of the sexual economy. We also need to grasp it in the context not only of the agonizing end-game in Apartheid's last years but also against the backdrop of all those efforts to "stabilize" the black workforce of the mines that made of black women these means. This entails recognizing the folded nature of the relationship between the domestic and the political, and refusing all those efforts that would draw the line of social history at the perimeter of the compound, or at the sectoral boundary of the gold industry, or on the threshold between the visible public and the invisible underground.

Mimetic Violence or the Specter of War

A poignant and painfully revealing attempt to address these questions occurred in one of the TRC's hearings about the violence that women in the ANC's Women's League and Youth League were subject to by the police, including at the Carletonville police station.

> Maria, we want you to assist us to have the political context of the first story you told us about. You heard that Sheila Meintjies during her submission here, she said that at some of the days, there is a very thin line between domestic violence and political violence. When this Willard police, this policeman, Willard, called you to his house and attempted to rape you at gunpoint, did he do this because he knew you were a Comrade or he just did it because he wanted to have sex with you? Maybe because he did not, [he] despised your husband because he was a cripple or rather you were a Comrade and he was a policeman and that offended him that you were a Comrade or he just did it, because he had lust and because your husband was disable[d]?[26]

This exchange between Commissioner Seroke, a woman, and the witness, Ms. Mxathule, had been preceded by one with the chair, in which a similar effort at delineating the politically sexual from mere lust had occurred:

> *Ms Mxathule*: This person attempted to rape me, because he had lust for me.
> *Chairperson*: For how long had you known this person and in what context?
> *Ms Mxathule*: I attended school with this person from Grade A up till standard five. He left town and then he attended school in Transkei. That is how we could not continue our studies together, because he left for Transkei.
> *Chairperson*: But he was not doing that in a political context, he was just doing it as a man who wanted to do that to you as a person? I am trying to get that clarity.
> *Ms Mxathule*: Yes, because when I explained this to his father, he explained to my father that your child is, they are use [*sic*] to each other.
> *Chairperson*: Again, I would like us to be clear on this. So, this man wanted to rape you not because it was a, there was no political context. He was just doing it, because he is use [*sic*] to doing that.
> *Ms Mxathule*: The riots were not yet over in Jubatine at that time. We were still involved in the political struggle.

No clarity was obtained in the exchange. For Ms. Mxathule, the notion of political context was one of a general milieu within which all acts were signified; it was not possible to draw the line that the commissioners so desperately desired and that eluded them at every turn. Because it was against this backdrop of a Struggle between the police and anti-Apartheid forces, and because she had been among many women who were arrested, beaten, tortured, and raped in that context, those acts could not be separated from the political struggle. Nor were they mere side-effects. They manifested its inner structure. Such violence was politics by other means. If this was so, and the TRC implicitly claimed as much, the difference between domestic and political violence would have to be rethought. With it, the question of means comes to the fore once again.

To understand these ultimately undecidable but seemingly necessary categorical distinctions, we may be helped by turning to structural anthropological accounts of power and kinship, politics and familial relations. The analyses of structural anthropologists often resemble those of gangsters and their sociologists—at least when it comes to the question of war's objectives and the messaging value or media function of women's bodies. Classical structuralist anthropology—and a certain Freudianism, with which such anthropology sometimes appears to be opposed—operates on the basis of two axioms. According to the first, social life is structured through mandatory exchanges among men of key values and valuables. Such exchange objects are said to sublate within themselves and thereby contain a more agonistic possibility that would arise among such men. In other words, exchange substitutes for war. According to the second axiom, in some exchanges, women may be conceived, and they are indeed conceived by structuralism, as comprising valuable objects. Thus, in the organized reciprocation of women by and for men, fraternal bonds are said to be affirmed, even as the conditions for conflict over them are put into play. In other words, marriage is a mode of deferring war. In the exemplary writing of Pierre Clastres, the mark of this sublation and deferral is read in the rituals of matrimony (in this case, among the Guayaki Indians) in which an act of violence is rendered as a symbolic event wherein violence is suspended.[27] But to maintain the perfection of the structuralist model, Clastres finds himself having to code the punching of a woman as something other than violence, because it occurs as part of the expected procedure of a wedding rite. I do not want to linger too long on this now-antiquated discourse, to which so many feminist anthropologists have offered their rebuttal. But I want to note the persistence, and even the intransigence (given the feminist critique), of a tendency in social analysis to explain gangsterism's violence against women and the politicization of rape in terms that remain redolent of this old paradigm.

A key distinction should be noted here, and it becomes visible in those same transcripts of the TRC, concerned as they were with the events that unfolded in the shadow of the mine dumps, where, as the stories go, bodies could be hidden and violence concealed. In an especially vexing case, Peter Lebona and Solomon Lekitlane made application under the terms of the TRC for the murder of one Zenzile Jospeh Lamini (or Nglamini or Ndlameni—the spelling changes by document) in July 1991, in Orkney, a gold-mining town not far from Carletonville/Khutsong. The context was comparable: conflict between the ANC Youth League and local gangs had erupted into armed combat. In this case, the murder victim had been a comrade who had changed his affiliation and had attached himself to a local gang, called the Kofifi. Although Zenzile was murdered following a meeting of the ANC, both Lebona and Lekitlane commenced their narratives by identifying Zenzile as the perpetrator of a particularly violent rape, in which a local ANC woman was assaulted in her home by Zenzile and his companions. According to the men's TRC testimony, when she was commanded to pay the gangsters, and indicated that she could not do so, Zenzile allegedly bound her husband before raping her in his presence and then crushed her skull with a stone.

In his response to the Commissioner's question as to why Zenzile might have attacked the woman, Peter Lebona revealingly remarked that the act had been the manifestation of a broader aim: "This woman was a member of the ANC Women's League . . . and *Zenzile was really intending to kill the activists* of the ANC that is why he chose to do that act."[28] Effectively, he attributed to the rape a metonymic status. The rape and murder (the latter now questionable) were not, precisely, representational or even representative acts. Nor did they produce any possibility of a reciprocal relation. The brutality and gratuitous-ness of the violence, which included the alleged crushing of the skull, was not unlike that excessive violence of the gangs described in chapter 12, or the witch burnings from which they drew their tactics. In this respect, it perhaps beto-kened the sense that the rapist did not think that the woman was or could be an adequate embodiment or stand-in. If he could eliminate the ANC activists by eliminating her, there would be no need for the frenzied additional violence. But the woman's body did not function for this man as a representative of the ANC; the ANC remained, as did other political forces. In other words, there was still something opposing him, and his rage seems to have grown partly from this fact. She was not, in the end, his enemy—the other against whom he could consolidate himself.

The men claimed for the act a political motive and a political signification—retrospectively cladding their brutality in the image of lawfulness—albeit a law unwritten in any constitutional order. A structuralist reading might read the violence as a breakdown or even a refusal of the effort to communicate across political divisions. The violence would thus be seen arising where social exchange failed. But this is not what was said. And although the hearings were marred by extraordinary problems of translations and although the witnesses seem to have spoken only broken versions of their mother tongues—the symp-tom of social dislocation and the educational wasteland to which so many black subjects were consigned under Apartheid—a certain logic can be read in the hearing and others like it. For the rape did not occur when the possibility of political relation broke down. It occurred when other kinds of violence were blocked, forms of violence that were (wrongly) believed to have been capable of annihilating the threat and obstacles in his way. Zenzile wanted to kill the other ANC operatives as the source of everything that opposed him and his desire. He couldn't and so he raped the woman instead. Or so said Peter Lebona. And then Zenzile killed her. Or so Peter Lebona said.

If there is something representative and revelatory in this otherwise sin-gular but also commonplace story of the terrifying violence to which black women were subject during the period of the virtual civil war between pro- and anti-Apartheid forces, inflected as they were by the history and ethos of gang-sterism on the goldfields, it is that its sexual violence was, on the one hand, inseparable from contests in the political order (organized by enmity between groups of men) but also that it exceeded the presumptive opposition between war and violence. Grounded as it is on the idea that the symbolic mediation of violence mitigates overt conflict and promotes group coherence while gener-ating alliance—albeit sometimes at the expense of scapegoats—the vision of politics and organized violence or warfare gave way as each became its other. But that opposition has always rested on the effacement of women's histori-cal placement and function in this system. This is another way of saying that social orders in which this opposition is not only a description but an ideology demand the reduction of women to means. And this reduction is one of the principles that not only traverses the mine compound, the homeland, and the *skomplaas* (mediated by the pass system), as well as the project of stabilization, but a key thread by which they were knitted together.

There is also an affinity between a system in which the generic categorization of people gendered black and female becomes available for so-called random violence and a system wherein—as described earlier in this chapter, in the account of the Order of Death—the generic categorization of people as black makes them available for the violence, at once structured *and* random, meted out by white supremacists. The affinity lies in the abstraction and effacement of singularities—particular lived experience in given bodily forms and social contexts—in the notion of categorical identity, or social type. In the end, the stretching (or reduction) of the category of enemy to the level of race or gender makes a mockery of every effort to specify a rationale for any particular act of violence. This is surely why, despite its best and most heroic efforts, its noble aspirations and patient labors, its elegant rationale and its rigorous efforts at impartiality (and this, despite its limited capacities), the TRC was, above all, a stage on which the category of the political seemed to falter. The delimitation of political motive, claimed by all amnesty applicants in a context in which racial and sexual identity had been rendered a means, was of course imperative if the new state was to maintain its legitimacy. The corollary of this was that political violence would vanish. In its place would be only crime.

Recall here that the TRC amnesty process had no capacity to bring charges, nor to declare the innocence of anyone who had previously been found guilty or imprisoned. It could only grant amnesty to the guilty, and more particularly to the guilty who confessed the totality of their crimes. It was thus inscribed within that circle of guilt that, as we have seen, is the modus operandi of racialized capitalism. First, amnesty was contingent on crimes having been committed in the service of a political project and, as we have seen, political crimes had to be separated from those motivated by generic racism. This was especially difficult for those crimes committed by white supremacists. One can see in those hearings concerned with the activities of the right-wing paramilitary groups a laborious effort to distinguish between the two—with the result being that political crimes came to be understood primarily as those conducted within the command structure of a party. Second, crimes for which amnesty could be obtained could not have been conducted out of self-interest or personal animus. Here, too, the exclusion of personal interest meant that crimes had to be conducted at the behest of a larger organizational structure, typically a party, in which orders could be sent, received, and enacted or betrayed.

The resolution desired from the TRC, which, as a nonjudicial institution, was never empowered to address the socioeconomic consequences of segregation or the organization of industrial society to promote tribalism, artificial rurality, and ethnic conflict, was riven by these twin limit structures and by the aporia at the heart of the personal political. Racism was the condition of Apartheid, but it could not constitute a rationale for amnesty. A capacity for decision making and personal responsibility were goals of liberation, but its exercise seemed to foreclose amnesty. In the end, and perhaps against the best intentions of its most ardent advocates, the fetishization of the party (and especially party leadership) and the understanding of the political as a structure of commandment were the TRC's ironic outcomes. Its successes, not to be undervalued, include the validation of the testimony of those whose words had previously been treated as counterfeit, and the acknowledgment in public of the nature and extent of the violence endured in the Apartheid era. One of the most significant accomplishments of the TRC was the theatricalization of a difference between law and justice. But the paucity of amnesties granted attest to the degree to which the TRC remained beholden to the notion that guilt in one domain (deed) was redoubled by guilt in another domain (representation), and the TRC made absolutely no claims about the innocence of the victims. Perhaps its leadership assumed that reconciliation would be a natural outgrowth of truth and the adequacy of representation. Almost thirty years later, few South Africans seem to believe that to be the case, and the country has been ravaged by waves of xenophobic violence and calls for more severe punishment of criminals—if also a newfound suspicion of party political structures. These gestures share the sense that a menace remains at large and needs to be ejected. The police are often said to be part of that menace, if only because they have failed to contain it. And to this extent, we may say that the present is yet haunted, and the era 1976–1986 is not closed.

And yet, what did not happen in 1964 did finally happen. The regime of formal Apartheid came to an end, and the gold mines, whose existence had provided the motive and alibi for its structure, and much of the administrative technology for its operation, persisted in its absence, although they would increasingly be oriented toward the horizon of their eventual closure. The meaning of Brenda Fassie's album, "Black President," acquired a new dimension. In light of the preceding chapters, the following questions come to mind most pressingly: How did people learn to live otherwise? What forms of preparation could possibly enable the survival and transformation of that legacy? What institutional and social practices could come to bear on that wounded world in such a manner as to permit something other than the persistence of death in life—whether as ghostliness or a kind of zombified existence in which the forms of appearance of life are mere masks for death? Let us now consider what has surfaced in the decades since, returning again to the aboveground world, and to the people who, from the start, have oriented this effort to grasp the lives, deaths, and afterlives of gold in South Africa.

PART III

SURFACING

CHAPTER 14

TERRAIN OF THE FETISH

Dislocations, Relocations, and the Difficulty of Moving On

Since the powers-that-be view qualification certificates as talismans, everyone materially able to do so chases after them and seeks to enhance his own monopoly value as much as possible.

—Siegfried Kracauer, *The Salaried Masses*

One day they will give her a certificate and a heart of stone.

—Yvette Christiansë, "Spring, for Martha"

"Here comes the new. Look out. There goes the sad stuff. The bad stuff. The things-nobody-could-help stuff. The way everybody was then and there. Forget that. History is over, you all, and everything's ahead at last." These lines from the opening chapter of Toni Morrison's *Jazz*, an American novel set in the years immediately following World War I, seem at first glance to bespeak the euphoria that comes at the end of strife, and the desire for oblivion that sometimes comes with it. One could have expected such a response to the fall of Apartheid, even in the small towns around gold mines. And certainly, the consumer pleasures that were being advertised in the new shopping malls, on television, and on the LoveLife billboards identifying the new era as one of sexual freedom—and secret danger—suggested as much. *Jazz* was published in 1992, two years after Nelson Mandela was released from prison and just as a national referendum was asking South Africans to finally put Apartheid behind them. In March 1992, Eugene Terre'Blanche of the Afrikaner Resistance Party (AWB) and, as we have seen, inspiration of the white supremacist underground—had rallied more than a thousand white people in the shadow of Carletonville's mine dumps and had argued that the end of white rule would mean the end of civilization in South Africa. The previous three years had seen, as discussed in chapter 13, a significant intensification of white-supremacist political violence against ANC youth, with the local police station as the scene of some of its most brutal torture, but the paramilitary right had been carrying out its own regime of terror underground, as it were.[1] The more mainstream but still rightist Conservative Party had argued that the ANC intended to redistribute wealth and thus poverty—an experience that Apartheid had been designed to prevent for whites.[2] When the "Yes" vote (to end Apartheid) won the day, many of those people would start speaking of Carletonville's "going down." Nor was this idiom the preserve of extreme white supremacists. I heard it spoken by residents of an elder care facility, who otherwise disavowed violence; in mixed-race churches where sermons advocated forgiveness; in shops, petrol stations, and funeral parlors. The trope of the sinkhole was, as noted in chapter 7, reborn as a signifier not only of decline but also of ressentiment—first of the white community that was about to lose its privilege and then for the black community that was about to be disappointed in its ambitions for a full transformation.

This ambivalence, and the copresence of joy and fear in freedom, was integral to Morrison's novel as well. The mysterious spectral narrator of *Jazz* thought that the only oblivion coming for the disenfranchised was going to be achieved in momentary drunkenness or the equally momentary acts of violence perpetrated by those whose experience of power was limited to holding a gun—or, alternatively, in the delirium, sometimes sweetly sensuous, sometimes wildly dissonant, of jazz. Most people were going to either hold on to the old ways or be burdened by them. This is why Morrison's text ironizes the discourse of the new by attributing it to the so-called "smart people," the people who write. Nonetheless, her narrator observes, "In the halls and offices people are sitting around thinking future thoughts about projects and bridges and fast-clicking trains underneath."[3] That depiction of exuberant planning, tinged with the same utopianism that had saturated the advertising for Carletonville's first real estate brochures, was indeed evident in the early post-Apartheid era, when government officials, mine management, and various representatives of civil society seemed constantly to be convening conferences on topics such as entrepreneurialism and human capital development, new sectoral management, skills development, and technology transfer and scaling appropriate to the "projects and bridges and fast-clicking trains underneath." From the vantage point granted by two more decades, it is possible to discern a certain pattern in which the talk of the new was counterposed to the oblivion for which music and violence represent the extreme counterposed examples. Having now considered the complex and uneven effort to overcome the opposition between the mental and the manual, and after having examined the nonsynchronized development of movements aimed at radical democracy in the townships and in the labor sector of the mines, I now want to reconsider a related opposition between education and the aesthetic domain, on one hand, and that kind of violence that expresses the blockage of political aspiration, on the other (the kind that so often took the form of sexual violence, as described in chapter 12). The scene for this drama—no longer a mourning play so much as a tragedy, in which individuals struggled against forces that came from the past—is the effort to reorganize political space by the post-Apartheid government in the early days of hoped-for liberation. Like so much of the history of South Africa, the areas around the gold mines of the Far West Rand, provided this drama with its stage, and gold was its recurrent theme: as ground, as metaphor, as the object of desire.

The sense of liberation from the strictures of Apartheid took many forms at the center of the gold-mining world. Learners in townships who harbored professional ambitions dreamt of accessing schools and colleges where they would finally be instructed in the curriculum with which the powerful had been fed for decades. People who had been forcibly relocated under the terms of the Group Areas Act hoped they would be able to return to, and reoccupy, the homes they recalled, or at least that they would be eligible to purchase real estate in those areas. Wage earners in the minerals sector hoped for a larger share of the industry's wealth. Poor farmworkers hoped they would no longer have to live as sharecroppers. Despite his promise from the dock at the Rivonia Trial in 1964, the new president Mandela made it clear that there would be no quick nationalization of the natural resources or agrarian sectors. Nonetheless, many people thought a radical redistribution was coming. Ellen Mabile, the first mayor of Merafong (after it was incorporated in 2001 to include Carletonville, Khutsong, Fochville, Kokosi, and Wedela), promised land redistribution—and was removed from office shortly thereafter, ostensibly on grounds of fiscal incompetence, to be replaced by Des van Rooyen (whom we met in chapter 12). But business owners who had been forced to sell their establishments or who had had to work with white merchants serving as fronts for the bureaucratic purposes of maintaining Apartheid's appearance of separation, clamored at the chance to restore themselves as the rightful owners and managers of their operations. Not unrelated to this, given that many merchants who had been displaced during the era of the Group Areas Act, were of Indian descent (many of the Gujarati diaspora), there was hope for the restoration of places of Islamic worship and education where they had been abolished.

During the ordeal of West Driefontein (which we considered in chapter 7), various congregations devoted their services to prayers for the miners. Among these were the Muslim community members who worshipped at the Mosque at Bank, an area at the perimeter of Khutsong that was prone to sinkholes.[4] Most of these Muslims were identified as "Indians," under the racial classificatory system of the time. A year later, when dewatering caused massive subsidence and instability in the area of Bank, its Indian residents, many of whom were patrons of the mosque, were simply told they would have to be relocated. Paltry recompense was given to the owners of land in the vicinity—not enough to even purchase stands elsewhere—and, moreover, the areas to which people designated as Indian could move had been radically restricted. Nearby Lenasia, the largest suburb allocated to people so designated, and another Indians-only area near Randfontein, were said to be without any available space. The Indian community of Carletonville attempted to bring legal action to defer the dewatering and complained that the Far West Rand Dolomitic Water Association, which we may recall had been formed following the disasters of 1964, had been in earnest negotiations with white farmers whose inconveniences seemed to many of their neighbors far less severe.[5] In the end, however, the Indians of Carletonville lost their mosque when the area was demolished. They also lost most of their residential area and their rights to the businesses that they had nourished over generations. Nor was the mosque restored or replaced with another comparable edifice elsewhere—at least not until well into the new millennium.[6]

As late as 1989, white residents had erected "Whites Only" signs in the park at the city's center in front of the old city hall, precipitating a rigorously enforced boycott of businesses by Khutsong's residents. Indian shop owners were exempted, although they too suffered the consequences of vacating the main shopping areas by boycotting residents from Khutsong (who accounted for the largest percentage of shoppers, if not the most monied). Not all white residents supported the exclusionary gesture, which was nonetheless addressed to them in a coded invitation to solidarity against the coming transformation (none of the signs were written in any African languages). But even the international press took note of the intransigence in this small town.

Throughout this era, the mecca of discount fabric shops, Edura, Pvt., had been located in Carletonville, on Emerald Street, just behind the old city hall. It attracted shoppers from throughout the region seeking everything from cheap linens to rare exquisite prints from India and East Africa. During the latter years of Apartheid and afterward, it achieved special renown as the place to which the elite women of the ANC (both officials and the wives of officials) went or sent buyers for the beautiful prints and textures with which they adorned themselves on special occasions. The aisles beneath its vaulted ceilings were, and still are, a kaleidoscope of print and pattern, with every color of the world—from its sparkling gems to its oceanic hues. Founded in 1961, its owners had to operate the business from an Indian-designated township closer to Johannesburg, but as democracy dawned, they were able to return to the visible world as owners of that institution. Having assumed significant political and economic clout despite their official marginalization, they agitated and organized funding for the establishment of a major new (Sunni) mosque and masjid (Masjid Al Islam) at the very center of town, where it now stands opposite the school library and where once was located the seat of municipal governance. Partly supported by the Institute for Islamic Services, the mosque's arrival into the midst of the otherwise conservative Christian communities of Carletonville and Khutsong, was hotly contested, although the later establishment of a smaller and more conservative mosque in Khutsong seemed to go relatively unopposed.

The refiguration of the old town center—now absent its "Whites Only" signs—as a scene of both minority religious and secular learning might seem like an extraordinary realization of the dreams thwarted in 1976. It was a belated and improbable but symbolically potent testimony to the revolutionary promise of liberty for all who had been oppressed by a Christianity bent toward white supremacy and then turned against it by the radical black Christian traditions stretching (at least) from Charlotte Maxeke to Desmond Tutu.

In 2008, on the other end of the municipality from where the boys we met in chapter 11 had been toyi-toyi-ing on the eve of National Youth Day, near the main artery leading from Carletonville to Johannesburg, older black school children in the high school named for the town's founder strolled in claques of three or four along the sidewalks, their burgundy blazers and dark slacks or short skirts, their neat backpacks and confident gait announcing their membership in the middle-class world of the New South Africa. Perhaps, I thought, they are the elder versions or the brothers and sisters of the young students I had visited years earlier, when I had been taken to an elementary school to "see the progress," as the teacher hosting me had described it. That was in 1998. Then, cheerful young black faces had greeted me as their proud teacher commanded them to say hello to the visiting professor, and they had shouted their salutation in perfect unison. The teacher had beamed. They had beamed. As I left, the faint but acrid smell of Jay's fluid swirled in the well-mopped hall, which was lit by the cool light of winter passing through the barred windows. The exercise of questioning and answering, reciting the lesson that was written on the clean blackboard and in the pages of the textbooks, recommenced as we exited. This was old-school schooling, newly opened to be sure, but in some profound ways unchanged. Still, as the teacher said, it was progress.

Impressive though the integration of schools was and is, it had been the librarian at the public library in the center of town who had especially moved me with her efforts to make reading a practice of learning for the poorest children of Khutsong. Long before the democratic elections and in the face of significant skepticism from her peers, she had commenced a lending program simply by bundling books into bags and circulating them among learners who wanted them, asking each to pass the books on to fellow students when they could, but with an expectation of regular transfer. She would drive across that desolate terrain between town and township, where most white women of her generation would never dare to tread, pulling volumes in their plastic sacks from her car upon arrival. There were no fees, nor penalties, and it was, she said, the responsibility of each for the other that had ensured that the books did not go missing. Library "lending" was in this sense premised on a form of economy in which everyone would learn not only to read but also to share responsibility for others' access to reading, and this responsibility would, if betrayed, incur a form of another kind of guilt if not yet a debt. When a small public library was established in the township by the municipal government, however, it required borrowers to register. Their parents were also required to register, and to affix their signature or leave their fingerprint if they could not write, as guarantee. There was also a small fee for membership. Responsibility and the possibility of its betrayal, as well as guilt for that betrayal, was thus transformed into a possible debt, the library's schema having been marked, or better phrased, haunted by the homology and indeed the identity of the two—recall that *skuld* is both debt and guilt in Afrikaans, as is *Schuld* in German.

I was surprised by how numerous were the fingerprints in the library's registry—mute testimony to Apartheid's educational inequality, and to the faith in fingerprinting that had taken root during the period of colonial segregationism's consolidation as a regime of bureaucratic policing (discussed in chapter 13). They were kept in a filing box that resembled a card catalog. I never counted them, but it never ceased to amaze me that people who could not sign their names, and who must certainly have had very little disposable income, would nonetheless pay the fee for their children to have access to books. This act was also testimony to the belief in education that Apartheid had both disseminated and selectively withheld. And here, as everywhere in the gold-made world (which includes elite universities in the Global North), the commodity form worked its awe-inducing magic. The fee, the price of education—the sign of education as that which can have a price—was the congealed form of expression of faith in its transformative power, and of its transformation into a powerful Thing. In a word, a fetish. Not for nothing do so many educational institutions and tutorial services use the phrase, "education is gold."

The library was beloved by many but also resented by some, and a few parents stayed away or kept their children away because of the confrontation it staged between the schooling of the children and the exposure of what was felt by learners and authorities alike to be parental ignorance. When I visited, the young black librarian of the township library was attentive to this risk, but she could not entirely contain it and believed that the fees and signatures promoted "respect" for the library's holdings—for things that are free, she said, are not treated with the same care as when they cost something. Hers was a verily Simmelian concept of value as a function of what one is prepared to sacrifice.[7] The white librarian who oversaw Carletonville's main branch continued to believe that it was her responsibility and perhaps even her calling to encourage reading—for its own sake, she said—and to ensure that people came to the library for reasons other than searching the internet, downloading data, and mistaking its possession for knowledge (although that was a relatively nascent possibility at the time). Her tools in that project were limited. And so, with the ready-made of contemporary celebrity culture, she put a cutout of Oprah Winfrey at the library entrance and ordered Oprah's Book Club bestsellers in the hopes of persuading black patrons that reading was not simply a white person's pastime. Fortuitously, Oprah's Book Club had been founded in the year when the country's new constitution had been ratified, when the Truth and Reconciliation Commission (TRC) had commenced its work, and when the National Union of Mineworkers (NUM), then a mere fourteen years old, had settled a major new wage agreement with the Chamber of Mines. No doubt, the librarian knew that Oprah's Book Club risked transforming reading into an apparent passageway to wealth and celebrity, but this did not mean that it could not be used. One never knows. And hope was in the air.

During the redemarcation protests, the windows of the library in Khutsong were broken and it was set ablaze, its collection devastated. Saddened by the thought of that modest but hard-won place of reading in flames, I asked people about what had led to the destruction of this particular target. Although many thought the attack had been sheer vandalism—which is to say, politically unmotivated destruction—others suggested that the books in its collections did not speak to the experiences of Khutsong residents, even if that had not been the motive rationale for the attacks. Some saw it as a symbol of whiteness or colonial education and of elitism more generally: of epistemic violence. Some with workerist sympathies accused it of valorizing mental over manual labor, and thus reproducing the antinomy that had afflicted both dominant and oppositional movements in earlier eras. For the latter, it was a lure as dangerous as any shadow in Plato's cave—and for related reasons, namely for promising an adequate representation while in fact projecting mere silhouettes of the masters. From this perspective, the conflagrations were refusals of this history and this experience of exclusion, expressed in and enabled by the racialized division between the mental and the manual. These commentators included several high-placed politicians and activists. They did not appear to deem the library or literature to be sites of an emancipatory experience, or to think that reading could enable liberation through encounters with others, with alterity. The imagination of the place of the other was not their aim, for they felt themselves to have been cast in the role of the Other throughout South African history. Rather, they wanted reflections of themselves. Perhaps it could not be otherwise, although the tragedy of this inevitability, as Frantz Fanon showed us so long ago, is the fact that not only was the longed-for authenticity, priority, and exteriority of a precolonial society inaccessible but also the very dream of a coherent "native society" was itself an artifact of colonization.[8] It is the impasse between the sense of having been captured by colonial "systems of reference" and the desire for that which it enabled in and as capitalism that afflicted the young arsonists and, in some sense, fueled these fires.[9]

As it happens, by the time it was razed in 2007, the Khutsong library had acquired a fine collection of African literature and videos. According to Saebo Gaeganelwe, its shelves hosted Wally Serote, Es'kia Mphahlele, Ngũgĩ wa Thiong'o, Wole Soyinka, Tsitsi Dangarembga, Ali Mazrui, and others. Its videos included *The Rise and Fall of Idi Amin*, *The Children of Soweto*, and *What Happened to Mbuyisa?* Gaeganelwe recalls that the library "inspired [him] so much that [he] even started reading Afrikaans novels" and that his daughter was moved by her experience of watching its video documentaries to ask to be taken to the Apartheid Museum and the Hector Pietersen memorial.[10] But such knowledge of the library and such a worldly imagination of its possible openings depends on having used it and thus on having the skills and desires to use it. For many, its status as bearer of colonial and Apartheid knowledge systems is related not to its content but to its institutional facticity. The young man who led the arson, David Thikeso, told the press, "I destroyed the library because the government had to be corrected for a big mistake it made." He did not regret it.[11] It was merely a medium in a war of messages demanded by a failure to attempt communication.

It is hard not to think that those windows (of the library, and of the schools destroyed in the uprisings of 1986, described in the previous chapter) has been repeatedly broken and then boarded over. Gwendolyn Brook's remarkable poem, "Boy Breaking Glass," written in 1968 in the midst of a youth insurrection that would ultimately be echoed in Soweto, captures some of the outrage and enigma of a scene that also unfolded in Carletonville and Khutsong. The poem commences with a description of the child "whose broken window is a cry of art." Deprived of every opportunity to make a world, he responds, defiantly: "I shall create! If not a note, a hole./If not an overture, a desecration."[12] Thus is the aesthetic and an aesthetic education both sacralized and counterposed to what would travesty it. Often, surveying the scene amid the boycotts of the mid-2000s, I felt something of the sentiment in Brooks's poem, and like many who resided in the area, I worried that the cost of what had become a form of general strike was being borne mainly by those who had the least. As schools and medical clinics burned, as shops closed and the houses of town councilors were burned or abandoned, as the township library's little collection became ash, and as learners stayed home while older young men roamed the streets or gambled in the pall, even the police conceded their right to guard the perimeter of the area and to determine the order of local things. Amid it all, it was hard to resist the rhetorical tradition that would code such protracted demonstrations as the antithesis of education. As riots.

Some months after the library was burned down, while discussing this epistemological chasm, Steve Mokwena, then part of the Trace team that was working to renew museology for the purpose of democratic education, asked me to consider why, in so many of South Africa's political protests, it is the library that is specifically burned (unlike other targets, such as liquor stores and shops, which are often the objects of looting). To understand South Africa, he suggested, this fact had to be grasped and understood. I agree. Doing so means understanding how and in what ways—and quite independently of its collections—the library came to represent the contradictions internal to the gold-made economy that, on one hand, promised a universe of perfect equivalences and representations of true value, and on the other, depended on the constant creation, extraction, and secreting of surpluses. It also means understanding how education institutionalized in schools and libraries was implicated in the racialized division between mental and manual labor that structured the gold industry.

We have seen how the struggle over education and the division between mental and manual labor infused and inflected the political scene in 1976 and 1986, differentiated as it was between the township and the mines. Against that backdrop, an understanding of how and why libraries became the object of incendiarist rage also means understanding how, in the vacillation between struggles in the two realms that we can represent through the tokens, "education" and "extraction-production," another order of desire emerged, only to be captured or recaptured by the fetishism that the financialized economy disseminated across the entire social field. The form of that recapture in the two domains can be summarized as follows: In the first, the aspiration for universal access to education and the belief in its transformative capacities gives way to a faith in the matriculation certificate and certification in general as a means of accessing opportunities for movement within the economic hierarchy. Education becomes like gold. In the process, a possible movement toward both equality and individual self-surpassing (becoming more and other than what one was as a subject and social actor) becomes its opposite (education becomes a confirmation of who one is, by birth, understood in the idiom of identity, whether racial, ethnonational or sexual). In the second, the critique of monopolistic and monopsonistic (financialized) capital gives way to an aspiration for wealth. Redistribution and economic justice become black capital formation. In each case, the social surplus threatens to become mere excess, to be channeled, appropriated, hoarded, secreted, or displayed. In the tragedy of these commons, it is sometimes difficult to discern the intuition of a capacity to generate something more liberatory. This is not surprising given that so many townships and informal settlements, and certainly Khutsong and its environs, were, for much of South African history, pedagogical scenes in which individuals were supposed to learn how to be useful for capitalism. They learned by observing and learning from capitalist practice, as well as by miming its forms *without* having access to capital. As previously argued, the spatial and legislated economic destitution of the township made it a scene of capitalism without capital. We should not be surprised then that what people learn in such a place is a desire for capitalism. And of course this is the desire *of* capitalism. That is how people become useful for it. If true and emancipatory education (as opposed to training into the habits of economism and the entrepreneurialism of the self) can succeed here, its promise lies in redirecting this desire toward something more.

The tokens, "education" and "extraction-production," in the previous summary suggest the existence of discreet domains or sectors, but there was a complex communication between education and extraction-production. Or rather, both were marked by a perceived lack of communication. It is a familiar story by now. But we must still grasp how the fetishism I have just described appeared in the redemarcation protests, and why these protests constitute such a significant event in the history of both the gold-mining region and South Africa more generally.

Frontier Wars

In 2005, the ANC-dominated national government oversaw the implementation of a program to integrate "cross-border municipalities" in line with constitutional provisions aimed at fiscal rationalization and the standardization of service delivery. This process emerged from a deeper history of governmental restructuring which, in the period 1994–2000, had been primarily aimed at extending resources to black townships and former "Bantustans" without reducing the standards in white communities. Beginning in 2000, and faced with insufficient resources to accomplish this task, municipal demarcations were redrawn to mitigate white dominance in some areas, to integrate rural and urban populations in others, and overall, to generate commensurable territories, and thus comparable voting blocs. To this end, the national government engaged in a series of apparently contradictory gestures, both devolving the costs of service delivery to local governments and exercising more and more surveillance over them. In many areas, this led to resentment of the national government on the part of local authorities, and percolating outrage among residents. Given the burgeoning costs of addressing needs and expectations at the local level, including those of long historical duration and more recent needs associated with the HIV/AIDS pandemic (see chapter 15), as well as the limited tax bases in most townships and poorer communities, the results were often disastrous. As Gillian Hart has persuasively argued, the demarcation process inaugurated a new crisis for the country and for the ruling ANC in particular, and opened onto a new era of populist insurrection.[13] It would unfold with special virulence in Khutsong.

Twelve municipalities in six provinces were affected by the more ambitious provincial demarcation program instituted in 2005, in response to which the Congress of South African Trade Unions (COSATU) offered early warnings about the risks of popular revolt if consultations with local residents in the affected areas were not undertaken, which in general they were not.[14] It is unlikely, however, that even COSATU could foresee the response that would be generated in Khutsong, where news of the decision was greeted with rioting, electoral boycotts, school closures, the eviction of ANC councilors, and a three-year-long state of siege in which virtually all elements of government operations came to a halt. The opposition to redemarcation was not all violent, to be sure. Petitions were made to the national government, and a case was taken to the Supreme Court—although it was rejected. But as the first and most persistent instance of sustained black opposition to the ANC, in which tactics of "ungovernability" developed against the Apartheid regime in the 1970s were renewed, Khutsong was and still is often figured in the national press as the locus of a terrifying populist opposition to the rule of law, and as a sign of future times in which the nation "falls apart," or, as many locals say, "goes down." It is easy to understand why.

As already stated, during the periodic uprisings that occurred in Khutsong after 2005, the homes of nearly all ANC councilors were razed, the local library and other municipal offices were burned to the ground, schools were vandalized and teachers assaulted, and the threat of necklacing hanged in the pall of smoke above the fires stoked by angry youth. Shops owned by people not supportive of the movement were looted. Despite the appearance of chaos, the crowds had their coherence, however. The street theater of opposition had its script—however improvised its delivery. And a coalition of local activists, including Communist Party members, ANC Youth League members, school teachers, and others, sustained a remarkable and remarkably long-lived alliance (which is not yet to say unity). The most vocal of the activists, Jomo Mogale, was himself a teacher, and former learner from Khutsong, who had memories of 1976 as well as 1986 and an oratorical zeal that made him the focal point of the movement.

There is much to be said about this oppositional formation. To begin with, it acquired its status as a mass less in the street than at the intersection, where the infrastructure of power met the tangled network of perpetual but also perpetually obstructed movement. For, as we have seen, the layout of Khutsong at the time was such that it could only be entered and exited by one of two roads, both of which were the location of police stations. But surely among the most interesting elements of this formation was the slogan under which opposition rallied, namely: "We won't go" or "We won't be moved." I heard this slogan daily over the years of insurrection—in seven different languages, in myriad contexts, and in the discourses of teachers and students, church workers and sangomas, unemployed miners, and highway prostitutes. This proclamation of a refusal to move, to travel, to be expelled from one's place seemed, initially, odd to me, even if the slogan had a long history. For redemarcation, at least as specified in the legislation, entails no redistribution of land or title, no eviction from any territory, no movement in any literal sense. The residents of Khutsong and Carletonville were to remain physically in place. But their remaining was of a different order than that of the other towns in the municipality of Merafong, namely Fochville and Kokosi, which, at the time of the new legislation's enactment, were already part of Northwest Province rather than Gauteng.

The feared movement was that which distances people from the centers of power, from the resources that accrue there, and from the personal networks through which they are distributed and accessed. Yet, the intensity of opposition indicates both the profundity of attachment to the idea of Gauteng and the need for a deeper interrogation of what redemarcation signified in this world. The government spokesperson who initially responded to the Khutsong revolt against redemarcation, Joel Netshitenzhe, told reporters in Pretoria that "we are talking about boundaries and not borders."[15] In doing so, he expressed a concern that provincial status and national identity were merging in people's minds, and he gave voice to a fear that nationalism(s) *within* the nation, rather than *of* the nation, is almost invariably the sign of the latter's demise. Yet, the opposition that oriented people's conversations in Khutsong had no nationalist inflections; rather it expressed what I can only describe as a township cosmopolitan disdain for the perceived rurality of Northwest Province. The irony of this contempt for rurality (as opposed to agrarian and village life) in a township where the very idea had been fabricated cannot be lost on us. Khutsong is a plurilingual, pluricultural world. This plurality is not of the order envisaged by Apartheid; it does not manifest the simultaneity of ongoing and separately developed "cultural" traditions, although these can be discerned in everything from the circumcision rites of the Xhosa still practiced after hospital-based surgery, to the shebeens whose female proprietors claim to be heirs to one or another tradition of beer-making. Nonetheless, the township cosmopolitanism to which I refer reflects something else: a constant and thorough-going transgression of the boundaries presumptively operating in and between ethnolinguistic groups. Although the Reverend (see chapter 8) had narrated a childhood of brutal interethnic conflict, most of the black people I interviewed over the years (including, as we saw, the mayor) have not claimed a genealogy in which all members of their parents' and grandparents' generation were from the same ethnic or language group (though Afrikaners often make this claim). And this fact played a role in Khutsong's resistance to the anti-black xenophobic rioting that afflicted so many townships in South Africa in 2008.[16] It is from this perspective, then, that rurality is reviled, as it was indeed reviled by the opponents to redemarcation in Khutsong. For them, Northwest Province signified the antithesis of the township life with which they identified. This rurality was not conceived only as the site and essence of life in an agrarian economy, or even village life. As we have seen, the mining industry's ruralization of its migrant population (in the interest of nourishing patriarchal tribalism and obedience to cultural leaders) was at odds with the more diverse economic life and social consciousness of Khutsong's first residents. Over the decades, a fierce opposition to the Apartheid state's efforts to identity urbanity with whiteness, as well as the program of residential stabilization advocated by the NUM, intensified the suspicion of rurality, which was also associated in many people's eyes with Bantustan politics and a general acquiescence to the idea of separate development.

Equally important, redemarcation implied the new placement of Khutsong (and Carletonville) in the geopolitical territory of Northwest Province, whose provincial capital was relatively far from the national capital city. Rurality was thus not so much a zone or territory in the economic order as it was a matter of distance from power. Thus, when explaining their opposition to redemarcation, people repeatedly compared the distance to Johannesburg or Pretoria with that to Mafikeng, the capital of Northwest. "I can get to Johannesburg in forty-five minutes, by car, an hour and a half by taxi," explained one after another young man, "but it's three or four hours to Mafeking. How can I access the government of Northwest Province if I have to travel all that distance?" Two things can be said about this statement. The first, perhaps obvious one, is that it operates in terms of a spatiotemporal calculus that requires actual travel, the body's movement in space: invariably, a journey in a packed minibus. It is marked in hours of sunlight and darkness, and it is traced in the muscular memory and mental fatigue of the traveler. Although cellphones were a ubiquitous part of life in Khutsong by 2005, electronic communication through computers and internet access was not. Relatively few people had bank accounts. Even the paying of utilities bills entailed a trip to Carletonville (and hence was more expensive for the poor residents of the township than the wealthier residents of the town).

The other remarkable aspect of the statements just quoted, is that they are recited, almost verbatim, by different people. Let me go so far as to say that these clichés and slogans resemble possessing spirits. Like ideology, that discourse without a subject, that language without a body, they speak through people in a citationality that knows few bounds and that is never entirely localized. And what they reproduce is a spatiotemporal consciousness oriented by a rural–urban opposition cast in the idiom of bureaucratic efficiency, which, in South Africa, is the idiom of "service delivery." But this is partly because service delivery means more than that; it is an idiom that condenses the aspiration for redistributive justice and the extension of what had been privileged access to state functions by whites under Apartheid to the general population.[17] Accordingly, arguments over service delivery are always also arguments about historical justice, although these arguments are also always vulnerable to being mired in media-infrastructural determinism.

There was some truth in the claims made by activists in Khutsong, that the infrastructure of service delivery in Northwest Province was less developed than in Gauteng. Thus, for example, there was a real and substantial diminution in the funding for AIDS education programs in Merafong after the redemarcation. This is at least partly a function of the fact that international and local nongovernmental organizations (NGOs) have historically been clustered in Johannesburg/Pretoria (Gauteng), Durban (KwaZulu-Natal), and Cape Town (Western Cape Province). Under Mbeki's regime, when HIV/AIDS management was substantially transferred to NGOs on account of his refusal to accede to the viral model of AIDS causality, they became not only necessary but also relatively well-developed alternative infrastructures. Northwest Province had relatively undeveloped infrastructures of this sort. Moreover, the patronage networks through which grant applications were submitted and prioritized, and resources distributed in health and education, were largely contained in and by the fiscal structures of the province—and were often passed through university and research-institution affiliations, which were themselves clustered in the major regional cities. Knowledge of one practical network, which includes personal intimacies, cannot necessarily be transferred to another. Still, the rhetorical repudiation of Northwest Province, which often entailed its denigration as a "Tswana homeland," exceed these questions of resource management and lead one to ask, once again, what is implied in and by the rhetoric of movement and by the framing of redemarcation as a forced relocation. The rhetoric of the homeland is a sign, of course. In speaking of Northwest Province this way, Khutsong residents invoked the entire history of forced relocation, and thus of personal and social dislocation that was the effect of the Group Areas Act of 1950, the Bantu Authorities Act of 1951, and the Promotion of Black Self-Government Act of 1958, among other legislation. The sign "homeland" activates a whole set of readings, summoning forth the past as an object of disavowal but also as a source of power. It is an act of conjuring. But it does not take much to summon the specters.

In the middle of the first decade of the new millennium, there were several major eruptions of discontent over national governmental decisions to redemarcate provincial boundaries and to eliminate cross-border municipalities. These included, most infamously, Bushbuck Ridge, Matatiele, and Merafong.

In all these cases, the zones in contention were previously frontier areas between South Africa's white regions and the Bantustans.[18] They were thus the places at which differential distributions of wealth and forms of life were most intensely visible, in which racial distinction and spatial separation redoubled each other.

In Khutsong, the organization of opposition to the proposed "move" was almost instantaneous and led to the formation of a civic organization called the Merafong Demarcation Forum (MDF), with Jomo Mogale as its spokesperson and chief agitator. Mogale in particular articulated the position that because Merafong's gold mines had contributed so much to the national economy, it was worthy of remaining at the center of power, but above all, this legacy legitimated the community's demands to participate in the decision making and to exercise and not merely to be proximate to power. The MDF had initially persuaded the mayor to make the case for nonintegration with the Northwest, and Des van Rooyen had indeed carried that message to the party leadership. But when this was refused by provincial and regional structures, he assumed the burdened role of enacting the reintegration, and this fact had made him the object of unrelenting opprobrium by the forum's members. Many assumed that both van Rooyen and the Gauteng provincial delegates to the National Council of Provinces (NCOP) who had voted against the municipality's declared majority position (i.e., that Carletonville and Khutsong remain in Gauteng) had betrayed the local population in exchange for promised promotions and kickbacks from Northwest Province. That provincial administration, in turn, was assumed to want the tax revenues from the larger populations of Carletonville and Khutsong, which accounted for about 71 percent of Merafong's 215,860 souls (although rate-paying was higher in Fochville and Kokosi—the communities already under Northwest Provincial jurisdiction—than in the other towns and townships of the municipality).[19]

Although much of the support for the MDF's resistance to the new redemarcation mandate came from the South African Communist Party, Khutsong, as the largest entity in Merafong (it accounted for 32 percent of the official population and its informal settlements were a significant additional demographic) had been a significant base for the ANC. At rallies that were held at the Soccer Stadium, for example, the slogans chanted ("The People Shall Govern") and the colors worn were those of the ANC.[20] The leverage exercised by threatening to boycott elections was significantly undervalued in the initial stages of the protest, coming as they did so soon after the first democratic elections—when the very fact of the franchise had been coveted and exercised by the great majority. But when less than 5 percent of Khutsong's residents turned out to vote in the municipal elections in October 2006, this power was no longer to be ignored. Six months before national elections were held in 2009, the provincial boundary decision was revoked, Carletonville and Khutsong were restored to

Gauteng. Residents spoke of being glad to be "back home" and agreed to throw their support behind the ANC once again.[21]

In the interim, however, schools had been closed for months on end. Medical services had become nearly impossible to access. One of the few means of accessing the township and of obtaining even basic medical services was with the vans and accompaniment of the area's inventive and indefatigable HIV/AIDS education NGO, Mothumsimpilo, led by Yodwa Mzaidume. It was she who drove me through the township on those days of smoke and fire, and who introduced me to its many players, often recalling as we drove the bitter 1980s, as the youth once again threw stones, burned tires, and threatened war. The logo on the van provided protection, partly because it was not a government-associated vehicle but mainly because of the enormous faith Yodwa had garnered after years of devoted care. I will discuss that program in chapter 15.

Beyond Borders

Most of the journalistic accounts and scholarly analyses of the anti-redemarcation protests remain captured by the discourse of the protestors, who treat it as a struggle over the form of politics—its participatory nature, the baroque hierarchies of provincial and national party executive committees, and the assignation of the region's place within the conceptual and cartographic imagination of the state.[22] Certainly these were its primary elements. A former Member of the Executive Committee (MEC) of the provincial government and long-time ANC activist explained to me that the decision to redemarcate the provincial boundaries had been partly motivated by the sense that there had accrued to Gauteng too much electoral power, the swelling demographics of Khutsong being one source of that bloc. But it was also part of a rationalization process the aim of which was actually to mitigate the service delivery and management burden that was falling on Pretoria as a result of this growth. The irony of this is, of course, that it was to keep the relatively capacious services of Gauteng that the people of Khutsong refused Northwest Province. My interlocutor, who spoke on condition of anonymity at the time, feared that the failure to communicate this rationale to residents had risked the ANC's base, and she predicted that many local political careers would be destroyed. And indeed, it was toward the subject of communication—its failures and its blockages, omissions, and dissimulations—that much of the discourse of anti-redemarcation oriented itself.

In my experience, there were three profoundly significant aspects of the dispute over borders, namely: communication, education, and economic justice. Overwhelmingly, the latter two were shaped by a concern with the question of access—to administrative centers, to power, and to wealth. It is not merely ironic that the activists conceived of themselves as "stakeholders," borrowing the language of colonial prospecting and land enclosures as the idiom for asserting their rights. They made their claims from within that economy, or rather they made them as the excluded interior of that economy. In this respect, of course, they are no different than the millions organized by international civil society as rights-bearers. But note the degree to which the desire for access to every power reproduced the promise that gold had held out to the earliest gold-minded investors of the industry's early days. Those dreamers wanted gold as a medium more than as a commodity. And it was the absence of mediation that the protestors in Khutsong so bewailed.

Whether a precipitating or exacerbating factor, failed communication was frequently adduced in people's commentary on the developing conflicts. Sometimes, people condemned poor or slow communication, and sometimes secrecy, and equally often they denounced the lack of opportunity to dispute the decisions made on high, lamenting the absence of fora for doing so. It was indeed for this reason that local activists led by Mogale established the MDF (with the D sometimes referring to Democratic, sometimes to Demarcation): to institutionalize an otherwise absent or inoperative public sphere. In local parlance, the term for the desired relation was "consultation." So, they complained, "we were not consulted" or "there was no consultation." As one survey respondent in a study conducted by M. E. Chapitso said, "The information was kept in the briefcase, meaning that the people were not informed about the decision that was taken by the government."[23]

Only a mistranslating literalism can condemn such a remark to conspiracy thinking. For this figuring of the secreting of information in the image of bureaucratic officialdom conveys not only the pathos of a community that feels oppressed by state machinery but also the displacement of communication into a documentary mode. It is thus an exemplary statement, more revealing in its metaphoricity than any simple description of lethargic information dissemination could ever be. According to many denizens of Khutsong, and not only protestors, neither had residents been invited to speak for themselves and express their own desires, nor had they been spoken to in a manner that recognized their capacity to do so. Everything had come as edict, as legislative fiat. Yet, exiled from the dreamed ideality in which spoken language is the medium of the will's externalization and materialization, they talked. They talked at great length. Many of the interviews that I conducted at this time lasted for hours. On one occasion, when my associate, Songezile Madikida and I arrived at a small township church to videotape a community discussion about the redemarcation, our car was blocked in by several other vehicles, and we were politely told that we would have to record until everyone had spoken. This was a democratic process, they said. No one would be silenced. We were in this sense to be captive to a need for expression. When we explained that we had limited battery life (there being no electricity at the site) our hosts conceded that we could then leave when our batteries were dead. How many hours? We were both anxious, Khustong's reputation for brutal "popular justice," not to mention less political violence, having created an aura of tense mutual suspicion to which we were not immune.

The day grew late. And people spoke, one by one by one—passionately, angrily, sadly. Voices rose and broke in a multitude of languages: isiXhosa, isiZulu, Sepedi, SeSotho, and English. "That night all the members of the community raised their voices and wept aloud."[24] People spoke in desperation, and they spoke in grief:

"What we have seen in the past years was a very abnormal situation."
"The community members were forcefully moved into a province that they did
    not want to fall in."
"We have seen young people getting arrested as part of trying to silence them."
"Teachers have been dismissed because of voicing out their grievances."
"They did not talk to us, . . . They should at least came to talk to the people
    concerned."
"They made us to sign papers that they did not explain to us."
"Our children do not have sports here—what is available here?—they live in the
    mud day and night."
"Children are no longer interested in education. Life in Khutsong is miserable
    because of the province [the provincial redemarcation.]
"I was . . . called by the so-called district director of the education department
    of North West telling me not to participate in this or he will fire me from the
    education system.
"Our township is bad, it stinks."
"I would like to ask that the roads of Khutsong be fixed because our cars are in
    danger because they need to be fixed."
"Hospitals . . . are not maintained, but at least in Gauteng at least I knew that if
    I need pills I go to the clinic and get them. Our grandmothers were getting
    pills every month and now the clinics under North West are not giving them
    because they do not have them."
"In the North West, the hospital has no water, and the people from the North
    West come and say that when they are done in the hospital, the child cannot be
    washed because there is no water, there is no food. Even here, our clinics are
    in the North West, and people die while going to the clinic down here. The [X]
    hospital is a mortuary because people die there and there is no food, we have to
    bring food and clothing to our people in the hospital."
"I saw the police involved in the protests here, I asked one captain how the police
    are involved in the politics of the place, he laughed at me."
"The government says 'Batho Pele' [People First] but it seems they are first and
    batho are last. They instruct, they tell."[25]

"I am very angry with the mayor of this place because we grew up together,
toyi-toyied together, and at the end of the day, he abandoned his own
constituency. His own people that brought him to power, he treats us like shit."

"Everything that we need we must fight for it."

"Our president is always on flights going to places while everything is going
expensive in his country. I think the money they spend on flights and petrol
can help us on the ground where the government can look at staple food like
bread, but the bread is very expensive today and there are no jobs."

"I feel the people of South Africa in the cabinet are enjoying themselves while we
remain peasants on the ground. I am saying this because our president who
goes to many countries and looks like he is doing well for his people in his
country. . . . But coming to us we are crying and he does not listen to us."

"With the current government I feel like I am an Israelite among Egyptians.
They are talking about better life for all but it is only for the people in
parliament alone."

"I am pained to open the wounds inside of me about this."

Language welled up in them. Sometimes, they spoke nostalgically, of a
period before, a period called "normal." Often, they spoke words that came
from the past: slogans, formulae, and the rituals of political piety. Again and
again, they made reference to "the democratic right of voicing (out) their grievances," the right being that of "people on the ground," and the right to be "consulted." In other conversations with Khutsong's residents these same phrases
recurred, along with those of a more overtly party-political sort.

This speaking in the idiom of another time, which is now thought of in
generational terms, was sometimes its own form of accessing that presence
of which Fredric Jameson spoke, and that magic of which Benedict Anderson wrote (see chapter 11). And it sought the kind of power in speaking that
was perhaps once the attribute of the *imbongi* but now supposed to have been
made available to all in and through schooling. But such a historical narrative
and the substitution it describes also implies a radical alteration in the idea of
collective representation. For, historically, the *imbongi* is one in whom a collective voice speaks with the authority of tradition—often to and against power.
Historically, the collective nature of this marked speech as a transmission of
inherited powers, in some ways immunized the *imbongi* against wrath and
retribution from chiefly authority. This kind of collective representative is very
different from the collective representation that is imagined to be possible by
virtue of every person acquiring a voice, as liberal political theory would imagine, and even in the dream of class-based self-representation, as certain Marxist
theory proposes. The demands of 1976 were for access to schooling that would
enable an empowered speaking and thus the capacity for self-representation
(rather than mere technical instruction as preparation for servitude). And the
movement's leaders were often virtuosic and erudite orators—or, in the case

of the gangsters, they were people whose words were to be obeyed. This is no doubt one of the reasons why the redemarcation protest also implicated schools at every level. Opposition meetings were held in schools, classes and examinations were boycotted, schools were vandalized, teachers threatened, the mayor's office intervened to bus students to other districts for exams (with considerable resistance), and learners experienced the conflict as an interruption of their studies. Let us then try to understand why these issues were deemed so salient to so many people and why the school was so central to the protests about territorial jurisdiction, although they were frequently passed by in much formal discourse.[26] We should do so while bearing in mind the earnest pleas of some township residents when, after two years of protracted insurrection and suspended life, they expressed not only their sense of exhaustion, their anger at having been made afraid, and their grief over lost property and educational opportunity, but also their desire for a return to the prior conditions of life:

> Everyone expects the government to come to us and correct the mistakes that they have done and hopefully life will go back to normal you know. There will be proper schooling, those who have been dismissed from work because of them participating in the protests in defending their democratic right of voicing out their grievances will be reinstated and life back to normal, seeing more development especially targeting the serious problem of unemployment, illiteracy amongst young people and also hierarchy of unemployment and also crime. Those are major challenges that the residents of Khutsong are facing; issues of crime, illiteracy, high HIV rate among young people as a result of lack of recreational activities, your libraries and the stuff.

This testimony from an especially articulate woman at the community forum can stand as representative of this current in the more nostalgic discourse of protestors—some two and a half years after their commencement. But her nostalgia was also, and at the same time, a kind of utopian vision of the future, and normal was not simply the name of a bygone period, it was also the name of a still-to-come improved life.

"Normalization" had meant the stabilization of the black workforce and the securing of patriarchal family life in urban contexts for the NUM when it had been formed in this area. But "normal" had seemed, when I heard it, a strange word to use in a place that had, before the protests, been so deprived of amenities, so far from the dreams purveyed in those marketing pamphlets of the Carletonville real estate brokers and updated in the shopping malls described by Achille Mbembe and Sarah Nuttall. Yet, it circulated widely in Khutsong as the conflict dragged on. Often, it signified a simple lack of overt conflict. In negative terms, it named a state of no boycotts and no closures, a state without blockades and checkpoints, of no fire and no ash. In positive terms, it signified a space and state of flows and movement. This aspiration for the flows and movements to and from power, possible only in that homogeneous now-time of the new nation (a now-time that is nonetheless still to come) sat in awkward proximity to the punctual repetitions and interruptions of the past that official culture staged and that protests constantly performed.[27]

School for Scandal

A persistent element of protests since 1976 has been that universal access to good education has been a goal, and, at the same time, schools have been targeted for destruction on the grounds that they have housed the mediocre or duplicitous failure to deliver this desired good. This doubled fact, and the grief that has accompanied it for students who want to learn, cannot easily be explained away as the mere expression of frustration, the targeting of the failed object, or the resentful destruction of institutions that constitute a source of negative judgment for the academically disinclined and those who, having studied, nonetheless face desolate labor markets for their certified skills. In Khutsong, as in other places in South Africa, the boycotts and strikes directed against the redemarcation led to the closure of schools and suspension of matriculation exams. It was not lost on some that the advocate of the protests was himself a teacher. Teachers were no longer viewed as representatives of the state or embodiments of authority. They were the ironic beneficiaries of that repudiation of mastery that had indicted the principal of Badirile Secondary School two decades previously and those in Soweto the decade before that. But they were also aspirants to the status of leader in the moral economy of insurrectionary celebrity.

When, during the second year of protests, after two lost matriculation exam seasons, the disgraced mayor determined to bus students to a rural educational "boot camp" in the Northwest, so that learners might receive compensatory tutoring and preparation to write their exams, he was drawing on his own experience. But the circumstances were profoundly different, and they entailed sending students into the very conditions that the protestors were attempting to resist. In the end, 435 students were bused to Taung, where they were boarded in a camp set up by Northwest Province department of education, with the support of their parents—who bore some of the considerable costs. Initially, these young argonauts were referred to as "child soldiers" in the struggle for education.[28] But circumstances deteriorated quickly. Protestors against redemarcation torched the homes of parents of the transported students, stoned others, and ostracized all who had transgressed the boycotts.[29] Moreover, the camp location, a deserted teacher's training college, was near a community whose own children had relatively poor educational experience. And conflict between the two seemed almost predestined.

The Khutsong Democratic Forum opposed the busing, in any case, and accused the mayor of fomenting divisions and undermining Khutsong's own schools. Mogale, having been fired from his teaching job for advocating the boycotts, was especially bitter about the fact that more than thirty teachers—"Khutsong's finest"—had been taken to Taung, while the schools in the township were shuttered. At the camp, far from home and the semblance of urbanity that it provided, Khutsong students explored the freedom that distance from parental authority enabled. Their drinking and the alleged sexual liaisons between some of the young women and local men (for which the visiting female students were held culpable) led to outrage. Tensions percolated until the assault of a local resident by one of the Khutsong learners incited rage among the inhabitants, who retaliated en masse, apparently charging the camp with pangas and stones. In the aftermath, one of the learners was accused of inciting riots and was expelled.[30] It was perhaps predictable: the condescension of the township youth toward their more rustic counterparts and the flouting of traditional mores on sexual and public decorum, as well as the fact that the residents of Taung, like those of Khutsong, had not been consulted in the matter, fed resentment and suspicion of the politicians who seemed, to them, to live in thrall to the trope of rescue. And then, there was the fact that education, which had come to appear like a limited good, was being offered to people from outside the province, people who, it seemed, disapproved of the very province providing their newfound opportunities.

And even so, and in the end, most of the matriculants from Khutsong passed, and moreover, passed with exceedingly good grades. I had met one of the young camp-bound students before the journey, and she had been desperate to attend classes. Awkward, precocious, with a love of mathematics, and yearning to escape the little world in which she had been raised, she was not interested in the struggles over provincial jurisdiction. Born and raised in Kokosi, a township that had long been under the Northwest Province jurisdiction, but dependent on the high schools in Khutsong, her own township bereft of similar institutions, education was for her a way out. A means to entering another world, the world of otherness. Of more. She was nonetheless concerned about how her matriculation results would "read" to others if certified by the Northwest Province government rather than Gauteng.

At issue, not only for her but also for many of the most strident opponents of the redemarcation (and she was not one) was the fact that the matriculation certifications of learners in Carletonville and Khutsong would, if redemarcation went ahead, be issued under the imprimatur of Northwest Province rather than Gauteng. Their education would thus be stamped with a now-naturalized value of rurality, with distance from authority and power, and with naïveté and a lack of all the values and virtues that had been associated with Gauteng. They described this stamp, the provincial seal at the top of their certificates, in visceral terms, as a kind of mark of the damned or at least the excluded. How could a matriculation certification from the Northwest Province, said many, open the way to a job in Johannesburg or Pretoria? Who would respect such a certificate? It could only signify belatedness and backwardness.

In essence, education, as a signifier and in a form that was increasingly commoditized, partook of the logic of a fetish that had been disseminated throughout this world in and through the gold economy. By fetish, I mean here to designate the concept-metaphor that aims to explain the overvaluation of objects or ideas, such that something that substitutes for a primary force of value comes to seem like an improved or enhanced replacement: a fetish is a locus of value and investment, a beguiling supplement that captures the imagination and interrupts other social processes by allowing power to be concentrated, captured, and, in some cases, used over others.[31] Gold is, as Marx once said, one such fetish, insofar as it seems to permit access to all other commodities. The phallus is another such fetish, insofar as it promises not only to organize but also to explain the order of gendered inequality. It is in the nature of the fetish to appear as the power of powers, the value of values, the ground of an otherwise groundless system. In the case of education, the fetish took the form of the certificate standing for an education that may or may not have been received.

With as much pathos as poignance, the perception of lost symbolic value in the education sphere reveals the degree to which education had become, as the colonial authorities, the missionaries, and the apologists for European Enlightenment values had hoped for more than a century, the privileged site and signifier of social value. There is a caveat to this statement, however. The ideal of education as a transformation machine and more, a site and process not only for knowledge acquisition but also for character formation and thus the basis for full membership and capacity to participate in the polis, orients what, in another time and context, was termed *aesthetic education*. And of course this was not offered to black or colored pulis under Apartheid, but only to white learners. Soweto's students wanted that kind of education for themselves. During the redemarcation struggles, the significance of education was constantly avowed. But in a history that commences with protests against the pass system and culminates in the embrace of documented life (as discussed in chapter 4), the conception of education that had come to dominate the municipality of Merafong was one in which the certificate had displaced the cultivation of the imagination as the goal of schooling. One might say, therefore, that the education project of the settler colonial state had succeeded, and moreover, that it had succeeded in excess. This excessive success, however, was also and at the same time its subversion and its dissipation, if not its ruin.

Education had come to appear as that which would grant the one who could claim and demonstrate it, access to new worlds: worlds of stable jobs, good income, public recognition, and more. But this presumption was increasingly focused in and on the realm of the signifier, namely the certificate. Given the demand for the performance of value and identity that had been cultivated under Apartheid, and reinflected with the collapse of the gold regime, the need to "show" one's education not only to those in power but also to those without it acquired more and more propulsive force. What Siegfried Kracauer observed about the process of certification among the newly salaried workers of Weimar Germany can be seen in South Africa in the democratic era.[32] The school document has, in many places, and certainly for many among the "formerly disadvantaged," acquired the characteristics of a magical device that, in itself, is thought to be capable of transforming the world, or at least the subject's relationship to and control over it. It promises to be almost as good as gold. Yet, another fifteen years after the conclusion of the experiment in Taung, with unemployment rates nearing 50 percent in the township, and educated youth among the most disappointed, Gustave Flaubert's lesson seems most apposite: one must be careful of one's fetishes, for the gold often rubs off on one's fingers.

Learning the Past of the Future

After the revocation of the legislation and the restoration of Carletonville and Khustong to the jurisdiction of Gauteng, there was much celebration. Even people who lost homes to arson could say it had been worth it, although Jomo Mogale was ill and exhausted. Other activists in other communities took the lessons seriously and threatened to turn their own locations into "another Khutsong," if their demands were not met. The costs had indeed been high, but amid it all, as South Africa was gripped by spasms of xenophobic violence, Khutsong, a township that had seen significant anti-Mozambiquan sentiment and interethnic strife in recent history, was calm. Mogale explained, and could claim some credit for the fact that, during the crisis, the oppositional community had reached out to the residents of the informal settlements, and, in exchange for their support of the anti-redemarcation struggle, offered them protection. It was a more or less contractual arrangement, born neither of humanist solidarity nor the generosity of *ubuntu*. Support meant immunity to violence. It was payment or repayment for a guilt that had been the corollary of included exclusion in the capitalist economy. And it worked. In some ways, the contract was the outcome of an improbably functional public sphere in which the negotiation of interests leads to compromise and to the appearance of agreement. In other ways, it was a spectacle of coercion whose outcome—the mitigation of acute violence—came at a price that illegalized immigrants could not afford to not pay. Those who had been raised in this economy had been trained, or educated, into its protocols. They had learned its lessons well. But other youths struggled to find other lessons in the experience or to offer them.

I recall, with special clarity, a slender young man who used to hang about while I was doing oral histories in Khutsong. One day, he asked, soberly, "Is it true that societies must pass through capitalism in order to get to socialism? Is that what Marx says?" The other boys with him were impressed, if also perhaps peeved by his academicism and his anxious desire to please the visiting scholar. The young man insisted that there must be a way to hasten "the revolution." He was not about to be robbed again. He wanted his piece of the pie, and his impatience was a function of that noted impasse between the sense of capture and the desire to escape in the jouissance of consumption.

Such conversations were not uncommon with the teenage boys I met in Khutsong at that time. I was often struck by the rigorous formulae, and the formulaic rigor of their discourse. The party (or the party concept) speaks in them, I thought. They were themselves media organs of the structures, possessed or at least haunted by the promise of access to a universe far from their experience. At times that discourse seemed entirely amenable to being recoded in more neoliberal terms. A young man interviewed by Molema Moiloa after the redemarcation protests explained his passionate attachment to the protests' cause by stating that "the working class . . . deserve a very reasonable living wage. People must not be exploited." The syllogism of the conditional is here an expression of political desire. If there is justice, then work will be reasonably compensated. But reason is cunning, and the conditional slides into the imperative and is carried forward in a humanist cloak on the wings of the young man's confidence. He continued, "People must earn according to his or her ability and contribution to the wealth, that's what communism says, you see." Wrapped in the banner of communism, Marx's principle, as elaborated in the *Critique of the Gotha Programme*, is here inverted. Rather than each person receiving according to his or need and contributing according to his or her ability, as Marx writes— describing a situation that is possible only in a radically transformed society, namely one in which the idling and parasitism of the capitalist class has been put behind, *with capitalism*—this young man wanted people to receive according to the ability that they exercised. In essence, he was advocating that isomorphism between labor time, value, and wage that Marx, in the "Working Day" chapter of *Capital*,[33] had staged as the desire of the hypothetical worker whose voice rose above the factory floor to confront the capitalist in his own terms. But that was a characterological fiction in the melodrama of a compromised, liberal struggle for the limited working day (which Marx referred to as limited Magna Carta). It was not the discourse of revolution. The chasm between the two appears in the young man's assertion that proper compensation (and the goal of political action) should be measured by workers' access to those goods whose display will constitute a source of cultural capital. This is perhaps another dimension of that display value that Walter Benjamin had identified in the new museums and Arcades of the industrializing world (chapter 1), that

Beit's Ball had theatricalized, and that du Maurier's novel, *Trilby*, had narrated (chapter 4). The Chamber of Mines had given form to this constantly renewing and renewed value in the moment (1972–3) that it substituted the image of a woman wearing gold jewelry for the scene of counting bullion (chapter 10), and in this sense its advertising had provided a pedagogy that was, to repeat the formula I have used previously, successful in excess.

In any case, it is difficult not to notice that the young communist's discourse had reverted to, or been haunted (perhaps contaminated) by, the biblical parable that Marx was invoking and overturning, namely, the parable of the talents. Nor is this surprising, given the ubiquity of Christological discourse and its axioms in this space. But one task of learning to read might be to acquire the capacity to recognize and disentangle the threads that together bind a biblical and a Marxian tradition in a manner that permits one to read their identity-in-difference. Doing so one might make an intervention that prevents the latter from reverting to the former in a vision that reduces economic justice to getting just what you paid for or getting paid for just what you did. It is in Matthew (25:15), that a rich man leaves his slaves to tend his wealth, the talents being given "to each according to his ability." These talents (whether money, ability, or knowledge of God—and exegesis on this is extensive) were supposed to be nurtured, and failure to do so results in the condemnation of the one who has merely saved what he got. The one entrusted with the most, because of his gifts, reaps most in this parable. All are subject to the master's severe judgment, but there is no sense of shame (or guilt) in the accumulation that results therefrom. On this point, Molema Moiloa's interlocutor seems entirely in agreement: "Communism does not say you must not drive a Range Rover or you mustn't drive a BMW, the latest one, or Mercedes Benz, no. It says people must earn as per their ability and their contribution, you see." Communism, for him would take the form of a perfect commensuration between individual (not average socially necessary) labor and wage. It would mean that talent is rewarded. It would also be a question of affect: "Being a communist is being someone who is sympathetic to the poor people who are being exploited on a daily basis. . . . You must be able to afford basic things. I mean things that . . . [give] human dignity you see."[34] The young man's communism looked a lot like neoliberalism.

The young man's discourse was vivid. Nonetheless, this is deadly speech. Its rigidity has all the attributes of a corpse. It is, moreover, deadly in the sense that Theodor Adorno described: it represents the indignity of death, which, once the supreme experience of the individual on whom bourgeois society erected its system of value, now "shares the ruin of the socially defunct individual." For, even beyond the replaceability of the individual that Adorno thought to define the society of mass production, it expresses the disposability of individuals in the necropolitical order.[35] For, it is in the face of such disposability that the young man cited by Moiloa imagines the latest model BMW to promise the afterlife of renown and recognizability. It is important to emphasize that the mortifying abstractions and substitutions that, in Adorno's (and Marx's) analysis, were thought to be so dehumanizing are, in South Africa's poorest communities not only, and often not at all, the result of being subjected to the system of wages and the reduction of bodily life to quantities of labor time. Where most youth are unemployed and where the prospects for continuous employment are almost nonexistent for the majority, capitalism's undermining of the individual's social capacities takes place in the spaces beyond labor, and neither the factory not the plantation are adequate structural metaphors for thinking this predicament. In this context, neoliberal capitalism not only colonizes the space of boredom with the desire to be employed (which so many youths profess), but it makes individuality appear accessible through forms of personal style and patterns of consumption. And of course, it makes success appear to be a function of self-motivated self-actualization. Often, it speaks in the idiom of human capital.

The death that affects and infects the young man's speech cited here is therefore not the dying of any individual; it is death as pure abstraction. It would be all too easy to find failure, or to accuse this speech, with its combination of literalism and masculine bravado, its lack of lyricism, and its seeming automaticity, of a totalitarian tendency or a neoliberal misreading. But it may also be read as the expression of ideology, that is to say of the untrue truth of this distorted universe.

It is by no means easy to understand the text from which the misquoted passage of Marx comes, namely the letter on the Gotha Programme. In that critical epistle (we are still receiving letters), Marx made the nearly scandalous statement that all rights are, substantively, ones of inequality. He made this statement in answer to the Programme's principle, which adduced an "equal right of all members of society" to share in "the proceeds of labor." This attribution of right, argued Marx, consists in the "application of a single standard" to "unequal individuals." But the individual was, for him, singular and thus incommensurable. So, what is commensurate in the notion of individual right is an abstracted dimension of being.

Peter Fenves rightly notes that the right of which Marx speaks is an economic right that depends on the transformation of society; in the absence of that transformation, it is simply an assertion of equivalence. He explains that the equalizing function of "labor time" was the instrument for thinking an equivalence among different and thus unequal subjects and, indeed, for negating the singularity of those people who are not, after all, reducible to their labor function. He might well have been describing the Swazi system or Patterson's schema (described in chapter 11). A truly communist society would have no need for this redistribution and would not reduce everyone to their labor power. Nor would work be entirely alienating. It would liberate people from the mere function of satisfying needs but also from the need to generate someone else's profits, and this would enable both self-making and social generation. "Setting things right means not only doing away with rights in general [as artifacts of a legal formalism], not only doing away with the legal structure that legitimizes itself through its appeal to the 'equal rights of the individual,' but, in the end also doing away with labor-time as a standard, that is, with labor in the service of quantifiable time."[36] In the national chronotope of the "new South Africa," punctuated as it is by memorial rites that celebrate "The Struggle" for and acquisition of new rights, the state puts on display its own commitment to a belief that, as the youth in Khutsong said, the revolution must run through capitalism.

This is precisely the topic of Njabulo Ndebele's exemplary essay, written on the cusp of the democratic transition. In that essay, Ndebele observes that "the brazen oppression of the past can now become the seductive oppression of having to build and consolidate and enjoy what was achieved at our expense. There will be the attractive tendency to accept all this as the spoils of struggle. The situation is likely to split the black community into those who seek immediate relief and those who wish to press ahead." He continues, "we can choose between absorption and accommodation on the one hand, and, on the other hand, the quest for a self-created reality." But he adds that the price to pay for "choosing the illusion of freedom" is forgetting the past in order to "enjoy the present as much as we can."[37] Of course, the past can be invoked in many competing ways. Andrew Nash rightly warns that it can be summoned as alibi for the present when it is the object only of a recovery rather than an interrogation.[38] The oblivion of commodity consumption when it is understood as a right and recompense for both labor and participation in the struggle is one form in which that alibi structure works. This doesn't mean that all consumption is complicit with such logics; as Jacob Dlamini has shown, the pleasures of personal style and the enjoyment of luxury commodities were not absent in townships during the Apartheid era, and did not preclude political participation.[39] It is the understanding and fetishization of these as the markers of social transformation that constitutes their alluring danger.

As for Moiloa's young interlocutor, in the mouth of a more powerful figure, such speech becomes the alibi for self-enrichment. It is marked and marred by the distance in proximity to Marx's suggestion, in the letter on the Gotha Programme, that communism will permit and nurture individual difference because the boundary between mental and manual labor will have been dissolved. But, as Fenves says, every right is contingent; it arises in and expresses its own time, and "for this reason, it demands the most vigilant critique." Every new form of appearance of the commensurating instrument (i.e., money made worldly through gold) risks reverting to an earlier stage: the "certificates of labor-time" can at any time turn into something else: the representative of money, the recurrence of currency, a fiscal return. "These *Scheine* [appearances] can show up (and have in a sense already done so) as ghosts of money and, therefore as specters of the fetish, reminders and remainders of its conjuring power."[40]

Nonetheless, the capitalism operative in South Africa today does not operate its commensurations and deracinations mainly through the wage-system. Massive unemployment and exclusion from credit are the conditions for most of the youth like Moiloa's informant and my young interlocutor. Yet, the abstraction that Marx saw as a function of the wage system and its commensurating abstraction continues, partly as a function of the still powerful ideology of individual rights and equality before the law that operates nationally, and partly as a negative attribute of those who are equally exposed to precarity. The deeper transformation to which Marx (and Fenves) points remain a project for the future. If the township was a space in which people were encouraged to desire capitalism without being granted access to capital, the youth previously cited seem to think that history's progress should permit them this access to money and consumer commodities, which they also confuse with capital. In the absence of a transformation that would eliminate the abstracting and violating commensuration of each individual—whether that occurs via the wage system, the juridical system or as serial exposure to precarity in "wageless life," to use Michael Denning's term—the desire for *both* a redistributive justice *and* a representation of singularity, is diverted into the aesthetics of distinction. Into fashion and commodity consumption.[41] This too is a capture of what might have been developed for the purposes of critical judgment, including that kind of judgment that expressed itself in Brenda Fassie's beautifully brazen songs, discussed in chapter 13. The "latest model" Land Rover or Mercedes Benz is justified as the appropriate compensation for a worker's "contributions." That *Scheine* that shines, that bling and brand-name beguilement, whose excesses stand in for the more of value, the beyond of equality, that is what haunts the space where the specter of a more profound change might have been and might yet be. Of course, for the young man speaking thus, such a car is almost impossibly inaccessible—even though there are such cars owned by people in the townships and not only by those with four-bedroom brick houses and the latest appliances, with good jobs and pension plans. Such cars are also the sign of gangster power and the lure of indebting sharks. Jabu, as Moiloa names him, is also justifying the party leadership's (every party leadership's) conspicuous consumption. He is naming an excess. If he is reducing it to the letter of capitalism's vulgar law, there is in this desire for more also an intuition of what the whole economic structure rests upon and that it also represses. It is implicit in the very term for surplus value in Marx's writing, *Mehrwert* (*mehr* meaning more).[42] This is why the demand for the latest model of car as the proper recompense for labor is not merely a surrender to commodity logics and the system of objects that Baudrillard describes—in which combat takes place in the order of signifiers and commodities are ammunition for the battle.[43] It is not a mere misunderstanding of a real revolutionary program, so much as it is the disclosure, the true image, of the system that it would like to change, from which it has not yet departed, and whose constraints are materialized in the term "*post*-Apartheid," as Michael Cawood Green claimed (see chapter 7). Yet, this attitude, what Ndebele so elegantly describes as the enjoyment of what was achieved at his own expense, is also complicit with kleptocracy. It codes corruption and personal wealth as the just compensation for collective historical injury. The first tragedy of that coding is that it subordinates the project of transforming the world to the dream of an individual's right to pursue inequality and reads it as the mark of a political success. The second tragedy is that this is the end toward which education is so frequently imagined as medium in the neoliberal order. The ubiquitous slogan, "education is gold," distills that principle.

The ambivalent status of schools in the townships near the gold mines, where they were sometimes the site of political mobilization, sometimes the object of glass-breaking rage, sometimes the locus of rote instruction, and sometimes the place of learning from each other, tells us that there is nonetheless still some room for hope. And the discourse of the redemarcation protesters, while often bespeaking the brokenness of natal languages and the desperation of township residents, also shows that people, however "unlettered," knew well how to operate the powers of metaphor. In effect, they turned the state's powerful and indeed, nearly magical language (its capacity to make things happen through edict) back on itself, exposing the violence that is possible when metaphors are treated literally. This is also a form of critical reading. By using the idiom of "forced relocation," the residents mobilized history and momentarily refused the price of forgetfulness about which Ndebele and Nash warned their readers. For this reason, one can yet hope that an aesthetic education, which would above all cultivate the faculties and reading practices necessary for a critical interrogation of and resistance to the systematic extraction-production of inequality, might take place despite all else, in the margins, the interstices, and the undergrounds of townships and cities and villages. And, indeed, it does, as I shall consider in concluding this book. Such faculties, one notes, might or might not include a reading of the *Critique of the Gotha Program* (and probably not). But they would permit an understanding of the difference between surplus value and excess, and that other capacity for surplus through which what Ndebele calls "self-created reality" might be activated. It would also mean an interrogation of history and a questioning of the values of "the leader," as well as the related "obedience to authority" that the Chamber of Mines cultivated as the core of so-called "tribalism" and that the gangsters embrace with such enthusiasm. As Fanon wrote, "political education means opening up the mind, awakening the mind, and introducing it to the world. . . . To politicize the masses is not and cannot be to make a political speech. It means driving home to the masses that everything depends on them, that if we stagnate the fault is theirs, and that if we progress, they too are responsible, that there is no demiurge, no illustrious man taking responsibility for everything."[44]

CHAPTER 15

RUSH, PANIC, RUSH

A New Book of the Dead

Clouds wept
the sun wore a black gown
mourning beforehand
for my death
and I heard the footsteps
of my coffin
coming towards me.

—Mangaliso Buzani, "I Will Be Gone"

But I who am bound by my mirror
as well as my bed
see causes in colour
as well as sex
and sit here wondering
which me will survive
all these liberations.

—Audre Lorde, "Who Said It Was Simple?"

I f every revolutionary moment must labor to find that poetry of the future with which to think and make the world anew, few have had to do so in more difficult circumstances than South Africa. The "traditions of the dead generations" were redoubled by a series of contingencies that added their own nightmares to the burdensome tasks of transformation. In the decade following Mandela's 1996 anniversary speech, when much of the world looked to South Africa for a model of belated decolonization and interracial reconciliation, the gold-mining region was submerged in a doubly abyssal space. The price of gold dropped in 2000 to its lowest point since 1979, although it would begin a remarkable recovery and upward journey in just a few years. As debilitating as the depression in the gold industry, however, was the fact that the region had become the epicenter of the HIV/AIDS epidemic and was suffering some of the highest rates of seropositivity in the world. This double burden must be borne in mind every time one asks whether the trajectory followed by South Africa could have been different, and every time one attempts to assess the success or failure of the first black-majority governments to deliver the economic liberation and social justice that they had promised and that they had struggled for the right to attempt.

Critiques of South Africa's neoliberal turn, of its failure to undertake a more radical redistributive program after the end of Apartheid, and of the virtual exemption of the minerals industry from demands for reparation or compensation to historically disadvantaged subjects who had toiled in the mines or endured their toxic effects are numerous. There is much to commend these critiques. And investigations into the origins of the neoliberal turn, including the revelation of Nelson Mandela's private meetings with Harry Oppenheimer, then CEO of the Anglo American Corporation, during the early 1990s as well as the sponsorship by Consolidated Gold Fields of meetings to plan a transitional government with the ANC, suggest that the determination to protect white capital as a means of enabling black majority rule long predated Thabo Mbeki's government and his policies of Growth, Employment and Recovery (GEAR). This produced the ironic situation described by Gillian Hart as "denationalization," by which she means an insertion of South Africa into global financial networks and a mitigation of limits on both white capital's movement out of the country and foreign ownership of local industries and interests—all in the name of forging a new nation.[1] In the early years of the post-Apartheid era, large portions of the public purse being diverted into the purchase of armaments rather than social service delivery as well as those that permitted the extraordinary accumulation of wealth by a few members of the black elite including through the private acquisition of former state enterprises, have received appropriate condemnation. The preservation of white capital's relative accumulations and power as well as its flight in the years before and after the transition have also been subject to vigorous interrogation, and their role in perpetuating the inequities that Apartheid organized and cultivated are well documented. More recently, a sustained investigation of "state capture" has found evidence that numerous senior members of the ruling party and its allies sold influence, accepted bribes, and corrupted the processes of accountable government. Attacks on the judiciary and assassinations of opponents, whistle-blowers and members of investigative bodies have become painfully common and mark a continuity rather than a departure from the mode of governance that defined the Apartheid era. But these too have been subject to rigorous condemnation, partly because of the scrupulous investigative journalism, if not always satisfactory police investigation, that has been nurtured by South Africa's robust multilingual press, and partly because of the endurance of a relatively independent judiciary.

Yet, beyond or below questions of policy and political transformation is the fact, blunt and bruising, that in the moment when it might have thrown off the yoke of so much oppression, when it might have opened the avenues for access to new forms of life, the state and its subjects were afflicted by a world-historical burden of uncommon dimensions: an epidemic that would rob its presumptively most robust (often called most productive) generation of countless lives and that would invite fear and loathing at the heart of a sexual economy, which was otherwise being invested as the locus of social restoration. It would lead to accusation and desperation. It would be answered with brave and creative responses by many, and by neglect, ignorance, and willful denial by others, including many in power and especially Thabo Mbeki himself. But the infrastructure of health service delivery had been so distorted by segregation and Apartheid that the capacity to care for the most afflicted communities was radically insufficient for even "normal conditions," never mind those of the HIV/AIDS epidemic. The need to scale up the health system's capacities in response to the epidemic came at precisely the same time as the nation was attempting to extend what had been a limited welfare state outward from the white population it had been designed to serve. And as already discussed, redemarcation processes exacerbated the inability of local communities to respond to the emergent needs—even when people agreed to do so (an agreement that was by no means uniformly expressed and that was in any case difficult to achieve in the face of so much fear and stigma). The scarcity of resources for healthcare services was intensified by diminished revenues and taxes from the gold industry, which by that point was a shadow of its former self. The number of workers employed in the gold mines in 1999 (194,567) was less than 50 percent of what it had been only a decade previously (406,192).[2] Large-scale layoffs, subcontracting, and reduced deep-level activities in no-longer-payable mines defined the millennial turn. Partnerships between corporate health programs in both the retail and mining sectors and international nongovernmental organizations (NGOs) provided essential stopgap funding and expertise, delivered services, and provided care and education, but these were small plugs in an enormous wall, behind which was a catastrophe of oceanic proportions, one whose tides have continued to ebb and flow but not to be stilled. In 2019, 20 percent of the world's HIV-positive population still resided in South Africa.[3]

At times, and especially in the early stages of the epidemic, it seemed as though the old order of death (Apartheid), for which the right-wing Order of Death had provided the allegorical emblem, had found a new form of appearance. Yet, there was life everywhere. Intense, exuberant, self-affirming and desirous life. It called from the billboards in the imagery of new consumers and new faces in offices of authority, cultural production, and sports. It coursed through the lyrics of the multilingual rappers and kwaito artists, whose driving rhythms and confident bravado suggested power and energy, and indeed freedom.[4] It sparkled on newly proud bodies, in locally designed fashion, and it filled the projects of memorialization, which, far from being exclusively melancholic, seemed to constantly affirm the possibility of transformation. Museums in former prisons repudiated state violence and exalted the quiet bravery of women and political prisoners; ecstatic conferences trumpeted the success of constitutional reform and reflected the glow of a globally admired bill of rights. New urban developments in major cities exuded luxury and the integration of formerly separated worlds, making them feel as vibrant and exciting as any anywhere else in the world—despite, or perhaps because, at the same time, stories about rising tides of violence and an epidemic constituted the ground against with their figures of escape and triumph were drawn. Such exuberance was less palpable in the smaller towns to which tourists did not flock, where foreign currency did not flow, and where unemployment was the condition and destiny of so many youth. The chasm between the imagery that circulated in the dream-space of the mass-mediated public sphere of metropolitan South Africa, where pride and possibility glittered goldly, and the still-destitute townships and informal settlements, where sewerage took the form of drop-pit latrines, electricity was unstable, and water hard to obtain, made the former seem grander and the latter—places like Khutsong in Merafong—seem poorer.

Stop/Limit?

I do not know if I imagined that the epidemic would persist for decades, as it has, or that it would also vanish into the ether of the normal when, in 2000, a group of black youths about sixteen years old, most of them self-professed Christians, answered my question about how they saw the AIDS epidemic in Merafong. Then, when explaining the situation they believed they had to confront, they spoke of HIV infectivity rates exceeding 95 percent. They were confident about the numbers, and they did not evidence even the slightest doubt about the viral etiology of AIDS.[5] But treatments, including those that organizations like the Treatment Action Campaign (TAC) would struggle to access and distribute, did not yet figure in their imaginations. They prophesied death for all the infected.[6]

This was, at the time, probably the most epidemiologically well-surveyed community in southern Africa, given the twin facts that it was the destination of a majority of South Africa's migrant labor and that sexual activity associated with migrancy was considered to be the primary vector of most HIV transmission in the sub-Saharan region. At the time of the conversation, levels for HIV infection in this group's age-cohort ranged from 2 percent for boys and 13 percent for girls fifteen years old, and 35 percent for men and 68 percent for women twenty-five years old. The overall community average was estimated at about 28 percent, although there were competing assessments that put the rates as high as 41 percent.[7] The rate of HIV infection was, in short, astronomical, and it betokened a future of enormous suffering and grief—if not that absolutized space of total death spoken by the youths. Moreover, the traffic in such numbers was part of everyday discourse, which was inflected by dramatic inflation coupled with the apparent certitude of epidemiological rhetoric and a strange kind of ennui. Huge numbers (as such) shifted from one locus to another, so that a massive percentage in one area (e.g., South Africa's caseload as a percent of African cases) was transposed into another (e.g., mortality rates or total seropositivity rates). Only the number, it seemed, moved—not its referent. It was as though a monstrous creature was roving across the landscape of fear, inscribing itself on the pages of an almanac of loss. Epidemiologists reported that about 70 percent of all new HIV infections in 1999 were in sub-Saharan Africa.[8] And these numbers then circulated along the arteries of formal media and rumor and then leaked into adjacent analytical categories. They were disapproved by Thabo Mbeki's government and many anticolonial health experts, who accused the Western press and the international (imperial) medical establishment of stoking racist stereotypes. Of course, Mbeki's denialism only intensified the crisis, and deferred a more robust response. It also inhibited the use of antiretroviral medications and incited interest in and use of unverified alternative therapeutic regimes, which, masquerading as traditional medicine, were often useless at best and toxic at worst. It was interesting, in this context, that youth in Merafong were so unpersuaded by the denialism—their exposure to researchers having shaped their awareness but also having stoked their terrified imagination. They were, as they had fantasized themselves to be, children of the modern, of science. But even in the worst-case scenarios of the epidemiologists, the prevalence rates did not approach those invoked by the youths with whom I spoke.

Two questions arose in this context, each more urgent than the other: What was the source of the inflation, by which an already bad epidemiological profile came to be translated into the prophecy of an absolute catastrophe? And how did this inflationary translation affect the capacity of those who believed such statistics to orient themselves toward a future horizon? In short, what did it mean for those who, only recently, had been recognized as the bearers of political subjectivity—however compromised it had become during the TRC, when, as we saw, political subjectivity and personal responsibility were construed as distinct and indeed antithetical categories?

One of the mechanisms by which this predicament was surmounted, or at least accommodated, was by subjecting inflation to calculation, and thus by converting a panic into the possibility of value and, even, a rush. Such a pattern was not uncommon in the history of the gold industry. But the process of actuarialization is always afflicted by contradictions, and in this case, it subjected the youth and others in the communities visited by HIV in South Africa (and elsewhere, no doubt) to a brutal double bind. In many ways it promised to stabilize everyday life (the specter of stabilization returns) and to offer individuals a means to appropriate agency as well as to experience the vitalizing effect of hope. At the same time, it entailed an often violent, if also value-producing, differentiation between those whose futures fell under the pall of HIV and those who, fortunately, would escape its effects. In what follows, I consider this dialectic between panic and rush (rush and panic) as it took hold in the changing landscape of epidemic South Africa. Before proceeding further, however, I want to return to the youths who expressed this seemingly inexpressible anticipation of mortality.

Surprisingly, I think, the faces of these young men and women, newly liberated for a future that was far less certain than the teleologies of either anticolonial nationalism or socialist transnationalism could have predicted, did not belie either fear or grief. But I would not invoke the word *resignation* to describe their demeanor either. Although some of the townsfolk were, at the time, proffering fantastical visions of apocalyptic ends, with rapturous escapes for the believers, these youths did not. Perhaps, we can say, they had adapted themselves, in the sense given that word by Max Horkheimer and Theodor W. Adorno, to what they believed was their predicament.[9]

At the time, and despite the NUM's successful efforts to obtain for mineworkers alternatives to the single-sex residential system, 25 percent of the mineworking population continued to reside in mine hostels or on mine-owned compounds.[10] Migrant labor, although diminished in scope and significance, continued to dominate the local economy. The municipality had only been newly renamed Merafong (Sesotho for "place of mines") in 2000. Some sections of Khutsong, those originally erected to house professionals and government workers, had by this time reasonable roads, electricity, and plumbing. The recent construction of state-financed Reconstruction and Development Program (RDP) houses had added two and three room brick houses for some of those who previously resided in shacks on the larger properties or in squatter settlements on nearby farm land.[11] Today, a huge overpass and multilaned highway system links the towns and can be watched on livestream at every hour of the day and night (electricity permitting). But then, much of the township remained unpaved; sewerage still ran in open ditches in some areas. And although many houses were electrified, this was by no means universally the case. As of 2023, this had remained true. The informal settlements that had accreted to the periphery of the township were a knot of tin and cardboard shacks laced together with wire and cobbled into masses rather than neighborhoods. In those locations, there was limited electricity, no running water, and no sewerage facilities beyond pit latrines. Less than twenty thousand people lived in the historically white town. The population in the black township and the informal settlement was officially one hundred and seventy thousand but probably exceeded two hundred thousand. In the most recent census, it had the highest number of wards with the highest rates of poverty in Gauteng.

The youth with whom I met in a local high school on that blue-skied day did not speak in a manner that seemed exceptional. Similarly catastrophic profiles were often proffered to me in conversations, and if, upon my questioning of these fantastic estimates, individuals replaced their more extreme assessments with slightly more sober ones, it was clear that, on some level of habitual consciousness, such extremities were indeed assumed. They constituted the intuition of what would soon begin to emerge as the object of overt and overtly interested discourse: let us call it the intuition of an actuarial unconscious. But they also constituted the basis for demanding that the terms of the language game be changed.[12] They required that a different set of demands be brought to the fore—those oriented not toward the transformation of personal behavior and cultural practice, but toward the amelioration of economic conditions in which unemployment is as pressing as is epidemic.[13] The simultaneous assumption and disavowal of a future catastrophe was expressed when young men resisted questions about AIDS with justly acidic rebukes. One could condense them as follows: Without a job and, hence, without food or shelter, everyone is going to die anyway, so perhaps the foreign researchers should focus on jobs instead of AIDS.

There are other idioms for articulating this sentiment: "You are saving us for dying. We want to make a living." These haunting words from a haunted young man were spoken at an experimental bakery in Khutsong, where the goal had been (it was then defunct) to provide "daily bread" to those who lacked means to obtain it any other way. Let us not turn away from the invitation to read beyond the obvious question of need. We are asked here to think the difference between a living and a life. This seemingly simple play of words effects a potent and powerfully critical juxtaposition, undertaken from within the linguistic repertoire of a multiply inflected English. It is an appropriation and a deployment of a linguistic contradiction within an emergent (and still far from generalized) actuarial discourse, which calculates risk and assigns monetary value to a life by estimating the likely time of its expiry.

In Fredric Jameson's typological analytics, such gestures emerge only if one reads at the level of the "mode of production."[14] And it is well to note that the kind of criticism offered by youths like those in Merafong (who so often speak in Marxist idioms) were grounded in an implicit demand for the recognition of their interests, but these interests were somewhat spectral. They were not the interests of labor so much as they expressed an aspiration to enter the space of labor as the condition of possibility for full subjectivity. In this sense, the alienated discourse of youth may have been among the last and most intransigent repositories of class consciousness in a world (the neoliberal world) for which the idiom of class conflict has lost much of its persuasiveness.[15] To be sure, there is a pathos to this discourse—which recognizes that being exploited by capital seems, at this point in history, better than not being exploited by capital. The consciousness of these youths is thus not class consciousness in the classical sense, and derives from wagelessness as much as waged life.

Still, I was taken aback by the seeming lack of panic in the words and voices of these youths. Nor was my experience idiosyncratic. A similar lack of panic can be discerned in much of the testimony gathered and analyzed by Catherine Campbell in her account of AIDS in the same community.[16] Campbell's evidence, like mine, revealed the simultaneous projection of catastrophe, and something like a developing accommodation to it. How can we understand this affective economy, and its relationship to the phenomenon of epidemic, without simply falling back on clichés that would attribute a lack of attachment to life among those who live in morbid environments and who have been relegated to the disposable? For, if it is true that people who inhabit worlds ravaged by dangers of natural and humanmade sorts often develop discourses that appear to naturalize these dangers, then it is also true that the form of their accommodation varies markedly—sometimes tending to fatalism, sometimes to the metaphysics of retribution, and sometimes to economism (the latter expressing itself in the rhetoric of opportunities amid the ruins).[17] How did the histories and social forms of the gold economy inflect this response?

Most narratives of the AIDS epidemic in South Africa at that time (e.g., as opposed to those in Uganda) emphasized the contradiction between a relatively successful civil society organized against both international pharmaceutical capital and local (national) governmental reticence to address the epidemic in terms that were consistent with international epidemiological and treatment protocols, and the relative paucity of success in tempering the rates of infection.[18] Many people remarked that, at least following the capitulation of Thabo Mbeki's African National Congress (ANC) government to the viral model of HIV and the demand for a programmatic distribution of antiretrovirals, especially to pregnant women, South Africa seemed to have been afflicted by a paradox. It had one of the most loquacious and trenchant public debates about AIDS, and one of the most persistent problems in the world. In this context, it was frequently remarked that "behaviors have not changed."[19]

The behaviorist model, which largely underwrites public health discourse, and certainly that emanating from the United States, tends to attribute the failure to change practice to either poor information transmission on the part of public health institutions and people or to the incapacity of those receiving such information to assimilate it and implement it in the form of changed behavior. Anthropological or generically culturalist apologetics for putatively African masculinities, African sexualities, and various other cultural factors are then offered by way of explanation. Sometimes these are supplemented by a recognition of the burden that poverty places on women in severely patriarchal contexts.[20] These are occasionally and sometimes contradictorally allied with religious discourses that emphasize both moral failure and personal respon-sibility and that advocate abstinence, thereby making the sexual practices of the infected the explanatory factor of epidemic.[21] Nor is this inadvertent alli-ance completely undermined when political economists retort by remarking, quite correctly, that in contexts of disproportionate male migrant labor and single-sex residential structures, the demand for abstinence and monogamous fidelity is unlikely to be viable as a strategy for mitigating the spread of the virus. But even these apparently condemning discourses can be appropriated for contrary purposes, as we shall see.

Whatever the merits or limitations of these individual approaches, none of them manages to escape the structure of representation within which sexu-ality is imagined as a matter of identity that orients people's pursuit of sexual satisfaction, a pursuit that expresses both the desire and the will of the indi-vidual agent. The same structure of representation conceives of epidemic as the consequence of a sociality in which the management of this agential sexual activity has been either inadequate or undermined. I would like to approach these issues from a different perspective and ask not what is the link between personal behavior and epidemic disease, but rather how we might think about the more complex linkage between the gold economy and sexuality in ways that illuminate AIDS as something more than a disease or vulnerability to other dis-eases (although it is, of course, also and even primarily this) and more than an illness as metaphor.[22] In this way, I hope to extend the analysis of the sex-gender system of the gold-made world, which has thus far entailed a critical reading of the spatial logic of the compound and *skomplaas*, as well as the instrumental-ization of women within the program of "stabilization" and the deployment of women as means in the conflict among gangs in the space between the town-ship and the unionizing mines after Soweto. If we want to understand AIDS as it was experienced at the turn of the millennium, we need to understand the apparent simultaneity of two discourses—one of panic and the other of accommodation through investment. By extension, an analysis of the representational economy of AIDS requires that we reconceive the relationship between "panic" and "rush." And this in turn helps us to understand what was happening across the entire social field, determined as it now is by an economy in which surplus value generation no longer depends exclusively on labor.

The rush is the effect of a speculative economy, and it has a lengthy history in mining communities (and in metropolitan centers from which investment in natural resources is drawn) and especially those oriented around highly industrialized deep-level mining where the joint stock form of finance capital has been so historically central. This speculative economy, however, developed a new medium in South Africa in the years following Apartheid's demise, namely insurance. And insurance, as a form of finance capital, sought out new territories of accumulation on the threshold of the newly emergent, if still modestly proportioned, black middle classes. The adaptation to premature death—as a natural rather than a political phenomenon—which was being solicited from so many (South) Africans, although not the conscious aim of capitalists, was nonetheless required by capital at that juncture. What we might call speculation on and investment in death occurred—in complex and highly mediated ways—through new forms and domains of risk management. This management took place, as it continues to do, in the insurance sector, where it enacted the value-producing dimension of risk while seemingly offering techniques with which to contain it. And this was achieved through a complex set of temporalizations, which distributed risk without eliminating it, and which cultivated a new oppositional structure between the HIV-positive and -negative people in the stead of older racial structures even as it recalled and, in some ways, reinstalled the latter.

We could offer a tentative, and inevitably reduced, schematization to describe the historical trajectory of this relationship between rush and panic in South African history. The first rush was that of the diamond economy, quickly followed by that of gold (with the minor phenomenon of the Ostrich feather boom of 1875–1895 in between). But more than any other, the gold rush was accompanied by panic and threatened to dissolve into panic from its inception—a tendency that only intensified with the increased capitalization of the industry. Nor has this rhythmic vacillation been put behind; it is, as it was in Charles van Onselen's account of its ealier era, a structural dimension of this special form of extractive capitalism.[23] Initial assay results may turn out to be unmatched by the content of actual deposits, or the cost of labor may increase and render mines unpayable. In periods when the gold standard was not operative, and especially after 1971, the prices of gold could fall and, once again, make mines unpayable even when there was gold to be mined. The history of the mines' stuttering progress toward closure reflects this multifactoral vulnerability and volatility. And then, there is the likelihood of accident and illness. The panics that these eventualities incite can be converted into value if they can be made the basis of a calculus that estimates risk and differentiates exposure to it, without eliminating danger altogether. Indeed, such a transformation of danger into value occurs in and through the category of risk.

It would not be entirely wrong to say that it is the work of the insurance industry to transform panic into a rush for capital, but it would be incomplete as a description. Nor would it be entirely wrong to say that in the early era of AIDS and in other epidemic conditions, the insurance industry reduced some people, those who can no longer sell their labor, or for whom there are no opportunities for such sale, to producing value by dying. This does not mean that they sell their death, or that death has become a kind of labor, even in an economy that traffics in services and in futures, and that makes speculation a source of value through such instruments as hedges and derivatives. This economy is not entirely reducible to disposability, although it is not unrelated to that concept either. Let me then explain what I mean.

Lessons from Elsewhere?

By now, of course, there have been hundreds, if not thousands, of studies of the structure of AIDS in the United States, where the first wave of something that was recognized as an epidemic arose and where the plethora of strategies for discursive management, population control, and treatment options arose. Much has been said about the differences between the epidemic in its American and European forms, and those in Asia (especially Southeast Asia) and Africa (specifically sub-Saharan Africa). These differences tend to be reduced to vectors of transmission—namely, heterosexual versus homosexual, sexual versus intravenous drug-related—and the different forms of medical treatment with which the epidemic is addressed, depending on financial and infrastructural resources in various locations. In general, wealth (including class structure and its racialization) and sexuality are the axes along which the epidemic has historically been differentiated.

These analyses reveal the degree to which sexuality and the economy are linked, and this linkage is both recognized and mobilized in the discourses about AIDS. For Linda Singer, one of the most incisive if underquoted thinkers on the matter, AIDS is a discourse with particular effectivities, one in which the old adage and the ideology it embodies, namely that "sex costs," was made a new source of profitability for capital.[24] She writes that "the anxiety that becomes mobilized around the connection of sex to death in AIDS entails an increased fetishization of life as such. Hence, the anxiety produced through the epidemic is displaced and condensed in the regulation of sexual reproduction and the promotion of the family as the supposedly exclusive site of safe sex."[25] This logic found fertile ground in the shadow of stabilization that the gold industry had been promoting at precisely the same time.

At the time that I was meeting with young people in Carletonville, there hung above the entrance to the town and the floral median in which the town's name was spelled in seasonal blossoms, a billboard on which a huge cross was wreathed with an AIDS ribbon. The sign called to the passerby in the name of Jesus and advocated abstinence and godliness as protection against infection. It cited "Biblical Principles" to prevent AIDS, namely Corinthians 7.2: "to avoid fornication, let every man have his own wife, and let every woman have her own husband." Thus, the stabilization program of the Chamber of Mines and the National Union of Mineworkers (NUM) had found its anticipatory echo in the old testamentary text, with family values seemingly enshrined as both a divinely sanctioned right of return (to patriarchy) and a public health panacea.

The apparent similarity in response to HIV/AIDs in the United States and South Africa (especially with regard to the Christian moralizing of its origin and effect), however, expresses the traveling nature of the moral discourse about AIDS more than it expresses the forms and social conditions within which the linkage of sexuality and economy have occurred in either place. Although both economies operate in terms of a single principle, namely that the goal of "multiplying and extending profit centers" occurs when "reproduction is organized . . . with the least investment of social resources,"[26] the ideal means for accomplishing that end have differed profoundly from continent to continent, and within the history of South Africa. We have already seen how the coerced movement of migrants and the single-sex hostel system distorted sociosexual relations. The securing of the perimeters of ideal patriarchal spaces, through the creation of *skomplaases* and then gang-controlled margins of informal settlements, all worked by attributing to black women an instrumental function. Both the formal migrant system and its informal peripheries converged in an understanding of Apartheid as a structure of black emasculation whose overcoming required the restitution of that same masculinity, without at the same time calling into question the norms of gendered hierarchy that continued and continue to render women as means. The long-term effects of family dislocation and the interruption of generational transmission have not been entirely reversed, but neither has this overturning been completely displaced as goals. It is in this context that we can recall Charlotte Maxeke and the women of the pass protests for whom the valorization of chastity could, in the terms of an avowed Christianity, provide women with the means to claim autonomy with divine sanction.

This does not mean that the sign hanging above the road in Carletonville was not also complicit with a biblical tradition that underscored male prerogative and rendered women in the idiom of property, or that it could not be used by conservatives to oppose women's autonomy. Its double signification, however, was both meaningful and usable for a more radical purpose, as Yodwa Mzaidume, the indefatigable leader of the local HIV/AIDS project, *Mothusimpilo*, would teach me. This radicality depended on reading—perhaps even that kind of reading that the older communists discussed in chapter 11 recalled as the condition of possibility of their political activism. It was easy to assume that the biblical citation was a simple instance of Christian moralism and a repudiation of the sexual desire that so much queer AIDS activism was otherwise attempting to liberate from fear and stigma. Certainly, I had initially read the sign this way. But I had had to learn from Yodwa Mzaidume to think otherwise.

In her history of sexual economies in the United States, Singer notes that, to the extent that the strategy of minimizing the cost of reproduction succeeded in the United States, "reproduction generate[d] profits in the form of commodity consumption." The result was a shift in the "signification of the reproductive unit (the biological family) from a site of production to that of consumption."[27] She was not arguing that consumption displaced production as a source of value production, as many have claimed in their analysis of postmodern financial forms; she was speaking of signification. Nonetheless, the shift she describes is not uniformly available for those who have been officially designated as "historically disadvantaged South Africans." For them, unemployment (then estimated at 40 percent), familial dislocation, and poverty inhibit the possibility of becoming consumers on the scale available in the United States, with enormous consequences for epidemic management. This does not mean that there was or is no desire for such consumption or, indeed, that a great deal of disposable income, however minimal, does not go into consumer goods. It does, and we have seen how much such consumption figured in the dreams of liberation among event stridently Marxist youth. But the transformation of black subjects into market consumers has been contradicted by a powerful counternarrative that runs alongside the explanation of commodity consumption as just reward for political labor. This other narrative reads commodity desire among the impoverished as excessive, an aspiration beyond means that is blamed for both economic crime and frivolous expenditure. This contradiction was already present in the early twentieth-century discourse of the Chamber of Mines, which lamented the failure of black male workers to develop the acquisitiveness that would make them eager wage seekers, even as it undermined their rights to accumulate capital and condemned their expenditures on entertainments.

In North American and, although perhaps to a lesser extent, European contexts, the transformation of the family into a unit of consumption and hence profitability for capital depended on both the cultivation of desire and the containment of its excesses. This containment occurred not by repressing excessive desire, but by distributing it across a wide range of objects and projecting it into the future (through the promise of deferred pleasure). This, says Singer, was accomplished through two strategies: "condensation and displacement, which correspond to genital primacy and commodity fetishism."[28] Under epidemic conditions, the demand for a displacement of desire from the bodily and especially genital domain to the commodity becomes both a quasi-moral, quasi-medical imperative and an opportunity for profit. And it is in this context that both pornography and advertising (especially of fashion) became so important in the era of AIDS, according to Singer. "Advertising is the mechanism for mobilizing [the] transferential network in the direction of particular commodities. In pornography, the commodity is a sexual semiotic, that is, a phenomenon of sex without bodies."[29] It is not always possible to draw a line between these domains, and advertising—including the television serials and movies that function mainly as platforms for product placement—is the space of their convergence. Commodity consumption does not simply satisfy a sexual desire that would otherwise find its outlet in reproductive sex, however. Rather, in its proliferation of objects and its multiplication of avenues of substitution, it opens the possibility of satisfaction in ways that are at least partly de-cathected from reproductivity. Nor is desire a limited quantity. The capacity for more, to both want more and to become more, is its core—and this has political potential beyond what can be satisfied in the realm of objects.

How, then, was this epidemic managed in those contexts in which the means of enacting such a proliferation of transferential possibilities through commodity consumption was limited by unemployment and poverty. What happened in South Africa, where the simultaneity of liberation from Apartheid and the end or at least the limitation of a socialist option, as well as the enormous coercive power of the minerals industry, ensured that the new regime would undertake the transformation of society in a neoliberal mode?[30] This latter fact, which was and continues to be accompanied by policies promoting the creation and enlargement of black capital, has had as one of its corollaries a saturation of the public sphere by advertising that solicits consumer desire and that holds out commodity consumption as a primary index of liberated existence (see also chapter 14). Fashion and technological accessorization, even in the poorest of the informal settlements, were and remain preoccupations for most youth.[31] Cellphones, expensive athletic shoes, and brand-name fashion (particularly that which comes from abroad) have been as crucial to the self-fashioning of the post-Apartheid generation in South Africa as they have been anywhere else in the world. And in South Africa as elsewhere, soap operas and reality television shows dedicated to unreal housewives exalt the tawdry phantasmagoria of suburban unreality and township plenitude: swimming pools and luxury cars, well-manicured nails and gold lamé. The invitation to transference has been made, and even incited, but its means of accomplishment is differentially distributed. So, we might say, there is desire in excess—of excess, for excess.

Those who are solicited as consumers but who lack means are often read as the bearers of this desire in excess, and, moreover, as subjects who are excessive in many other ways: not only hypersexual and hyperconsumerist but also gratuitously violent and antisocial. The mark of this excess is typically said to be visible in the disproportionate willingness to sacrifice a great deal for a small commodity: to sell sex for a bag of potato chips or to kill for a cellphone. The same logic that has always afflicted the African accused of fetishism operates here. This is the terrible underside of the phenomenon for which Gwendolyn Brooks's poem, discussed in chapter 14, provides the poetic expression: the child "whose broken window is a cry of art."[32] That poem suggested an awful alternation between aesthetic and desecrative possibilities when there is desire and/in excess, and no means for the sublation of that "more" (that *mehr* of *mehrwert*, as Peter Fenves reminded us). Desecration—Brooks's word—is not destruction. It names the power of defacement to reinvest the mutilated object, rather than to merely annihilate it. And we will want to bear this in mind when thinking about how and why the victims of HIV/AIDS are asked, as are the poor rioters, why they do not preserve (for) themselves that which instead they seem to destroy and to lament at the same time.

In the United States, we know, the success of the safe sex movement relied on the capacity of its target audience to take up the demand for transference or substitution to respond to the demand that eros be both diversified and displaced through commodities—not only in the form of sexual commodities, from phone sex to sex toys, pornography, and sadomasochistic paraphernalia, but also in eroticized commodities of a less obviously sexual nature (fitness club memberships, athletic clothing, and, of course, fashion in general). And it is not incidental that the safe-sex strategy worked best in relatively affluent white gay male communities; its early relative failure in African American communities must be explained at least partly by the relatively limited means for satisfying desire through commodity transference, at least in poorer areas, as well as by the dominance of heteronormatively reproductive erotic economies and the suspicion of transferential projects that might divert or redirect its desire away from reproduction.

A far more generalized situation of this latter sort can be seen in South Africa. Many of the techniques for combating the epidemic were derived from epidemiological and health models that presumed a different context and far more developed infrastructures for education and service delivery. But in their mediatic form, they also operated through the cultivation of new desires. The display of beautiful bodies through which desire was cultivated could, for example, be seen in those promotional advertisements of LoveLife, the Kaiser Foundation–backed anti-HIV/AIDS campaign, which, in its early years, used publicly placed billboards featuring ambiguous messages about sexual practice (often conservative ones), while showcasing attractive young black men and women attired in beautiful clothes and accessorized with hip technology and the tokens of metropolitan access.[33] These ads, praised by some for their contemporaneity and their attentiveness to youthful fantasy, and condemned by others as either lacking in informative content or being covertly allied with conservative heteronormative forms, can be helpfully understood in the terms that Singer makes available, as part of a semiotic system that both incites desire and makes it available for transference. But there is the rub, so to speak. For the transfer to consumer commodities demands trade-offs with, for example, payment of rents, cooking oil and foodstuffs, personal care products, school fees, and medical costs. As in the United States, the project of political emancipation in South Africa has been accompanied by a comprehensive effort on the part of cultural producers to resignify blackness and to reclaim Africanity from its denigrated status within the historical perspective of white settler colonialism through aesthetic valorization. The necessary task of making blackness eligible for recognition as beautiful, hip, worldly, or cosmopolitan thus converged, or was structured in its conjuncture, with a moment in which the twin facts of epidemic and poverty threatened to transform the erotic transference (so essential to safe sex) into debt.

Consider, then, the conversations I had with both young women in the township and HIV/AIDS educators. Both described the situation of young women who, desiring commodities and without means, sought them from boyfriends. An eighteen-year-old Zulu-speaking woman from the township, who nonetheless had managed to get into a university, said:

> Girls in the township want many boyfriends. [She describes someone in particular.] She'll be faithful to one, but the others, she'll just keep them hidden. Each one gives her something. Maybe she gets a cell-phone from one boyfriend, and clothes from the other. The more boyfriends she has, the more she gets. That's what makes her "hot." She has to keep them hidden, though. If one of them finds out about the other boyfriends, he might beat her. Then, she has to hide the bruises. She uses a condom with the second boyfriends. But she'll be faithful to her main boyfriend.

Mzaidume recognized this fact when she took it upon herself to rewrite the surveys being used to assess sexual behavior.[34] Her survey, always addressed to women in their own languages, commenced with the following questions:

> Do you have a boyfriend? If, yes, what does he give you?
> Do you have a second boyfriend? If yes, what does he give you?
> Do you have another boyfriend?

Frustrated with the language of foreign NGOs, and their insistence on what was, locally, a foreign vocabulary of "multiple partners" that presumed the isomorphism between sexual contact and partnership, she recognized the degree to which women conceived of their many relationships in which a lover and a set of needs were correlated without being reduced to each other. The incapacity to achieve satisfaction with a lover was not, primarily, a sexual matter, although it had sexual implications. Poor women may have sexual relations with several different men to obtain commodities or money while nonetheless conceiving of those relations as being subject to strict limits. The acknowledgment of those limits was, for Mzaidume, because for them, a kind of fidelity.

We are not, therefore, talking about an economy in which mutuality and multiplicity are opposed, in which need obliterates the capacity for contracts of mutual trust. Faithfulness is construed within a set of practical exigencies, and it is as highly valorized as desirability is. But here, desire, which is being incited by the same apparatus of consumer culture that mobilizes it in more affluent contexts, overflows the opposition of sex and commodity in a reverse direction. Instead of allowing for a multiplication of possible satisfactions and thus freedom from or supplementation of reproductive sexuality, it demands it.

One might expect the response to this situation to be rage or frustration. And perhaps these affective tendencies are partly to blame for the rise in sexual violence, the emergence or intensification of intergenerational sexual violence (including that directed at infants and elders), and other forms of domestic dysfunction so well documented in the local media and the international press. But that response, or at least the imagination of it, is conceived from the vantage point of a male subject. Women's forms of responding to the contradictions between their commodity desires, their erotic aims, and the limitations imposed on them by poverty, lack of employment, and the need to care for others, may express themselves in violence, sometimes directed at others, sometimes at themselves, but rarely in sexual violence.

But there is always a limit, a perimeter within which these pseudo-social logics operate. And as often as not, that limit of the normative, the one in whom the norm is disclosed by its transgression, is the prostitute. The women, some of whom we have already met, who worked at the Truck Stop brothels before being recruited as peer educators in the local HIV/AIDS prevention program, spoke of poignantly complex relations to their own health status, the revelation (or not) of their HIV status to partners, parents, and children. Sisipho, for example, had initially spoken to their own mother about possibly being HIV positive. She had watched others, apparently robust and full of health, begin to waste and gradually to die, their skin acquire a gray pallor, and their hair to thin, but not before retreating inward and withdrawing from the social world. And despite her concern for and even contempt for her daughter's prostitution, the elder woman had urged her to be tested and to seek out whatever medications were available (this even before antiretrovirals became widely accessible). Sisipho's mother referred to AIDS (as reported by Sisipho), already in 2000, as a common disease and one that no one could be certain to escape. Akhona's mother had died in 1978, only two years after she herself had given birth (amid the riots of 1976, it will be remembered) and she could not ask her mother's advice. It was to her daughter, and her daughter alone, that she spoke after testing positive, hoping that her example would be instructive for the child, whose studying she encouraged as the means to avoid prostitution and the life of disappointment that she herself had endured.

Both Sisipho and Akhona, though HIV educators, had lovers with whom they continued to have unprotected sex, in addition to the clients with whom they had, over the years, engaged. Sisipho remembered her first encounter with a client in terms of what he had bought her—a bag of chips and some bread—and recalled the fact that he had taken her to OK Bazaar to buy groceries for the woman with whom she stayed. Not exactly luxury commodities. But OK Bazaar, with its aisles of stacked food and refrigerated drinks, its detergents and small domestic appliances, was grand relative to the little tuk shops run out of township houses, which often had stock limited to a few tins of beans and pilchards fish, candy-colored sodas and beer, matches, candles, and batteries.

Sisipho's narrative about commodities and sex in some ways paralleled that of the young woman cited peviously, but it was in other respects inverted. Having more than one partner was not just a matter of accessing goods (including minimal necessities) that were entirely unavailable to her otherwise. She inserted herself into a web of relations on the presumption that migrant men who maintained two or more residential commitments would want "wives" in both locations. She resided with her lover, a Zulu man from KwaZulu-Natal, whose primary wife would occasionally visit. She was aware of Sisipho's presence, which the man in question explained as essential to a man's existence in Johannesburg, and agreed that he needed someone to "cook and wash for him," a phrase that stood in for the range of needs and desires that Sisipho agreed to satisfy in exchange for money. When the lover's wife would visit, Sisipho remained at the house, and enjoyed friendly relations with her, but she explained, proud of her magnanimity, that "I do give them a chance together at night and sleep out with my cousin." Sisipho claimed she "did not have a problem with that. It could be because I do not get any stress from him, because when I want money he gives, and his wife also does not fight with me. Even when his children come to visit, we understand each other. I think he gave us good discipline and we also do not want people from outside to see us fighting over a man. He taught us as his wives, discipline. His wife cooks for us and I also cook when it is my turn, so we are just a happy family together."

No one will likely read this statement as testimony of a woman's liberation even within polygamous contexts. And feminist critique in South Africa must contend with the question of how this position could come to seem so normal and, indeed, so desirable for so many. But it begins with the recognition that someone like Sisipho could experience this relation as a kind of freedom—from worry, from fear, from want. And even from prostitution. Although there was money involved, this relationship was not coterminous with Sisipho's life as a prostitute; that had ended, she said, when she met the members of the HIV/AIDS peer education program. The apparent mimesis between domestic life and prostitution, where the management of the household economy veers toward the exchange of sexual services for monetizable values, is perhaps only perceptible from within a moralizing discourse for which monogamy is of the order of the gift. Nonetheless, this mimed domesticity was not entirely devoid of the debt and guilt that afflicts the rest of the economy.

Sisipho's lover knew of her previous life as a prostitute but had asked her to stop seeing other men, on the condition that he alone provide her with money when she needed it. Perhaps for this reason, when she was diagnosed with HIV, she did not inform her lover, who she assumed would leave her upon learning this. Nor did she tell her son about her status, although he was aware of her work with the HIV/AIDS project. She did, however, urge him to use condoms and was in fact pleased when she found a condom in his bedroom one day. Perhaps suspecting his mother's status, he had told her and her mother that, in the event she should become ill, they should care for her at home lest she be stigmatized by the community and subjected to violence. And Sisipho took comfort in this. Her desire to help others avoid the illness that she was battling, and for which she took daily medication, did not, however, produce a completely coherent publicness. She was riven by fear and doubt; she was beholden to her lover, and she cared for him; but she also feared the violence that drunken retribution would inflect on her if word about her seropositivity status got out. So, she lived in public with a secret whose weight was measured in the coins she did not have.

I confess that I was initially concerned to learn of Sisipho's ongoing and unprotected sexual relations with her lover. To educate is not to judge, Mzaidume constantly reminded me, without ever indulging such didacticism. Intervention for change makes its gestures where it can, leaves a mark where it can be received, and keeps going. That was her approach. Songezile Madikida and I nonetheless wondered why Sisipho continued to have an unprotected sexual relations with her lover, whom she likened to a husband and whom she knew to be in a relationship with another woman. And she demurred, matter-of-factly, that if he refused to use a condom that was his choice, and the consequences would be his to bear. What could she do about it? He did not like to use a condom, but he was willing to have sex in the "old way of doing it between the thighs without penetrating" her. Whether he did so out of some acknowledgment of the risk, is unclear. What is clear is that from within heteronormative reproductivity, rather than against it, she had found a way to minimize her risk and that of her lover and his wife as well. What is also clear is that it was the stipend that she received from the project that had made even that compromised gesture possible. If Sisipho's example can be generalized at all, one can imagine that a program of universal basic income might offer some women a comparable opportunity.[35]

Akhona had also struggled with the burden of telling a lover of her HIV-positive status. When she had initially informed him, he was so shocked that she retracted her confession, and told him that it was a "lie" to test him. Later, when he became ill and was diagnosed with AIDS, he was shocked again, and she reminded him that she had tried to tell him of her status. Once again, she said, he had been shocked. The menace within him was entirely unassimilable. But her willingness to continue in a relationship, premised on the agreement that they wear a condom to save each other from reinfection, seemed to be a relief to both of them. And they clasped each other in the secret embrace of that shared ailment. But like Sisipho, she believed the best HIV-mitigating strategy was for men to invest in wives in each of the locations where they lived and worked. Migration was still an axiomatic dimension of life near the mines for many, and living out allowances, which the NUM had encouraged as a mechanism of stabilization and as a means to escape the debasements of the single-sex hostel system, only exacerbated the demands for more cash.

On the side of both the NUM and the mine management, the entire stabilization narrative was modeled on the presumption of monogamy, and on the movement of women from their natal homes to their husbands' places of work. But contracts were not eternal, mines were constantly downsizing, and women did not always want to leave home. Nor did men desire this, for they too, had invested in the notion of a functional rurality as the mise-en-scene for their own restabilized masculinity. Equally important, the cost of living far from metropolitan centers was cheaper, and accumulations in those areas could be invested in houses and other property, whereas the same money in the urban areas was barely enough to enable the little spectacles of *dépense* that came at the weeks' ends. In this context, and surely against the expectations and aspirations of reformists, massive indebting of mineworkers became a phenomenon of stabilization, for the maintenance of two or three households demanded enormous financial resources (and as we will see). The accumulations of debt and the investment in such debt by the union itself would be a source of growing hostility to the NUM and was implicated in the catastrophe of Marikana in 2012 (to be discussed in chapter 16).

But for Akhona, voicing the sentiment of so many in the mid-2000s, HIV seemed to demand an enclaved multiple monogamy, rather than either exclusive or serial monogamy. Abstinence was not viable as a strategy and not desirable as a mode of relation, but it was the name of a refusal that women constantly invoked as the horizon of possible autonomy. Survival in this world was not a matter of binary choices or completely transformed modes of being; it was an ethically taxing and often frightening set of negotiations of personal status, as approval or opprobrium by others, dependency, and sometimes (but rarely) personal choice. Choice itself was exercised mainly in relation to children. All of the female sex workers I met hoped that their knowledge and willingness to discuss HIV, even if they could not enact it themselves, could save their children its experience. But that required regular HIV testing for pregnant women and the administration of nevirapine to women to prevent maternal-infant transmission. Here, too, combating AIDS was to be conceived from within the framework and against the background of a naturalized mandate for heter-onormative reproductivity. But the sex workers who had taken on the labor of educating their peers had come to believe in the future—if not for themselves, then for their children and, equally importantly, for other people's children.

Only the teenagers not yet exiled from habitability could indulge the rhe-torical absolutization of death in the impossible statistics of near-complete infectivity. But then, these were precisely the subjects-as-market for the new actuarial order, the ones who had to believe in death to value life and whose transference of desire to commodities was being cultivated in and through pub-lic health campaigns like LoveLife.

Not Literally

Considered from another perspective, the extraction of a surplus desire from the youth, one that risks leading them toward death, is in itself an extraction of surplus value from death. Here, we begin to see what it might mean to say that the interests of capital in the situation of an epidemic under neoliberalism entail an investment in death. But let us not refer to it as a uniformly necrotic economy. Or at least, let us recognize that this investment will also bring with it an investment in life. Moreover, the investment in death is not yet a situation of "letting them die," as Catherine Campbell terms it, or "disposability," as Achille Mbembe phrases it.[36] This disposability is not entirely generalized. Rather, the investment in death entailed the insertion of a cut, or an opposition within the categories of the living and the dying organized in terms of temporal prox-imity. To make that argument, I would like to consider some of the contexts in which the investment in death is literalized, and, in particular, to consider the operations and discourses of the funerary and life insurance industries—which make speculation on death a source of value—for they are an integral part of life in mining towns and throughout South Africa. Under Apartheid, their dif-ferential distribution was also one of the ways of marking and enforcing racial difference; it was a technique of governmentality operated beyond the state. After the end of Apartheid, this distributive function changed; it was no longer operating primarily as an indicator and boundary marker of race. Nor did it work by replacing racial difference with class difference—and class no longer operated as it had in earlier eras of (relatively) high employment. But differentiation remained its effective outcome.

The first thing to note in this context is the extraordinary growth in participation in burial societies and insurance schemes in those areas where AIDS infectivity rates grew most spectacularly and most visibly—which is also to say in ways that have been researched and documented.[37] This growth was limited by two factors: the exhaustion of the financial viability of funeral societies in areas with very high mortality rates, and the seeming decline of participation among those groups with the highest rates of infection (over 50 percent), and the least durable and least legitimated social relations (prostitutes). At the same time, the resultant vulnerability of funeral societies, long a source of solace and connectivity for migrant workers who would otherwise have remained isolated from their homes even in death, provided the occasion for a concerted move by the capitalized insurance industry to begin soliciting lower-income clients and to begin cultivating a new oppositional structure within social categories that once seemed to provide the basis for political solidarities.

By way of historical background, one can turn to the work of R. J. Thomson and D. B. Posel for the contemporary period, and that of H. Kuper and S. Kaplan, for the early twentieth century. The narrative they generate can be summarized roughly as follows: burial societies developed among migrant laborers in urban contexts throughout the twentieth century as a means of ensuring proper funerals for the deceased—who were otherwise distant from the homes to which they wished their remains to be consigned—and of providing social support for the living.[38] The latter received not only monetary contributions from a shared purse that was both managed and dispersed by the society on the basis of need but also assistance with funeral preparations, including the provision of food, the expression of solidarity in grief, and the social sustenance that comes from collectivity.[39] Dominated by women, these societies were historically connected to churches, and they shared the habits of dress and moral piety that characterized many African Christian congregations. Their ethos of collectivity and reciprocity was aptly captured in the name of a burial society in Khutsong, the Mahata Mmoho society, meaning "those who walk together side by side."[40]

The emphasis placed in these societies on consensual decision making, remarked by M. Brandel-Syrier,[41] and reiterated by Thomson and Posel, permits us to consider them as instances of a local public sphere and as crucial institutions within which the habits of democratic life were produced long before the body politic assumed its democratic form.[42] Buti Kulwane, writing about such organizations in Khutsong township, considers them to be crucial elements of civil society and an inadequately recognized resource for political transformation.[43] But he notes, as do other writers, that this same emphasis on public discussions of fiscal management and personal need made them vulnerable to conflict and resulted in the collapse of many societies, even when they had been listed with the Registrar of Friendly Societies.[44] The persistence of societies and the emergence or growth of new societies, as occurred in Mera-fong, thus attests to their ongoing importance even when they fail.

A little over one fourth of people in townships are estimated to be mem-bers of burial societies, a number that seems not to have changed radically over the years—although it declined during the pandemic.[45] According to Thomson and Posel, the most significant, but not the only, motivation for joining a society is the financial costs that attend death. Burial societies redis-tribute this burden over a longer period, and they do so through a process of collectivization, but they are limited in their capacities to absorb radical changes in the temporalities of death, which is to say in mortality rates. For this reason, some predicted that the HIV/AIDS pandemic would both cripple families and bankrupt burial societies.[46] In a milieu so saturated by talk about AIDS, Thomson and Posel nonetheless found (in the early 2000s) that people did not discuss AIDS in burial societies, whether because of lack of personal exposure to death by AIDS, lack of willingness to address it as the cause of death, or some other factor. Yet, one notes, upon rereading their ethnographic data, that these people spoke about not speaking about AIDS.[47] This speaking about not speaking of AIDS constitutes something of a peri-performative, in Eve Sedgwick's sense, and partakes of the logic of negation in speech as Sigmund Freud analyzed it. In other words, it expresses unconscious recog-nition. Although not precisely analogous to the more overt disavowals that I encountered among Merafong youths, such speech raises the question of whether we need to expand our understanding of how AIDS was incorporated into everyday consciousness and to acknowledge that the opposition between denialism and action—articulated by many activists—is inadequate as an ana-lytic framework.

If burial societies were threatened by the increasing financial burden posed by AIDS, they were also assaulted by proponents of new corporate logics, many of which were undertaken from within the discourses of transparency. Thus, for example, Thomson and Posel discuss an administered burial society in Johannesburg in which members neither knew the other members, nor under-stood the financial practices with which their monies were being managed. They imply that the society not only mimicked the structures of capitalized insurance companies but also suffered from the problems associated with bureaucratization and depersonalization.[48] These were somewhat mitigated at the local level, where the "books were open," but at the regional level, the oper-ations were largely occulted.

The new kind of society described by Thomson and Posel became possible only after the removal of Apartheid-era restrictions on capital accumulation by people designated as Africans. It was in this transformed legal context that large-scale societies and competition between insurance schemes and burial societies arose. In addition, the meaning of being in societies changed. Thus, for example, Erik Bähre notes that, among male Xhosa migrants of Cape Town, membership in burial societies, as well as savings and credit groups, diminished after the end of Apartheid, when coresidency among men from the same district ceased to describe patterns of residence.[49] In contrast, women's membership in societies increased, as the societies came to be seen as mechanisms for protecting earnings against the claims of kin in distant areas.[50] Bähre adds that social grants and the state-based provision of social services mitigated the need for these institutions to work as redistributive mechanisms, as in the old funeral societies, and instead, they became associated with more permanent migration to the city and with new forms of acquisitiveness and the desire to accumulate in urban areas.

It is not incidental that many if not most of the analyses of burial societies were undertaken at the behest of the insurance industry at the turn of the millennium.[51] In 2006, Bähre could remark the emergence of a targeted marketing of insurance to previously excluded groups, particularly mid- and low-income black South Africans. At that point, the penetration of the insurance industry in South Africa was estimated at 14.5 percent of gross domestic product (GDP), a very high rate compared with other developing countries, such as Indonesia (1.19 percent) and India (0.62 percent). But it also exceeded the rates in the United States by nearly three times—the U.S. rates was then 5.23 percent of GDP.[52] The South African rates bespeak an extraordinary generalization of actuarial consciousness and testify to the fact that life there was increasingly saturated by the anticipation of death. This penetration of the insurance industry rate was already high before the AIDS epidemic, but it has increased enormously since then. The relationship between the two is complex, however, mediated as it is by the expansion of insurance schemes beyond the previous groups of racially delimited consumers. Indeed, this targeting of new black and especially lower-income black consumers has continued to be a major concern of the insurance industry. Although unemployment continues to foreclose such possibilities for many, there has nonetheless been a gradual expansion of the working poor, and lower-middle-class black populations, and not just the black bourgeoisie, and these people are among the new targets of insurance companies.

In 2000, Gary Hartwig proposed to the Actuarial Society of South Africa that the low-income market was a viable frontier for expansion by assurance schemes. He harnessed a culturalist anthropological understanding to make this case, arguing for the development of "products" that acknowledge the importance of community, the short time horizons of people with low salaries or uncertain wages, and the demand for trust-based negotiations rather than contractual forms that substitute legal guarantees for interpersonal commitment.[53] He also identified "conspicuous consumption" and language (i.e., lack of literacy or proficiency in English and Afrikaans) as obstacles to the industry. And he offered a few strategies to accommodate an otherwise presumably suspicious population, namely the provision of credit, tolerance for missed or irregular premium payments, and low transaction costs.

It is in his discussion of HIV/AIDS as risks for the industry that we discern the social consequences of this new actuarialization. To begin, Hartwig assessed the cost of HIV/AIDS for those who were seeking insurance in terms of antiselection. Because seropositivity testing for low-income groups was said to be impractical, he advocated waiting periods, underwriting that included questions that could detect likely HIV infection, and so forth. Revealingly, he stated that "the HIV/AIDS pandemic threatens to raise the cost of products like funeral cover to such an extent that healthy lives are no longer prepared to subsidise sick lives. Healthy individuals would then prefer to undergo thorough underwriting, including an HIV test, in order to pay much lower premiums for a given level of cover. There is thus a need to understand the degree of cross-subsidisation that the market is prepared to accept."[54] In other words, one of the reasons that the life insurance industry might wish to intervene in the low-income market was that it would generate a desire among those would previously have been financially responsible for costs that attend the deaths of the HIV-positive members of their community to abandon them in favor of reduced costs and enhanced benefits for themselves. This too constitutes a moment of bounding, a bounding of a reduced and newly circumscribed social self. And however reticent it was to endorse public health policies advocating condom use, Bähre reminds us that the South African state remained committed to the idea of a social contract, and, for a time, it continued to inhibit this new drive toward new divisions. Legislation prohibiting discrimination, especially the Promotion of Equality and Prevention of Unfair Discrimination Act, was a major resource in this effort to interrupt what, from the insurance industry's perspective, are highly atomistic cost-benefit analyses—despite the rhetoric of cultural relativity and the advocacy of products designed for African sensibilities.[55]

It may be helpful to summarize the rhetorical and logical case being made by the insurance industry, as part of its efforts to reduce the risk of offering risk management products to a population described as being always already "at risk." The industry had both to disseminate a consciousness of death as potentially imminent and to cultivate a tendency to displace that imminence onto others. Ultimately, this displacement had to produce a division between those who were HIV negative and those who were HIV positive, or rather those who could prove their seronegativity and its likely maintenance and those who could not. What the insurance company had to repress was the error of presuming a permanent HIV status. But it could do so only by bringing that possibility to consciousness for the consumer; hence, it became an advocate of something like a privatized (neoliberalized) biopolitical regime. It also became the purveyor of panic as the condition of investment. And this panic was the source of the industry's own rush.

In Bed with Death

When I first went to Carletonville in 1998, I visited the local cemetery, a handsome, well-manicured space that one approaches along a narrow road lined with neatly spaced cypress trees. The road passes through fields of grasses and has for its horizon the nearly incandescent white dumps excavated from the mines. Its older graves bear the names of mainly Afrikaner dead, but there is a monument to the NUM with a wall of names associated with mine accidents, and increasingly, there are other African names on the headstones as well. Some of the old Afrikaner graves bear the wrought-iron beds that so hauntingly mark the impossibility of physical intimacy between the living and the dead, but that are invariably adorned with the tokens of longing: flowers, photographs, glasses of water. Most other graves have modest stone markers.

In 1998, when I wandered through the cemetery, there were fresh flowers at some grave sites, but there were only two open graves, the mounds of red soil at their perimeter indicating by inversion the chasm into which the coffins would be placed. When I returned two years later, there were more than a dozen open graves, each awaiting the corpse of another deceased resident. Some of the graves were tiny—their smallness indicating the destiny of a child. There had not been an accident in the mines, nor in the town and its township. To the contrary, a readiness for death had become a routine part of the cemetery's "life." The situation was much, much worse in the townships. Some people began to suggest that the very digging of graves in anticipation of death was causing it, and this was accompanied by a belief, prevalent in many areas, that AIDS was being caused by witchcraft. Walking between the graves of Khutsong's cemetery with Yodwa, I could not help—and nor could she—but take note of the extraordinary number of deaths among those in young adulthood and early middle age. These graves, with the names etched on stones or wooden crosses bracketed between birth dates of the late 1970s (birth) and the deaths at turn of the millennium (death) foretold the increasing prevalence of AIDS. Among other things, this also revealed either that migrant labor no longer accounted for the growth in deaths or that there were no longer sufficient resources (either personal resources or resources collectivized by burial societies) or desires to send the bodies home. The young Xhosa poet Mangaliso Buzani somehow captures the sense of that moment: "Clouds wept/the sun wore a black gown/

mourning beforehand/for my death/and I heard the footsteps/of my coffin/ coming towards me."[56]

The burgeoning business of the gravediggers was soon matched by the affective labor of the ANC officials, who attended funerals as a means of recognizing the contributions of community members. In 2000, when I visited the ANC office in town, the whiteboard was a mass of names mapped onto dates, shadowed by another set of names and dates that had been erased, but whose traces could not be entirely effaced. I initially imagined these to be weekly work schedules, and in some ways they were. In fact, they expressed the assignment of mourning duties among the representatives and office workers. A few years later, even the mayor told me he was exhausted by funerals, but also that he was afraid to start choosing among them, lest this be read as an immoral distribution of political favors. He was not able to maintain his policy of universality, however, and soon had to share this labor with lower-ranking members of the party.

In ways that mirror but invert this concern to maintain universalism in the face of AIDS (even if such universalism has always been a fiction), a mine manager told me that the biggest source of concern for him about HIV in the mines was the fear that it induced in team bosses, who became reticent to help injured miners for fear of contracting the virus. In this way, he articulated the consciousness that the insurance industries precisely cultivated, namely a set of social distinctions organized by the principle of infection, and operationalized by the category of risk. For this manager, the principle still appeared to manifest the older, racialized structures of Apartheid. But elsewhere in the community, it was becoming clear that the discursive strategy of Africanizing AIDS was losing its purchase. At the local hospital, a nurse estimated that 25–30 percent of those who died at the facility were victims of the disease. This rate was not, she said, racially specific, although she admitted that few of the white deaths were acknowledged to be related to HIV. In 2007, an undertaker with access to death certificates confirmed these numbers, in which more than 80 percent of deaths of people under the age of thirty-seven were listed as "natural," which is to say, caused by disease rather than accident of violence. It was at the time not acceptable practice to name HIV/AIDS as a cause of death in South Africa, and so although there remained some doubt as to the cause of these deaths, it is highly probably that many were the result of AIDS.[57]

In 2000, the national government had not begun its rollout of antiretrovirals, and the task of providing testing, counseling, and treatment was only slowly being assumed by the mining companies and large retailers. These corporate entities, but especially the mines, began to shift policy in the late 1990s. Where previously a diagnosis of HIV had led to automatic dismissal, as a diagnosis of tuberculosis (TB) or phthisis had in previous years, AngloGold determined that the cost of replacing the workforce, a workforce with increasing skills levels, had outstripped that of caring for it. Unable to demand that the relatively underresourced state assume the burden of reproducing the workforce, extractive capital took it upon itself to extend its biopolitical regime.[58] This regime was limited insofar as it depended on voluntary accession to the testing and treatment regime, and initially, only about 30 percent of miners made use of this opportunity.[59] Nonetheless, it provided some grounds for resisting the temptation to generalize the condition of the South African postcolony as one dominated by "necropolitics." According to a spokesperson of Anglo-Gold Ashanti, testing rates rose and death rates declined, thanks mainly to better treatments and care (a decline that was not initially matched by government facilities). Although many subjects of the South African state were indeed granted the means to only bare life, that was not entirely true at the mines, and this fact alone demands a careful specification of the ways in which the social body was differentiated by and for investment. We need to account for the degradations that attend the organization of African social and economic life, but AIDS cannot be understood in terms of the figure of the living dead. It must also be understood in terms that recognize how an investment in death becomes the means for investing in life, and how, at the same time, a seeming investment in life becomes the means for investing in death.

Parlor Games

In 2005, there were sixteen major funeral service providers in Merafong, most of which had offices within a few blocks of each other, not far from the commercial center of town. I used to drive through this part of time upon each new visit to the area; it was a key index of historical change. Green or red signage displaced the blue. The logos were the same everywhere. The largest of these, the national provider AVBOB, claimed the vast majority of business (nearly 95 percent), being the exclusive provider to the mines, with premiums being paid for by the corporations on the basis of contracts negotiated by the NUM and Solidarity. Of course, as has been repeatedly argued in the preceding pages, not everyone worked in the mines. Indeed, most did not, and there were many other, smaller providers to offer them services. There were also at least ten insurance retailers. As it was widely said throughout the gold-mining areas, where the gold deposits were gradually being depleted, death was the biggest growth industry. The proprietors of both large and small funerary businesses disagreed with this, and noted the accelerating rates of payout as a liability. Many had adopted a stern practice (quite contrary to those advocated by the Actuarial Association) that revoked policies when a premium was missed. These policies could not be restarted; the contributions already made were forfeited. In one case, the proprietor of a funerary business serving Khutsong exclusively, remarked that services would be denied in the event of the death unless the full amount of the funeral costs had already been met by the policy holder. Even if a client had invested 1,500 of 1,600 rand committed under the terms of the contract before the death occurred, the funeral services would be withheld (although they would be offered if the difference could be made up). Needless to say, the interest accrued on the monies already invested was not calculated toward the policy.

In any case, death is everywhere, and everywhere it is imbricated with the world of profit making. It is also imbricated in risk management, and the two had become increasingly inseparable by the turn of the millennium. It will come as no surprise, given what we heard from the youths with whom I introduced this chapter, that at that time, membership in burial societies and investment in insurance schemes escalated at dramatic rates. Among miners, membership in church groups and burial societies increased from 27 percent to 42 percent and from 37 percent to 47 percent, respectively, between 1998 and 2001. Overall membership, higher among women than men, as is typical, nonetheless declined in the three-year period of the study, which fact the authors attributed to diminished income levels.[60] But the statistics for women were also distorted by the fact that the group includes prostitutes. Suffering from infectivity rates of more than 60 percent, local prostitutes' membership in these kinds of societies decreased from 26 percent to 11 percent and in stokvels from 16 percent to 13 percent during the same period, although membership in church organizations remained constant.[61] As everywhere else in the world, prostitutes account for a group in which the acuity of the crisis was so severe and in which illness and poverty were so rife that risk management appeared to have been entirely abandoned—except in relation to children. Indeed, the testimony recorded by researchers for the Mothusimpilo project confirmed this and observed that the lack of social connectedness signified by diminished membership was another risk factor—one that redoubled that afflicting prostitutes in particular. Its most extreme expression was found in those who lacked the resources even to participate in a burial society and who, because of both poverty and social dislocation, in some senses could no longer afford to die socially (bearing in mind the distinction between biological and social death that anthropology has always insisted on). Indeed, this latter problem was so acute that it had entered formal political debate. Accordingly, the municipal government established among its priorities for the "Multi-Sectoral HIV/AIDS Programme," the development of a strategy to deal with indigent burials.

In these circumstances, it is not surprising that youths would be overwhelmed by the omnipresent fact of AIDS. But if the statistics about burial societies suggest that their parents' generation still believed that they could and should insure against the costs of death, and hence, that they could invest in their families' futures (by relieving them of the financial burden that death will entail), the inflationary discourse about AIDS among youths revealed something else. What is this something else if not the very demand for something else, something outside of risk management, something beyond actuarialization? Something more? We have encountered this question before.

Many factors come into play in this context, including the intergenerational memory of having had very limited access to social goods and the ameliorative technologies by which suffering could be addressed—whether in the short term, through health care, or in the long term, through education. These were supplemented by the enormous force of grief, emerging from the generalized experience of loss, which the AIDS pandemic brought about. Add to this the political disappointment that attends not only the slow transfer of resources (when compared with the transfer of rights) but also the lethargic or nonexistent expansion of employment opportunities. All told, we have many ingredients with which to explain a general affective disorientation. The question is, how could this disaffection be overcome? The insurance industry responded not by disavowing the reasons for such malaise but by rendering the idea of total death as a future possibility (here it partook of the structure of deferral and displacement illuminated by Singer) and then subjecting it to a calculus of probability, which estimates the likely exposure to and progress toward this end for each individual.

The burial societies might be considered to be forms of risk management, as Thomson and Posel assert. But this is true in a limited sense. Certainly, when compared with the capitalized insurance industry, the burial society comes to appear like an old-fashioned savings account, although the transformation of the local society into nationally integrated corporate-style entities suggests that this has changed somewhat, without eliminating the older forms. The primary mutation in habit that is performed by the insurance industry differs precisely in its social distribution of risk. Its goal, recall, is not merely to sell its product but to get people to differentiate among themselves—that is, between those who will be able to buy cheaply and those who will have to pay dearly. This is, one must admit, entirely contrary to the logic expressed in the name Mahata Mmoho (those who walk together side by side), and the enormity of the transformation being solicited cannot be underestimated. For profitability for the corporation requires that individuals construe life as an opportunity for profiting in relation to others' deaths—if only as relative survival, of outlasting all the rest. If pornography is sex without bodies, insurance of this sort is death without bodies. And the excess that it generates for consumers makes further commodity consumption possible. Here, the sequence of desire's incitement and displacement is played against a desire whose obstruction is inseparable from that death which makes the HIV-negative or the non-HIV-positive person a source of profit in the first instance.

This subjection of all to the principles of risk management has taken place against a backdrop of intensified financialization. Although intrinsic to the gold industry from its inception, this was also a crucial element in the ANC regime's retreat from a more socialist project to a more neoliberal policy, which entails the marketization of all and the introjection into individual subjects of the responsibility for managing risk. That movement was itself a response to the attribution of risk to South Africa. As Edward Lipuma and Benjamin Lee note, the decision taken by the South African government to mitigate capital flight and halt the fall of the rand by privatizing state-owned firms was partly dictated by the international business community's assignment of risk based on the country's racial composition and the ANC's historical sympathy to socialism. And even so, it took place to a limited degree. Nonetheless, financialization and marketization were, at this macroeconomic and political level, a risk-reduction strategy, intended to mitigate international aversion. Those processes worked by subjecting the entire economy and all of its subjects to risk-management calculations along with the recruitment of more and more individuals into capitalized insurance markets.[62] Moreover, these calculations have been disseminated at the individual and interpersonal level. And risk management has been supplemented by a more extreme kind of risk-taking, from which surplus value is once again being sought.

One can see the effects of this move in a variety of contexts and not simply in the sphere of public health and death services. In Merafong, a particularly dramatic instance can be seen in the 2005 agreement that DRDGold (which at the time operated the Blyvooruitzicht mine) struck with the NUM. The agreement introduced an unprecedented pay strategy, according to which miners would be paid on a sliding scale, with their wages linked to gold prices. At times of high gold prices, this would benefit the miners, but it would also ensure economic difficulties at other times, and the overall volatility of gold prices—which exceeds that of most commodities—ensured a highly unpredictable pay experience of workers. As it happens, the price of gold began to rise in the middle of the new millennium's new decade, but it varied month to month, and costs of production also grew as ores were depleted.

The extraordinary risks agreed to by the NUM were unthinkable ten years previously. Yet, risk was quickly generalized within a new epistemic orientation in post-Apartheid South Africa. It summoned strategies that increasingly invested in risk, rather than its management, or that at least paired risk management and risk investments in a manner analogous to the balancing of a portfolio with hedge funds. It is not coincidental that, in the same venue in which Hartwig presented his proposal for generating self-selection through voluntary HIV seropositivity testing, S. J. B. Peile and W. S. van der Merwe proposed that hedge funds should assume a greater role in the South African investment economy.[63] Hedge funds are typically uninsured and therefore risky investments, which cannot be marketed; they depend on individual consumers seeking them out. And unlike most other financial products, they often rely on short selling. Peile and van der Merwe describe short selling in succinct terms, which make clear what is at stake—namely, profit through loss. They write: "Short selling involves borrowing a security that you do not own, in order to sell the security in the open market with the objective of buying it back later at a price lower than it was sold for in order to return it to its original owner, whilst profiting from the fall in price. Conventional trading strategies focus on first buying low and then selling high. Short sellers merely reverse this order—first sell high, then buy low."[64] Despite being exposed in terms of liability, the Financial Services Board of South Africa refers to short selling as a means to reduce risk and volatility. This is because such funds try to minimize "down-side risk" and endorse a "cut your losses and let your profits run" strategy.[65]

Hedge funds are typically construed in terms of those who trade in them, and those who manage them. In cases in which short selling is involved, the question of risk and profit is premised on the loss of value elsewhere, and hence on the experience of other shareholders suffering losses. The entire schema of financialization works this way, not merely in terms of fictitious capital, as Rudolf Hilferding once noted, or through the production of relative values, but through the mobilization of loss, as the condition of possibility of gain. It is important to recognize this if we are to understand the question of sexual economy in the age of AIDS, which is also the era of so-called stabilization. Far too often, the deployment of finance capital's idioms—and especially that of risk management—occlude this bitter fact. In so doing, these gestures also occlude the degree to which surplus extraction under finance is connected to death, as well as the manner in which the fantasy of risk management is always also a fantasy of risk-taking—and that the latter must exceed the former.

More than twenty years into the new millennium, South Africa remains relatively afflicted by HIV/AIDS. Yet the subject of AIDS, in the sense of both topic and agent, has receded from the horizon of discourse. After 2020, of course, public health discourse was dominated entirely by the COVID-19 pandemic, and as with HIV/AIDS, a deficient health infrastructure and living conditions that made most preventive measures impracticable for large portions of the population impeded mitigation strategies (residential density prohibiting social distancing was accompanied by a lack of running water, as well as the absence of masks and personal protective equipment). Yet, and for reasons not yet fully understood, fatality rates appear to have been less catastrophic than might have been feared, given past experience with HIV/AIDS and prevalence rates of both HIV and drug-resistant forms of TB.

Before 2019, however, the discourse of the insurance industry, which is divided between life and nonlife insurance sectors, continued to emphasize expansion of its markets to include formerly disadvantaged and impoverished populations, treating access to insurance products and financial instruments as a key means of accessing civil rights in general. Among these new instruments were agricultural insurance and state-mandated third-party motor insurance.

In 2019, however, the issue looming largest above the industry's shifting policy was not HIV/AIDS but climate change. In fact, the 2019 Annual Review of the South African Insurance Association does not even mention HIV or AIDS.[66] If the early millennium was clotted with studies, programs, analyses, and conferences about HIV/AIDS in South Africa and elsewhere, the second decade saw a growing silence on the virus and associated disease. Partly, this was a function of the development of new medications, regimes of testing, and the gradual accommodation to prophylactic practices, such as the use of preexposure prophylaxis (PrEP) and postnatal nevirapine treatments. A generation learned to consider death in terms of deferral rather than imminence. This is, then, partly a success story.

But HIV/AIDS did not leave South Africa, and the consciousness cultivated in relation to its prevalence was too valuable or rather too value-generating to relinquish. There was still a rush to be found in every panic. A McKinsey report of 2020, already taking cognizance of the pandemic, was silent on HIV/AIDS but offered a wildly enthusiastic prognostication of market growth. In "Africa's Insurance Industry Is Ready for Take-off,"[67] McKinsey's authors noted that personal life insurance and pensions were the likely objects of most investment and interest in what it construed as a still-untapped potential reservoir of fantastical value—a veritable gold mine—in Africa. Before the pandemic, Africa's insurance markets were expected to grow at annual rates of more than twice their American and European counterparts—at about 7 percent per year. The African industry already accounts for $68 billion per year and quite remarkably, more than 70 percent of that comes from South Africa. Yet, it was less life insurance than funeral insurance that continued to sell in South Africa. Tellingly, in 2019, only 10 percent of South Africans had life insurance, whereas 53 percent had funeral cover, although this number dropped to 42 percent in 2021, after two years of pandemic, with its attendant job losses.[68]

It is not easy to assess the effects of the insurance industry's effort to redirect conceptions of life and death as sites of differential and differentiating investment, but the pattern that was established in the 1990s and early years of the new millenium—of rush, panic, rush—persists. Nonetheless, as HIV/AIDS receded into the background of public health discourses and assumed the status of a more manageable disease, the structuring of desire that educators had attempted to cultivate was also redirected. In retrospect, it seems clear that the desire in excess that capital requires constantly threatens to turn back on itself, and in times of epidemic or pandemic, under the conditions of extreme inequality (racial, sexual, and regional), this tendency is intensified. A similar surfeit afflicts the mining communities where the depletion of ores and the finitude of the deposits lead to closures, reduced work forces, and increased automation, as well as the conversion of mining operations from underground extraction to reclamation of the dumps. Here, the specter of finitude demands or is addressed in analogous postures, and with similar attitudes. More and more is the frenzy of reclamation overtaking that of extraction. The investment in waste and margins has become the object of newly fastidious calculation, just as the notion of securitizing the perimeters between formality and informality, between nation and ethnic or corporate community, between capital and new social forms beyond waged labor, has become a new conceptual and political task. Borders are being redrawn between large-scale corporate activities and the autonomous scavenging of the newly itinerant migrants as well as between the organized syndicates and transnational but still ethnicized gangs. Local governments and organized labor converge and diverge in support and opposition of these forces. Everything once past appears to live again. One can live, perhaps one always lives, in the ruins of what has gone before. But this does not mean that everything past is ruin, only that it persists in a form that bears the mark of time.

CHAPTER 16

MAGIC MOUNTAIN

Debt and the Ancestors

White people are white people
They must learn to listen
Black people are black people
They must learn to talk.

—Wally Mongane Serote, "Ofay-Watchers, Throbs-Phase"

I n 2024, national elections saw the African National Congress lose its majority control of the country's government. In Gauteng, the ANC had had a slender majority, of merely 50.19 percent following the 2019 elections. In 2024, that percentage had dropped to 34.76. In Merafong, which had been restored to the province following the Khutsong insurrection and electoral boycotts, the ANC had lost its majority of the popular vote in municipal elections in 2021, but it had retained 27 of the 55 available ward seats, most of the others going to the Democratic Alliance (DA, 9) and the Economic Freedom Fighters (EFF, 9). A far right white supremacist party, the *Vryheidsfront Plus* (Freedom Front Plus, or VF Plus), an ideological heir to the militant right wing movements discussed in chapter 13, came in fourth, obtaining just short of 7 percent of the vote, and securing four seats). A few other minority parties received a little more than one percent of the vote.[1] In 2024, Jacob Zuma's new populist Zulu party, uMkhonto weSizwe (MK, not to be confused with the older paramilitary wing of the ANC, of the same name), displaced the VF in

Merafong for fourth place, although the VF Plus fared better in Merafong than nationally, with 2.3 percent of the count.[2] The turn-out for the 2024 national elections in this municipality, this "place of mines," was exceptionally high, and unexpectedly so in light of the earlier disaffection, but the reason for voting in 2024 was parallel to the reasons for *not* voting eighteen years previously: to voice discontent and to communicate that discontent to the powers that be. "*Through our votes, we can tell the people on top what is happening. This makes us very powerful,*" said one voter when interviewed by the *Carletonville Herald*. Another explained, "*It is very important to vote as it is the only way you can show you are not happy. Your vote is your voice.*"[3]

Above all, the protests against redemarcation in Merafong and especially Khutsong were against the exclusion (coded in the metaphors of displacement) of those who believed that their labor in and around the gold mines had been at the center of nation formation, and that, for this reason, they had a right to access power in the new era. This was not a right a priori; it was grounded in the historical consciousness of labor's share in the creation of that fantastical surfeit that the zama zama Mwanga would later describe in the idiom of beds of cash (on which the rich sleep). This claim was made by those who had never entered a gold mine, at a time when the gold industry was contributing a relatively small share of the nation's gross domestic product (GDP). Being in the place of gold (the very name of the municipality) was to be an heir to its histories and its production. The fruits of such labor were in this sense to be socialized—and this was the form in which people intuited that the organization of the social field was the condition of possibility of the industry's success, even if that meant that most people had no contact with the mines and did not receive wages from them. The dissident representatives of Khutsong refused to accept the notion that only employees could be producers of value. And, accordingly, every act of exclusion, every refusal to attend the calls of local residents, was for them an experience of subalternization and of inclusion in the form of exclusion. This is what Benjamin meant when de described capitalism as a cultic religion; it requires no particular faith, for one is subject to its force and logic whether one is employed or not.[4] Recognizing this, and their position as the included excluded, the disenfranchised people of Merafong were concerned to at least have a voice. They lived and expressed the contradiction that Gillian Hart has described between a politics of democratic nationalism and an economic policy of "denationalizing" finance capitalism.[5] This is why, beyond the question of jobs and service delivery, so much of their discourse was concerned with the fact that they were not being consulted, not being listened to, not being heard. The same themes would continue to reverberate as the shape of labor organizing in the goldfields began to change, in the second decade of the new millennium. But this time, accusations would be extended from the corporations to the labor aristocracy, and then to the forebears of the dispossessed, who would increasingly be indicted for not having opposed the old regime with sufficient force. In the shadow of "The Struggle," then, there emerged the specter of acquiescence and complicity, of a shameful need rather than an affirmative desire.

This was the milieu in which, on the eve of the twentieth anniversary of South Africa's democratic transition, I returned to Merafong and visited the same HIV/AIDS nongovernmental organization from which I had been led so carefully by Yodwa Mzaidume through the labyrinths of protest—against redemarcation and those earlier insurrections she recalled from her own days as a student. It was winter; the light was severe and low, and the iron bars threw carceral shadows on the walls. The heat, such as it was, emanated from portable electric heaters. Lace curtains covered the windows, and a second door made of latticed ironwork provided security. A new keypad, with its faint glow, announced a distant electronic sentry. The time of hopeful resistance to fortification and electric fences had passed. But the twin aspirations for transformation through education and economic restructuring had not disappeared. Indeed, they had acquired a new sense of urgency, tinged with fear. This urgency was intensified in 2012 by the bloody events of Marikana and the reconfiguration of the union movement in the gold and platinum sectors, where the struggle for that transformative power that we have been tracing throughout this book, took on yet another dimension.

The events at Lonmin's platinum mine in Marikana were transformed into a national spectacle because of the ways in which they were relayed through mass and social media, including cellphone technologies. As the first major police action against striking and protesting civilians in the post-Apartheid era (thirty-four miners were shot and killed in front of news cameras, after ten had been killed by security forces of the mines and union), Marikana quickly became symbolic of the new alliance of state and capital, and the events shook the foundational claim of the African National Congress (ANC) of having created a new and different kind of state. Moreover, Marikana became representative of a political crisis "located" in the minerals sector because the striking protestors staged the problem that we have seen so repeatedly through the history of the gold-made world, namely the pursuit of full political subjectivity as the assumption of a voice capable of making things happen.

On that cool winter day, I overheard a conversation between two isiXhosa speaking women. The women were speaking about the then-sitting president Jacob Zuma (still a member of the ANC), who, at the time, was the subject of official corruption inquiries for his use of government funds to build a highway to his private estate, a multihome, highly securitized compound called Nkandla. Both of the women were veterans of the anti-Apartheid movement. But both had become disaffected with the ANC, and especially by the privileging of *Umkonto we Sizwe* (MK, the ANC paramilitary organization rather than

Zuma's party) veterans in government employment and black capital formation schemes.[6] But on that day, seated at a large conference table in an otherwise modest room, the walls of which were unadorned by anything but posted work schedules, they were not talking about corruption, or unfair employment practices, or the self-aggrandizement and enrichment of former militants. They were talking about Jacob Zuma's English.

Against what they deemed to be Zuma's execrable pronunciation, they lauded Barack Obama's rhetorical grace. Not Mandela's, note, but Obama's. Mandela's authority exceeded his famed rhetorical prowess. For these women, his charisma emanated from his identification with a righteous struggle, with his survival of Apartheid, with his being more than himself; it would be improper to explain his authority through recourse only to his oratory, and hence to his own skills. To the extent that he spoke for South Africans, Mandela did so in their voice, lending his tongue and his performance of moral fortitude. But it was his life more than his speech that grounded his authority. The contrast with Obama allowed the women to both include me in the terms of the conversation and to emphasize that it was Zuma's oddly accented pronunciation of English, a stand in for his "illiteracy" that not only irked them but that symptomatized his political failure, his incapacity to be one with the people. In veritable unison, they mimicked his most recent address to the nation, landing on the word *development*, and breaking into derisive laughter. This was not because development was being realized in its breach more than its application in a country with the highest Gini coefficient in the world, nor because the idea of the developmental state had been evacuated or, worse, become an alibi for neoliberal economic policy (though this had happened). Their most urgent criticism was not directed at the signification of his discourse, but at the signifier. It was the wrong distribution of emphasis, the heavy first syllable, rather than the accented second syllable that elicited their contempt and distilled the essence of his failure: Dev' *el op ment*. They brought themselves to tears of intimate hilarity in this mime of Zuma's improper troche, treating the missing iamb as though it contained the secret of Zuma's intellectual and political incapacity.

The jokes about Zuma's ostensibly poor English would be insignificant if it weren't for the fact that speech and violence were constantly being linked and opposed in the conversations being woven in that lace-curtained room—just as they had been in the conflicts of the 1980s. As cellphones buzzed and one or another of the women withdrew from conversation to respond to a distant call, the women's talk shifted from Zuma to a violent assault experienced by a program director. As she recounted her harrowing tale, a young man, also sitting at the table with us, was typing in a stuttering fashion on a laptop. I recognized him as someone whom I had met and interviewed years earlier, in an informal settlement near the mines where he both lived and worked as a peer educator among sex workers. At the time, he had told me of three elderly women who had been killed after he accused them of witchcraft. In the face of my horror and incredulity, he had claimed that the accusation had not demanded the women's execution by a mob and that he was innocent of their deaths, if guilty of the accusation. He did not claim any authority nor grant to his own words the force to make something happen. Instead, he narrated his flight from the police prosecuting this crime, and described how, while hiding in the informal settlement near the mine that would become his temporary home, he had himself been attacked by his neighbors who suspected him of sexual impropriety. A deep scar across his face testified to the accusation and the retributive injury.

On this day, so many years later, he would tell me that he had left the settlement, not because he had earned the means to do so, but because he feared conflict with the new pirates of a deindustrializing mining economy, the zama zamas who had recently staked their claim on his broken shack community. I had not yet met anyone of these new "criminals," as he described them, had not come to know their struggles or their inheritances of the migratory imaginations bequeathed by the mineworkers of an earlier era. I had not yet accompanied Mwanga to the schools where he was seeking admission for his daughter and where he would judge the teachers on the basis of their English pronunciation, just as these Xhosa women were judging Zuma. I simply listened to this scarred young man deride them because "they cannot even sign their own name." In his imagination, zama zamas, as uneducated, are ineligible for a public sphere that depends on literacy. For, without literacy they cannot submit to the law. The essence of their criminality was, for him, this illiteracy. Once again, the stereotype has little to do with reality—for although I have met unschooled young men who work as zama zamas, I have also met college students trying to earn money to pay off school fees through illicit gold mining.

In this and countless other conversations about zama zamas, reproduced and circulated in the public sphere, they are described as men for whom language provides no alternative to violence. They speak only to threaten. They thus abuse language by treating it as a weapon. For the most part, the two women spoke without regard to this protégé of the program, although his eyelashes betrayed his continued if distracted interest in our conversation. The women nonetheless paused when he described the zama zamas' putative illiteracy, shaking their head in agreement with his condemnation of the men who ostensibly cannot sign their own names. A signature, after all, would be a form of writing recognizable across all of South Africa's languages, and in some ways, it represented the condition of possibility of recognition from within its constitutional order.

Language As and Beyond Mediation

It is a truism of all materialist analysis of language that dialect bears the evidence of social history: of class position, regional origin, gendered identification, ethnic or national affiliation, education, and professional training.[7] The ridicule heaped on Zuma by these two educated women was partly a derogation of those who lack education, partly a Xhosa bias against Zulu-ness, partly a repudiation of the antiquated (if constantly self-renewing) form of patriarchy that Zuma incarnates, and partly a deep resentment that they were not the recipients of opportunities they felt they deserve. But it also pointed to other issues.

For the women, Zuma's speech represented a political failure precisely because it had become so visible, audible, and obstructive. His efforts at communication failed, and in this context, there was all manner of illegality, corruption, and violence. If the political sphere was functioning as it should, then he would be a great communicator; mediation would occur but only by virtue of its self-effacement. Now, this ideal of political speech is different from immediacy, which would describe the aspiration of properly performative or magical speech, and which would be associated with the politics of the commandment and thus sovereignty rather than representationalism. Performative speech is not always of this type, however. It is known in the form of witchcraft and prophecy to these devout Christian religious women and to the young man, who had feared the powers of the old women enough to call for their expulsion. The self-effacing mediation of ideal political speech in a representational order is that in which there appears to be an identity between the saying and the said, but not a causal relation. We can call this the truth effect of such speech, but colloquially, it is simply the perceived sincerity or honesty of that speech. In Zuma's case, an audibly marked pronunciation inserted a division between the saying and the said, the medium and the message of communication. And this opened his speech to suspicion. But such suspicion about a possible gap between the saying and the said is everywhere to be seen in South Africa. It is associated with the experience of deferral and delay, and the perception of mendacity. Perhaps only in the realm of humor—the fabular cross-lingual play that is so characteristic of South African discourse—is the ambiguity of the signifier treated as a value and made the basis of playful or combative jouissance.

Otherwise, across a vast and heterogeneous field, and running alongside or directly counter to the efforts to shore up a public sphere based in ideals of representationalism (of truthfulness and pacific self-effacement), one sees tactics that aim to bypass former structures for the representation of interests, and to access or deploy power immediately—without delay, without the risk of dissemination or dispersion. In this context, one cannot help noticing that a remarkable uniformity can be heard in the slogans and ossifications of the discourse purveyed by the same protesting aspirants to power. On the one hand, the fantasy of immediacy manifests itself in messianic movements and direct-action politics and in various kinds of violence. On the other, as though to short-circuit its essential characteristics, there is language hollowed out of ambiguity, pried away from subjectivity, and reduced to the most instrumental dimension. As we saw in chapter 14, slogans and phrases from obsolescent ideological programs often seem to possess communities of protestors. They need not even be spoken, but they are often worn in the form of mass-produced placards. Whether vocalized or only visualized, these reified linguistic forms are both instantaneously recognizable and oddly awkward, making the most ardent professions of belief seem unbelievable, and bathing testimonies to the personal experience of oppression in an acid bath of suspicion. Because they are simultaneously both so overly full and so empty of meaning, these slogans (congealed word-things) can move from site to site, discourse to discourse—gathering force and reinflecting attachment as they go. One can see this in the case of the slogan "we want the money," a slogan of long-standing provenance in strikes, the term *mali* or *imali*, meaning value and valuables, money or cash, and also gold. It was the clarion call of strikers at Marikana and was repurposed by the (EFF) when they demanded in Parliament that Zuma repay the hundreds of millions of rand that had been used to renovate and pave the highway to his private residence. It has also become a tacit slogan of the new capitalist classes formed under the auspices of Black Economic Empowerment (BEE). But at Marikana, the slogan became something more than words on a placard. The awkwardly inscribed "voice" of the strikers was transformed into a "cry," even a battle cry, in the sense that that term has acquired over many decades in the phrases "Yakhal'Inkhomo," "Jolinkomo," and "Jol'Iinkomo"—expressions that refer at once to the bovine cry in the moment of sacrifice, the suffering of black subjects under colonialism and Apartheid, and militant opposition to it.[8] It has spawned volumes of poetry (Wally Serote and Mafika Gwala, and—somewhat more critically—Lesego Rampolokeng), songs (Miriam Makeba, Winston Mankunku Ngozi, and Fela Kuti), and paintings (Ayanda Mabulu). But before we consider them, we need to recall the event of Marikana.

An Unoriginal Slogan

On August 16, 2012, police and armed security forces of the Lonmin platinum mine opened fire on striking mineworkers at Marikana, killing thirty-four of them. The killings followed on weeks of strikes, deemed illegal because they were off schedule, and were followed by mass protests, and further strikes, as well as additional violence leading to numerous deaths among the mine workforce, the management's security personnel, the ANC, and the two unions representing miners—namely, the National Union of Mineworkers (NUM), formed in 1982, and the younger Association of Mineworkers and Construction Union (AMCU), formed in 2001. The years since then have seen the displacement of NUM by AMCU as the dominant organ of mineworking labor on most of the mines in the platinum and gold-mining sectors. The EFF, an increasingly powerful political party led by former African National Congress Youth League (ANCYL) firebrand, Julius Malema, emerged against the backdrop of Marikana and quickly joined those proffering a public critique of corruption in the previously dominant unions and the governing political party. During parliamentary inquiries into Zuma's Nkandla financing, Malema and the EFF recited the slogan of the strikers, "we want the money," which implied that he and the ANC, including the current president and former NUM leader, Cyril Ramaphosa, were partly to blame for the murderousness at Lonmin's "mountain."

At least three major documentary films and several extended televisual reports, numerous books, scholarly and journalistic articles, and even a musical (*Marikana, the Musical*) have been produced with Marikana as its subject matter. A Commission of Inquiry established on August 23, 2012, deliberated for nearly three years before issuing its report on March 31, 2015, having amassed thousands of pages of testimony and documentation. Its conclusions exempted top political officials from culpability but found fault with Lonmin's management as well as with the police at all levels; it also impugned the leadership of both the NUM and AMCU and called for an investigation into the actions of individuals in each of these organizations.[9]

The conditions in the mines that led to the strikes and the violent effort to suppress them are widely recognized: low wages and a bonus system encouraging risky overtime work, the labor brokerage system, a lack of linkage between cost of living and wage increases, appalling living conditions, resentment of the labor aristocracy in the NUM and its use of bureaucratic proceduralism to protect privilege, ethnic tension, the perception of exorbitant profit rates in the platinum sector, and usurious informal lending practices that indebt workers. But two elements in particular bear recalling: (1) the place of debt in the shaping of the striking mineworkers' grievances, and (2) the identification of the most vulnerable and poorly recompensed mineworkers with illiteracy. We should not be surprised that these attributes—indebtedness and illiteracy—have been braided together.

Gavin Hartford has argued that a main "driver" of this crisis was a new kind and intensity of indebtedness, in which the union (NUM) as well as the mining companies are the demanding creditors, and in which indebtedness is not simply a function of low wages but also of the mining companies' transformation of the wage gap into a source of rent.[10] This is possible, argues Harford, because of the continued importance if not centrality of the migrant labor system, abetted by "living out" allowances (rather than the closure of hostels) that have encouraged migrant laborers to maintain two households, one in the shack-lands where they reside (often beyond the *skomplaases*, see chapter 10) and one in the labor-sending community. According to Hartford, this pattern has been associated with the renewed splitting of familial solidarities. In making this analysis, he assumes, somewhat anachronistically, the prior integrity of black households in the peripheral provinces (a postulation that has not been sustainable at least since the 1970s). By contrast, Keith Breckenridge notes that, despite the attachments of migrant laborers to the still-bucolic image of a resid-ual "commons" in Pondolond and other labor-sending areas, the fantasy of an intact, not-yet-alienated world in such places is extremely distorted.[11] We have already discussed the complexities of the rural—its artificially reified status, buttressed by legislative mandates, and its imbrication with sharecropping and other forms of dependency. Deborah James has further noted how the with-drawal of formal credit to black householders under Apartheid led to borrowing from both relations and informal lenders and that the disparity between the provision of credit to new consumer groups and generalized expectations of access to debt precipitated extreme forms of both borrowing (informal lending in South Africa often entails interest rates of 1 percent per day) and intensi-fied inequality.[12] What needs to be added to these observations is the role of "stabilization" and its post-Apartheid iterations in multiplying obligation and doubling the figure of the one household—key drivers of the desperation of so many of the lower-ranked and lesser-paid workers. I emphasize that the dream of the one (the mime and legacy of the gold standard) was doubled by stabili-zation rather than split; in each locus, the fantasy of patriarchal command over a coherent reproductive unit was given form and substance. But we should also emphasize that this was indeed a dream image. As we saw with Akhona, com-plex strategies are employed to negotiate doubled and regionally distributed households. Sometimes, they take the form of triadic solidarity rather than counterposed dyads.

Nonetheless, Hartford rightly emphasizes the intensifying indebtedness of migrant laborers, who are often able to sustain two households and two spouses only through borrowing. And this doubled and dispersed topogra-phy of migrant domesticity is nonetheless also a single terrain—migrant men cannot be in two places at once. Hence, the strange sense that they are both overrepresented in the public imagination and in the social scientific literature, and absent too, as both subjects in the debate about what mineworkers want and in the households where their alternatively spectral and corporeally dense occupation is felt by the women who depend on them—women like Akhona and Sisipho—most acutely in their absence.

Hartford notes that education in the labor-sending regions is frequently dys-functional or nonexistent; hence, the general fact of alphabetic illiteracy among the rock-drill operators (RDOs), which entails both their exclusion from

16.1 *Tina Funa Lo Mali*, striking workers at Marikana, August 2012.

Photo by Greg Marinovich.

upward mobility and their dependency on (increasingly remote) representatives who, because they are literate, can negotiate the bureaucratic labyrinth of contracts and labor-management relations. This latter is said to be the source of their dependency on and resentment toward union structures.[13] Again, it is a question of education and of how people might communicate their desires in such a fashion as to become legible, audible, and deserving of response. This is not a question of merely alphabetic literacy—although such literacy (or lack thereof) did become a key signifier of the broader problems confronting the mineworkers during and after the strike.

Then, widely circulated images of striking miners, bearing knobkerries and placards, circulated in the mass media. Unlike the neatly printed, mass-produced posters with English-language slogans carried by women and others opposing the police violence that followed the strikes and that were also disseminated by international labor and human rights organizations, the placards borne by the striking men were often written in rough script and in the mine pidgin, Fanakalo. These placards were blunt and explicit: "*Tina funa lo mali* [We want the money]: 12,500 Rand" (figure 16.1).

It is not surprising that the clumsiness and illegibility of the script on the latter placard drew attention beyond the miners' ostensibly intended signification, namely their demand for a subsantial increase in the monthly recompense for RDOs. This crude script was widely read as proof of the RDOs' uneducated status, which was at the same time a partial explanation for both their pursuit of work in the mines and their vulnerability to predatory lenders. But other questions—concerning the nature and form of address, and the aspiration to political subjectivity understood as the acquisition of a voice—arise here as well. The ridicule of Zuma's accented speech has prepared us to recognize how the awkward trace of an unstable claim to literacy reveals itself and thereby introduces resistance into the communicative process. In this context, a number of questions arise: Who speaks? Or, even "what speaks"? And to whom?

The women who bore placards printed by the Marikana Support Campaign were addressing anyone in an internationalized media sphere of anonymous potential readers. Their signs took the form of an imperative and a double negative: "DO NOT LET THE POLICE GET AWAY WITH MURDER." The language on the men's placard was addressed to those within the mining sphere, and especially mine management.[14] The women's placard was addressed to an open-ended you. The striking men's use of a first-person plural pronoun emphasized the collective being of the mineworkers. So minimal and unambiguous was its message that it bordered on telegraphic code. And, yet, the code dissipates at the perimeter of the language's functionality. To be sure, it wants to be read from afar, but the circumference of the sphere being addressed is narrow, local. It is the sphere of Fanakalo.

With their placards and their slogans, both the men and the women were attempting to enter a public sphere and to actualize their right to "have a voice." The placards were indeed the graphic form of a chant, itself the vocalization of a slogan. The fact that anyone can speak such phrases without losing their recognizability also enables their resignification and redeployment.[15] When the EFF took up the slogan "We want the money" in Parliament, it was no longer spoken in Fanakalo as *tina funa lo mali*. In chanting its translated form, however, the EFF partook of the mineworkers' moral authority and that of all the strikers who had chanted these words before. Inserting their speech into the chain of iterations and themselves into the place of an always receding origin, they produced (or attempted to produce) the appearance of identity with the mineworkers. In so doing, they also restored the mineworkers to the metonymic function of representative workers—even as they claimed to be the necessary representatives of those workers, whose voices, they implied, would not otherwise be heard. Whether or not they supported the EFF, many of the mineworkers seemed to agree.

An Other Call

The striking mineworkers of Lonmin did not get their money. Those whose testimonies are recorded in the volume *Marikana: A View from the Mountain and a Case to Answer* repeatedly asserted that "we only wanted to talk"

(Mineworker 1) and that they could not understand why "the management did not want to talk to the drill operators. . . . The management refused to talk to them" (Mineworker 3, 96).[16] When they had gathered on the mountain, awaiting news of a possible address from Lonmin, a miner by the name of Tholakele Bhele Dunga explained the refusal of NUM to address the workers as a response to this very aspiration for direct address: "A word came that our claims should not [have] been taken into consideration because we went behind our lawyer's back to come and address our employer ourselves" (67). Then he relayed to those who already knew the story, that they had decided not to "pitch for work until our cries were heard" (67).

Other strike leaders expressed their outrage at the white management's refusal to talk face to face, but to address the workers, instead, from inside a police vehicle: "The white man refused to come and speak to them directly" (69). Even NUM President Zenzile Zokwana was derided for remaining in the armored vehicle and stating that he "did not come here to address us," as one worker put it (70). Mineworker 1 said that "Zokwana was not in a right place to talk to us as a leader, this thing of him talking to us while he is in a Hippo [armored car]" (84). He was careful to distinguish the speech attributed to Zokwana and which had been overheard only via the radio from that which they had heard from him directly (95). Other miners similarly reviled the use of the loudspeaker from the Hippo (99).

Every mediation of the relation between mineworkers and their addressees appeared as an interruption and a blockage of the relation that was being sought. As with the discourse of the young radical described in chapter 14, this relation might appear to resemble that ideal (and indeed fictive) reciprocity imagined by Marx in the "Working Day" chapter of *Capital*, wherein the voice of the worker arises to confront the capitalist and demand the "modest magna carta" of a reasonable working day.[17] But such a resemblance would be false. The aim was not reciprocity but rather the transformation of the addressee, the effecting of that desire expressed in the mineworkers' speech. This speaking was to be confined neither to expressivity (the exteriorizing of an inner state) nor to representation (the doubling of that inner state). It strove toward performativity. Unable to ground its force in a shared belief that would traverse racial and institutional hierarchies, however, the mineworkers summoned another ear and another hearing, to give to their words the force that would then be mimed in the deployment of sticks as, alternatively, musical instruments and weapons.

Speaking out, if it is to be heard, requires one of three conditions. Either everyone speaks separately and is thus heard in the particularity of their utterance, or everyone speaks in unison and is heard in the unanimity of their discourse. Both of these forms of speaking occurred at Marikana. The placards exemplified the latter type of speaking. The careful orchestration of sequential speaking that embodies the first took place at the mountain, as one after another mineworker stood to address his comrades. But there is also a kind of speech in which the unanimity of the group can be given its token, it representative vehicle, its substitution, and its medium. In this regard, there is always the possibility that the representation opens a space for doubt about the coherence of the group in whose name this speech is uttered. Such speech also took place in the initial confrontation between strike and union officials, when the five "madoda" or spokespeople were chosen to address the police and union officials. Initially, the mineworkers rejected the demand for such spokespeople, asserting that "we do not have representatives," but they were nonetheless told to "pick five men who will come to speak to [the police]" (92).

The contributors to *Marikana: A View from the Mountain and a Case to Answer*, indulge their own messianic fantasy of a transparent representationalism when they say that the five madoda "are the voices of the masses behind them" (2). In fact, as one mineworker put it, madoda was the name given to the men by the police, men whose selection was entirely determined by the demand for spokespeople: "You see, my brother, the five madoda, the word used by the police, they said they wanted the five madoda, that is the language they used. And that is the language we use in the mines, but they were using police cars, so that name five madoda was given to us by the police. . . . They wanted to speak to only five people, they did not want to speak to all of us" (104).

Unison took two forms at Marikana. In the first, it took the form of song. The workers narrated their experience at Marikana as an occasion at which they were constantly singing—to give themselves courage, to express their anger, and to inhabit the sensation of the one. A female mineworker somehow distills the essential difference between song and the individuated utterance summoned by the police, when she gives her own account of the election of the madoda: "We do not all speak at once, . . . but we do all sing at once. So, we . . . they" —she equivocates—"decided that there [would] be people elected to go, to go and talk" (130). She insists that the election was unrelated to status or wealth but that the madoda were chosen for their speaking abilities. Back on the *koppie* (mountain), there was singing.

This singing is extremely significant. I understand it to be a form in which speech reverts to chant, and where weapons, in turn, revert to communicational devices in the form of drumming sticks. When I say revert, I mean to imply the impossibility of any priority of war over communication. Nonetheless, the reading of singing as either "war chant" and "encouragement" of militarism or as expressive cultural practice congeals the entire problematic of Marikana as a problem of signification and as a crisis of representation. The mineworkers sang war chants, to be sure: *makuliwe* in isiXhosa is a chant meaning "let there be a fight." At the same time, mineworkers repeatedly asserted the linkage between singing and *not* fighting—as though they, too, could be doing the pata pata. Mineworker 10 explained: "We were singing and no one was holding any weapon" (24). Mineworker 8 claimed, "We were singing, talking and sharing ideas, and encouraging each other" (27). Indeed, when asked whether the sticks and spears were themselves not weapons announcing and inciting violence, one mineworker explained as follows: "The spears and sticks [is] what we came with from back home. It is our culture, as black men, as Xhosa men, as I am Xhosa . . . even back home we have our spears and stocks. Even here, like when I wake up in the morning or I wake up at night . . . going to look at the cows, when I go look at anything I always have my spear or stick . . . or here at night or when I have to go urinate . . . I never go out without it" (88). And again, "many workers here . . . when they march or sing they carry, what do they call these things, the sticks like the spears and so on" (88).

It may seem odd to hear a mineworker speaking about taking a spear out at night when going to look at cows, but bovines can indeed be seen crossing the highways in the lull between timber-bearing trucks or shift buses at night and dawn, with the mine dumps in the distance. They wander in dispersed herds, tended by men clad in blankets who also carry knobkerries and spears. The isiXhosa-speaking man who defends his carrying of objects, which might be either weapons or musical instruments, depending on circumstance, comes from Pondoland, in the Eastern Cape. Consciously or unconsciously, he is also citing the lengthy tradition of offering cultural stereotypes to the journalist or white liberal as cover for more radical insurrectionary projects. And often enough, these Trojan Horses come in the form of song, and especially that kind of song that vacillates on the threshold between lamentation and war anthem.

Miriam Makeba, whose song "Jolinkomo" appeared on the album *Pata Pata*, used to introduce the song with what Brendon Nicholls calls a touristic framing, intended for a Hollywood-consuming audience (recall that cinema but not television was available to South Africans of all races before 1976). In her English-language explanation of the song, young maidens sing praises to the "braves" departing for war, and the audience is assumed to be dreaming of Westerns—the kind that were parodied in *A Man Called Sledge* (see chapter 11). The opening phrase of her song refers to the bellow of the cow or bull whose sacrifice summons the ancestors, but it could also be translated as a dedication or praise. In Brendon Nicholls's analysis, Makeba's transformation of a song more typically sung with a chorus borrowed Apartheid's ethnic clichés to encourage political opposition and even violence against the regime (*Jolinkomo* was recorded in 1967, after Sharpeville and the Rivonia Trial, but before Soweto). In so doing, it summoned listeners into the role of participants in both song and struggle.[18] Over the years, the concept of the bull's bellow (or what Fela Kuti referred to in the title of his own song as the "Black Man's Cry") has had many iterations, including Mankunku's wordless jazz elegy for John Coltrane, and Wally Serote's verse collection, both under the title *Yakhal'Inkhomo* (1968). In fact, Serote's poem references Mankunku's saxophone in its prosaic preface, in which he explains that it was Dumile Fene (the modernist artist) who inspired the poem with a description of the sorrow of the cattle in the slaughterhouse who are bereft upon seeing their animal brethren fall. The cattle, writes Serote, "raged and fought, they became a terror to themselves; the twisted poles of the kraal rattled and shook. The cattle saw blood flow into the ground." Invoking this framing scene in Serote's volume, and the doubled reference to both music and sculpture, David Attwell has referred to Serote's "yakhal'inkomo" as a "sound-image," and reads it within a Romantic and modernist aesthetic tradition.[19] In the context of Marikana, sound-image remains a relevant descriptor of the placard as a slogan-becoming-cry, albeit one now stripped of its modernist ambitions and absorbed into the teletechnological relay of the mass media. Many iterations of this "cry" have been written into the poetry and music of South African protests over the years, across media and genre forms. We have already encountered Mafika Gwala's later "Gumba, Gumba, Gumba," which, not incidentally, was first published in a volume also titled *Jolinkomo*. All are part of a complex circuitry by which political language is given additional force by being transformed into song at the point at which it either reverts to or lifts off toward—in any case is infused by the qualities of—a cry. We can understand this cry as song seeking transcendence, as speech desperate for recognition.

It is in this vein that the chanting of slogans verged on singing at Marikana as at every political protest in which a mass of people gives themselves to be seen and heard in their massness. The standardization of placards is the visual analog of the sung lyric. As with song, there is in the slogan a speaking without subjectivity, or at least a speaking that exceeds individual subjectivity. With the slogan, however, those who bear the placard or chant its percussive words, abandon their bodies to a discourse that comes from elsewhere and leaves them behind. With the slogan (more than with any song), there is also a reduction of this speaking to a language that disavows dissemination. It is language aspiring to unidirectional, univocal movement. It seeks the most direct route, endeavoring to minimize semantic loss and to reach its target uninhibited in force or meaning. Somewhere on the other side of speech, however, there is the cry that might be heard by the ancestors, a cry that would be recognizable by those to whom it is addressed even in the moment of the wailer's sacrificial expiry.

Song, Slogan, and Sublimity

A few days after my encounter at the HIV/AIDS office, I met up with the new leadership of the AMCU in their new offices on Palladium Street. The regional secretary was a young man with a mellifluous voice who spoke slowly in educated English, although it was not his native language. He was accompanied by the union's regional chair, an older man with a coal-colored complexion who insisted that the "protocol" of our meeting required me to place his name before that of his secretary in all notations and references, although the latter would be doing the talking. AMCU's rise to power in Merafong came quickly and without much forewarning. Barely six weeks after the massacre at Marikana, workers on AngloGold Ashanti's mines staged a month-long strike, organized largely against the advice of their NUM representatives, and shortly thereafter, the mineworkers migrated en masse to the upstart union, which had been formally instituted barely a decade earlier. Within six months, virtually every shaft had transferred its allegiance to AMCU, which was consequently recognized with official bargaining status by the Chamber of Mines and the mining companies. Fifteen years into fieldwork in this area, I was shocked by the rapidity of the conversion, and I sought out the new union's representatives for an account of how and why they had been able to displace what had been, for so long, the heroized organ of mineworking labor.

A few doors from Wimpy's, the diner where I had met the former mayor in our last encounter and where much political wheeling and dealing took place, the new office was still without much furniture, and what furniture there was seemed to be too large for the rooms. We sat pushed against the walls, separated by an enormous conference table in a room with humming florescent lights, as office staff paced by the door and peered in. After the initial instruction in protocols, about which we all laughed a little, I asked the secretary to explain what had happened. He commenced with a verily Spartican parable: "For a long time workers have been feeling that they have no power . . . not only in terms of wages or money or salary but in terms of their dignity." There is no way I could understand this he said, if I had not been underground, and when I affirmed that I had indeed been down, he continued, now more hastily, in a crescendo of moral indignation:

> Yeah, it's another world. It's a kind of system in which people are being seen as slaves. Their dignity is reduced drastically. Ah, their safety . . . in terms of money . . . it led to desperation. It led to some deep desperation . . . a human being will work close to 12 hours a day underground without seeing the sun, . . . so that he can meet his monthly needs. . . . The current union at that time, which was the NUM, was becoming distant from the mandate of the workers, in terms of daily issues. Workers did not see—I personally did not see NUM, even though I was a member—I personally did not see NUM as a party that can represent me.[20] Ah, in my daily disputes made with management, I wouldn't go to NUM because I knew very well that I'm not going to get assistance. The mass meetings' mandates were not implemented, leaders started to see workers as stepping stones to getting to higher positions in [the] municipality, in [the] parliament. . . . When you do not listen to your constituency, the very same people that put you there . . . you're looking [at an] erupting volcano if I can put

it in that manner. After, after . . . in 2012, as you know, after thirty-four of the workers were killed, I think that was the last straw . . . where workers decided that we are not going to sit back and watch while our brothers are being murdered like it is still Apartheid.

Passionate and forceful, the secretary's accelerating narrative, moving from working conditions to the fact of state and corporate violence against workers, made clear the rationale for change and for the displacement of the NUM. But the massacre was not the origin of the radicalization; it is only that which brings to fruition and visibility what was already in process, namely a failure of representation: "We elected a government democratically and they slaughter the very same people who put them in the parliament. They slaughter the very same people who put them in power. Most of the people in government come from the NUM; they were elected by the very same workers, so it was quite a shock, that they could be slain, the very same workers could be slain like that. Before the uprising in 2012, the workers started joining AMCU, even before the Marikana Massacre, they were joining AMCU drastically, in many numbers."

Later, the secretary would speak of the ways in which labor disputes were recoded as disciplinary hearings, by virtue of management's contestation of worker grievances. In these proceedings, he argued, a combination of the history of racism and the drive for institutional power (and the salaries associated with it) on the part of the NUM representatives materialized itself in the demand that workers confess to supervisors' charges against them so that management might be lenient in its penalties. The mitigation of penalties then constituted a victory in NUM's representations, despite the fact that it was a betrayal of workers' real needs and interests. The pseudo-juridical form of these hearings bears discussion—but not here. What must be noted is the progression from a failure of representation at the level of the elected officials to an overt enactment of coercion in the place of representation by those officials and against those who are the origin of their power. Already, it is clear that the representative function has been confused with a governing function, and speaking has been confused with the exercise of power. But in an institution that construes itself as a more adequate representational vehicle, beneath signs with the slogan, "AMCU will make the difference," there was also an aspiration to something beyond this representation, a power that would, in fact, exceed all representationalism.

When I first asked the secretary for a history of AMCU, he initially surprised me with a fabular gesture, one that continues to haunt me with its resonant pairing of song and slogan, and one that I have taken seriously in these efforts at theorization. Without preamble or preface, he said, "There's a song, professor, which basically states that—it's a Xhosa song, a slogan—it states that AMCU found us in the bushes while we were lost, you see, and it took us to the promised land." His voice trailed off. And then he commenced his history, which I have already quoted: "for a long time workers have been feeling that they have no power."

Did the biblical metaphor, uttered in this strangely insular office, five kilometers from the mines, imply an identification on the part of the mineworkers with the foundling prince and the Mosaic legend? Did it imply that the surviving minerworkers had been spared a massacre precisely to establish a moral order on an analogy with Moses, who, among all the infants of his generation, had been saved by being hidden in the reeds? Would it entail their own exclusion at the threshold of liberation? And who or what would be AMCU's Joshua? In this social space, where, as we have seen, biblical narrative circulates as common sense, and where Zionism names the largest denomination of African Christianity, readings are at once on the surface and at the same time unconscious, mythopoetic structures. Few mineworkers profess overt religiosity, and yet, the messianism of this fable suffuses the post-Marikana political sphere, not only in the rhetoric of the mountain, which binds Marikana and other locations (the secretary says "we have our own Marikana") with the prophetic traditions of the Eastern Cape and KwaZulu-Natal, but also in the understanding of the strike as an ecstatic experience of collectivity and self-presencing rather than self-representation.

"And was Jerusalem builded here . . . among these dark Satanic Mills?" I wondered, the Blakeian lyric flitting across my mind as I asked the secretary to recommend the names of mineworkers he thought could help me understand their experience.[21] Soon thereafter, I met with a shop steward in an empty parking lot of AngloGold Ashanti's properties. We talked in the shadowed back seat of my car, as the sun set on the tailings dumps. This was to avoid the "eyes," which, my interlocutor told me, were always looking, always seeking him out. Later, he would tell me to "Google" him, but this belated indulgence of the desire for celebrity disclosed itself only after several days of theatrical secrecy and cellphone-organized appointments, most of them missed. After the fact, the elaborate tales and gestures of clandestinity appeared to have been a technique of the shop steward's power, but this does not mean, at the same time, that there was not surveillance. For, as a labor activist at a time of volatile and violent competition among unions, he had established himself as a magnetic force on the mountain, which he too referred to as "our Marikana," although Carletonville is more than 100 kilometers away from Rustenburg, and 150 or so via the shortest route to Marikana. One could easily imagine the array of forces that might make his elimination, or at least silencing, desirable.

The steward had previously worked at a platinum mine in Rustenburg, near Marikana, having entered the mines on the advice of an uncle after his father's death "in the mines." But he had quit, horrified at the intensity of the labor underground, only to be forced back when he could not obtain alternative work from the municipality, which he presumed to be a preferable source of employment. When he moved from the platinum belt to the gold mines of Carletonville, following dismissal during a strike, the steward was shocked by what he perceived to be the complaisance of the workforce in his new home, and he took it upon himself to "inform" them: "I think there was a lack of information. People didn't get a clear picture of what is happening within the mining industry. They were remote controlled, they were remote controlled indeed." The phrase stood out: a remarkably poetic registration of industrial capitalism's compulsive force, cast in the idiom of contemporary media and thus in the appearance of immediacy, which is to say secular magic. I asked the steward how things had changed after Marikana, recalling the AMCU secretary's insistence that Marikana did not originate but had rather catalyzed an incipient disaffection in this area, bringing to the surface a radicalism immanent to the conditions of labor. "When I arrived here," he answered, "I could see that there is a lot of things that's not going well." To remedy the situation, he started "to engage people individually and explain to them what is happening in the mining industry. The gold sector as it was, the operation and the system that was used in the mine that I was employed at before, it was a different thing, and you can see that people don't have information of actually what is happening." As he described his efforts to explain to them "how things should be," he meditated with obvious excitement on the "fortunate" events of "2012, when things happened in Marikana. The people started to realize that they got power in their hands. And that is when we decided to go at the hill, on the 25th of September."

The strike at AngloGold Ashanti lasted a month and generated a mere 2 percent wage increase. But the paucity of economic gains was in some way compensated for by the sense of empowerment that came with the experience of being on the mountain. I asked the steward what it was like, during those days of anxious anticipation, so soon after the massacre of workers in the neighboring town. He responded, smilingly, "It was fun. It was fun to be in that mountain. We took a month, on the strike. . . . It was fun. We took it like fun, but it was very difficult. . . . We were very much militant on the engagement with management . . . we used our own intelligence so that people can't lose their jobs." When I questioned what made the experience fun, he paused and reflected before continuing, with a verily tremulous sense of self-importance: "I was a, I was the pillar of around 12,500 people, that were on strike. Not only this shaft. Not only this shaft. There are three shafts at AngloGold Ashanti, so we gathered at the mountain, the three shafts. So, I could realize that I've got, I've got this, I've got this power mentality [mental power], and this power, ways that I can say to people, to convince people. . . . It's not easy to convince people that this is what is happening and we are going to stand for what we are actually here for."

Initially, the steward appeared to be an ordinary labor organizer, a man who would exercise his rhetorical skills in acts of suasion. And he had a knack for the uncanny—the 12,500 people paralleled the 12,500 rand being demanded by strikers—a resonance so perfect that it strained credibility. His skills, he explained, were necessary because something had blocked the other workers in what should have been a verily automatic recognition of their interests, and moreover, of the system that would otherwise obstruct their capacities to recognize those interests. Precisely because they were blocked, however, he had to speak to and for them, in order that they could discover their own voice. Gayatri Spivak's analysis of subalternity and her incisive critique of the workerism subtending European radical discourse, drawn from Marx's reading of the crisis of peasant producers in *The Eighteenth Brumaire*, can help us grasp what is at stake in this effortful appropriation of the workers' possible but interrupted capacity for self-representation.[22] In *The Eighteenth Brumaire*, Marx describes how the identity of the workers' interests does not become the basis of a sense of community. This is why, he asserts, they must be represented. In his account of the peasants' superstitious adoration of Louis Napoleon, the figure of the emperor is shown to provide, for the poor peasants, an image and a trope (*Darstellung*) that absorbs into itself the act of representation as persuasion, a coming to consciousness of an identity of interests (*Vertretung*). The shop steward appeared to recognize the difference between these two elements of representation (concealed in English as "representation," but usefully distinguished by Spivak through recourse to the original German). This difference, however, was for him a gap to be closed, as much as it was to be mediated or maintained in its difference. It was, indeed, to cover over this gap that he offered himself in the role of "leader" in the process that I have described as a pursuit of immediacy. His claim to identity, and to a metonymic status vis-à-vis the class of mineworkers (a profession that he nonetheless felt himself above), moves his gesture from what might have been organic affiliation, à la Antonio Gramsci, to a presumption of the tropological function grounded in the claim to full identity. In this respect, his function was extraordinary and its origins were also extraordinary: "I believe that I was sent to, I was sent here to come and actually rescue the mineworkers that are oppressed."

Even before he arrived among these workers, blocked in their capacities for self-representation because they had not yet grasped their own lack, "there were signs" that came from beyond, he intimated. To be sure, he said, he "was always in the lead" (i.e., at school, in relation to his age-mates), but the incitement to come to this community came in the form of something like a commandment: "it was like an ancestor." It was to assuage the unease of the ancestor, namely his father, that he now spoke, and it is because the ancestor heard him, that it (and not the workers) was now "at ease." Up until this point, the father/ancestral figure had been described by the steward only in terms of its/his failure to fulfill the paternal function ("he has done *nothing* for me").

The steward's speech restores to the father that ideal function, which is, above all, the function of conferring recognition. In this way, however, there is a kind of detour in the representational dramaturgy of the working-class accession to self-representation, a detour and a substitution. As the workers are replaced by the father as the origin of the steward's communicative and thus social power, the labor of history is transferred to a narrative of origins. A patriarchal and phallocentric sublimity overwhelmed the steward, who, in the course of our conversation, with its accelerating sense of excitement, abandoned his earlier self-presentation as a skilled rhetorician charged with the task of educative persuasion and asserted, instead, that he was the recipient of a gift, a quality of leadership at once inborn and compulsive: "leadership . . . it's not something I actually learned, it's something that I was born with."

During our second meeting, this one in the residential section of the compound, where minivans beeped and fruit vendors offered their produce to the men coming off shift, the steward's speech grew increasingly elaborate. He was lustrous with this tale and waved repeatedly to the mineworkers who watched, warily, from afar. His power assumed mythic proportions as he conjured the specter of a company conspiracy to torture him, but it was in his narration of escape form security forces that he finally arrived at the point of delirious self-apotheosis.[23]

On the mountain, he said, he had been chased by security forces in a helicopter, from which he escaped repeatedly, each time returning to his fellow strikers on the mountain, where he "ma[de] that it was a joke." Questioned about whether he had not felt any fear in the face of helicopters after the horrible violence of Marikana ["wasn't it frightening?" I asked], he responded with alacrity, "No, it wasn't. It wasn't. Because I believed that, eh . . . I am untouchable. I believed that I am untouchable. And I was preaching that." What conferred this untouchability, this nearly divine sense of immunity to the violence that is deployed by the company in the interest of crowd-management and the protection of private property, was, in the end, the paternal gaze: "I believe that wherever my father is, he's watching over me. And I said that to the employees, that 'I know that my father is watching over me, wherever he is, because I am doing this for you, because he has done nothing.'" This is why, he said, his words became true. He no longer concealed the substitutional logic, the conflation of *Darstellung* with *Vertretung*, and in this very moment, he described a potent, corporeal sensation of limitlessness, of being the locus of power and not merely its explanatory vehicle. His most thrilling recollection was the sensation of a pure power in speaking, a speaking so potent that it traverses the boundaries separating the living and the dead, not only persuading workers and management to accept new terms of employment but also conferring immortality. It is in this sense that I speak of messianism, a messianism neither religious nor secular, which partakes of Christological myth as well socialist metaphysics while casting them both in the idiomaticity of Xhosa (and southern African more generally) genealogical convention.[24]

The Political Instance

The problem on the mines, from AMCU's perspective, and that of so many of AMCU's members, is that the elders were uneducated and, despite this, presumed authority. They presumed authority but did not exercise it, especially with regards to the treatment that black workers have received at the hands of the white establishment. According to the young men, foreign elders— migrant laborers who entered the mining system during the Apartheid era and who accustomed themselves to being boss-boys and living in hostels—were insufficiently radical and allowed management to tell them when they could strike and what they could negotiate. They accepted the bureaucratic obstructions and institutional degradations that the old union elite still performs in their mimicry of the whites. In contrast, the young mineworkers say they have the right to speak on their own and to thereby demand and command a hearing. Despite all of the critical literature that explains the poverty of the mineworkers at Marikana in terms of their poor access to education in rural areas, the mineworkers' claim to be able to speak on their own behalf is almost always introduced with an explanation of their changed historical circumstances: today, mineworkers are educated, at least relative to their forebears. They can, they say, read the legislation and critique the dissimulations that are encoded in the text of mining capital.

And, yet, the diagnosis does not, it turns out, materialize itself in the capacity to make of one's words the source of transformation in the world. At every turn, there is blockage, interruption, or something obtruding between what should have been and what is, where the dialectic of history ought to have closed that gap. In the place of that satiety that would express the identity between desire and being, there is lack. Where people ought to have found their voice, they find themselves newly muted, excluded, marginalized, and abjected. The presumption, widely shared in this context, is that political (as opposed to economic—and the cleaving of the two) power consists of making oneself heard, and heard in a manner to which others must respond. In liberal, electoral democratic orders, of course, having a voice is the mark of political subjectivity, but this is exercised mainly in the delegation of that speaking function to a representative, who speaks not in one's voice but on one's behalf. Etymology in both English and Afrikaans links vote and voice, and this is lexicalized into most regional languages, as "ukuvota" (X, Z) or "ho vouta" (S). More precisely, elected and designated representatives should articulate the interests of those who have so delegated their speaking function. The perceived failure of such a representative function by union officials was a crucial motivating factor in the disputes at Marikana. Dissatisfaction was also intensified by the NUM's vectoral use of cellphone technology to transmit information in lieu of mass meetings. AMCU had used text messaging to crowdsource such meetings, but it had quickly recognized that the absence of face-to-face engagement was a critical failure on the NUM's part. The desire for that thrilling exchange between the one and the many would not be satisfied by a branched tree of text messages. AMCU and its agents recognized and gathered to themselves the desire for a transcendent experience of communication and even communion in which the sensation of presence and immediacy is particularly heightened. The point of efficacious speech is, of course, that there should be no loss or dissipation between speaking and being heard, whether by one's coworkers or by the ancestors.

Here, the questions that press on the minds of the youth are not so much "Who speaks? And for whom?" but "Who did not speak?" and "Whose silence condemned us to voicelessness?" In this context, the attribution to foreign elders of a retrograde consciousness, a complicitous or cowardly submission to the status quo, echoes the steward's condemnation of his father's failures. But it is not unique to the discourse of mineworkers, and intergenerational conflict that takes this form—the accusation of insufficient radicalism—now envelopes Mandela and the old young lions of the ANC. Such accusations were already being leveled before the events of Soweto, and even at the protest poets, such as Oswald Mtshali. In a remarkable interview in 1973, he acknowledged that black youth of the 1970s were disappointed by the "lack of revolutionary fire in [his] poems" and that some "found them platitudinous."[25] Not incidently, Mtshali's breakthrough volume was titled *Sounds of a Cowhide Drum*. When, in 2013, the infamously irreverent poet Lesego Rampolokeng reflected on the radical tradition and the rhetoric of the cry that the ancestral tradition and its bovine sacrifice have been summoned to provide as the idiom for political insurrection, he rejected it entirely. For him, it is not possible to separate the bovine metaphor and the identification of men with cattle from the long history by which colonial and Apartheid governments named black people as animals and committed them to the margins of the urban, to the peri-industrial zones of the mine compounds (and the *skomplaases*), and to the reservations that resemble agrarian lifeworlds in form only. Instead, in the poem entitled "Writing the Ungovernable," he embraced the practice of pirating commuter trains, called Staffriding:

COLONIAL LITERATURE . . . GOT ME THINKING BLUE

. . . several blues . . . the blue of eyes, of collars, of some blood . . . & I bled til Mista Gwala sang me 'no more lullabies' but Liberation blues 1974, mourning of Onkgopotse Tiro parcel-bombed up in the murder-church service of the god of pigmentation (& yessah, I realized then that 'me listening to jazz is not leisure / it is a soul operation' & I knew then that I had to choose between Jol'inkomo (that is, in his words 'bringing lines home to the kraal of my black experience' or Yakhal'inkomo, to OUTCRY with Mutabaruka . . . to bawl the anguish like a cow being slain . . . & decided there was nothing bovine about me . . . & so . . . I took to Staffriding . . . all the way from Phefeni to HERE.[26]

Rampolokeng's incandescent poem takes up the archive of black radicalism—and other insurrectionary texts, from Antonin Artaud to Marx—in a genre-defying gesture of denunciation. It is an incantation and an invocation, an indictment and a calling to account. Among other referents, he is addressing the Rhodes Must Fall movement, and the call by university students to decolonize tertiary education. In 2016, Rampolokeng was commissioned by Salim Washington to write the lyrics for a song, "Tears of Marikana," which the saxophonist premiered at the Orbit in Johannesburg. A response to the massacre of August 2012 that we have been discussing, Washington's suite (which also included *Imlilo*, or Fires, about xenophobic violence) was partly an homage to Abby Lincoln's and Max Roach's "Tears for Johannesburg," which was written and recorded to honor the victims of the Sharpeville Massacre in 1960. That work had been banned in South Africa in 1962. Washington, who had been inspired by Coltrane (the object of Mankunku's elegiac *Yakhal'Inkomo*) was teaching at the University of KwaZulu-Natal at the time of the Marikana Massacre, and although his music materializes the circuit that links South Africa to the United States, he praised Rampolokeng specifically for not being an "African-American wannabe."[27] The difference within the circuit is marked by the lexical shift in the title—from "*for* Johannesburg" to "*of* Marikana"; "for" designates a distance and perhaps even a speaking for, whereas "of" implies that the tears arise within and are proper to Marikana—and are not the mark of a sympathetic gesture of "distant suffering," to invoke Luc Boltanski, or an identification born of the effacement of that difference.[28]

Rampolokeng would leave the bovine metaphor behind, but Ayanda Mabula, a painter known for his parodies of classical masterpieces, turned to *Yakhal'Inkomo* for the idiom of his accusation against the new black elite and their complicity with the violence at Marikana. In a hyperbolically naturalist style, it borrows the scenography of Cezanne's and Picasso's bullfights, and it depicts a white matador spearing not a bull but a man wearing horns. The murderous sport is observed by then-president Jacob Zuma and is cheered on from the galleries by then-reigning Queen Elizabeth and Prince Charles, and on the other side, Cyril Ramaphosa (then Lonmin's Board chair and not yet president of South Africa). Julius Malema, with a characteristic red beret, appears to be giving a kind of benediction—or perhaps anticipating victory—and the nationalization of the mines that he and his party promise. A dog menaces the miners, who are seen scrambling for money, or marching and shouting (singing?) across the picture plane. A photographer lays almost prostrate, seeking the most proximate position from which to picture the wounded man-bull. Hanging above it all is the emblem of the ANC, with its spear, shield, and flag. The matador also carries a flag, a bit like the billowing fabric of the party emblem. But this red, green, white, gold, and black banner hangs limp. Directly beneath the ANC emblem, in the hand of a mineworker, is the text of the strikers' placard: "*Thina Funa Lo* R12,500." There is no need for the word "money." The number says it all. The events at Marikana reflected the ascendance of the platinum economy over the gold, and as we have seen, although AMCU would claim the mantle that the NUM had worn when it arose on the goldfields near Carletonville, gold would for the foreseeable future be a mere shadow of the new minerals economy in which platinum currently reigns.

In the same 2013 volume of *New Coin*, where Rampolokeng's blues-poem, "Writing the Ungovernable" appeared, Ari Sitas, dramatist-poet and radical sociologist, published his poem "Marikana."[29] It is a meditation born of watching the shootings unfold on television, and as such, it performs the awful rhyme between traumatic repetition and televisual replay. As a poet of an elder generation, Sitas continues to embrace the figuration of the rural and the ancestral, although it appears in his poem as an inaccessible domain. After the news coverage, the poet-narrator remarks, "The night is quiet as the smelter has been closed,/the only music is of the wind on razor wire/the ears are too shut to hear the ancestral thuds on goatskin." One of the most well-known figures of Marikana was a man known for the green blanket he wore. Named Mgcineni 'Mambush' Noki, he was among those who led the so-called charge from the *koppie* where the striking mineworkers had gathered in the long winter nights of the conflict, and he was among those shot and killed. Forensic evidence later showed that the strikers' exit routes had been blocked and that they had effectively been corralled, like cattle, and shunted into the line of fire. Sitas's poem refers to this green-blanketed man, whom he describes as wearing a shroud, even before his death: "The image of the man in the green shroud endures/ . . . The loom endures too, the weaver is asleep/The land of the high winds will receive the man naked/The earth will eat the stitch back to a thread/What will remain is the image and I in vain/Reversing him back to life to lead the hill to song."[30] Sitas, who, with the Junction Avenue Theater Company, acquired fame as the playwright of *Randlords and Rotgut* (1978) about the early days of the gold rush, concludes his elegy for Marikana with reference but little or no faith in the ancestors; it is only "impassive nature that has heard their songs," he writes. Nor did the mineworkers, and especially the RDOs, receive their money—despite the international outcry, the professions of workerist solidarity, the films, and plays and, yes, that musical, not to mention the Commission of Inquiry. Accordingly, Sitas ends his poem with three bitterly terse lines that recall Benedict Wallet Vilakazi's reference to the underground where men, whom one expects could only be there if dead, nonetheless walk, in a macabre afterlife: "The strike is over/The dead must return/to work."[31] If they can find it.

CHAPTER 17

GAMBLING ON GOLD AGAIN

> There are some of them who have left a name,
> so that men declare their praise.
> And there are some who have no memorial,
> who have perished as though they had not lived;
> they have become as though they had not been born,
> and so have their children after them.

—Sirach 44: 8–9

> There's always a return to ruins, only to the womb is there no return.

—Solomon Tshekisho Plaatje, *Mhudi*

Francis Wilson concluded the penultimate chapter of his 1972 book *Labour on the South African Gold Mines* with speculations on what would happen after the closure of the gold mines.[1] He prophesied "some ghost towns," but despite having documented what he termed systematic "social destruction" among the black working classes, whose deprivations and dislocations had been caused by coerced migration, and despite his belief that "whites [had] chosen to move toward the equilibrium of slavery," he knew that the processes by which the violence of a new system are normalized over time would ensure that a second dislocation, caused by mine closures or a national-ization process that excluded noncitizens from employment under a more dem-ocratic dispensation, could also be destructive.[2] Hence, the nearly apocalyptic tone of his conclusions. Remonstrations accumulate at the end of his book, where the word "peril," reappropriated but not entirely cleansed of the taint of its origins in white supremacy, menaces his contemporary reader in the tense of future anteriority. Wilson asked his readers, whose actions might have introduced that event capable of changing the direction of the future (the one that Green tells us did not occur), by asking not merely, What is to be done? But what will this moment have been? Entailed in this urgent but still implicit query, which submitted his present to the hallucinatory gaze of a future if not final judgment, is the recognition that history is best understood as being writ-ten from the point of view not of a vanishing past but of an always already van-ishing present.[3] Wilson could not yet anticipate the debates that would engage historians in the aftermath of the turn to memory studies, including those emerging from South Africa's Truth and Reconciliation Commission (TRC), which would see a modern and progressivist historiography supplemented and partially displaced by a concern with the persisting force of the past in the lives of contemporary subjects. Nonetheless, his simultaneous reference to a prior history, shrouded in mystery but propelling the boom in gold prospecting, and the future closure of gold mines, shares something of their ambivalence.[4]

Two years after Wilson made his plea, the South African government, through The Employment Bureau of Africa (TEBA) began, although not for the first time, a program of replacing foreign labor with domestic recruits.[5] Between 1966 and 1979, the foreign component of labor on the gold mines was reduced from 37 percent to 16 percent.[6] The most dramatic contraction took place over a period of less than four years when, between 1973 and 1977, the foreign labor component on the gold mines dropped from 337,000 to 208,000, almost all of whom were black workers.[7] There was a corollary growth in domestic labor (in the sense of South African-born workers), which initially was recruited with enhanced wages and benefits (partly enabled, as we have seen, by the U.S. abandonment of the gold standard, and the subsequent rise of gold prices on the international market but also by militant labor action), but then increasingly enabled by the desperation associated with rising poverty and unemployment. Not all of this was a function of the mining industry's and government's nationalist efforts, however. The withdrawal of permission to work in South Africa in response to the Apartheid regime's brutalities, by Zambia and other African states, constituted the mirror image and codriver of this "internalization" process.[8] A brief recovery in the global economy follow-ing the oil crisis of the late 1970s saw the overall numbers of people employed in the gold mines swell to their highest levels ever in the late 1980s. But in 1994, the year of the official transition out of Apartheid, productivity had dropped to its lowest level since 1958. There followed a precipitous shedding of employees. Among the most dramatic reductions occurred among Mozambiquans, whose numbers in the gold mines dropped by more than half after 1985.[9] Indeed, their relative expulsion from this economy accounted for much of the overall contraction in the workforce. But output and employment were moving in opposite directions. The total number of black workers employed in the gold mines declined between 1985 and 2000 by almost 50 percent, while gold output increased by some 250 percent.[10] Even as gold prices continued their upward trend in the mid-teens of the new millennium, the reduction of the labor force continued. By 2023, the total numbers of employees had dropped to 93,589, from a high in 1988 of just over 750,000.[11]

It is against this backdrop of fluctuating but general decline that, nearly half a century after Wilson's book was published, the Chamber of Mines issued a report estimating that formal gold mining using traditional methods would likely cease in South Africa by the year 2033.[12] And as the numbers just cited indicate, much of what he feared has come to pass, including the increasing exclusion of noncitizens from formal employment in the gold mines of the black majority-ruled country—an eventuality that Wilson had described as "particularly inappropriate," given that the mines' "development [had] been so enormously dependent on labour from other countries."[13] Another way of saying this is that, from the 1980s on, a de facto (re)nationalization has been taking place in South Africa's gold mines as ores have been depleted, although this has taken place within a value bubble in which human labor has increasingly been substituted for by the dead labor of technology.[14] This renationalization has taken place without socialization, however; it is private nationalization, in the interest of national capital formation. In this sense, as in so many others, the gold mines have been the site and scene on which more general processes have become visible, where indeed they are anticipated and summoned.

That said, the apotheosis of industrial (gold) mining is not its end. Moreover, general processes are lived, perhaps one should say suffered, by individuals. If, as Walter Benjamin says, "it is more difficult" for the historian "to honor the memory of the anonymous than it is to honor the memory of the famous, the celebrated," it is the task of an anthropologist to pay testimony to the perceptions of those unheroized figures and especially to their own sense of being in time.[15] The purpose of doing so is not to make the present available for a future historiography in which the past could be made present in an illusory fullness and artificial accessibility (this was the hubristic aim of salvage ethnography, or the kind of uncritical memory projects that Andrew Nash warned against), but rather to learn from people who inhabit a specific history how they understand it or will have understood it; to understand what questions they pose of it. This is not simply a question of recognizing the "agency" of the formerly excluded subjects of history. Nor can it satisfy the still-to-be realized task of transforming a universalist "history from below" through recourse to the generically "vernacular" and the "ordinary."[16] What I have tried to do in the preceding chapters and what I hope to show in the following concluding pages of this book is that if there is a counterhistory being produced in this space—and I think there is—it is split and doubled. It has been differentially marked by race and ethnicity, and always by gender, but it is irreducible to them. Its assertions are often implicit, gestural, and imagistic, although they are also, and often explicitly, narrative. On the one hand, this counterhistory emerges in a simulacrum of preindustrial life, which is brought to consciousness *in the image of the past*, in the very gestures of postindustrial mining, although such gestures are neither continuous with, nor identical to, that distant precedent. On the other hand, and at the same time, it declares the newness of the forms of life that are being generated in the space of deindustrialization where, nonetheless, a constant recursion to technology occurs.

This duality gives to life in the space of deindustrialization and what I call remanualization, an aura of belatedness, and of being "out-of-joint" with time. And it is accompanied by specific affects. In the world of informal secondary extraction, what follows industrialization—in the sense of both coming after and pursuing the routes and paths laid down by industrialization—is saturated by an attitude of anticipation that, bereft of any faith in progress, assumes the sense of fatalism common to much gambling. Not for nothing are the informal miners of South Africa referred to as zama zamas, one of the meanings we now know is "gamblers." Let us then turn to that scene, that plane above prehistoric waters, where mine dumps stand in for the rocks of temptation, singing their siren song. We have been here before. In a way, we have been coming here all along. Recall Muriel Rukeyser: "These roads will take you into your own country."[17] From the Witwatersrand into the United States, into Britain, into Germany, France, the United Arab Emirates, Panama, China, and India.

Back to the Future of a Memory

In 2008, more than three decades after Wilson speculated on the matter, I asked people living in Merafong what they imagined would happen when the inevitable depletion of ores occurred and the mines closed. It is not that such a question had gone unasked before my interrogation. The mining companies operative in the area had publicly floated a few proposals for sustaining life in a postextraction economy. These included a rose farming initiative modeled on similar enterprises in Kenya and a lion park to be built on rehabilitated mine dumps.[18] Both were transparently incapable of absorbing the labor force to be rendered obsolete by mine closures. Nonetheless, and perhaps because of the improbability of the proposals that had been laid forth, my questions about a future after gold seemed to provoke perplexity. The rhyming bond between metal and settle(ment) seemed irreducible: each the raison d'être for the other, and both together perceived as the condition of possibility not only for the municipality but also for the nation's historical being.

Eventually, one after another person proffered a potential means of survival of living after gold. The community could be sustained, I was told, if mining could become the object of a museological project, one that would make the *history* of gold's mining, rather than its ongoing extraction, the object of a touristic industry. Because the area was the foundational home of the National Union of Mineworkers (NUM)—the Association of Mineworkers and Construction Union (AMCU) had not yet displaced it on these mines—and to the extent that people conceived of the museum in anything more than generic terms, they imagined that labor history and the place of the NUM in the struggle against Apartheid would be central features of its narrative. The museum would thus counter that heroic account of national capital enunciated by the large corporations whose partnership with the South African state had been a feature of governance since even before the Anglo-Boer War with a workerist alternative, equally saturated with romantic overtones, and not without tragedy.[19] By 2008, moreover, the memorial function of testimony that South Africa's TRC had established as a means to enlarge and correct nationalist historiography had lifted off from its original purpose and acquired a reified value within the emergent economy of the heritage industry, one that was also being mobilized by corporatized ethnic formations.[20] It was against that backdrop that I asked my question and received in answer the dream image of that strange form of afterlife—at once preserved and suspended—that the museum grants to the dead and the past more generally.

The future anteriority that I solicited generated a form of *Nachträglichkeit*, that split and doubled temporality that is both belated and anticipatory, and that is linked to the retrospective assignation of traumatic significance to events, which become both foundational and haunting as a result.[21] In 2008, in much of the formal gold-mining sector, or at least that portion of it still resting on substantial reserves, both the gesture toward future anteriority and the sense of belatedness that it would call forth were somewhat premature, although the relative decline in the workforce was continuing apace. Gold prices were rising significantly again, deferring the closure of some mines, enabling the industrial reclamation of the tailings, and tempting a few scavengers to find what they could in the refuse and abandoned shafts. Yet, not far away, the future of loss whose anticipation I had summoned, was already past. We can recall from chapter 10 the film *Joe Bullet*, which, already in 1973, as gold was losing its status as South Africa's largest source of gross domestic product (GDP) and as the country was beginning to extrude its foreign labor force, could depict some of these great mines as ghost structures. Such disappearances would recur.

Even so, the generalized process of termination still seemed far off for most South Africans at that time. Large-scale closures and consistent shrinkage in the workforce have taken place mainly and consistently since the 1990s, since the Apartheid era came to a formal close.

One need not postulate an immediate causal relation between these phenomena to grasp what Virgil-Umholi and Dante-Xolani, whom we met in chapter 2, believed: namely, that the simultaneity of the gold industry's final denouement and the end of Apartheid discloses the truth of their mutual imbrication. Recall that they attributed the closure of the mines directly to white capital flight, motivated by a fear of Nelson Mandela and the African National Congress (ANC)'s rise to power. They did not share the recent critical scholarship's assignation to Mandela of a complicitous role in the neoliberal compromise. Rather, they saw his assumption of power as the primary reason and inciting factor of that flight. For them, black political power was the cause of white economic anxiety. Why, they asked, would you leave gold behind, if not for political reasons? Economy knows only money; if it was a matter of money, *imali*, you could continue to mine.

> V-U: There's still a lot of money in the mines and . . .
> D-X: There's still a lot of money?
> V-U: These mines were just closed when a black man came into power.
> D-X: They just shut down.
> . . .
> V-U: They were upset because a black man was in power.
> V-U: And they shut down, just like that.
> D-X: Oh, they shut down when they heard, freedom is coming.
> V-U: Freedom. And they closed. (Z-N)

Indeed, there was money left in the mines. I have already mentioned that the material infrastructure of the mine to which they referred was initially disabled by the owners either as punishment for nonpayment of rent, or to discourage squatters, who nonetheless ransacked its remaining ruins for electrical cable, bricks, beams, and recyclable fixtures. It was clear to everyone that the old mine had much to offer: both residual gold and that which could be sold for cash. As I write these words, its last bricks and the rusted remnants of its old train station are being disassembled.

This deliberately ruined landscape of the mine and its compounds soon became the destination of new waves of migrants who moved not only to squat in the wrecked remnants but also to descend into the now-closed but unsealed shafts in pursuit of the gold that some claim is growing back, and that others claim as their right, or simply as the only alternative to more violent forms of theft.[22] Once again, these migrants come mainly from Lesotho, Zimbabwe, and

Mozambique, although itinerants from Swaziland, Malawi, and occasionally, from the Sepedi- and Sesotho-speaking parts of South Africa also join them. Some have experience in mining, but many do not; their previous occupations include fishing, farming, carpentry, domestic work, gardening, and a variety of relatively unskilled jobs. Some undertake zama zama work on a seasonal basis, between planting and harvesting or, in the case of those who are university students, during semester breaks. Some have other jobs—as domestic employees of nearby residents or as security guards for local businesses.[23] Many have come to join relations—brothers and sisters, cousins and uncles—and many send a portion of their modest earnings home to sustain other family members. They have nonetheless established secondary households, married or taken up with locals or other migrants, and many have children in South Africa. Some have been in South Africa for decades. Largely undocumented, and thus bereft of formal recognition in the papered world, including that which would permit them access to credit, banking services, and other social benefits, these migrants have traversed the borders at the points at which those dividing lines dissolve into the natural landscape or become the smoothed surface across which deterritorializing capital moves. They have walked through the bush, crossed the Limpopo River on foot, or, equally clandestinely, hidden in taxis or lain prostrate in flatbeds trucks, concealed by blankets or, if that has failed, they have resorted to bribes, which buy from the border guards and the police a temporary invisibility.

This book has been an effort to answer the question, How did they get here? Underground, a great deal of conversation among both friends and new acquaintances concerns the journeys taken from towns and villages in neighboring countries. Listening to sound recordings made by miners as they hammer away at the rock, or while taking meals during breaks between such labor, I have been astonished by the fantastic cartographic narratives that each seems ready to offer. These are not lists of points on maps, designating places of origin or residence. They are marvelous accounts of the personally named buses (which the others recognize), their decorated interiors, and their drivers. They are stories about the pastors who mount the buses at stations and deliver sermons on the temptations of the flesh that befall the travelers, the gamblers. They are descriptions of the bends in rivers, the trees and streetlamps at the ends of roads, and the corner stores in dusted towns where one or another miner gets down from his bus to greet an aunt, an uncle, a lover, a child. They are tales of the drivers who race and of those who are more sedate, of the music listened to, and, of course, the ticket prices at each station, the willingness of a driver to give credit, and the costs of bribing the guards, soldiers, or police at checkpoints. And they are stories of terrible accidents and murderous robberies. Or sexual threats and rapes of the women traveling the same routes.

This relentless recall of traveling as a dimension of lived experience and the medium of a bond is one reason to call these people migrants, but this nomination is not framed in opposition to the refugee—that figure of displacement in the aporia between national and international legality, that Hannah Arendt described as the one who lacks the right to have rights.[24] "I am free. No one tells me when to work, what I must do." "I work for no one." "Every man works for himself." Such phrases resound throughout the many conversations I have had with zama zamas over the years, and they are not uncommonly heard among informal and artisanal miners elsewhere on the continent. Nonetheless, although these migrants often assert their autonomy, the predicament of these men and, to a lesser extent, these women, will not be captured in the idiom of mobility. They move, true, but they do not enjoy the recognized freedom to *not move* and *to not be moved*. That is to say, although there is a constant traffic between the informal settlements around mines and hometowns in Zimbabwe, Lesotho, Malawi, or Mozambique, enabled by vast networks of kin-based and other kinds of credit, these journeys are, for undocumented people, typically made in fear, using clandestine routes and transport that are always vulnerable to intercession and subject to diversion. It is thus in the political sense that one can speak of a lack of mobility, or, to repeat, an absence of the right to *not be moved*. Deprived of the negative ground of meaning, the ability that is implicitly inscribed in the term *mobility*, loses its sense and force.[25] It was indeed this shared experience of a vulnerability to forced removal that led the long-standing, legally recognized residents of Merafong who were protesting against redemarcation to recognize in the illegalized migrants of Khutsong possible allies (see chapter 14). And it was this shared experience of a vulnerability to what they perceived as forced removal that led Merafong's protest organizers to promise protection against xenophobic violence to these migrants, if they would throw in their lot with the local residents and oppose the ANC's redistricting efforts—which they did.[26] In 2008, as already noted, Merafong remained notably free of such violence, which swept the rest of the country.

As was the case during the days of high Apartheid, but differently, precarity in the ruins of the mines often expresses itself in a relentless movement without mobility.[27] This movement conjoins spaces—at once material and social—but it also entails a disjointing of time. Or, rather, it involves a double displacement—such that the postindustrial has the preindustrial as its *form of appearance*. Appearance is not identity, however. No matter how "primitive" the techniques of the zama zamas seem (and this language saturates virtually all public discourse about their activities), their works and lives are entirely conditioned in their possibility and are shaped in their forms by the historically particular forms of industrialized mining that preceded the mines' ruination.[28] And, of course, they live in the world of mundane technology: with cellphones and cars, and, when possible, electric appliances, and especially televisions. What thus looks like a restituted continuity with the past, which is often written under the heading of the "artisanal" in studies of informal mining in Africa, demands recognition as something profoundly novel.[29] It is predicated on resemblance to, *and* an often-times explicitly avowed departure from, the past.

Consider the actual practices of these ragpickers of industrial waste, and the spaces where they work. I have described them elsewhere, but they bear recounting. The vast network of involuting networks of tunnels that stitch the underground world together, and that make it vulnerable to collapses, were fabricated in the heyday of deep-level mining. The formal mines' operations depended on the use of pneumatic drills and blasting explosives, automotive removal equipment, and electrified rail transport—not to mention large-scale dewatering and ventilation as well as cyanide- and mercury-based communition processes and industrial smelting. Zama zamas note that the difference between what they do and what the industrial mines do can be reduced in some sense to their use of chemicals. The zama zamas may use mercury, but they do not have access to cyanide. So, their mining of the remainder continues to leave what is, under the current conditions of gold's valuation, another remainder.

As I observed them in the years before 2020, zama zamas descended with no more than picks, hammers, "cheesa sticks" (used to make holes in the rock for dynamite), battery-operated headlamps (the kinds often used by cyclists), and, on occasion, rubber boots and protective clothing ("outer-pants") woven from jute or plastic sacks. They followed the same routes as industrial miners did, but they did so without the assistance of mechanized carriages and transport vehicles (trains and conveyor belts for persons and ore). They slid down the shafts with old and fraying cable as their guide, traversing gaping holes on beams that once served as vertical supports. Upon finding a vein in the rock, they used small amounts of dynamite (about the size of a cigar) purchased on an illicit market to blast rock that they then sorted by hand and carried on their backs in bags that once held mealie-meal (cornmeal) or rice. The men—and they are *almost* exclusively men—stayed underground for days and weeks at a time, leaving briefly to obtain food or carrying it with them. This duration also depended on how their teams were organized, whether they were self-formed and self-governed or part of more systematically ordered groups under the authority of international gangs. Among the self-organized teams, whose members worked in small groups of friends and relations, or as men from the same region who shared a language, and even among those who were less freely deployed, these scavengers slept and ate, worked and rested, listened to music stored on cellphones, made offerings to the ancestors, smoked cigarettes, and told jokes about women and stories of home.

Above ground, the labor of crushing was, then, generally highly structured and distributed among socially less powerful actors: either women or young men, and sometimes adult men who, for reasons of injury or personal choice, did not go underground. In this area, women received the miners when they arrived from underground, if they had managed to pass out of the shafts, unmolested by police or *tsotsis*, back to the "crushes." Immediately, they set about breaking rock with hammers or other rocks, then ground the broken stone into powder using only corporeal energy, returning it to the men who claimed it as their individual property. If they arrived voluntarily, they worked in teams without freedom, under the severe authority of the men who were recognized by other such men as the temporary owners of both the grinding territories and the women's dependency. These "overseers" regulated the women's labor and even their conversations with others through threats, intimidation and, sometimes, assault. The men observed the women and tested the consistency of the powder, not infrequently demanding that it be reground to produce a finer texture. Those same men mixed the powdered rock with water and then poured it over sluicing tables made of mud, old planks and ribbed towels, gathering visible gold nuggets and flakes from the table before consolidating and sifting the runoff. This was finally amalgamated with mercury, which the men passed between their bare fingers, feeling the silt for those sparkling elements that signify the presence of gold. The residue of the sluicing processes constituted the payment for the women, who then reprocessed it, transforming the mud into mineral cake by drying it in the sun and then smelting it on wood fires. Each of these substances was referred to as "money," and it was precisely the absence of money in their place of origin that everyone laments. "There are jobs, yes, but no money," they often said.

At the end of these gendered processes, which differed in both the time they took and the amount of gold they generated, tiny nuggets were sold into the market, through local intermediaries who kept track of spot prices on the international commodities market and paid in cash. Thence, the gold traveled along the capillary networks that extend from Johannesburg to China and Pakistan, the United States, and Europe. One of the most common ports of illicit entry into the international market is Dubai, which has relatively lax hand-carry gold importation laws. As though to testify to this fact, the Dubai International Airport hosts an enormous palm tree, the trunk of which is made of gold bars. It is topped by palm fronds of hammered gold, which shimmer beneath the permanently unreal skies of fluorescent blue in that shopping arcade-cum-entrepot. Most of the gold that passes through that "nonplace" of petrochemical futurism ends up as jewelry.

Return to Laughter?

I have written this description in the past tense, to mark the fact that much has changed in the years since the pandemic, not least because of the South African state's efforts to repress the activity of zama zamas since 2023. Much nonetheless continues in this same manner and is structured by the same logics. What I have narrated as a practical and methodological sequence, decomposable into elementary units, takes place in a scene that is by turns meticulously rationalized and exuberantly ludic. But it is part of an ongoing flow. At least before 2020, and persisting in some places, the outdoor sites where rock was pulverized and sluices operated, that flow had a particular tempo; it pulsed between the conserving, reserving dimensions of women's labor and the expenditures that follow the men's. The men who came up from beneath the earth, ghostlike thanks to the dust that caked their bodies, were quickly bathed and reattired, and in the euphoria that attended their emergence into the living day, they ate and drank heavily. While waiting for the women to complete their grinding, they gambled: threw dice, played checkers, and bet their earnings on chance. To a certain extent, the ante was itself a remainder, that left over after rents were paid and monies sent home, but because so much of remittance life is itself mortgaged to the future, and because so much of these essential expenses were covered with loans—from friends and informal lenders, many of them charging 1 percent a day—the ante was a kind of fictive money. Yet, as with all debt, what can be imagined can be wagered. Once again, zama zamas are those who keep on trying or seeking, gambling as they do, and more with each passing day. This makes zama zamas those who have not yet lost—at least not everything.

If life underground demands of the men that they wager everything, all the time, their struggle lacks the dimension of a dialectic insofar as the only escape from the dependency of life underground is through an irruption of fate: an extravagant discovery, guided by ancestors perhaps. but always surprising. Yet, it is less that possibility—which looms as a wishful specter on the imaginary horizon of every underground sojourner—than the ordinary recompense of labor that holds people here. The gambling of the zama zamas is not like the lottery, they insist; here, they know that they will get "something."[30] A young zama zama puts the matter succinctly: "You go there to look for money. But sometimes, you can't find money . . . you can't go outside without money. You have to sacrifice yourself, stay underground for three, four, five days, until you get what you want."

This something is irreducibly linked to effort, to both time and the accumulated knowledge that working in the mines generates. That knowledge does not so much lead to efficiency as it enables the men to recognize the opportunities that arise in the spaces abandoned by industry. There, they say, they look for the traces of the old mine's operational centers, seeking out the rock pillars near former blasting sites where, they believe, gold is likely to be found, and then remining the area while using old timbers to balance and support the increasingly unstable internal spaces. In such spaces, one is always in need of assistance and is always *en face* of death. The opening scene of this book was, of course, the aftermath of such a confrontation, a confrontation for which the word accident is entirely insufficient. Death had been the outcome, and there is still more death to narrate. But fortunately, this is not the near-term destiny of all the informal miners who descend into the pits. And it is to stave off the former possibility that many zama zamas solicit the ears of their ancestors, those ancestors who await them in the future. That and the desire for money, of course. Between death and the dream of escape in the plenitude of gold, there is laughter. It echoes in the antechambers of the deep.

What makes all of this possible, beyond the irrepressible desire for gold and the dream of metamorphosis, is the fact that decommissioned mines are not always sealed. The shafts are also often open, and in any case, new openings can be established aboveground and made to transect existing tunnels. It is not uncommon to hear people who live near the old mines say that they can hear the voices of zama zama working in the spaces directly beneath their homes. And some shafts have been in fact made from within shacks and other domestic buildings. If this description verges on the apocryphal, its repetition implying the status of urban rumor, it is nonetheless the case that, in 2020, there were more than six thousand such mines—"derelict or ownerless"—in South Africa.[31] And although there are laws governing the stoppage of mining operations, which require environmental remediation and sealing of shafts, this has been very poorly enforced and is poorly complied with. So, the closures are also an opening, or at least a possible opening, to both the earth and to wealth, if also to death. We should thus not be surprised to hear the ancestors invoked at the precipice. For they are often called on to assist in transforming a mere hole into a true opening, an opportunity:

> We are going in, my Sibanda forefathers. My very own people.
> You, the Great Warriors. We are calling upon you.
> We are here, asking for good luck.
> We are asking you to open the way for us.
> We are going down, into the hole right here.
> Deep, down, down.
> Please, give us your help. Be with us. Show us your favor.
> Here are the coins we give you.
> This corn-beer is for you, we also drink it for you.
> We offer it to you.
> We are saying, "Be with us, and look kindly on us."
> We are crying before you,
> Oh Pathmakers, oh Great Chiefs, the Crushers,
> the jaws that cannot be defeated by any bone,
> you who open and close all paths.
> We are asking you because you are our own people,
> we offer it to you.
> We are saying, Open the way . . .
> to the fortune in the place of the ancestors.[32]

The address to the ancestors is a solicitation of assistance but, as at Marikana, it is also a plea for recognition. Not all informal miners working the abandoned industrial spaces of South Africa's gold mines make such rites. Some even ridicule them as sentimental archaisms. But those who do enact them are anything but pious about this relation.

The prayer just cited was made at the entry to one of the disused shafts by a group of Chitonga-speaking zama zamas from northern Zimbabwe. Some two days into the underground journey that commenced with this incantation, the men performed a second similar rite. It was both improvised and prepared for. The men had carried their beer, and they had brought candles and coins to accompany the verbal rites. Alongside the formal poetry and the theatrical enunciation, the second rite was accompanied by jokes about drinking the beer away. One of the men asked, half seriously, if his companion thought the ancestors would hear their call, and the other man rejoined sardonically, and said "Nah." They were offering mere pennies, only enough for snacks he said, not enough to merit the attention of the ancestors. And laughter erupted to bind the men in that momentary experience of self-transcendence that accompanies its involuntary but liberating release.

Often, the invocation of the ancestors among these men vacillated in this manner: from solemnity to levity, from the grandiose performance of respect for intergenerational authority and power, to the jocular assertion of more immediate concern. After a shared but improvised underground meal, the men joked about the fact that their meal would have been complete if only it had had meat. And there was laughter. One said he was buttering his bread and jested in a manner that anticipated his own future recall, "You could even say he buttered it for tomorrow." Laughter, again. The bread crumbled, and one of the men said, "This is shit." The others laughed. One of them took a bit of the plastic wrap shrouding his piece of bread into his mouth. Derisive laughter followed. Another had assembled his "kit" of food in front of him like it was a banquet. The men ridiculed this elaborate setup with more laughter.

This laughter was a veritable condiment of the meal, accompanying every course, as each man took turns to ridicule another's hunger and to find company for his own. The hilarity was often tempered by bitter reflection, however, as when one of the men sighed and said (in that incandescent carnal idiom that defines so much of these unlettered men's speech), "the mouth has been dreaming." As they finished the meal and fatigue overtook them, another of the miners, bitten by conscience, said, quite suddenly, "We forgot to thank the ancestors." After a brief pause, laughter punctuated his sentence.

Mealtimes are often occasions for talk about other things, of course. And one of the favored topics among zama zamas concerns what might happen if the men "strike it rich." Here is a citation from one such conversation: "If I hit it big, I am going to park a car. Then I'm going to buy groceries. After that, I'm going dancing. That will be the end of my Christmas." The men laughed at this strange litany. Why would you park a car if you struck gold? Wouldn't the first thing be to buy a car? Perhaps a very fancy car? Often enough, these men talk about their poverty as being indexed by their lack of a car, of being dependent on their legs. In this land of automobility, in which cars and other vehicles have for decades provided the symbolic infrastructure within which racialization and class differentiation takes place, the car is an index of wealth and the medium of spatial and social mobility (even when it is not the Mercedez Benz invoked by Moiloa's informant, discussed in chapter 14). So, it is important that the young zama zama described his hoped-for wealth in an image of parking and repose. Not speed, or the thrilling velocity that violates the laws of the highway, not the rush of acceleration, or the cinematic sequence of the passing trees. The dream of a parked car is a dream of economy's transcendence. It is a picture of surfeit, a dialectical image of a stasis achievable only after having entered and exited the world of movement, including the movement *out* of the immobility that acute poverty entails. It is a passage beyond (recall our earlier perambulation with Virgil-Umholi and Dante-Xolani) economy and economization.

The other men understood this. But they scoffed when the young man said he would buy groceries: "Why are you always talking about groceries. I want money! Everything!" If, however, they derided the descent into practicalities, actual exchanges, and the consumption of use values, which is to say the satisfaction of needs, their own fantasies followed the same sequences. Only secondarily did they enumerate the purchases they would make, typically starting with new cellphones. Women, when they imagined receiving a boon, tended to do the opposite: to imagine the necessities that could be taken care of, and only subsequently, the luxuries that might be indulged.

The dream of sudden, magically emergent surplus arises at the point of differentiation between waste and surfeit. Yet, if the hope for a big strike is compelling, it is also curbed by the worry that too much success could attract thieves. And even the most fantastic discovery underground must be shared among coworkers and, at rare best, will amount to a few hundred dollars. So, the dream of wealth beyond calculation must come from elsewhere. Not surprisingly, the shining images of bejeweled cultural icons and glittering toilets in the metropolitan centers of the Global North travel back to the abandoned mines in conversations about the extravagant wealth of mining magnates, politicians, drug dealers, and sports stars. The licit and the illicit, the famous and the infamous. These figures of superabundant means appear in conversations among those who have almost nothing, conversations about inequality in which people seek—without finding—the explanation for their relative impoverishment and the wealth garnered by the beneficiaries of the highest Gini coefficient in the world.

The police are constant figures in these conversations and are one of the triad of expropriative forces, which also included tsotsis and buyers. For the undocumented are doubly exposed to the violence of the law. Accordingly, the risks they take must be in the dark: underground, as it were, and, if contrary to the law of the state, at least in conformity with the law of capital. The discourse of actuarialization does not completely saturate or displace the ways in which life is wagered, however, even when it provides the idiom for negotiating the challenges of survival and for expressing the hope for a terminus—a parking—to the unrelenting demands of the gold-made world. In that context, risk is a relation to death rather than a source of value (death has no value for the dead), and its other is not saving, or redemption in calculation, but luck.

Consider, for example, the following conversation, opened by the youngest of the two cousins, Mwanga and Benefit: "Some people have big money, eh! I can't even tell myself that I'm a person, but some people they're doing a lot of money [selling drugs]." Benefit (whom we met in chapter 5) says he wouldn't risk his life to do that, even if it meant getting rich. There are moral limits to the risks one should take, limits that intensify for those who are undocumented. It is also necessary to acknowledge that luck and risk are axes of inequality; the zama zamas, at least those I have met, are not advocates of egalitarianism. They hope to inhabit a stratified world, and occupy a slightly higher position in the hierarchy, but the idea that all should have similar means, regardless of ability, birth, or effort expended, is anathema to them, as it was to the earnest young radicals of Khutsong.

Mwanga sagely observed, in English, "There's always risk if you're going to get money."

Benefit answered, "Yeah, if you're risky, at the end of the day, you'll get rich."

Comparing their situation to that of someone like Christiano Ronaldo, Mwanga said, "He can buy a small country. Whereas some of us we don't have enough to buy t-shirts." But in his estimation, Ronaldo is "not risking. Some people, they are luck(y). Like if we're talking about these players, they didn't even risk even one of the days." It is not enough to have potential, not enough to work for a living—even if only as an athlete. Something else must enter the "equation" for wealth to be legitimate. Luck can be desired, but it cannot be admired. Risk is something else.

His younger cousin retorted, "Sometimes it's luck, sometimes it's potential."

But Mwanga insisted: "Why does luck always go to some people?" And then he shouted, "Does God have favor? [does God show favor to some over others?]"

His younger cousin, briefly silenced, slowly demurred, "No, God doesn't have favor, but let me tell you. . ." Benefit condemned the athletes because they "didn't even risk even one of the days." He continued in speculative reverie: "If I can be Christiano, I can do *mati* [make a carpet] of money. Even my blankets can be made of money." The literalization of the idiomatic metaphor provides the inverse image of that parked car in which the lucky man expresses his freedom from need as repose rather than frenzied consumption. Here, money is not only that which buys the carpet or the bed, it *is* the carpet and the bed. One is hard-pressed to imagine a more perfect expression of the fetish-character of the money commodity. The image has banished from its body the memory of labor as well as exchange, while disclosing a truth about money's capacity to transmogrify into absolutely anything.

The men knew that this is what they were doing: imagining that money could become anything. They laughed with deep and self-satisfied irony as they slid between the idiom of "walking on cash" and the fanciful depiction of blankets woven from paper currency. Their line of flight into the absurd was no more or less self-conscious than that of any surrealist. And their laughter, as Freud remarks, was not unrelated to the kind of expenditure that they dream of making, the kind made by the "poor wretch," who, "by winning some large sums of money, is suddenly relieved from chronic worry about this daily bread."[33] Their laughter thus traverses the boundaries between dreaming and waking life and brings back into the everyday the momentary experience of a surplus wasted in joyous abandonment. This surplus is not merely the excess, the remainder, or the waste described in early chapters. It is not the endlessly revalorized residue of industrial technologies, although it emerges there. It is the limit and transcendence of waste.

Sometimes, laughter is also mockery. On another occasion, the zama zama miners with whom I had been working concluded their meal with a tribute to the ancestors of the woman who was serving them. She was the common-law wife of the host and eldest of the miners. She had prepared the meal of fish curry and rice that she watched them eating before taking her own repast as her young daughter learned the art of teasing when the men suggested she was eating a snake and then cajoled her into doing so by saying that it would make her live as long as Mugabe or a white person (which, mentioned in my presence, also elicited laughter).[34] The men's gestures, which might sound on the surface to be a recognition of the woman's value, given that it was her ancestors rather than her common-law husband's who were invoked, raised an eyebrow and she asked, laceratingly, "And what about me?" She had, after all, prepared the meal, had done the work of shopping and cooking, and would wash the dishes and pots with water that she had to fetch from the communal tank before stacking them neatly in the eight-by-ten abode the three family members shared.

This woman's sardonic remark did nothing to dispel the ancestors from the scene, and certainly it did not call their existence into question. It merely demanded some acknowledgment of her contributions, while opening the question of why the ancestors are so constantly on the side of patriarchy.

The gesture also retriangulated the conversation, inviting an at least tacit solidarity from the other women in the compound where the meal had been prepared, and effecting the momentary exclusion of the men.

Images of the Past?

One of the men who seemed always to be the butt of everyone else's joke was also the least adept in English. Unlike the other men in his circle, most of whom speak five or six languages, he was nearly monolingual in a minority language of Zimbabwe and thus constantly at sea in the languages of power in South Africa. Frequently arrested for lack of papers and for his zama zama activity, he was also vulnerable to that symbolic violence that the mineworkers otherwise revel in and that is part of the verbal game underground. It is expressed in the adage, "I could kill you with words and you wouldn't even know it," a possibility opened when one person cannot comprehend the languages spoken by others in the group wherein he finds himself.

Now, as it happens, this young man, frequently mocked if also tenderly supported, was also a deeply nostalgic man, and it was he who most often spoke of home with longing, he who invoked the clichés of "back in the day" or "in the olden days," and who, despite describing his own childhood as one of severest deprivation, nonetheless conjured images of primal plenitude with every description of the Zambezi River where he had grown up. For such sentimentality, he was often laughed at. Without dismissing the hurtfulness of that derision, we may nonetheless derive a question from it and ask whether the laughter and verbal play of the other men, which dislodged and interrogated everything to which it was directed, might also help us understand the general practice of ironizing and thus displacing, if not entirely negating, the urge to invoke origins with every apparent resemblance to the past.

The temptation of this tendency is indeed difficult to resist. For the spaces underground often seem to be reverting to the status of caves (a familiar trope, as already discussed), partaking of a regression that is attributed to the miners when, for example, people remark that their practice differs little from that of imperial Roman or Medieval times. For zama zamas, however, the risk of regression is precisely a function of trying to occupy technological infrastructures that are now bereft of what makes them work. The difference between the worlds above- and belowground was described to me in terms of an opposition between smooth straight paths and broken labyrinthine tunnels, the latter of which reduce men to a verily animal nature (recall Mwanga's description of his own movements as resembling those of a cow, in chapter 5). Yet, the ideal of smooth space was not limited to the aboveground world in these conversations; it also referred to the subterranean routes of the industrial mines, whose railroads and straight paths were also frequently remarked, if only as the now-inaccessible framework for zama zamas' improvisational journeys. In this manner, a temporal conflation took place, such that the time of infrastructural modernity was divided: underground, it was but a trace of a ruined past; aboveground, and despite the erosion and decrepitude of township roads, it was the material of contemporaneity and the literal ground of freedom, however limited.

Despite the contrast between them, both the above- and belowground worlds are in shadow, negatively shaped by the history of industrialized extraction. The evacuated earth has as its skeletal support the geometries and regularities of machinic fabrication—and their collapse—and these combinations of ideal emptiness and rocky occlusion shape the routes and possible itineraries of the miners. The artificial folds introduced into the rock by blasting, which, as I noted earlier, mimic natural caves, provide places of rest. The pile of rocks interrupting the path—the result of a blast or a collapse—is but another layer in the dense residue of material traces that, in their accumulation, simultaneously distance the zama zama miner from the last moment of the industrial mine's forms and bind him to it in the shape and tempo of his movements, his tactics and his strategies. As much as the closure of the mine, then, the functioning prehistory of that closure—what is often referred to as the life of the mine—demands that the zama zamas conform their actions to technology's forms. This means not merely following the routes already established but also negotiating the abyssal gaps and severe angles that traction cables, hoists, and pumps had once enabled miners to traverse in the time of electricity.

What was true belowground is also true aboveground. The women or boys who broke the rock and ground it with other stones or handmade hammers did so on the cement foundations of ruined buildings. They dried their pats of sluice on the same horizontal planes, grateful for the uncracked surfaces that made the sweeping of powdered stone easier and less vulnerable to loss in the crevasses and furrows where grasses grow and rainwater pools. Nonetheless, the infrastructure of the mines is irreducible to these solidities, for it includes, in addition to the system of financial capital already discussed, the social—racialized and gendered—organization of the migrant economy and its histories. It is here, in the domain of a social life riven by hierarchies of gender and seniority that one must confront not merely the fact of shadows but also of simulations. The question of simulation poses itself along a double axis: that of historicity and especially the historicity of racialized and ethnicized labor, and that of sexual difference, but the two are related. And it is also at their point of convergence that the simulacrum dissolves and change enters.

Many who look at the women grinding stone are gripped by the uncanny sensation that this grinding is, in its form, its rhythm, and its product, almost indistinguishable from the grinding of corn as it is done in many poor, rural parts of this world. The fact that rock can be ground into a powder so fine that it can hardly be differentiated from corn, except by smell or taste, comes as a surprise to afflict the consciousness of any observer with the sting of the Real. But this powder, in its infinitesimal fineness, clouds the air and enters the lungs of the women and the infants strapped to their backs or crouched at their sides, just as the dust that rises from the blasted rock enters the lungs of the underground miners, scarring and thickening the passages of their lungs and infiltrating them with death. The oracle of that death writes her prophecy in the indecipherable lines made by sweat or tears on the dusted faces of the men and women and the children who accompany them.

The women seem, on the surface, to be bearing within their corporeal techniques the memory of a verily prehistorical form of work, one passed from one generation of women to another, through processes of mimesis that are integral to all learning. Indeed, the histories that attributed to women the function of preserving the (artificial) rural also demanded that they signify it and rendered the generalized and generalizing figure of the "African woman" as a kind of hieroglyph whose outline is that of a female form, grinding corn. We might therefore say that what migrancy has both posited and alienated in the women (what it has forced them to be and to leave behind), the mines of the deindustrializing world seem to have recalled, thus transforming the women's very movements into the statements of a bodily archive. This is a tempting reading, but it is contaminated by the same misrecognition that leads people to find in the men's remanualized mining a return of the archaic practice of artisanal mining.

Certainly, the women draw on the forms of labor that they or, just as likely, other women in agrarian areas performed in other times. But any postulation of an identity between these forms, an identity that rests on the effacement of difference between both the product and consequences of grinding corn or stone, as well as the relative intensities of energy that must be expended for one rather than the other, is guilty of substituting that "copula in effigy" whose burning Luce Irigaray invited us to think in her condemnation of the Platonists and the aesthetics of representationalism.[35] That this grinding has as its support the foundations of ruined buildings, making a modern infrastructure the base for an action that arises in its ruins and in the image of its past, can provide an allegory with which to think the "shadowed memory of these bodies"—but only if the very status of that allegory remains foremost in our mind. One could say, of course, that the difference is to be found in the material, in the stuff being ground. Does the stone and cement not remake these female bodies by transforming their habitus? Perhaps. But the most concrete and materially determining force in this world is an absent presence. It is the fetish of gold, which continues to function as both a representation and its own referent within the economic system where it is both image and ground of support.

In 2017, just after I first began working with the zama zamas, the South African headlines reported decisions by the Russian government to purchase gold and to sell its U.S. dollar reserves. Such eruptions into the formal economic domain of a popular belief that gold is a good hedge against the vagaries of international monetary systems and financial volatility are not infrequent today, although the gold standard is ostensibly a relic of the past, and finance depends less on the phantasm of a real store of value than on the infinitely expanding circulation of digital signifiers. There are reasons for this. In a 2024 lecture, Keith Breckenridge described the massive proliferation of informal mining across the continent, in which an estimated eight million individuals are now directly involved, as an "infrastructure of trust."[36] In his analysis, people who have no faith in formal banking systems, or who have been excluded or ejected from them on the grounds of immigration status or poor credit ratings, have created a global market for extralegally generated gold, which remains, despite all else, a mobile vehicle and store of value. From Russia and the former Soviet states, to China, to Africa, and to South Asia, the accumulating exiles from the formal economy have ensured the growth of the market for this product, and thus the proliferation of the activity. Moreover, as he notes, the value that producers, or at least intermediaries, in this dispersed underground system get as a proportion of its actual worth (as listed on the international gold exchanges) is much higher than in other sectors, whether agricultural or manufacturing. Thus, in addition to the laundering of criminal activity, from drug trafficking to terrorism, so remarked by the mining corporations and institutions of international civil society, zama zamas are the counterparts and helpmeets of the radically indebted and formally excluded global precariat, many of whom have been forced into illegality not by states but by banking and financial institutions that refuse them credit or the means to legitimately transfer remittances across international borders. It is thus additionally important to recognize the degree to which even this source of last resort is so increasingly hostile to women. It is one more instance of the ceaseless regendering of precarity.

The Cave, the Womb: Returning Once More

Things appear slightly different in the formal sector, but this difference also belies the continuity and contiguity between the formal mines and the marginal zones where zama zamas operate. Among the many gestures made in the interest of overturning the iniquities of the Apartheid era, the South African government began to enact policies opening mining to women as early as 1996. In 2002, it announced targets according to which 10 percent of the workforce in the minerals sector would be female by 2009.[37] By 2020, that target had been exceeded, although it was lowest in the gold sector, where 11,271 women (12 percent of the workforce, above- and belowground) were employed.[38] A path-breaking dissertation by Asanda Benya recounts her experiences conducting doctoral research on the predicament of women in this new occupational space, during which she worked underground on the platinum mines near Rustenburg (not far from Marikana) for several months, variously employed as a general laborer, a winch operator, and an assistant to other mineworkers. Benya's vivid and illuminating text recounts the corporeal and psychic attunement that was required of her, and the fear that stalked her and other women underground—despite the mining corporations' discourse (from in-mine posters to public relations campaigns) promoting safety, mitigating and measuring accident rates, and promising to rein in sexual harassment.[39] The fear described by Benya encompasses the disabling and fatal accidents that can afflict all miners, male and female; it also reflects the sexual vulnerability that, for men, is deemed exceptional, but for women, is a presumptive if repudiated dimension of being in both public and private domains, especially those that have, historically, been said to belong to men by right.

Readers may recall from chapter 5 that Benefit, a zama zama miner, had quit working underground after being exposed to a threat of sexual violation by gangsters. He said the gangsters wanted to make him and his coworkers into *mfazi* (Z, wives), using an idiom that has been widely deployed to describe the institutionalized sexual services demanded by elder men of juniors in the same-sex hostel milieu (a much-remarked feature of South Africa's mining world).[40] I noted then that he comprehended this violence as a becoming-woman, thereby indicating a certain plasticity of sexed identity or at least a vulnerability to its coerced transformation. Benya also describes the ambiguous position of women in the formal mining sector, where their entry into the workforce is, on one hand, a signifier of enhanced opportunities and more equitable hiring *for women*, and, on the other hand, a relentless double inscription as beings who are both feminized *and* masculinized. In the formal mines, as elsewhere, women often receive unwanted sexual attention, from verbal harassment to physical assault. Although rape is apparently rare in formal mines, women describe having their breasts and buttocks grabbed or being masturbated on while squeezed into the transport cages that take them between levels. The mandated darkness of these cages, where dozens of bodies are compressed between the walls, and where workers may not turn on their headlamps or are scorned for doing so, makes them spaces of intense intimacy and also dangerous mystery.[41] For women, they are caverns of concentrated vulnerability. Yet, the insistence on women's feminine incapacities—as an indelible mark of the female-sexualized body—is coupled with what many female mineworkers themselves describe as a requirement that they become "as men" while underground. Benya quotes a typical statement: "I'm a miner at work and a woman at home. . . . I'm a man at work."[42] Nor is this a metaphoric idealization; many women described by Benya and others also comport themselves in this way and recount their affective and corporeal transformations as a corollary of time spent underground. This does not imply nonheterosexuality, although as Zaneli Mahole has so brilliantly depicted, there is a deep tradition and elaborated aesthetic of masculinism among lesbian women in South Africa.[43] The women of whom Benya writes are generally women living in heteronormative households, and they often are mothers and wives or lovers of men.

If there is a male affect that runs parallel to women's fear and envelopes this residually masculinist space beyond that which inheres in and palpates throughout the bodies of these female workers, it is perhaps ressentiment.[44] Benya rightly notes that the entry of women into the mines *as mineworkers* (they had long been present, as sweepers, cooks, beer brewers, and, as we have seen, sexual service providers) took place at the same time that there was a downturn in the gold industry's output and a major reduction in its waged workforce.[45] For some, then, women's arrival was correlated with men's displacement and of the gold industry's dissipation. The same may be said of the zama zama whose appearance on the margins of the increasingly broken world of the older mines is frequently read not only as a symptom but also as a causal force in the process of decay and ruination. The ressentiment that has been addressed to both women in formal mining, and zama zamas in the industry's declining peripheries, is inseparable from that long history of compensatory "stabilization" and the accompanying structures of heteronormative desire discussed in earlier parts of this book. Both are read as threats by partisans of the old or neotraditional order, and the discursive mechanism for stabilization often entails coding the zama zamas as a special threat to women. The ambivalent demand that women in the formal mines become masculinized to obtain recognition and to evade the harassment and discrimination that is otherwise normed aboveground, also has some parallels in the realm of zama zamas, where underground teams are *almost* uniformly male, and where the discourse of that subterranean space so often turns to questions of women's desirability, and also, to their powers—to enchant, to seduce, to usurp authority, or to redirect expenditures away from pleasure and toward utility. Nonetheless, there are a very few women who do go underground in the ruins and who form exclusively female zama zama teams. Although I have not spoken to any myself, I have heard from those who have, and who report their toughness, their self-confidence, and the fact that some have previously worked in the formal mines before turning to more piratical practices after losing employment. In the circumstances to be described henceforth, however, it is the double-displacement of women on the threshold of an increasingly reduced circuit of remanualization and technization, rather than their inclusion, that accompanies and marks the final denouement and the most recent effort at resurrection in spaces of gold's decline.

"We Eat the Mines, the Mines Eat Us"

To understand this circuit, by turns constricting and widening, we need to repose the question of the industrial, go back to that image of the deep industrial mine as the inverted arcade where technology is placed on the pedestal of display value. For hovering above that image is the allegorical figure of a serpent, turning on itself, swallowing its tail. It is a widespread belief among zama zamas that underground accidents are the expression of a serpent spirit, whose explosive breath fills the tunnels with death. This spirit is not to be placated and, as far as I know, receives no obeisances. Some miners, who disavow the existence of such spirits, and cleave to a more exclusive Christianity, invoke this spirit in a self-consciously metaphorized way. But I have also heard zama zamas refer, after an accident, to the possibility that someone has been throwing the corpses of animals into the mines and that these gestures are indeed malevolent acts, forms of negative magic intended to bring harm. The miners say that "someone has thrown death in the hole." They can smell it. Later, when someone dies, as inevitably someone will, they say they have proof. As Marcel Mauss has observed, magical thinking always confirms its own axioms.[46] Upon the heels of such assertions, I have heard people adduce the name or location of one or another old woman as the possible witch whose hostile magic is responsible for recent deaths. It invariably follows that someone urges the punishment of that woman. And such gestures are made even by those who claim to oppose the attacks on women that occur in the worlds of both the formal mines and of their margins. Nor is it uncommon, following a collapse, when bodies have not yet been located, for *sangomas* to be summoned, and for those same *sangomas* to charge handsome sums to the bereft widows and mourning friends for information about the location of the bodies whose corpses reside where the serpent has dropped them. And still, and at the same time, others mock such beliefs, avowing a scientized worldview, which is to say a view of the world as that which can be apprehended by science in the mode of a diagram, a cross-section, a map, and a plan.

One might be tempted to read this technologized view of the world as being entirely antipathetic to what is apparently a more animist relation to the world, one that conceives of the earth as enlivened and incessantly renewed by spiritual forces, the kind that can even regenerate gold. But these are not counterposed ontologies, or historically sequential epistemic orientations. Rather, the question of technology in the gold mines is a question of the constant overwriting of one way of worlding by another, and of the persistence of technicization even in the midst of remanualization. Indeed, it constitutes the very condition of possibility of the latter. Each overwriting entails a mutual contamination of both by each other. The ruins of technology do not give way to a simple resurgence of past forms any more than they are the scene of a simple return to earlier ways. There is regression, to be sure, but this is not the result of a violent contest between specific modes of production (the coherence of which has already been questioned), so much as it discloses a conflict between the forces of property and the aesthetics of power that mediate them; the conceptions of law, order, and justice that orient them; and the vision for the future that they find in the past. Above all, this ever-expanding circuit materializes the dialectic of productivity and waste that sustains the extractionist economy, extending beyond the material excavated to the bodies and lives of those who live in the shadow cast by gold's luminous but diminishing halo. In this context, the change of self, of consciousness, of desire, and of social form is a profoundly daunting task. And yet, it is constantly happening. Some women go underground. Some men try to imagine being otherwise.

Despite every invocation of the ancestors, which occur daily—in both colloquial gestures of greeting, and on the cusp of descent into the mines— the young men who call themselves zama zamas frequently draw a distinction between what they believe their parents desired, namely, continuity and self-reproduction in place, and what they desire, namely, to go beyond familiarity and to be with others in a manner that is as full of opportunity as it is of threat: "Our parents did not want to know about others, how they do things; we are interested in the new things." To be interested in new things brings with it considerable pressures. These include the pressures to demonstrate a certain up-to-datedness with commodity consumption that will testify to both one's means and one's knowledge of what is current, what has not yet passed out of fashion. That pressure, as we have seen, was actively mobilized by the Chamber of Mines in its early days, as a means to encourage wage labor, and it remains the engine of soft power inciting a willingness to work or a sense of need for employment and consumption today. It also informs the tsotsi's drive to expropriate the little accumulations of other poor people. And for all the talk and fear of nationalization and of the uncompensated takeover of capitalist enterprises, the most common form of expropriation around the old gold mines takes place as the vindictive mimesis of power: in the robbery of poor people, by slightly less poor people, and by very wealthy people.

But the subterranean rumblings of a wished-for self-transformation can also be heard in the mines. Among those conversations that the zama zamas permitted me to overhear by recording themselves while underground was one between young men of different ethnic groups in Zimbabwe and southern Zambia. As far as I could tell, they had not previously met, but they seemed to recognize in each other a certain experience of marginality associated with their minority status in their countries of origin, a status indexed by language. The conversation commenced with questions about origins—where people were from, and what ancestral clan claimed them. Upon discovering the origin of his new companions, one of the young men remarked, in a gesture of accusative anthropological typing, that he had heard they practiced a marital tradition in which the father of the groom is given the right of sexual access to the bride the night before her wedding. This legitimated rape of the bride-to-be, in which the paternal authority of her new family takes and then passes on to a husband the unlimited right to her body, is a source of curiosity and shame among some young people today.[47] So, the young man who was called out for his membership in a "culture" of such sexist and sexual brutality joined his accuser in denouncing the tradition as one of the to-be-forgotten practices of the elders. "We don't do that anymore," he shouted. What followed the back and forth of accusation, mockery and self-defense was an extended discussion of the difficulty of change when one feels partly obligated to parents whose beliefs and practices seem, from the perspective of their children, not only incomprehensible but morally wrong. This critical judgment extended to many issues surrounding marriage, especially with regard to the payment of *lobola*, the right or not to establish one's own household, and what kind of respect and care is owed to elder parents when they are no longer able to support themselves. Above all, it concerned the question of how men should treat women.

In a society suffused by patriarchal values, where tradition is often an alibi for the reclamation of masculine privilege, and where sexual violence is rife, this extended conversation is evidence of a tentative opening and a possible movement toward equity, or at least a mitigating of inequity, from within. This opening takes place at a distance from law and formal industrial policy, which does not mitigate its significance. If any sector of the economy, in South Africa and more globally, functions as a theater of hierarchical sexual difference, it is surely that of mineral extraction, and this is true at the level of the metaphors with which mining is coded (the tropology of penetration, the earth as womb, and so forth), in the organization of its labor forces, or, as we have seen in our contemplation of the *skomplaas*, the repeated representation of the violence of Apartheid's mineral industry as a process of emasculation whose remedy is the restoration of heterosexual male prerogative in an integral household. In the world of zama zamas, this theater of sexual difference is no less invested than in the formal mines, and this investment has intensified as the sector has come under more and more pressure from both the state and gangs. As though in direct proportion to the opportunities for capital accumulation in this realm, women are excluded. Or, to put the matter differently, in remanualized contexts, the moment of technicization is also the moment of women's effacement. Where they can be replaced by mechnization, they often are. This too is a shadow in the cave in which the projection of the past as tradition and authenticity is relentlessly inscribed.

In fact, the ruination or at least closure of the mines has its own movements, and this is related to the fact that the oldest and shallowest mines of the

Witwatersrand are generally on the East Rand, with the newest and deepest on the West Rand. The general pattern of closure moves along the arc of the Witwatersrand, westward. The populations of zama zamas follow. With them, come all the predatory forms of piratical extraction that feed off illegalized economic activity: the forms that depend on that lack of mobility described earlier, as well as the lack of access to police protection, and of course, the control over arms. Given the long history of gangsterism on the Witwatersrand, we can also say that what follows and preys on the zama zamas has also been here all along, awaiting their arrival like a prophesy. The little accumulations of money that accrue to lucky miners and low-level buyers, and then to the higher-level buyers interlinked with international criminal gangs—these accumulations have enabled modest technical interventions, which is to say capitalizations. In some areas, the work of crushing is increasingly mechanized with hand cranked or electrical grinding tubes called *penduka*. Costing relatively little, but more than most can afford, they are more "efficient" than the hand-grinding done by the women and youths, and they permit the concentration of control over the production process. The axis of this efficiency is less the fineness of the grind, although uniformity in this respect is important, than it is the rapidity of the process. Equally important, because it ensures that crushing can be accomplished in compressed periods, the use of *pendukas* enables more nimble and flexible evasion of the police raids. It is not surprising, then, that the *pendukas* are coveted by and often expropriated by armed gangsters and are operated in territories that can be fenced, surveilled, and, if necessary, hidden, whether in shacks or shallow shafts. The *pendukas* and the spaces of their operation are in this sense sites of concentrated value production or extraction, and vulnerable choke points in the web of relations that stretch from the lowliest digger to the most powerful members of the illicit extractionist economy. Evasion of the police is not always possible, however. Police raid these sites either to confiscate the machines or to extract bribes—and sometimes both, charging fees for the return (or ransom) of the *pendukas*. Competing gangs similarly raid these sites—to obtain the machinery for their own operations or simply to take over the territory through armed sieges. Against the backdrop of such developments, the specter of the zama zama as a violently piratical figure and threat to the legitimate economic order, has been redoubled in recent years, to such an extent that, in October 2023, the South African government launched a nationwide effort to eliminate zama zamas in the name of national prosperity. That operation, titled "Operation Prosper," has entailed joint military and policing operations and a show of armed force that has not been seen in South Africa since the Apartheid era—with the possible exception of Marikana.[48] In December 2023, a more local operation in Roodeport (one of the areas discussed in this book), but with similarly multiforce elements, was initiated under the name *Operation Vala Umgodi* (Close the Hole/Pit), and commenced parallel raids.[49]

The raids were inevitably preceded by pronouncements by politicians and police officials. The same convergence between the discourse of state and capital that had characterized the heyday of the Chamber of Mines's influence in the Apartheid era can be heard in their statements, which bemoaned the loss of gold from the corporations, and the loss of tax revenues for the state. The South African president's announcement of Operation Prosper, which was to employ 3,300 army personnel to supplement local and national police forces, at an estimated cost of 492 million rand, claimed that zama zamas rob the mines of "7 billion rand annually and the economy tens of billions of rand more in lost export earnings, taxes and royalties."[50] The siege undertaken with this rationale brings to mind and echoes Mgqwetho verse: "Here are the leaders of the nation who bleated in Johannesburg and the cops trotted down the mountain!"[51] News broadcasters followed them and ventriloquized police policy, filming the men lined up for police processing and showing the accouterments of the alleged criminality—not just hammers and chisels, but old rice sacks and bottles of orange soda, which were said to be evidence of underground life. Meanwhile, the WhatsApp networks of the zama zamas were abuzz with warnings about the specific targets of sieges, conveying tips from one or another informer in the police and armed forces.

The October announcements of Operation Prosper and Operation Vala Umgodi in many ways seemed belated. Already, in August of that same year, armed raids on zama zamas and the informal settlements where they resided were in full swing. When I drove along the routes to the mines in the early mornings, as the first spring breezes began to moderate the winter chill, caravans of armored trucks, with black-clad operatives carrying automatic weapons could be seen preparing their assaults on the settlements along the roadside. And occasionally, the Main Reef Road and arteries in other mining towns were closed or shrouded with smoke, as residents in the settlements nearby protested their ceaseless exposure to theft, infrastructural ruin, and violence, which they blamed upon the zama zamas, hauling tires onto the fissured and cratered pavement and setting them alight. The black plumes that billowed over the reef carried in their metamorphosing shapes the remembered images of other protests, other blocked roads, other struggles for recognition, justice, and relief from impoverishment. This time, however, the protestors were not opposing the state, as under Apartheid; they were calling for its explicit arrival, its exercise of most potent force, its termination of violence with absolute violence. Meanwhile, the word zama zama had expanded outward to encompass all forms of illegality, theft, piracy, and especially violence by non-nationals. The word had become a floating signifier, lifting off from every referent to designate, without specifying, everything that could cause lost value, everything that could transform mines into sinkholes, as is said of areas that can no longer generate a return on investments. Popular discourse has its reasons, of course, and a general condition of fear and infrastructural decrepitude informs this discourse. But a social analysis of the "formal" mining industry that did not differentiate among investors and shareholders, upper- and middle-level management, and labor recruitment and brokerage organizations, or between team bosses and the finely calibrated ranks of skill and function, would be risible. One should not accept anything less of the so-called informal industry, even as we recognize the instability of the ground that would oppose these two (and more) dimensions of extractivism.

The State of Things, Now

Before 2023, the police appeared in the vicinity as much to threaten a future arrival and an imminent enactment of those laws enabling the arrest and deportation of the undocumented migrants, as to enforce property laws under which zama zamas could be prosecuted. Daily bribes deferred this promised intervention and ensured for the zama zama a condition of visible invisibility, if I may borrow Foucault's felicitous language.[52] If the police occasionally staged raids, rounding up or arresting a few dozen men and women at a time, this was only because there was no ongoing police presence that could claim the function of preserving order. In fact, the police raids were often and increasingly militarized operations: of strikes, captures, and withdrawals. They worked to "secure the perimeter" of what was otherwise a zone of abandonment.[53] Even so, they seemed less aimed at terrorizing the illegalized residents than demonstrating a capacity to exercise force for a South African citizenry for whom the term zama zama had come to connote a profound antisocial violence, a menace whose elimination they constantly avowed. The state does not maintain many other outposts in the areas where zama zamas tend to operate and live—even in the form of information-gathering for population management purposes. The numbers of zama zamas, which are said to have grown from thirty thousand to several hundred thousands in the past decade, are but rough estimates. This is not a site of biopolitical governmentality. And yet, life is concentrated here, as much as is death.

As in many other places, the receding horizon of governmentality returns in the dream image of lawfulness.[54] The longing for recognition and the investment in documents, the impugning of the police—these are the many forms in which this desire has already been described in the foregoing chapters. And this is true among both zama zamas and other, legal residents of the gold-mining region. But that lawfulness is often less the ideal of a world unmarred by crime than it is the scene of a widely hoped-for retribution, where violence would be the occasion for the state's materialization as an authority that responds to individuals while foreclosing the specter of ethnocidal war, which is to say political violence *within* its bounds. In the wake of the history we have traced, such violence constantly threatens to erupt both aboveground and underground. When the state fails to materialize in the scene where it is desired, and where it is conceived as the only entity capable of mediation, a society is faced with two apparently contradictory options: politicized violence which, in South Africa, would take the form of ethnocidal war; or sacrificial violence, in which groups turn inward and affirm themselves in spectacles of sacrificial self-purification that also aim to prevent intergroup conflict structured by vengeance.

In the frayed and heterogeneous spaces of the ruined mines, abandoned by the state and by the corporate pseudo-state, untethered from any overarching political institutions, and lacking a shared set of ideological commitments, the transcendentalized grounds on which a distinction between vengeance, sacrificial violence, and legal punishment might be made, are tenuous at best. As René Girard has taught us to expect, the absence of these distinctions often shows itself in virulent and intensifying cycles of vengeance and in the avowal of vengeance as the necessary and only effective response to violence. I can think of no more potent enunciation of this principle than that which followed a conversation among zama zamas about one of their members who, after having been stabbed, decided—against the advice and beyond the understanding of his fellows—not to seek vengeance.

Half-jokingly, one of them said, "A person who doesn't take revenge is good to rob," and then mused, "Unbelievable! A person who doesn't take revenge."

In Girard's reading, it is not that a more formally juridical system of punishment lacks the violence that is clearly present in the brutal executions meted out by mobs, but that such systems can enact violence on a scale so much beyond that of vindictive individuals or groups that they can at least appear to have the power to contain it, to interrupt it for a sufficient period as to appear to have brought it to a halt. Such is the monopoly on violence: the appearance of a power so concentrated that it could outdo every other violence arising from within the social body. To the extent that the symbolic forms and mimetic processes of religions dilute the force of that originary violence in rituals that claim to be the mere simulations or symbolic reenactments of violence, they aim at containment without ever promising an escape from violence, according to Girard. The substitution of representational violence for a more primal and more immediate brutality, however, is insufficient to save society from itself. In Girard's analysis, the work of producing unity is achieved by substituting a new kind of victim, the foreigner, for that which would otherwise come from within the community.[55] This argument sometimes seems to come close to an avowal of nationalist violence, and I do not endorse that tendency, but what remains of great utility in Girard's account is his recognition that "the surrogate victim . . . appears as a being who submits to violence without provoking a reprisal; a supernatural being who sows violence to reap peace."[56] This is better understood not so much as a voluntary submission, as the acknowledgment of an already lost cause. In such circumstances, no one can or would come to the accused's defense. This is why Girard refers to the surrogate as "the final victim."[57] If, however, there is a final victim, there must also be a final perpetrator who is unsullied by the fact of bloodletting, one whose judgment goes unjudged, whose executions demand no reprisal. Such is sovereignty.

Elsewhere I have described the desperate efforts undertaken in one informal community where the state failed to materialize as the bearer of this sovereignty and where the residents feared the consequent eruption of ethnocidal warfare.[58] After it was ostensibly discovered that a series of rapes and murders had been perpetrated by members of one ethnic group against another, and after the police failed to intervene, the community members determined that the alleged perpetrators should be killed by members of their own group. That is to say, they were to become the victims of a sacrificial violence that would mime the state's imagined function and thereby interrupt what could otherwise become a cycle of revenge killings structured by ethnic enmity. Such efforts are rare, and inevitably the "peace" they engineer is short-lived. Far more common is the demand for vengeance and the sacrifice of the foreigner who is said to have been the cause of the social menace—as in xenophic purges. As James Siegel has shown, an amorphous menace can provide the alibi for purgative violence, which operates by designating the supposed culprit or culprits with a name that is semiotically capacious enough to be applied to many.[59] Such would appear to be the case at present, as the term "zama zama" becomes ever more broadly signified.

Between April and August of 2023, there were, officially, some 4,067 people arrested for illegal mining across the nation—and not only in the gold sector, but also in the coal and diamond fields—although only 329 had been convicted of these offenses. An additional 7,351 people were arrested for contravening immigration laws as a result of the sweeps, revealing the close entanglement of national border maintenance, the protection of national capital, and opposition to illegal mining. Defense Minister Thandi Modise was willing to brook diplomatic incident when he announced: "I don't think it is our jobs as ministers to protect the image of other countries when ours is going to the tatters [sic] because other people are coming in and disregarding the laws within our borders. . . . We should take a hard stance against any foreign national who comes into this country with the sole intention of breaking our laws."[60]

One of the most powerful narratives enabling these sieges, which perhaps even Francis Wilson could not foresee in their theatrical nationalism, is that which holds the zama zamas responsible for the virulent sexual violence that has afflicted both the marginal communities of undocumented migrants and the peripheries of the urban and periurban townships near the mines. The double threat that they are said to pose is one of lost value and the economic viability of the nation, on one hand, and sexual violence, on the other. What held this dyad together in the nationalist rhetoric of the 2023 government, and even that of its opponents on both the left and the right, was the insistence on the foreignness, the illicit migrancy of the presumed perpetrators. If, however, for the state, the question could be posed in terms of law's violation, and thus as a problem of its sovereignty, for people who reside in the communities being raided, the problem to be addressed is of another order and concerns the exposure to violence. Women in these communities have gone to the police—including to the same police who so often failed to intervene in the past—and reported numerous cases of rape and sexual assault, robbery, and intimidation. Some to whom I spoke reported that they had taken in lodgers involved in illicit mining, and that these men, largely members of Sotho gangs (including the famed Marashea, discussed earlier), had refused to pay rent, on the grounds that these impoverished landlords had received their housing as a state benefit and therefore had no right to profit by it. They had not only ceased paying rent, but also demanded of the women who headed these households, that they provide services ranging from the provision of food to sexual access to them and their daughters. Groups of women in some informal settlements had even gone so far as to take their children to police stations at night, demanding protection and refusing to leave until dawn.

In the past, these women's pleas for assistance had gone largely unanswered by the South African state. But in late July 2022, eight women who were part of a crew making a music video near an illegal mine in Krugersdorp were attacked and gang-raped. The women—if not celebrities then at least part of a more visible class—survived their horrific experience and described their assailants as being zama zamas, whom they also said were wearing blankets (an ethnically marked form of Sotho male attire). Fourteen men were arrested relatively quickly, but not before the residents of the nearby neighborhoods went on a rampage of vengeance and outrage, undertaking citizen's arrests, beating, and brutalizing anyone they deemed a zama zama, burning their shacks and destroying their property.[61] It is necessary here to note that zama zamas do not typically wear blankets while working, even if Sotho, and that their attire is rather obviously chosen to permit their activity, the particular marker being the wearing of additional "overpants" woven from durable plastic or jute, and of course the presence of kneepads and headlamps. Some say, too, that they wear the earth, the dirt that covers them when they come aboveground. It is not impossible that these men perpetrate crimes, of course—they are not innocents—but the alacrity with which they were identified on the basis of an ethnically stereotypical attire, thus confusing ethnicity with illegality and conflating all dimensions of this economy, demands some skepticism. In the end, all of those arrested were acquitted. Popular desires for justice remained unfulfilled, and of course, the injured women's trauma was unsalved by any of this.

The desire for justice simmered, however, and gave energy to Operation Prosper, which gathered stories of similar violence as if to appropriate their force. In August 2023, it was reported on national radio that zama zamas were taking refuge in school grounds and that gangsters, who were also referred to as zama zamas, were waging armed wars with each other, exposing children not only to the danger of cross fire but also leaving them traumatized when one or another corpse was found in the yard. By all accounts, something beyond ruination has occurred in these territories.

One might understand Operation Prosper, and initiatives of this sort, to be an effort to reestablish the boundaries between formal and informal, internal and external (although these boundaries have never been secured). Certainly, it was underwritten by a fantasy of restabilization—of national value, domestic innocence, and female vulnerability. Much is overshadowed in this braided narrative fantasy, which is nonetheless not without its truths; zama zamas are generally illegalized migrants, and women are especially vulnerable to sexual violence (both materially and as a structural condition of possibility of patriarchal order). One can nonetheless ask for an analysis that does not simply recapitulate the xenophobic tropes that operated during the earlier days of the mining industry and that have led to the eruption of purgative violence aimed at foreigners with such tragic frequency in the years since Apartheid fell. Such an analysis must confront the limits of the line between formal and informal, licit and illicit mining, which only a technological fetishism can sustain. As in the past, that limit of the limit showed itself in the account of a sinkhole.

That Sinking Feeling: Déjà Vu?

Evidence from the inquiry following the collapse of a container into a sinkhole at Lily Mine in Mpumalanga, which in 2016 claimed three miners' lives, including two women—those women newly employed in the interest of employment equity[62]—revealed with special poignancy how in the mines, the line between the interior and the exterior, the formal and the informal, is porous and frayed. Following the disaster, hearings were held under the auspices of the Department of Mineral Resources, and a formal inquiry followed, with its final judgment being released only in October 2023. One of the witnesses at the inquiry was identified as a paid informant of Lily Mine, who had previously worked as an illegal miner or zama zama after losing his job in the formal sector. He testified that one of the deceased had been supplying illegal miners with batteries and other equipment, charging them 1,000 rand for their supplies. His brother, a police officer, had been a buyer of their product. The magistrate overseeing the inquiry accepted the evidence that the sinkhole might have formed as a result of zama zama activity, namely the mining of the crown pillar, which would otherwise have kept the surface even. But there was also evidence from a Mr. Ackerman, a long-standing employee of the mine, who claimed that to meet targets and obtain bonuses, the paid workers of Lily Mine sometimes also went back to scavenge what they had supposedly left behind:

> Dean Martin Ackerman, a solo rig operator in the mine at the time of the collapse, attempted to convey the idea that although mine management tried to convince the court otherwise, underground operations were not always according to plan, ring designs or requirements and that they were "stealing" from the pillars whenever production was low. He testified that they mined the "crown pillar" at 4 level on instruction after breaking down the no-entry barriers. The evidence however clearly shows that although the drilling was indeed into the crown pillar, it was not in the area where the failure occurred. The mining activities referred to by Mr Ackerman were east of the ventilation shaft whereas the failure happened to the west of the ventilation shaft.[63]

In other words, there had been illicit mining in the formal mine but it may not have been the source of the sinkhole. Justice van der Merwe did, however, note with some concern that although the original government (DMRE) inquiry had included discussion of zama zama activity, this did not appear in the formal report: "The DMRE inquiry into the incident appears to have completely ignored it [zama zama activity, referred to as the "pink elephant in the room] as there is no mention of it in the final Section 72(1)(b) report, even though the transcripts of the inquiry reflect that it did receive attention during the questioning of the witnesses."[64] The "judgment" indicated that it did not have responsibility for investigating illegal mining, in general, but only that which may have occurred at Lily Mine. Management claimed that it had actively attempted to control and mitigate illegal activities in the mine and that it was in the context of these conflicting stories, that the protected witness and informant, "Mr. X," was summoned:

> The gist of Mr X's evidence was that illegal mining at Lily mine got out of hand prior to the incident, with approximately 50 groups of between 10 and 20 people each, operating at the mine at the time of the incident. The gold buyers provided the illegal miners, also referred to as zamas, who were mainly foreigners from neighbouring countries, with the necessary drill equipment and generators and the zamas will then [sic] pay for the equipment in gold. These illegal miners would enter the worked out stopes, also referred to as old sites or madala sites, where they spend weeks and even months underground. The legally employed mine workers would provide them with food, mainly chicken, tinned food and bottled drinks in a bartering system where gold were [sic] received in exchange for the commodities. Entry into the underground

work areas were either through paying bribes to the Fidelity security guards who escorted them to the sites or by entering the mine dressed and equipped as legal mine workers. Solomon Nyirenda [one of the three who died] assisted by issuing the lamps and underground equipment of legal mine workers, who were on leave at the time, to the zamas against payment of up to R1000 per person. Entry without involving the formal mining sector included roping down make-shift shafts from the surface to the west of the mine entrance, directly into the madala sites.[65]

At once extraordinary and familiar, given what we have learned in the preceding pages, the testimony was followed by questioning of witness after witness, of both management and workers, most of whom denied knowing of any illegal activity.

In the end, the question of the sinkhole's cause remained open, and the elision of the testimony about the possible mirror relationship between the zama zamas and the employees vanished. Whether it was the result of excessive blasting by the zama zamas or the mine's employees, or both, the pillar below the surface collapsed, leading to a sudden implosion at the surface. It was on this surface that the double-capacity container, created by welding two regular-size containers together, had been standing when the earth subsided, causing it to split in half with one half falling into the hole. The report of the inquiry included a truckdriver's testimony of his observations as the sinkhole formed and swallowed the now-split container with its human cargo: "everything went dark, and the air became thick with choking dust. . . . He noticed the soil receding behind the truck as he turned around, and he found himself on a precipice. He realised, through the swirls of dust, that an avalanche of sinking earth was carrying the lamp room and other surface structures into the mine's depths."[66] The similarities between the descriptions of the sinkhole and that of earlier sinkholes in Carletonville is more than a little uncanny. It incarnates the full haunting force of history.

Just as the earth inverts, and the mine becomes the cave, as underground becomes sky and the earth rises to become a cloud above a sinkhole, so the itineraries of the informant would appear to have moved from formal to informal to formal again in the Lily Mine. The very word, "informant" seems to congeal this mutation and provide it with a figure. So, too, in the life of the accused "inside men," kinship enveloped and effaced the boundary between state, capital, and the illicit economy—a miner and police officer, both brothers "criminals," in the end both dead, the latter apparently killed (in 2009) in a tavern when a deal went bad. The report of the "Inquiry" included evidence on all of the factors that had, since the sinkhole of 1962, come to be recognized as possible sources of collapse: excessive or insufficient dewatering, open stopes leading to weakness, insufficient buttressing of pillars, geological fractures in the sills and hanging walls, and excessive blasting.

There is something tragic in this episode, and this tragic quality exceeds the question of how awful and saddening are the deaths of the women. It is classically tragic in the sense that Kierkegaard gives the term, which implies not merely guilt (Aristotle's *hamartia*) but also an "ambiguous innocence." This ambiguous innocence, says Kierkegaard, derives from the fact that the individual is not wholly and individually responsible for his own downfall and those which he causes, but is also to be understood as a member of a nation, family, and a community of friends. The men were underpaid employees of state and capital. They were brothers, using bonds with friends and coworkers to exploit those even further removed from power, those whom the history of the industry and its decline had cast into illegality. What historicism and anthropology transpose from aesthetics to the domain of social science is this recognition of social overdetermination, with the result being a problem for explanation, as well as for law, insofar as both attempt to account for the non-immediate, which is to say structural causal forces at play. Such forces have a certain timelessness to them, or rather, their temporality exceeds and undermines the fantasy of chronological progress, of linear, sequential movement. For this reason, structural analysis seems always to entail a certain problem of tense: of the present, the past perfect, the future and future anterior.

An ethnographic predilection for the present tense often converges with the projection of timeless and changeless, which is also to say futureless "culture" as a "way-of-being." This ethnographic present of allochronic perception, as Johannes Fabian described it, would be the opposite of that "now-time" or *Jetztzeit*, of which Walter Benjamin wrote in his effort to theorize the dialectical image.[67] The dialectical image in this formulation is less a picture than a mode of critical apprehension, and it becomes possible when circumstances in the present allow the historical contours and determinations of a given phenomenon to be revealed. It requires a keen attunement and an active seizure by the observer. In describing the underground mines as being analogous to the arcades of the nineteenth century, but with technology on display, I have attempted to generate a dialectical image of the deep industrial mines to show how the spectacular achievements of those underground structures were always already haunted by their decline, always already anticipating the scavengers who now roam on their peripheries and indeed in their interstices. But if this image and the images of the preceding pages are not to become ossified in themselves, it is necessary to keep taking account of the transformations in the ruins to which, as Plaatje wrote, people are always returning.

CHAPTER 18

AFTERWARD, AFTERWORD

Utopia, an end that does not cease to end.

—Louis Marin, "The Frontiers of Utopia"

In August 2023, I returned to Carletonville, in Merafong, and found, in the shadow of those still-monumental mines and their towering slime dumps, that the one-time dream town was relatively well-kempt. The lawns of those neat bungalows, now occupied by black and white residents, were clipped, the boulevards still spacious. The blazer-clad students who attended the desegregated Carleton Jones High School were walking in groups, distracted in apparently happy repartee. The roads in and out of town were fissured, it is true, but the city center was abuzz with shoppers. Buses of mineworkers, still mainly black, careened along the highways. The mines themselves were throbbing with activity. In most respects, it appeared to be a successful small town, unlike many such locations across the country. The local newspaper, the *Carletonville Herald*, depicted a somewhat more mixed world, however, running news of local crime, environmental degradation, and especially water problems, sinkholes, and illegal mining, along with advertisements for sports and cultural events, including spoken-word slams and musical concerts oriented toward youth.

It was with these advertisements in mind that I turned to the constantly forming archives of the internet to learn what these new young word artists and musicians might be saying or singing and to discover the sound of this new generation, heirs not only to *pata pata* and *gumba* and *kwela*, but also to *kwaito*, rap, hip hop, and much more. That journey continues, but two stops along the way may provide a punctuation mark to this text that has, all along, been motivated by a commitment to listening. The first is a music video by the Limpopo-born "Shangaan disco king," who also happens to have worked at the West Driefontein mine, near Carletonville. Now an African National Congress (ANC) council member, Penny Penny (Eric Kulani Giyani Nkovani) dropped his first hip-hop album, titled *Gold Bone*, in 2017. At the time, he was in his mid-fifties and was also starring in his own reality television show. The music video, in its form and sound, its lyrics and its ethos, was a distillation of gold's fetish in the era of reality television devoted to unreal housewives and lifestyles of the uber-rich. Clad in golden silk clothes of Indian style, his chest bare but bejeweled with gold chains, his fingers weighted with gems, Penny Penny mounts the stairs of his mansion, slides into his convertible, plays in a pool-cum-bubble-bath, and is surrounded by scantily clad women who twerk against him and frolic in the bubbles, as t-shirted younger men swagger with faux-gangster machismo. Here, perhaps, is one image of that "parking" of which the zama zamas spoke while sampling gold in the deep (see chapter 17).

Shot mostly in slow motion, the aura of the video is that of reverie, which is also myth (or self-mythification), although Penny Penny calls the genre of his video "heavy gum" to differentiate it from the "bubble gum" for which he was once known. Above the synth and canned rhythms, the lyrics repeatedly posit the identity of a generic "Africa" and gold, not as a locus of mining but rather as a dimension of racialized being: "What is your color, I'm a gold color. What is your color, I'm a goldbone. African, African, you're a gold color. . . . I'm not black, I'm a gold color."[1] As fetish, gold signifies the possibility of leaving behind the history of its making and the repeating process of racialization with which it has been so relentlessly associated in South Africa.

The social media response to Penny Penny's efforts to move with the times ranged from intergenerational ridicule to sheepishly guilty admiration. But his incarnation of excess, grounded in efforts to overcome the misery of mine labor, has its critical counterpoints, and among the most exemplary of these is *16 Khuts*,[2] a documentary about sixteen young creatives living in Khutsong. In that video, the task of art is avowed as the alternative to that boy's broken glass of which Gwendolyn Brooks wrote in 1968. The "16" of the documentary also places it in relation to the student revolts of June 16, 1976, South Africa's 1968. Like Brooks's poem, the testimony of these youths is in every way concerned with understanding the place of art as a redemptive practice and means of negating the racialized violence that assigns so many to the wastelands of the industrial world. It commences with a title sequence that includes the meaning of the name, Khutsong: "A place where there is peace, that is free from disturbance: associated with tranquility." The intertitles continue, "But . . . Khutsong has been everything but peaceful." Not anything, but everything. "But" is the term of refusal as well as disappointment here. As we have seen, Khutsong was never intended to have the luxuries that the 1940s and 1950s brochures advertising Carletonville promised to its residents, although it was supposed to have been a pacific community. But the video's montage lays media photographs of the riots and conflagrations that have been discussed in previous chapters, alongside headlines from more recent years in an accumulating sequence of brutality and insurrectionary defiance.

Another "But" introduces the subsequent sequence, this time opening with a title describing the sixteen creatives to be featured in the video as "like the youth of 1976 changing the status quo." Neo Influence and the Khutsong Literary Club are named as presenters. A stack of South African novels by black writers sits on the table next to the interviewees and performers and is passingly featured in shot after shot. These books are, in some senses, fugitive testimony to the burning of the library a decade earlier, and the figure of a ghostly repository where literature continues to incite. Nonetheless, the aesthetics of the intertitles shift from book to record album. And this shift, from the page to the audiovisual medium and from the library to the airwaves is a crucial element of the media-technological transformation that these young artists inherit—the analogue but also the inverse of that other, more violent set of developments in the ruins of the mines, where technicization and remanualization were and are the condition and effect of intensified inequality. Technology as pharmakon. Aesthetically, although the effects were generated in postproduction, the piece plays between eras of media technologies: from analogue and the handmade to digitality, from granular black and white (with bleaching, sun flares, and simulated scratches) to high-resolution color. Analogue is here the artifact of digitality, just as remanualization was the afterlife of technicization in the mines.

The featured artists of *16 Khuts* first appear in photographic portraits, high-contrast black-and-white images accompanied by a quotation.[3] The conceit of the fifty-five-minute documentary derives from the cross-lingual rhyme on the word *khut* from Khutsong, a name and a common noun, and the English cut. The young "creatives" have clearly been asked to explain how they are "a cut/Khut above the rest." They have also been asked to reflect on June 1976 and on the capacities of youth to effect change. Each answers questions about the challenges they face, a question that I myself asked young people when I interviewed them in the same township fifteen years before. Their discourse ranges from questions of craft to the pragmatics of professionalization. Bafana Puff Lecwamotse, one of the poets of the group, opens the sequence and speaks of the need for "start-up capital," but in the moment that he seems to veer in the direction of Penny Penny, he explains that he overcomes this challenge through the "power of collaboration." Each artist concludes his "spot" with the same gesture: "My name is . . . and I choose to be the solution." Collaboration is perhaps the trace of the discourse of "Ubuntu," stripped of its theological and culturalist significations. But if it appears to share something of the entrepreneurialization that afflicts that discourse throughout South Africa today, it also retains a capacity for resignification and remobilization. And if the video has something of a public service message in its reference to "solutions," the skill and charisma of the young artists ensure that they do not entirely vanish in this instrumentalizing gesture.

Lecwamotse's opening discourse is echoed by almost all of the artists, whether rappers, poets, musicians, or videographers. Each decries a lack of money, inadequate access to the means of (artistic) production, and, sometimes, a lack of understanding of their ambitions. These are, of course, sentiments also expressed by the zama zamas. I have wondered what Lecwamotse and his colleagues might say to Benefit and Mwanga, what conversations they might have, if they met. Would the young creatives recognize themselves in these other disenfranchised young people who, like them, long for a future of opportunity and imagine new forms of being and desire, while dreaming of recognition? Or would they reject them as foreign usurpers of their own aspirations and ambitions? An answer to the latter question is provided by one of the young artists.

The tendency to slogan is hard to resist, especially in rhymed verse form ("crime doesn't pay," "time cannot wait") but amid the clichés, the young rapper, "King Tjwereza" Lobakeng's rhymes denounce xenophobia and violence. He also talks about HIV and AIDS. Bontle BdaDji Matabane, Khutsong's first female DJ, starts her discourse about the challenges confronting her with a flashing smile beneath glamorous sunglasses, saying "don't even remind me, because I'm a woman." I wonder what conversations she might have with the women of the crushing fields or the partners of the zama zamas. Often, she and the other artists of *16 Khuts* shuttle between English and their native tongues, without translating either. They, like the zama zamas, also play across languages and take momentary flight in laughter.

Among the most remarkable episodes of the video is a performance by the young actor, poet, and musician Sipho Patoors. He speaks of himself in the third person and describes himself as "concentrated," "persevering," "focused," "spiritual," "patient," and "deep." His monologue, from a work of which he is coauthor, articulates the experience of a man who is accused of being an *impimpi* (informant), and whose daughter is murdered by three men when he is unable to provide them with information. Set against the backdrop of the riots of 1976, whose students Patoors has earlier praised, the performance seems also to summon the memory of the gang wars of the 1980s in Khutsong. It is a riveting breach of historical location, made all the more ambiguous by the styled black-and-white frame in which he appears. "I'll never forget that day," his character concludes, now speaking in first person, from the place of an imaginary other. "Never," he adds.

This gesture, an insistent promise to the future that takes the form of memory, is not unrelated to the museological aspirations of residents who, a decade earlier, had stumbled in imagining a post-mine world. But it also expresses a local experience through forms—international documentary and music video aesthetics—that come from afar. The allure of global aesthetics, licit and illicit, entering world markets, is redoubled in the young artists' referents, which draw on the national repertoire of images more than on municipal history or events. Reaching toward Johannesburg, but also further afield, one rapper, Prince Chronic Koena, chants and channels the Rhodes Must Fall movement: "Education comes with terms and conditions" and "They say education's key but fees ain't falling." The hope that was once invested in education as a medium of mobility and transformation is rekindled in Koena's incantation, if only to be staged as that which has been withdrawn. Another poet, Kgotsiesile Monoto, recites verses about storytelling: "we are stories to be told, not written but known." Isabel Hofmeyr had titled her book *We Spend Our Years as a Tale to Be Told*, to communicate a way of being that, although overwritten by colonial logics of fencing, is never fully effaced. With Monoto and Hofmeyr, then, one can speak of a persistence beyond the remainder.[4]

As I was typing these words, a flurry of images came, through WhatsApp, from Cora Bailey, am indefatigable provider of care and services in one of the most destitute areas of the West Rand. She has been yet another guide, and one of my most trusted, on my journeying in the ruins. The image that captured my attention most completely depicts the final destruction of the *skomplaas* where I learned so much about the lives and deaths, and afterlives of the ruined mines, and which features in my film *We Are Zama Zama* (figure 18.1). Amid the broken roads, and the bulldozers flattening the houses of squatters and long-settled residents, one photo in particular stands out. It shows the remnants of what was once the compound school, now missing its roof and one wall. Its windows are falling in, and in front is a pile of rubble. One can see on the remaining walls, painted letters forming the words, "read," "book," and, partially, "learn." In the rubble, a small three-dimensional letter can be seen. It might be an N, or it might be a Z. N for Nix, or nothing. Z for Zama. One for death, the other for living.

I peer at the image and am reminded of a young woman who sold snacks to the zama zamas and said of her eighteen-month-old son, "I want him to go to school and do something better . . . [than] be a zama zama." And of Mwanga and his wife, speaking of their desire for their daughter's education, the fact that they cannot know what she will desire in the future. Their willingness to let her become something or someone whom they could not have been or become moves me. I think of Benefit, asserting his belief that an education would free him. Once again, I imagine the conversation that might have taken place between these young people on either side of the Witwatersrand arc.

18.1 Ruins of School in *Skomplaas*, 2024.

Photo by Cora Bailey.

A year after this return to Merafong, in August 2024, I visited the areas around Roodepoort once again. The headgear of the Durban Roodepoort Deep mine that once loomed as icon of the region's history had been partly dismantled for scrap metal, and now stood like a wounded metal beast, one of the supports extended like an amputated limb. The gear itself was gone. Not far away, the industrial reclamation of the mine dumps proceeded, and enormous trucks shuttled along the broken roads, sometimes laden with mountains of sand, sometimes with timber, always throwing up clouds of dust. Nearby, a group of about twenty or twenty-five young men, mostly from Mozambique, were taking pickaxes and shovels to the roads, breaking into the tarmac and then the layers of gravel and sand beneath. They were sampling and assaying on the spot, filling bags with the rock they thought to be gold-bearing. Along the trail of their excavations, they left holes the size and depth of graves.

Many of the residents and squatters of the old bungalows had fled, and only a few remained—with Cora—to ask the men to leave them "in peace," with enough of the road intact to permit the passage of a vehicle, and enough of the ground untouched to keep the fences and walls of their homes and offices stable. The police raided periodically, their cars joining the stream of minibus taxis, trucks and construction equipment heading to the working mines and townships of the area, and the new residential developments that are rising, improbably, amid the ruins.

In that milieu, I could not help but be astonished, on a Sunday afternoon, to see three elegantly clad, stately older people, a woman and two men, striding over the rubble. The woman was wearing a pleated skirt, tightly buttoned blazer and high heels, and the men wore neatly pressed pants, patent dress shoes, with coats and ties. Coming from church on an unseasonably hot day, their habitual route a new labyrinth of stone, crater and snaking coils of metal rope, they walked in assertive defiance of the rubble about them. The woman held a black umbrella aloft to shield them against the sun. Normally, it would not have surprised me to see such refined attire on people who resided in these modest and often crumbling and squatted-in buildings. Normally. That sense of the "normal" is the mark of history and its forgetting. But maintaining even this hard-won and compromised sense of normality was beginning to feel impossible for these same people. Just as it had become impossible in Khutsong during the redemarcation process, and in earlier as well as subsequent conflicts. Once again, people were feeling displaced, and despite their lack of faith in the institution, and even their fear of it, they called on the police to protect them and in fact restore them to their ordinary routines for negotiating the violence of everyday life. Threatened with the elimination of the last shreds of this improbable ordinariness, some voiced a nostalgia for the days of Apartheid, when the police, they said, would at least not rest until they "got their man." These days (2024), they suggested, the police efforts were lackadaisical, despite the theater of force. The proof lay all around them, in the broken infrastructure, the interrupted flows, the constant detours to which they were subject. Such remarks from black subjects are not uncommon in South Africa today, the purest mark of that ostensibly overturned regime's persistence, its status as remainder rather than ruin. But they are not dominant, and even when they are, they manifest a desire for security and lawfulness, abstracted and empowered, as much as any particular political regime. As we have already seen, this desire for preemptive violence-cancelling power, materialized in law-and-order, is also a desire for a violence to end all violence in a world redeemed—beyond debt and perhaps beyond economy. Perhaps, this is also a desire to be beyond representation—or at least beyond the signs, symbols, simulacra and all the substitutes that permit dissimulation. In any case, such people want not only to be unmolested and unrobbed; they want others to simply let them be, in both the simplest and fullest sense of that phrase.

In response to the police raids, the new zama zamas, who had abandoned the underground as surely as Orpheus did, fled and returned, fled and returned. Yet another mutation in the ever-extending life of the Witwatersrand, these scavengers and the scene of their surface extraction summoned for me the memory of my first visit to Carletonville, when I had been shown the glittering pavement and told that, truly, the roads of the region were paved with gold (chapter 3). Here was the dream image made real, now deprived of glitter.

For these new zama zamas, the road was indeed gold. Treating it as the thing itself, the medium of exchange and the infrastructure of mobility were dissolved into the stuff of which they were made: stone and precious metal, and the labor of extracting it. The idea of the gold mine had dilated to encompass almost everything, or at least everything that could generate value and retain that value without having to pass through the metamorphoses of digital credit and institutional banking. This demetaphorization, when things become simply what they are, stripped of their associations and significations, is perhaps the most brutal tendency (never fully realized) in extractivism, although its condition of possibility is a metaphor: of the entire world becoming a mine.

In this context, it is interesting to note the absence of any mention of the gold mines in the discourse of *16 Khuts*, despite the fact that the lives of these young people are as overdetermined by the history of the gold mines as are those of the zama zamas—the migrants from Zimbabwe working under ground, and those from Mozambique plundering the roadways. In some cases, Khutsong is entirely dissolved in the penumbra of Johannesburg. Like their elders, these young people would refuse the demarcations of their world and their assignation to a "location" far from the centers of power. They want to transcend all of those distances that Apartheid materialized in the roads and the empty spaces between towns and townships. "Ghetto is code, city of gold, cause I'm in Joburg," thus raps Pat Lyx Matubatuba, from Khutsong. But as Charlotte Maxeke and Nontsizi Mgqwetho thought, the luster of gold also hides a sordid interior. And Matubatuba continues: "City of prominence where little girls get stripped of their innocence, Joburg, city of common sense where little boys get killed for their ignorance." Not all distance is freeing, of course, but taking distance is necessary for freedom.

It is indeed notable that, while the prosaic speech that is intercut with the more artistic performances in *16 Khuts* makes specific reference to Khutsong, all of these artists reach for forms and referents that are inflected by something foreign, and worldly or cosmopolitan in artistic practice. This is in fact the means of their claim on the aesthetic, and it is what commends their efforts to us, not merely as the outcome and reflection on all that has gone before in this text, but as the means of acting on their world and making something new. The distance that these youths seek is not the alienating distance of judgment, but rather it is a kind of freedom, and it is the liberating if limited inner lining of the processes that they inherit and that have been the subject of this book. For gold has been the historical condition of possibility for the worlding of their world. And, as we now know, the history of gold is the history of abstraction and delocalization, of alienation and colonization, of wealth and immiseration, and of chemical metamorphosis and forced movement. It is the history of accidents and lucky strikes, of waste and fantastic surplus and of sinkholes and caves in which all of these oppositions collapse inward. It is the ongoing history of violence and vengeance and of the desire for justice, of repetition and renewal, of lives and deaths, and of living afterward.

ACKNOWLEDGMENTS

A book that takes more than two decades to research and to write is the product of countless relationships, and is indebted to many. It is impossible to adequately recognize the contributions of all from whom I learned during this process. I can only name some of them here, and hope that such an act suffices to communicate my deep gratitude. Many must remain unnamed, however. My debt to them is no less profound for that reason.

In the early years of my field research in Carletonville and Khutsong, I was assisted by Renee Warrington, and then by Songezile Madikida. Songezile became my trusted counterpart, cameraman and translator for the oral histories project that I undertook in Khutsong—and as his oft-cited presence in this book attests, I am deeply indebted to him.

I was generously and wisely guided by several brave and passionately devoted women, whose work in the areas of education and community service shine as examples of committed intellectual activism. In particular, I am grateful to Yodwa Mzaidume—she is also frequently cited in the pages of this book. Buti Kulwane was another generous interlocutor. I am also grateful to Hlumela Sondlo, who helped with translations in several lanaguages, and introduced me to people from whom I learned much about the world of zama zamas. Cora Bailey, whose indefatigable work in the most destitute communities of the West Rand fills me with awe, has been a guide, a friend, and a mentor for nearly a decade. My debt to her is inseparable from my affection.

My first formal education about South Africa commenced long before I began field research in that country. It started at the University of Chicago in the classrooms of David Bunn, and of Jean and John Comaroff. Jean and John have remained friends and interlocutors from whose work and conversation I have benefitted for more than thirty years.

Some of the research for this book took place in conjunction with my making of a documentary film, entitled *We are Zama Zama*. The relationships and gift of understanding that grew out of that endeavor were both revelatory and inspiring. In particular, I would like to thank: Natalie Denbo, Bette Gordon, Ebrahim Hajee, Fanie (Ndozi) Magwaza, Sarah Muchimba, Bhekani Mumpande, Darren Munenge, Diana Neille, Noel Musokotwane, Tanya Nyathi, Musa Radebe, Richard Poplak, Hlumela Sondlo, and Pascal Troemel.

In South Africa, and in Southern African Studies, I have enjoyed conversations with, and learned much from, many. In particular, I would like to acknowledge Premesh Lalu, Isabel Hofmeyr, Njabulo Ndebele, Sarah Nuttall, Deborah Posel, and Lorena Rizzo.

Several institutions provided me with the support and, most precious of all, the time needed to write, think, and try out my ideas on subjects and materials related to this book. I thank: the Princeton Institute for Advanced Studies; the Stellenbosch Institute for Advanced Study; the Leuphana Institute for Advanced Studies in Culture and Society; the Institute for Cultural Technology and Media Philosophy, Weimar; the American Academy of Berlin. I am thankful to the many people at these institutions who steward their intellectual lives, and who enable the conversations that I participated in there, and especially to: Lorenz Engel, Erich Hörl, Gertrud Koch, Susanne Leeb, Joan W. Scott, and Bernard Siegert. Thanks also to Berit Ebert, Johana Gallup, Thomas Krutak, Aaron Levy, Katja Rieck, and Carol Scherer. I am also grateful for the support of the Guggenheim Foundation, whose fellowship permitted me to complete the final stages of this book.

Other institutions provided material and intellectual support that was hugely enabling. In particular, I wish to acknowledge, at Columbia University, the Department of Anthropology, the Institute for Social and Economic Policy Research, the Institute for Research on Women, Gender and Sexuality (now, the Institute for Gender and Sexuality Studies), the Institute for Comparative Literature and Society, and the Committee on Global Thought.

At Columbia University Press, I have had the brave support and enabling encouragement of Jennifer Crewe, as well as her excellent team. I thank Jennifer for her vision and for seeing this book through publication with such commitment. I also thank Kathryn Jorge for her wonderful editorial stewardship, Wren Haines for project supervision, and Maureen O'Driscoll for her marvelous copy-editing. It is an honor to have Clive van den Berg's painting, "The Big Koppie," a work that honors the victims of Marikana, as cover art, and I thank the designers at Columbia for using it so well, and Clive for allowing them to do so.

For intellectual comradeship, instructive provocation, and that most enabling of all gifts, friendship, I would like to thank: Emily Apter, Étienne Balibar, Shelly Barry, Heike Behrend, Anne Berger, Eduardo Cadava, Astrid Deuber-Mankowsky, Noam Elcott, Jörn Etzold, Brent Hayes Edwards, Zeynep Gürsel, Andreas

Huyssen, Marilyn Ivy, William Kentridge, Brian Larkin, Reinhold Martin, Joe Masco, Nora Nicolini, Stefania Pandolfo, John Pemberton, Jasmine Pisapia, Rose Razaghian, James Siegel, Gayatri Spivak, Patricia Spyer, Farzana Shaikh, Anne Stanwix, Rhiannon Stephens, Lisa Stevenson, Peter Szendy, Radhika Subramaniam, Liana Theodoratou, Daphne Winland, and Martin Zillinger.

Rudolf Mrázek and Andrew Willford read this manuscript from start to finish and gave me invaluable feedback. For their care and insight, I am infinitely indebted.

Ingrid Fiske, Antjie Krog, and John Samuel have been soul mates on this long journey, and I have learned as much from them as from anyone. And throughout these many years, and during periods that have been by times hopeful and despairing, both in South Africa and throughout the world, I have received the hospitality and been embraced and sustained by the friendship of Clive van den Berg and Rocco de Villiers, whose home has often felt like my own. My gratitude for this gift is enormous.

My sisters have provided constant support, despite the remoteness of this work from their lives, and my gratitude to them is profound. Beyond all, I have had the partnership, the intellectual engagement, and the steadying presence of Yvette Christiansë who has kept me going and made me want to write a better book.

Perhaps inevitably, a book that takes such a long time to produce is also scarred by the deaths and losses that occurred along the way. Its completion is burdened by the melancholy realization that those from whom I learned so much cannot receive the offering of this testimony to those lessons. During the writing of *Unstable Ground*, my mother, father, and grandmother died. In ways that cannot be explicated here, they enabled and summoned this exploration. One of my most cherished readers, Tony Morphet, passed away in 2021. Another, Rafael Sánchez died in 2024. In their memory and with a sense of their still-enabling presence in my life, I offer thanks, while accepting responsibility for all the errors and misunderstandings that remain despite their generous tutelage.

* * *

This book was completed during a nine-month fellowship at the Leuphana Institute for Advanced Studies in Culture and Society at Leuphana University, Lüneburg and published with the partial support of a publication grant, both funded by the Ministry of Research and Culture of Lower-Saxony Germany under the SPRUNG! funding scheme (grant number: 11-76251-36031-2021), with additional support from the Volkswagen Stiftung.

**Niedersächsisches Ministerium
für Wissenschaft und Kultur**

 VolkswagenStiftung

NOTES

1. Clearing Ground

Epigraphs to this chapter are from Muriel Rukeyser, "The Speed of Darkness," in *The Speed of Darkness* (New York: Random House), 111; and

Mazisi Kunene, "The Song of the Stone Clan," in *The Ancestors and the Sacred Mountain*. Heinemann Africa Writers Series, available at: http://gateway.proquest.com/openurl?ctx _ver=Z39.88-2003&xri:pqil:res_ver=0.2&res_id=xri:ilcs-us&rft_id=xri:ilcs:ft:aws_poetry :Z300850962.

1. Paul Celan, "Night," in *Paul Celan: Poems*, trans. Michael Hamburger (Manchester: Carcanet, 1980 [1959]), 108–9.
2. Jacques Derrida, "A Certain Impossible Possibility of Saying the Event," trans. Gila Walker, *Critical Inquiry* 33 (Winter 2007): 441–61. "Like the *arrivant*, the event is something that vertically befalls me when I didn't see it coming. The event can only seem to me to be impossible before it occurs [*arriver*]," 452.
3. Stanley Mogoba, "Cement," in *Voices from Within: Black Poetry from Southern Africa*, ed. with intro. Michael Chapman and Achmat Dangor (Johannesburg: A.D. Donker, 1982), 87.
4. On the importance of this process of socializing death, anthropologists have written a great deal. See especially Robert Hertz, "A Contribution to the Study of the Collective Representation of Death," in *Death and the Right Hand*, trans. Rodney and Claudia Needham (New York: Routledge, 2009 [1907]), 27–88; and Bronislaw Malinowski, "Baloma; the Spirits of the Dead in the Trobriand Islands," in *Magic, Science and Religion and Other Essays*, ed. Robert Redfield, (New York: Doubleday, 1954), 151–274.
5. Ovid, "Orpheus, and Eurydice," in *Metamorphoses*, trans. Arthur Golding, ed. Madeleine Forey (Baltimore: Johns Hopkins University Press, 2002), Book X: 57–59.
6. E. E. Evans-Pritchard, *Witchcraft, Oracles and Magic Among the Azande*, abridged ed., ed. Eva Gillies (Oxford: Clarendon Press, 1976).
7. Muriel Rukeyser, "The Speed of Darkness," in *The Speed of Darkness* (New York: Random House), 111.

8. Walter Benjamin, *The Origin of German Tragic Drama*, trans. John Osborne (1963; repr., New York: NLB 2023).

9. Freud wrote about trauma in many contexts, but especially in the analysis of the war neuroses. See Sigmund Freud, "Introduction" to *Psycho-Analysis and the War Neuroses*, in *SE*, vol. XVII, *1917–1919*, 205–16; and *Beyond the Pleasure Principle, Group Psychology and Other Works*, in *SE*, vol. XVIII, *1920–1922*, 1–64. The question of belatedness is brought out in Lacan's rereading of a dream that appears in Sigmund Freud, *The Interpretation of Dreams*, in *SE*, vol. V, *1900*–1901, 339–627, namely the dream of the burning child. See Jacques Lacan, "The Unconscious and Repetition," in *The Four Fundamental Concepts of Psycho-Analysis*, Seminar 1, trans. Alan Sheridan (New York: Norton, 1998 [1973]), 17–66.

10. The play across languages evoked in this reading of "mine" does not translate to all of the vernacular tongues spoken in the regions of which I write, and only partially in Afrikaans, the other dominant European language of the area. This despite the fact that mining is a space in which many European terms are lexicalized.

11. Shakespeare, *Julius Caesar*, III, i.

12. Muriel Rukeyser, "On Money and the Past," in *Body of Waking: Poems*, (New York: Harper and Brothers, 1949), 34–35.

13. There is considerable lexical sharing between the closely related Nguni languages of isiZulu, isiXhosa, and isiNdebele, in addition to a history of lexicalizing English and Afrikaans words. SeSotho, and especially that spoken in the rural areas of Lesotho, whence come many of the migrants to the mines, shares many lexical units and verb structures with the other languages but is otherwise part of a different subset of the larger Southeastern Bantu group, namely the Sotho-Tswana group of languages. Other languages spoken in this area include Chitonga (its speakers coming from northern Zimbabwe and Zambia), Chihlengwe, and Shangaan (from Zimbabwe, Mozambique, and Eastern South Africa; "Shangaan" is also a colloquial term used to refer generally to people from Mozambique). This taxonomy gives the impression that these languages are fixed and more or less discreet. But, as is discussed in chapter 17 of this book, this is not the case; many people speak creolized versions of these languages and move—sometimes with knowing punning and sometimes with a more direct pragmatism—across languages within a single sentence or set of locutions, depending on context and audience.

14. Benjamin Wallet Vilakazi, "Ezinkomponi" [On the Mine Compounds], in Francis Wilson, *Labour on the South African Gold Mines, 1911–1969* (Cambridge: Cambridge University Press, 1972), 192.

15. Peter Abrahams, *Mine Boy* (1946; repr., London: Heinemann, 1975), 42.

16. Revelation 9:2.

17. Muriel Rukeyser, "Murmurs from the Earth of this Land," in *Body of Waking*, 85.

18. Michael Cawood Green, "Older Than Time," in *Sinking: A Verse Novella*, (London: Penguin, 1997), 6.

19. Green, "Older Than Time."

20. Jacques Rancière, *The Politics of Aesthetics: The Distribution of the Sensible*, trans. Gabriel Rockhill (New York: Continuum, 2004 [2000]).

21. Foucault's theorization of visibility and sayability is elaborated in three volumes, beginning with *The Order of Things: An Archaeology of the Human Sciences* [*Les mots et les choses*] (New York: Vintage, 1970 [1966]); *The Birth of the Clinic: An Archaeology of Medical Perception*, trans. A. M. Sheridan Smith (New York: Vintage, 1994 [1963]); and *Discipline and Punish: The Birth of the Prison*, trans. A.M. Sheridan Smith (New York: Vintage, 1984 [1975]). See also Gilles Deleuze, *Foucault*, trans. Seán Hand, intro. Paul Bové (Minneapolis: University of Minnesota Press, 1988 [1986]).

22. Karl Marx, *The Eighteenth Brumaire of Louis Bonaparte*, trans. Ben Fowkes, in *Surveys from Exile*, ed. David Fernach (New York: Vintage, 1974 [1850]), 143–249. On the function of poetry as opposed to imagery in Marx's discourse on the imagination, see Dermot Ryan,

"The Future of an Allusion: "Poïesis," in Karl Marx, "The Eighteenth Brumaire of Louis Bonaparte," *SubStance* 41, no. 3 (2012): 127–46.

23. Lesego Rampolokeng, "The Word or the Head," in *The New Century of South African Poetry*, ed. Michael Chapman (Jeppestown: Jonathan Ball, 2002), 456.

24. Andrew Parker, "The Poetry of the Future," in "Conference Debates—Untiming the Nineteenth Century: Temporality and Periodization," *PMLA* 124, no. 1 (2009): 273–88, 283. Parker retains the capital letters used for nouns in Marx's German.

25. Muriel Rukeyser, "The Usable Truth," *Poetry* 58, no. 4 (July 1941): 206–9, 207.

26. The World Bank used this number, unchanged since 2017, in 2022, despite likely increases in poverty following the pandemic. Their statistics appear to be derived from "Poverty on the Rise in South Africa," Stats SA, August 22, 2017, http://www.statssa.gov.za/?p=10334,. For an explication of the procedures used to determine the poverty line in South Africa, see "National Poverty Lines," Stats SA, July 31, 2018, http://www.statssa.gov.za/publications /P03101/P031012018.pdf. Also see World Bank, *Poverty and Equity Brief*, South Africa, April 2020, https://databankfiles.worldbank.org/public/ddpext_download/poverty /33EF03BB-9722-4AE2-ABC7-AA2972D68AFE/Global_POVEQ_ZAF.pdf.

27. Marx, *Eighteenth Brumaire*, chap. 1.

28. Rukeyser, "Usable Truth," 206.

29. This reference is to Paul Celan, "Sand from the Urns," in *Paul Celan: Poems*, 35: "Green as mould is the house of oblivion."

30. Rukeyser, "Usable Truth," 206.

31. Ntongela Masilela, *An Outline of the New African Movement in South Africa* (Trenton, NJ: Africa World Press, 2013), 14.

32. Njabulo Ndebele, *The Cry of Winnie Mandela* (Cape Town: David Phillip, 2003).

33. Sandile Dikeni, "Night," in *Planting Water* (Durban: University of KwaZulu-Natal Press, 2007), 72.

34. Rukeyser, "Usable Truth," 208.

35. On Nietzsche's poeticization of philosophy, see Astrid Deuber-Mankowsky, "Nietzsche's Practices of Illusion," *Critical Horizons* 18, no. 4 (2017): 307–32.

36. Theodor Adorno, *Kierkegaard: Construction of the Aesthetic*, trans. and ed. Robert Hullot Kentor (Minneapolis: University of Minnesota Press, 1989 [1962]), 3.

37. Adorno, *Kierkegaard*, 3.

38. In this sense, ethnography shares something with the kind of documentary writing that James Agee described when he observed, in *Let Us Now Praise Famous Men*, that unlike the novel, in which characters depend entirely on the author for their being, documentary prose testifies to the autonomous existence of the people whom it describes. James Agee and Walker Evans, *Let Us Now Praise Famous Men* (1939; repr., Boston: Houghton Mifflin, 2001).

39. Johann Wolfgang von Goethe, *Faust*, Part II, ed and trans. Stuart Atkins, intro. David Wellerby (Princeton, NJ: Princeton University Press, 1984 [1832]), lines 4892–96.

40. Goethe, *Faust*, Part II, 6132.

41. Alain Badiou, "The Cultural Revolution: The Last Revolution?," *Positions: East Asia Cultures Critique* 13, no. 3 (2005): 481–514, 505, emphasis in original.

42. There is a double figuration here: of text and textile, on one hand, and of figure and ground, on the other. Gayatri Chakravorty Spivak refers to the text as a "safe figure" precisely insofar as it escapes the speech-writing opposition and the corollary temptation to imagine the individual as the author or creator of the language itself. "Feminism and Critical Theory," in *The Spivak Reader*, ed. Donna Landry and Gerald McLean (1985; repr., New York: Routledge, 1996), 53–74.

43. Compulsory education in Afrikaans was introduced in 1974, as an extension of the terms of the earlier Bantu Education Act (1953). It coincided with an increase in enrollments in secondary schools (from 12,656 to 34,656) and in an increase in agitation against the notion of unequal education by activist groups, especially the South African Students Association (SASO).

44. W. H. Auden, "In Praise, of Limestone," in *Collected Poems*, ed. Edward Mendelsohn (1948; repr., New York: Vintage, 1991), 540–42.

45. Octave Mannoni, "I know very well, but all the same . . .," trans. G.-M. Goshgarian, in *Perversion and the Social Relation*, ed. Molly Anne Rothenberg, Dennis Foster, and Slavoj Žižek (Durham, NC: Duke University Press, 2003), 68–92. This formulation underlies Slavoj Žižek's own account in *The Sublime Object of Ideology* (New York: Verso, 2009).

46. In Greek myth, the *obolus* or *danake* was a golden coin paid to Charon to cross the River Styx and enter the kingdom of death.

47. Walter Benjamin, *The Arcades Project*, trans. Howard Eiland and Kevin McLaughlin. (Cambridge, MA: Belknap Press, 1999), 160.

48. I use the concept of display by analogy with Walter Benjamin's concept of "exhibition value," which he counterposes to "cult value" in an account of the artwork's transformation by photography. In my case, which extends beyond the museum context, the notion of display value is also intended to provide a third term beyond exchange and surplus value, as Marx defined them. See Walter Benjamin, "The Work of Art in the Age of Mechanical Reproducibility: Second Version," trans. Edmond Jephcott and Harry Zohn. In *Selected Writings*. Vol. 3, *1935–1938*, ed. Howard Eiland and Michael W. Jennings (Cambridge, MA: Harvard University Press, 2002 [1935]), esp. 106–108.

49. Benjamin, *Arcades Project*, 496.

50. Theodor Adorno, *Minima Moralia: Reflections from Damaged Life*, trans. E. F. M. Jephcott (London: Verso, 1974 [1951]), 232.

2. Letters, Ruin: Migrancy's Remainders

The epigraph to this chapter is from S. M. Guma, *The Form, Content, and Technique of Traditional Literature in Southern Sotho* (Pretoria: J.L van Shaik, 1967); also quoted in David Coplan, *In the Time of Cannibals: The Word Music of South Africa's Basotho Migrants* (Chicago: University of Chicago Press, 1994), 107.

1. Defy was a brand of household appliance prized in working and middle-class households.

2. In many mythic narratives of southern African provenance, the messenger is both the bearer of a sacred message and the bringer of death. In contemporary idioms and the aesthetic practices of compound life, such as the Sesotho *lifela*, the traveler and the messenger are both doubled and split. The traveler is the migrant laborer, whereas the messenger is the bureaucratic functionary, he who can address the migrant from within the corporation-state and mediate the chasm between "rural" and urban worlds.

3. Jean Comaroff and John Comaroff, "The Madman and the Migrant," in *Ethnography and the Historical Imagination* (Boulder, CO: Westview, 1992), 155.

4. According to Simmel, "The stranger is close to us, insofar as we feel between him and ourselves common features of a national, social, occupational, or generally human, nature. He is far from us, insofar as these common features extend beyond him or us, and connect us only because they connect a great many people." See George Simmel, "The Stranger," in *The Sociology of Georg Simmel*, trans., ed. and intro. Kurt Wolff (New York: Free Press, 1950 [German original, 1921]), 448–53, 451.

5. The postal hour was the moment of delight or disappointment at the center of much English epistolary fiction—not a little of which was on the curriculum of the schools where the African elite were educated.

6. David Coplan, *In the Time of Cannibals: The Word Music of South Africa's Basotho Migrants* (Chicago: University of Chicago Press, 1994), 134.

7. These "intimate missives" sent between home and mine compound are to be distinguished from the political letter writing and petition-making made possible by mission-sponsored

literacy (see chapter 5). Examples of the latter can be found in Isabel Hofmeyr, *We Spend Our Years as a Tale That Is Told: Oral Historical Narrative in a South African Chiefdom* (Johannesburg: Witwatersrand University Press, 1993), 59–77. Also, see the remarkable letters of Emma Sandile addressed to Bishop Gray in 1860: "Emma Sandile, Letters and Land Submission," in *Women Writing Africa: The Southern Region*, eds. M. J. Daymond et al. (New York: Feminist Press, 2003), 92–96.

8. Keith Breckenridge, "Love Letters and Amenuenses: Beginning the Cultural History of the Working Class Private Sphere in Southern Africa, 1900–1933, *Journal of Southern African Studies* 26, no. 2 (2000): 337–48.

9. Breckenridge, "Love Letters," 341.

10. Isaac Schapera, *Married Life in an African Tribe* (New York: Sheridan, 1941). Also see Jeff Guy, "Making Words Visible: Aspects of Orality, Literacy and History in Southern Africa," *South African Historical Journal* 31 (1994): 3–27. Bechuanaland was a British protectorate established in 1885. In 1891, it came under the jurisdiction of the British High Commissioner in South Africa and was administered from Mafeking (now Mafikeng), before becoming part of Cape Colony—against the wishes of its chiefs (see also chapter 5). Part of the territory is now under South African jurisdiction, and the other constitutes Botswana, which achieved independence in 1966.

11. Jacques Derrida develops this notion of survival in his essay, "Sur-vivre," translated into English as "Living On." See chapter 13 for an exploration of this concept in relation to the phenomenon of ancestrality. Jacques Derrida, "Living On," in *Parages*, trans. James Hulbert, ed. John Leavey (Stanford, CA: Stanford University Press, 2011), 103–91.

12. Schapera, *Married Life*, 152.

13. Schapera, *Married Life*, 46, 54, 153–55.

14. Schapera, *Married Life*, 274.

15. Coplan, *Time of Cannibals*, 135.

16. Mazisi Kunene, "White People," in *Two Zulu Poets: Mazisi Kunene and B.W. Vilakazi.* Compiled by Dike Okoro (Milwaukee: Cissus World, 2015), 18. Kunene, a contemporary of the *sefela* artist, was a central member of the ANC during the 1970s and was, for a period, its director of finance as well as the convener of several international events aimed at generating solidarity for the struggle against Apartheid. See, Dike Okoro, "Introduction," to *Two Zulu Poets*, viii–xxi, xii.

17. Walter Benjamin, "The Storyteller: Observations on the Works of Nikolai Leskov," in *Selected Writings*, vol. 3, *1935–1938*, eds. Howard Eiland and Michael W. Jennings (Cambridge, MA: Harvard University Press, 2002), 146.

18. Raymond Williams. *The Country and the City* (London: Chatto and Windus, 1973).

19. Both Bell Telephone and AT&T commercials used the lyrics from Diana Ross's 1970 Motown hit by the same name.

20. Martin Hägglund, *Dying for Time: Proust, Woolf, Nabokov* Cambridge, MA: Harvard University Press, 2012), 133.

21. Witwatersrand Chamber of Mines, *Annual Report*, 1893, 11.

22. Mazisi Kunene, "Age of the Gods," *Anthem of the Decades* (1981; repr., London: Heineman, 2006), line 11, 3.

23. Kunene, "Age of the Gods," line 3027, 85.

24. Gwede Mantashe and the National Union of Mineworkers, *Contracting Out: The NUM View* (Johannesburg: National Union of Mineworkers, 1995), 153; Jonathan Crush et al., "Undermining Labour: The Rise of Sub-Contracting in South African Gold Mines," *Journal of Southern African Studies* 27, no. 1 (2001): 10. The crucial issue of bonuses tied to productivity is that workers are encouraged to work hastily and to extend their hours beyond what has been determined are excessive safety risks. Bonus pay is clearly linked to higher rates of accident.

25. Originally a representative and presiding territorial chief from Emigrant Tembuland, Kaizer Matanzima was prime minister of the Bantustan from 1976 to 1979 and was

president from 1979 to 1986. From the start, he opposed the ANC's strategies, and many in the ANC read Matanzima's affirmation of Verwoerd's agenda, recounted in his book, *Independence My Way* (Pretoria: Foreign Affairs Association, 1976), as acquiescence to white supremacy. Matanzima, for his part, claimed to be enacting a kind of reciprocal exclusion, and he repeatedly advocated for *both* sovereignty *and* equal treatment before the law of Black subjects in the Republic. He avowed "the cardinal principle of separate development with which we have consistently agreed" and asserted: "We shall have [the Europeans] when we need them but certainly we do not want to have a multi-racial government in the Transkei and we have repeatedly said so in this House. They have got their own parliament. Now if we are given our own parliament we must be alone." Transkeian Territorial Authority (TTA), *Proceedings of the Special Session Called to Consider a Draft Bill for the Granting of Self-Government to the Transkei* (Territorial Printers, 1983), 9–10. This led some to describe his position as "apartheid in reverse"; see "Vital Pointer to Trends in the Transkei," *Rand Daily Mail*, November 17, 1963. Matanzima shared the regime's antipathy toward communism as well as the Liberal Party (and especially its journalistic organ, *Contact*), which he described as a "danger coming from the North"; see TTA, *Proceedings*, 21; Douglas Irvine, "The Liberal Party, 1933–1968," in *Democratic Liberalism in South Africa: Its History and Prospects*, eds. Jeffrey Butler, Richard Elphick, and David Walsh (Middleton, CT: Wesleyan University Press, 1987), 131. He also opposed trade unions and proposed banning them in 1979. Steve Kgame, "Matanzima's Union Ruling Under Fire," *Rand Daily Mail*, April 25, 1975, 6.

26. Nahum 1:6.

27. Kerry Chance, *Living Politics in South Africa's Urban Shacklands* (Chicago: University of Chicago Press, 2018).

28. There is no doubt that some of his hesitation to indict the mines had to do with the fact that I, a white woman and obvious beneficiary of racial capitalism, was listening. Nonetheless, I do not believe that his wish and indeed his memory that things had been more plentiful in the past than they were at the time of our conversation were reducible to this fact. The awful truth of the matter is that, however atrocious had been the circumstances of the mineworkers in the Apartheid era—and they were atrocious—this desolate remnant where we stood had become the scene of even more degradation than had been the case in those years.

29. Ernest Cole, *House of Bondage: A South African Black Man Exposes in His Own Pictures and Words the Bitter Life of His Homeland Today*, with Thomas Flaherty, intro. Joseph Lelyveld (New York: Random House, 1967), 28–31 and 54, respectively.

30. Ovid, *Metamorphoses*, trans. Arthur Golding, ed. Madeleine Forey (Baltimore, MD: Johns Hopkins University Press, 2002), 1:125–150.

31. This distinction, between coercive and ideological state apparatuses, is most explicitly deployed by Louis Althusser, *On the Reproduction of Capitalism: Ideology and Ideological State Apparatuses*, trans. A. M. Goshgarian, preface Etienne Balibar, intro. Jacques Bidet (New York: Verso, 2014 [1971. 1995]). Contemporary service delivery protests in South Africa have made the lack of sanitation facilities a key node of opposition—making shit a signifier as well as a weapon of a movement aimed at the creation of habitable communities. See, for examples, Chance, *Living Politics*; Antina von Schnitzler, "Performing Dignity: Human Rights and the Legal Politics of Water," in *Democracy's Infrastructure: Techno-politics and Protest After Apartheid* (Princeton, NJ: Princeton University Press, 2016), 168–195; Steven Robins, "How Poo Became a Political Issue," *Cape Times*, July 2, 2013.

32. Alan Jeeves, "The Control of Migratory Labour on the South African Gold Mines in the Era of Kruger and Milner," *Journal of Southern African Studies* 2, no. 1 (1975): 17. The WNLA was established in 1900 and replaced the Rand Native Labour Association. The terminology of wastage persisted for as long as the WNLA operated (until 1968), but

it came to encompass those discharged at the end of service in addition to those who "deserted and [were] sent to goal," and those who died during the period of contract.

33. For example, the report of the WNLA's Board of Management counted 292,802 and 306,966 out of a total of 316,534 and 327,579 in 1944 and 1945, respectively, as "wastage." Of these, the deserters numbered 6,116 and 6,729 and the dead 1,723 and 1,858 for each year in the period. The wastage was also calculated as a percentage of workers employed: 7.71 and 7.81 percent. WNLA, "Annexure A," *Report of the Board of Management for the Period Ended December 31, 1945*, 1 and 8.

34. Karl Marx, *Grundrisse*, trans. Martin Nicolaus (New York: Penguin, 1993), 90–94.

35. Georges Bataille, "The Meaning of General Economy," in *The Accursed Share*, vol. 1, 19–26, trans. Robert Hurley (New York: Zone 1988 [1949]), 21; and *The Bataille Reader*, ed. Fred Botting and Scott Wilson, trans. Allan Stoekl with Carl R. Lovitt and Donald M. Leslie Jr. (London: Blackwell, 1997 [1993]), 184.

36. Emily Dixon, "Solid Gold Toilet Stolen from Blenheim Palace, Birthplace of Winston Churchill," *CNN Style*, electronic edition, accessed September 14, 2019, https://www.cnn.com/style/article/uk-blenheim-palace-gold-toilet-scli-gbr-intl/index.html. See also "Busted Flush: Gold Toilet Stolen from Blenheim Palace," *The Guardian*, September 14, 2019, https://www.theguardian.com/uk-news/2019/sep/14/gold-toilet-reportedly-stolen-blenheim-palace-cattelan.

37. Georges Bataille, "The Notion of Expenditure," in *The Bataille Reader*, 180.

38. Bataille, "Expenditure," 179.

39. I am taking some distance from the discourse of those Afropessimists and especially the followers of Agamben, as well as the prophets of disposability, who elide the difference between the negations of dominant discourse and the nihilism that takes that discourse for the truth of social life. See gamEdze and gamedZe, "Anxiety, Afropessimism, and the University Shutdown," *South Atlantic Quarterly* 118, no. 1 (2019): 215–25.

40. As Jacob Dlamini has observed, "native nostalgia," which is often simply the pleasurable recall of forms of social life enjoyed *despite* Apartheid, can appear to be a nostalgia *for* apartheid, but the two must be analytically separated. See Jacob Dlamini, *Native Nostalgia* (Johannesburg: Jacana, 2009).

41. Margaret Thatcher, "Speech to Conservative Women's Conference," May 21, 1980, available at: https://www.margaretthatcher.org/document/104368, accessed July 12, 2024. The phrase later became a slogan of neoliberalism. The phrase later became a slogan of neoliberalism.

42. A vast literature has emerged to offer analyses of this conjuncture, focusing by turns on the "Faustian bargain" that the ANC was forced to enter with white capital to bring about the end of Apartheid, and the intensification of inequality and precarity that accompanied its first two and half decades in power. The period has been described as "precarious liberation," and its structure has been aptly analyzed by Gillian Hart in terms of a dialectic of denationalization and renationalization. See Gillian Hart, *Rethinking the South African Crisis: Nationalism, Populism, Hegemony* (Athens: University of Georgia Press, 2013). On the assessment of rising inequality, see Haroon Bhorat and Ravi Kanbur, eds., *Poverty and Policy in Post-Apartheid South Africa* (Cape Town: Human Sciences Research Council, 2006). Also see Franco Barchiesi, *Precarious Liberation: Workers, the State, and Contested Social Citizenship in Postapartheid South Africa* (Binghamton: SUNY, 2011); Ari Sitas, *The Mandela Decade 1990–2000: Labour, Culture, and Society in Post-Apartheid South Africa* (Pretoria: Unisa Press, 2010); and Sampie Terreblanche, *Lost in Transformation: South Africa's Search for a New Future Since 1986* (Johannesburg: KMM Preview, 2012).

43. Anita Parbhaker-Fox, "Treasure from Trash: How Mining Waste Can Be Mined a Second Time," *The Conversation*, June 28, 2016, https://theconversation.com/treasure-from-trash-how-mining-waste-can-be-mined-a-second-time-59667.

44. My understanding of the need to read from the margins, and to recognize the constitutive role of the excluded part, including the detail, in the phenomenon, history, and discourse that would otherwise be excluded by the analytic frame, derives from Jacques Derrida. See *Truth in Painting*, trans. Geoff Bennington and Ian McLeod (Chicago: University of Chicago Press, 1987 [1978]). Derrida refers to "digging in" to Kant's texts on aesthetics, when developing his notion of the frame or parergon (92). On the question of the shadow cast by that which is excluded, see Samuel Weber, *Mass Mediauras: Form, Techniques, Media* (Stanford, CA: Stanford University Press, 1996).

45. Derrida, *Truth in Painting*, 17.

3. Gold Fools: Or, What Is a Gold Rush?

Epigraphs to this chapter are from Dante Alighieri, *Divine Comedy*, Book VII, lines 31–32; and Edouard Gourdon, *Faucheurs de la nuit* [Reapers of the Night], cited by Walter Benjamin, "On Some Motifs in Baudelaire," in *Walter Benjamin, Selected Writings*, ed. Michael W. Jennings, Howard Eiland, and Gary Smith (1940; repr., Cambridge, MA: Belknap Press, 2006), n58, 352.

1. A. S. Gray, *Payable Gold: An Intimate Record of the History of the Discovery of the Payable Witwatersrand Goldfields and of Johannesburg in 1886 and 1887*, Based on researches made in the State Archives, Pretoria by Ethel L. Gray, and containing "The Oosthuizen Papers," trans. B. De Coigny Marchange (South Africa: Central News Agency, 1937), 82.

2. R. T. Jones, "President's Corner," *Journal of the Southern African Institute of Mining and Metallurgy* 116, no. 1 (2016): vi–vii.

3. Ed Cropley, "Desperation and Death Beneath South Africa's City of Gold," Reuters, September 13, 2016, https://www.reuters.com/article/us-safrica-mining/desperation-and -death-beneath-south-africas-city-of-gold-idUSKCN11J1M6.

4. Advertisement from the *Port Elizabeth Telegraph and Eastern Province Standard*, November 13, 1886. Such advertisements appeared daily in virtually all of the English-language newspapers of the region, and in the Dutch language newspapers of the Republic. They also appeared in European papers.

5. Revelation 21:21.

6. In other words, it was "fool's gold." Typically, fool's gold is actually pyrite or chalcopyrite, but it may also be mica, especially if the latter is weathered. Gray, *Payable Gold*, 18. On the metals that may be mistaken for gold, see U.S. Geological Survey, "What Is 'Fool's Gold'?," accessed May 1, 2019, https://www.usgs.gov/faqs/what-fools-gold?qt-news_science_products =0#qt-news_science_products.

7. Georgius Agricola, *De Re Metallica*, trans. Herbert Clark Hoover and Lou Henry Hoover (New York: Dover, 1959), 1–2.

8. Agricola, *De Re Metallica*, 3–4.

9. Agricola, *De Re Metallica*, 26–29.

10. Chinese indentured labor was brought into South Africa between 1903 and 1908, but the duration of the contract ensured their presence on the mines until 1910. See Peter Richardson, "The Recruitment of Chinese Labour for the South African Gold Mines, 1903–1908," *Journal of African History* 18, no. 1 (1977): 85–108.

11. Bewick, Moreing was British-based, but its dominance was achieved in Western Australia, where its mines generated about 40 percent of the region's gold output in the early years of the twentieth century. Hoover saw Bewick, Moreing and Co. as a new form of corporation, in which mining engineers dominated the company directors in decision making, but in South Africa, he thought he recognized a new kind of mining company, in which groups of partners, largely men of finance, were controlling "the bulk of mining enterprise."

Herbert Hoover, Editorial, *Western Australian Mining, Building and Engineering Journal* 28 (April 1904), 670; see also J. J. van Helten and Y. Cassis, *Capitalism in a Mature Economy: Financial Institutions, Capital Export and British Industry, 1870–1939* (Aldershot: Algar, 1990), 175.

12. Thomas Baines, *The Gold Regions of Southeastern Africa* (London: Stanford, 1877), 162.

13. Francesco Guala, "Critical Notice: Review of *La Naissance de la Clinique*, by Michel Foucault," *Economics and Philosophy* 22 (2006): 429–39, 430.

14. Transvaal Chamber of Mines, *Gold in South Africa* (Johannesburg, 1969), 10B, quoted in Francis Wilson, *Labour in the South African Gold Mines* (Cambridge: Cambridge University Press, 1972), 20. This description would be reproduced verbatim in later editions of *Gold in South Africa*, well into the late 1980s, with the only difference being its shifting location from page 10B to 8B.

15. Antonio de Herrera y Tordesillas, *Descripcion de las Indias Ocidentales* (Madrid: Imprenta Real, 1601). On Herrera's account and its circulation in the critical scholarship on fetishism, from Charles de Brosses to Karl Marx, see my "After de Brosses: Fetishism, Translation, Comparativism, Critique," in *The Returns of Fetishism: Charles de Brosses and the Afterlives of an Idea*, with a translation of *The Worship of Fetish Gods*, by Daniel H. Leonard (Chicago: University of Chicago, 2017), esp. 153, 192.

16. The renowned gold rhinoceros that was found at Mapungubwe, near what is now the South African/Zimbabwe border, and which dates to the thirteenth century, was recovered from a royal burial only in 1934. And the era as well as its gold production and trade were largely effaced by Apartheid historians. Leo Fouché, reports on excavations at Mapungubwe (Northern Transvaal) from February 1933 to June 1935. Leo Fouché, *Mapungubwe, Ancient Bantu Civilization on the Limpopo*, edited on behalf of the Archaeological Committee of the University of Pretoria (Cambridge: Cambridge University Press, 1937). For a recent account of the debates about gold's place as a signifier in early state development, see Thomas N. Huffman, "Mapela, Mapangubwe, and the Origins of States in Southern Africa," *South African Archaeological Bulletin* 70, no. 201 (2015): 15–27.

17. Anthony Trollope, *South Africa*, ed. J. H. Davidson (1878; repr., Cape Town: Balkema, 1973), 311. In H. Rider Haggard's novel, the legendary city is imagined as the Ophir of the Bible. H. Rider Haggard, *King Solomon's Mines*, in *Three Adventure Novels of H. Rider Haggard: She, King Solomon's Mines, Allan Quartermain* (New York: Dover, 1951), 251. Haggard's association of diamonds and gold in these mines might be read as a thinly veiled transposition of the bond between the two forms of capital, and the men who controlled it, in the region's mining industry.

18. Owen Letcher, *The Gold Mines of Southern Africa: The History, Technology and Statistics of the Gold Industry* (London: Waterlow, 1936), 12.

19. Donald Denoon, "Capital and Capitalists in the Transvaal in the 1890s and 1900s," *Historical Journal* 23, no. 1 (1980): 117; and A. P. Cartwright, *Valley of Gold* (Cape Town: Timmins, 1961), 20.

20. Gray, *Payable Gold*, 20–30.

21. Agricola, *De Re Metallica*, 8.

22. Agricola, *De Re Metallica*, 6.

23. Thomas Collingwood Kitto, quoted in Gray, *Payable Gold*, 44. For Kitto's biography see "Thomas Collingwood Kitto," S2A3, *Biographical Database of Southern African Science*, accessed May 6, 2019, http://www.s2a3.org.za/bio/Biograph_final.php?serial=1544.

24. Gray, *Payable Gold*, 81; emphasis added. Gray, an analytical chemist was employed by the Langlaagte Estate and Gold Mining Company between 1905 and 1912. See "Gray, Mr. James," in S2A3, *Biographical Database of Southern African Science*, accessed May 6, 2019, http://www.s2a3.org.za/bio/Biograph_final.php?serial=1124.

25. Sigmund Freud, "Dreams in Folklore," in *SE*, vol. XII, *1911–1913*, 187. Freud was quoting Alfred Jeremias, *Das Alte Testament im Lichte des Alten Orients* (Leipzig: Hinrichs, 1904), 115n.

26. Freud, "Character and Anal Erotism," in *SE*, vol. 9, 174.

27. Freud, "Dreams in Folklore," 187.

28. On Marx's theory of productive consumption, see the "Introduction" to *Grundrisse*, trans. and intro. Martin Nikolaus (New York: Penguin, 1973), esp. 90–94.

29. John A. Hobson, *Imperialism: A Study* (New York: James Pott, 1902), 49.

30. Trollope, *South Africa*, 310.

31. Trollope, *South Africa*, 311.

32. Hannah Arendt, *The Origins of Totalitarianism* (New York: Harcourt, Brace, Jovanovich, 1973), 189.

33. Trollope, *South Africa*, 311

34. Arendt, *Totalitarianism*, 188. Arendt's analysis of South Africa depends, almost entirely, on her reading of Cornelius de Kiewiet's writings on the subject. De Kiewiet, who wrote as passionately against Apartheid as against communism, and who oversaw Cornell University's Area and Language Program for army personnel during World War II, had grown up in South Africa as the Dutch immigrant son of a prospector in both the diamond and gold fields.

35. Arendt, *Totalitarianism*, 189.

36. Cartwright, *Valley of Gold*, 20.

37. Such personalism is often associated with the specific dimensions of Kruger's rule and republican politics and treated as an artifact of the tensions between the Afrikaner agrarian capitalists and the Uitlander mining capitalists. One of the reasons adduced *against* annexation by the Transvaal of the Bechuanaland tribes was the fact that, in the Cape Colony, local powers had relatively direct access to political authority and could obtain their ends without having to pass through "an entanglement of red-tape." Sol (Solomon Tshekisho) Plaatje, "Article," *Bechuana Gazette*, December 13, 1902, in *Sol Plaatje: Selected Writings*, ed. Brian Willan (Johannesburg: Witwatersrand University Press, 1996), 64.

38. E. J. Kärrström, *Eighteen Years in South Africa. A Swedish Gold-Digger's Account of His Adventures in the Land of Gold (1877–1896)*, ed. Ione Rudner, trans. Ione and Jalmar Rudner (Cape Town: Africana, 2013), 155.

39. "Dawson, Mr. William E," in S2A3, *Biographical Database of Southern African Science*, accessed May 6, 2019, http://www.s2a3.org.za/bio/Biograph_final.php?serial=3290.

40. Fockens arrived in South Africa in 1883, and commenced his classes in 1886, a year before publishing *Beknopt leerboek der delfstofkunde, eene noodzakelijke handleiding voor allen die begerig zijn de delfstoffen der Z.A. Republiek te leeren kennen* [A brief textbook of mineral science, an indispensable manual for all who wish to learn about the minerals of the S.A. Republic] (Pretoria, 1887). Fockens was also commissioned to undertake a report of inquiry into the monopoly granted to Eduard Lippert for the supply of dynamite to the mines. See "Fockens, Dr Jabob Wilhelm," S2A3, *Biographical Database of Southern African Science*, accessed May 6, 2019, https://www.s2a3.org.za/bio/Biograph_final .php?serial=954. On Fockens's course offerings, see Gray, *Payable Gold*, 79–80.

41. Gray, *Payable Gold*, 32.

42. Gray, *Payable Gold*, 25. Participation in the gold industry entailed more substantial outlays from investors—£5 versus £25—than other joint stock ventures in the mining sector. The conversion rate at the time was approximately 1 pound sterling to 4.94 U.S. dollars; therefore this represents approximately $24.70 versus $123.50.

43. Baines, *The Gold Regions*, 96.

44. Cartwright, *Valley of Gold*, 53.

45. Charles van Onselen, *New Babylon, New Nineveh: Everyday Life on the Witwatersrand 1886–1914* (Cape Town: Jonathan Ball, 1982), 2. Adjusted for inflation, that amount would be equivalent to £17,661,675,500 or US$21,370,626,750 in October 2023.

46. Van Onselen, *New Babylon*, 2.

47. *The Port Elizabeth Telegraph and Eastern Province Standard*, Thursday, November 1886, 2.

48. *Cape Times*, Wednesday, November 3, 1886, 1.

49. *In the Common Interest: The Story of the Transvaal and Orange Free State Chamber of Mines*, Public Relations Series No. 94 (Johannesburg: TOFS Chamber of Mines, 1967?), 4.

50. Sol (Solomon Tshekisho) Plaatje, "Native Affairs: After Four Years?," *Selected Writings*, 317–18.

51. V. L. Allen, *The History of Black Mineworkers in South Africa*, vol. 1, *The Techniques of Resistance, 1871–1948* (Keighley, UK: Moor Press, 1992), 45. According to Rob Turrell, Tyamzashi owned three claims in the Dutoitspan mine in 1879. See Robert Vicat Turrell, *Labor and Capital on the Kimberley Diamond Fields, 1871–1890* (London: Institute of Commonwealth Studies, 1987), 256, n127. Also see Rob Turrell, "Kimberley: Labour and Compounds, 1871–1888," in *Industrialisation and Social Change in South Africa: African Class Formation, Culture and Consciousness, 1870–1930*, ed. Shula Marks and Richard Rathbone (London: Longman, 1982), 47.

52. Henri Lefebvre, *The Critique of Everyday of Everyday Life*, trans. John Moore, pref. Michel Trebitsch (New York: Verso, 1991 [1958]), 104.

53. Karl Marx, *Contribution to the Critique of Political Economy*, ed. Maurice Dobb (New York: International Publishers, 1970), 155; emphasis added.

54. Marx also mentions the rush in Colombia, but insofar as British imperial ambitions were focused on the deposits in the territories of the settler colonies, these were the more relevant levers of exploration in southern Africa (including the Cape Colony, and what is now Zambia and Zimbabwe). See Marx, *Contribution*, 157.

55. Marx, *Grundrisse*, 166.

56. George Bernard Shaw, "Karl Marx and *Das Kapital*," *National Reformer*, August 14 1887, in *Bernard Shaw and Karl Marx: A Symposium, 1884–1889* (New York: Random House, 1930), 105–18.

57. Georg Simmel, *Philosophy of Money*, trans. Tom Bottomore and David Frisby, with Kathe Mengelberg (New York: Routledge, 1978), 67 and 85.

58. Karl Marx, *Capital*, vol. 1, intro. Ernst Mandel, trans. Ben Fowkes (London: Penguin, 1976 1867]), 189; emphasis added.

59. Despite this important historicist revision of Marx's analysis, Stemmet retreats into positivism when he argues that, in most places, gold has throughout history been mined from placer deposits (or conglomerate outcrops) and as such was technologically similar and thereby "comparable" throughout the world. In his analysis, this technological comparability ensured that "gold would not only come to serve as the measure of all value, but that the unit of that measure would be universally understood to mean the same thing: x amount of labour-time." Farouk Stemmet, *Golden Contradiction: A Marxist Theory of Gold, with Particular Reference to South Africa* (Aldershot, UK: Avebury, 1996), 31.

60. Stemmet, *Golden Contradiction*, 39.

61. Marx, *Capital*, 199.

62. Marx, *Grundrisse*, 166.

63. Marx, *Grundrisse*, 166; emphasis added. It is not true that silver is inoxidizable. Here Marx is treating silver, oddly enough, as a species of gold. On the linkage between gold and superfluity, see also Jean-Joseph Goux, *Symbolic Economies: After Marx and Freud*, trans. Jennifer Curtiss Gage (Ithaca, NY: Cornell University Press, 1990 [1972], esp. 27–28.

64. Marx, *Contribution*, 107.

65. Marx, *Contribution*, 107.

66. These lines from Act 4, Scene 3, appear in *Grundrisse*, 163. Slightly different lines, from the same scene are invoked in *Capital*, 230.

67. Marx, *Contribution*, 125.

68. Marx, *Capital*, 187.

69. Marx, *Capital*, 188; emphasis added.

70. Marx, *Capital*, 195.

71. Marx, *Contribution*, 114.

72. Johanne Wolfgang von Goethe, *Faust*, ed. and trans. Stuart Atkins, intro. David Wellerby. (Princeton, NJ: Princeton University Press, 1984 [1832], part II, lines 6083–6089 and 6198, respectively. Goethe was writing at a time when the Prussian state was attempting to impose a uniform standard but in silver. However, it pushed Europe toward gold after the Franco-Prussian War. See Ted Wilson, *Battles for the Standard: Bimetallism and the Spread of the Gold Standard in the Nineteenth Century* (New York: Routledge, 2000).

73. Marx, *Contribution*, 49.

74. Marx, *Contribution*, 75; emphasis added.

75. Marx, *Contribution*, 115.

76. Marx, *Contribution*, 114–16.

77. Marx, *Contribution*, 145.

78. Pliny, the Elder, *Natural History*, Book XXXV, trans. Henry Rackham, (Cambridge, MA: Harvard University Press, 1952), chap. 36, 309.

79. Marx, *Contribution*, 111.

80. Marx, *Contribution*, 111–12.

81. Marx, *Contribution*, 113.

82. Marx, *Contribution*, 114.

83. Marx, *Contribution*, 115.

84. This popular English rendition of Goethe is differently and more correctly translated by Stuart Atkins as "what you don't coin, you think of no account" (Goethe, *Faust*, line 4922). The original German is: "*Was ihr nicht münzt, das, meint ihr, gelte nicht.*" The English substitution of gold for money of account is itself revealing of the structure that Marx is describing.

85. Walter Benjamin, *The Arcades Project*, trans. Howard Eiland and Kevin McLaughlin (Cambridge, MA: Belknap Press, 1999), 495.

86. Marx, *Contribution*, 149.

87. Jean Comaroff and John L. Comaroff, "The Madman and the Migrant," in *Ethnography and the Historical Imagination* (Boulder, CO: Westview, 1992), 157. This ambition was widely shared during the 1980s and 1990s, when, in a variety of idioms, a nonpsycho-analytic problem of the unconscious was formulated in anthropology. The notions of "tacit knowledge" (Polanyi) and unconscious resistance (Scott) were partly adduced in an effort to evade the dilemmas of vulgar Marxism (not to be confused with Marx's own writings), which conceived of ideology as false or inverted (representational) conscious-ness, on one hand, and those of symbolic culture associated with Clifford Geertz, which privileged the notion of shared meanings over antagonistic or dissonant perspectives, on the other. See Clifford Geertz, "Religion as a Cultural System," in *The Interpretation of Cultures*" (New York: Basic Books, 1973), 87–125; Michael Polanyi, *Personal Knowledge: Towards a Post-Critical Philosophy* (Chicago: University of Chicago Press, 1974); and James Scott, *Weapons of the Weak: Everyday Forms of Peasant Resistance* (New Haven, CT: Yale University Press, 1987).

88. In an especially protracted exchange between the attorney-general and Mr. Labouchere, Kruger's after-dinner speech of January 28, 1895, was adduced in evidence. The issue was whether Kruger had gone to Germany and signed a treaty with Germany without obtaining sanction from the Queen, as required under the terms of the London Conven-tion. Kruger's statement that the Queen had "relinquished suzerainty" was seen by the English defenders of the Raid as proof of his political threat to the Crown and Empire. UK House of Commons, "Second Report from the Select Committee on British South Africa, Together with Proceedings of the Committee and Evidence" (London: Her Majesty's Sta-tionery, 1897), lxi, 72.

89. Rosalind Morris, "Dialect and Dialectic in 'The Working Day' of Marx's *Capital*," in "Music, Sound, Value," eds. Jairo Moreno and Gavin Steingo, special issue, *Boundary 2* 43, no. 1 (February 2016): 219–48.

90. J. A. Hobson, *Capitalism and Imperialism in South Africa* (New York: Tucker, 1900). Hobson's rhetoric of internationalism is belied by his repeated insistence that the majority of the owners were foreign Jews: "most of them are Jews for the Jews are *par excellence* the international financiers" (9). This was not in fact true, although relative to their proportional membership of the population, the Jewish financiers had a large representation, a fact that Arendt explains in *On Totalitarianism*. See also, Allen, *History of Black Mineworkers*, vol. 1, 138–39.

91. Robert V. Kubicek, "The Randlords in 1895: A Reassessment," *Journal of British Studies* 11, no. 2 (1972): 90.

92. Wayne Graham, "The Randlord's Bubble, 1894–1896: South African Gold Mines and Stock Manipulation" (Discussion Papers in Economic and Social History No. 10, University of Oxford, 1996), 7.

93. Denoon, "Capital and Capitalists," 132.

94. Rudolf Hilferding, *Finance Capital: A Study in the Latest Phase of Capitalist Development* (New York; Routledge, 2019 [1919]), 221

95. Hilferding, *Finance*, 221.

96. Francis Wilson, *Labour*, 15. Also, E. B. Jeppe, *Gold Mining on the Witwatersrand* (Johannesburg: Transvaal Chamber of Mines, 1946), 64B.

97. Francis Wilson, *Labour*, 15.

98. Peter Richardson and Jean-Jacques van Helten, "The Development of the South African Mining Industry, 1895–1918," *Economic History Review* 27, no. 3 (1984): 319–40, 322; also S. Herbert Frankel, *Capital Investment in Africa: Its Course and Effects* (London: Oxford University Press, 1938), 85.

99. Van Onselen, *New Babylon*, 2; also see the history of the Minerals Council of South Africa (formerly the South African Chamber of Mines), accessed May 1, 2019, https://www.mineralscouncil.org.za/about/history.

100. Denoon, "Capital and Capitalists," 118. See also Graham, "Randlord's Bubble," 8.

101. Denoon, "Capital and Capitalists," 117.

102. Richard Mendelsohn, "Blainey and the Jameson Raid: The Debate Renewed," *Journal of Southern African Studies* 6, no. 2 (1980): 157–70, 168.

103. Kubicek, "The Randlords in 1895," 86.

104. Denoon, "Capital and Capitalists," 117–18. In making this claim, Denoon is arguing against Mendelsohn's assertion that the "stock-jobbers" could be categorically differentiated from those capitalists who, interested in long-term profits and deep-level mining, had participated in the Jameson Raid that sought to oust Kruger (Mendelsohn, "Blainey," 170). This debate was inaugurated by G. Blainey with his essay, "Lost Causes of the Jameson Raid," *Economic History Review*, 18, no. 2 (1965): 350–66. Blainey's argument is that the raid was not primarily motivated by Rhodes's political ambitions but instead by a combination of his economic interests and those of Alfred Beit. By Blainey's account, these two were only subsequently joined by others who also sought to eliminate the Kruger regime's limitations on mining and the associated legislative and other political sources of costs that could inhibit deep-level mining.

4. Cyanide Dreams and the Redemption of Waste: Or, Snowballs in Hell

Epigraphs to this chapter are from Steve Biko, "The Righteousness of Our Strength," in *I Write What I Like* (1978; repr., Chicago: University of Chicago Press, 2002), 129; George du Maurier, *Trilby* (New York: Harper and Brothers, 1894), 90; Mazisi Kunene, "The Age of Fantasy," in *Anthem of the Decades* (London: Heineman, 1981), lines 5415–16, 153; and Douglas Blackburn, *Richard Hartley, Prospector* (London: Blackwood, 1905), 318.

1. In Marx's analysis, bimetallism was inherently flawed. In evidence, he adduced the history of disturbances in both England (from the reign of Edward III to that of George II) and France, during the period his writing. Despite the legal sanction of both metals, he argued, that "it is always one of them only which actually maintains this position." Karl Marx, *Contributions to the Critique of Political Economy*, ed. Maurice Dobb (New York: International Publishers, 1970 [1859]), 77.

2. U.S. Government, "Appendix to the Congressional Record," *Proceedings and Debates of the Fifty-Second Congress, First Session*, 1892, 362.

3. This number rose to 40 percent by the beginning of World War I. Charles van Onselen, *New Babylon, New Nineveh: Everyday Life on the Witwatersrand 1886–1914* (Cape Town: Jonathan Ball, 1982), 1.

4. *Official Proceedings of the Democratic National Convention Held in Chicago, Illinois*, July 7, 8, 9, 10, and 11, 1896, Logansport, Indiana, 1896), 226–34, in *The Annals of America*, vol. 12, *1895–1904: Populism, Imperialism, and Reform* (Chicago: Britannica, 1968), 105.

5. John dos Passos, *The Forty-Second Parallel* (1930; repr., New York: Houghton, Mifflin, Harcourt, 2000), 136.

6. Peter Richardson and Jean-Jacques van Helten, "The Development of the South African Mining Industry, 1895–1918," *Economic History Review* 27, no. 3 (1984): 320.

7. The analogy of the ore deposits to a comma in a thick book comes from Transvaal Chamber of Mines, *Gold in South Africa* (Johannesburg, 1969), 10B, quoted in Francis Wilson, *Labour in the South African Gold Mines* (Cambridge: Cambridge University Press, 1972), 20. See also Chapter 3.

8. Britain would double its reserves by 1896, thanks in no small part to the growing production in Africa, but saw nearly 40 percent of that disappear when it had to pay the indemnity on Chinese War bonds, and from then on, it worried that India's switch to the gold standard would introduce competition for still limited gold. Shula Marks and Stanley Trapido, "Lord Milner and the South African State," *History Workshop* 8 (1979): 50–80. Marks and Trapido stop short of saying the need for gold led to the Anglo-Boer War, but they do note that Milner worked under Lord George Goschen when he was chancellor of the exchequer, before being posted to South Africa as high commissioner for South Africa and governor general of the Cape Colony in 1897. Goschen had advocated that Baring Brothers be bailed out, and Marks and Trapido imply that he exercised considerable influence on Milner's approach to the conception of the gold industry within the imperial project. Equally important is their claim that political opposition to British imperialism *did not* lead to support (from Germany, France, or the United States) for the Boer Republic in the war because the interests of capital and emergent financial institutions took precedence in geopolitical decision making. It is thus notable that there *was* support for the Republic against the British from distant anti-imperial movements, many of them anarchist, including those in the Philippines and Cuba, despite its white supremacism. See Benedict Anderson, *Under Three Flags: Anarchism and the Anticolonial Imagination* (New York:Verso, 2007).

9. Peter Abrahams, *Mine Boy* (1946; repr., London: Heinemann, 1975), 68.

10. Abrahams, *Mine Boy*, 60. In the novel, Xuma cannot read what is on this piece of paper, although the narrator tells his readers and the typography of the novel's text reproduces the stern categorization that is written there: "PASS NATIVE XUMA GANG LEADER FOR MR. PADDY O'SHEA" (61).

11. Pass cards and identity documents were retained under Apartheid, of course, but Abrahams's novel predates that development.

12. Other accounts of this color and its imbrication with political history have been written for other contexts. Cyanide was accidentally discovered as a "byproduct" of a new pigment,

namely 'Prussian Blue', by the Swiss pigment-maker, Johann Jakob Diesbach, in 1792. That color turned out to be less costly than the lapis lazuli-based 'ultramarine,' a color associated since the time of ancient Egypt with the depiction of royalty on account of its expense. According to Benjamin Labatut, Diesbach's effort to link the new color with the Germanic empire by calling it 'Prussian Blue', would presage the complex linkage between the Nazi Reich and cyanide, which chemical was used for both mass murder and the pre-emptive suicides of its leadership. Before that, however, 'Prussian Blue' was a huge profit-maker, leading Benjamin Abatut to write that the financier behind the pigment's marketing, Johann Leonhard Frisch, "turned blue to gold" (14). See, Benjamin Labatut, *When We Cease to Understand the World*, trans. Adrian Nathan West (New York: New York Review of Books, 2021), 12–16. Also, Joshua Cohen, "Thirty-Six Shades of Blue," *Triple Canopy*, Issue 9, March 17, 2010. Accessed July 14, 2024: https://canopycanopycanopy.com/contents /thirty_six_shades_of_prussian_blue?q=Joshua%20Cohen%20Prussian%20Blue.

13. Van Onselen, *New Babylon*, 13.

14. J. S. MacArthur, "The MacArthur-Forrest Method of Gold Extraction," *Journal of the Society of Chemical Industry* (March 31, 1890): 14.

15. Labatut, *When We Cease to Understand the World*.

16. "S.A. Parliaments," *Johannesburg Times*, July 26, 1895, 8.

17. "Cyanide Poisoning," *Johannesburg Times*, September 4, 1895, 9.

18. "The Cyanide Question," *Johannesburg Times*, February 2, 1895.

19. "Evidence of G. H. Goch, January 30, 1901," in *Report of the Transvaal Concession Commission* (Pretoria, April 19, 1901), 237–38. Goch was advocating the use of water from Wonderfontein as an alternative.

20. Walter Benjamin, *The Arcades Project*, trans. Howard Eiland and Kevin McLaughlin (Cambridge, MA: Belknap Press, 1999), 391.

21. Lionel Phillips, "Letter to Julius Wernher," May 28, 1894, in *All That Glittered: Selected Correspondence of Lionel Phillips, 1890–1924*, ed. Maryna Fraser and Alan Jeeves (Cape Town: Oxford University Press, 1977), 77.

22. Lionel Phillips, "Letter to Alfred Beit," June 16, 1894, in *All That Glittered*, 78. When the Jameson Raid was being investigated in 1897, this letter was adduced as evidence because in it, Phillips asserted that "I have no desire for political rights, and believe, as a whole, that the community is not ambitious in this respect." The report of inquiry redacted the letter to omit the following portion of the letter, quoted above in my own text. It says only "There follow opinions on the cyanide monopoly" (Cape of Good Hope (South Africa), Parliament, House, *Report of the Select Committee of Cape of Good Hope House of Assembly on Jameson Raid into Territory of South African Republic*, Appendix A, Command Papers, C.8380, 1897), 66. Phillips's letter was deemed so scandalous for its claim that Uitlanders were not in fact seeking the franchise, that it was reported in colonial newspapers as far away as Melbourne. "Letters of Mr. Lionel Phillips, A Candid Opinion," *The Argus* (Melbourne), May 25, 1986, 15.

23. C. J. Joubert, "Government Notice: To Managers and Directors of Gold Mining and Exploration Companies and Syndicates," *Transvaal Argus*, July 12, 1894, 1.

24. "Cyanide Once More," *Johannesburg Times*, August 3, 1895, 3.

25. Chamber of Mines, "Executive's Monthly Report," *Transvaal Argus*, August 10, 1894.

26. "Mr. Leonard's Evidence Before the Select Committee on British South Africa," in *Papers on the Political Situation in South Africa, 1885–1895*, ed. Charles Leonard (London: Arthur Humphreys, 1903), 363–420. Charles Leonard was president of the South African Union, the body seeking representation of Uitlander political interests. Adjusted for inflation, this amount would be equivalent to more than $5,110,500 in 2024.

27. "The Position of the Uitlanders in the Transvaal, with History of the Franchise," A Statement Prepared for the Committee of the House of Commons Made by Mr. Charles Leonard," in Leonard, *Papers on the Political Situation*, 89.

28. "The Position of the Uitlanders," 89.
29. "Patent Law," in "Report of The Volksraads," *Johannesburg Times*, August 13, 1895, 5.
30. "The McArthur-Forrest Patent [*sic*]," *Johannesburg Times*, August 16, 1895, 6.
31. "Manifesto of 1895," in Leonard, *Papers on the Political Situation*, 21–38.
32. Under a law passed in 1890, only those resident for fourteen years could be naturalized, and for a fee.
33. "Appendices to the Statement of Mr. Charles Leonard, Report from *The Star*, July 21, 1894," in Leonard, *Papers on the Political Situation*, 265.
34. Testimony of Mr. Labouchere, in Leonard, *Papers on the Political Situation*, 369.
35. Robert V. Kubicek, "The Randlords in 1895: A Reassessment," *Journal of British Studies* 11, no. 2 (1972): 90.
36. "Mr Leonard's Evidence," 369.
37. "Select Committee Report," in Leonard, *Papers on the Political Situation*, 265, 445. The capitalists, especially those in the organization referred to as the "Reform Committee," were nonetheless held accountable. Rhodes's strategic leadership of the Raid led to his being forced to resign the governorship; both he and Beit were compelled to resign from the British South Africa Company. With the other members, including Phillips and Leonard, but also Rhodes's brother, Frank, the two were also charged with and found guilty of high treason, a crime demanding capital punishment, but all of the sentences were commuted within a day. Jameson himself was sentenced only to fifteen months' imprisonment but was released early. He went on to be prime minister of the Cape Colony, a privy counsellor of the Conference of Colonial Premiers, and head of the Union Party. Ultimately, he was granted a baronet.
38. Carl Schmitt, *The Concept of the Political*, trans. George Schwab (Chicago: University of Chicago Press, 2007 [1932]).
39. "Extract from the *Standard and Diggers News*," August 22, 1892, in Leonard, *Papers on the Political Situation*, 181. Leonard was citing Thomas Babington Macauley's "Virginia," in *Laws of Ancient Rome*, 88–105, ed. William J. Rolfe and John C. Rolfe (New York: American Book Company, 1888), first published in 1842.
40. *Die blaue Stunde* is a German expression referring to the last blue before the darkness of night.
41. Wayne Graham, "The Randlords' Bubble, 1894–1896: South African Gold Mines and Stock Manipulation" (Discussion Papers in Economic and Social History No. 10, University of Oxford, 1996), 5.
42. C. Harz and S. B. Beauhbock, "Is the Manufacture of Cyanide of Potassium Rationally Possible in the Transvaal?," WCM, *Annual Report, 1895*, 109.
43. WCM, "Labour Returns, 1895," *Annual Report, 1895*, 180.
44. One finds traces of such accidents in the newspapers, as when a worker named Welcome had his leg crushed between two loading trucks at the cyanide works of Langlaagte Estate in August 1894; see "Accident at the Langlaagte," *Johannesburg Times*, August 8, 1895, 4.
45. James Bryce, *Impressions of South Africa*, rev. 3rd ed. (London: MacMillan, 1899), 627.
46. "The Great Cyanide Case: Text of the Judgement, Summing-up Dead Against the Patents," December 6, 1896, *African Review* IX (October-December 1896): 465. Also see Albert H. Welles, "Patents of Interest to Chemists," *Journal of the American Chemical Society* 15 (1893): 180–81.
47. WCM, "Treatment of Rand Ores," *Annual Report, 1895*, 162–63.
48. "Slimes: The Cost of Treatment; The Probable Financial Results," October 17, 1896, *African Review* 9 (October–December 1896): 122–23.
49. John 11:43.
50. Karl Marx, *Capital*, vol. 1, intro. Ernest Mandel, trans. Ben Fowkes (London: Penguin, 1976 [1867]), 169; emphasis added.

51. WCM, "Return of Stores Consumed for the Year, 1895," *Annual Report, 1895*. Adjusted for inflation, these values would be equivalent to (in 2024) $30,273,833.43 and $1,141,263.13, respectively.

52. My analysis differs here from that of Gabrielle Hecht, who, in a recent book that covers related issues, argues that the South African gold and uranium industries operate and form the basis of what she terms "residual governance." I share Hecht's belief that the minerals complex in South Africa was constituted through technopolitical means, and in my analysis of excremental politics, I have proposed a reading of racialization in South Africa that similarly accords black people the status of excess. Nonetheless, Hecht's claim that "residual governance treats people and places as waste" seems to me too simple. What one sees, when one descends a little from the perspective of the stratosphere (Hecht's chapter is titled, "You can see apartheid from space") is a complex and vacillating relation to waste that treats it above all as the source of surplus value, and not merely as discard. These terms—waste and discard—identify distinct relations to what I have variously described throughout this book as surfeit, superfluity, and surplus. See Gabrielle Hecht, *Residual Governance: How South Africa Foretells Planetary Futures* (Durham, NC: Duke University Press, 2023), esp.29–31.

53. "British Capital," *Johannesburg Times*, August 23, 1895, 5.

54. "Foreign Miscellany: Finance—Banking." The article originated in the French press and was "specially translated and prepared" for *Rhodes Journal of Banking, A Practical Banker's Magazine* 16 (July 1889): 645. There was no immediate relationship between the editor of the journal, Bradford Rhodes, and the Rhodes brothers of British South Africa, Cecil and Frank. Bradford Rhodes was a founder of the 34th Street National Bank in New York, an editor and publisher of banking journals and books, and a contributor on financial matters to the *Encyclopedia Britannica* of 1911.

55. "Is a Commercial Panic Impending?," *News Letter, San Francisco*, in *Rhodes Journal of Banking, A Practical Banker's Magazine* 16 (August 1889): 773–74.

56. "Amusements," *Johannesburg Times*, December 14, 1895, 5.

57. "The Share Market: A Dreary Day," *Johannesburg Times*, December 14, 1895, 5.

58. George du Maurier, *Trilby* (New York: Harper, 1894), 389–90.

59. For Mbembe, Johannesburg was a "pale imitation" of an "English town." And he claims, citing John Hyslop, that the mimicry that defined it led to both a sense of "falsehood" and "a mélange of and a deep antagonism between provincial and cosmopolitan ways." Achille Mbembe, "The Aesthetics of Superfluity," *Public Culture* 16, no. 3 (2004): 376. That said, London was a city unlike other English towns, precisely because it was the locus of so much international commercial traffic, the home of so many foreign-born subjects, and the origin of so many exiles.

60. du Maurier, *Trilby*, 489–90.

61. Thelma Gutsche, "Roaring Nineties and Darkling Days: 1891–1895," in *Old Gold: The History of the Wanderers Club 1888–1968*, 2 accessed July 5, 2019, https://www.thewanderersclub.co.za/wp-content/uploads/2012/03/chapter5.pdf.

62. The column was split into two sections, the first being "Mr. A. Beit 'At Home': A Brilliant Function. Four Hundred Guests." The second was "What the Ball Was Like: From a Woman's Point of View." It is not clear who the author was, nor whether there were in fact two—a man and a woman, or only one, a man or a woman. There is only one byline for the double entry, and it was common in South Africa for male writers to assume female pseudonyms (the well-documented case of *Voorslag* [whiplash]), being a case in point). *Johannesburg Times*, June 22, 1895, 5.

63. Gertrude Stein, *Paris, France* (1940; repr., New York: Liveright, 1996), 11.

64. Morrisby, though his name was misspelled by the columnist, as Morisby, came from a mining family. His brother, Arthur Calyton Morrisby, was the owner of the Hamburg mine in Rhodesia—part of the Rhodes/Beit empire.

65. Stephen Spender, "Beethoven's Death Mask," in *Collected Poems, 1923–1953* (New York: Faber and Faber, 1946), 27.

66. Benjamin, *Arcades*, 69.

67. Benjamin, *Arcades*, 609.

68. Fitts would acquire a reputation as an ardent nationalist, working to find legal arguments against the Industrial Workers of the World (IWW) and condemning World War I passivism. See Fred Ragan, "Obscenity or Politics: Tom Watson, Anti-Catholicism and the Department of Justice," *Georgia Historical Quarterly* 70, no. 1 (1986): 17–46, 17; and see also Steven Parfitt, "The Justice Department Campaign Against the IWW, 1917–1920," accessed June 25, 2020, https://depts.washington.edu/iww/justice_dept.shtml#_edn9. On Fitts's judicial opinions, see Rayman L. Solomon, "The Politics of Appointment and the Federal Courts' Role in Regulating America: U.S. Courts of Appeals Judgeships from T.R. to F.D.R.," *American Bar Foundation Research Journal* 9, no. 2 (Spring 1984): 285–343.

69. Mark Twain, *Following the Equator* (New York: Doubleday and McLure, 1897), 687.

70. J. Campbell, "The Americanization of South Africa" (seminar paper no. 44, University of Witwatersrand, Institute for Advanced Social Research, 1998), 6.

71. A. Scheidel, *The Cyanide Process: Its Practical Application and Economical Results* (Bulletin No. 5, California State Mining Bureau, Sacramento, 1894), 5, 13, emphasis added.

72. Scheidel, *Cyanide*, 34.

73. Scheidel, *Cyanide*, 58–60.

74. Scheidel, *Cyanide*, 39.

75. For example, *Punch Magazine* published a caricature of two women riding on horseback in their May 18, 1904, edition and titled it, "A Modern Woman: Innocence up to Date" (357). Not incidentally, the women are seen over the shoulder of a gentleman viewer, who, one might say, "takes in the image" of the transformed women and provides the vantage point for the magazine's reader to appropriate it.

76. On Ernst's *La Femme 100 têtes*, see Rosalind Krauss, *The Optical Unconscious* (Cambridge, MA: MIT Press, 1993), esp. 35–36.

77. A.L. Fom, "Mr. A. Beit 'At Home.' A Brilliant Function. Four Hundred Guests." *Johannesburg Times*, June 22, 1895, 5.

78. Carl Maria Pielsticker, "Application for Letters Patent for Improvements in the Extraction of Gold and Silver from Ores," December 14, 1893, in Scheidel, *Cyanide*, 129; emphasis added.

79. Benjamin, *Arcades*, 70.

80. Georg Simmel, *Philosophy of Money*, cited in Benjamin, *Arcades*, 662.

81. Roy Campbell, "Notes from Fetish Worship in South Africa," *Voorslag* 1, no. 2 (1926): 3–18. On the difference between African and settler colonial witch-hunting, Campbell noted the difference between the African "selection" of its victims and the European drive for rationalized principles, which merely ensured the generalization and consequent indiscriminateness of the accusation and the violence it unleashes (6–7).

82. Mbembe, "Aesthetics of Superfluity," 382.

83. Fom, "Mr. A. Beit 'At Home,' 5. All further quotes describing Beit's ball are from this same newspaper review.

84. Joyce posed this question in the story entitled "The Dead": "What is a woman, standing on the stairs and listening to distant music, a symbol of?" In James Joyce, *The Dubliners* (1914; repr., New York and London: Penguin Classics, 2014), 210.

85. Fom, "Mr. A. Beit 'At Home,' 5

86. Mangaliso Buzani, *A Naked Bone* (Durban: Deep South Pres, 2019), 14.

87. Buzani, "It Is Thursday," in *Naked Bone*, 80.

88. Van Onselen, *New Nineveh*, 209.

89. Van Onselen, *New Nineveh*, 212.

90. *South African Native Affairs Commission, 1903–1905*, vol. 1 (Cape Town: Government of the Colonies and Territories in British South Africa, 1906), 83.

91. Michel Foucault, "The Lives of Infamous Men," in *Power*, vol. 3 of *The Essential Works of Michel Foucault, 1954–1984*, ed. James Faubion, trans. Robert Hurley and others (New York: New Press, 2001 [1967]), 157–75.

92. Carolyn Steedman, "Something She Called a Fever: Derrida, Michelet, and Dust," *American Historical Review* 106, no. 4 (2001): 1176–77.

93. J. Bryce, *Impressions of South Africa* (New York: 1897), 316, quoted in Harri R. J. Mäki, "Development of the Supply and Acquisition of Water in South African Towns in 1850–1920," in *Environmental History of Water*, eds. Petri Juuti, Tapio S. Katko, and Heikki Vioerinen (London: IWA, 2007), 173–96.

94. On the aleatory as a mode of historiographical reading, see Nancy Rose Hunt, *A Nervous State: Violence, Remedies, and Reverie in Colonial Congo* (Durham, NC: Duke University Press, 2016), 5.

5. "We're Ground Underfoot": Movements Without Mobility

Epigraphs to the chapter are from William Shakespeare, *Timon of Athens*, Act 4, Scene 1, 429–31; and Nontsizi Mgqwetho, "Go and We'll Follow You," trans. Jeff Opland, in *The Nation's Bounty: The Xhosa Poetry of Nontsizi Mgqwetho*, ed. Jeff Opland (Johannesburg: Wits University Press, 2007), 208–9.

1. On a tour of the underground caves in northern Thailand many years ago, the very caves that became famous in June 2018 when a team of soccer-playing youth were stranded there by a flood, the guide performed this same, edifying prank. I have never forgotten the sense of absolute vulnerability.

2. Muriel Rukeyser, "Mearl Blankenship," in *The Book of the Dead* (New York: Covici Friede, 1938), 24.

3. Louis Althusser, *On the Reproduction of Capitalism: Ideology and Ideological State Apparatuses*, pref. Etienne Balibar, trans. G. M. Goshgarian (London and New York: Verso, 2014 [1995]), 264.

4. Benjamin writes further that, "Unlike law, which acknowledges in the 'decision' determined by place and time a metaphysical category that gives it a claim to critical evaluation, a consideration of the police institution encounters nothing essential at all. Its power is formless, like its nowhere-tangible, all-pervasive, ghostly presence in the life of civilized states." However, in the borderlands where people like Benefit and Mwanga live, the police never vanish into such intangibility, even if their spectral presence exceeds their material manifestation in the daily anxieties and dreaming unconscious of these undocumented migrants. Walter Benjamin, "Critique of Violence," trans. Edmund Jephcott, in *Selected Writings*, vol. 1, *1913–1926*, ed. Marcus Bullock and Michael W. Jennings (Cambridge, MA: Belknap Press, 1996 [1921]), 243.

5. Althusser, *Reproduction of Capitalism*, 264, n.18.

6. Franz Kafka, *The Trial*, trans. Breon Mitchell (New York: Schocken, 1998 [1925]), 55.

7. Walter Benjamin, "Franz Kafka: On the Tenth Anniversary of His Death," in *Selected Writings*, vol. II, 797. Also see Astrid Deuber-Mankowsky, "Rhythms of the Living: Conditions of Critique: On Judith Butler's Reading of Benjamin's 'Critique of Violence,'" trans. Catharine Diehl, in *Walter Benjamin and Theology*, ed. Colby Dickinson and Stéphane Symons (New York: Fordham University Press, 2016), 257.

8. What Teresa de Lauretis argued long ago—that Woman figures as an impasse or an obstacle to be overcome or transcended in the narratological tradition of both classical myth and Hollywood cinema—applies here. See Teresa de Lauretis, "Desire in Narrative," in *Alice Doesn't: Feminism, Semiotics, Cinema* (Bloomington: Indiana University Press, 1984), 103–57.

9. This formulation, of a "right to have rights," is, of course, Hannah Arendt's and its lack is what she identified as the very core of the post–World War II refugee experience. The practical impossibility of human rights, she notes, is related to the structures of enforcement, namely the nation-state, but also the evacuation of the concept of the human in the aftermath of the "Final Solution." As she writes, "The conception of human rights, based upon the assumed existence of a human being as such broke down at the very moment when those who professed to believe in it were for the first time confronted with people who had indeed lost all other qualities and specific relationships—except that they were still human." Hannah Arendt, *The Origins of Totalitarianism* (New York: Harcourt, Brace, Jovanovich, 1973), 299. Without making recourse to the perilous discourse of comparative victimage, it is possible to argue that the pass system in South Africa anticipated some of the mechanisms by which the Final Solution was realized. One thinks of the iron armband, for example, demanded of workers going to the mines.

10. Because there is often confusion among contemporary U.S. readers about this term and the status of Zionism as a tradition of black Christianity, and its relationship to contemporary Jewish Zionism associated with the state of Israel, it is important to know that Zion was a widely circulating and broadly signifying term in South Africa. It is a name often reported in the list of baptisms in the Cape Press, starting in its earliest days. There were chapels named for Zion, and citations of the Bible referring to Zion appear in the newspapers both in printed Christian sermons and in reports about Jerusalem (e.g., "The Place of Wailing," *Natal Witness*, Pietermaritzburg, March 22, 1850, 3). It functions as the name of the Christian community as well as of paradise in many editorials in English and Afrikaans newspapers throughout the nineteenth century, as well as in the African language presses, where it features in "Sunday School lessons" with elaborate exegetical commentary. It is both the name of a unity threatened by schism and the name of specific and even secessionist churches, as well as Masonic lodges. In 1898, long before the American Church arrived, the *Christian Express* published an article, "The Mission Field: Missions In South Africa," and listed among the various recognized societies "The Church of Zion" (*Christian Express*, May 2, 1898, 69). Earlier, in 1892, the paper also featured an article about the emergent Zionism among Jews seeking a return to Palestine. "The colonization of Palestine is no longer a doubtful experiment but already in part a proved success" (*Christian Express*, April 1, 1892, 63). Later, the same paper reported on "the New Spirit of Judaism," reviewing Herzl's *The Jewish State*, and analyzing antisemitism and "the Jewish Question" (*Christian Express*, September 6, 1897, 132). In the same year, the Grahamstown-based *Journal* saw fit to print a piece titled "More Bismarckiana," in which it quoted his statement (so important to Hannah Arendt's analysis of antisemitism) that "the Jews have still no true home but are a sort of universal Europeans, or cosmopolitan nomads. Their fatherlands is Zion" (*Supplement to the Journal*, September 6, 1898, 6). There was increasing interest among the South African Christians (and Jews, of course) in the question of Zionism, and many reports of the Kaiser's tour of Palestine. When the Jewish Colonial Trust was established to raise money for the project of colonizing Palestine, it advertised in *De Express en Oranjevrijstaatsch* in Bloemfontein ("The New Zion Jewish Trust Floated," March 23, 1899, 8). But this does not mean that the African Christian churches were easily allied to that project. The name Zion was a floating signifier, amenable to a variety of readings and capable of being attributed to competing referents. Indeed, it is that which was the object of such competition. In 1904, it even became the name of a brand of cigarettes.

11. George Chetwynd Griffith, *Briton or Boer: A Tale of the Fight for Africa*, 2 vol. (London: F. V. White, 1897). In fact, bribes were far less important than the threat brought by the Rand Lords of closing the mines in protest against the detentions. Had they brought the gold industry to a halt, the economy would have collapsed, but so too would have the companies, and their shareholders would not likely have endorsed such action. Nor would the Bank of England have survived it.

12. Griffith, *Briton or Boer*, 4.

13. Griffith, *Briton or Boer*, 4–5.

14. "Death of Reverend G. Tyamzashe," *Christian Express* (Lovedale, South Africa), November 2, 1896, 2–3.

15. Tyamzashe, whose father had been a "councillor" in the royal court of the Rudula clan of the amaXhosa, was a Wesleyan Methodist minister educated at the Lovedale mission. He was described by Solmon T. Plaatje as the first ordained black minister he had encountered, and one of his roles at Kimberley was to minister at the executions of convicted criminals of color. Tyamzashe's article, "Life at the Diamond Fields," was published in *Outlook on a Century* in 1874, some years before he went to Zoutpansberg to establish a mission station in 1884, at the beginning of the gold rush. Tyamzashe resided there for several years before returning in 1890 to Kimberley where he died. Gwayi Tyamzashe, "Life at the Diamond Fields. August 1874," in *Outlook on a Century. 1870–1970*, ed. Francis Wilson and Dominique Perrot (Cape Town: Lovedale Press and Spro-cas, 1973), 19–21. Trevor Mweli Skota, who also edited the newspaper *Abantu-Batho* and served as general secretary of the African National Congress, which published the paper in the 1920s and 1930s, wrote his biographical note. See T. D. Mweli Skota, "Prince Gwayi Tyamzashe," in *African Yearly Register*, Wits Historical Papers, Series C (ZA HPRA A1618-C2_01), 105–6.

16. "The Pass System," [1907] in *Outlook on a Century*, eds. Francis Wilson and Dominique Perrot (Cape Town: Lovedale Press and Spro-cas, 1974), 221–24. This editorial from *South African Outlook* lamented precisely the danger faced by Tyamzashe, namely that, leaving the Cape Colony, black men found themselves suddenly in need of a pass to travel (221).

17. Julia C. Wells, *We Now Demand: The History of Women's Resistant to Pass Laws in South Africa* (Johannesburg: Wits University Press, 1993), 5. The first pass laws of the Cape Colony, whence Tyamzashe came, were originally addressed to so-called Khoisan servants of European colonists, and were extended in 1828 to cover those who had been enslaved, first during their period of mandatory apprenticeship (a virtual indenture), effectively binding apprentices to their employers. Labor contracts were virtual passes, but although enforced by local police, they were not necessarily issued by the state bureaucracy.

18. Skota, "Tyamzashe," in *African Yearly Register*, 104–5.

19. Skota's dates vary slightly from those in the *Christian Express* obituary. Skota dates Tyamzashe's completion of his theological studies to 1874, the *Christian Express* to 1872, with his ordination in 1873. Note, in this context, that the new principal of Lovedale dropped Greek and Hebrew from the curriculum in 1870, in favor of book-binding and wagon-making—an early gesture of de-intellectualizing the Bantu curriculum. See Jeff Opland, *The Nation's Bounty: The Xhosa Poetry of Nontsizi Mgqwetho* (Johannesburg: Wits University Press, 2007), xx.

20. Tyamzashe wrote about the difficulty of missionizing among the diverde "tribes" of the region, and noted that "Many of these can hardly understand each other, and in many cases they have to converse through the medium of either Dutch, Sisutu [sic], or Kaffir." Tyamzashe, "Life at the Diamond Fields," 20.

21. Ntongela Masilela, "African Intellectual and Literary Responses to Colonial Modernity in South Africa," in *Grappling with the Beast: Indigenous Southern African Responses to Colonialism, 1840–1930*, ed. Peter Limb, Norman Etherington, and Peter Midgley (Leiden: Brill, 2010), 247.

22. Skota, "Tyamzashe," in *African Yearly Register*, 105.

23. Revelation 6:8.

24. Zechariah 1:10.

25. The best historical account of the cattle killing is that by J. B. Peires. See J. B. Peires, *The Dead Will Arise: Nongqawuse and the Great Cattle-Killing of 1856–7* (Bloomington: Indiana University Press, 1989). Zakes Mda's novel about this historical event is intertextually woven, though not directly cited, with the isiXhosa novel by S. E. K Mqhayi, titled *Ityala*

Lamawela [Lawsuit of the Twins], as well as Peires's archivally based history. See Zakes Mda, *The Heart of Redness* (New York: Picador, 2003); S.E.K Mqhayi, *Lawsuit of the Twins*, trans. Thokozile Mabeqa (Cape Town: Oxford South Africa, 2018 [1914]).

26. It is remarkably difficult to find any mention, never mind any substantial information about MacKriel. Her name appears in Skota's biography as Mrs. Gwayi Tyamzashe, but she is omitted in the obituary published by the *Christian Express*, and she is almost only ever mentioned, if at all, in her son's (the composer Benjamin John Peter Tyamzashe) biography. See *New Dictionary of South African Biography*, vol. 1, ed. E. J. Verwey (Pretoria: HSRC, 1995), 247. Also see T. D. Mweli Skota, "notes for biographies for inclusion in the 'African Register,'" in "T. D. Mweli Skota Papers," ZA HPRA A1618-C-C2-C2.1, Accession No. A1618, Wits Historical Research Papers, (University of Witwatersrand, Johannesburg), 104–5. A notable exception can be found in Leo Spitzer, "The Beginnings of African Protest Journalism at the Cape," in *South Africa's Alternative Press: Voices of Protest and Resistance, 1880–1960* (Cambridge: Cambridge University Press, 1997), 57–78, 74, 81.

27. This becoming animal-like is to be distinguished from the notion of "becoming-animal" as Gilles Deleuze and Félix Guattari describe it. While I am refering to a process of transformation that is born of deconstruction and that cannot be transmitted or inherited, the notion of animality is here still in a hierarchy and is lower than human. Moreover, imperceptibility in Slindile's case is an undesired condition of invisibility or non-recognition, rather than escape from power's structures. See, Gilles Deleuze and Félix Guattari, "*Becoming-Intense, Becoming-Animal, Becoming-Imperceptible*," trans. and foreword Brian Massumi (Minneapolis: University of Minnesota Press, 19877 [1980]), 232–309.

28. "South African Chamber of Mines Re-Named: Minerals Council of South Africa," *Mining Review*, May 23, 2018, https://www.miningreview.com/top-stories/sa-chamber-mines -renamed-minerals-council-south-africa/.

29. It changed its name to the Chamber of Mines of the South African Republic in 1897 and then to the Transvaal Chamber of Mines in 1902, following the end of the South African War. In 1953, its title was again revised with the addition of the Orange Free State.

30. WCM, Articles of Association, in *Eighth Annual Report, 1896*, v.

31. The difference between monopoly and monopsony is that a monopoly controls prices by functioning as the only producer of goods and services, whereas a monopsony controls them by functioning as a single buyer. Transvaal Chamber of Mines, Article 3, Paragraph 8. "Constitution," in *Fifty-Seventh Annual Report, 1946* (Parow: Cape Town, 1951), 143. Hereafter, authorship of the annual reports of the Transvaal Chamber of Mines is indexed by the acronym TCM, and, following 1953 when the Orange Free State mines were included, TOFSCM. The report is referenced by the year to which it refers rather than the publication date, which was occasionally deferred.

32. Parenthetical numbers refer to articles and paragraphs of the Chamber's constitution.

33. In 1897, the subscription rate for representative status and voting rights was £75 ($365 US).

34. WCM, *Annual Report, 1897*, vi–vii. The subscription rate also jumped to £105 ($511 US).

35. WCM, Articles of Association, Nos. 18–23, vi–vii.

36. Alan Jeeves, *Migrant Labour in South Africa's Mining Economy: The Struggle for the Gold Mines' Labour Supply, 1990–1920* (Montreal: McGill/Queens University Press, 1985), 41.

37. Jeeves, *Migrant Labour*, 42.

38. On this analogy, see W. J. T. Mitchell, *Iconology: Image, Text, Ideology* (Chicago: University of Chicago, 1987). My own rereading of Marx's concept appears in Rosalind C. Morris, "After de Brosses: Fetishism, Translation, Comparativism, Critique," in *The Returns of Fetishism: Charles de Brosses and the Afterlives of an Idea*, with a translation of *The Worship of Fetish Gods*, by Daniel H. Leonard (Chicago: University of Chicago, 2017), esp. 187–203. It should go without saying that the old presumption of an inverted image predates digital technologies.

39. Luce Irigaray, *Speculum of the Other Woman*, trans. Gillian G. Gill (Ithaca, NY: Cornell University Press, 1985 [1974]), 250.

40. WCM, *Annual Report, 1897*, 6–7.

41. Peter Limb, "Representing the Labouring Classes: African Workers in the South African Nationalist Press, 1900–1960," in *South Africa's Resistance Press: Alternative Voices in the Last Generation Under Apartheid*, ed. Switzer, Les, and Mohamed Adhikari (Athens: Ohio University Press, 2000), 95.

42. "Pass Legislation, 1889," *Outlook on a Century*, eds. Francis Wilson and Dominique Perrot (Cape Town: Lovedale Press and Spro-cas, 1974), 123–25.

43. WCM, *Annual* Report, *1897*, 4. Also see correspondence about the reduction of wages, and "Revised Schedule of Native Wages," Witwatersrand Chamber of Mines, April 24, 1897, *Annual Report 1897*, 110–13. This meant that the black laborers, categorized as "boys" and "assistants" would earn between one shilling and two cents, and two shillings, sixpence (about US$85–190 when adjusted for inflation and converted).

44. Jeeves, *Migrant Labour.*

45. Even so, dividends for 1899 were paid out in the amount of £2,933,251 (US$14,600,000). Chamber of Mines of the Republic of South Africa (CMRSA), *Annual Report, 1899*, 196–216.

46. CMRSA, *Annual Report, 1899*, 223.

47. TCM, "A Descriptive and Statistical Statement of the Gold Mining Industry of the Witwatersrand, Annexure to the Thirteenth Report of the Transvaal Chamber of Mines for the Year 1902," 24, 20.

48. TCM, Annexure, 21, emphasis in original.

49. TCM, Annexure, 21.

50. TCM, Annexure, 21.

51. *Correspondence Relating to Conditions of Native Labour Employed in Transvaal Mines*, 1904, 111.

52. Anthony Trollope, *South Africa*, ed. J. H. Davidson (1878; repr., Cape Town: Balkema, 1973), 367–68.

53. Sol (Solomon Tshekisho) Plaatje, "Equal Rights," *Bechuana Gazette*, September 13, 1902, in *Sol Plaatje: Selected Writings*, 64; and "The Leadership Cult from Another Angle," *Umteteli wa Bantu*, in *Selected Writings*, 346.

54. Mbuyiseni Oswald Mtshali, "The Detribalised," in *The Lava of this Land: South African Poetry 1960–1996*, ed. Denis Hirson (Evanston: TriQuarterly Books, 1997), 86.

55. Isaac Schapera, *Married Life in An African Tribe* (New York: Sheridan, 1941), 124. Rosa Luxemburg used this phrase to describe the forms of social life permitted on the diamond fields, where she thought the satisfaction of both traditional needs and new commodity desires was enabling new forms of surplus value extraction, South Africa being a part of that colonial exteriority on which the expansion of capital was dependent. Rosa Luxemburg, *The Accumulation of Capital*, trans. Agnes Schwarzchild (New York: Routledge, 2003 [2013]), 343–44, n10. Luxemburg relied for much of her information on James Bryce, *Impressions of South Africa*, rev. 3rd ed. (London: MacMillan, 1899).

56. Florence Nolwandle Jabavu, "Bantu Home Life," in *Women Writing Africa: The Southern Region*, vol. 1, ed. M. J. Daymond et al. (New York: Feminist Press, 2003), 192. "Bantu Home Life" was originally solicited for and published in *Christianity and the Natives of South Africa: A Yearbook of South African Missions*, ed. Rev. James Dextor Taylor (Cape Town: Lovedale Press, 1928), 164–77.

57. In the isiXhosa speaking-world, the tension between traditionalists and modernists was (and still is) coded through color, with "redness" signifying adherence to tradition.

58. Ernst Bloch, "Nonsynchronism and the Obligation to Its Dialectics," trans Mark Ritter, *New German Critique* 11 ([1932] 1977): 22–38.

59. This idiom, of being consumed by the mines, is omnipresent in the *sefela* recorded by Coplan, as mentioned. And, of course, it is echoed elsewhere in the mining world, as June

Nash's ethnography so vividly demonstrates. See June Nash, *We Eat the Mines, the Mines Eat Us* (Baltimore, MD: Johns Hopkins University Press, 1980).

60. The historical analysis of the Chinese labor on the Rand is extensive and growing. The locus classicus is Peter Richardson's, *Chinese Mine Labour in the Transvaal* (London: Mac-Millan, 1982). See also Rachel K. Bright, *Chinese Labour in South Africa, 1902–10* (London: Palgrave, MacMillan, 2013); John Higginson, "Privileging the Machines: American Engineers, Indentured Chinese and White Workers in South Africa's Deep-Level Gold Mines, 1902–1907," *International Review of Social History* 52, no. 1 (2007): 1–34; Jeeves, *Migrant Labour*, esp. 59–84; Alan Jeeves and Johnathan Crush, "The Failure of Stabilization Experiments and the Entrenchment of Migrancy to the South African Gold Mines," in "Transformation on the South African Gold Mines," special issue, *Labour, Capital and Society* 25, no. 1 (1992): 18–45, esp. 23–25; Gary Kynoch, "'Your Petitioners Are in Mortal Terror': The Violent World of Chinese Mineworkers in South Africa, 1904–1910," *Journal of South African Studies* 31 (2005): 531–46, and "Controlling the Coolies: Chinese Mineworker and the Struggle for Labor in South Africa 1904–1919," *International Journal of African Historical Studies* 36, no. 2 (2003): 309–29; William Kentridge and Rosalind Morris, *Accounts and Drawings from Underground* (Kolkata: Seagull Books, 2012); Mae Ngai, "Trouble on the Rand: The Chinese Question on the Rand and the Apogee of White Settlerism," *International Labour and Working Class History* 91 (2017) 59–78; and Bridglal Pachal, "Indentured Chinese Immigrant Labour on the Witwatersrand Goldfields," *India Quarterly* 21, no. 1 (1965): 58–82. It should be acknowledged, however, that there was never any intent to completely substitute Chinese for black labor, and in fact, at the same time as recruiting the former, the Chamber sought permission to import an additional five thousand black mineworkers from select locations throughout the imperial region. See Peter Richardson, "The Recruiting of Chinese Indentured Labour for the South African Gold Mines, 1903–1908," *Journal of African History* 18, no. 1 (1977): 89, n15.

61. Richardson, "Recruiting of Chinese Indentured Labour," 86.

62. *Mafeking Mail and Protectorate Guardian*, May 25, 1904, 2.

63. House of Lords, "Transvaal (Chinese Labour)," May 16, 1905, vol. 146, cc407–58. See Kynoch, "Your Petitioners Are in Mortal Terror," and Ngai, "Trouble on the Rand," on the protests.

64. House of Lords, "Transvaal (Chinese Labour)," cc409–10; emphasis added.

65. Edward Dicey, "Last Month II," *The Nineteenth Century and After: A Monthly Review* 55 (January–June 1904): 702.

66. *Mafeking Mail and Protectorate Guardian*, May 25, 1904, 2.

67. Roderick Jones, "The Black Peril in South Africa," *The Nineteenth Century and After* 37 (1904): 712–23.

68. "The Black Peril: Fruits of Native Indolence; Chinese the Only Alternative," *Rand Daily Mail*, April 9, 1904, 7. This discourse circulated throughout the press, as one or another advocate of the Chinese importation scheme weighed the relative risks of either "yellow" or "black" perils. See, for example, "Black Peril More to be Feared; Earl Percy's View," *Cape Daily Telegraph*, April 14, 1904, 7; and "The Black Peril: A Trade Commissioner's Observations," *Cape Times*, April 14, 1904, 7. But the black peril was a phrase that migrated and was used to address every form of threat deemed to emanate from the so-called African community. Thus, it was also adduced to repudiate the rise of "Ethiopianism" ("'The Black Peril': Native Question Discussed in London; The Ethiopian Movement," *Rand Daily Mail*, April 29, 1904, 7); and to explain interracial sexual assault by black men (e.g., "The Black Peril: Indecent Assault at Pretoria; Five Years and the Lash," *Rand Daily Mail*, July 28, 1904, 7; and "The Black Peril: Outrages on Women; The Guild's [Guild of Loyal Women] Petition," *Rand Daily Mail*, December 5, 1906, 7). In some cases, the black peril was a codeword for the argument to disenfranchise black voters in the Cape Colony, where land

ownership had enabled some to acquire that right ("The Black Peril: Cape Natives Must Be Disenfranchised," *Cape Daily Telegraph*, May 2, 1904, 5). It is in fact impossible to count the ways or frequency with which the phrase was adduced. But it is especially notable that in 1905 when a motion was put forth in the British parliament calling for the imperial government to protect all Natives within its territories, and that promised to veto any legislation that "infringed on the fundamental traditions of British liberty," Winston Churchill, argued that he "hoped by the presence of the black peril the two European races of South African would be drawn together," and he urged that special consideration be given to Indians, given the "high status of civilisation," that they could claim. It was in this context, that he announced that the imperial government was contemplating the allocation of funds to underwrite a Native department in the "Transvaal and Orangia" [*sic*], and that one million hectares were to be allocated to "Natives" in Swaziland. The latter number represents less than 6 percent of the total land in that country ("Future Treatment of Natives: Interference by Imperial Government Hinted at [Reuter's Colonial Service], *Cape Daily Telegraph*, March 2, 1906, 7). This was a rehearsal for the Native Lands Act of 1913.

69. Jones, "Black Peril," 712.
70. Jones, "Black Peril," 715.
71. W. Gumede, "Summer School e-Cabhane: An Address by Jabavu," *Abantu-Batho*, c. April 1923," in *The People's Paper: A Centenary History and Anthology of Abanto-Batho*, ed. Peter Limb (Johannesburg: Wits University Press, 2012), 451–52.
72. Indeed, the famous lines spoken by Marc Antony had appeared in a number of *Abantu-Batho* when they were used by R. V. Selope Thema to open a deeply ironic editorial about the white community's celebration of the Battle at Blood River, on December 16, 1920 (now celebrated as the Day of Reconciliation). R. V. Selope Thema, "Dingane a Senzangakana," *Abantu-Batho*, December 16, 1920, in *People's Paper*, 442. Thema, a member of the South African National Native Congress, precursor of the ANC, was a delegate sent to Versailles in 1919 to represent Black South African interests.
73. Gumede, "Summer School," 451. Further references to this article appear in parentheses in text.
74. Jones, "Black Peril, 723.
75. Jones, "Black Peril, 721.
76. Sigmund Freud, *The Psychopathology of Everyday Life: Forgetting, Slips of the Tongue, Bungled Actions, Superstitions and Errors*, SE VI (1901): vii-296.
77. Georg Wilhelm Friedrich Hegel, *The Phenomenology of Spirit*, trans. Terry Pinkard (Cambridge: Cambridge University Press, 2018 [1807], esp. 102–35; Jacques Lacan, *The Other Side of Psychoanalysis [L'envers de psychanalyse, 1969–70]: The Seminar of Jacques Lacan, Book XVII*, trans. Richard Grigg, ed. Jacques-Alain Miller (New York: Norton, 2007 [1991]); Alexandre Kojève, *Introduction to the Reading of Hegel: Lectures on the 'Phenomenology of Spirit*, trans. James. H. Nichols, comp. Raymond Queneau, ed. Allan Bloom (Ithaca, NY: Cornell University Press, 1980 [1947]).
78. Frantz Fanon, *Black Skin, White Masks*, trans. Richard Philcox (New York: Grove, 2008 [1952]), 84, emphasis in original.
79. Fanon, *Black Skin, White Masks*, 68.

6. Down, in Africa: Women Surpassing Protest

The chapter epigraph is from Nontsizi Mgqwetho, "Go and We'll Follow You," trans. Jeff Opland, in *The Nation's Bounty: The Xhosa Poetry of Nontsizi Mgqwetho*, ed. Jeff Opland (Johannesburg: Wits University Press, 2007), 208–9.
1. Jean Comaroff, *Body of Power, Spirit of Resistance: The Culture and History of a South African People* (Chicago: University of Chicago Press, 1985), esp. 166–93.

2. Zubaida Jaffer, *Beauty of the Heart: The Life and Times of Charlotte Maxeke* (Bloemfontein: Sun Press, 2016), 102.

3. Jaffer, *Beauty of the Heart*, 20–22.

4. Typically, she is recognized for having a bachelor of science, except in the writings of Mgqwetho, who accords her a bachelor of arts.

5. W. E. B. Du Bois, "Foreword," in Alfred Xuma, "Charlotte Manye (Mrs. Maxeke): "What an Educated African Girl Can Do," pamphlet (Women's Parent Mite Missionary Society of the AME Church, 1930, Wits Historical Research Papers, AD2186), 8. Du Bois used the orthography then in practice, but "Manye" is now written "Mannya" by her descendants.

6. On the choir's British journey, see Veit Erlmann, "Spectatorial Lust—the African Choir in England 1891–1893," in Bernth Lindfors, ed., *Africans on Stage; Studies in Ethnological Show Business* (Bloomington: Indiana University Press, 1999); Veit Erlmann, " 'A Feeling of Prejudice': Orpheus M. McAdoo and the Virginia Jubilee Singers in South Africa, 1890–1898," in *African Stars: Studies in Black South African Performance* (Chicago: University of Chicago Press, 1991), 21–53; and also see Jaffer, *Beauty of the Heart*, esp. 38–58.

7. Roderick Jones, "The Black Peril in South Africa," *The Nineteenth Century and After: A Monthly Review* 37 (1904): 712–23, 716.

8. Jones, "Black Peril," 719.

9. Sol (Solomon Tshekisho) Plaatje, "The Colour Bar," *Diamond Fields Advertiser*, March 10, 1925, in *Sol Plaatje: Selected Writings*, ed. Brian William (Johannesburg: Witwatersrand University Press, 2001), 345.

10. T. R. H. Davenport, "The Triumph of Colonel Stallard: The Transformation of the Natives (Urban Aras) Act Between 1923 and 1937, *Suid-Afrikaanse historiese joernaal* (South African Historical Journal), 2, no. 1 (1970): 77–96, 79.

11. Davenport, "Triumph of Colonel Stallard," 78.

12. Davenport, "Triumph of Colonel Stallard," 78.

13. Julia C. Wells, *We Now Demand: The History of Women's Resistance to Pass Laws in South Africa* (Johannesburg: Wits University Press, 1993), 38.

14. Wells, *We Now Demand*, 38–9.

15. A. Serrero and C. Mallela, "A Resolution: Native Women Pass Law," *Abantu-Batho*, December 6, 1917," in *The People's Paper: A Centenary History and Anthology of Abanto-Batho*, ed. Peter Limb (Johannesburg: Wits University Press, 2012), 391.

16. "A Fabulous Snake Suddenly Appears at the Scene," *Abantu-Batho*, April 22 (?), 1920, in *People's Paper*, 432. Questions of date in original reference.

17. "What Shall We Do?," in *People's Paper*, 456; capitalization in original, emphasis added.

18. Wells, *We Now Demand*, 38.

19. I derive this concept of the feminine as a structure of "to-be-looked-at-ness" from Laura Mulvey, "Visual Pleasure and Narrative Cinema," *Screen* 16, no. 3 (1975): 6–18.

20. Quoted in Wells, *We Now Demand*, 17.

21. Union of South Africa, *Report of the Interdepartmental Committee on the Native Pass Laws*, 1920, 10.

22. Jaffer, *Beauty of the Heart*, 79–80.

23. Quoted in Jaffer, *Beauty of the Heart*, 80.

24. "Native Women's Brave Stand," *Abantu-Batho*, July? 1913, in *People's Paper*, 343–44; questions of date in original reference.

25. "Native Women's Brave Stand."

26. Hannah Arendt, *The Human Condition*, 2nd ed. (Chicago: University of Chicago Press, 1958), 198. I thank Astrid Deuber-Mankowsky for conversations enabling this analysis.

27. Arendt, *Human Condition*, 199.

28. I use the term *mass strike* in Rosa Luxemburg's sense. In Luxemburg's analysis, which I follow here, the mass strike represented the unity of two struggles, one economic and

the other political, with each "fertilizing" the ground of the other. See "The Mass Strike, the Political Party, and the Trade Unions," trans. Patrick Lavin, in *The Essential Rosa Luxemburg: Reform or Revolution and The Mass Strike*, ed. Helen Scott (1906; repr., Chicago: Haymarket, 2008), esp. 142–45.

29. Luxemburg, "Mass Strike," 142–45.

30. Wells, *We Now Demand*, 1.

31. "Ruin of Native Girls. How They Flock to the Rand: A Social Evil. Mrs. Maxeke on Remedial Measures. White Landlords Who Ask No Questions." Maxeke is quoted as saying, "There must be many thousands of native girls along the Reef—young girls of from twelve upwards—who by stress of circumstances are driven into immorality," *Rand Daily Mail*, July 14, 1922, 5. The story was then reported in in *South African Outlook*, August 1, 1921, 159.

32. "Women and Pass Law," *Abantu-Batho*, December 20, 1917, in *People's Paper*, 392.

33. "Women's Suffrage Bill: Protest of Bantu Women," *Umteteli Wa Bantu*, April 9, 1921, 3.

34. Correctly written (the typo probably originates with the newspaper), "Dux Femina Facti" is a line from Vergil's *Aeneid*, referring to the deeds of women, in that case Dido. It has often been invoked in reference to women's leadership.

35. Michael Savage, "The Imposition of Pass Laws on the African Population in South Africa, 1916–1984," *African Affairs* 85, no. 339 (April 1986): 181–205.

36. This would be one of the issues on which South African opposition to African American and especially Garveyite "back to Africa" movements were based, although there was also much interest in it. African Americans were entitled to exceptions, and the radical presses insisted that if they wanted to express solidarity with people in South Africa, they would have to relinquish their expectation of being treated differently than their Black counterparts. Many writers for *Abantu-Batho* likened Garveyism to Jewish Zionism, given its discourse of a return to origins. They also resented the notion that any but themselves would be the authors of African emancipation. See Robert Trent Vinson, "Garveyism, *Abantu-Batho* and the Radicalisation of the African National Congress During the 1920s," in *People's Paper*, 282–97. See also "Back to Africa Movement," *Abantu-Batho*, November 11, 1920, in *People's Paper*, 435–31. As might be expected, the South African authorities encouraged the local suspicion.

37. This is the position of Julia Wells (*We Now Demand*), as well as Deborah Gaitskell. See Gaitskell's "Power in Prayer and Service: Women's Christian Organizations," in *Christianity in South Africa: A Political, Social and Cultural History* (Oxford: Oxford University Press, 1997), 253–67; and "Housewives, Maids or Mothers: Some Contradictions of Domesticity for Christian Women in Johannesburg 1903–39," *Journal of African History* 24, no. 2 (1983): 241–56.

38. Wells, *We Now Demand*, 30.

39. Wells (*We Now Demand*, 31) may overstate the matter when she says that "Black men objected mostly to the fact that their wives were subject to abuse from any passing policeman," but certainly complaints were made.

40. Wells, *We Now Demand*, 36.

41. Hortense J. Spillers, "Mama's Baby, Papa's Maybe: An American Grammar Book," in Black, White and in Color: Essays on American Literature and Culture, 203–29. Chicago: University of Chicago Press, 2003.

42. Nontsizi Mgqwetho, "Unity, Black Workers!" [*Imanyano! Basebenzi Abantsunda*], in *Nation's Bounty*, 100.

43. Natasha Erlank, "*Umteteli wa Bantu* and the Constitution of Social Publics in the 1920s and 1930s," *Social Dynamics: A Journal of African Studies* 45, no. 1 (2019): 75–102, 80.

44. Mgqwetho, "Chizama the Poet" [*Umbongi u Chizama*], in *Nation's Bounty*, 4–5. Opland explains that Chizama was Mgqwetho's clan name, and she wrote her earliest poems under it, before adopting Nontsizi Mgqwetho.

45. Mgqwetho, "Listen, Compatriots" [*Pulapulani! Makowetu*], in *Nation's Bounty*, 76–77. On Mgqwetho's use of masculine and feminine personae, see Isabel Hofmeyr, "Foreword," in *Nation's Bounty*, xi; and Opland, "Introduction," *Nation's Bounty*, xxi. Opland notes, too, that she often feminizes and Africanizes both Jehovah and Jesus ("Introduction," xxiv).

46. Mgqwetho, "The Vale of Tears" [*Iziko Ie Nyembezi*], in *Nation's Bounty*, 30–31.

47. Mgqwetho, "A Long Lying-In, Then the Python Uncoils and Leaves" [*Yacombuluka! Inamba u 1923 ebisoloko ifukamele ukunduluka*], in *Nation's Bounty*, 64–65.

48. Mgqwetho, "Mama's Death" [*Umpanga ka Mama*], in *Nation's Bounty*, 48–49.

49. "Pass office" is in English.

50. Mgqwetho, "Alas! Africa, You Fade Into the Horizon!," trans. Jeff Opland and Pamela Maseko, in *People's Paper*, 414.

51. Ndlovukadsi (or Ndhlovukadzi), the name of the Swazi Queen mother and regent, translates as the Great She-Elephant.

52. Opland, "Introduction," *Nation's Bounty*, xiii–xxx.

53. Opland, "Introduction," *Nation's Bounty*, xxiii–xxiv.

54. Jean Comaroff, *Body of Power*, esp. 181–86. See also B. Zundkler, *Zulu Zion and Some Swazi Zionists* (London: Oxford University Press, 1976). As already noted, this was only one of several Zionist congregations. Before Dowie's church was invited to Natal, its leader visited the country but was ridiculed by the editors of the *Rand Daily Mail* as a "charlatan." See "The 'Prophet of Zion' Makes Many Converts in Australia," *Rand Daily Mail*, February 3, 1903, 7. Somewhat later, an editorial in the *Mafikeng Mail* accused Dowie of a mercantile rather than missionary interest. See "Rival Messiahs and Elijah," in *Mafeking Mail and Protectorate Guardian*, April 16, 1904, 3–4.

55. I thank Yvette Christiansë for this reference

56. Charlotte Maxeke, quoted in Jeff Opland, "Abantu-Batho and the Xhosa Poets," in *People's Paper*, 201–2, 205.

57. Opland, "Abantu-Batho and the Xhosa Poets," in *People's Paper*, 206.

58. Opland, "Introduction," *Nation's Bounty*, xviii.

59. Opland suggests that her English name was Elizabeth and that the name Nontsizi may either have been given at birth or assumed by her as a *nom de plum*. See Jeff Opland, "Introduction" to *Nation's Bounty*, xxi–xxii.

60. Mgqwetho, "Unity," in *Nation's Bounty*, 102–103.

61. John Tengo Jabavo had edited the first isiXhosa newspaper, *Sigidimi samaXhosa* [The Xhosa Messenger] and founded another (i.e., *Imvo Zabantsundu*). Davidson took over the editorship of *Imvo Zabantsundu* when his father died. Davidson Jabavu was not always disapproved by *Abantu-Batho*. In fact, the paper had celebrated his return to South Africa after ten years' absence, in 1915, when he became the first Black professor in a teacher's college. "Native College Staffing, *Abanto-Batho*, February? 1915, in *People's Paper*, 360–61.

62. Mgqwetho, "Unity," in *Nation's Bounty*, 102–103.

63. Luce Irigaray, *Speculum of the Other Woman*, trans. Gillian C. Gill (Ithaca, NY: Cornell University Press, 1985 [1974]), 252.

64. Irigaray, *Speculum*, 254.

65. Irigaray, *Speculum*, 255.

7. Figure, Ground, and Sinkhole

This chapter draws partly from Rosalind C. Morris, "The Miner's Ear," *Transition* 98 (2008): 96–115. Epigraphs to this chapter are from Michael Cawood Green, "Falling (Hettie's Love Song)," in *Sinking: A Verse Novella* (London: Penguin, 1997), 16–17; Moses Bopape and Stephen Ratlabala, "Diepegauta" [The Gold-Diggers], in *Ithute Direto* (Pretoria: J.L. Van

Schaik, 1968), 36; and Jacques Derrida, *The Beast and the Sovereign*, vol. 2, 2002–2003, trans. Geoffery Bennington (Chicago: University of Chicago Press, 2011 [2010]), 130–31.

1. "Down in the Dumps Over Sand," *Rand Daily Mail* (hereafter referred to as *RDM*), January 8, 1980, 4.
2. A Wikipedia entry on Carleton Jones linked to the entry on Carletonville confuses him with another Carleton Jones, a Canadian physician who became the country's fourth surgeon-general.
3. Schalk Daniël van der Merwe, "The Dynamics of the Interaction Between Music and Society in Recorded Popular Afrikaans Music, 1900–2015" (PhD diss., University of Stellenbosch, 2015), 127.
4. E. S. Van Eeden, "The Effect of Mining Development on the Cultural Experience of the Carletonville Community," *South African Journal of Cultural History* 12, no. 1 (1998): 75–89.
5. Green, *Sinking*, 112.
6. Green, *Sinking*, 111.
7. Goldreich and Wolpe (whose scholarship on labor migration has been so important to the analysis of Apartheid and its relationship to the mining industry) escaped before the trial. It was at their house on Liliesleaf Farm in Rivonia, purchased to serve as a safehouse and base for planning operations, that the men were all arrested.
8. "The ideological creed of the ANC is, and always has been, the creed of African Nationalism. . . . It is by no means a blueprint for a socialist state. It calls for redistribution, but not nationalization, of land; it provides for nationalization of mines, banks, and monopoly industry, because big monopolies are owned by one race only, and without such nationalization racial domination would be perpetuated despite the spread of political power. It would be a hollow gesture to repeal the Gold Law prohibitions against Africans when all gold mines are owned by European companies. . . . The ANC has never at any period of its history advocated a revolutionary change in the economic structure of the country, nor has it, to the best of my recollection, ever condemned capitalist society." Nelson Mandela, "Nelson Mandela's Speech from the Dock at the Opening of the Defense Case in the Rivonia Trial," accessed January 3, 2020, http://db.nelsonmandela.org/speeches/pub_view .asp?pg=item&ItemID=NMS010&txtstr=prepared%20to%20die.
9. John Oxley, *Down Where No Lion Walked: The Story of Western Deep Levels* (Johannesburg: Southern Book Publishers, 1989), 100.
10. Muriel Rukeyser, "Murmurs from the Earth of This Land," in *Body of Waking: Poem* (New York: Harper, 1958), 85.
11. Green, "From Structure to Event: Willie Britz," in *Sinking*, 36–38.
12. Green, *Sinking*, 94.
13. Hendrik Vorster, "Sinkhole Swallows Family," *RDM*, August 3, 1964, 1.
14. "Westonaria Bid for Hospital," *RDM*, February 1, 1963, 3
15. "Sinkholes Answer Likely Soon," *RDM*, May 29, 1963, 3.
16. "Sinkhole Threat," *RDM*, September 24, 1963, 3.
17. Oxley, *Down Where No Lion Walked*, 101.
18. Oxley, *Down Where No Lion Walked*, 102.
19. "West Wits Income Continues to Grow," *RDM*, November 29, 1963, 28.
20. To be sure, real estate values vacillate in all economies, and with far less dire sources of loss. I am merely summarizing the position of the financial interests that were calculating necessary write-offs within a specific time horizon so as to maximize profits in the long run. I thank Rudolf Mrázek for arguing this point with me.
21. "West Wits Income Continues to Grow," 28.
22. Green, "Older Than Time," in *Sinking*, 6.
23. H. J. Van Niekerk and I. J. Van der Walt, "Dewatering of the Far West Rand Dolomitic Area by Gold Mining Activities and Subsequent Ground Instability," *Land Degradation and Development* 17 (2006): 331–52.

24. Green, "Older Than Time," in *Sinking*, 5.

25. Jacques Derrida, "Plato's Pharmacy," in *Dissemination*, trans. and intro. Barbara Johnson, (Chicago: University of Chicago Press, 1981 [1972]), 63–171.

26. "Geologists Race Against Time to Study Cave," *RDM*, October 5, 1963, 9.

27. Green, "Older Than Time," in *Sinking*, 6.

28. Mark 4:10.

29. "Landslip at Springs. Treacherous Mine Ground. Two Houses Engulphed. Marvellous [sic] Escape of Inmates. Child Buried Alive," *RDM*, March 22, 1907, 11.

30. Derrida, *The Beast and the Sovereign*, 130–31.

31. A. P. Cartwright, *West Driefontein—Ordeal by Water* (J.G. Ince and Sons, for Gold Fields of South Africa, Ltd., 1969?), 4.

32. Cartwright, *West Driefontein*, 4.

33. Cartwright, *West Driefontein*, 7.

34. Genesis 7:19.

35. Jonah 2:5.

36. Cartwright, *West Driefontein*, 8.

37. Cartwright, *West Driefontein*, 8.

38. Transvaal Chamber of Mines (TCM), *Annual Report for 1951*, 39.

39. Chamber of Mines of South Africa (CMSA), *Annual Report*, 1968, 29.

40. Benjamin Wallet Vilakazi, "Ezinkomponi." This quotation from the translation by F. L. Friedman originally appeared in *Amazle 'Zulu* in Bantu Treasury Series No. 8, in Francis Wilson, *Labour in the South African Gold Mines* (Cambridge: Cambridge University Press, 1972), 190–94, 193. The poem had been earlier translated by A. C. Jordan, for Bantu Treasury Series No. 3, 115–19, https://disa.ukzn.ac.za/sites/default/files/pdf_files/asjan57.17.pdf. This passage is translated by Jordan as follows: "Thunder away, machines of the mines,/Thunder away from dawn till sunset;/I will get up soon: do not pester me;/Thunder away, machines. Heed not/The groans of the black labourers" (115).

41. A. C. Jordan's translation: "Rumble softly, O machines;/Because the white man feels not for others,/Must you treat me as heartlessly too?/Thunder not so loud in the mines;/Be pleased to hear what we have to say" (Bantu Treasury Series No. 3, 118).

42. Cartwright, *West Driefontein*, 10.

43. Cartwright, *West Driefontein*, 13.

44. Cartwright, *West Driefontein*, 80.

45. Cartwright, *West Driefontein*, 71.

46. Cartwright, *West Driefontein*, 70.

47. CMSA, *Annual Report*, 9.

48. CMSA, *Annual Report*, 16.

49. Grietjie Verhoef, "Nationalism and Free Enterprise in Mining: The Case of Federale Mynbou, 1952–1965," *South African Journal of Economic History* 10 (1995): 89–107.

50. Gayatri Chakravorty Spivak, "Can the Subaltern Speak?," in *Can the Subaltern Speak: Reflections on the History of an Idea*, ed. Rosalind C. Morris (New York: Columbia University Press, 2010), 237–91.

51. CMSA, *Annual Report*, 10.

52. The phrase is likely a loose citation of Acts 17:26. On the destruction of the plaque, see *Carletonville Herald*, August 19, 1994.

53. I am indebted to Antjie Krog for an understanding of this phrase's resonances. Antjie Krog, personal communication, August 1, 2021.

54. Derrida, *Beast*, 2:131.

55. Derrida, *Beast*, 2:129.

56. I thank Rudolf Mrázek for helping me grasp this dimension of Defoe's narrative. Rudolf Mrázek, personal communication, November 16, 2021.

57. Benjamin Wallet Vilakazi, "In the Gold Mines," 192. I quote here the translation that appears in Wilson, *Labour in the South African Gold Mines*. The Zulu original reads: *Wake wakubonaphi ukungcwatshwa/ubheke ngawo womabil' uzihambela?* (l:71–72). It has been retranslated as "Where have you ever seen a person buried alive?" by Nompumelelo Zondi. The retranslation has the merit of precision but loses the line break and the rhyming of the original. See Nompumelelo Zondi, "Three Protagonists in B. W. Vilakazi's Ezinkomponi'" (On the mine compounds), *Literator* 32, no. 2 (August 2011): 177–78. Jordan translated these lines as follows: "Where was it ever done to bury a man/While he walks and sees with both his eyes?" (117).

58. Bopape and Ratlabala, "Diepegauta [The Gold-Diggers]," 36.

59. It seems necessary to remark here that the protocols of university ethics boards, which demand anonymization in the name of protection and the safety of "human subjects" involved in research, are woefully inadequate to the complex and ambiguous desires of ethnographers' interlocutors, for whom recognition is often desired in the (inevitably transferential and countertransferential) relationships with the anthropologist.

60. Eddy Mazembo Mavungu, "Frontiers of Power and Prosperity: Explaining Provincial Boundary Disputes in Postapartheid South Africa," *African Studies Review* 59, no. 2 (2016): 195. Mavungu made this claim in 2011 as part of a doctoral dissertation and it has been widely cited since, although he does not indicate on what basis he makes this assertion, which echoes popular sentiment but may be exaggerated.

61. Loyiso Tunce was given similar narratives and similarly shown damaged homes while conducting research a decade after I undertook my own research. For dramatic amateur images of those cracked and sinking structures, see Loyiso Tunce, "The Dynamics of Mining Towns: The Case of Khutsong Township, Carletonville" (master's thesis, University of Witwatersrand, School of Architecture and Planning, 2016), esp. 35–37.

62. Jacques Derrida, "Passions," in *On the Name*, trans. David Wood, John P. Leavey Jr., and Ian McLeod (Stanford, CA: Stanford University Press, 1995 [1993]). I have discussed this conception of the secret in relation to traumatic narratives in South African literature more broadly. See Rosalind C. Morris, "In the Name of Trauma: Notes on Testimony, Truth-Telling and the Secret of Literature in South Africa," *Comparative Literature Studies* 48, no. 3 (2011): 388–416.

63. "Bultfontein," Mindat.org, accessed August 3, 2021, https://www.mindat.org/min-800.html.

64. I have in mind here the processes of condensation and displacement described by Sigmund Freud in his analysis of the dreamwork. Sigmund Freud, *The Interpretation of Dreams*, in *SE*, vol. IV, *1900–1901*.

65. Luce Irigaray, *Speculum of the Other Woman*, trans. Gillian C. Gill (Ithaca, NY: Cornell University Press, 1985 [1974]), 246.

66. Irigaray, *Speculum*, 115, 125.

67. "Sinkhole Causes Water Chaos," *Carletonville Herald*, August 8, 2016, https://carletonvilleherald.com/7616/sinkhole-causes-water-chaos.

68. "Sinkhole Causes Water Chaos," *Carletonville Herald*, August 8, 2016, https://carletonvilleherald.com/7616/sinkhole-causes-water-chaos.

8. The Sky's the Limit: Visions and Divisions of the World

The chapter epigraph is from Michel Foucault, "Utopias and Heterotopias," in *Architecture/Mouvement/Continuité* October, 1984; ("Des Espaces Autres," trans. Jay Miskowiec, March 1967), 1, accessed August 19, 2001, https://web.mit.edu/allanmc/www/foucault1.pdf.

1. These interviews were partly facilitated by Buti Kulwane, who at that time worked for one of the mining companies in the area while also helping to run the HIV/AIDS hospice where

we were recording. He had previously written an excellent thesis on municipal governance in Khutsong (see note 24) based on oral histories conducted in 2002. Our interviews were conducted in multiple languages and were video-recorded with the assistance of the artist and translator Songezile Madikida. I have chosen not to identify the interviewees by name because of the sensitivity of the information they provided and the possibility that those referenced in their discourse may wish to have remained untraceable. Where I discuss individuals whose names and deeds are a matter of public record, actual names are used.

2. Green, "Older Than Time," in *Sinking: A Verse Novella* (London: Penguin, 1997), 4.

3. Antjie Krog, *A Change of Tongue* (Johannesburg: Random House, 2003), 27.

4. Immanuel Kant, *Critique of the Power of Judgment*, trans. Paul Guyer and Eric Matthews, ed. Paul Guyer (Cambridge: Cambridge University Press, 2000 [1790]).

5. Roderick Jones, "The Black Peril in South Africa," *The Nineteenth Century and After* 37 (1904): 712–23.

6. Siegfried Kracauer, "Those Who Wait," in *The Mass Ornament: Weimar Essays*, trans. Thomas Y. Levin (Cambridge, MA: Harvard University Press, 1995), 129–40; also see Andrew McCann, "Melancholy and the Masses: Siegfried Kracauer and the Media Concept," *Discourse* 43, no. 1 (Winter 2021): 150–70.

7. John Ruskin, "The Storm-Cloud of the Nineteenth Century. Two Lectures Delivered at the London Society. February 4th and 11th, 1884," in *The Complete Works of John Ruskin*, vol. 34, ed. E.T. Cook and Alexander Wedderburn (London: George Allen, 1908), 4–80, 23. Here is Ruskin's description: "It looks partly as if it were made of poisonous smoke; very possibly it may be: there are at least two hundred furnace chimneys in a square of two miles on every side of me. But mere smoke would not blow to and fro in that wild way. It looks more to me as if it were made of dead men's souls—such of them as are not gone yet where they have to go, and may be flitting hither and thither, doubting, themselves, of the fittest place for them."

8. Ernst Bloch, "Nonsynchronism and the Obligation to Its Dialectics," trans Mark Ritter, *New German Critique* 11 ([1932] 1977): 22–38.

9. In his introduction to the collection, *Black Villagers in an Industrial Society* (Cape Town: Oxford University Press, 1980), Philip Mayer is careful to define the "traditional" villages of the Nguni world, typically composed of homesteads "strung out along ridges." This understanding emphasizes a certain spatial separation, compared with the dense proximity of residents in colonial contexts, but even in precolonial times, he says, "compact villages" were not uncommon, at least in Sotho communities (xiii). Among the Xhosa, he notes, independent landholders were dominant. Philip Mayer, *Townsmen or Tribesmen: Conservatism and the Process of Urbanization in a South African City* (Cape Town: Oxford University Press, 1971), 1.

10. This is a more heterogenous and less typologically oriented characterization than that which Legassick proposed in his analysis of merchant colonialism, although it bears some resemblance to his description of African societies defined by "hunter-trader-pastoralist" activities. The difference is one that can both accommodate women, who are elided by Legassick's typology, and that does not represent a precolonial condition so much as a complexly transformed one. See Martin Legassick, "South Africa: Forced Labour, Industrialization, and Racial Differentiation," in *The Political Economy of Africa*, ed. Richard Harris (Boston: Schenkman, 1975), 241 and 234, respectively.

11. Raymond Williams, *The Country and the City* (London: Chatto and Windus, 1973).

12. Mamdani understands this investment in authoritarian culture within the paradigm of a split governmental logic: on one side, the withholding of rights from racialized subjects; on the other side, the forced incorporation of ethnicized citizens. His argument, that apartheid constituted the logical paradigm for all colonial governance in Africa rather than an exception need not detain us here. More important is Mamdani's observation,

anchored in a reading of General, and then Prime Minister, Jan Smuts's claim that migrant labor in South Africa actually risked undoing the principles of racial rule, and that the territorialization of ethnicity—as rurality—was a mechanism to prevent the collapse of racial difference that urbanization would otherwise have generated as the economy grew. See Mahmood Mamdani, *Citizen and Subject: Contemporary Africa and the Legacy of Late Colonialism* (Princeton, NJ: Princeton University Press, 1997), esp.5–7.

13. Jacob Dlamini, *Native Nostalgia* (Johannesburg: Jacana, 2009), 45–46.
14. Francis Wilson, *Labour in the South African Gold Mines* (Cambridge: Cambridge University Press, 1972), 135.
15. Mayer, *Townsmen or Tribesmen*.
16. T. Dunbar Moodie, *Going for Gold: Men, Mines and Migration* (Berkeley: University of California Press, 1994), 13.
17. Mayer, *Townsmen or Tribesmen*, 1. Also, Ruth First, *Black Gold: The Mozambican Miner, Proletarian and Peasant* (New York: St Martin's Press, 1977).
18. Transvaal Chamber of Mines (TCM), *Annual Report*, 1952, 67; emphasis added.
19. TCM, *Annual Report*, 1952, 68.
20. There is an enormous literature on the concept of racial capitalism commencing with Cedric Robinson's *Black Marxism: The Making of the Black Radical Tradition*, foreword by Robyn Kelley (Chapel Hill, NC: University of North Caroline Press, 2000 [1983]). I do not aim to argue with or contribute to the ongoing debate about the concept and its terminology so much as to offer an empirically rigorous analysis of how it (racial capitalism) operated in South Africa, partly because many of the assumptions and caricatures of that operation have inhibited an understanding of the challenges faced in overcoming it.
21. Quoted in J. A. Gemmill, "Native Labour on the Gold Mines," in *Transactions of the Seventh Commonwealth Mining and Metallurgical Congress*, vol. 1 (Johannesburg: South African Institute of Mining and Metallurgy, I961), 298; emphasis added.
22. For Foucault ("Utopias and Heterotopias," 3), the crisis heterotopia, which he associates with simple societies, is largely displaced by the deviation heterotopias of the modern administrative states, although he acknowledges that they may be mixed at different times. The situation in South Africa was one of relative heterogeneity and does not admit of such ideal-typical separations. Bloch's notion of synchronous nonsynchronicity is helpful as a supplement and corrective to the linearity of Foucault's genealogy.
23. Foucault, "Utopias and Heterotopias," 7.
24. Buti Kulwane, "Civic Competence in Khutsong" (master's thesis, Faculty of Management, University of the Witwatersrand, 2002), 54.
25. Kulwane interviewed the former mayor in 2002. See "Civic Competence in Khutsong," 50.
26. I consider the prison to be an ideological and not merely a coercive apparatus insofar as it was such an important locus for exposure to discipline, to rationalized labor regimes, and to the educative relationships inscribed within the often ethnically or regionally specific orders of gangsterism that extended beyond the prisons. More than this, the regular experience of youth in prison, as a result of pass law violations, ensured that they were sites for learning the codes of the settler colonial state, in addition to being loci of exposure to its violence.
27. Such a grounding is not uniquely South African of course; the feudality of the European colonies, and the United States, often took this form.
28. Martin Legassick's original formulation of this argument appeared in 1972 in the widely circulated essay, titled "South Africa: Forced Labour, Industrialization, and Racial Differentiation" (cited in note 9). He later accepted much of Wolpe's critique, particularly Wolpe's claim that it was not merely the extension of segregation as a strategy to maintain low wages to secondary industry but also the transformation and evisceration of the conditions in the Bantustans, and the erosion of their "precapitalist" forms, that characterized Apartheid and enabled its intensified and increasingly brutal operation. Martin Legassick,

"South Africa: Capital Accumulation and Violence," *Economy and Society* 3, no. 3 (1974): 253–91.

29. Harold Wolpe, "Capitalism and Cheap Labour-Power in South Africa," *Economy and Society* 1, no. 4 (1972): 432. Also see Claude Meillassoux, *Maidens, Meal and Money* (Cambridge: Cambridge University Press, 1975), 115. Albert Memmi and Lucy Mair shared this broad analysis. See Albert Memmi, *The Colonizer and the Colonized* (1957; repr., Boston: Beacon, 1966) and Lucy Mair, *Primitive Government* (Gloucester, MA: Peter Smith, 1975).

30. Jonathan Crush, "Inflexible Migrancy: New Forms of Migrant Labour on the South African Gold Mines," "Transformation on the South African Gold Mines" (*Numéro thématique: Évolution de la situation dans les mines d'or sud-africaines/Evolution of the situation on the South African gold mines*), special issue, *Labour, Capital and Society* (*Travail, capital et société*) 25, no. 1 (April 1992): 46–71; and "Restructuring Migrant Labour on the Gold Mines," in *South African Review*, ed. Glen Moss and Ingrid Obery, vol. 4 (Johannesburg: Ravan Press, 1987), 283–91. Also see Wilmot G. James, *Our Precious Metal: African Workers in South Africa's Gold Industry, 1970–1990* (Cape Town: David Philip, 1992). The industry's repudiation of the cheap labor hypothesis appears in A. I. Beck, G. H. Henderson, R. N. Lambert, and R. A. Mudd, "Stoping Practice on the Transvaal and Orange Free State Goldfields," in *Transactions of the Seventh Commonwealth Mining and Metallurgical Congress*, vol. 2 (Johannesburg: South African Institute of Mining and Metallurgy, 1961), 660.

31. Mayer, *Black Villagers*, 7. For Mayer, the crucial element of urbanization is the transformation of consciousness that is linked to new forms and loci of association and attachment, whereby people's "basic social ties" are rooted in the urban rather than rural context.

32. See Jean Comaroff and John L. Comaroff, "The Madman and the Migrant," in *Ethnography and the Historical Imagination* (Boulder, CO: Westview, 1992), 155–78.

33. This pattern extends beyond the migrant mining economy and into the future. As John L. and Jean Comaroff observe for the emergent ethnic tourist industries of the new millennium, often "new sources of profit exacerbate 'traditional' privilege." Jean Comaroff and John L. Comaroff, *Ethnicity, Inc.* (Chicago: University of Chicago Press, 2009), 14–15, 24. This does not mean, as they concede, that outsiders are not also profiting or, as the local idiom has it, "feeding off" people whose value consists in their capacity to signify tradition.

34. The lexical and conceptual binarity between *mmereko/bereka* and *tiro* (S/T), or *ukwakha* and *pangela* (Z/X) is well documented in the literature on the historical development of commodity exchange and capitalist relations in southern Africa. Comaroff and Comaroff read the terms as indicative of two mutually exclusive modalities of being; T. Dunbar Moodie claims individuals used one to support the other. In my experience, these terms may sometimes be used to imply the opposite of their historically prior meaning, depending on the generational cohort of the speakers. Thus, there is linguistic documentation to suggest that *pangela* originally implied theft or booty, which indicates that working for whites was a way to get what was desired at home but that was not otherwise accessible through traditional work. At the same time, it could be read critically to imply that wage-work was theft by whites from black laborers. Today, some youth feel that *bereko* is the theft by their parents of what they would like to retain. They understand *tiro* as the watchword of entrepreneurial self-fashioning rather than socially oriented building. See Comaroff and Comaroff, "Madman and the Migrant"; and Moodie, *Going for Gold*, 24. Also see Hoyt Alverson, *Mind in the Heart of Darkness: Value and Identity among the Tswana of southern Africa* (New Haven, CT: Yale University Press, 1978), 117–44; Philip Mayer, "The Origin and Decline of Two Rural Resistance Ideologies," in *Black Villagers*, 1–80; and P. A. McAllister, "Work, Homestead, and the Shades: Home Friend Networks in the Social Life of Black Migrant Workers in a Gold Mine Hostel," in Mayer, *Black Villagers*, 205–53.

35. Dunbar Moodie, *Going for Gold*, 21.

36. William Beinart, "Worker Consciousness, Ethnic Particularism and Nationalism: The Experiences of a South African Migrant, 1930–1960," in *Politics of Race, Class and Nationalism in Twentieth Century South Africa*, ed. Shula Marks and Stanley Trapido (London: Routledge, 1987), 286–309.

37. Lucy Mair, "Review of *Black Villagers in an Industrial Society* by Philip Mayer; *Ciskei: A South African Homeland* by Nancy Charton," *African Affairs*, 81, no. 323 (1982): 292.

38. William Eksteen, general manager of Gold Fields, testified before the Myburgh Commission into ethnic violence in the mines and very clearly stated that the company allotted jobs on the basis of ethnicity, and attributed to different social groups different propensities and skill sets. See Justice J. F. Myburgh, "Report on the Commission of Enquiry Into the Violence on Three Gold Fields Mines" (1996), 470–71. This report would later feature in the TRC's consideration of the corporate role in Apartheid. See "Hearings of the Business Sector, Truth and Reconciliation Commission," SABC, November 13, 1997," https://sabctrc.saha.org.za /hearing.php?id=56249&t=Hearings+of+the+Business+Sector%2C+Truth+and+Reconciliation+Commission&tab=hearings, 49. Also, Jeff Guy and Motlatsi Thabane, "Technology, Ethnicity and Ideology: Basotho Miners and Shaft-Sinking on the South African Gold Mines," in "Culture and Consciousness in Southern Africa," special issue, *Journal of Southern African Studies* 14, no. 2 (1988): 257–78; and T. Dunbar Moodie, "Ethnic Violence on South African Gold Mines," Special Issue: Political Violence in Southern Africa *Journal of Southern African Studies* 18, no. 3 (1992): 584–613.

39. J. A. Gemmill, "Native Labour on the Gold Mines," 291. Gemmill's anthropology is not naïve. He cites among others, Marvin Harris's study of Thongan labor migration from Mozambique as a basis for thinking about the ways in which ostensible cultural propensities and intergenerational competition could explain attraction to migrant labor (290). He also quotes Harris on the substitution of cash for cattle as brideprice. And his essay includes a comprehensive chart of tribal affiliation, languages spoken, and areas of residential concentration that extends from South Africa to the High Commission Territories (Basutoland, Bechuanaland and Swaziland), Portuguese East Africa, Nyasaland, Pafuri, Northern Bechuanaland, Caprivi Strip, the Zambezi Area, and Tanganyika (293–95).

40. David Bunn, "Art Johannesburg and its Objects," in *Johannesburg, the Elusive Metropolis*, eds. Sarah Nuttall and Achille Mbembe (Durham, NC: Duke University Press, 2008), 139.

41. It was nonetheless from David Bunn that I first learned of these debates when, in 1990, I took a class with him at the University of Chicago. In my opinion, he underestimates the degree to which the social historians, and especially Charles van Onselen, did account for the complexity of urban life in Johannesburg.

42. V. Y. Mudimbe, *The Invention of Africa: Gnosis, Philosophy and the Order of Knowledge* (Bloomington: Indiana University Press, 1988), 5. Here, Mudimbe is quoting Samir Amin, *Accumulation on a World Scale: A Critique of the Theory of Underdevelopment* (New York: Monthly Review, 1974), 377. For a different reflection on the limits of Amin's conception of originary accumulation, see my article: Rosalind Morris, "*Ursprüngliche Akkumulation:* The Secret History of an Originary Mistranslation," in "Marxism, Communism, and Translation," ed. Nergis Ertürk and Özge Serin, special issue, *Boundary* 2 43, no. 3 (August 2016): 29–77.

43. Mudimbe, *Invention of Africa*, 6.

44. Dlamini, *Native Nostalgia*, 63.

45. On the false analogies linking the prison and the city, see Philippe Artières, "Lignes de fuite," in *Hautes Surveillances*, ed. Mathieu Pernot (Arles: Actes Sud, 2004), 9, cited in Gregory Salle, "How We Got from Prisons Located in Cities to City-Like Prisons: A Relationship between Metamorphoses and Contradictions," *Politix* 97, no. 1 (2012): 75.

46. Gold Producers' Committee, "Evidence of the Gold Producer's Committee of the Chamber of Mines," Statement No. 8, "The Social Aspect of Migratory Labour as Opposed to

Stabilized Native Mining Communities," Minutes of Evidence (Native Laws Commission of Enquiry, Chamber of Mines, 1947), 39.

47. Dan O'Meara, "The 1946 African Mine Workers' Strike and the Political Economy of South Africa," *Journal of Commonwealth and Comparative Politics* 13, no. 2 (1975): 146–73. According to O'Meara the strike was a "watershed event," despite its brevity and failure to elicit any improvements in conditions or wages of black and colored mineworkers. In his estimation, "the policies of the Nationalist government since 1948 have been a reply to questions about the nature of South African social formation posed by the strike" (146).

48. On the recruitment of urban laborers for the mines, see James, *Our Precious Metal*, 72–73. For its part, the Chamber of Mines reports for 1976 and 1977 note the volatility of gold prices during this period, with gold plummeting in 1976 when the International Monetary Fund had commenced gold auctions and, after two auctions, the world market had been "unable to absorb the Fund's offerings" (TCM, *Annual Report*, 1976, 8–9). At the same time, the white mineworkers struck to demand a five-day work week (the Chamber offered eleven days a fortnight). As gold prices began to rebound in 1977, the Chamber complained that productivity was declining but asserted that national efforts to absorb local unemployed populations as mine labor also demanded an end to "job reservation based on racial discrimination." It feared a lack of skilled labor, and it lamented the loss of the foreign labor supply, which it deemed much more productive (TCM, *Annual Report*, 1977, 11).

49. Gold Producers' Committee, "Evidence," 37.

50. Marcel Mauss, *The Gift*, annot. and trans. Jane Guyer, expanded ed. (Chicago: Hau Books, 2016 [1925]).

51. British Pathé, "Deep Shaft Sets Record—South Africa," ID 1595.4 (newsreel film, 1959).

52. John Oxley, *Down Where No Lion Walked: The Story of Western Deep Levels* (Johannesburg: Southern Book Publishers, 1989), 89; Neil Orpen, with H.J. Martin, *Salute the Sappers*, vol.8, pt. 2 (Johannesburg: The Sappers Association, 1981), esp.328–30.

53. In this case "colored" refers to black workers and not the mixed-race category that was operative under the terms of the Group Areas Act.

54. Etienne Balibar, "The Basic Concepts of Historical Materialism," in Louis Althusser and Etienne Balibar, *Reading Capital*, trans. Ben Brewster New York: Verso, 1997 [1968]), 199–208. See my discussion of this argument in Rosalind Morris, "After de Brosses: Fetishism, Translation, Comparativism, Critique," in *The Returns of Fetishism: Charles de Brosses and the Afterlives of an Idea*, Rosalind Morris and Daniel Leonard (Chicago: University of Chicago Press, 2017), esp. 187–204.

55. Morris, "After de Brosses,'" esp. 179–86.

9. Utopia on the Highveld

Epigraphs to this chapter are from Ingrid de Kok, "Into the Sun," in *Terrestrial Things* (Cape Town: Kwela/Snail Press, 2002), 56; and Muriel Rukeyser, "The Road," in *US 1* (New York: Covici Friede, 1938), 9.

1. Toni Morrison, in conversation with Jim Lehrer, March 9, 1998. https://pr.princeton.edu/news/98/c/0312-clips.htm.

2. Botha's narrative exactly reproduces many sentences and phrasings of Cartwright's text. An especially telling example is the opening question of chapter 14: "What was Krahmann's theory? It was simplicity itself." These words appear verbatim in Botha's little history along with hand-drawn versions of the accompanying maps (152–3). As for Cartwright's text, it was published the year before the ordeal at West Driefontein, of which he was also the chronicler. In *Gold Paved the Way*, he notes that West Driefontein had made

a profit of £2,000,000 within one year of starting milling, and was the largest producer on the West Rand. At the time of his writing, the profits of the five mines of the West Wits line were approaching £20,000,000 per annum (242–3). The majority shareholder in these mines was the West Witwatersrand Areas, Ltd, which was itself a holding company of Gold Fields. A. P. Cartwright, *Gold Paved the Way: The Story of the Gold Fields Group of Mines* (London: Palgrave Macmillan London, 1967).

3. Merensky is also credited with discovering the platinum deposits in Rustenburg and Lydenburg (Cartwright, *Gold Paved*, 154).

4. In Botha's account, Krahmann and Reinecke met with Carleton Jones and Douglas Chris-topherson at the Gold Fields building in Johannesburg. For Cartwright's account of the meeting, see *Gold Paved*, 156. Reinecke and Carleton Jones later worked together at the Sub Nigel mine and were credited with transforming it from a so-called problem mine into one of enormous profitability. Shareholder dividends rose from 7.5 percent in 1924–1925 to an astonishing 65 percent in 1927–1928 (*Gold Paved*, 134).

5. Carleton Jones's "vision" nonetheless had to be approved and pitched to shareholders. Cartwright credits John Agnew and Robert Annan with approving the proposal, despite the risks (202–3). Buying up the stakes meant purchasing them from other financiers who had acquired the land but not developed it. In this case, most of the area was actually owned by Colonel James Donaldson and W. Carlis, under the company title of West Areas. They had bought up the area when Western Rand Estates had been liquidated for £80,000 but soon become cash-strapped and, in Cartwright's estimation, were easily persuaded by Gold Fields's offer of £225,000 (144, 159). This is yet another example of how many mining companies made their profits without ever mining.

6. The West Witwatersrand Areas, Ltd. holding company was simply announced to share-holders in the June 1932 annual meeting, where it was revealed that it had been established with an initial capital of £500,000 (Cartwright, *Gold Paved*, 162).

7. Cartwright, who had access to Krahmann's correspondence, largely dismisses this fact as well: "He was also a most patriotic young German of the post-war generation and, like most of that generation, a supporter of Hitler's Nationalist-Socialist party. But Krahmann's thought were not on politics when he arrived in Johannesburg in March 1930" (Cartwright, *Gold Paved*, 150).

8. Transvaal Chamber of Mines (TCM), *The Gold Standard. Report of the Proceedings at a General Meeting of the Transvaal Chamber of Mines held on Friday, 13th November, 1931. Mr. John Martin in the Chair* (Johannesburg, 1931), 1–3.

9. TCM, *Gold Standard*, 3.

10. William Beinart, *Twentieth Century South Africa* (Oxford: Oxford University Press, 2001), 116.

11. Beinart, *Twentieth Century*, 116.

12. TCM, *Annual Report*, 1941, 100. These Chamber-originating numbers approximate but do not precisely match Beinart's figures. Beinart, however, does not indicate his source, nor state whether he was including all of the mines (coal, diamonds, and gold), only the gold mines, or only the mines of the Witwatersrand.

13. Although Hertzog presided over a split Anglo-Afrikaner government, he is often described as an intense Germanophile opposed to British imperialism. He supported Germany's position on war reparations in relation to the Treaty of Versailles, and he was sympathetic to Hitler, his Foreign Minister and several members of his cabinet being openly supportive of Nazism and antisemitism.

14. Beinart, *Twentieth Century*, 120. Beinart's text is marked by a scrupulous insistence that the "reasons for the headway made by D. F. Malan's *Geswuiwerde* (purified) National Party . . . are not self-evident" and that each phase in the development of Apartheid needs to be examined in terms of the historically and regionally particular battles being waged for "hearts, minds and pockets of Afrikaners" (119). Nonetheless, in retrospect, we

may observe a certain analogy between the tendency he describes and that of our own moment, when ethnonationalism arises among the least disenfranchised who then mobilize the beneficiaries of welfare statism in opposition to the government, and often in the name of antistatism.

15. In invoking this phrase, "heart of the heartless world" from Marx's writing on religion, I mean to imply that the industry had something of a cultic dimension. See Karl Marx, "Contribution to the Critique of Hegel's Philosophy of Law [Recht]," in Collected Works, vol. 3, trans. Jack Cohen et al. (New York: International, 2005), 175.

16. Michael D. Bordo, "The Bretton Woods International Monetary System," in The Gold Standard and Related Regimes (Cambridge: Cambridge University Press, 1999), 395.

17. "West Witwatersrand Areas, Ltd. Oppressive Level of Taxation: Exhaustive Review of Company's Financial Position," RDM, Thursday, November 14, 1946, 4. All future references to Jones's speech are from this text.

18. Elize van Eeden, "So Long, Gold Mines, Long Live Industries? A Case Study of Carletonville's Battle for Economic Survival," South African Journal of Economic History 12:1–2 (1997): 103–127, 107.

19. "West Witwatersrand Areas, Ltd. Oppressive Level of Taxation: Exhaustive Review of Company's Financial Position," RDM, Thursday, November 14, 1946, 4.

20. The earliest version of this ad that I could locate appeared in the Rand Daily Mail in August 1947 and was repeated every week. See RDM, August 29, 1947, 11.

21. "Driefontein Brick and Potteries Co., Ltd. Report of the Ordinary General Meeting of Shareholders," RDM, October 24, 1947, 3

22. "Report of the Ordinary General Meeting of Shareholders, The Ryan Nigel G.M. and Estate C., Limited," RDM, December 16, 1947, 4.

23. Katharina Pistor, The Code of Capital (Princeton, NJ: Princeton University Press, 2019).

24. "The Standard Bank of South Africa," Legal Notices, RDM, April 2, 1948, 4.

25. Notices emanated from the office in Pretoria, but most meetings were held on site. See for example, "Notice No. 47/1949, September 30, 1949: Peri-Urban Health Board Pretoria," RDM, October 12, 1949, 3.

26. "West Driefontein Gold Mining Company: Outlook for Development and Production," RDM, November 10, 1949, 5.

27. "Prospects Materially Enhanced by Devaluation, West Witwatersrand Areas, Ltd.," RDM, November 11, 1949, 5

28. "Prospects Materially Enhanced," 5.

29. "Report on the Company Meetings, West Witwatersrand Areas, Ltd.," RDM, November 30, 1950, 5.

30. "Prospects Materially Enhanced," 5.

31. "Prospects Materially Enhanced," 5.

32. "Report on the Company Meetings, West Witwatersrand Areas, Ltd.," RDM, November 30, 1950, 5.

33. Gertrude Stein, Brewsie and Willie (New York: Random House, 1946), 98.

34. TCM, Annual Report, 1957, 48.

35. "West Wits: Chairman on Prospects of Higher Price of Gold," RDM, November 27, 1952, 15.

36. "Chairman's Review: Consolidated Gold Fields of South Africa," RDM, December 15, 1952, 4. Note that the meetings were held in London, not in South Africa.

37. TCM, Annual Report, 1954.

38. South Africa, Report of the Commission of Inquiry Into the Riots at Soweto and Elsewhere from the 16th of June 1976 to the 28th of February 1977. Vol 1 (Pretoria, 1980), 137.

39. Thomas More, Utopia, intro. Richard Marius (1516; repr., London: Everyman, 1981), 79.

40. More, Utopia, 132.

41. Louis Marin, "Frontiers of Utopia," Critical Inquiry 19, no. 3 (Spring 1993): 397–420, 406–8.

42. Marin, "Frontiers of Utopia," 399.

43. Michel de Certeau, "Walking in the City," in *The Practice of Everyday Life*, trans. Steven Rendall (Berkeley: University of California Press, 1984 [1974]), 91–110. For de Certeau, the phenomenon of "atopia-utopia" must be grasped as an effort to overcome, by rising above, urban agglomeration. It is a belated, compensatory project based on an abstraction from the actual movements (which he terms "mobilities") of subjects. In de Certeau's case, the gesture toward the empirical is belied by the fact that the rule-breaking bearer of enunciation is a universalized, racially unmarked and degendered subject whose access to space and capacities to transgress its boundaries is undifferentiated and unconstrained by social histories of racialization or sexualization—precisely those dimensions of differentiation upon which the women pass protestors insisted.

44. Marin, "Frontiers of Utopia," 402.

45. Louis Marin, "The Frontiers of Utopia," short version, in *Utopias and the Millennium*, eds. K. Kumar and S. Bann (London: Reaktion Books, 1993), 11.

46. Jean Comaroff and John Comaroff, *Theory from the South: Or, How Euro-America Is Evolving Toward Africa* (New York and London: Routledge, 2011).

47. Marin, "Frontiers of Utopia," 413. Marin is citing his own earlier elaboration of this concept "in homage to Ernst Bloch." See Louis Marin, "Reveries: La pratique-fiction utopie (1976)," *Lectures Traverieres* (Paris: 1992).

48. Gilles Deleuze and Felix Guattari, *Anti-Oedipus: Capitalism and Schizophrenia*, trans. Robert Hurley (New York: Penguin, 2009 [1972]).

10. Good as Gold: Standards and Margins of Value

Epigraphs to this chapter are from Muriel Rukeyser, "The Book of the Dead," in *US 1* (New York: Covici Friede, 1938), 66; and Ingrid de Kok, "Truck Stop," in *Terrestrial Things* (Cape Town: Kwela Books, 2002), 60.

1. Rukeyser, "Book of the Dead," 66.

2. Linda Singer, "Sex and the Logic of Late Capitalism," in *Erotic Economy: Sexual Theory and Politics in the Age of Epidemic*, eds. Judith Butler and Maureen MacGrogan (New York: Routledge, 1993), 34–61.

3. The relative portion of mineworkers permitted to live in nonhostel circumstances (i.e., "living out") varied in time and by sector. Women had been prohibited from working underground in 1898 and again in 1911 under terms set by the Chamber of Mines, on the model of the English prohibition, laid down in 1842. But this did not exclude women from surface activities. In the asbestos sector, women formed a relatively high percentage of the mine labor force (about half), although this came under restriction in the early Apartheid era. In the coal industry, women also accounted for a significant portion of the aboveground labor force and worked in open-pit and surface extraction activities. In the gold-mining sector, where hostels were much larger, women were far fewer in number. This was not true of deep mines in the gold sector, from which they were largely absent, until well into the post-Apartheid era. Dhiraj Kumar Nite, "Refashioning Women's Self and Mining Homemakers and Producers on the South African Mines, 1976–2011," *Essays on Social History and the History of Social Movements* 54 (2015): 7–36. On women in the coal sector, see Peter Alexander, "Oscillating Migrants, Detribalised Families, and Militancy: Mozambicans on Witbank Collieries: 1918–1927," *Journal of Southern African Studies* 27, no. 3 (2001): 505–25. Also see Angela V. John, *By the Sweat of Their Brow: Women Workers at Victorian Coalmines* (London: Routledge and Kegan Paul, 1984); and Jock McCulloch, "Women Mining Asbestos in South Africa: 1893–1980," *Journal of Southern African Studies* 29, no. 2 (2003): 413–33.

4. Louis Molamu, *Tsotsi-taal: A Dictionary of the Language of Sophiatown* (Pretoria: Unisa, 2003), 95.

5. Glen S. Elder, *Hostels, Sexuality, and the Apartheid Legacy: Malevolent Geographies* (Athens, OH: Ohio University Press, 2003).

6. For example, a report about the opening of a new technical high school in Wedela referred to it as having been transferred from the "schoonplaas" at Western Deep Levels in 1983. Only after the transfer, did it come under the authority of the Ministry of Education and Training. Funded by Anglo American and de Beers, it initially had 140 students registered. Sophe Tema, "5m Technical High School Is Handed Over," *Rand Daily Mail*, June 26, 1984.

7. These distinctions orient Mark Hunter's account of concurrent sexual relations in KwaZulu-Natal. Although I do not share his taxonomic ambition, shared by many of the isiZulu speakers whom he interviewed, I agree that the acute material vulnerability of women in informal settlements is made usable in discourses of masculinity that make gifts the means of securing women's dependency. The apparent "choice" exercised by such women when compared with the lobola system, which Hunter describes as being "based on male-to-male transactions" (112), is correlated with the effort to code prostitution as a total vocation: "Whether using sex for subsistence, more common in the informal settlement, or for consumption, more common in the township, women sew themselves into the very fabric of masculinity through their own agency. Women actively *qoma* (choose) men—while operating through patriarchal structures they rarely see themselves as "victims." See Mark Hunter, "The Materiality of Everyday Sex: Thinking Beyond 'Prostitution,'" *African Studies* 16, no. 1 (2002): 99–120. In a more recent article, Hunter acknowledges and rebuts the critique of the literature on transactional sex in Africa, namely that it overemphasizes and misidentifies material exchanges in conjunction with sexual intimacy as narrowly transactional. See Mark Hunter, "The Political Economy of Concurrent Partners: Toward a History of Sex-Love-Gift Connections in the Time of AIDS," *Review of African Political Economy* 42, no. 145 (2015): 362–75.

8. N. Chabani Manganyi, "The Migrants' Burden," in *Looking Through the Keyhole: Dissenting Essays on the Black Experience* (1981; repr., Johannesburg: Ravan, 2001), 128. Also see N. Chabani Manganyi, *Apartheid and the Making of a Black Psychologist* (Johannesburg: University of Witwatersrand Press, 2016).

9. Manganyi, "Migrants' Burden," 129.

10. Manganyi, "Migrants' Burden," 127, 129.

11. Jean Comaroff and John L. Comaroff, "The Madman and the Migrant," in *Ethnography and the Historical Imagination* (Boulder, CO: Westview, 1992), 192.

12. Manganyi, "Migrants' Burden," 129.

13. "World Gold Rush Still On, but Paper Boom Possible," *Randy Daily Mail*, August 11, 1971, 4. In fact, premium sales by gold producers in South Africa generated more revenue in 1970 than ever before, and while profits declined from 1969, total revenue was trumpeted as having reached unprecedented levels in stores early in 1971. See "Record Output, Revenue, but . . . Gold Mine Profits Hit by Premiums Sale Fall," *Randy Daily Mail*, February 12, 1971, 12.

14. Joanne Gowa, *Closing the Gold Window: Domestic Politics and the End of Bretton Woods* (Ithaca, NY: Cornell University Press 1983), esp. 60–87.

15. Giorgio Agamben, "Capitalism as Religion," trans. Nicholas Heron, in *Agamben and Radical Politics*, ed. Daniel McLoughlin (Edinburgh: Edinburgh University Press, 2021 [2018]), 15.

16. Agamben, "Capitalism," 21–22.

17. John Maynard Keynes, "Auri Sacra Fames (1930)," in *Essays in Persuasion* (New York: Classic House, 2009), 101.

18. Joseph Gold noted in 1975 that the United States was the only country with a sufficient voting block to effect a veto over other states' proposals. Joseph Gold, *Legal and Institutional Aspects of the International Monetary System: Selected Essays* (Washington, DC: International Monetary Fund, 1979), 92.

19. The articles were published together in Gertrude Stein, *Writings and Lectures*, ed. Patricia Meyerowitz (New York: Penguin, 1971). Perhaps more to Agamben's point would have been Stein's writings on a possible identity between money and words: "Money is what words are./Words are what money is" and "Is money what words are/Are words what money is?"; see Solveig Daugaard, "Anybody Living a Private Life Is a Believer in Money: Gertrude Stein, The Great Depression, and the Abstraction of Money," *Nordic Journal of Aesthetics* 60 (2020): 26–47. Also see Gertrude Stein, *The Geographical History of America, Or the Relation of Human Nature to the Human Mind*, in *Writings 1932–1946*, eds. Catherine R. Stimpson and Harriet Chessman (New York: Library of America, 1998), 461.

20. Keynes, "Auri," 99. Keynes was less concerned with the imperial connection.

21. Gowa, *Closing the Gold Window*, 35.

22. Gowa, *Closing the Gold Window*, 35.

23. Lawrence B. Krause, *Sequel to Bretton Woods: A Proposal to Reform the World Monetary System* (Washington, DC: Brookings Institute, 1971), 10; cited in Gowa, *Closing the Gold Window*, 36.

24. Richard Nixon, "The Challenge of Peace," presidential address, August 15, 1971, https://www.presidency.ucsb.edu/documents/address-the-nation-outlining-new-economic-policy-the-challenge-peace.

25. Michael D. Bordo, *The Gold Standard and Related Regimes: Collected Essays* (Cambridge: Cambridge University Press, 1999), 453–54.

26. Richard Nixon, "The Challenge of Peace." Presidential address, August 15, 1971. https://www.presidency.ucsb.edu/documents/address-the-nation-outlining-new-economic-policy-the-challenge-peace.

27. As already noted, the United States was the only country with a sufficient voting block to effect a veto over other states' proposals. Gold, *Legal and Institutional Aspects*, 86.

28. Beginning in the late 1970s, the Carter administration took a relatively hard line in opposition to the Apartheid regime. The Reagan regime embraced the concept of "constructive engagement," although grassroots opposition to Apartheid in the United States and transnational alliances with forces in South Africa led to boycotts and divestment. Alex Thompson has argued that the policy was never in fact implemented. See Alex Thompson, "Incomplete Engagement: Reagan's South Africa Policy Revisited," *Journal of Modern African Studies* 33, no. 1 (1995): 83–101.

29. Adam Martin, "Remembering Nixon's Gold-Standard Gamble: Interrupting *Bonanza*," *The Atlantic*, August 15, 2011, https://www.theatlantic.com/politics/archive/2011/08/nixon-gold-standard-gamble-interrupting-bonanza/354136/. *Bonanza* was also one of the earliest television serials to play on South African television after it commenced broadcasting in 1976 (permission to develop television in South Africa had been granted in 1971, but the first broadcasts did not occur until five years later).

30. CMSA, *Annual Report*, 1971, 12.

31. Ernst Bloch, *Traces*, trans. Anthony A. Nassar (Stanford, CA: Stanford University Press, 2006), 12. Thanks to Rudolf Mrázek for leading me to this text.

32. Jonathan Crush and Wilmot James, "Depopulating the Compound: Migrant Labor and Mine Housing in South Africa," *World Development* 19, no. 4 (1991): 304. Also see Jonathan Crush, Alan Jeeves, and David Yudelman, *South Africa's Labor Empire: A History of Black Migrancy to the Gold Mines* (Boulder, CO: Westview, 1991), 16.

33. Crush and James, "Depopulating the Compound," 304.

34. According to Crush, Jeeves, and Yudelman, less than 1 percent of the black labor force was in married accommodations in 1984. Jonathan Crush, Alan Jeeves, and David Yudulman, *South Africa's Labor Empire: A History of Black Migrancy to the Gold Mines* (Boulder, CO: Westview, 1991), 171–72.

35. Crush and James, "Depopulating the Compound," 303. Wedela was built between Western Deeps and Elandsrand—two of the world's deepest and richest gold mines. See "Western

Deep Levels: Further Comment by Mr. G. Langton," Business Mail, *Rand Daily Mail*, March 22, 1979, 15.

36. Crush, Jeeves, and Yudelman, *South Africa's Labor Empire*, 173.

37. An electrical company's advertisement of 1980, for example, sought qualified black electricians for the "township" of Wedela, "near Carletonville" (*Rand Daily Mail*, September 16, 1980, 25).

38. G. W. F. Hegel, *Phenomenology of Spirit*, trans. A. V. Miller (Oxford: Clarendon, 1977 [1807]). For an excellent analysis of this dynamic, see Patricia J. Mills, "Hegel's Antigone," *The Owl of Minerva* 17, no. 2 (1986): 131–52.

39. Immanuel Kant, "What Is Enlightenment," in *On History*, trans. Lewis White Beck (New York: Macmillan 1963), 10. On the limits but also the generalized deployment of this understanding, see also the note by Gayatri Spivak in Mahasweta Devi, *Imaginary Maps: Three Stories by Mahasweta Devi*, trans., ed., and intro. Gayatri Chakravorty Spivak (New York: Routledge, 1995), n10, 213.

40. Hortense Spillers, "Mama's Baby, Papa's Maybe: An American Grammar Book," in *Black, White and in Color: Essays on American Literature and Culture* (Chicago: University of Chicago Press, 2003), 203–29.

41. I am here re-invoking the description of a guest at Beit's Ball (see chapter 4). See A.L. Fom, "Mr. A. Beit 'At Home.' A Brilliant Function. Four Hundred Guests." *Johannesburg Times*, June 22, 1895, 5.

42. In this sense, there are limits to which the prostitute represents commodified labor in the abstract. As Andrew McCann says, in a critical engagement with Benjamin's analysis, "the figure also introduces something wholly exceptional into conceptions of labour— an irreducible corporeality at the heart of the contract that threatens to undo the status of prostitution as a representative figure." See Andrew McCann, "Walter Benjamin's Sex Work: Prostitution and the State of Exception," *Textual Practice* 28, no. 1 (2014): 110. Also Carol Pateman, *The Sexual Contract* (Palo Alto, CA: Stanford University Press, 1988).

43. Walter Benjamin, *The Arcades Project*, trans. Howard Eiland and Kevin McLaughlin (Cambridge, MA: Belknap Press, 1999), 69. See also chapter 4.

44. Keynes, "Auri," 101.

45. Keynes, "Auri," 100.

46. Jean-Joseph Goux, *Symbolic Economies: After Marx and Freud*, trans. Jennifer Curtiss Gage (Ithaca, NY: Cornell University Press, 1990 [1973]), 115–16.

47. Keynes, "Auri," 100.

48. Astrid Deuber-Mankowsky, "Rhythms of the Living: Conditions of Critique: On Judith Butler's Reading of Benjamin's 'Critique of Violence,'" trans. Catharine Diehl, in *Walter Benjamin and Theology*, ed. Colby Dickinson and Stéphane Symons (New York: Fordham University Press, 2015), 253–71.

49. Walter Benjamin, "Capitalism as Religion," trans. Rodney Livingstone, in *Selected Writings*, vol. 1, *1913–1926*, ed. Marcus Bullock and Michael W. Jennings (Cambridge, MA: Belknap Press, 1996 [1921]), 288.

50. Benjamin, "Capitalism as Religion," 290.

51. The most sustained of these histories is that by Jean Comaroff and John L. Comaroff, *Of Revelation and Revolution*, 2 vols. (Chicago: University of Chicago Press, 1987, 1991).

52. I have explored this dimension of "originary accumulation" in Rosalind C. Morris, "'Ursprüngliche Akkumulation: The Secret History of an Originary Mistranslation,'" in "Marxism, Communism, and Translation," ed. Nergis Ertürk and Özge Serin, special issue, *Boundary 2* 43, no. 3 (August): 29–77.

53. Benjamin, *Arcades Project*, 346. For criticism on Benjamin's treatment of the prostitute as figure, see Esther Leslie, "Ruin and Rubble in the Arcades," in *Walter Benjamin and the Arcades Project*, ed. Beatrice Hanssen (London: Continuum, 2006), 87–112; McCann,

"Walter Benjamin's Sex Work"; Angela McRobbie, *Postmodernism and Popular Culture* (London: Routledge, 1994); and Susan Buck-Morss, "The Flâneur, the Sandwichman and the Whore: The Politics of Loitering," in *Walter Benjamin and the Arcades Project*, ed. Beatrice Hanssen (London: Continuum, 2006), 33–65.

54. Benjamin, *Arcades Project*, 348.

55. See, for example, Clement Greenberg, *Art and Culture: Critical Essays* (1961; repr., Boston: Beacon Press, 1989); T. J. Clark, *Farewell to an Idea: Episodes from a History of Modernism* (New Haven, CT: Yale University Press, 1999); Walter Benn Michaels, *The Gold Standard and the Logic of Naturalism* (Berkeley: University of California Press, 1987), esp. 157–63; and Frederic Jameson, *Postmodernism. Or, the Cultural Logic of Late Capitalism* (Durham, NC: Duke University Press, 1992), esp. 197–99.

56. On the figure and fashion of the Tsotsi, Rosalind C. Morris, "Style, Tsotsi-style and Tsotsitaal: The Histories, Politics and Aesthetics of a South African Figure," *Social Text* 28, no. 2 (Summer 2010): 85–112.

57. Peter Wilhelm, "Like a Troubled Dream: *A Man Called Sledge*," *Rand Daily Mail*, May 25, 1971, 9.

58. At the time, the official rendition of Verwoerd's assassination was that Dimitri Tsafendas had been insane when he committed the act. He, however, had long been politically active, including as a member of the South African Communist Party, and asserted that he killed Verwoerd out of hatred for his racial policies.

59. Tonie van der Merwe was named one of KwaZulu-Natal's "heroes and legends" for his Apartheid-era film work in 2014. Norimitsu Norishi, "Honoring a Filmmaker in the Shadow of Apartheid," *New York Times*, July 29, 2014, https://www.nytimes.com/2014/07/30/world /africa/honoring-a-filmmaker-in-the-shadow-of-apartheid.html.

60. Teresa De Lauretis, "Desire in Narrative," in *Alice Doesn't: Feminism, Semiotics, Cinema* (Bloomington: Indiana University Press, 1984), 103–57.

61. Contemporary film students in South Africa, better trained in neoliberalism than were the censors of 1973, have sometimes praised *Joe Bullet*'s autonomy and read the film as testimony to the notion that crime and "success" are mutually exclusive. The film was banned in 1973 because of its depiction of black men bearing guns, which was illegal at the time. Norishi, "Honoring a Filmmaker."

62. In European moral philosophy from the seventeenth century on, this primitivism was partly sustained by the long-standing obsession with African fetishism, especially as represented by the snake cult of Whydah. See Rosalind C. Morris, "After de Brosses: Fetishism, Translation, Comparativism, Critique," in *The Returns of Fetishism: Charles de Brosses and the Afterlives of an Idea*, with a translation of *The Worship of Fetish Gods*, by Daniel H. Leonard (Chicago: University of Chicago, 2017), 161.

63. I am borrowing the language of Raymond Williams, "Dominant, Residual and Emergent," in *Marxism and Literature* (Oxford: Oxford University Press, 1977), 121–27.

11. Catalytic Conversions: Becoming Organized

Epigraphs to this chapter are from J. P. Rieckert, *Commission of Inquiry Into Legislation Affecting the Utilisation of Manpower (excluding the Legislations administered by the Departments of Labour and Mines)* (Pretoria, 1978), 83; and Oupa Thando Mthimkulu, "Nineteen Seventy-Sex," *Staffrider* 7, nos. 3 and 4 (1988): 173.

1. Fredric Jameson, *Valences of the Dialectic* (New York: Verso, 2009), 525.

2. Benedict Anderson, *Imagined Communities: Reflections on the Origin and Spread of Nationalism* (London: Verso, 1983), 19.

3. Joseph Lelyveld, "South African Gold Boom Has Diverse Implications," *New York Times*, June 7, 1981.

4. V. L. Allen, *The History of Black Mineworkers in South Africa*, vol. 2 (Keighley, UK: Moor Press, 1992), 295.

5. Tony Morphet, "Brushing History Against the Grain: Oppositional Discourse in South Africa," in Richard Turner, *The Eye of the Needle* (Calcutta: Seagull Books, 2015), esp. 209–10.

6. *Isisebenzi* (Zulu), is not to be confused with *Umsebenzi* (The Worker, Xhosa), the journal of the South African Communist Party, mainly edited by Moses Kotane.

7. *Isisebenzi*, vol. 1, "Pietermaritzburg's Own Workers' Pamphlet," April 1973.

8. I heard this too many times to count. It is confirmed by others investigating the redemarcation protests. See, for example, M. E. Chapitso, "The Community Response to the Demarcation of the Merafong Municipality Into the North West Province" (master's thesis, Nelson Mandela Metropolitan University, Port Elizabeth, 2016).

9. Allen, *Black Mineworkers*, vol. 2, 285–90.

10. The dockworkers strike of 1972 was an early instance of national labor-based insurrection, moving from Durban to Cape Town and virtually stalling imports, as ships were idled and goods rotted while awaiting processing.

11. During the period 1968–1977, the black population accounted for 70.4 percent of the total, but only 3 percent of its physicians. See Anne Digby, "Black Doctors and Discrimination Under South Africa's Apartheid Regime," *Medical History* 57, no. 2 (2013): 269–90; and P. V. Tobias, "Apartheid and Medical Education: The Training of Black Doctors in South Africa," *Journal of the National Medical Association* 72, no. 4 (1980): 407. More shockingly the doctor-to-patient ratio was 1:400 for whites and 1:40,000 for blacks. See Harold Nelson, ed., *South Africa: A Country Study* (Washington, DC: U.S. Government, Foreign Area Studies, American University, 1981), 154.

12. Allen, *Black Mineworkers*, vol. 2, 300.

13. Allen, *Black Mineworkers*, vol. 2, 297.

14. Jonathan Crush, "Migrancy and Militance: The Case of the National Union of Mineworkers of South Africa," *African Affairs* 88, no. 350 (1989): 5.

15. Allen, *Black Mineworkers*, vol. 2, 296.

16. For accounts of the IIE's efforts and the development of the Federation of South African Trade Unions (FOSATU), see Alec Irwin, "Interview," Wits Historical Papers, ZA HPRA A3402-B-B4, accessed July 25, 2022, http://historicalpapers-atom.wits.ac.za/b4-41.

17. Tony Morphet, "The Intellectual Reach of *The Eye of the Needle*," in Richard Turner, *The Eye of the Needle* (Calcutta: Seagull, 2015), 224.

18. In fact, Turner's own radicalism was based in Christian theology tempered by Sartrean existentialism and initially emerged from SPRO-CAS (The Study Project on Being Christian in an Apartheid Society). Although there was much debate about how much *Eye of the Needle* was an expression of his own faith or a strategic address to the dominant Christian majority, he concluded his essay on participatory democracy with the assertion that "there is no reason why Christian business people should not practice Christianity by handing their own enterprises over to the workers" (Turner, *Eye of the Needle*, 125).

19. Allen, *Black Mineworkers*, vol. 2, 297.

20. These entities had slightly different constituencies, and if, in the long run, they generated powerful alliances, they did not share uniform analyses of the situation. See Kally Forrest, *Metal That Does Not Bend: National Union of Metalworkers of South Africa* (Johannesburg: Wits University Press, 2011), 320.

21. Refilwe Ndzuta, "Interview 2010," Wits Oral History Project, ZA HPRA A3402-B-B108.

22. According to D. G. Clarke, "managed acclimatisation" was a key variable in determining productivity and profits: "The requirements as such as to significantly pre-pattern labour

demand considerations, making essential the existence *for the industry* of a 'relative sur-plus' of 'eligible workers.'" See D. G. Clarke, "The South African Chamber of Mines: Policy and Strategy with Reference to Foreign African Labour Supply" (DSRG Working Paper No. 2, Pietermaritzburg, Development Studies Research Group, 1977), 12–15.

23. Horner and Kooy mention an earlier strike at Solver mine in the Cape in late 1972, which they construe as a possible harbinger, but they date the onset of true compound conflict to the events in September. Like most commentators, however, they neglect what the news-papers reported, namely a rising tide of discontent over a week, rather than a sudden con-frontation. Dudley Horner and Alide Kooy, "Conflict on South African Mines, 1972–1976" (Saldru Working Paper No. 5., Cape Town, 1976), 4https://www.opensaldru.uct.ac.za /bitstream/handle/11090/580/1976hornerswp5.pdf?sequence=1.

24. "African Miners Slain," *Southern Africa: A Monthly Survey of News and Opinion* 6, no. 9 (1973): 8.

25. "The Start of the Tragedy," *Rand Daily Mail*, September 12, 1973, 2.

26. "Striking Miners Go Home," *Rand Daily Mail* (hereafter referred to as RDM), September 6, 1973, 2. The conflict was represented unequivocally as a wage dispute: "11 Shot Dead: Police Shoot on Miners' Pay Riot," *RDM*, September 12, 1973, 1.

27. Allen, *Black Mineworkers*, vol. 2, 339; emphasis added.

28. Daluxolo Jekwe, "Interview," Wits Oral History Project, 2010, ZA HPRA A3402-B-B19.

29. Allen, *Black Mineworkers*, vol. 2, 338–40.

30. "We May Have Bungled Wages, Mine Chief Admits," *RDM*, September 13, 1973, 1.

31. SACM, *Annual Report*, 1973, 10, 14–15. In fact, Plumbridge hardly mentioned the strikes at Western Deep Levels and instead focused his remarks on the other "tragic" events, namely the crash of a WENELA plane transporting workers to Malawi, in which seventy-four employees died, and "several severe accidents" (10).

32. Michael Bray, *Powers of the Mind: Mental and Manual Labor in the Contemporary Political Crisis* (Bielefeld: Transcript Verlag, 2019), 53.

33. Transvaal Chamber of Mines, "A Descriptive and Statistical Statement of the Gold Min-ing Industry of the Witwatersrand, Annexure to the Thirteenth Report of the Transvaal Chamber of Mines for the Year 1902," 24.

34. Hortense Spillers, "Mama's Baby, Papa's Maybe: An American Grammar Book," in *Black, White and in Color: Essays on American Literature and Culture* (Chicago: University of Chicago Press, 2003), 206.

35. Allen, *Black Mineworkers*, vol. 2, 333.

36. Louis Althusser, *On the Reproduction of Capitalism: Ideology and Ideological State Appara-tuses*, trans. A. M. Goshgarian, pref. Etienne Balibar, intro. Jacques Bidet. (1971, 1995; repr., New York: Verso, 2014), 186.

37. Some former miners claim that this time was longer. Osborne Galeni, for example, said that he had spent eighteen days in acclimatization. See Osborne Galeni, "Interview," Wits Oral History Project, ZA HPRA A3402-B-B98, accessed July 26, 2022, http://historicalpapers -atom.wits.ac.za/b98-3.

38. This is a somewhat colloquial rendition of Bataille's concept of expenditure, which I aim to separate out from the paradigm of phallic jouissance. Georges Bataille, "The Notion of Expen-diture," in *The Bataille Reader*, ed. Tom Bottomore and Scott Wilson, trans. Allan Stoekl, with Carl R. Lovitt and Donald M Leslie Jr. (1933; repr., Oxford: Blackwell, 1997), 167–81.

39. Julie Livingston, *Self-Devouring Growth: A Planetary Parable as Told from Southern Africa* (Durham, NC: Duke University Press, 2019).

40. *Commission of Inquiry Into the Riots*, 46.

41. P. J. Riekert, *Report of the Commission of Inquiry into Legislation Affecting the Utilisation of Manpower (Excluding the Legislation Administered by the Departments of Labour and Mines)* (Pretoria, 1978), 81.

42. Pam Christie and Colin Collins, "Bantu Education: Apartheid Ideology of Labour Repro-
    duction," *Comparative Education* 18, no. 1 (1982): 68. Verwoerd trained in Germany before
    being appointed to the department of psychology at Stellenbosch University, where he
    propagated the elements of what would become Apartheid ideology. He was Minister of
    Native Affairs from 1950–1958, and Prime Minister from 1958 to 1966, when he was assas-
    sinated, having survived an earlier assassination attempt in 1960.

43. Ali Khangela Hlongwane, "The Mapping of the June 16 1976 Soweto Student Uprisings
    Routes: Past Recollections and Present Reconstruction(s)," "Performing (In) Everyday
    Life," special issue, *Journal of African Cultural Studies* 19, no. 1 (2007): 10.

44. Hlongwane, "Mapping," 12.

45. Hlongwane, "Mapping," 12.

46. Jabulani Mayaba, "Interview," Wits Oral History Interviews, ZA HPRA A3402-B-B48,
    accessed July 25, 2022, http://historicalpapers-atom.wits.ac.za/b48-18.

47. This reading is indebted to that of James T. Siegel, who describes the revolutionary
    national independence movement in Indonesia as well as the witchcraft trials reported
    by Matilda Coxe Stevenson and analyzed by Claude Lévi-Strauss, as phenomena in which
    people are ensorcelled by the force of language in which something foreign operates. This
    foreignness has the capacity to transform the listener, to make him or her do something
    she or he might not otherwise do. See James T. Siegel, *Fetish, Recognition, Revolution*
    (Princeton, NJ: Princeton University Press, 1997) and *Naming the Witch* (Stanford, CA:
    Stanford University Press, 2005).

48. Walter Benjamin, "The Storyteller: Observations on the Works of Nikolai Leskov," trans.
    Harry Zohn, in *Selected Writings*, vol. 3, *1935–1938*, ed. Howard Eiland and Michael W.
    Jennings (Cambridge, MA: Harvard University Press, 2002), 144.

49. Zolani Ngwane, "'Christmas Time' and the Struggles for the Household in the Country-
    side: Rethinking the Cultural Geography of Migrant Labour in South Africa," *Journal of
    Southern African Studies* 29, no. 3 (September 2003): 681–99.

50. *Report of the Commission of Inquiry Into the Riots at Soweto and Elsewhere from the 16th of
    June 1976 to the 28th of February 1977*, vol. 1, 114.

51. *Annexure, Report of the Commission of Inquiry Into the Riots at Soweto and Elsewhere*, vol.
    2, 85–87.

52. *Commission of Inquiry Into the Riots*, vol. 1, 522–23. For the descriptions of student versus
    migrant conflicts, see the *Annexure*, vol. 2.

53. *Commission of Inquiry Into the Riots*, vol. 1, 135.

54. Chris Dlamini, "Interview," 2011, ZA HPRA A3402-B-B118, 9, accessed July 26, 2022, http://
    historicalpapers-atom.wits.ac.za/uploads/r/historical-papers-research-archive-library
    -university-of-witwatersrand/d/8/4/d8473abcd9ce33d31ee1a3b9d0487577cf27c13678678592a-
    c1eec8c1bf909c9/A3402-B18-001-jpeg.pdf. An extreme description of opposition between
    students and workers within the opposition occurs in an interview with Special (David)
    Radebe, a former union organizer with FOSATU. He states that on the East Rand, union
    workers had commenced engagements with students in 1975, as part of an effort at conscien-
    tization, but says that "truthfully we should say Soweto hijacked the East Rand programme."
    See Special (David) Radebe, "Interview," Wits Oral History Project, ZA HPRA A3402-B-B133,
    2, accessed July 26, 2022, http://historicalpapers-atom.wits.ac.za/uploads/r/historical
    -papers-research-archive-library-university-of-witwatersrand/e/d/0/ed020e73946
    abfa347df7a404cc727bcc7db5c19a5028ac3c3b153c02aa95648/A3402-B133-001-jpeg.pdf.

55. Gayatri Chakravorty Spivak, *Critique of Postcolonial Reason: Toward a History of the Van-
    ishing Present* (Cambridge, MA: Harvard University Press, 1999), 257.

56. Joe Matthews, "Interview, 2009." Historical Papers Research Archive, University of the
    Witwatersrand. Wits Oral History Project, ZA HPRA A3402-B-B58. Accessed July 21,
    2024: http://historicalpapers-atom.wits.ac.za/uploads/r/historical-papers-research-archive
    -library-university-of-witwatersrand/7/7/7/7771422e72970403d8da320c31903296
    527a034af17d6095fd47c242e727f249/A3402-B58-001-jpeg.pdf

57. In a scathing rebuke to Matthews's daughter, an ANC party member whose speech at the party centenary celebration passed by her father's abandonment of the ANC for the Zulu nationalist Inkatha Freedom Party, Isaac Mpho Mogotsi invokes the Soviet agent Vladimir Shubin's criticism of Matthews as a self-interested turncoat and writes that he "failed to consistently honour the great legacy of his father, 'ZK,' of unswerving loyalty and commitment to one political home, the ANC." Such party loyalty is precisely what Matthews identified as mindless subservience. But many other ANC leaders saw Matthews as the party intellectual and mediator of ANC-IFP conflicts. See Isaac Mpho Mogotsi, "Naledi Pandoor and Joe Matthews," *Politics Web*, January 17, 2012, https://www.politicsweb.co.za/news-and-analysis/naledi-pandor-and-joe-matthews. Also see Vladimir Shubin, *ANC: A View from Moscow*. On Matthews's status as theoretician and on his move to the IFP, see Mondli Makhanya, "No Fly-by-Night Intellectual," *Sunday Times*, August 22, 2010.

58. Hlongwane, "Mapping," 12.

59. Matthews, "Interview, 2009," 13.

60. Mayaba, Jabulani. "Interview." Historical Papers Research Archive, University of the Witwatersrand. Wits Oral History Project, ZA HPRA A3402-B-B48. Accessed July 25, 2022, thttp://historicalpapers-atom.wits.ac.za/b48-18, 5–6.

61. Mayaba, "Interview, 2012," 6.

62. Mayaba, "Interview, 2012," 17.

63. Mabaya, "Interview, 2012," 17.

64. Mabaya, "Interview, 2012," 2.

65. Mayaba, "Interview, 2012," 2.

66. Mattews, "Interview, 2009," 5.

67. Raymond Suttner, *The ANC Underground in South Africa* (Johannesburg: Jacana, 2008), 55–57.

68. There were conflicting reports about Motapanyane's possible participation in meetings at Winnie Mandela's home before the uprisings, although it has been argued that this claim was part of an effort to incriminate Mandela by both the state and the ANC. See Helena Pohlandt-McCormick, "Controlling Woman: Winnie Mandela and the 1976 Soweto Uprising," *International Journal of African Historical Studies* 33, no. 3 (2000): 585–614. As for his age, this was not unusual, given the deferred or inconstant attendance of schools that was sometimes a corollary of parents' poverty and the need to work or to care for junior siblings.

69. *Commission of Inquiry Into the Riots*, vol. 1, 547.

70. *Commission of Inquiry Into the Riots*, vol. 99, 4730 (evidence of inquiry held on February 7, 1977), 30.

71. J.M.L. Lentsoane, "Laboraro le lesoleso," translated from the Sepedi by Biki Lepota, as "Black Wednesday," in *Stitching a Whirlwind: An Anthology of Southern African Poems and Translations*, fwd. by Gabeba Baderoon, intro. Antjie Krog (Oxford: Oxford University Press, 2018), 196–205 (lines 65–78).

72. "The Voice of South Africa's Young Generation: 'Go Underground and Organize.' New African Talks to TEBELLO MOTAPANYANE, Secretary General of the Banned South African Students' Movement," *New African*, December 1977, 1188

73. "How June 16 Demo was Planned," Interview with Tebello Motapanyane, January 1977, 59. Accessed July 21, 2024: https://www.sahistory.org.za/archive/how-june-16-demo-was-planned.

74. "The Voice of South Africa's Young Generation," 1188. When he died in 2006, it was reported that he had become embittered and ill during his exile, which ended only in 1991. Living in penury, he was granted no formal state honors. Kamogelo Seekoei, "Student Leader Dies Heartbroken," *Sowetan*, December 21, 2006.

75. See Gayatri Chakravorty Spivak on the misprision inherent to authoritarian populism that conflates the two dimensions of representation—that of the proxy and that of the imaginal figure. *Critique of Postcolonial Reason*, 260.

76. "How the June 16 Demo was Planned," 58.
77. Walter Benjamin, "On the Language of Man and Language as Such," in *Selected Writings*, vol. 1, *1913–1926*, ed. Marcus Bullock and Michael W. Jennings (1916, repr., Cambridge, MA: Belknap Press, 1996), 62–75.
78. CMSA, *Annual Report*, 1976, 9.
79. CMSA, *Annual Report*, 1976, 5.
80. CMSA, *Annual Report*, 1977, 11.
81. N. E. Wiehahn, *The Complete Wiehahn Report, Parts 1–6, and the White Paper on Each Part* (Pretoria: Lex Patria, 1982), 711.
82. Wiehahn, *Complete Report*, 711
83. Government of South Africa, "White Paper on Part 6 of the Report of the Commission of Inquiry Into Labour Legislation," in Wiehahn, *Complete Report*, 755–61; emphasis added.
84. Jeremy Baskin, "Mass Strike on the Mines," *Worker Struggles on the East Rand: The Labour Bulletin* 7, no. 8 (1982): 61.
85. Crush, "Migrancy and Militance," 10.
86. The phrase is a euphemism for the dictatorship of the proletariat, but the latter phrase— saturated as it is by a history of misrecognizing efforts to grab power—at least recognizes the communicative dimension of the project. Dictatorship of the proletariat is the dictation, the powerful speaking, which is to say legislative authority, of the workers.
87. Crush, "Migrancy and Militance," 11.
88. Crush, "Migrancy and Militance," 13.
89. Crush, "Migrancy and Militance," 13.

12. Go Underground: Or, When Was Youth?

The epigraph to this chapter is from William Shakespeare, *Merchant of Venice*, Act 1, Scene 3, 52.
1. Cited in Peter Fenves, "Marx, Mourning, Messianicity," in *Violence, Identity, and Self-Determination*, ed. S. Weber and H. D. Vries (Stanford, CA: Stanford University Press, 1997), 259.
2. Achille Mbembe, *On the Postcolony*, trans. A. M. Berrett et al. (Berkeley: University of California Press, 2001), 201. For an example of the more common reference to Apartheid racial classification as baroque, see Paul N. Edwards and Gabrielle Hecht, "History and the Technopolitics of Identity: The Case of Apartheid South Africa," *Journal of Southern African Studies* 36, no. 3 (September 2010): 625.
3. Fenves, "Marx, Mourning, Messianicity," 259.
4. Walter Benjamin, *The Origin of German Tragic Drama*, trans. John Osborne (repr., New York: New Left Books, 2023 [1928]), 65.
5. Benjamin, *Origin of German Tragic Drama*, 66.
6. Benjamin, *Origin of German Tragic Drama*, 66.
7. John L. Comaroff and Jean Comaroff, "Law and Disorder in the Postcolony: An Introduction," in *Law and Disorder in the Postcolony* (Chicago: University of Chicago Press, 2006), 1–56.
8. Fenves, "Marx, Mourning, Messianicity," 260.
9. Mark Shaw, *Crime and Policing in Post-Apartheid South Africa: Transforming Under Fire* (Cape Town: David Philipps, 2002).
10. Fenves, "Marx, Mourning, Messianicity," 261.
11. Raymond Suttner, *The ANC Underground in South Africa* (Johannesburg: Jacana, 2008), 93.
12. Thabiso Thakali, "Finance Minister Has a Sting in his Tail," *Cape Argus*, December 13, 2015.
13. Pierre Clastres, *Chronicle of the Guayaki Indians*, trans. Paul Auster. New York: Zone, 1998 [1972], esp.105–107.

14. Clifton Crais, for example, describes the coexistence of incendiarism and belief in muti powers among opponents of the Bantu Authorities and in popular movements, such as the Congo movement in Apartheid-era Pondoland. See Crais, *The Politics of Evil: Magic, State Power, and the Political Imagination in South Africa* (Cambridge: Cambridge University Press, 2002), esp. 204–5. Others have argued that witchcraft beliefs and accusations were incited rather than curbed by modernist developments and bureaucratic statecraft. See Jean Comaroff and John Comaroff, eds. *Modernity and its Malcontents: Ritual and Power in Postcolonial* Africa (Chicago: University of Chicago Press, 1993). Some, such as Peter Geschiere, have linked the proliferation of witchcraft accusation specifically to ethnic politics in postcolonial states. See *Witchcraft and Modernity: Politics and the Occult in Postcolonial Africa*, trans. Janet Roitman and Peter Geschiere (Charlottesville, VA: University of Virginia Press, 1997).

15. In this sense, "on the roof," likely means "toward the ceiling, given that the teacher had to take cover and the event took place inside.

16. Truth and Reconciliation Commission, *Truth and Reconciliation Commission of South Africa Report*, vol. 7 (Johannesburg: Juta for the TRC, 1998), 871.

17. His official biography on the website of the South African government describes him as a former MK operative. It also states that he was born in Khutsong.

18. Ephraim Jonas Israel Motsumi, Truth and Reconciliation Commission, SABC, accessed February 9, 2024, https://sabctrc.saha.org.za/victims/motsumi_ephraim_jonas_israel .htm?tab=hearings.

19. S. Lesotho, "Testimony at Human Rights Violations Hearings," Truth and Reconciliation Commission, Krugersdorp, November 11, 1996, https://sabctrc.saha.org.za/hearing.php?id =55438&t=S.+Lesotho&tab=hearings.

20. This incident was reported in the *Daily Mail* by Philippa Garson and cited by Steve Mokwena, "The Era of the Jackrollers: Contextualising the Rise of Youth Gangs in Soweto and Khutsong," Seminar No. 7 (Johannesburg: University of the Witwatersrand, 1991), 26. Mokwena's account renders the Gadaffi as primarily organized against the Khutsong Youth Congress. In the TRC hearings about conflict in the area, Johannes Stephanus Kriel claimed that Eugene Terre'Blanche instructed his militants, that "if they [referring specifically to the ANC] haven't got ears, if they don't listen, cut their ears off. That was a general command or saying." See Andre Stephanus Kriel, "Testimony in the Case of Cornelius Johannes Lottering," Amnesty Hearings, Truth and Reconciliation Commission, March 23–28, 1998, https://sabctrc.saha.org.za/hearing.php?id=54885&t=Kriel+&tab=hearings.

21. A. de. V. Minnaar, *An Analysis of the Scope and Extent of Conflict in South African with Specific Reference to the Identification of High Conflict Areas* (Pretoria: Centre for Socio-political Analysis, Human Sciences Research Council, 1994), 11, 16, 18. These figures are confirmed by the Independent Board of Inquiry, *Fortress of Fear* (Braamfontein, 1993), which reported hostel violence levels on the West Rand to be substantially lower than those on the East Rand, but significantly higher than those in the Johannesburg area (48).

22. Wayne Safro, *Special Report on Violence Against Black Town Councillors and Policemen* (Johannesburg; South African Institute of Race Relations, 1990).

23. J. K. McNamara, "Inter-Group Violence Among Black Employees on South African Gold Mines, 1974–1986," *South African Sociological Review* 1, no. 1 (1988): 33.

24. Gary Kynoch, "*Marashea* on the Mines: Economic, Social and Criminal Networks on the South African Gold Fields, 1947–1999," *Journal of Southern African Studies* 26, no. 1 (2000): 79–103.

25. Kynoch does not use the word prostitution. He says, "The Russians kept strict control over the women in their areas and it was difficult for men to have a relationship with resident women close to the mine unless they joined the group or paid protection fees"

("*Marashea,*" 87). Thabang argues against Kynoch's more accommodationist reading of the role of women. See his review of Kynoch.

26. Kynoch, "*Marashea* on the Mines," 89.

27. Kynoch, "*Marashea* on the Mines," 90.

28. Motlatsi Thabane, "Marashea Gangs in South Africa: Review of Gary Kynoch, *We Are Fighting the World: A History of the Marashea Gangs in South Africa, 1947–1999,*" *Journal of Southern African Studies* 32, no. 3 (2006): 629–31.

29. Such postmortem violation is also mentioned by Crais as a feature of political combat amid the fight against Apartheid, as these were leavened by muti beliefs. See *The Politics of Evil,* 205.

30. Ineke van Kessel was in this case discussing the killing of those who *dingaka* (N) who were deemed to be unsympathetic to the UDF youth. See Ineka van Kessel, *Beyond our Wildest Dreams: The United Democratic Front and the Transformation of South Africa* (Charlottesville, VA: University of Virginia Press, 2000), esp. 132. Also see Nechama Brodie, *Femicide in South Africa* (Cape Town: Kwela Books, 2020), 151–3; and Isak Niehaus, "Witchcraft and the South African Bantustans: Evidence from Bushbuckridge," *South African Historical Journal,* vol.41., no1 (March 2012): 48–61.

31. James T. Siegel, *Naming the Witch* (Stanford, CA: Stanford University Press, 2006), esp.111–70.

32. South African Labor Board, "Mine Struggles in the Carletonville Region," Digital Innovation South Africa Portal, University of KwaZulu-Natal, July 1985, 20, https://disa.ukzn.ac.za/sites/default/files/pdf_files/LaJul85.0377.5429.010.008.Jul1985.15.pdf.

33. T. Mvudle, "Testimony at the Hearings on Human Rights Violations," Krugersdorp, November 11, 1996, https://sabctrc.saha.org.za/hearing.php?id=55447&t=T.+Mvudle&tab=hearings.

34. Allistair Sparks, "S. [South] African Township Gangs: Murder and Firebombing in the Cause of Freedom," *Washington Post,* January 5, 1990.

35. Sparks quotes Cross as saying, "The uprising popularized the political struggle. Then the detention of the political leadership created space for the expression of gang culture." See Sparks, "S. African Township Gangs."

36. Michael Cross, "Culture and Identity in South African Education, 1880–1990" (PhD diss., University of Johannesburg, 2015), esp. chap. 2 and 6.

37. Cross, "Culture and Identity," 301.

38. Cross, "Culture and Identity," 307.

39. Cross, "Culture and Identity," 307

40. "COSATU Cracks CP [Conservative Party]: Carletonville Shows How," *Cosatu News,* March 2, 1989, 4.

41. Sparks, "S. African Township Gangs."

42. Frantz Fanon, *Wretched of the Earth,* trans. Richard Philcox, intro. Jean-Paul Sartre and Homi K. Bhabha (New York: Grove, 2004 [1961]), 48.

43. W. S. Goliath, "Testimony at the Hearings on Human Rights Violations," Truth and Reconciliation Commission, Krugersdorp, November 11, 1996, https://sabctrc.saha.org.za/hearing.php?id=55436&t=Goliath%2C+W.S.+&tab=hearings.

44. "Report of the Independent Board of Inquiry for the Month of September 1991," Wits Historical Research Papers, AG2543.2.2.18, 2.

45. "Report of the Independent Board of Inquiry for the Month of September 1991," 14.

46. Truth and Reconciliation Commission, "TRC Appeal to Victims of AWB Bombings," South African Press Association, May 12, 1998, https://www.justice.gov.za/trc/media/1998/9805/s980512c.htm.

47. Walter Benjamin, "Critique of Violence," trans. Edmund Jephcott, in *Selected Writings,* vol. 1, *1913–1926,* ed. Marcus Bullock and Michael W Jennings (Cambridge, MA: Belknap Press, 1996 [1921]), 239.

48. Benjamin, "Critique of Violence," 239.

49. T. Dunbar Moodie, "Managing the 1987 Mineworkers' Strike," *Journal of Southern African History* 35, no. 1 (2009): 51.

50. Moodie, "Managing," 55.
51. Moodie, "Managing," 45.
52. Benjamin, "Critique of Violence," 239.
53. Benjamin, "Critique of Violence," 248.
54. Benjamin, "Critique of Violence," 242.
55. Astrid Deuber-Mankowsky, "Rhythms of the Living: Conditions of Critique: On Judith Butler's Reading of Benjamin's 'Critique of Violence,'" trans. Catharine Diehl, in *Walter Benjamin and Theology*, ed. Colby Dickinson and Stéphane Symons (New York: Fordham University Press, 2015), 265.
56. Deuber-Mankowsky, "Rhythms of the Living," 265.
57. Dhlomo, one of the major Zulu writers of the early twentieth century, was editor of the *Bantu World* newspaper and he contributed under the pseudonym of "Rollie Reggie" to the Zulu-language *Ilanga Lase Natal*, with which it merged in 1935. His reputation as a conservative nativist derives mainly from his novels, and especially *An African Tragedy* and *Ndlela yababi* (The Way of the Wicked), which condemns the supposed moral decay associated with urban life. Dhlomo, however, also wrote more ambiguous first-person columns for the *Bantu World* under the nom de plume of "R. Roamer, esq." These were organized around the conceit of a flaneur who meanders in the shadows of the urban landscape. More than local travelogue, these columns range from critical observational sociology, to moralizing satire, and literary essay.
58. R. R. R. Dhlomo, "Murder on the Mine Dumps," *English in Africa* 2, no. 1 (March 1975): 33–35. The story originally appeared in *The Sjambok*, December 12, 1930.
59. Dhlomo, "Murder on the Mine Dumps," 33.
60. Dhlomo, "Murder on the Mine Dumps," 34.
61. Dhlomo, "Murder on the Mine Dumps," 34
62. Dhlomo, "Murder on the Mine Dumps," 35.
63. Benjamin, "Critique of Violence," 250.

13. Zombies Sing Pata Pata: The Impossible Subject of Political Violence

This chapter draws partly from Rosalind C. Morris, "The Mute and the Unspeakable: Political Subjectivity, Violent Crime, and 'the Sexual Thing' in a South African Mining Community," in *Law and Disorder in the Postcolony*, ed. Jean Comaroff and John Comaroff, 57–101 (Chicago: University of Chicago Press, 2006).

Epigraphs to this chapter are from Truth and Reconciliation Commission, *Truth and Reconciliation Commission of South Africa Report*, vol. 1 (Johannesburg: Juta for the TRC, 1998), 40; and Ingrid de Kok, "Parts of Speech," in *Terrestrial Things* (Cape Town: Kwela Books, 2002), 21.

1. Alick Macheso, "Masasi A Jonas Kasamba," Facebook, February 4, 2013, https://www.facebook.com/chesomusic/posts/-masasi-a-jonas-kasamba-1-once-upon-a-time-there-was-a-music-propheta-alick-mach/10150278363929970.
2. Gwen Ansell, *Soweto Blues; Jazz, Popular Music and Politics in South Africa* (New York: Continuum, 2004), 93.
3. Mafika Pascal Gwala, "Gumba, Gumba, Gumba," in *Jol'inkomo: Poems* (Johannesburg: Ad. Donker, 1977).
4. Sheridan Jones and R. Hunt Jr., *Mandela, Tambo and the African National Congress: The Struggle Against Apartheid, 1948–1990: A Documentary History* (New York: Oxford University Press, 1991), cited in Njabulo Ndebele, *Thinking of Brenda. The Desire to Be* (1996; repr., Vlaeberg, South Africa: Chimurenga, 2009), 15–16.
5. Lyrics for Brenda Fassie's "Shoot Them Before They Grow" available at: https://genius.com/Brenda-fassie-shoot-them-before-they-grow-lyrics.

6. Cornelius Johannes Lottering, "Testimony in the Case of Cornelius Johannes Lottering at the Amnesty Hearings," Pretoria, March 23–27, 1998, https://sabctrc.saha.org.za/hearing .php?id=54885&t=Cornelius+Lottering&tab=hearings.

7. James Wheeler, "Testimony in the Case of James Wheeler at the Amnesty Hearings," Pretoria, March 23–27, 1998, https://sabctrc.saha.org.za/hearing.php?id=54886&t=James +Wheeler&tab=hearings,

8. Lottering, "Testimony."

9. Andries Stephanus Kriel, "Testimony in the Case of Cornelius Johannes Lottering at the Amnesty Hearings," Pretoria, March 23–28, 1998, https://sabctrc.saha.org.za/hearing.php?id =54885&t=Kriel+&tab=hearings.

10. Carl Schmitt, *The Concept of the Political*. Trans. George Schwab (Chicago: University of Chicago Press, 2007 [1932]).

11. Barend Strijdom, "Testimony in the Case of Cornelius Johannes Lottering" Pretoria, March 23–27, 1998, https://sabctrc.saha.org.za/hearing.php?id=54885&t=Kriel+&tab=hearings.

12. Phila Martin Dolo, "Testimony in the Matter of the Zastron Mayaphuthi Bridge Shooting at the Amnesty Hearings, Aliwal North," Aliwal North, April 20, 1998, https://sabctrc .saha.org.za/hearing.php?id=54585&t=Testimony+of+Phila+Martin+Dolo%2C+Case +No.+3485%2F96.+Amnesty+Hearings%2C+Aliwal+North.+April+20%2C+1998&ta b=hearings; see also Greg Rosenberg, "Battle Is on Against Legacy of Apartheid," *The Militant* 60, no. 8 (February 26, 1996).

13. Kriel, "Testimony."

14. Kriel, "Testimony."

15. Truth and Reconciliation Commission (hereafter referred to as TRC), *Truth and Reconciliation Commission of South Africa Report*, vol 1. (Johannesburg: Juta for the TRC, 1998), 103.

16. TRC, *Report*, vol 1, 84; emphasis added.

17. Rosalind C. Morris, "The Mute and the Unspeakable: Political Subjectivity, Violent Crime, and 'the Sexual Thing' in a South African Mining Community," in *Law and Disorder in the Postcolony*, ed. Jean Comaroff and John Comaroff (Chicago: University of Chicago Press, 2006), 57–101.

18. Keith Breckenridge, "The Allure of Violence: Men, Race and Masculinity on the South African Goldmines, 1900–1950," *Journal of Southern African Studies* 24, no. 4 (1998): 669.

19. Clive Glaser, "The Mark of Zorro: Sexuality and Gender Relations in the Tsotsi Subculture on the Witwatersrand," *African Studies* 51 (1992): 62.

20. Catherine Campbell, "Learning to Kill? Masculinity, the Family and Violence in Natal," *Journal of Southern African Studies* 18 (1992): 625. Campbell's argument is more ambiguous than that of Belinda Bozzoli, who first took leave of materialist orthodoxy (and the presumption that indigenous cultural logics had been radically effaced by mining capital) when she described the condition of social life in South Africa as a "patchwork of patriarchies," in which competing forms of masculinist authority coexisted, overlapped, and reinforced each other. See Belinda Bozzoli, "Marxism, Feminism, and South African Studies," *Journal of Southern African Studies* 9, no. 2 (1983): 149.

21. Clive Glaser, "Swines, Hazels and the Dirty Dozen," *Journal of Southern African Studies* 24, no. 4 (December 1998): 719; emphasis added.

22. Gary Kynoch, "A Man Among Men: Gender, Identity, and Power in South Africa's Marashea Gangs," *Gender and History* 13, no. 2 (2001): 252.

23. Kynoch, "A Man Among Men," 252–53.

24. In addition to Casanova gang, the area became the operational base of several other gangs, including the Creatures, Delta, and Mavandal. See Fhumulani Khumela, "Khutsong on the Boil Again," *Sowetan*, September 19, 2014, https://www.pressreader.com/south-africa /sowetan/20140919/281638188415135.

25. Nozibonelo Maria Mxathule, "Testimony of Nozibonelo Maria Mxathule, Case No. JB01840/03NW—Women's Hearings, Human Rights Violations," SABC, July 29, 1997, https://sabctrc.saha.org.za/hearing.php?id=56406&t=Nozibonelo+Maria+Mxathule&tab=hearings.

26. Pierre Clastres, *Chronicle of the Guayaki Indians*, trans. by Paul Auster (New York: Zone, 1998 [1972]).

27. "Amnesty Hearings in the Matter of the Murder of David Maseko," SABC, September 9–13, 1996, https://sabctrc.saha.org.za/hearing.php?id=54856&t=Lebona&tab=hearings. See also Amnesty Hearings of the Truth and Reconciliation Commission, "Decision, Case Number AC/97/0006," SABC, March 13, 1997, https://sabctrc.saha.org.za/hearing.php?id=58493&t=Lebona&tab=hearings.

14. Terrain of the Fetish: Dislocations, Relocations, and the Difficulty of Moving On

Epigraphs to this chapter are from Siegfried Kracauer, *The Salaried Masses: Duty and Distraction in Weimar Germany*, trans. Quintin Hoare (London: Verso, 1998), 34; and Yvette Christiansë, "Spring, for Martha," *Staffrider* 10, no. 4 (1992): 20.

1. A good index of this trend can be seen in the TRC's report on unknown victims, which details the occasions when several and even "scores" of people were killed in the conflict in Carletonville—most of the events taking place between 1986 and 1991; see https://www.justice.gov.za/trc/report/finalreport/victims_10to300_vol7.pdf.

2. Scott Kraft, "South Africans Hear Final Call for 'Yes' on Reform,'" *Los Angeles Times*, March 17, 1992.

3. Toni Morrison, *Jazz* (New York: Penguin, 1992), 7.

4. "Prayers for the Mine," *Rand Daily Mail*, October 30, 1968, 5.

5. "Residents at Bank to Take Legal Action," *Rand Daily Mail*, December 22, 1969, 4.

6. Elize van Eeden, "The Effect of Mining Development on the Cultural Experience of the Carletonville Community," *South African Journal of Cultural History* 12, no. 1 (1998): 75–89, esp. 8–89.

7. George Simmel, *The Philosophy of Money*, trans. Tom Bottomore and David Frisby, with Kathe Mengelberg (London: Routledge, 1978 [1907]).

8. Frantz Fanon, *Wretched of the Earth*, trans. Richard Philcox, intro. Jean-Paul Sartre and Homi K. Bhabha (New York: Grove, 2004 [1961]), 40.

9. Frantz Fanon, "Medicine and Colonialism," in *A Dying Colonialism*, trans. Haakon Chevalier, intro. Adolfo Gillay (New York: Grove, 1965 [1959]), 123. I am grateful to Chloé Faux for guiding my reading of this text.

10. Saebo Gaeganelwe, "Burning Down Libraries Deprives People of Reading," *Sowetan*, March 30, 2007.

11. Rowan Philp, "The Khutsong rebellion," *Sunday Times* (Johannesburg, South Africa), March 15, 2009.

12. Gwendolyn Brooks, "Boy Breaking Glass (1968)," in *Blacks* (Chicago: Third World Press, 1987), 438.

13. Gillian Hart, *Rethinking the South African Crisis: Nationalism, Populism, Hegemony* (Athens, GA: University of Georgia Press, 2013).

14. The "Cross-Border Municipalities Laws Repeals Act" (B-36, 2005) was introduced into Parliament on September 23, 2005. A copy of the bill can be found at http://www.info.gov.za/view/DownloadFileAction?id=66085. The COSATU response to the bill was submitted on September 27, 2005. The text may be obtained at http://www.cosatu.org.za/docs/2005/Cross-boundary.pdf.

15. Joel Netshitenzhe, quoted in: Parliament of South Africa, "Minutes of the Proceedings of the National Council of Provinces," December 14, 2005, 127pp, 29.

16. Pumla Dineo Gqola, "Brutal Inheritances: Echoes, Negrophobia and Masculinist Violence," in *Go Home or Die Here: Violence, Xenophobia and the Reinvention of Difference in South Africa*, eds. Shireen Hassim, Tawana Kuta and Eric Worby (Johannesburg: Wits University Press, 2008), 209–222, 213.

17. Anne Mc Lennan, "The Delivery Paradox," in *The Politics of Service Delivery*, eds. Anne Mc Lennan and Barry Munslow (Johannesburg: Wits University Press, 2009), 19–42.

18. Eddy Mazembo Mavungu, "Frontiers of Power and Poverty: Explaining Provincial Boundary Disputes in Postapartheid South Africa," *African Studies Review* 59, no. 2 (2016): 190.

19. Joshua Kirshner and Comfort Phokela, "Khutsong and Xenophobic Violence: Exploring the Case of the Dog That Didn't Bark" (Johannesburg: University of Johannesburg, Center for Social Research and Atlantic Philanthropies Foundation, 2010), 7, http://www.atlanticphilanthropies.org/wp-content/uploads/2010/07/5_Kutsong_c.pdf.

20. Mavungu, "Frontiers of Power and Poverty," 195.

21. Pokolo Tau, " 'Hola GP, Hola,' " *Independent Online* (IOL), South Africa, March 20, 2009.

22. M. E. Chapitso's formal survey confirms my own conversations. See M. E. Chapitso, "The Community Response to the Demarcation of the Merafong Muncipality into the North West Province" (master's thesis, Nelson Mandela Metropolitan University, 2016).

23. Chapitso, "The Community Response," 43.

24. Numbers 14.1

25. Batho Pele was an initiative of the Mandela government, which was started in 1997 and continues today. It originally aimed to provide a framework for service delivery, and included the following principles: (1) regular consultation; (2) set service standards; (3) increase access to services; (4) ensure higher levels of courtesy; (5) enhance information dissemination; (6) increase openness and transparency; (7) remedy failures and mistakes; and (8) give the best possible value for money. See Department of Development, Government of South Africa, "Batho Pele," accessed July 20, 2022, https://www.dsd.gov.za/index.php/about/batho-pele.

26. An exception to this bypassing is the study by Kirshner and Phokela, "Khutsong and Xenophobic Violence."

27. Peter Fenves, "Marx, Mourning, Messianicity," in *Violence, Identity, and Self-Determination*, edited by Samuel Weber and Hent de Vriest (Stanford, CA: Stanford University Press, 1997), 253–70; and Walter Benjamin, *The Origin of the German Tragic Drama*, trans. John Osborne (New York: New Left Books, 2023 [1928]). The mourning play of which Benjamin writes is mistranslated as tragic drama insofar as he opposes the Baroque mourning play to the "authentic" tragedy of classical Greece.

28. "The Taung Children," *Sowetan* (online), October 16, 2007. Accessed July 23, 2024: https://www.sowetanlive.co.za/news/2007-10-16-the-taung-children/.

29. Mfundekelwa Mkhulisi, "Kids at Taung Camp Threatened," *Sowetan* (online), August 17,2007, https://infoweb.newsbank.com/apps/news/document-view?p=WORLDNEWS&docref=news/132F2374CFFE21A8.

30. Kingdom Mabuza, "Pupil Thrown Out," *Sowetan*, October 8, 2007.

31. Rosalind C. Morris, "After de Brosses: Fetishism, Translation, Comparativism, Critique," in *The Returns of Fetishism: Charles de Brosses and the Afterlives of an Idea*, with a translation of *The Worship of Fetish Gods*, by Daniel H. Leonard (Chicago: University of Chicago, 2017), 133–319. Also see William Pietz, *The Problem of the Fetish*, ed. Francesco Pellizzi, Stefanos Geroulanos, and Ben Kafka (Chicago: University of Chicago Press, 2022).

32. Kracauer, *Salaried Masses*, 34.

33. Marx, *Capital*, 340–416. See also my analysis of this characterological drama in Rosalind C. Morris, "Dialect and Dialectic in 'The Working Day' of Marx's Capital," in "Music,

Sound, Value," ed. Jairo Moreno and Gavin Steingo. Special issue, *Boundary 2* 43, no. 1 (February 2016): 219–48.

34. Molema Moiloa, "Youth in Khutsong, South Africa: Nostalgia for a Different Political Present," *Peace and Conflict: Journal of Peace Psychology* 18, no. 3 (2012): 332.

35. Theodor Adorno, *Minima Moralia: Reflections from Damaged Life*, trans. E. F. M. Jephcott (London: Verso, 1974 [1951]), 148–49.

36. Fenves, "Marx, Mourning, Messianicity," 255.

37. Fenves, "Marx, Mourning, Messianicity," 255.

38. Njabulo Ndebele, "Guilt and Atonement: Unmasking History for the Future," *New Nation* (Johannesburg), December 1991, 9. See also Anthony O'Brien's excellent discussion of Ndebele's argument in Anthony O'Brien, *Against Normalization; Writing Radical Democracy in South Africa* (Durham, NC: Duke University Press, 2001), esp.76–102.

39. Andrew Nash, "The Moment of Western Marxism in South Africa," *Comparative Studies in South Asia, Africa and the Middle East* 19, no.1 (1999): 66–81.

40. Jacob Dlamini, *Native Nostalgia* (Johannesburg: Jacana, 2009).

41. Michael Denning, "Wageless Life," *New Left Review* 66 (December 2010), 79–97.

42. Fenves, "Marx, Mourning, Messianicity," 257.

43. Jean Baudrillard, *The System of Objects*, trans. James Benedict (New York: Verso, 1996 [1968]).

44. Frantz Fanon, *Wretched of the Earth*, trans. Richard Philcox (New York: Grove, 2004 1961]), 138.

15. Rush, Panic, Rush: A New Book of the Dead

This chapter draws on an earlier essay: Rosalind C. Morris "Rush/Panic/Rush: Speculations on the Value of Life and Death in South Africa's Age of Aids," *Public Culture* 21, no.2 (2008): 199–231.

Epigraphs to this chapter are from Mangaliso Buzani, "I Will Be Gone," in *A Naked Bone*, 37–39 (Durban: Deep South Press, 2019), 39; and Audre Lorde, "Who Said It Was Simple?," in *Chosen Poem: Old and News* (1973; repr., New York: Norton and Norton, 1982), 49.

1. Gillian Hart, *Rethinking the Crisis in South Africa: Nationalism, Populism, Hegemony* (Athens, GA: University of Georgia Press, 2013), esp.160–66.

2. C. Tshitereke, "GEAR and Labour in Post-Apartheid South Africa: A Study of the Gold Mining Industry, 1987–2004" (PhD diss., Queen's University, 2004), cited in Jonathan Crush and Belinda Dodson, "Another Lost Decade: The Failure of South Africa's Post-Apartheid Migration Policy," *Tijdschrift voor Economische en Sociale Geografie* 98, no. 4 (2007): 436–54.

3. UNITAID, "South Africa to Introduce State-of-the-Art HIV Treatment" (press release, November 17, 2019).

4. On the linkage between the politicization of sexual and consumer pleasures as symptomatic of the transition out of Apartheid, see Deborah Posel, "Sex, Death, and the State of the Nation: Reflections on the Politicization of Sexuality in Post-Apartheid South Africa," *Africa: Journal of the International African Institute* 75, no. 2 (2005): 125–153.

5. At the time that these interviews were conducted, there was considerable debate about the viral etiology of AIDS, not least because of the skepticism expressed about it by President Thabo Mbeki and his two health ministers, Nkosazana Zuma and Manto Tshabalala-Msimang. Mbeki and his health ministers famously sided with medical dissidents, who either disputed the existence of the virus or argued that it was a merely passive passenger in patients whose illnesses had other causes. However, as Didier Fassin has shown, their

suspicion about the viral etiology of AIDS was conflated in the press with their skepticism about some of the treatments being offered and were mediated by long experience with pathologizing discourses and inequitable health-care service provision under Apartheid. While these debates were playing out at the national center, they did not seem to sway thought about AIDS in the scenes where I worked—which nonetheless was strongly devoted to the ANC at that time. See Didier Fassin, *When Bodies Remember: Experiences and Politics of AIDS in South Africa* (Berkeley: University of California Press, 2007).

6. It is perhaps this sentiment, as much as any objectively discernible strategic orientation on the part of the national government, that explains Catherine Campbell's decision to title her book on the AIDS crisis in Carletonville, *Letting Them Die: Why HIV/AIDS Intervention Programmes Fail* (Cape Town: Double Storey/Juta, 2003).

7. Catherine Campbell, *Letting Them Die*, 17. According to a report published in 2003, "prevalence of HIV among men and women in the general population, mineworkers, and sex workers, was 20 percent, 37 percent, 29 percent and 69 percent, respectively." See Brian Williams et al., "Changing Patterns of Knowledge, Reported Behaviour and Sexually Transmitted Infections in a South African Gold Mining Community," *AIDS* 17, no. 14 (September 2003): 2099–107. Relative to the provincial averages, these numbers were high, but they conformed to the general patterns seen elsewhere. According to the Actuarial Society of South Africa, HIV prevalence rates in 2002 were estimated at 20.6 percent for all women ages fifteen to forty-nine, with the rate of presentation at antenatal clinics being 31.9 percent. The rates for men ages fifteen to forty-nine was calculated at 17.5 percent. In 2003, the total number of deaths caused by AIDS exceeded those caused by all other factors for the first time. By 2006, according to the South African National AIDS committee, prevalence levels were at 33.3 percent for females ages twenty-five to twenty-nine, and 12.1 percent in the same age-group for men. See South African National AIDS Committee, "HIV and AIDS and STI Strategic Plan for South, 2007–2011," 24.

8. Elizabeth Pisani, "Aids Into the Twenty-First Century: Some Critical Considerations," *Reproductive Health Matters* 8, no. 15 (May 2000): 63.

9. Horkheimer and Adorno use the term adaptation to refer to a process coerced by capital, by which laborers come to treat their predicament as both necessary and natural. Max Horkheimer and Theodor W. Adorno, *Dialectic of Enlightenment*, ed. Gunzelin Schmid Noerr; trans. Edmund Jephcott (Stanford, CA: Stanford University Press, 1992 [1947]).

10. Buti Alfred Kulwane, "Civic Competence in Khutsong" (master's thesis, University of the Witwatersrand, 2002), 11.

11. As Kulwane notes, the proliferation of shacks even on the properties of township houses, was the result of extreme population growth, especially at the end of the 1980s, and a ban, placed by the Apartheid state, on further construction. There were, in fact, no new houses built with government support or licensing between 1973 and the end of Apartheid. See Kulwane, "Civic Competence," 33–34.

12. I use the term *language game* in Wittgenstein's sense, to suggest a contextual system according to which a term can be understood. The term(s) in question here are life and living. The games are those of epidemiology and actuarial science versus political economy. See Ludwig Wittgenstein, *Philosophical Investigations* (1953; repr., London: Blackwell, 2001).

13. Didier Fassin rightly notes the excessive degree to which questions of behavior, long the central concern of public health educators, are culturalized when these issues are discussed in African contexts. Fassin, *When Bodies Remember*, 2007.

14. Fredric Jameson, *The Political Unconscious: Narrative as a Socially Symbolic Act* (Ithaca, NY: Cornell University Press, 1981).

15. Jean Comaroff and John Comaroff, "Millennial Capitalism: First Thoughts on a Second Coming," in *Millennial Capitalism* (Durham, NC: Duke University Press, 2001): 11.

16. Campbell, *Letting Them Die*.

17. I use the term *danger* to apply to the actual events afflicting people, and the term *risk* to its representation in terms of calculable and incalculable probabilities.

18. The most visible of these civil society entities is, of course, the Treatment Action Campaign, the group which spearheaded the movement to demand generalized antiretroviral distribution. There have been numerous others, supplemented by a myriad foreign-financed NGOs. It is important to recognize, however, that, in the early period, civil society and state in South Africa were not opposed, and indeed they jointly opposed the international pharmaceutical lobby, although they were soon to fall into conflict. But even in this case, many civil society participants were themselves prominent members of the state apparatus. The most notable among these is Supreme Court Justice Edwin Cameron, who, along with Zachie Achmat and Mark Heywood, was a significant member of TAC for many years. An account of Cameron's involvement in the struggle against AIDS can be found in Edwin Cameron, *Witness to AIDS* (Cape Town: Tafelberg, 2005). For the history of the complex relations between civil society and the state in South Africa's epidemic see Fassin, *When Bodies Remember.*

19. What Yodwa Mzaidume communicated to me as a still-to-be confirmed decline in seropositivity in August 2007 was later confirmed. More recent numbers reveal a substantial decline, although a significant number of South Africans still live with HIV and AIDS. The Sixth South African National HIV Prevalence, Incidence, and Behaviour survey (SABSSM VI) found that the percentage of all people living with HIV in South Africa had decreased from 14.0 percent in 2017 to 12.7 percent in 2022, indicating that approximately 7.8 million people were living with HIV in 2022. Human Sciences Research Council, "New HIV Survey Highlights Progress and Ongoing Disparities in South Africa's HIV Epidemic" (Pretoria: HSRC, November 27, 2023), https://hsrc.ac.za/press-releases/hsc/new-hiv-survey-highlights-progress-and-ongoing-disparities-in-south-africas-hiv-epidemic/#:~:text=SABSSM%20VI%20found%20that%20the,to%207.9%20million%20in%202017.

20. The full range of these analytics can be found in Kyle D. Kauffman and David L. Lindauer, *AIDS and South Africa: The Social Expression of a Pandemic* (New York: Palgrave, 2004).

21. I am grateful to Yodwa Mzaidume for explaining to me in what ways abstinence might be thought differently as a preventive discourse. In her analysis, abstinence is a discourse with the broadest legibility, and hence it must be the frame within which other strategies, such as condom use, are addressed, particularly in the education of youth. If abstinence is the initial starting point in preventive education, then youths who are not sexually active can imagine themselves as the addressees, even though they are unlikely to maintain this posture indefinitely.

22. The reference here is to Susan Sontag, *Illness as Metaphor* (New York: Farrar, Strauss, and Giroux, 1978) much more than her later *AIDS and Its Metaphors* (New York: Farrar, Strauss and Giroux, 1988), but I also have in mind Emily Martin's work on immunology and late capitalism, wherein the apparent resemblance between the discourses of flexible accumulation and immunology comes in large part to substitute for an analysis of the relationship between the two. See Emily Martin, *Flexible Bodies: Tracking Immunity in American Culture from the Days of Polio to the Age of AIDS* (Boston: Beacon, 1994).

23. Charles van Onselen, *New Babylon, New Nineveh: Everyday Life on the Witwatersrand 1886–1914* (Cape Town: Jonathan Ball, 1982), 3.

24. Linda Singer, *Erotic Welfare: Sexual Theory and Politics in the Age of Epidemic,* ed. Judith Butler and Maureen MacGrogan (New York: Routledge, 1993), 40. The text was written in 1990, shortly before Singer's death and posthumously assembled and edited by Judith Butler.

25. Singer, *Erotic Welfare,* 29.

26. Singer, *Erotic Welfare,* 36.

27. Singer, *Erotic Welfare,* 36.

28. Singer, *Erotic Welfare,* 36.

29. Singer, *Erotic Welfare*, 38.

30. Like Jean and John Comaroff, I see this conjuncture as determinant of South African possibilities. See Comaroff and Comaroff, "Millennial Capitalism," 8.

31. Sarah Nuttall, "Stylizing the Self: The Y Generation in Rosebank, Johannesburg," *Public Culture* 16, no. 3 (2004): 430–52. Also, Posel, "Sex, Death and the State of the Nation."

32. Gwendolyn Brooks, "Boy Breaking Glass (1968)," in *Blacks* (Chicago: Third World Press, 1987), 438

33. Kylie Thomas, "A Better Life for Some: The LoveLife Campaign and HIV/AIDS in South Africa," *Agenda: Empowering Women for Gender Equity* 62 (2004): 29–35. Also Nuttall, "Stylizing the Self"; and Posel, "Sex, Death, and the State of the Nation."

34. Mzaidume, personal communication, August 2007.

35. James Ferguson may be right, that antipathy to the idea of basic social income (sloganized as "give a man a fish") stems from a belief that it would allow men, who have historically been considered wage-earners, to assume the feminized position of dependent. And he is surely correct in arguing (as I do) that there is no necessary opposition between money and intimate care as a motive force for people's economic activity. Here, however, I want to emphasize the decision-making capacities that money affords in the context where sex is not merely access to money but sometimes an invitation to death. See James Ferguson, *Give a Man a Fish: Reflections on the New Politics of Distribution*, Lewis Henry Morgan Lectures (Rochester, NY: University of Rochester, 2009), 41, 135.

36. Campbell, *Letting Them Die*; Achille Mbembe, *Necropolitics*, trans. Steven Corcoran (Durham, NC: Duke University Press, 2019).

37. It is difficult to overestimate the degree to which research on AIDS, and the publication of infectivity rates is involved in a complex feedback system, which is itself responsible for some of these phenomena, such as participation in funeral schemes. That question is beyond the purview of the present chapter, but it should be borne in mind as one considers the historical account being provided.

38. H. Kuper and S. Kaplan, "Voluntary Associations in an Urban Township," *African Studies* 3, no. 4 (1944): 178–86.

39. Thomson and Posel (6–7) differentiate between several types of societies and insist on the maintenance of categorical distinctions between those formations that work like credit unions or stokvels, and those that also provide social services (from emotional support to transportation and festivities at funerals). They further distinguish between "assured sum" societies, which tend to a multiplicity of needs, and "indemnifying societies," which cover set costs of essential goods such as caskets and food. Some work by managing collective resources, some by setting up savings accounts for members and then securing them against withdrawal (e.g., by holding bank pass books), and some by collecting monies and disbursing them to next of kin, who then spend it with or without supplementing the funds, for funerary rites. There are societies that are devoted exclusively to burial planning and others that take on this task as part of a much larger mandate. Some also provide for illness. These distinctions, while historically significant, nonetheless are of less concern to me than the general differentiation between such societies and other kinds of capitalized insurance. See R. J. Thomson and D. B. Posel, "Burial Societies in South Africa: Risk, Trust, and Commercialisation" (paper presented to the Actuarial Society of South Africa, Annual Convention, 2003).

40. Kulwane, "Civic Competence," 39.

41. M. Brandel-Syrier, *Black Women in Search of God* (London: Lutterworth, 1962).

42. Thomson and Posel ("Burial Societies," 7) also note the emergence of different kinds of societies, less likely to be premised on the consensual model. In particular, they mention administered societies, whose purpose is to generate profit for their administrators.

43. Kulwane, "Civic Competence."

44. Thomson and Posel, "Burial Societies," 4.
45. Bähre gave a much higher estimate for Kayelitsha, stating that 96 percent of the people who earn more than 4,000 rand had an insurance policy or were covered by a policy of their partner in the early 2000s. Respondents with an estimated income of less than 1,000 rand were quite often also covered by a policy (41 percent), sometimes because the partner took out the policy. See Erik Bähre, "New Sources of Wealth, New Sources of Conflict: A Historical Approach to Burial Societies and Insurance among the Xhosa in South Africa" (paper presented at the Actuarial Society of South Africa Annual Convention, Cape Town, October 12–13, 2006), 14.
46. P. Hoets et al., *Futurefact 2000* (Durban: Gitam, Absa and Unilever, 2000).
47. Thomson and Posel, "Burial Societies," 16.
48. Thomson and Posel, "Burial Societies," 55.
49. Bähre, "New Sources of Wealth," 8–9.
50. Bähre, "New Sources of Wealth," 9.
51. One of the best examples of this is the Uthini research group's report on the significance and management of funerals: Uthini Research, "Project Usizi: Management Report," for G:ENESIS, August 2004. The report, no longer accessible online, was originally available at the website of FinMark, an organization funded by the United Kingdom Department of International Development. It is devoted to the idea of "making financial markets work for the poor."
52. Bähre, "New Sources of Wealth," 12. He is citing the Q4 2004, *Business Monitor International* (London: Mermaid House), 3, and Tyler Cowen, "Is micro-insurance the next development revolution?," *Marginal Revolution*, February 19, 2005, http://www.marginalrevolution.com/marginalrevolution/2005/02/insurance_fact_.html.
53. Gary Hartwig, "The Low Income Sector—the Life Industry's Perspective" (paper presented at the Annual ASSA Convention, Cape town, October 13–14, 2000), 1–13.
54. Hartwig, "The Low Income Sector," 24.
55. Bähre, "New Sources of Wealth," 26.
56. Mangaliso Buzani, "I Will Be Gone."
57. At the time, there was considerable debate about whether the disclosure of HIV status, even as a cause of death on death certificates, violated rights to privacy. Many doctors and funerary workers believed it was indeed a violation of law to indicate status. David McQuoid-Mason, "Disclosing the HIV Status of Deceased Persons--Ethical and Legal Implications," *South African Medical Journal* 97, no.10 (2007): 920–23.
58. Despite the aesthetic appeal of the argument for disposability, it is my sense that HIV/AIDS may well have generated the occasion for an ironic containment of what Mbembe has called necropolitics.
59. AngloGold Ashanti, *Annual Report*, 2006.
60. Lewis Ndhlovu et al., "Reducing the Transmission of HIV and Sexually Transmitted Infections in a Mining Community: Findings from the Carletonville Mothusimpilo Intervention Project: 1998 to 2001" (Horizons Final Report, Population Council, Washington, DC, 2005), 31.
61. Ndhlovu et al., "Reducing the Transmission of HIV," 30.
62. Edward Lipuma and Benjamin Lee, *Financial Derivatives and the Globalization of Risk* (Durham, NC: Duke University Press, 2004), 182–84.
63. S. J. B. Peile and W. S. van der Merwe, "Hedge Funds in South Africa—The Investment Case" (paper presented to the Actuarial Society of South Africa, Cape Town, October 13–14, 2004).
64. Peile and van der Merwe, "Hedge Funds," 4.
65. Peile and van der Merwe, "Hedge Funds," 15.
66. South African Insurance Agency, "Annual Review," 2019. The theme of the 2019 review was "Pulling Together for a Sustainable Future for All."

67. Umar Bagus et al., "Africa's Insurance Market Is Set for Takeoff," *McKinsey*, December 2020, https://www.mckinsey.com/featured-insights/middle-east-and-africa/africas-insurance-market-is-set-for-takeoff.

68. Marc Bechard, "Only 19 Percent of South Africans Are Insured When Funeral Cover Is Excluded," Moonstone, April 11, 2022, https://www.moonstone.co.za/only-19-of-south-africans-are-insured-when-funeral-cover-is-excluded/.

16. Magic Mountain: Debt and the Ancestors

This chapter draws from Rosalind C. Morris, "Mediation, the Political Task: Between Language and Violence in Contemporary South Africa," *Current Anthropology* 58, Supplement 17 (February 2017): 123–134.

The epigraph to this chapter is from Wally Mongane Serote, "Ofay-Watchers, Throbs-Phase," in *Yakhal'inkomo* (Johannesburg: Ad Donker, 1972), 50–51.

1. Electoral Commission of South Africa, "Municipal Elections Results, 2021," https://results.elections.org.za/dashboards/lge/.

2. Electoral Commission of South Africa, "Detailed Results, National Election, 2024, GT484 - Merafong City," 3pp. https://results.elections.org.za/home/NPEPublicReports/1334/National%20Ballot/Results%20Report/GP/GT484/GT484.pdf.

3. "Merafong's Voters Ready for Election," *Carletonville Herald*, May 26, 2024. https://www.citizen.co.za/carletonville-herald/?p=75290.

4. Walter Benjamin, "Capitalism as Religion," trans. Rodney Livingstone. In *Selected Writings*. Vol. 1, *1913–1926*, ed. Marcus Bullock and Michael W. Jennings (Cambridge, MA: Belknap Press, 1996 [1921]), 288–91. See also chapter 10.

5. Gillian Hart, *Rethinking the South African Crisis: Nationalism, Populism, Hegemony* (Athens: University of Georgia Press, 2013).

6. *uMkhonto weSizwe* was the armed faction of the African National Congress. Today, MK veterans receive both official and unofficial recognition in government schemes aimed at assisting those from historically disadvantaged groups.

7. M. M. Bakhtin, *The Dialogic Imagination: Four Essays*, ed. Michael Holquist, trans. Caryl Emerson and Michael Holquist (Austin: University of Texas Press, 1981).

8. A succinct precis of the early history of the phrase as an artistic cris de coeur can be found at Chimurenga, and runs as follows: "An explosive bellow from the spiritual heart of the black experience, saxophonist and composer Winston Mankunku's Ngozi's Yakhal' Inkomo is at once a call to action, an open letter and a prayer. Recorded in 1968, as a cry mourning the Sharpeville massacre, and reinvoked in Mongane Wally Serote's 1972 collection of poems, it tasks us with imagining dispossessed feelings in common as the basis of a new community." "Yakal' Inkhomo," *Chimurenga Chronic*, accessed December 26, 2023, https://chimurengachronic.co.za/yakhal-inkomo/.

9. I. F. Farlam, P. D. Hemraj, and B. R. Tokota, *Marikana Commission of Inquiry: Report on Matters of Public and International Concern Arising out of the Tragic Incidents at the Lonmin Mine in Marikana, in the North West Province*, http://www.gov.za/sites/www.gov.za/files/marikana-report-1.pdf. See also Luke Sinwell, with Siphiwe Mbatha, *The Spirit of Marikana: The Rise of Insurgent Trade Unionism in South Africa* (Johannesburg: University of Witswatersrand Press, 2016); and Keith Breckenridge, "Revenge of the Commons: The Crisis in the South African Mining Industry," *History WorkshopOnline*, November 5, 2012, http://www.historyworkshop.org.uk/revenge-of-the-commons-the-crisis-in-the-south-african-mining-industry.

10. Gavin Hartford, "The Mining Industry Strike Wave: What Are the Costs and What Are the Solutions," *GroundUp*, 2012, https://groundup.org.za/article/mining-industry-strike-wave-what-are-causes-and-what-are-solutions.

11. Breckenridge, "Revenge of the Commons."
12. Deborah James, *Money from Nothing: Indebtedness and Aspiration in South Africa* (Stanford, CA: Stanford University Press, 2015).
13. Hartford also emphasizes the loss of representativeness in the National Union of Mineworkers and an intensifying gap between the rock face, on one hand, and the labor bureaucracy, on the other. The problem of a labor aristocracy had been well noted by Sakhele Buhlungu and is an indubitable source of resentment among mine laborers, who, according to worker surveys conducted by COSATU, are often less opposed to hierarchy per se than to the loss of personalistically responsible relations between levels of the hierarchy, and the blockage of access to upward mobility that such loss entails. See Sakhela Buhlungu, *A Paradox of Victory: COSATU and the Democratic Transformation in South Africa* (Durban: Kwa-Zulu Natal Press, 2010). Also Themba Masondo, "The Sociology of Upward Social Mobility Among COSATU Shop Stewards," in *COSATU: Contested Legacy*, ed. Sakhela Buhlungu and Malehoko Tshoaedi (Johannesburg: HSRC, 2012), 110–31; Sakhela Buhlungu and Malehoko Tshoaedi, "A Contested Legacy: Organizational and Political Challenges Facing COSATU," in *COSATU: Contested Legacy*, ed. Sakhela Buhlungu and Malehoko Tshoaedi (Johannesburg: HSRC, 2012), 1–31; and Andries Bezeidenhout and Sakhele Buhlungu, "Old Victories, New Struggles: The State of the National Union of Mineworkers," in *State of the Union*, ed. Sakhele Buhlungu, John Daniel, Roger Southall, and Jessica Lutchman (Johannesburg: HSRC, 2004), 245–65.
14. Indeed, the translation of Fanakalo into English was a contested issue in the Commission of Inquiry. The police commissioner, Lieutenant Colonial McIntosh, had required a translator to speak with the strike leaders and the Commission's report notes Lonmin's withholding of the name of the translator as an index of the fear that suffused the environment in August, before the violence (Farlam, Hemraj, and Tokota, *Marikana Commission of Inquiry*, 560).
15. In making this argument I am indebted to James T. Siegel, and especially his discussion of language and subjectivity, as well as political sloganeering in *Fetish, Recognition, Revolution* (Princeton, NJ; Princeton University Press, 1997).
16. Quoted testimony is from Peter Alexander, *Marikana: A View from the Mountain and a Case to Answe.* (Johannesburg: Jacana, 2013). Page numbers for further citations from this work appear in parentheses in the text.
17. Marx, *Capital*, 340–416. See also my analysis of this characterological drama in Rosalind C. Morris, "Dialect and Dialectic in 'The Working Day' of Marx's Capital," in "Music, Sound, Value," ed. Jairo Moreno and Gavin Steingo. Special issue, *Boundary 2* 43, no. 1 (February 2016): 219–48.
18. Brendon Nicholls, "Decolonization and Popular Poetics: From Soweto Poetry to Diasporic Solidarity," *English in Africa* 45, no. 3 (2018): esp. 52–55.
19. David Attwell, *Rewriting Modernity: Studies in Black South African Literary History* (Scottsville: University of KwaZulu-Natal, 2005), 146.
20. Technically, of course NUM is not a party, and yet, its role in the Congress of South African Trade Unions, which is part of the Tripartite Alliance that until 2024 governed South Africa, blurs this distinction. As can be seen throughout the interview, NUM's failures are construed in terms of a governmental logic as much as a syndicalist function.
21. William Blake (1970). The poem later became the basis of the hymn, widely sung in South Africa, "Jerusalem," with music by Sir Hubert Parry (1916). The semiotic proliferation of the signifier "Jersusalema" in both white and black South African Christianity is broad, and it ranges from the works of Antjie Krog, whose volume of poetry, *Jerusalemgangers* [The Jerusalemites or The Jerusalem-bound] (Cape Town: Human and Rousseau, 1985) narrates the mania of the "Great Trek," to the gangster film, *Gangster's Paradise: Jerusalema* (2008, dir. Ralph Zima, prod. Ralph Ziman and Tendeka Matatu). The latter features music by Alan Lazar as performed by Sipho Nxumalo. A traditional Zulu song by the

name of Jerusalem, made internationally famous by the Soweto String Quartet, features different lyrics in which Jerusalem is, not incidentally, described as a city with roads paved with gold. Finally, it is also the name of an informal settlement on the West Rand, where many zama zamas reside.

22. Gayatri Spivak, "Can the Subaltern Speak?," in *Can the Subaltern Speak: Reflections on the History of an Idea*, ed. Rosalind C. Morris (New York: Columbia University Press, 2010), 237–91.

23. In describing the steward in such terms, enchanted or ensorcelled by his narrative powers, and thus by the force available to him from within language, I am drawing on James T. Siegel's rereading of Matilda Coxe Stevenson's account of a Zuni boy's confession to witchcraft in his *Naming the Witch* (Stanford, CA: Stanford University Press, 2005), esp. 39–42.

24. A long tradition of messianism in this area makes the mountain the seat of transcendent powers. Largely associated today with the Nazarite church of Isaiah Shembe, this tradition has been broadly significant in the history of rebellions throughout the Eastern Cape and KwaZulu-Natal, especially among the Pondo. As many commentators have noted, the relatively impoverished Pondo ethnic group provides a high percentage of the Rock Drill Operators, who were at the center of the Marikana strikes. This deep resource of messianism is a necessary consideration in any account of the Marikana strikes, and anywere where the reference to the mountain orients liberationist discourse, or where the idea of "our Marikana" grounds itself in a spiritualized topography.

25. Oswald Joseph Mtshali, "Mtshali on Mtshali," *Bolt* 7 (1973), cited in Nicholls, "Decolonization and Popular Poetics," 46.

26. Lesego Rampolokeng, "Writing the Ungovernable," *New Coin* 49, no. 1 (2013): 99.

27. Gwen Ansell, "Salim Washington: Reedman Blows Fire and Tears," *Mail and Guardian*, January 21, 2016.

28. Luc Boltanski, *Distant Suffering: Morality, Media and Politics*, trans. Graham D. Burchell (Cambridge: Cambridge University Press, 1999 [1993]).

29. Ari Sitas, "Marikana," *New Coin* 49, no. 1 (2013): 36–38.

30. Sitas, "Marikana," 37.

31. Sitas, "Marikana," 38.

17. Gambling on Gold Again

Portions of this chapter have appeared in published essays, including: "Chronicling Deaths Foretold: The Testimony of the Corpse in De-Industrializing South Africa," in *Reverberations: Violence Across Time and Space*, eds. Yael Navaro, Zerrin Ozlem Biner, Alice von Bieberstein, and Seda Altug (Philadelphia, University of Pennsylvania Press, 2021) 33–61; "Conspiracies of Theory: Of Gold in the Shadow of Deindustrialization," in *Conspiracy/ Theory*, eds. Joseph Masco and Lisa Wedeen (Chicago: University of Chicago Press, 2024), 235–263; and "Shadow and Impress: Ethnography, Cinema and the Task of Writing History in the Space of South Africa's De-Industrialization," *History and Theory*, Theme Issue 56 (December 2018): 102–125;

The epigraph to this chapter is from Sol T. Plaatje, *Mhudi* (1930; repr., London: Heinemann, 1982), 186.

1. Walter Benjamin, "Paralipomena to 'On the Concept of History,'" in *Walter Benjamin: Selected Writings*, vol. 4, *1938–1940*, trans. Edmund Jephcott, eds. Marcus Bullock and Michael W. Jennings (Cambridge, MA: Harvard University Press, 2006 [1916]), 400; also see "On the Concept of History," trans. Harry Zohn, in *Selected Writings*, vol. 4, esp. 390–91.

2. Francis Wilson, *Labour in the South African Gold Mines* (Cambridge: Cambridge University Press, 1972), 139. The speculations about the end of the mines appears on 136–39.

3. Gayatri Chakravorty Spivak, *Critique of Postcolonial Reason: Toward a History of the Vanishing Present* (Cambridge, MA: Harvard University Press, 1999).

4. Berber Bevernage has persuasively argued that the double turn to memory that emerged from Holocaust and critical race studies, and the global phenomena of truth commissions as the institutional apparatuses of transitional justice in postconflict circumstances (he cites South Africa and Sierra Leone in particular) has generated a conflict between the drive to treat history as that which can be put behind one, and thus forgotten—a process ironically allied with positivist historiography—and a trauma-based conception of the effectivity or performativity of the past in contemporary circumstances. See Berber Bevernage, "Writing the Past Out of the Present: History and the Politics of Time in Transitional Justice," *History Workshop Journal* 69 (2010): 111–31; and "Time, Presence, and Historical Injustice, *History and Theory* 47, no. 3 (2008): 149–67.

5. Once the recruitment arm of the Chamber of Mines, TEBA was privatized in 2005, and 75 percent of the shares were bought by James Motlatsi, the former head of the National Union of Mineworkers. Motlatsi became CEO, and 25 percent were shared among company employees. Motlatsi quit the NUM in 2000 to work for AngloGold Ashanti.

6. J. S. Harington, N. D. McGlashan, and E. Z. Chelkowska, "A Century of Migrant Labor in the Gold Mines of South Africa," *Journal of the South African Institute of Mining and Metallurgy* (March 2004): 67.

7. Jonathan Crush, "The Extrusion of Foreign Labour from the South African Gold Mining Industry," *Geoforum* 17, no. 2 (1986): 164.

8. According to Crush, the "internationalization" process commenced with relative investments in wages, to attract local labor, but increasing poverty and unemployment among South Africa's black populations (constituting what he terms, in Marx's old idiom, a "reserve army" of potential labor) made this unnecessary after a while, while immunizing South Africa against the efforts of neighboring states to withdraw labor. With such a "reserve army," benefits could be withdrawn, and choices of place of employment limited. In this respect, Crush's analysis coincides with those of Wolpe and Legassick (cited earlier), who observed the intensifying coerciveness of the Apartheid state during this period. Crush, "Extrusion of Foreign Labour," 167.

9. Harington, McGlashan, and Chelkowska, "Century of Migrant Labor," 66.

10. Harington, McGlashan, and Chelkowska, "Century of Migrant Labor," 68.

11. In 1994, South Africa stopped maintaining employment statistics for the mines differentiated by race.

12. Chamber of Mines, *Mining SA 2016* (Johannesburg: Chamber of Mines, 2017).

13. Wilson, *Labour*, 153.

14. This renationalization can be understood as one of the material bases of the ideological projects and macro-financial policies that Gillian Hart describes under the same term. See, Gilliam Hart, *Rethinking the South African Crisis: Nationalism, Populism, Hegemony* (Athens: University of Georgia Press, 2013).

15. Benjamin, "Paralipomena," 406. He is surely paraphrasing the apocryphal biblical text, which would be recovered by James Agee and Walker Evans as the title of their volume about impoverished tenant farmers in the United States, namely *Let us now praise famous men*. The relevant biblical passage is cited as the first epigraph to this chapter.

16. Surren Pillay, "Translating 'South Africa': Race, Colonialism and Challenges of Critical Thought after Apartheid," in *Re-Imagining the Social in South Africa: Critique, Theory and Post-apartheid Society*, eds. Heather Jacklin and Peter Vale (Durban: University of KwaZulu-Natal Press, 2009), 225–67.

17. Muriel Rukeyser, "Book of the Dead," in *US 1* (New York: Covici Friede, 1938), 66–72.

18. Gold Fields actually commenced one on a small scale in 2003. Now (2024) controlled by Sibanyegold and Sozitime Investments (Pty) Ltd., and called "Living Gold," it is still active, with a total of ten hectares under cultivation.

19. For a brief period, I worked with the municipality on a proposal for such a mining museum, and consulted with Clive van den Berg, of TRACE, the design company behind much of South Africa's new museology. This possible project, however, fell into abeyance shortly after the eviction of the then-mayor, Des van Rooyen, following the debacle of redemarcation. See also chapter 14.

20. On the corporatization of ethnicity, see Jean Comaroff and John J. Comaroff, *Ethnicity, Inc.* (Chicago: University of Chicago Press, 2009). On the rise of the heritage industry, see Ciraj Rasool, "The Rise of Heritage and the Reconstruction of History in South Africa," *Kronos* 26 (2000): 1–21; and Annie Combes, "Witnessing History/Embodying Testimony: Gender and Memory and Post-Apartheid South Africa," *Journal of the Royal Anthropological Institute* 17 (2011): S92–112.

21. On the concept of *nachträglichkeit*, see Friedrich-Wilhelm Eickhoff, "On *Nachträglichkeit*: The Modernity of an Old Concept," *International Journal of Psychoanalysis* 87, no. 6 (2006): 1452–69. On the spectrality of the past, as well as the contradictory impulses within museology, to preserve but also contain and economize that spectrality, see Jacques Derrida, *Archive Fever: A Freudian Impression*, trans. Eric Prenowtiz (Chicago: University of Chicago Press, 1996). Derrida's remarks about the possible drive to forget within archivization, articulated in relation to the TRC ("Archive Fever in South Africa") and Verne Harris's trenchant response ("A Shaft of Darkness: Derrida in the Archive") appear in *Refiguring the Archive*, eds. Carolyn Hamilton, Verne Harris, et al. (Cape Town: David Philips, 2002), 38 and 61–82, respectively.

22. It is tempting to read this notion of earthly regeneration as the sign of an animist ontology, but the situation is more ambivalent than that. Although many claim that the fact of gold's constant discovery demonstrates that gold is an organic matter, germinated by a persistently fecund earth, they mock the attribution of personhood or even animate force to that earth. They often invoke the mine engineers' own terminology for the venting chimneys, namely "breathers," and insist that their own metaphoricity be granted equal status.

23. I have met Zimbabwean college students who, unable to pay their fees for lack of cash wages at home, work as zama zamas during semester breaks, and earn enough doing so to continue their studies. I have also met zama zamas working for residents in nearby suburbs of South Africa who asked their gardeners or private security guards to serve as proxy buyers for them.

24. On the refugee as one who lacks the right to have rights, see Hannah Ardent, *The Origins of Totalitarianism*.

25. In making this argument I am following Samuel Weber's analysis of the concept of "ability" in Walter Benjamin's writings. See Samuel Weber, *Benjamin's Abilities* (Cambridge, MA: Harvard University Press, 2008).

26. Joshua Kirshner and Comfort Phokela, "Khutsong and Xenophobic Violence: Exploring the Case of the Dog That Didn't Bark" (Johannesburg, University of Johannesburg, Center for Social Research and Atlantic Philanthropies Foundation, 2010), http://www.atlanticphilanthropies.org/wp-content/uploads/2010/07/5_Kutsong_c.pdf.

27. The terminology of precarity may be new, but the analysis of this structure by which violence is sublated in the economy, was crucial to Marx's analysis of *ursprüngliche Akkumulation*. On recent debates about this concept, and the question of precarity, see my "*Ursprüngliche Akkumulation*: The Secret History of an Originary Mistranslation," "Marxism, Communism, and Translation," eds. Nergis Ertürk and Özge Serin, special issue, *boundary* 2 43, no. 3 (August 2016): 29–77.

28. The category of the artisanal is often used, in South African contexts and more broadly, in the conjunction "artisanal and small-scale mining," which is indicated with the acronym ASM. The literature is suffused with reference to the "traditional" nature of the practice or the "rudimentary" status of the technology. ASM was formally recognized in 1994, under the terms of the post-Apartheid Reconstruction and Development Program, but the referent of that legislation was mainly licit, small-scale mineral entrepreneurialism undertaken by citizens. Recent policy continues to advocate the legalization of such activity: "The department is working to legalise the small-scale mining operations that currently exist, and find ways to help make them economically viable in a way that is relevant, understandable and affordable to small—scale miners" (see DMRE, https://www.dmr.gov .za/mineral-policy-promotion/small-scale-mining). Several thousand licenses have been granted under this legislation, but in addition, and despite state efforts and professions of a desire to bring the sector under regulatory authority, many thousands of itinerant miners, grinders, and informal processors of tailings dump operate "outside of the legal framework." The South African Human Rights Commission has estimated that some thirty thousand people had been involved in illegal ASM mining by 2015, and Ledwaba has calculated a tenfold increase of such activity in the decade before 2017, noting that poverty, unemployment, and the high cost of licensing for ASM has ensured the relative growth of what I would prefer to call the illegalized (rather than illegal or criminal) sector. Some writers, including Ledwaba, distinguish between informal miners working without licenses, and hence illegally, and those who are involved in overt or organized criminal activity, particularly those who operate in abandoned shafts. He refers only to the latter as zama zama, while conferring on the former the legitimating moniker of "traditional" informal workers. Other writers distinguish among informal miners on the basis of scale. See P. F. Ledwaba, "The Status of Small-Scale and Artisanal Mining Sector in South Africa: Tracking Progress," *Journal of the Southern African Institute of Mining and Metallurgy* 117 (January 2017): 33–40. Also see Kgothatso Nhlengetwa and Kim Hein, "Zama Zama Mining in the Durban Deep/Roodepoort Area of Johannesburg, South Africa: An Invasive or Alternative Livelihood?," *Extractive Industries and Society* 2, no. 1 (2014); Nellie Mutemeri and Francis W. Peterson, "Small-Scale Mining in South Africa: Past, Present and Future," *Natural Resources Forum* 26, no. 4 (2002): 286–92; and Robert Thornton, "*Zamazama* 'Illegal' Artisanal Miners, Severely Misrepresented by Press and Government," *Extractive Industries and Society: An International Journal* 1 (2014): 127–29. Before 2018, protests in favor of the legalization of zama zama miners and statements by representatives of the Department of Mineral Resources suggested a softening of national policy with regard to some people involved in so-called ASM activity, but this did not extend to zama zamas for reasons that cannot easily be dismissed as disingenuous. Thus, Godfrey Oliphant, while announcing the amendment and relaxation of legislation on ASM, has stated: "There is no ways that we, as the DMR, can in good conscience grant permits to artisanal miners for deep-level mines, that in most cases are being accessed using old, abandoned shaft infrastructure, which are unsafe [*sic*]. We would essentially be sending people to their deaths." See Ilan Solomons, "Government to 'Amend and Relax' Legislation for Small-Scale Miners to Combat Illegal Mining," *Mining Weekly*, March 24, 2017.

29. A notable exception in this literature comes from Elizabeth Hull and Deborah James. While still using the terminology of the "artisanal," they depart from much of the discourse on this topic when they claim that the "informality" that has arisen in the mining sector in South Africa is "neither a throwback to some pre-capitalist past, nor an accidental fall-out from a dominant structure" (5). They argue, further, that "it is the result of intentional retractions of governmental regulation." See Elizabeth Hull and Deborah James, "Introduction: Popular Economies in South Africa," "Popular Economies in South Africa," *Africa: International Journal of the Africa Institute* 82, no. 1 (2012): 1–19.

30. Ironically, a lottery game called "zama zama" was introduced in South Africa in 1994.

31. Vincent Cruywagen, "Illegal Mining Crackdown—Minister Fires Warning to Foreigners 'Wreaking Havoc,' as National Drive Racks up 4,000 Arrests," *Daily Maverick*, November 10, 2023.

32. Translated from the Chitonga by Tanya Nyathi and Noel Musokotwane, with Rosalind Morris.

33. Sigmund Freud, "Mourning and Melancholia," in *SE*, vol. XIV, *1917*, 263.

34. The associations are important. Mugabe, whose longevity was often a source of frustration for his political opponents (including those, like my interlocutors, who are members of an ethnic minority in Zimbabwe), is often likened by them to a snake. His repeated evasions of justice and the common violent fates of the people around him sometimes also leads him to be likened to a white man, despite his rise to power in the anticolonial struggle.

35. Luce Irigaray, *Speculum of the Other Woman*, trans. Gillian C. Gill (1974; repr., Ithaca, NY: Cornell University Press, 1985), 252.

36. Keith Breckenridge, "Can Trust Be Engineered?" (lecture delivered at Leuphana University, Lüneburg, Germany, January 31, 2024).

37. Asanda Benya, *Women in Mining: Occupational Culture and Gendered Identities in the Making* (PhD diss., University of the Witwatersrand, 2016), 7.

38. Minerals Council of South Africa, "Women in Mining in South Africa" (Johannesburg, 2020), 2.

39. Benya, *Women in Mining*, 43.

40. The word, *mfazi/umfazi* (X/Z) can be used to refer to wife or, generically, any black woman.

41. Benya, *Women in Mining*, 157–61.

42. Benya, *Women in Mining*, 358.

43. Zanele Muholi's work has been widely seen in South Africa and internationally. Photographic exhibitions specifically concerned with lesbian and trans life include "Only Half the Picture" (2004), "Faces and Phases (2006–ongoing), *Zanele Muholi: Only Half the Picture* (Cape Town: Michael Stevenson, 2006), "Innovative Women," "Brave Beauties" (2014). See Zanele Muholi, *Faces + Phases 2006–14* (Göttingen, Germany: Steidel, 2014), and Zanele Muholi, *Zanele Muholi: Only Half the Picture* (Cape Town: Michael Stevenson, 2006).

44. Several South African feminists have addressed the question of a sexual violence, and its culturalization, or normativization, as well as the fear that accompanies it. See Pumla Dineo Gqola, *Rape: A South African Nightmare* (Johannesburg: MF Books/Jacana, 2015) and Pumla Dineo Gqola, *Female Fear Factory: Unravelling Patriarchy's Cultures of Violence* (Abuja, Nigeria: Cassava Republic, 2022); and Redi Tlhabi, *Beginnings and Endings* (Johannesburg: Jacana, 2012).

45. Benya recounts both the presence of women in early mining contexts as well as their historical displacement, both in actuality and in the literature that redoubled the masculinist bias of the mineral extraction world. See Benya, *Women in Mining*, esp. 59–61.

46. Marcel Mauss, *A General Theory of Magic*, trans. Robert Brain (New York: Routledge, 2001 [1902]).

47. Lest this tradition be misrecognized as something essentially "African," it should be remembered that a comparable set of assumptions was embedded in the *droit de seigneur* in Europe. It may be found in many other settings—from West to South Asia, as well.

48. An operation in the Western Cape, aimed primarily at gang violence, had the same name, "Operation Prosper." "That operation had, however, culminated in complaints by South African Defense Force members that they were under supplied with vehicles and even underfed." Rebecca Davis, "Soldiers Claim Operation Prosper a Shambles, with Lack of Food, Vehicles and Uncertainty Around Who Is in Charge," *Daily Maverick*, July 24, 2021.

49. "Operation Vala Umgodi Clamping Down on Illegal Mining in Matholesville, Roodepoort," *Truck and Freight News*, February 2, 2024.

50. "South African President Deploys Army to Tackle Illegal Mining," *Daily Maverick*, November 9, 2023.

51. Nontsizi Mgqwetho, "Alas, Africa, You Fade Into the Horizon!," trans. Jeff Opland and Pamela Maseko. In *The People's Paper*, ed. Peter Limb, 413–16.

52. Foucault developed this terminology in his account of clinical medicine's development: Michel Foucault, *The Birth of the Clinic: An Archaeology of Medical Perception*, trans. by A. M. Sheridan Smith (New York: Vintage, 1994 [1973]).

53. I take this phrase from Joao Biehl, *Vita*. I owe this conception of township policing, as a form of "securing the perimeter," to Abdoumaliq Simone, personal communication, May 4, 2018.

54. As Jean Comaroff and John Comaroff have recently argued, "criminality [has become] the vernacular in which politics is increasingly conducted" and "citizens tend increasingly to construe social reality . . . through the allegory of law-making and law-breaking" (Jean Comaroff and John L. Comaroff, *The Truth About Crime: Sovereignty, Knowledge, Social Order* (Chicago: University of Chicago Press, 2016), 7.

55. René Girard, *Violence and the Sacred*, trans. Patrick Gregory (New York and London: 2005 [1972]), 102.

56. Girard, *Violence*, 86.

57. Girard, *Violence*, 86. Giorgio Agamben's argues that such a condition is the drive but also the origin of the *homo sacer*, the being whose death is permitted to anyone, for which no one will be prosecuted, and which cannot generate sacral value. Giorgio Agamben, *Homo Sacer, Homo Sacer*, trans. by Daniel Heller-Roazen (Stanford, CA: Stanford University Press, 1998 [1995]).

58. Rosalind C. Morris, "Chronicling Deaths Foretold: The Testimony of the Corpse in De-Industrializing South Africa,' in *Reverberations: Violence Across Time and Space*, ed. Yael Navaro, Zerrin Ozlem Biner, Alice von Bieberstein, and Seda Altug (Philadelphia: University of Pennsylvania Press, 2021), 33–61.

59. James T. Siegel, *Naming the Witch* (Stanford, CA: Stanford University Press, 2005).

60. Cruywagen, "Illegal Mining Crackdown."

61. The press coverage of the stories was prolific and changed dramatically over the course of the case's unfolding in the courts. For examples, see Shiraaz Mohamed, "Police Stop Violent Kagiso Residents' Group from Hunting Down Zama Zamas," *Daily Maverick*, August 4, 2022; Nonkululeko Njilo, "Krugersdorp Rapes—Frustration as Media Blocked from Court, Police Deny DNA Backlogs to Blame for Delays," *Daily Maverick*, September 30, 2022; Nonkululeko Njilo, "Krugersdorp Victim's Ordeal: 'I Closed My Eyes, Crying. Moments Later, I Was Also Raped, by Three Men,'" *Daily Maverick*, August 5, 2022; and Phumza Fihlani and Tiffany Wertheimer, "South Africa: Illegal Miners Cleared of Gang Rape," *BBC News*, October 27, 2022.

62. Intensifying the sense of tragic fatality in this case is the fact the one of the women, Pretty Winnie Nkambule, was not supposed to have been on shift. According to the report of the inquiry, she "was supposed to have knocked off with the previous shift. Her relief never reported for duty and she thus remained on duty in the lamp room at the start of the Friday morning shift. She never returned to her family or her four children after the incident." A. van der Merwe, presiding officer, "Inquest Proceedings in Terms of the Provisions of the Inquiry Act 58 of 1959 Into the Circumstances Attending to the Presumed Death of: Solomon Emmanuel Nyirenda, Yvonne Mnisi, Pretty Winni Nkambule," Inquest Number 26/2021 (Barberton Magistrate, Barberton, South Africa, October 19, 2023), 9.

63. van der Merwe, "Inquest," 29.

64. van der Merwe, "Inquest," 29.

65. van der Merwe, "Inquest," 32.

66. van der Merwe, "Inquest," 8. Also cited in Vincent Cruywagen, "'Mr X's' Testimony at Lily Mine Inquest Paints Chilling Picture of Illegal Mining Facilitated by Employees," *Daily Maverick*, October 24, 2023.

67. Johannes Fabian, *Time and the Other: How Anthropology Makes Its Objects* (1983; repr., New York: Columbia University Press, 2014).

18. Afterward, Afterword

The epigraph to this chapter is from Louis Marin, "The Frontiers of Utopia" (short version), in *Utopias and the Millennium*, eds. K. Kumar and S. Bann (London: Reaktion Books, 1993), 11.

1. Penny Penny ft Rafiki, "Goldbone," composed by Gezani E. Khobane/Gorden Netshikweta/ Julius Dlamini, written by Penny Penny and Rafiki, Penny Penny, accessed February 8, 2022, https://www.youtube.com/watch?v=NEPN9ExVx6E.

2. Omphile Neo Makiri and Bafana Lecwamotse, dirs., *16 Khuts*, executive producer Bhabile Mithani (Neo Influence and the Khutsong Literary Club, 2017), accessed February 12, 2024, https://www.youtube.com/watch?app=desktop&v=thmZJHGZ3Kk.

3. They are Bafana Puff Lecwamotse, Bafana Subsir Mtini, Bhabile Slim Mithani, Kgotsiesile Monoto, Sphiwe Mo Touch Khumalo, Bontle BdaDji Matabane, Itumeleng Matha, Kagiso Vibration Segone, Kgomotoso Nxz Dinake, Thmelo T. J. Selepe, Pat Lyx Matubatuba, Sipho Patoors, Moreno Rex Maboe, Thabo Putsoa, Mosimanegape "King Tjwereza" Lobakeng, and Prince Chronic Koena.

4. Isabel Hofmeyr, *We Spend Our Years as a Tale That Is Told: Oral Historical Narrative in a South African Chiefdom* (Johannesburg: Witwatersrand University Press, 1993).

REFERENCES

Chamber of Mines Annual Reports and Other Publications

Annual Reports of the Chamber of Mines are referenced by year and appear under the authorship of the Chamber. Special publications and annexures also appear under the Chamber's name. However, the Chamber's full name changed over the years and is abbreviated after first mention according to the title operative at the time of publication. These include the following:
Chamber of Mines of South Africa (CMSA)
Transvaal Chamber of Mines (TCM)
Transvaal and Orange Free State Chamber of Mines (TOFSCM)
Witwatersrand Chamber of Mines (WCM)
Minerals Council of South Africa (MCSA)

Commissions of Enquiry and Other Government Publications

South Africa

Cape of Good Hope (South Africa) Parliament. House Select Committee on the Jameson Raid. *Report of the Select Committee of Cape of Good Hope House of Assembly on Jameson Raid into Territory of South African Republic*, Appendix A, Command Papers, C.8380, 1897.

Farlam, I. F., P. D. Hemraj, and B. R. Tokota. *Marikana Commission of Inquiry: Report on Matters of Public and International Concern Arising out of the Tragic Incidents at the Lonmin Mine in Marikana, in the North West Province*, 2015.

Goldstone, Justice Richard, chair. *Report of the Commission of Inquiry Regarding the Prevention of Public Violence and Intimidation*. Pretoria, 1994.

Government of the Colonies and Territories in British South Africa. *South African Native Affairs Commission*. Vol. 1, *1903–1905*. Cape Town, 1906.

Independent Board of Inquiry. "Report of the Independent Board of Inquiry for the Month of September 1991." Wits Historical Research Papers, AG2543.2.2.18.

Independent Board of Inquiry. *Fortress of Fear*. Braamfontein, 1993.

Myburgh, Justice J. F., chair. "Report of the Commission of Enquiry into the Violence on Three Gold Fields Mines." 1996.

Rieckert, Justice J. P., chair. *Report of the Commission of Inquiry Into Legislation Affecting the Utilisation of Manpower (excluding the Legislations administered by the Departments of Labour and Mines)*. Pretoria, 1978.

South Africa. *Report of the Commission of Inquiry Into the Riots at Soweto and Elsewhere from the 16th of June 1976 to the 28th of February 1977*. 2 vols. Pretoria, 1980.

South African Native Affairs Commission, 1903–1905. Vol. 1. Cape Town: Government of the Colonies and Territories in British South Africa, 1906.

Safro, Wayne. *Special Report on Violence Against Black Town Councillors and Policemen*. Johannesburg: South African Institute of Race Relations, 1990.

Transkeian Territorial Authority. *Proceedings of the Special Session Called to Consider Draft Bill for the Granting of Self-Government to the Transkei*. Territorial Printers, 1983.

Union of South Africa. *Report of the Interdepartmental Committee on the Native Pass Laws*. Cape Town, 1920.

van der Merwe, A, presiding officer. "Inquest Proceedings in Terms of the Provisions of the Inquiry Act 58 of 1959 Into the Circumstances Attending to the Presumed Death of: Solomon Emmanuel Nyirenda, Yvonne Mnisi, Pretty Winni Nkambule." Inquest Number 26/2021. Barberton Magistrate, Barberton, South Africa, October 19, 2023.

Wiehahn, N. E., chair. South Africa. *Report of the Commission of Inquiry Into Labour Legislation*. Johannesburg: Lex Patria, 1982.

United Kingdom

Great Britain. Transvaal Concessions Commission. *Report of the Transvaal Concession Commission*. Pretoria: April 19, 1901.

UK House of Commons. *Second Report from the Select Committee on British South Africa, Together with Proceedings of the Committee and Evidence*. London: Her Majesty's Stationery, 1897.

UK House of Lords. "Transvaal (Chinese labour)." Vol. 146, cc407–58. May 16, 1905.

United Kingdom. *Correspondence Relating to Conditions of Native Labour Employed in Transvaal Mines*. Blue Book. London: Printed for His Majesty's Stationery Office by Darling & Son, 1904.

United States

U.S. Government. "Appendix to the Congressional Record." *Proceedings and Debates of the Fifty-Second Congress, First Session*. Washington, DC, 1892.

Truth and Reconciliation Commission Testimony and Evidence

General Hearings and Publications

"Hearings of the Business Sector, Truth and Reconciliation Commission." November 13, 1997. https://sabctrc.saha.org.za/hearing.php?id=56249&t=Hearings+of+the+Business+Sector%2C +Truth+and+Reconciliation+Commission&tab=hearings.

Truth and Reconciliation Commission. "TRC Appeal to Victims of AWB Bombings." South African Press Association. May 12, 1998. https://www.justice.gov.za/trc/media/1998/9805 /s980512c.htm.

Truth and Reconciliation Commission, *Truth and Reconciliation Commission of South Africa Report*. 7 vols. Johannesburg: Juta for the TRC, 1998.

Personal Testimony and Individual Cases

"Amnesty Hearings in the Matter of the Murder of David Maseko." September 9–13, 1996. https://sabctrc.saha.org.za/hearing.php?id=54856&t=Lebona&tab=hearings.

Amnesty Hearings of the Truth and Reconciliation Commission. "Decision, Case Number AC/97/0006." March 13, 1997. https://sabctrc.saha.org.za/hearing.php?id=58493&t=Lebona&tab=hearings.

Dolo, Phila Martin. "Testimony at the Amnesty Hearings, Aliwal North." April 20, 1998, https://sabctrc.saha.org.za/hearing.php?id=54585&t=Testimony+of+Phila+Martin+Dolo%2C+Case+No.+3485%2F96.+Amnesty+Hearings%2C+Aliwal+North.+April+20%2C+1998&tab=hearings.

Goliath, W. S. "Testimony at the Hearings on Human Rights Violations." Krugersdorp. November, 11, 1996. https://sabctrc.saha.org.za/hearing.php?id=55436&t=W.S.+Goliath&tab=hearings.

Kriel, Andre Stephanus. "Testimony at the Amnesty Hearings." March 23–28, 1998. https://sabctrc.saha.org.za/hearing.php?id=54885&t=Kriel+&tab=hearings.

Lesotho, S. "Testimony at Human Rights Violations Hearings." November 11, 1996, https://sabctrc.saha.org.za/hearing.php?id=55438&t=S.+Lesotho&tab=hearings.

Lottering, Cornelius Johannes. "Testimony at the Amnesty Hearings." March 23–27, 1998.https://sabctrc.saha.org.za/hearing.php?id=54885&t=Cornelius+Lottering&tab=hearings.

Motsumi, Ephraim Jonas Israel. "Testimony at the Special Victims Hearings." Accessed February 9, 2024. https://sabctrc.saha.org.za/victims/motsumi_ephraim_jonas_israel.htm?tab=hearings.

Mvudle, T. "Testimony at the Hearings on Human Rights Violations." Krugersdorp. November 11, 1996. https://sabctrc.saha.org.za/hearing.php?id=55447&t=T.+Mvudle&tab=hearings.

Mxathule, Nozibonelo Maria. "Testimony of Nozibonelo Maria Mxathule, Case No. JB01840/03NW—Women's Hearings, Human Rights Violations." July 29, 1997. https://sabctrc.saha.org.za/hearing.php?id=56406&t=Nozibonelo+Maria+Mxathule&tab=hearings.

van der Merwe, A. "Inquest Proceedings in Terms of the Provisions of the Inquiry Act 58 of 1959 Into the Circumstances Attending to the Presumed Death of: Solomon Emmanuel Nyirenda, Yvonne Mnisi, Pretty Winni Nkambule." Barberton, South Africa, 2023.

Articles and Books

Wherever possible, dates of original publication are included in square parentheses following the date of publication of the text referenced. Books and articles that first appeared in a language other than English include date of publication in first language and the cited translation. Works that appeared originally in English but for which a different edition is cited, are identified as reprints.

"11 Shot Dead: Police Shoot on Miners' Pay Riot." *Rand Daily Mail*, September 12, 1973, 1.

Abrahams, Peter. *Mine Boy*. 1946. Reprint, London: Heinemann, 1975.

"Accident at the Langlaagte." *Johannesburg Times*, August 8, 1895.

Adorno, Theodor. *Kierkegaard: Construction of the Aesthetic*. Trans. and ed. Robert Hullot-Kentor. Minneapolis: University of Minnesota Press, 1989 [1962].

Adorno, Theodor. *Minima Moralia: Reflections from Damaged Life*. Trans. E. F. M. Jephcott. London: Verso, 1974 [1951].

"African Miners Slain." *Southern Africa: A Monthly Survey of News and Opinion* 6, no. 9 (1973): 8–9.

Agamben, Giorgio. "Capitalism as Religion," trans. Nicholas Heron. In *Agamben and Radical Politics*, ed. Daniel McLoughlin, 15–26. Edinburgh: Edinburgh University Press, 2021 [2018].

Agamben, Giorgio. *Homo Sacer*. Trans. Daniel Heller-Roazen. Stanford, CA: Stanford University Press, 1998 [1995].

Agee, James, and Walker Evans. *Let Us Now Praise Famous Men.* 1939. Reprint, Boston: Houghton Mifflin, 2001.

Agricola, Georgius. *De Re Metallica.* [On the Nature of Metals] 1556 ed. Trans. Herbert Clark Hoover and Lou Henry Hoover. New York: Dover, 1959.

Alexander, Peter. "Oscillating Migrants, Detribalised Families, and Militancy: Mozambicans on Witbank Collieries: 1918–1927." *Journal of Southern African Studies* 27, no. 3 (2001): 505–25.

Alexander, Peter, *Marikana: A View from the Mountain and a Case to Answer.* Johannesburg: Jacana, 2013.

Allen, V. L. *The History of Black Mineworkers in South Africa.* Vol. 1, *The Techniques of Resistance, 1871–1948.* Keighley, UK: Moor Press, 1992.

Allen, V. L. *The History of Black Mineworkers in South Africa.* Vol. 2. *Dissent and Repression in the Mine Compounds, 1948–1982.* Keighley, UK: Moor Press, 2003.

Althusser, Louis. *On the Reproduction of Capitalism: Ideology and Ideological State Apparatuses.* Trans. A. M. Goshgarian, pref. Etienne Balibar, intro. Jacques Bidet. New York: Verso, 2014 [1971, 1995].

Alverson, Hoyt. *Mind in the Heart of Darkness: Value and Identity Among the Tswana of Southern Africa.* New Haven, CT: Yale University Press, 1978.

"Amusements." *Johannesburg Times,* December 14, 1895.

Amin, Samir. *Accumulation on a World Scale: A Critique of the Theory of Underdevelopment.* New York: Monthly Review, 1974.

Anderson, Benedict. *Under Three Flags: Anarchism and the Anticolonial Imagination.* New York: Verso, 2007.

Anderson, Benedict. *Imagined Communities: Reflections on the Origin and Spread of Nationalism.* London: Verso, 1983.

AngloGold Ashanti. *Annual Report.* 2006.

Ansell, Gwen. "Salim Washington: Reedman Blows Fire and Tears." *Mail and Guardian,* January 21, 2016.

Ansell, Gwen. *Soweto Blues: Jazz, Popular Music and Politics in South Africa.* New York: Continuum, 2004.

"Appendices to the Statement of Mr. Charles Leonard, Report from *The Star,* July 21, 1894." In *Papers on the Political Situation in South Africa, 1885–1895,* ed. Charles Leonard, 254–88. London: Arthur Humphreys, 1903.

Arendt, Hannah. *The Human Condition.* 2nd ed. Chicago: University of Chicago Press, 1958.

Arendt, Hannah. *The Origins of Totalitarianism.* New York: Harcourt, Brace, Jovanovich, 1973.

Artières, Philippe. "Lignes de fuite (Lines of Flight)" In *Hautes Surveillances,* ed. Mathieu Pernot. Arles: Actes Sud, 2004.

Attridge, David and Rosemary Jolly, eds. *Writing South Africa: Literature, Apartheid, Democracy.* Cambridge: Cambridge University Press, 1998.

Attwell, David. *Rewriting Modernity: Studies in Black South African Literary History.* Scottsville: University of KwaZulu-Natal, 2005.

Attwell, David, and Derek Attridge, *The Cambridge History of South African Literature.* Cambridge: Cambridge University Press, 2012.

Auden, W. H. "In Praise of Limestone" [1948]. In *Collected Poems,* ed. Edward Mendelsohn, 540–42. New York: Vintage, 1991.

"Back to Africa Movement." *Abantu-Batho,* November 11, 1920. In *The People's Paper: A Centenary History and Anthology of Abanto-Batho,* ed. Peter Limb, 435–41. Johannesburg: Wits University Press, 2012.

Badiou, Alain. "The Cultural Revolution: The Last Revolution?" *Positions: East Asia Cultures Critique* 13, no. 3 (2005): 481–514.

Bagus, Umar, François Jurd de Girancourt, Raées Mahmood, and Qaizer Manji. "Africa's Insurance Market Is Set for Takeoff." *McKinsey,* December 2020. https://www.mckinsey.com /featured-insights/middle-east-and-africa/africas-insurance-market-is-set-for-takeoff.

Bähre, Erik. "New Sources of Wealth, New Sources of Conflict: A Historical Approach to Burial Societies and Insurance Among the Xhosa in South Africa." Paper presented at the Actuarial Society of South Africa Annual Convention, Cape Town, October 12–13, 2006.

Baines, Thomas. *The Gold Regions of Southeastern Africa*. London: E. Stanford, 1877.

Bakhtin, M. M. *The Dialogic Imagination: Four Essays*. Trans. Caryl Emerson and Michael Holquist. Ed. Michael Holquist. Austin: University of Texas Press, 1981.

Balibar, Etienne. "The Basic Concepts of Historical Materialism." In Louis Althusser and Etienne Balibar, *Reading Capital*, trans. Ben Brewster, 199–208. New York: Verso, 1997 [1968].

Barchiesi, Franco. *Precarious Liberation: Workers, the State, and Contested Social Citizenship in Postapartheid South Africa*. Binghamton, NY: SUNY University Press, 2011.

Baskin, Jeremy. "Mass Strike on the Mines." *Worker Struggles on the East Rand: The Labour Bulletin* 7, no. 8 (1982): 59–66.

Bataille, Georges. "The Meaning of General Economy." In *The Accursed Share*. Vol. 1, trans. Robert Hurley, 19–26. New York: Zone 1988 [1949].

Bataille, Georges. "The Notion of Expenditure." In *The Bataille Reader*, ed. Tom Bottomore and Scott Wilson, trans. Allan Stoekl, with Carl R. Lovitt and Donald M Leslie, Jr., 167–81. Oxford: Blackwell, 1997 [1933].

Baudrillard, Jean. *The System of Objects*. Trans. James Benedict. New York: Verso, 1996 [1968].

Bechard, Marc. "Only 19 Percent of South Africans Are Insured When Funeral Cover Is Excluded." Moonstone. April 11, 2022. https://www.moonstone.co.za/only-19-of-south-africans-are-insured-when-funeral-cover-is-excluded/.

Beck, A. I., G. H. Henderson, R. N Lambert, and R. A. Mudd. "Stoping Practice on the Transvaal and Orange Free State Goldfields." In *Transactions of the Seventh Commonwealth Mining and Metallurgical Congress*, Vol. 2, 655–95. Johannesburg: South African Institute of Mining and Metallurgy, 1961.

Beinart, William. *Twentieth Century South Africa*. Oxford: Oxford University Press, 2001.

Beinart, William. "Worker Consciousness, Ethnic Particularism and Nationalism: The Experiences of a South African Migrant, 1930–1960." In *Politics of Race, Class and Nationalism in Twentieth Century South Africa*, ed. Shula Marks and Stanley Trapido, 286–309. London: Routledge, 1987.

Benjamin, Walter. *The Arcades Project*. Trans. Howard Eiland and Kevin McLaughlin. Cambridge, MA: Belknap Press, 1999.

Benjamin, Walter. "Capitalism as Religion," trans. Rodney Livingstone. In *Selected Writings*. Vol. 1, *1913–1926*, ed. Marcus Bullock and Michael W. Jennings, 288–91. Cambridge, MA: Belknap Press, 1996 [1921].

Benjamin, Walter. "Critique of Violence," trans. Edmund Jephcott. In *Selected Writings*. Vol. 1, *1913–1926*, ed. Marcus Bullock and Michael W. Jennings, 236–52. Cambridge, MA: Belknap Press, 1996 [1921].

Benjamin, Walter. "Franz Kafka: On the Tenth Anniversary of His Death," trans. Harry Zohn. In *Selected Writings*. Vol. 2, Part 2, *1931–1934*, ed. M. W. Jennings, H. Eiland, and G. Smith, 794–818. Cambridge, MA: Belknap Press, 1999 [1934].

Benjamin, Walter. "On the Concept of History," trans. Harry Zohn. In *Selected Writings*. Vol. 4, *1938–1940*. ed. Michael W. Jennings, Howard Eiland, and Gary Smith, 389–400. Cambridge, MA: Belknap Press, 2003 [1940].

Benjamin, Walter. "On Some Motifs in Baudelaire," trans. Harry Zohn. In *Walter Benjamin, Selected Writings*, Vol. 4, ed. Michael W. Jennings, Howard Eiland, and Gary Smith, 313–55. Cambridge, MA: Belknap Press, 2003 [1940].

Benjamin, Walter. "On Languages as Such and on the Language of Man," trans. Edmund Jephcott. In *Walter Benjamin: Selected Writings*. Vol. 1, *1913–1926*, ed. Marcus Bullock and Michael W. Jennings, 62–75. Cambridge, MA: Belknap Press, 1996 [1916].

Benjamin, Walter. *The Origin of German Tragic Drama*. Trans. John Osborne. New York: New Left Books, 2023 [1928].

Benjamin, Walter. "Paralipomena to 'On the Concept of History,'" trans. Edmund Jephcott and Howard Eiland. In *Walter Benjamin: Selected Writings*. Vol. 4, *1938–1940*, ed. Marcus Bullock and Michael W. Jennings, 421–24. Cambridge, MA: Harvard University Press, 2003 [1940].

Benjamin, Walter. "The Storyteller: Observations on the Works of Nikolai Leskov," trans. Harry Zohn. In *Selected Writings*. Vol. 3, *1935–1938*, ed. Howard Eiland and Michael W. Jennings, 142–66. Cambridge, MA: Harvard University Press, 2002 [1936].

Benjamin, Walter. "The Work of Art in the Age of Mechanical Reproducibility: Second Version," trans. Edmond Jephcott and Harry Zohn. In *Selected Writings*. Vol. 3, *1935–1938*, ed. Howard Eiland and Michael W. Jennings, 101–33. Cambridge, MA: Harvard University Press, 2002 [1935].

Benya, Asanda. "Women in Mining: Occupational Culture and Gendered Identities in the Making." PhD diss., University of the Witwatersrand, 2016.

Bevernage, Berber. "Writing the Past Out of the Present: History and the Politics of Time in Transitional Justice." *History Workshop Journal* 69 (2010): 111–31.

Bevernage, Berber. "Time, Presence, and Historical Injustice." *History and Theory* 47, no. 3 (2008): 149–67.

Bezeidenhout, Andries, and Sakhele Buhlungu. "Old Victories, New Struggles: The State of the National Union of Mineworkers." In *State of the Union*, ed. Sakhele Buhlungu, John Daniel, Roger Southall, and Jessica Lutchman, 245–65. Johannesburg: HSRC, 2004.

Bhorat, Haroon, and Ravi Kanbur, eds. *Poverty and Policy in Post-Apartheid South Africa*. Cape Town: Human Sciences Research Council, 2006.

Biehl, Joao. *Vita: Life in a Zone of Abandonment*. Updated ed. Berkeley: University of California Press, 2013.

Biko, Steve. "The Righteousness of Our Strength." In *I Write What I Like*, 120–37. 1978. Reprint, Chicago: University of Chicago Press, 2002.

"The Black Peril. Fruits of Native Indolence: Chinese the Only Alternative." *Rand Daily Mail*, April 9, 1904.

"The Black Peril. Cape Natives Must Be Disenfranchised." *Cape Daily Telegraph*, May 2, 1904.

"The Black Peril. Indecent Assault at Pretoria: Five Years and the Lash." *Rand Daily Mail*, July 28, 1904, 7.

"Black Peril More to Be Feared: Earl Percy's View." *Cape Daily Telegraph*, April 14, 1904.

"'The Black Peril.' Native Question Discussed in London. The Ethiopian Movement." *Rand Daily Mail*, April 29, 1904.

"The Black Peril. Outrages on Women: The Guild's [Guild of Loyal Women] Petition." *Rand Daily Mail*, December 5, 1906.

"The Black Peril: A Trade Commissioner's Observations." *Cape Times*, April 14, 1904.

Blackburn, Douglas. *Richard Hartley, Prospector*. London: William Blackwood, 1905.

Blainey, G. "Lost Causes of the Jameson Raid." *Economic History Review* 18, no. 2 (1965): 350–66.

Bloch, Ernst. "Nonsynchronism and the Obligation to Its Dialectics." Trans. Mark Ritter. *New German Critique* 11 ([1932] 1977): 22–38.

Bloch, Ernst. *Traces*. Trans. Anthony A. Nassar. Stanford, CA: Stanford University Press, 2006.

Boltanski, Luc. *Distant Suffering: Morality, Media and Politics*. Trans. Graham D. Burchell. Cambridge: Cambridge University Press, 1999 [1993].

Bopape, Moses, and Stephen Ratlabala. "*Diepegauta*" [The Gold-Diggers]. In *Ithute Direto*, 36. Pretoria: JL. Van Schaik, 1968.

Bonner, Phillip. "The Russians on the Reef, 1947–1957: Urbanisation, Gang Warfare and Ethnic Mobilisation." In *Apartheid's Genesis, 1935–1962*, ed. Phillip Bonner, Peter Delius, and Deborah Posel, 160–94. Johannesburg: Ravan Press, 1993.

Bordo, Michael D. "The Bretton Woods International Monetary System." In *The Gold Standard and Related Regimes: Collected Essays*, 395–500. Cambridge: Cambridge University Press, 1999.

Bozzoli, Belinda. "Marxism, Feminism, and South African Studies." *Journal of Southern African Studies* 9, no. 2 (1983): 139–71.

Brandel-Syrier, M. *Black Woman in Search of God*. London: Lutterworth, 1962.

Bray, Michael. *Powers of the Mind: Mental and Manual Labor in the Contemporary Political Crisis*. Bielefeld: Transcript Verlag, 2019.

Breckenridge, Keith. "The Allure of Violence: Men, Race and Masculinity on the South African Goldmines, 1900–1950." *Journal of Southern African Studies* 24, no. 4 (1998): 669–93.

Breckenridge, Keith. "The Book of Life: The South African Population Register and the Invention of Racial Descent, 1950–1980." *Kronos: Southern African Studies* 40 (2014): 225–40.

Breckenridge, Keith. "Can Trust Be Engineered?" Lecture delivered at Leuphana University, Lüneburg, Germany, January 31, 2024.

Breckenridge, Keith. "Love Letters and Amenuenses: Beginning the Cultural History of the Working Class Private Sphere in Southern Africa, 1900–1933." *Journal of Southern African Studies* 26, no. 2 (2000): 337–48.

Breckenridge, Keith. "Revenge of the Commons: The Crisis in the South African Mining Industry." *History Workshop Online*, November 5, 2012. http://www.historyworkshop.org.uk/revenge-of -the-commons-the-crisis-in-the-south-african-mining-industry.

Breckenridge, Keith. "Verwoerd's Bureau of Proof: Total Information in the Making of Apartheid." *History Workshop Journal* 59 (2005): 83–108.

Bright, Rachel K. *Chinese Labour in South Africa, 1902–10*. London: Palgrave, MacMillan, 2013.

"British Capital." *Johannesburg Times*, August 23, 1895.

Brodie, Nechama. *Femicide in South Africa*. Cape Town: Kwela Books, 2020.

Brooks, Gwendolyn. "Boy Breaking Glass (1968)." In *Blacks*, 438–39. Chicago: Third World Press, 1987.

Bryce, James. *Impressions of South Africa*. Rev. 3rd ed. London: MacMillan, 1899.

Buck-Morss, Susan. "The Flâneur, the Sandwichman and the Whore: The Politics of Loitering." In *Walter Benjamin and the Arcades Project*, ed. Beatrice Hanssen, 33–65. Continuum: London, 2006.

Buhlungu, Sakhela. *A Paradox of Victory: COSATU and the Democratic Transformation in South Africa*. Durban: KwaZulu-Natal Press, 2010.

Buhlungu, Sakhela, and Malehoko Tshoaedi. "A Contested Legacy: Organizational and Political Challenges Facing COSATU." In *COSATU: Contested Legacy*, ed. Sakhela Buhlungu and Malehoko Tshoaedi, 1–31. Johannesburg: HSRC, 2012.

"Bultfontein." Mindat.org. Accessed August 3, 2021. https://www.mindat.org/min-800.html.

Bunn, David. "Art Johannesburg and Its Objects." In *Johannesburg, the Elusive Metropolis*, ed. Sarah Nuttall and Achille Mbembe, 137–69. Durham, NC: Duke University Press, 2008.

Gayle, Damien. "Busted Flush: Gold Toilet Stolen from Blenheim Palace." *The Guardian*, September 14, 2019. https://www.theguardian.com/uk-news/2019/sep/14/gold-toilet-reportedly-stolen -blenheim-palace-cattelan.

Buzani, Mangaliso. *A Naked Bone*. Durban: Deep South Press, 2019.

Cameron, Edwin. *Witness to AIDS*. Cape Town: Tafelberg, 2005.

Campbell, Catherine. "Learning to Kill? Masculinity, the Family and Violence in Natal." *Journal of Southern African Studies* 18 (1992): 614–28.

Campbell, Catherine. *Letting Them Die: Why HIV/AIDS Prevention Programs Fail*. Bloomington: Indiana University Press, 2003.

Campbell, J. "The Americanization of South Africa." Seminar paper no. 44, University of Witwatersrand, Institute for Advanced Social Research (Johannesburg, South Africa), 1998.

Campbell, Roy. "Fetish Worship in South Africa: A Skirmish on the Borders of Popular Opinion." *Voorslag* 1, no. 2 (1926): 3–18.

Cartwright, A. P. *Gold Paved the Way: The Story of the Gold Fields Group of Mines*. London: Palgrave Macmillan, 1967.

Cartwright, A. P. *Valley of Gold*. Cape Town: Timmins, 1961.

Cartwright, A. P. *West Driefontein—Ordeal by Water*. Cape Town: J. G. Ince for Gold Fields of South Africa, 1969?

Celan, Paul. "Night." In *Paul Celan: Poems*, trans. Michael Hamburger, 108–9. Manchester: Carcanet, 1980 [1959].

Celan, Paul. "Sand from the Urns." In *Poems of Paul Celan*, trans. Michael Hamburger, 43–44. New York: Persea Books, 1988 [1952].

"Chairman's Review: Consolidated Gold Fields of South Africa." *Rand Daily Mail*, December 15, 1952.

Chamber of Mines. *Mining SA 2016*. Johannesburg: Chamber of Mines, 2017.

Chance, Kerry. *Living Politics in South Africa's Urban Shacklands*. Chicago: University of Chicago Press, 2018.

Chapitso, M. E. "The Community Response to the Demarcation of the Merafong Muncipality into the North West Province." Master's thesis, Nelson Mandela Metropolitan University, (Port Elizabeth, South Africa), 2016.

Christiansë, Yvette. "Spring, for Martha." *Staffrider* 10, no. 4 (1992): 20.

Christie, Pam, and Colin Collins. "Bantu Education: Apartheid Ideology of Labour Reproduction." *Comparative Education* 18, no. 1 (1982): 59–75.

Clark, T. J. *Farewell to an Idea: Episodes from a History of Modernism*. New Haven, CT: Yale University Press, 1999.

Clarke, D. G. "The South African Chamber of Mines: Policy and Strategy with Reference to Foreign African Labour Supply." DSRG Working Paper No. 2, Development Studies Research Group, Pietermaritzburg, 1977.

Clastres, Pierre. *Chronicle of the Guayaki Indians*. Trans. Paul Auster. New York: Zone, 1998 [1972].

Cohen, Joshua. "Thirty-Six Shades of Blue," *Triple Canopy*, Issue 9, March 17, 2010. Accessed July 14, 2024: https://canopycanopycanopy.com/contents/thirty_six_shades_of_prussian_blue?q=Joshua%20Cohen%20Prussian%20Blue.

Cole, Ernest. *House of Bondage: A South African Black Man Exposes in His Own Pictures and Words the Bitter Life of His Homeland Today*, with Thomas Flaherty. Intro. Joseph Lelyveld. New York: Random House, 1967.

"Colonization of Palestine Is No Longer a Doubtful Experiment but Already in Part a Proved Success." *Christian Express*, April 1, 1892, 63.

Comaroff, Jean. *Body of Power, Spirit of Resistance: The Culture and History of a South African People*. Chicago: University of Chicago Press, 1985.

Comaroff, Jean, and John L. Comaroff. *Ethnicity, Inc*. Chicago: University of Chicago Press, 2009.

Comaroff, Jean, and John L. Comaroff. "The Madman and the Migrant." In *Ethnography and the Historical Imagination*, 155–78. Boulder, CO: Westview, 1992.

Comaroff, Jean, and John Comaroff. "Millennial Capitalism: First Thoughts on a Second Coming." In *Millennial Capitalism*, 1–56. Durham, NC: Duke University Press, 2001.

Comaroff, Jean, and John Comaroff., eds. *Modernity and its Malcontents: Ritual and Power in Postcolonial Africa*. Chicago: University of Chicago Press, 1993.

Comaroff, Jean, and John L. Comaroff. *Of Revelation and Revolution*. 2 vols. Chicago: University of Chicago Press, 1987, 1991.

Comaroff, Jean, and John L. Comaroff. *Theory from the South: Or, How Euro-America Is Evolving Toward Africa*. New York and London: Routledge, 2011.

Comaroff, Jean and John L. Comaroff, *The Truth About Crime: Sovereignty, Knowledge, Social Order*. Chicago: University of Chicago Press, 2016.

Comaroff, John L., and Jean Comaroff. "Law and Disorder in the Postcolony: An Introduction." In *Law and Disorder in the Postcolony*, 1–56. Chicago: University of Chicago Press, 2006.

Coombes, Annie E. "Witnessing History/Embodying Testimony: Gender and Memory in Post-Apartheid South Africa." *Journal of the Royal Anthropological Institute* 17 (2011): S92–112.

"COSATU Cracks CP [Conservative Party]. Carletonville Shows How." *Cosatu News*, March 2, 1989, 4.

Coplan, David. *In the Time of Cannibals: The Word Music of South Africa's Basotho Migrants.* Chicago: University of Chicago Press, 1994.

Crais, Clifton. *The Politics of Evil: Magic, State Power, and the Political Imagination in South Africa.* Cambridge: Cambridge University Press, 2002.

Cropley, Ed. "Desperation and Death beneath South Africa's City of Gold." Reuters, September 13, 2016. https://www.reuters.com/article/us-safrica-mining/desperation-and-death-beneath-south-africas-city-of-gold-idUSKCN11J1M6.

Cross, Michael. *Culture and Identity in South African Education, 1880–1990.* PhD diss., University of Johannesburg, 2015.

Crush, Jonathan. "The Extrusion of Foreign Labour from the South African Gold Mining Industry." *Geoforum* 17, no. 2 (1986): 161–72.

Crush, Jonathan. "Inflexible Migrancy: New Forms of Migrant Labour on the South African Gold Mines." In "Transformation on the South African Gold Mines" [Évolution de la situation dans les mines d'or sud-africaines]. Special issue, *Labour, Capital and Society* (*Travail, capital et société*) 25, no. 1 (April 1992): 46–71.

Crush, Jonathan. "Migrancy and Militance: The Case of the National Union of Mineworkers of South Africa." *African Affairs* 88, no. 350 (1989): 5–23.

Crush, Jonathan. "Restructuring Migrant Labour on the Gold Mines." In *South African Review.* Vol. 4, ed. Glen Moss and Ingrid Obery, 283–91. Johannesburg: Ravan Press, 1987.

Crush, Jonathan, and Belinda Dodson. "Another Lost Decade: The Failure of South Africa's Post-Apartheid Migration Policy." *Tijdschrift voor Economische en Sociale Geografie* [Journal for Economic and Social Geography] 98, no. 4 (2007): 436–54.

Crush, Jonathan, and Wilmot James. "Depopulating the Compound: Migrant Labor and Mine Housing in South Africa." *World Development* 19, no. 4 (1991): 301–16.

Crush, Jonathan, Alan Jeeves, and David Yudelman. *South Africa's Labor Empire: A History of Black Migrancy to the Gold Mines.* Boulder, CO: Westview, 1991.

Crush, Jonathan, Theresa Ulicki, Teke Tseane, and Elizabeth Jansen van Veuren. "Undermining Labour: The Rise of Sub-Contracting in South African Gold Mines." *Journal of Southern African Studies* 27, no. 1 (Mar. 2001): 5–31.

Cruywagen, Vincent. "Illegal Mining Crackdown—Minister Fires Warning to Foreigners 'Wreaking Havoc,' as National Drive Racks up 4,000 Arrests." *Daily Maverick,* November 10, 2023.

Cruywagen, Vincent. "'Mr X's' Testimony at Lily Mine Inquest Paints Chilling Picture of Illegal Mining Facilitated by Employees." *Daily Maverick,* October 24, 2023.

"Cyanide Once More." *Johannesburg Times,* August 3, 1895.

"Cyanide Poisoning." *Johannesburg Times,* September 4, 1895.

"The Cyanide Question." *Johannesburg Times,* February 2, 1895.

Daugaard, Solveig. "Anybody Living a Private Life Is a Believer in Money: Gertrude Stein, The Great Depression, and the Abstraction of Money." *Nordic Journal of Aesthetics* 60 (2020): 26–47.

Davenport, T. R. H. "The Triumph of Colonel Stallard: The Transformation of the Natives (Urban Aras) Act Between 1923 and 1937." *Suid-Afrikaanse historiese joernaal* (South African Histrical Journal) 2, no. 1 (1970): 77–96.

Davis, Rebecca. "Soldiers Claim Operation Prosper a Shambles, with Lack of Food, Vehicles and Uncertainty Around Who Is in Charge." *Daily Maverick,* July 24, 2021.

Daymond, M. J., Dorothy Driver, Sheila Meintjes, Leloba Molema, Chiedza Musengezi, Margie Orford, and Nobantu Rasebotsa, eds. *Women Writing Africa: The Southern Region.* New York: Feminist Press, 2003.

"Death of Reverend G. Tyamzashe." *Christian Express* (Lovedale, South Africa), November 2, 1896, 2–3.

de Certeau, Michel. "Walking in the City." In *The Practice of Everyday Life,* trans. Steven Rendall, 91–110. Berkeley: University of California Press, 1984 [1974].

de Lauretis, Teresa. "Desire in Narrative." In *Alice Doesn't: Feminism, Semiotics, Cinema,* 103–57. Bloomington: Indiana University Press, 1984.

de Kok, Ingrid. "Into the Sun." In *Terrestrial Things*, 56. Cape Town: Kwela Books, 2002.

de Kok, Ingrid. "Parts of Speech." In *Terrestrial Things*, 21–24. Cape Town: Kwela Books, 2002.

de Kok, Ingrid. "Truck Stop." In *Terrestrial Things*, 60. Cape Town: Kwela Books, 2002.

Deleuze, Gilles. *Foucault*. Trans. Seán Hand. Minneapolis: University of Minnesota Press, 1988 [1986].

Deleuze, Gilles, and Félix Guattari, *Anti-Oedipus: Capitalism and Schizophrenia*. Trans. Robert Hurley. New York: Penguin, 2009 [1972].

Deleuze, Gilles and Félix Guattari, "Becoming-Intense, Becoming-Animal, Becoming-Imperceptible." In *A Thousand Plateaus: Capitalism and Schizophrenia*, trans. and foreword Brian Massumi, 232–309. Minneapolis: University of Minnesota Press, 1987 [1980].

Denning, Michael. "Wageless Life." *New Left Review* 66 (December 2010), 79–97.

Denoon, Donald. "Capital and Capitalists in the Transvaal in the 189s and 1900s." *Historical Journal* 23, no. 1 (1980): 111–32.

Department of Development, Government of South Africa. "Batho Pele." Accessed July 20, 2022. https://www.dsd.gov.za/index.php/about/batho-pele.

Derrida, Jacques. "A Certain Impossible Possibility of Saying the Event," trans. Gila Walker. *Critical Inquiry* 33 (Winter 2007): 441–61.

Derrida, Jacques. *Archive Fever: A Freudian Impression*. Trans. Eric Prenowtiz. Chicago: University of Chicago Press, 1996.

Derrida, Jacques. *The Beast and the Sovereign*. Vol. 2, ed. Trans. Geoffrey Bennington. Chicago: University of Chicago Press, 2011.

Derrida, Jacques. "Living On" [1977]. In *Parages*, trans. James Hulbert, ed. John Leavey, 103–91. Stanford, CA: Stanford University Press, 2011.

Derrida, Jacques. "Passions." In *On the Name*, trans. David Wood, John P. Leavey Jr., and Ian McLeod, 3–34. Stanford, CA: Stanford University Press, 1995 [1993].

Derrida, Jacques. "Plato's Pharmacy." In *Dissemination*, trans. and intro. Barbara Johnson, 61–173. Chicago: University of Chicago Press, 1981 [1972].

Derrida, Jacques. *Truth in Painting*. Trans. Geoff Bennington and Ian McLeod. Chicago: University of Chicago Press, 1987 [1978].

Deuber-Mankowsky, Astrid. "Nietzsche's Practices of Illusion." *Critical Horizons* 18, no. 4 (September 2017): 307–32.

Deuber-Mankowsky, Astrid. "Rhythms of the Living, Conditions of Critique: On Judith Butler's Reading of Benjamin's 'Critique of Violence,'" trans. Catharine Diehl. In *Walter Benjamin and Theology*, ed. Colby Dickinson and Stéphane Symons, 253–71. New York: Fordham University Press, 2015.

Devi, Mahasweta *Imaginary Maps: Three Stories by Mahasweta Devi*. Trans., ed., and intro. Gayatri Chakravorty Spivak. New York: Routledge, 1995.

Dhlomo, R. R. R. "Murder on the Mine Dumps." *English in Africa* 2, no. 1 (March 1975): 33–35.

Dicey, Edward. "Last Month II." *The Nineteenth Century and After* 55 (January–June 1904).

Digby, Anne. "Black Doctors and Discrimination Under South Africa's Apartheid Regime." *Medical History* 57, no. 2 (2013): 269–90.

Dikeni, Sandile. "Night." In *Planting Water*. Durban: University of KwaZulu-Natal Press, 2007.

Dikeni, Sandile. *Soul Fire: Writing the Transition*. Intro. Antjie Krog. Pietermaritzburg: University of Natal Press, 2002.

Dixon, Emily. "Solid Gold Toilet Stolen from Blenheim Palace, Birthplace of Winston Churchill." *CNN Style*, September 14, 2019, https://www.cnn.com/style/article/uk-blenheim-palace -gold-toilet-scli-gbr-intl/index.html.

Dlamini, Chris. "Interview, 2011." Historical Papers Research Archive, University of the Witwatersrand. Wits Oral History Project, ZA HPRA A3402-B-B118. Accessed July 26, 2022. http://historicalpapers-atom.wits.ac.za/uploads/r/historical-papers-research-archive-library -university-of-witwatersrand/d/8/4/d8473abcd9ce33d31ee1a3b9d0487577cf27c13678678592 ac1eec8c1bf909c9/A3402-B18-001-jpeg.pdf.

Dlamini, Jacob. *Native Nostalgia*. Johannesburg: Jacana, 2009.

dos Passos, John. *The Forty-Second Parallel*. 1930. Reprint, New York: Houghton, Mifflin, Harcourt, 2000.

"Down in the Dumps Over Sand." *Rand Daily Mail*, January 8, 1980.

"Driefontein Brick and Potteries Co., Ltd. Report of the Ordinary General Meeting of Shareholders." *Rand Daily Mail*, October 24, 1947.

Du Bois, W. E. B. "Foreword." In Alfred Xuma, "Charlotte Manye (Mrs. Maxeke): "What an Educated African Girl Can Do." Pamphlet. The Women's Parent Mite Missionary Society of the AME Church, 1930. Wits Historical Research Papers, AD2186.

du Maurier, George. *Trilby*. 1895. Reprint, New York: Broadview Press, 2003.

Edwards, Paul N., and Gabrielle Hecht. "History and the Technopolitics of Identity: The Case of Apartheid South Africa." *Journal of Southern African Studies* 36, no. 3 (September 2010): 619–39.

Eickhoff, Friedrich-Wilhelm. "On *Nachträglichkeit*: The Modernity of an Old Concept." *International Journal of Psychoanalysis* 87, no. 6 (2006): 1452–69.

Elder, Glen S. *Hostels, Sexuality, and the Apartheid Legacy: Malevolent Geographies*. Athens, OH: Ohio University Press, 2003.

Electoral Commission of South Africa. "Municipal Elections Results, 2021." https://results .elections.org.za/dashboards/lge/.

Erlank, Natasha. "*Umteteli wa Bantu* and the Constitution of Social Publics in the 1920s and 1930s." *Social Dynamics: A Journal of African Studies* 45, no. 1 (2019): 75–102.

Erlmann, Veit. "Spectatorial Lust—the African Choir in England 1891–1893." In *Africans on Stage: Studies in Ethnological Show Business*, ed. Bernth Lindfors, 107–34. Bloomington: Indiana University Press, 1999.

Erlmann, Veit. "'A Feeling of Prejudice': Orpheus M. McAdoo and the Virginia Jubilee Singers in South Africa, 1890–1898." In *African Stars: Studies in Black South African Performance*, 21–53. Chicago: University of Chicago Press, 1991.

Evans-Pritchard, E. E. *Witchcraft, Oracles and Magic Among the Azande*, abridged edition. Ed. Eva Gillies. Oxford: Clarendon Press, 1976.

"Evidence of G. H. Goch, January 30, 1901." *Report of the Transvaal Concession Commission*, 236–38. Pretoria, April 19, 1901.

"Extract from the *Standard and Diggers News*, August 22, 1892." In *Papers on the Political Situation in South Africa, 1885–1895*, ed. Charles Leonard, 157–89. London: Arthur Humphreys, 1903.

Fabian, Johannes. *Time and the Other: How Anthropology Makes Its Objects*. 1983. Reprint, New York: Columbia University Press, 2014.

"A Fabulous Snake Suddenly Appears at the Scene." *Abantu-Batho*, April 22 (?), 1920. In *The People's Paper: A Centenary History and Anthology of Abanto-Batho*, ed. Peter Limb, 432. Johannesburg: Wits University Press, 2012.

Fanon, Frantz. *Black Skin, White Masks*. Trans. Richard Philcox. New York: Grove, 2008 [1952].

Fanon, Frantz. "Medicine and Colonialism." In *A Dying Colonialism*, trans. Haakon Chevalier, intro. Adolfo Gillay, 121–46. New York Grove, 1965 [1959].

Fanon, Frantz. *Wretched of the Earth*. Trans. Richard Philcox. Intro. Jean-Paul Sartre and Homi K. Bhabha. New York: Grove, 2004 [1961].

Fassin, Didier. *When Bodies Remember: Experiences and Politics of AIDS in South Africa*. Berkeley: University of California Press, 2007.

Fenves, Peter. "Marx, Mourning, Messianicity." In *Violence, Identity, and Self-Determination*, ed. Samuel Weber and Hent de Vriest, 253–70. Stanford, CA: Stanford University Press, 1997.

Ferguson, James. *Give a Man a Fish: Reflections on the New Politics of Distribution*. Durham, NC: Duke University Press, 2015.

Fihlani, Phumza, and Tiffany Wertheimer. "South Africa: Illegal Miners Cleared of Gang Rape." *BBC News*, October 27, 2022.

First, Ruth. *Black Gold: The Mozambican Miner, Proletarian and Peasant*. New York: St Martin's, 1977.

Fockens, Jakob Wilhelm. *Beknopt leerboek der delfstofkunde, eene noodzakelijke handleiding voor allen die begerig zijn de delfstoffen der Z.A. Republiek te leeren kennen* [A brief textbook of mineral science, an indispensable manual for all who wish to learn about the minerals of the S.A. Republic] (Pretoria, 1887).

Fom, A.L. "Mr. A. Beit 'At Home.' A Brilliant Function. Four Hundred Guests." *Johannesburg Times*, June 22, 1895, 5.

"Foreign Miscellany: Finance—Banking." *Rhodes Journal of Banking, A Practical Banker's Magazine* 16 (July 1889): 645.

Forrest, Kally. *Metal That Does Not Bend: National Union of Metalworkers of South Africa*. Johannesburg: Wits University Press, 2011.

Foucault, Michel. *The Birth of the Clinic: An Archaeology of Medical Perception*. Trans. A. M. Sheridan Smith. New York: Vintage, 1994 [1973].

Foucault, Michel. *Discipline and Punish: The Birth of the Prison*. Trans. A. M. Sheridan Smith. New York: Vintage, 1984 [1975].

Foucault, Michel. "The Lives of Infamous Men." In *Power*. Vol. 3 of *The Essential Works of Michel Foucault, 1954–1984*, ed. James Faubion, trans. Robert Hurley et al., 157–75. New York: New Press, 2000 [1967].

Foucault, Michel. "Nietzsche, Genealogy, History." In *Aesthetics, Method, and Epistemology*. Vol. 2 of *The Essential Works of Michel Foucault, 1954–1984*, ed. James Faubion, trans. Robert Hurley and others, 369–91. New York: New Press, 1998 [1971].

Foucault, Michel. *The Order of Things: An Archaeology of the Human Sciences*. New York: Vintage, 1970 [1966].

Foucault, Michel. "Utopias and Heterotopias." In *Architecture/Mouvement/Continuité* October, 1984 [1967], trans. Jay Miskowieci. Accessed August 19, 2021. https://web.mit.edu/allanmc/www/foucault1.pdf.

Fouché, Leo. *Mapungubwe, Ancient Bantu Civilization on the Limpopo*. Reports on excavations at Mapungubwe (Northern Transvaal) from February 1933 to June 1935. Edited on behalf of the Archaeological Committee of the University of Pretoria. Cambridge: Cambridge University Press, 1937.

Frankel, S. Herbert. *Capital Investment in Africa: Its Course and Effects*. London: Oxford University Press, 1938.

Freud, Sigmund. *Beyond the Pleasure Principle, Group Psychology and Other Works*. In *SE*, Vol. XVIII, *1920–1922*, 1–64.

Freud, Sigmund. "Character and Anal Erotism." In *SE*, Vol. 9, 167–76.

Freud, Sigmund. "Dreams in Folklore." In *SE*, Vol. XII, *1911–1913*, 175–204.

Freud, Sigmund. "Introduction." In *Psycho-Analysis and the War Neuroses*. In *SE*, Vol. XVII, *1917–1919*, 205–16.

Freud, Sigmund. *The Interpretation of Dreams*. In *SE*, Vol. V, *1900–1901*, 339–627.

Freud, Sigmund. "Mourning and Melancholia." In *SE*, Vol. XIV, *1917*, 263.

Freud, Sigmund. "On Transformations of Instinct as Exemplified by Anal Eroticism." In *SE*, Vol. XVII, *1917–1919*, 125–34.

Freud, Sigmund. *The Psychopathology of Everyday Life: Forgetting, Slips of the Tongue, Bungled Actions, Superstitions and Errors*. In *SE*, Vol. VI, *1901*, vii–296.

"Future Treatment of Natives. Interference by Imperial Government Hinted at (Reuter's Colonial Service). *Cape Daily Telegraph*, March 2, 1906.

Gaeganelwe, Saebo. "Burning Down Libraries Deprives People of Reading." *Sowetan*, March 30, 2007.

Gaitskell, Deborah. "Housewives, Maids or Mothers: Some Contradictions of Domesticity for Christian Women in Johannesburg, 1903–39." *Journal of African History* 24, no. 2 (1983): 241–56.

Gaitskell, Deborah. "Power in Prayer and Service: Women's Christian Organizations." In *Christianity in South Africa: A Political, Social and Cultural History*, ed. Richard Elphick and Rodney Davenport, 253–67. Oxford: Oxford University Press, 1997.

Galeni, Osborne. "Interview." Historical Papers Research Archive, University of the Witwatersrand. Wits Oral History Project, ZA HPRA A3402-B-B98. Accessed July 26, 2022. http://historicalpapers-atom.wits.ac.za/b98-3.

gamEdze and gamedZe. "Anxiety, Afropessimism, and the University Shutdown." *South Atlantic Quarterly* 118, no. 1 (2019): 215–25.

Geertz, Clifford. "Religion as a Cultural System." In *The Interpretation of Cultures*, 87–125. New York: Basic Books, 1973.

"Geologists Race Against Time to Study Cave." *Rand Daily Mail*, October 5, 1963.

Gemmill, J. A. "Native Labour on the Gold Mines." In *Transactions of the Seventh Commonwealth Mining and Metallurgical Congress*, Vol. 1, 289–306. Johannesburg: South African Institute of Mining and Metallurgy, I961.

Geschiere, Peter. *Witchcraft and Modernity: Politics and the Occult in Postcolonial Africa*. Trans. Janet Roitman and Peter Geschiere. Charlottesville, VA: University of Virginia Press, 1997.

Giliomee, Hermann. *The Afrikaners: Biography of a People*. Cape Town: Tafelberg, 2003.

Girard, René. *Violence and the Sacred*. Trans. Patrick Gregory. New York: 2005 [1972].

Glaser, Clive. "The Mark of Zorro: Sexuality and Gender Relations in the Tsotsi Subculture on the Witwatersrand." *African Studies* 51 (1992): 47–67.

Glaser, Clive. "Swines, Hazels and the Dirty Dozen." *Journal of Southern African Studies* 24, no. 4 (December 1998): 719–36.

Goethe, Johanne Wolfgang von. *Faust*, Part II. Ed. and trans. Stuart Atkins, intro. David Wellerby. Princeton, NJ: Princeton University Press, 1984 [1832].

Gold, Joseph. *Legal and Institutional Aspects of the International Monetary System: Selected Essays*. Washington, DC: International Monetary Fund, 1979.

Gold Producers' Committee. "Evidence of the Gold Producer's Committee of the Chamber of Mines." Statement No. 8, "The Social Aspect of Migratory Labour as Opposed to Stabilized Native Mining Communities," 37–40. Minutes of Evidence. Native Laws Commission of Enquiry, Chamber of Mines, 1947.

Gowa, Joanne. *Closing the Gold Window: Domestic Politics and the End of Bretton Woods*. Ithaca, NY: Cornell University Press, 1983

Goux, Jean-Joseph. *Symbolic Economies: After Marx and Freud*. Trans. Jennifer Curtiss Gage. Ithaca, NY: Cornell University Press, 1990 [1973].

Gqola, Pumla Dineo. "Brutal Inheritances: Echoes, Negrophobia and Masculinist Violence." In *Go Home or Die Here: Violence, Xenophobia and the Reinvention of Difference in South Africa*, eds. Shireen Hassim, Tawana Kuta and Eric Worby, 209–222. Johannesburg: Wits University Press, 2008.

Gqola, Pumla Dineo. *Rape: A South African Nightmare*. Johannesburg: MF Books/Jacana, 2015.

Gqola, Pumla Dineo. *Female Fear Factory: Unravelling Patriarchy's Cultures of Violence*. Abuja, Nigeria: Cassava Republic, 2022.

Graham, Wayne. "The Randlord's Bubble, 1894–1896: South African Gold Mines and Stock Manipulation." Discussion Papers in Economic and Social History No. 10, University of Oxford, 1996.

Gray, James, A. S. *Payable Gold: An Intimate Record of the History of the Discovery of the Payable Witwatersrand Goldfields and of Johannesburg in 1886 and 1887*. Based on research made in the State Archives, Pretoria by Ethel L. Gray, and containing "The Oosthuizen Papers." Translations of Photographic Reproductions by B. De Coigny Marchange. South Africa: Central News Agency, 1937.

"Gray, Mr. James." *Biographical Database of Southern African Science*. S2A3. Accessed May 6, 2019. http://www.s2a3.org.za/bio/Biograph_final.php?serial=1124.

"The Great Cyanide Case: Text of the Judgement. Summing-up Dead Against the Patents." *African Review* 9 (October–December 1896): 464–66.

Green, Michael Cawood. "Falling (Hettie's Love Song)." In *Sinking: A Verse Novella*, 16–17. London: Penguin, 1997.

Green, Michael Cawood. "From Structure to Event: Willie Britz." In *Sinking: A Verse Novella*, 36–38. London: Penguin, 1997.

Green, Michael Cawood. *Novel Histories: Past, Present and Future in South African Fiction*. Johannesburg: University of Witwatersrand Press, 1997.

Green, Michael Cawood. "Older Than Time." In *Sinking: A Verse Novella*, 4–12. London: Penguin, 1997.

Greenberg, Clement. *Art and Culture: Critical Essays*. 1961. Reprint, Boston: Beacon Press, 1989.

Griffith, George Chetwynd. *Briton or Boer: A Tale of the Fight for Africa*. 2 vols. London: F. V. White, 1897.

Guala, Francesco. "Critical Notice. Review of *La Naissance de la Clinique*, by Michel Foucault." *Economics and Philosophy* 22 (2006): 429–39.

Guma, S. M. *The Form, Content, and Technique of Traditional Literature in Southern Sotho*. Pretoria: J. L. van Shaik, 1967.

Gumede, W. "Summer School e-Cabhane: An Address by Jabavu." *Abantu-Batho*, c. April 1923. In *The People's Paper: A Centenary History and Anthology of Abanto-Batho*, ed. Peter Limb, 451–52. Johannesburg: Wits University Press, 2012.

Gutsche, Thelma. "Roaring Nineties and Darkling Days: 1891–1895." In *Old Gold: The History of the Wanderers Club 1888–1968*. Accessed July 5, 2019. https://www.thewanderersclub.co.za /wp-content/uploads/2012/03/chapter5.pdf.

Guy, Jeff. "Making Words Visible: Aspects of Orality, Literacy and History in Southern Africa. *South African Historical Journal* 31 (1994): 3–27.

Guy, Jeff, and Motlatsi Thabane. "Technology, Ethnicity and Ideology: Basotho Miners and Shaft-Sinking on the South African Gold Mines." In "Culture and Consciousness in Southern Africa." Special issue, *Journal of Southern African Studies* 14, no. 2 (1988): 257–78.

Guy, Jeff, and Motlatsi Thabane. "The Ma-Rashea: A Participant's Perspective." In *Class, Community and Conflict: South African Perspectives*, ed. Belinda Bozzoli, 436–56. Johannesburg: Ravan, 1987.

Hadfield, Leslie Ann. "Restoring Human Dignity and Building Self-Reliance: Youth, Women, and Churches and Black Consciousness Community Development, South Africa, 1969–1977." PhD diss., Michigan State University, 2010.

Haggard, Rider. *King Solomon's Mines*. In *Three Adventure Novels of H. Rider Haggard: She, King Solomon's Mines, Allan Quartermain*, 240–415. New York: Dover, 1951.

Hägglund, Martin. *Dying for Time: Proust, Woolf, Nabokov*. Cambridge, MA: Harvard University Press, 2012.

Hansen, Deirdre. *The Life and Work of Benjamin Tyamzashe: A Contemporary Xhosa Composer*. Grahamstown: Rhodes University, Institute for Social and Economic Research, 1968.

Harington, J. S., N. D. McGlashan, and E. Z. Chelkowska. "A Century of Migrant Labor in the Gold Mines of South Africa." *Journal of the South African Institute of Mining and Metallurgy* 104, no. 2 (March 2004): 65–71.

Harris, Verne. "A Shaft of Darkness: Derrida in the Archive." In *Refiguring the Archive*, ed. Carolyn Hamilton et al., 61–82. Cape Town: David Philips, 2002.

Hart, Gillian. *Rethinking the South African Crisis: Nationalism, Populism, Hegemony*. Athens, GA: University of Georgia Press, 2013.

Hartford, Gavin. "The Mining Industry Strike Wave: What Are the Costs and What Are the Solutions." *GroundUp*, 2012. https://groundup.org.za/article/mining-industry-strike-wave -what-are-causes-and-what-are-solutions.

Hartwig, Gary "The Low Income Sector—the Life Industry's Perspective." Paper presented at the Annual Actuarial Society of South Africa Convention, Cape Town, October 13–14, 2000.

Harz, C., and S. B. Beauhbock. "Is the Manufacture of Cyanide of Potassium Rationally Possible in the Transvaal?" In WCM, *Annual Report, 1895*, 108–10.

Hecht, Gabrielle. *Residual Governance: How South Africa Foretells Planetary Futures*. Durham, NC: Duke University Press, 2023.

Hegel, Georg Wilhelm Friedrich. *The Phenomenology of Spirit*, trans. Terry Pinkard (Cambridge: Cambridge University Press, 2018 [1807].

Herrera y Tordesillas, Antonio de. *Descripcion de las Indias Ocidentales* [Description of the West Indies]. Madrid: Imprenta Real, 1601.

Hertz, Robert. "A Contribution to the Study of the Collective Representation of Death." In *Death and the Right Hand*, trans. Rodney and Claudia Needham, 27–88. New York and London: Routledge, 2009 [1907].

Higginson, John. "Privileging the Machines: American Engineers, Indentured Chinese and White Workers in South Africa's Deep-Level Gold Mines, 1902–1907." *International Review of Social History* 52, no. 1 (2007): 1–34.

Hilferding, Rudolf. *Finance Capital: A Study in the Latest State of Capitalist Development*. Trans. Morris Watnick and Sam Gordon. Ed. Tom Bottomore. New York: Routledge, 2019 [1919].

Hirson, Baruch. *Year of Fire, Year of Ash: The Soweto Revolt: Roots of a Revolution?* London: Zed Books, 1979.

Hlongwane, Ali Khangela. "The Mapping of the June 16 1976 Soweto Student Uprisings Routes: Past Recollections and Present Reconstruction(s)." In "Performing (In) Everyday Life." Special issue, *Journal of African Cultural Studies* 19, no. 1 (2007): 7–36.

Hobson, John A. *Capitalism and Imperialism in South Africa*. New York: Tucker, 1900.

Hobson, John A. *Imperialism: A Study*. New York: James Pott, 1902.

Hoets, P., T. Langschmidt, E. Metton, D. Milne, C. Oakenfull, C. Platt, R. Roux, J. Simpson, and J. Van Wyk. *Futurefact 2000*. Durban: Gitam, Absa and Unilever, 2000.

Hofmeyr, Isabel. "Foreword." In *The Nation's Bounty: The Xhosa Poetry of Nontsizi Mgqwetho*, ed. Jeff Opland, x–xii. Johannesburg: Wits University Press, 2007.

Hofmeyr, Isabel. *We Spend Our Years as a Tale That Is Told: Oral Historical Narrative in a South African Chiefdom*. Johannesburg: Witwatersrand University Press, 1993.

Hoover, Herbert. "Editorial." *Western Australian Mining, Building and Engineering Journal* 28 (April 1904): 670.

Horkheimer, Max, and Theodor Adorno. *Dialectic of Enlightenment*. Trans. Edmund Jephcott. Ed. Gunzelin Schmid Noerr. Stanford, CA: Stanford University Press, 1992 [1947].

Horner, Dudley, and Alide Kooy. "Conflict on South African Mines, 1972–1976." Saldru Working Paper No. 5. Cape Town, 1976, 4, https://www.opensaldru.uct.ac.za/bitstream/handle/11090/580/1976hornerswp5.pdf?sequence=1.

"How June 16 Demo was Planned," Interview with Tebello Motapanyane, January 1977. Accessed July 21, 2024: https://www.sahistory.org.za/archive/how-june-16-demo-was-planned.

Huffman, Thomas N. "Mapela, Mapangubwe, and the Origins of States in Southern Africa." *South African Archaeological Bulletin* 70, no. 201 (2015): 15–27.

Hull, Elizabeth, and Deborah James. "Introduction: Popular Economies in South Africa." In "Popular Economies in South Africa." Special issue, *Africa: International Journal of the Africa Institute* 82, no. 1 (2012): 1–19.

Human Sciences Research Council. "New HIV Survey Highlights Progress and Ongoing Disparities in South Africa's HIV Epidemic." HSRC. November 27, 2023. https://hsrc.ac.za/press-releases/hsc/new-hiv-survey-highlights-progress-and-ongoing-disparities-in-south-africas-hiv-epidemic/#:~:text=SABSSM%20VI%20found%20that%20the,to%207.9%20million%20in%202017.

Hunt, Nancy Rose. *A Nervous State: Violence, Remedies, and Reverie in Colonial Congo*. Durham, NC: Duke University Press, 2016.

Hunter, Mark. "The Materiality of Everyday Sex: thinking beyond 'prostitution.'" *African Studies* 16.1 (2002): 99–120.

Hunter, Mark. "The Political Economy of Concurrent Partners: Toward a History of Sex-Love-Gift Connections in the Time of AIDS." *Review of African Political Economy* 42, no. 145 (2015): 362–75.

Irigaray, Luce. *Speculum of the Other Woman*. Trans. Gillian C. Gill. Ithaca, NY: Cornell University Press, 1985 [1974].

Irwin, Alec. "Interview." Historical Papers Research Archive, University of the Witwatersrand. Wits Oral Historical Project, ZA HPRA A3402-B-B4. Accessed July 25, 2022. http://historicalpapers-atom.wits.ac.za/b4-41.

Irvine, Douglas. "The Liberal Party, 1933–1968." In *Democratic Liberalism in South Africa: Its History and Prospects*, ed. Jeffrey Butler, Richard Elphick, and David Walsh, 116–33. Middletown, CT: Wesleyan University Press, 1987.

"Is a Commercial Panic Impending." *News Letter, San Francisco*, in *Rhodes Journal of Banking, A Practical Banker's Magazine* 16 (August 1889): 773–74.

Jabavu, Florence Nolwandle. "Bantu Home Life." In *Women Writing Africa: The Southern Region*, ed. M. J. Daymond et al. 189–95. New York: Feminist Press, 2003 [1928]. Originally published in *Christianity and the Natives of South Africa: A Yearbook of South African Missions*, ed. Rev. James Dextor Taylor (Cape Town: Lovedale Press, 1928).

Jaffer, Zubaida. *Beauty of the Heart: The Life and Times of Charlotte Maxeke*. Bloemfontein: Sun Press, 2016.

James, Deborah. *Money from Nothing: Indebtedness and Aspiration in South Africa*. Stanford, CA: Stanford University Press, 2015.

James, Wilmot G. *Our Precious Metal: African Workers in South Africa's Gold Industry, 1970–1990*. Cape Town: David Philip, 1992.

Jameson, Fredric. *The Political Unconscious: Narrative as a Socially Symbolic Act*. Ithaca, NY: Cornell University Press, 1981.

Jameson, Fredric. *Postmodernism. Or, the Cultural Logic of Late Capitalism*. Durham, NC: Duke University Press, 1992.

Jameson, Fredric. *Valences of the Dialectic*. New York: Verso, 2009.

Jeeves, Alan. "The Control of Migratory Labour on the South African Gold Mines in the Era of Kruger and Milner." *Journal of Southern African Studies* 2, no. 1 (1975): 3–29.

Jeeves, Alan. *Migrant Labour in South Africa's Mining Economy: The Struggle for the Gold Mines' Labour Supply, 1890–1920*. Montreal: McGill/Queens University Press, 1985.

Jeeves, Alan, and Johnathan Crush. "The Failure of Stabilization Experiments and the Entrenchment of migrancy to the South African Gold Mines." In "Transformation on the South African Gold Mines." Special issue, *Labour, Capital and Society* 25, no. 1 (1992): 18–45.

Jeppe, E. B. *Gold Mining on the Witwatersrand*. Johannesburg: Transvaal Chamber of Mines, 1946.

Jekwe, Daluxola. "Interview, 2010." Historical Papers Research Archive, University of the Witwatersrand. Wits Oral History Project, ZA HPRA A3402-B-B19. Accessed July 29, 2022. http://historicalpapers-atom.wits.ac.za/b19-15.

Jeremias, Alfred. *Das Alte Testament im Lichte des Alten Orients* [The Old Testament in Light of the Ancient Orient/Middle East]. Leipzig: Hinrichs, 1904.

John, Angela V. *By the Sweat of Their Brow: Women Workers at Victorian Coalmines*. London: Routledge and Kegan Paul, 1984.

Jones, R. T. "President's Corner." *Journal of the Southern African Institute of Mining and Metallurgy* 116, no. 1 (2016): vi–vii.

Jones, Roderick. "The Black Peril in South Africa." *The Nineteenth Century and After* 37 (1904): 712–23.

Jones, Sheridan and R. Hunt Jr. *Mandela, Tambo and the African National Congress: The Struggle Against Apartheid, 1948–1990: A Documentary History*. New York: Oxford University Press, 1991.

Joubert, C. J. "Government Notice: To Managers and Directors of Gold Mining and Exploration Companies and Syndicates." *Transvaal Argus*, July 12, 1894.

Joyce, James. *The Dubliners*. 1914. Reprint, New York: Penguin Classics, 2014.

Judy, R. A. *Sentient Flesh: Thinking in Disorder, Poiēsis in Black*. Durham, NC: Duke University Press, 2020.

Kafka, Franz. *The Trial*. Trans. Breon Mitchell. New York: Schocken, 1998 [1925].

Kant, Immanuel. *Critique of the Power of Judgment*. Trans. Paul Guyer and Eric Matthews. Ed. Paul Guyer. Cambridge: Cambridge University Press, 2000 [1790].

Kant, Immanuel. "A Perpetual Peace: A Philosophical Sketch." In *Philosophical Writings*, trans. Lewis White Beck, ed. Ernst Behler, 270–311. New York: Continuum, 1991.

Kant, Immanuel. "What Is Enlightenment?" In *On History*, trans. Lewis White Beck, 3–10. New York: Macmillan, 1963 [1784].

Kärrström, E. J. *Eighteen Years in South Africa. A Swedish Gold-Digger's Account of His Adventures in the Land of Gold (1877–1896)*. Trans. Ione and Jalmar Rudner. Ed. Ione Rudner. Cape Town: Africana, 2013.

Kattago, Siobhan. "Statelessness, Refugees, and Hospitality: Reading Arendt and Kant in the Twenty-First Century." *New German Critique* 41, no. 1 (2019): 15–40.

Kauffman, Kyle D., and David L. Lindauer. *AIDS and South Africa: The Social Expression of a Pandemic*. New York: Palgrave, 2004.

Kentridge, William, and Rosalind Morris. *Accounts and Drawings from Underground*. Rev. ed. Calcutta: Seagull, 2021.

Keynes, John Maynard. "Auri Sacra Fames (1930)." In *Essays in Persuasion*, 99–101. New York: Classic House, 2009.

Kgame, Steve. "Matanzima's Union Ruling Under Fire." *Rand Daily Mail*, April 25, 1975.

Khoapa, B. A. "Introduction." *Black Review*. Durban: Black Community Programs, 1971.

Khumela, Fhumulani. "Khutsong on the Boil Again." *Sowetan*, September 19, 2014. https://www.pressreader.com/south-africa/sowetan/20140919/281638188415135.

Killingray, David. "Significant Black South Africans in Britain Before 1912: Pan-African Organizations and the Emergence of South Africa's First Black Lawyers." *South African Historical Journal* 64, no. 3 (2012): 393–417.

Kirshner, Joshua, and Comfort Phokela. "Khutsong and Xenophobic Violence: Exploring the Case of the Dog That Didn't Bark." University of Johannesburg, Center for Social Research and Atlantic Philanthropies Foundation, 2010. http://www.atlanticphilanthropies.org/wp-content/uploads/2010/07/5_Kutsong_c.pdf.

"Kitto, Thomas Collingwood." *Biographical Database of Southern African Science*. S2A3. Accessed May 6, 2019. http://www.s2a3.org.za/bio/Biograph_final.php?serial=1544.

Kojève, Alexandre. *Introduction to the Reading of Hegel: Lectures on the 'Phenomenology of Spirit'*. Trans. James. H. Nichols, comp. Raymond Queneau, ed. Allan Bloom. Ithaca, NY: Cornell University Press; 1980 [1947].

Kracauer, Siegfried. *The Salaried Masses: Duty and Distraction in Weimar Germany*. Trans. Quintin Hoare. London: Verso, 1998.

Kracauer, Siegfried. "Those Who Wait." In *The Mass Ornament: Weimar Essays*, trans. Thomas Y. Levin, 129–40. Cambridge, MA: Harvard University Press, 1995.

Kraft, Scott. "South Africans Hear Final Call for 'Yes' on Reform." *Los Angeles Times*, March 17, 1992.

Krause, Lawrence B. *Sequel to Bretton Woods: A Proposal to Reform the World Monetary System*. Washington, DC: Brookings Institute, 1971.

Krauss, Rosalind. *The Optical Unconscious*. Cambridge, MA: MIT Press, 1993.

Krog, Antjie. *A Change of Tongue*. Johannesburg: Random House, 2003.

Krog, Anrtjie. *Jerusalemgangers*. Cape Town: Human and Rousseau, 1985.

Kubicek, Robert V. "The Randlords in 1895: A Reassessment." *Journal of British Studies* 11, no. 2 (1972): 84–103.

Kulwane, Buti. "Civic Competence in Khutsong." Master's thesis, University of the Witwatersrand, 2002.

Kunene, Mazisi. *Anthem of the Decades*. 1981. Reprint, London: Heineman, 2006.

Kunene, Mazisi. "Emergences". In Ntongela Masilela, "The Return of Mazisi Kunene to South Africa: The End of an Intellectual Chapter in Our Literary History." *Ufahamu: A Journal of African Studies* 21, no. 3 (1993): 7–15.

Kunene, Mazisi. "The Song of the Stone Clan." In *The Ancestors and the Sacred Mountain*. Exeter: Heinemann Africa Writers Series, 1982.

Kunene, Mazisi. "White People." In *Two Zulu Poets: Mazisi Kunene and B. W. Vilakazi*, comp. Dike Okoro, 18. Milwaukee, WI: Cissus World, 2015.

Kuper, H., and S. Kaplan. "Voluntary Associations in an Urban Township." *African Studies* 3, no. 4 (1944): 178–86.

Kynoch, Gary. "Controlling the Coolies: Chinese Mineworker and the Struggle for Labor in South Africa 1904–1919. *International Journal of African Historical Studies* 36, no. 2 (2003): 309–29.

Kynoch, Gary. "A Man Among Men: Gender, Identity, and Power in South Africa's Marashea Gangs." *Gender and History* 13, no. 2 (2001): 249–72.

Kynoch, Gary. "*Marashea* on the Mines: Economic, Social and Criminal Networks on the South African Gold Fields, 1947–1999." *Journal of Southern African Studies* 26, no. 1 (2000): 79–103.

Kynoch, Gary. "'Your petitioners are in Mortal Terror': The Violent World of Chinese Mineworkers in South Africa, 1904–1910." *Journal of South African Studies* 31 (2005): 531–46.

Kynoch, Gary. *We Are Fighting the World: A History of the Marashea Gangs in South Africa, 1947–1999*. Athens, OH: Ohio University Press, 2005.

Labatut, Benjamin. *When We Cease to Understand the World*, trans. Adrian Nathan West. New York: New York Review of Books, 2021.

Lacan, Jacques. "The Function and Field of Speech and Language in Psychoanalysis." In *Ecrits*, trans. Bruce Fink, 197–268. New York: Norton, 2006 [1966].

Lacan, Jacques. *The Other Side of Psychoanalysis [L'envers de psychanalyse, 1969–70]: The Seminar of Jacques Lacan*, Book XVII, trans. Richard Grigg, ed. Jacques-Alain Miller. New York: Norton, 2007 [1969–70].

Lacan, Jacques. "Seminar on 'The Purloined Letter.'" In *Ecrits*, trans. Bruce Fink, 6–48. New York: Norton, 2006 [1957].

Lacan, Jacques. "The Unconscious and Repetition." In *The Four Fundamental Concepts of Psycho-Analysis*, Seminar 1, trans. Alan Sheridan, 17–66. New York: Norton, 1998 [1973].

"Landslip at Springs. Treacherous Mine Ground. Two Houses Engulphed. Marvellous [sic] Escape of Inmates. Child Buried Alive." *Rand Daily Mail*, March 22, 1907.

Lazarus, Neil. "Modernism and Modernity: T. W. Adorno and Contemporary White South African Literature." *Cultural Critique* 5 (1986–1987): 131–55.

Ledwaba, P. F. "The Status of Small-Scale and Artisanal Mining Sector in South Africa: Tracking Progress." *Journal of the Southern African Institute of Mining and Metallurgy* 117 (January 2017): 33–40.

Lefevre, Henri. *The Critique of Everyday of Everyday Life*. Trans. John Moore, pref. Michel Trebitsch. New York: Verso, 1991 [1958].

Legassick, Martin. "South Africa: Capital Accumulation and Violence." *Economy and Society* 3, no. 3 (1974): 253–91.

Legassick, Martin. "South Africa: Forced Labour, Industrialization, and Racial Differentiation." In *The Political Economy of Africa*, ed. Richard Harris, 229–70. Boston: Schenkman, 1975.

Lelyveld, Joseph. "South African Gold Boom has Diverse Implications." *New York Times*, June 7, 1981.

Lentsoane, J.M.L. "Black Wednesday" [original Sepedi, "Laboraro le lesoleso"]. Trans. Biki Lepota. In *Stitching a Whirlwind: An Anthology of Southern African Poems and Translations*. Fwd. Gabeba Baderoon, intro. Antjie Krog, 196–205. Oxford: Oxford University Press, 2018.

Leonard, Charles. "Mr Leonard's Evidence Before the Select Committee on British South Africa," in *Papers on the Political Situation in South Africa, 1885–1895*, ed. Charles Leonard, 363–420. London: Arthur Humphreys, 1903.

Leonard, Charles, ed. *Papers on the Political Situation in South Africa, 1885–1895*. London: Arthur Humphreys, 1903.

Leonard, Charles. "The Position of the Uitlanders in the Transvaal, with History of the Franchise. A Statement Prepared for the Committee of the House of Commons Made by Mr. Charles Leonard." In *Papers on the Political Situation in South Africa, 1885–1895*, ed. Charles Leonard, 63–129. London: Arthur Humphreys, 1903.

Leslie, Esther. "Ruin and Rubble in the Arcades." In *Walter Benjamin and the Arcades Project*, ed. Beatrice Hanssen, 87–112. London: Continuum, 2006.

Letcher, Owen. *The Gold Mines of Southern Africa: The History, Technology and Statistics of the Gold Industry*. London: self-published, printed by Waterlow and Sons, 1936.

"Letters of Mr. Lionel Phillips, A Candid Opinion." *The Argus* (Melbourne), May 25, 1986.

Limb, Peter, ed. *The People's Paper: A Centenary History and Anthology of Abanto-Batho*. Johannesburg: Wits University Press, 2012.

Limb, Peter. "Representing the Labouring Classes: African Workers in the South African Nationalist Press, 1900–1960." In *South Africa's Resistance Press: Alternative Voices in the Last Generation Under Apartheid*, ed. Les Switzer and Mohamed Adhikari, 79–127. Athens, OH: Ohio University Press, 2000.

Lipuma, Edward, and Benjamin Lee. *Financial Derivatives and the Globalization of Risk*. Durham, NC: Duke University Press, 2004.

Livingston, Julie. *Self-Devouring Growth: A Planetary Parable as Told from Southern Africa*. Durham, NC: Duke University Press, 2019.

Lorde, Audre. "Who Said It Was Simple." In *Chosen Poems: Old and News*, 49. 1973. Reprint, New York: Norton, 1982.

Luxemburg, Rosa. *The Accumulation of Capital*. Trans. Agnes Schwarzchild. New York: Routledge, 2003 [1913].

Luxemburg, Rosa. "The Mass Strike, the Political Party, and the Trade Unions." In *The Essential Rosa Luxemburg: Reform or Revolution and The Mass Strike*, trans. Patrick Lavin, ed. Helen Scott, 111–82. Chicago: Haymarket, 2008 [1906].

MacArthur, J. S. "The MacArthur-Forrest Method of Gold Extraction." Reprinted from the *Journal of the Society of Chemical Industry* (March 31, 1890): 1–14.

"The McArthur-Forrest [*sic*] Patent." *Johannesburg Times*, August 16, 1895.

Mabuza, Kingdom. "Pupil Thrown Out." *Sowetan*, October 8, 2007.

Macauley, Thomas Babington "Virginia," in *Laws of Ancient Rome*, ed. William J. Rolfe and John C. Rolfe, 88–105. New York: American Book Company, 1888.

Mair, Lucy. *Primitive Government*. Gloucester, MA: Peter Smith, 1975.

Mair, Lucy. "Review of *Black Villagers in an Industrial Society* by Philip Mayer; *Ciskei: A South African Homeland* by Nancy Charton." *African Affairs* 81, no. 323 (1982): 291–93.

Makhanya, Mondli. "No Fly-by-Night Intellectual." *Sunday Times*, August 22, 2010.

Mäki, Harri R. J. "Development of the Supply and Acquisition of Water in South African Towns in 1850–1920." In *Environmental History of Water*, ed. Petri Juuti, Tapio S. Katko, and Heikki Vioerinen, 173–96. London: IWA, 2007.

Malinowski, Bronislaw. "Baloma; The Spirits of the Dead in the Trobriand Islands." In *Magic, Science and Religion and Other Essays*, ed. Robert Redfield, 151–274. New York: Doubleday, 1954.

Mamdani, Mahmood. *Citizen and Subject: Contemporary Africa and the Legacy of Late Colonialism*. Princeton, NJ: Princeton University Press, 1997.

Mandela, Nelson. "Speech from the Dock at the Opening of the Defense Case in the Rivonia Trial." Accessed January 3, 2020. http://db.nelsonmandela.org/speeches/pub_view.asp?pg=item&ItemID=NMS010&txtstr=prepared%20to%20die.

"Manifesto of 1895." In *Papers on the Political Situation in South Africa, 1885–1895*, ed. Charles Leonard, 21–38. London: Arthur Humphreys, 1903.

Manganyi, N. Chabani. *Apartheid and the Making of a Black Psychologist*. Johannesburg: University of Witwatersrand Press, 2016.

Manganyi, N. Chabani. "The Migrants' Burden." In *Looking Through the Keyhole: Dissenting Essays on the Black Experience*, 126–33. 1981. Reprint, Johannesburg: Ravan, 2001.

Mannoni, Octave. "I Know Very Well, But All The Same. . . . ," trans. G. M. Goshgarian. In *Perversion and the Social Relation*, ed. Molly Anne Rothenberg, Dennis Foster, and Slavoj Žižek, 68–92. Durham, NC: Duke University Press, 2003.

Mantashe, Gwede and the National Union of Mineworkers. *Contracting Out: The NUM View*. Johannesburg: National Union of Mineworkers, 1995.

Marin, Louis. "The Frontiers of Utopia." Critical Inquiry 19, no. 3 (Spring 1993): 397–420.

Marin, Louis. "The Frontiers of Utopia" (short version). In *Utopias and the Millennium*, ed. Kumar and S. Bann, 9–16. London: Reaktion Books, 1993.

Marin, Louis. "Reveries: La pratique-fiction utopie (1976). [Reveries: Utopian Fiction-Practice]" *Lectures Traverieres*. Paris: 1992.

Marks, Shula, and Stanley Trapido. "Lord Milner and the South African State." *History Workshop* 8 (1979): 50–80.

Martin, Adam. "Remembering Nixon's Gold-Standard Gamble: Interrupting *Bonanza*." *The Atlantic*, August 15, 2011. https://www.theatlantic.com/politics/archive/2011/08/nixon-gold -standard-gamble-interrupting-bonanza/354136/.

Martin, Emily. *Flexible Bodies: Tracking Immunity in American Culture—From the Days of Polio to the Age of AIDS*. Boston: Beacon, 1995.

Marx, Karl. *Capital*. Vol. 1, intro. Ernst Mandel, trans. Ben Fowkes. London: Penguin, 1976 [1867].

Marx, Karl. "Contribution to the Critique of Hegel's Philosophy of Law [*Recht*]." In *Collected Works*. Vol. 3., trans. Jack Cohen et al., 175–87. New York: International, 2005,

Marx, Karl. *Contribution to the Critique of Political Economy*, ed. Maurice Dobb. New York: International, 1970 [1859].

Marx, Karl. *The Eighteenth Brumaire of Louis Bonaparte*, trans. Ben Fowkes. In *Surveys from Exile*, ed. David Fernach, 143–249. New York: Vintage, 1974 [1952].

Marx, Karl, *Grundrisse*. Trans. Martin Nicolaus. New York: Penguin, 1993.

Masilela, Ntongela. "African Intellectual and Literary Responses to Colonial Modernity in South Africa." In *Grappling with the Beast: Indigenous Southern African Responses to Colonialism, 1840–1930*, ed. Peter Limb, Norman Etherington, and Peter Midgley, 245–75. Leiden: Brill, 2010.

Masilela, Ntongela. *An Outline of the New African Movement in South Africa*. Trenton, NJ: Africa World, 2013.

Masilela, Ntongela. "The Return of Mazisi Kunene to South Africa: The End of an Intellectual Chapter in Our Literary History." *Ufahamu: A Journal of African Studies* 21, no. 3 (1993): 7–15.

Masondo, Themba. "The Sociology of Upward Social Mobility Among COSATU Shop Stewards." In *COSATU: Contested Legacy*. Ed. Sakhela Buhlungu and Malehoko Tshoaedi, 110–31. Johannesburg: HSRC, 2120.

Matanzima, Kaizer. *Independence My Way*. Pretoria: Foreign Affairs Association, 1976.

Matlou, Joel. "Man Against Himself." *Staffrider* (November/December 1979): 24–28.

Matthews, Joe (Vincent Joseph Gaobakwe). "Interview, 2009." Historical Papers Research Archive, University of the Witwatersrand. Wits Oral History Project, ZA HPRA A3402-B-B58. Accessed July 21, 2024: http://historicalpapers-atom.wits.ac.za/uploads/r/historical-papers -research-archive-library-university-of-witwatersrand/7/7/7/7771422e72970403d8da320c319 03296527a034af17d6095fd47c242e727f249/A3402-B58-001-jpeg.pdf

Mauss, Marcel. *A General Theory of Magic*. New York: Routledge, 2001 [1902].

Mauss, Marcel. *The Gift*. Expanded ed. Selected, annot., and trans. Jane Guyer. Chicago: Hau Books, 2016 [1925].

Mavungu, Eddy Mazembo. "Frontiers of Power and Prosperity: Explaining Provincial Boundary Disputes in Postapartheid South Africa." *African Studies Review* 59, no. 2 (2016): 183–208.

Mayaba, Jabulani. "Interview, 2012." Historical Papers Research Archive, University of the Witwatersrand. Wits Oral History Project, ZA HPRA A3402-B-B48. Accessed July 25, 2022, thttp://historicalpapers-atom.wits.ac.za/b48-18.

Mayekiso, Mzwanele. *Township Politics: Civic Struggles for a New South Africa*. New York: Monthly Review, 1996.

Mayer, Philip, ed. *Black Villagers in an Industrial Society*. Cape Town: Oxford University Press, 1980.

Mayer, Philip. "The Origin and Decline of Two Rural Resistance Ideologies." In *Black Villagers in an Industrialized Society*, 1–80. Cape Town: Oxford University Press, 1980.

Mayer, Philip. *Townsmen or Tribesmen: Conservatism and the Process of Urbanization in a South African City*. Cape Town: Oxford University Press, 1971.

Mbembe, Achille, *Necropolitics*. Trans. Steven Corcoran. Durham, NC: Duke University Press, 2019 [2016].

Mbembe, Achille. "The Aesthetics of Superfluity." *Public Culture* 16, no. 3 (2004): 373–405.

Mbembe, Achilel. *On the Postcolony*. Trans. A. M. Berrett et al. Berkeley: University of California Press, 2001.

McAllister, P. A. "Work, Homestead, and the Shades: Home Friend Networks in the Social Life of Black Migrant Workers in a Gold Mine Hostel." In *Black Villagers*, ed. Philip Mayer, 205–53. Cape Town: Oxford University Press, 1980.

McCann, Andrew. "Melancholy and the Masses: Siegfried Kracauer and the Media Concept." *Discourse* 43, no. 1 (Winter 2021): 150–70.

McCann, Andrew. "Walter Benjamin's Sex Work: Prostitution and the State of Exception." *Textual Practice* 28, no. 1 (2014): 99–120.

McCulloch, Jock. "Women Mining Asbestos in South Africa: 1893–1980." *Journal of Southern African Studies* 29, no. 2 (2003): 413–33.

Mc Lennan, Anne. "The Delivery Paradox." In *The Politics of Service Delivery*, eds. Mc Lennan, Anne and Barry Munslow, 19–42. Johannesburg: Wits University Press, 2009.

McNamara, J. K. "Inter-Group Violence Among Black Employees on South African Gold Mines, 1974–1986." *South African Sociological Review* 1, no. 1 (1988): 3–38.

McQuoid-Mason, David. "Disclosing the HIV Status of Deceased Persons—Ethical and Legal Implications." *South African Medical Journal* 97, no.10 (2007): 920–23.

McRobbie, Angela. *Postmodernism and Popular Culture*. London: Routledge, 1994.

Mda, Zakes. *The Heart of Redness*. New York: Picador, 2003.

Meillassoux, Claude. *Maidens, Meal and Money*. Cambridge: Cambridge University Press, 1975.

Memmi, Albert. *The Colonizer and the Colonized*. Trans. Howard Greenfeld. Boston: Beacon, 1966 [1957].

Mendelsohn, Richard. "Blainey and the Jameson Raid: The Debate Renewed." *Journal of Southern African Studies* 6, no. 2 (1980): 157–70.

"Merafong's Voters Ready for Election." *Carletonville Herald*, May 26, 2024. https://www.citizen.co.za/carletonville-herald/?p=75290.

Mgqwetho, Nontsizi. "Alas! Africa, You Fade Into the Horizon!" [*Yeha Watshona Afrika! ELundini*] trans. Jeff Opland and Pamela Maseko. In *The People's Paper: A Centenary History and Anthology of Abanto-Batho*, ed. Peter Limb, 410–16. Johannesburg: Wits University Press, 2012.

Mgqwetho, Nontsizi "Chizama the Poet" [*Umbongi u Chizama*], trans. Jeff Opland. In *Nation's Bounty: The Xhosa Poetry of Nontsizi Mgqwethu*, ed. Jeff Opland, 2–5. Johannesburg: Wits University Press, 2007.

Mgqwetho, Nontsizi. "Go and We'll Follow You," trans. Jeff Opland. In *The People's Paper: A Centenary History and Anthology of Abanto-Batho*, ed. Peter Limb, 208–9. Johannesburg: Wits University Press, 2007.

Mgqwetho, Nontsizi. "A Long Lying-In, Then the Python Uncoils and Leaves" [*Yacombuluka! Inamba u 1923 ebisoloko ifukamele ukunduluka*], trans. Jeff Opland. In *Nation's Bounty: The Xhosa Poetry of Nontsizi Mgqwethu*, ed. Jeff Opland, 64–69. Johannesburg: Wits University Press, 2007.

Mgqwetho, Nontsizi. "Listen, Compatriots" [*Pulapulani! Makowetu*], trans. Jeff Opland. In *Nation's Bounty: The Xhosa Poetry of Nontsizi Mgqwethu*, ed. Jeff Opland, 76–81. Johannesburg: Wits University Press, 2007.

Mgqwetho, Nontsizi. "Mama's Death" [*Umpanga ka Mama*], trans. Jeff Opland. In *Nation's Bounty: The Xhosa Poetry of Nontsizi Mgqwethu*, ed. Jeff Opland, 42–49. Johannesburg: Wits University Press, 2007.

Mgqwetho, Nontsizi. "Unity, Black Workers!" [*Imanyano! Basebenzi Abantsunda*], trans. Jeff Opland. In *The Nation's Bounty: The Xhosa Poetry of Nontsizi Mgqwethu*, ed. Jeff Opland, 100–105. Johannesburg: Wits University Press, 2007.

Mgqwetho, Nontsizi. "The Vale of Tears" [*Iziko Ie Nyembezi*], trans. Jeff Opland In *Nation's Bounty: The Xhosa Poetry of Nontsizi Mgqwethu*, ed. Jeff Opland, 30–37. Johannesburg: Wits University Press, 2007.

Michaels, Walter Benn. *The Gold Standard and the Logic of Naturalism*. Berkeley: University of California Press, 1987.

Mills, Patricia J. "Hegel's Antigone." *Owl of Minerva* 17, no. 2 (1986): 131–52.

Minerals Council of South Africa. "Women in Mining in South Africa." Johannesburg, 2020.

Minnaar, A. de. V. *An Analysis of the Scope and Extent of Conflict in South African with Specific Reference to the Identification of High Conflict Areas*. Pretoria: Centre for Socio-political Analysis, Human Sciences Research Council, 1994.

"The Mission Field. "Missions In South Africa." *Christian Express*, May 2, 1898, 69.

Mitchell, W. J. T. *Iconology: Image, Text, Ideology*. Chicago: University of Chicago, 1987.

"(A) Modern Woman: Innocence up to Date." *Punch Magazine*, May 18, 1904, 357.

Mkhulisi, Mfundekelwa. "Kids at Taung Camp Threatened." *Sowetan*, August 17, 2007. https://infoweb.newsbank.com/apps/news/document-view?p=WORLDNEWS&docref=news/132F2374CFFE21A8.

Mogoba, Stanley. "Cement." In *Voices from Within: Black Poetry from Southern Africa*, ed. Michael Chapman and Achmat Dangor, 87. Johannesburg: A. D. Donker, 1982.

Mogotsi, Isaac Mpho. "Naledi Pandoor and Joe Matthews." *Politics Web*, January 17, 2012. https://www.politicsweb.co.za/news-and-analysis/naledi-pandor-and-joe-matthews.

Mohamed, Shiraaz. "Police Stop Violent Kagiso Residents' Group from Hunting Down Zama Zamas." *Daily Maverick*, August 4, 2022.

Moiloa, Molema. "Youth in Khutsong, South Africa: Nostalgia for a Different Political Present." *Peace and Conflict: Journal of Peace Psychology* 18, no. 3 (2012): 329–40.

Mokwena, Steve. "The Era of the Jackrollers: Contextualising the Rise of Youth Gangs in Soweto and Khutsong." Paper presented at the Centre for the Study of Violence and Reconciliation, Seminar No. 7. Johannesburg: University of the Witwatersrand, 1991.

Molamu, Louis. *Tsotsi-taal: A Dictionary of the Language of Sophiatown*. Pretoria: Unisa, 2003.

Moodie, T. Dunbar. *Going for Gold: Men, Mines and Migration*. Berkeley: University of California Press, 1994.

Moodie, T. Dunbar. "Ethnic Violence on South African Gold Mines." In "Political Violence in Southern Africa." Special issue, *Journal of Southern African Studies*, 18, no. 3 (1992): 584–613.

Moodie, T. Dunbar. "Managing the 1987 Mineworkers' Strike." *Journal of Southern African History* 35, no. 1 (2009): 45–64.

More, Thomas. *Utopia*. Intro. Richard Marius. 1516. Reprint, London: Everyman, 1981.

"More Bismarckiana." *The Journal. Supplement to the Journal*, September 6, 1898, 6.

Morris, Rosalind C. "After de Brosses: Fetishism, Translation, Comparativism, Critique." In *The Returns of Fetishism: Charles de Brosses and the Afterlives of an Idea*, with a translation of *The Worship of Fetish Gods*, by Daniel H. Leonard, 133–319. Chicago: University of Chicago, 2017.

Morris, Rosalind C. "Chronicling Deaths Foretold: The Testimony of the Corpse in De-Industrializing South Africa." In *Reverberations: Violence Across Time and Space*, ed. Yael Navaro, Zerrin Ozlem Biner, Alice von Bieberstein, and Seda Altug, 33–61. Philadelphia: University of Pennsylvania Press, 2021.

Morris, Rosalind C. "Crowds and Powerlessness: Reading //kabbo and Canetti with Derrida in (South) Africa." In *Demenageries [Animals]*, ed. Anne Berger and Marta Segarra, 167–212. Amsterdam: Rodopi, 2011.

Morris, Rosalind C. "Conspiracies of Theory: Of Gold in the Shadow of Deindustrialization." In *Conspiracy/Theory*, eds. Joseph Masco and Lisa Wedeen, 235–63. Chicago: University of Chicago Press, 2024.

Morris, Rosalind C. "Dialect and Dialectic in 'The Working Day' of Marx's *Capital*." In "Music, Sound, Value," ed. Jairo Moreno and Gavin Steingo. Special issue, *Boundary 2* 43, no. 1 (February 2016): 219–48.

Morris, Rosalind C. "In the Name of Trauma: Notes on Testimony, Truth-Telling and the Secret of Literature in South Africa." *Comparative Literature Studies* 48, no. 3 (2011): 388–416.

Morris, Rosalind C. "Learning to Learn: Linking Marikana and Labour History." *South African Labour Bulletin* 37, no. 2 (Summer 2013): 18–21.

Morris, Rosalind C. "Mediation, the Political Task: Between Language and Violence in Contemporary South Africa," *Current Anthropology* 58, Supplement 17 (February 2017): 123–134.

Rosalind C. Morris, "The Miner's Ear." *Transition* 98 (2008): 96–115.

Morris, Rosalind C. "The Mute and the Unspeakable: Political Subjectivity, Violent Crime, and 'the Sexual Thing' in a South African Mining Community." In *Law and Disorder in the Post-colony*, ed. Jean Comaroff and John Comaroff, 57–101. Chicago: University of Chicago Press, 2006.

Morris, Rosalind C. "Rush/Panic/Rush: Speculations on the Value of Life and Death in South Africa's Age of Aids," *Public Culture* 21, no.2 (2008): 199–231.

Morris, Rosalind C. "Shadow and Impress: Ethnography, Cinema and the Task of Writing History in the Space of South Africa's De-Industrialization," *History and Theory*, Theme Issue 56 (December 2018): 102–125.

Morris, Rosalind C. "Style, *Tsotsi*-style and *Tsotsitaal*: The Histories, Politics and Aesthetics of a South African Figure." *Social Text* 28, no. 2 (2010): 85–112.

Morris, Rosalind C. "*Ursprüngliche Akkumulation*: The Secret History of an Originary Mis-translation." In "Marxism, Communism, and Translation," ed. Nergis Ertürk and Özge Serin. Special issue, *Boundary 2* 43, no. 3 (August 2016): 29–77.

Morrison, Toni. *Jazz*. New York: Penguin, 1992.

Morphet, Tony. "Brushing History Against the Grain: Oppositional Discourse in South Africa." In Richard Turner, *The Eye of the Needle*, 203–20. Calcutta: Seagull, 2015.

Morphet, Tony. "The Intellectual Reach of *The Eye of the Needle*." In Richard Turner, *The Eye of the Needle*, 221–47. Calcutta: Seagull, 2015.

Mqhayi, S.E.K. *Lawsuit of the Twins*, trans. Thokozile Mabeqa. Cape Town: Oxford South Africa, 2018 [1914].

Mrázek, Rudolf. *Engineers of Happy Land: Technology and Nationalism in a Colony*. Princeton, NJ: Princeton University Press, 2002.

Mtshali, Oswald. "Black Poetry in South Africa: Its Origin and Dimension." *Iowa Review* 7, no. 2/3 (1976): 199–205.

Mtshali, Mbuyiseni Oswald. "The Detribalised." In *The Lava of this Land: South African Poetry 1960–1996*, ed. Denis Hirson, 85–88. Evanston: TriQuarterly, 1997.

Mtshali, Mbuyiseni Oswald. "Mtshali on Mtshali." *Bolt* 7 (1973).

Mthimkulu, Oupa Thando. "Nineteen Seventy-Six." *Staffrider* 7, nos. 3 and 4 (1988): 173.

Mudimbe, V. Y. *The Invention of Africa: Gnosis, Philosophy and the Order of Knowledge*. Bloomington: Indiana University Press, 1988.

Muholi, Zanele. *Faces + Phases 2006–14*. Göttingen, Germany: Steidel, 2014.

Muholi, Zanele. *Zanele Muholi: Only Half The Picture.* Cape Town: Michael Stevenson, 2006.

Mulvey, Laura. "Visual Pleasure and Narrative Cinema." *Screen* 16, no. 3 (1975): 6–18.

Mutemeri, Nellie, and Francis W. Peterson. "Small-Scale Mining in South Africa: Past, Present and Future." *Natural Resources Forum* 26, no. 4 (2002): 286–92.

Nash, Andrew. "The Moment of Western Marxism in South Africa." *Comparative Studies in South Asia, Africa and the Middle East,* 19, no.1 (1999): 66–81.

Nash, June. *We Eat the Mines, the Mines Eat Us.* Baltimore, MD: Johns Hopkins University Press, 1980.

"National Poverty Lines." Stats SA. July 31, 2018. http://www.statssa.gov.za/publications/P03101 /P03102018.pdf.

"Native Women's Brave Stand." *Abantu-Batho,* July?, 191. In *The People's Paper: A Centenary History and Anthology of Abanto-Batho,* ed. Peter Limb, 343–44. Johannesburg: Wits University Press, 2012.

Ndebele, Njabulo. *The Cry of Winnie Mandela.* Cape Town: David Phillip, 2003.

Ndebele, Njabulo. "Guilt and Atonement: Unmasking History for the Future." *New Nation* (Johannesburg), December 1991.

Ndebele, Njabulo. *Thinking of Brenda: The Desire to Be.* 1996. Reprint, Vlaeberg, South Africa: Chimurenga, 2009.

Ndhlovu, Lewis, Catherine Searle, Johannes van Dam, Yodwa Mzaidume, Bareng Rasego, and Solly Moema. "Reducing the Transmission of HIV and Sexually Transmitted Infections in a Mining Community: Findings from the Carletonville Mothusimpilo Intervention Project: 1998 to 2001." Horizons Final Report, Population Council, Washington, DC, 2005.

Ndzuta, Refilwe. "Interview, 2010." Historical Papers Research Archive, University of the Witwatersrand. Wits Oral History Project, ZA HPRA A3402-B-B108. Accessed July 29, 2022. http://historicalpapers-atom.wits.ac.za/b108-3.

Nelson, Harold, ed. *South Africa: A Country Study.* Washington, DC: U.S. Government, Foreign Area Studies, American University, 1981.

New Dictionary of South African Biography. Vol. 1, ed. E. J. Verwey. Pretoria: HSRC, 1995.

"The New Zion Jewish Trust Floated." *De Express en Oranjevrijstaatsch* [The Orange Free State Express], March 23, 1899, 8.

Ngai, Mae. "Trouble on the Rand: The Chinese Question on the Rand and the Apogee of White Settlerism." *International Labour and Working Class History* 91 (2017): 59–78.

Ngwane, Zolani. "'Christmas Time' and the Struggles for the Household in the Countryside: Rethinking the Cultural Geography of Migrant Labour in South Africa." *Journal of Southern African Studies* 29, no. 3. (September 2003): 681–99.

Nhlengetwa, Kgothatso, and Kim Hein. "Zama Zama Mining in the Durban Deep/Roodepoort Area of Johannesburg, South Africa: An Invasive or Alternative Livelihood?" *Extractive Industries and Society* 2, no. 1 (2014): 1–3.

Nicholls, Brendon. "Decolonization and Popular Poetics: From Soweto Poetry to Diasporic Solidarity." *English in Africa* 45, no. 3 (2018): 41–78.

Niehaus, Isak. "Witchcraft and the South African Bantustans: Evidence from Bushbuckridge." *South African Historical Journal* 41, no.1 (March 2012): 48–61.

Nikolaus, Martin. "Introduction." In *Grundrisse,* trans. and intro. Martin Nikolaus, 83–111. New York: Penguin and New Left Books, 1973.

Nite, Dhiraj Kumar. "Refashioning Women's Self and Mining Homemakers and Producers on the South African Mines, 1976–2011." *Essays on Social History and the History of Social Movements* 54 (2015): 7–36.

Nixon, Richard. "The Challenge of Peace." Presidential address, August 15, 1971. https://www .presidency.ucsb.edu/documents/address-the-nation-outlining-new-economic-policy-the -challenge-peace.

Njilo, Nonkululeko. "Krugersdorp Rapes—Frustration as Media Blocked from Court, Police Deny DNA Backlogs to Blame for Delays." *Daily Maverick,* September 30, 2022.

Njilo, Nonkululeko. "Krugersdorp Victim's Ordeal: 'I Closed My Eyes, Crying. Moments Later, I Was Also Raped, by Three Men.'" *Daily Maverick*, August 5, 2022.

Norishi, Norimitsu. "Honoring a Filmmaker in the Shadow of Apartheid." *New York Times*, July 29, 2014. https://www.nytimes.com/2014/07/30/world/africa/honoring-a-filmmaker-in-the-shadow-of-apartheid.html.

"Notice No. 47/1949, September 30, 1949. Peri-Urban Health Board Pretoria." *Rand Daily Mail*, October 12, 1949, 3.

Nuttall, Sarah. "Stylizing the Self: The Y Generation in Rosebank, Johannesburg." *Public Culture* 16, no. 3 (2004): 430–52.

O'Brien, Anthony. *Against Normalization; Writing Radical Democracy in South Africa*. Durham, NC: Duke University Press, 2001.

Official Proceedings of the Democratic National Convention Held in Chicago, Illinois, July 7, 8, 9, 10, and 11, 1896 (Logansport, Indiana, 1896). Reprinted in *The Annals of America*. Vol. 12, *1895–1904: Populism, Imperialism, and Reform*, 100–105. Chicago: Encyclopedia Britannica, Inc., 1968.

Okoro, Dike. "Introduction." In *Two Zulu Poets*, viii–xxi. Milwaukee, WI: Cissus World, 2015.

O'Meara, Dan. "The 1946 African Mine Workers' Strike and the Political Economy of South Africa." *Journal of Commonwealth and Comparative Politics* 13, no. 2 (1975): 146–73.

"Operation Vala Umgodi Clamping Down on Illegal Mining in Matholesville, Roodepoort." *Truck and Freight News*, February 2, 2024.

Opland, Jeff. "Abantu-Batho and the Xhosa poets." In *The People's Paper: A Centenary History and Anthology of Abanto-Batho*, ed. Peter Limb, 201–25. Johannesburg: Wits University Press, 2012.

Opland, Jeff, ed. *The Nation's Bounty: The Xhosa Poetry of Nontsizi Mgqwetho*. Johannesburg: Wits University Press, 2007.

Orpen Neil and H.J. Martin. *Salute the Sappers*. Vol.8, pt.2. Johannesburg: The Sappers Association, 1981.

Ovid. *Metamorphoses*. Trans. Arthur Golding. Ed. Madeleine Forey. Baltimore: Johns Hopkins University Press, 2002 [c8AD].

Oxley, John. *Down Where No Lion Walked: The Story of Western Deep Levels*. Johannesburg: Southern Book Publishers, 1989.

Pachal, Bridglal. "Indentured Chinese Immigrant Labour on the Witwatersrand Goldfields." *India Quarterly* 21, no. 1(1965): 58–82.

Parbhaker-Fox, Anita. "Treasure from Trash: How Mining Waste Can Be Mined a Second Time." *The Conversation*, June 28, 2016. https://theconversation.com/treasure-from-trash-how-mining-waste-can-be-mined-a-second-time-59667.

Parfitt, Steven. "The Justice Department Campaign Against the IWW, 1917–1920." University of Washington. Accessed June 25, 2020. https://depts.washington.edu/iww/justice_dept.shtml#_edn9.

Parker, Andrew. "The Poetry of the Future." In "Conference Debates. Untiming the Nineteenth Century: Temporality and Periodization," ed. Emily Apter. *PMLA* 124, no. 1 (2009): 273–88.

Parliament of South Africa, "Minutes of the Proceedings of the National Council of Provinces," December 14, 2005, 127pp

"Pass Legislation, 1889." In *Outlook on a Century*, eds. Francis Wilson and Dominique Perrot, 123–25. Cape Town: Lovedale Press and Spro-cas, 1974 [1889].

"The Pass System." In *Outlook on a Century*, eds. Francis Wilson and Dominique Perrot, 221–24. Cape Town: Lovedale Press and Spro-cas, 1974 [1907]), 221–24.

Pateman, Carol. *The Sexual Contract*. Palo Alto, CA: Stanford University Press, 1988.

"Patent Law." In "Report of The Volksraads." *Johannesburg Times*, August 13, 1895.

Peile, S. J. B., and W. S. van der Merwe. "Hedge Funds in South Africa—The Investment Case." Paper presented to the Actuarial Society of South Africa, Cape Town, October 13–14, 2004.

Peires, J. B. *The Dead Will Arise: Nongqawuse and the Great Cattle-Killing of 1856-7*. Bloomington: Indiana University Press, 1989.

Phillips, Lionel. *All That Glittered: Selected Correspondence of Lionel Phillips, 1890–1924*. Ed. Maryna Fraser and Alan Jeeves. Cape Town: Oxford University Press, 1977.

Phillips, Lionel. "Letter to Alfred Beit, June 16, 1894." In *All that Glittered: Selected Correspondence of Lionel Phillips, 1890–1924*, ed. Maryna Fraser and Alan Jeeves, 78. Cape Town: Oxford University Press, 1977.

Phillips, Lionel. "Letter to Julius Wernher, May 28, 1894." In *All That Glittered: Selected Correspondence of Lionel Phillips, 1890–1924*, ed. Maryna Fraser and Alan Jeeves, 77. Cape Town: Oxford University Press, 1977.

Philp, Rowan "The Khutsong Rebellion." *Sunday Times* (Johannesburg, South Africa). March 15, 2009.

Pielsticker, Carl Maria. "Application for Letters Patent for Improvements in the Extraction of Gold and Silver from Ores, December 14, 1893." In A. Scheidel, *The Cyanide Process: Its Practical Application and Economical Results*, 129–32. Bulletin No. 5. Sacramento: California State Mining Bureau, 1894.

Pietz, William. *The Problem of the Fetish*. Ed. Francesco Pellizzi, Stefanos Geroulanos, and Ben Kafka. Chicago: University of Chicago Press, 2022.

Pillay, Surren. "Translating 'South Africa': Race, Colonialism and Challenges of Critical Thought after Apartheid." In *Re-Imagining the Social in South Africa: Critique, Theory and Post-apartheid Society*, eds. Heather Jacklin and Peter Vale, 225–67. Durban: University of Kwa-Zulu-Natal Press, 2009.

Pisani, Elizabeth. "AIDS Into the Twenty-First Century: Some Critical Considerations." *Reproductive Health Matters* 8, no. 15 (May, 2000): 63–76.

Pistor, Katharina. *The Code of Capital*. Princeton, NJ: Princeton University Press, 2019.

Plaatje, Solomon (Sol) Tshekisho. "Article." *Bechuana Gazette*, December 13, 1902. In *Sol Plaatje: Selected Writings*, ed. Brian Willan, 64–65. Johannesburg: Witwatersrand University Press, 1996.

Plaatje, Solomon (Sol) Tshekisho. "The Colour Bar." *Diamond Fields Advertiser*, March 10, 1925. In *Sol Plaatje: Selected Writings*, ed. Brian Willan, 343–46. Johannesburg: Witwatersrand University Press, 1996.

Plaatje, Solomon (Sol) Tshekisho. "Equal Rights." *Bechuana Gazette*, September 13, 1902. In *Sol Plaatje: Selected Writings*, ed. Brian Willan, 61–64. Johannesburg: Witwatersrand University Press, 1996.

Plaatje, Solomon (Sol) Tshekisho. "The Leadership Cult from Another Angle." *Umteteli wa Bantu*. In *Sol Plaatje: Selected Writings*, ed. Brian Willan, 346–48. Johannesburg: Witwatersrand University Press, 1996.

Plaatje, Solomon (Sol) Tshekisho. *Mhudi*. 1930. Reprint, London: Heinemann, 1982.

Plaatje, Solomon (Sol) Tshekisho. "Native Affairs: After Four Years?" In *Sol Plaatje: Selected Writings*, ed. Brian Willan, 313–20. Johannesburg: Witwatersrand University Press, 1996.

"The Place of Wailing." *Natal Witness*. Pietermaritzburg, March 22, 1850, 3.

Pliny, the Elder. *Natural History*, Book XXXV. Trans. Henry Rackham. Cambridge, MA: Harvard University Press, 1952 [AD c.77-79].

Pohlandt-McCormick, Helena. "Controlling Woman: Winnie Mandela and the 1976 Soweto Uprising." *International Journal of African Historical Studies* 33, no. 3 (2000): 585–614.

Polanyi, Michael. *Personal Knowledge: Towards a Post-Critical Philosophy*. Chicago: University of Chicago Press, 1974.

Posel, Deborah. *The Making of Apartheid, 1948–1961: Conflict and Compromise*. Oxford: Clarendon Press, 1991.

Posel, Deborah. "The Apartheid Project: 1948–1970." In *The Cambridge History of South Africa*, ed. Robert Ross, Annie Kelk Mager, and Bill Nasson, 319–68. Cambridge: Cambridge University Press, 2011.

Posel, Deborah."Sex, Death, and the State of the Nation: Reflections on the Politicization of Sexuality in Post-Apartheid South Africa." *Africa: Journal of the International African Institute* 75, no. 2 (2005): 125–153.

Poulantzas, Nicos. *State, Power, Socialism*. London: Verso, 1978.

"Poverty on the Rise in South Africa." Stats SA. August 22, 2017. http://www.statssa.gov.za/?p=10334.

"Prayers for the Mine." *Rand Daily Mail*, October 30, 1968, 5.

"The 'Prophet of Zion' Makes Many Converts in Australia." *Rand Daily Mail*, Feb 3, 1903, 7.

"Prospects Materially Enhanced by Devaluation, West Witwatersrand Areas, Ltd." *Rand Daily Mail*, November 11, 1949.

Radebe, Special (David). "Interview (undated, circa 2009–2012)." Historical Papers Research Archive, University of the Witwatersrand. Wits Oral History Project, ZA HPRA A3402-B-B133, 2. Accessed July 26, 2022, http://historicalpapers-atom.wits.ac.za/uploads/r/historical-papers-research-archive-library-university-of-witwatersrand/e/d/o/edo20e73946abfa347df7a404cc727bcc7db5c19a5028ac3c3b153c02aa95648/A3402-B133-001-jpeg.pdf.

Ragan, Fred. "Obscenity or Politics: Tom Watson, Anti-Catholicism and the Department of Justice." *Georgia Historical Quarterly* 70, no. 1 (1986): 17–46.

Rampolokeng, Lesego. "The Word or the Head." In *The New Century of South African Poetry*, ed. Michael Chapman, 456. Jeppestown: Jonathan Ball, 2002.

Rampolokeng, Lesego. "Writing the Ungovernable." *New Coin* 49, no. 1 (2013): 92–102.

Rasool, Ciraj. "The Rise of Heritage and the Reconstruction of History in South Africa." *Kronos* 26 (2000): 1–21.

Rancière, Jacques. *The Politics of Aesthetics: The Distribution of the Sensible*. Trans. Gabriel Rockhill. New York: Continuum, 2004 [2000].

"Record Output, Revenue, but . . . Gold Mine Profits Hit by Premiums Sale Fall." *Rand Daily Mail*, February 12, 1971.

"Report of the Ordinary General Meeting of Shareholders, The Ryan Nigel G. M. and Estate C., Limited." *Rand Daily Mail*, December 16, 1947.

"Report on the Company Meetings, West Witwatersrand Areas, Ltd." *Rand Daily Mail*, November 30, 1950.

Resch, Robert Paul. *Althusser and the Renewal of Marxist Social Theory*. Berkeley: University of California Press, 1992.

"Residents at Bank to take Legal Action." *Rand Daily Mail*, December 22, 1969, 4.

"Ruin of Native Girls. How they Flock to the Rand. A Social Evil. Mrs. Maxeke on Remedial Measures. White Landlords Who Ask No Questions." *Rand Daily Mail*, July 14, 1922, 5.

Richardson, Peter. *Chinese Mine Labour in the Transvaal*. London: MacMillan, 1982.

Richardson, Peter. "The Recruiting of Chinese Labour for the South African Gold Mines, 1903–1908." *Journal of African History* 18, no. 1 (1977): 85–108.

Richardson, Peter, and Jean-Jacques van Helten. "The Development of the South African Mining Industry, 1895–1918." *Economic History Review* 27, no. 3 (1984): 319–40.

"Rival Messiahs and Elijah." *Mafeking Mail and Protectorate Guardian*, April 16, 1904, 3–4.

Robins, Steven. "How Poo Became a Political Issue." *Cape Times*, July 2, 2013. https://www.iol.co.za/dailynews/opinion/how-poo-became-a-political-issue-1541126#.Ukv1KYYmvNE.

Robinson, Cedric. *Black Marxism: The Making of the Black Radical Tradition*. Foreword by Robin Kelley. Chapel Hill, NC: University of North Caroline Press, 2000 [1983].

Ronell, Avital. *The Telephone Book*. Lincoln: University of Nebraska Press, 1991.

Rosenberg, Greg. "Battle Is on Against Legacy of Apartheid." *The Militant* 60, no. 8. February 26, 1996.

Rukeyser, Muriel. "The Book of the Dead." In *US 1*, 66–72. New York: Covici Friede, 1938.

Rukeyser, Muriel. "The Road." In *US 1*, 9. New York: Covici Friede, 1938.

Rukeyser, Muriel. "Mearl Blankenship." In *The Book of the Dead*, 24–26. New York: Covici Friede, 1938.

Rukeyser, Muriel. "Murmurs from the Earth of this Land." In *Body of Waking: Poems*, 85. New York: Harper, 1958.

Rukeyser, Muriel. "On Money and the Past." In *Body of Waking: Poems*, 34–35. New York: Harper, 1958.

Rukeyser, Muriel. "The Speed of Darkness." In *The Speed of Darkness*, 111. New York: Random House, 1968.

Rukeyser, Muriel. "The Usable Truth." *Poetry* 58, no. 4 (July 1941): 206–9.

Ruskin, John. "The Storm-Cloud of the Nineteenth Century. Two Lectures Delivered at the London Society. February 4th and 11th, 1884." In *The Complete Works of John Ruskin*, vol. 34, ed. E.T. Cook and Alexander Wedderburn, 4–80. London: George Allen, 1908.

Ryan, Dermot. "The Future of an Allusion: 'Poïesis' in Karl Marx's 'The Eighteenth Brumaire of Louis Bonaparte.'" *SubStance* 41, no. 3 (2012): 127–46.

"S. A. Parliaments." *Johannesburg Times*, July 26, 1895.

Saghafi, Kas. "Dying Alive." *Mosaic* 48, no. 3 (2015): 15–26.

Salle, Gregory. "How We Got From Prisons Located in Cities to City-Like Prisons: A Relationship between Metamorphoses and Contradictions." *Politix* 97, no. 1 (2012): 75–98.

Sandile, Emma. "Emma Sandile, Letters and Land Submission." In *Women Writing Africa: The Southern Region*, ed. M. J. Daymond et al., 92–96. New York: Feminist Press, 2003.

Savage, Michael. "The Imposition of Pass Laws on the African Population in South Africa, 1916–1984." *African Affairs* 85, no. 339 (April 1986): 181–205.

Schapera, Isaac. *Married Life in An African Tribe*. New York: Sheridan, 1941.

Scheidel, A. *The Cyanide Process: Its Practical Application and Economical Results*. Bulletin No. 5. Sacramento: California State Mining Bureau, 1894.

Schmitt, Carl. *The Concept of the Political*. Trans. George Schwab. Chicago: University of Chicago Press, 2007 [1932]

Scott, James. *Weapons of the Weak: Everyday Forms of Peasant Resistance*. New Haven, CT: Yale University Press, 1987.

Seekoei, Kamogelo. "Student Leader Dies Heartbroken." *Sowetan*, December 21, 2006.

"Select Committee Report." In *Papers on the Political Situation in South Africa, 1885–1895*, ed. Charles Leonard, 427–58. London: Arthur Humphreys, 1903.

Senatore, Mauro. "The Drive to Drive: The Deconstruction of the Freudian *Trieb*." *Derrida Today* 12, no. 1 (2019): 59–79.

Serote, Wally Mongane. "Ofay-Watchers, Throbs-Phase." In *Yakhal'inkomo*, 50–51. Johannesburg: Ad Donker, 1972.

Serrero, A., and C. Mallela. "A Resolution: Native Women Pass Law." *Abantu-Batho*, December 6, 1917. In *The People's Paper: A Centenary History and Anthology of Abanto-Batho*, ed. Peter Limb, 391. Johannesburg: Wits University Press, 2012.

Shakespeare, William. *Julius Caesar*. In *The Norton Shakespeare*, ed. Stephen Greenblatt, Walter Cohen, Suzanne Gossett, Jean E. Howard, Katharine Eisaman Maus, and Gordon McMullan, 1685–750. New York: Norton, 2015.

"The Share Market: A Dreary Day." *Johannesburg Times*, December 14, 1895.

Shaw, George Bernard. "Karl Marx and *Das Kapital*." *National Reformer*, August 14 1887. https://www.marxists.org/subject/economy/authors/fabians/earlyenglishvalue/gbs-nationalreformer-18870814.htm.

Shaw, Mark. *Crime and Policing in Post-Apartheid South Africa: Transforming Under Fire*. Cape Town: David Philipps, 2002.

Shubin, Vladimir. *ANC: A View from Moscow*. Cape Town: Mayibuye Center, 1999.

Siegel, James T. *Fetish, Recognition, Revolution*. Princeton, NJ: Princeton University Press, 1997.

Siegel, James T. *Naming the Witch*. Stanford, CA: Stanford University Press, 2005.

Sinwell, Luke, with Siphiwe Mbatha. *The Spirit of Marikana: The Rise of Insurgent Trade Unionism in South Africa*. Johannesburg: University of Witswatersrand Press, 2016.

Sitas, Ari. *The Mandela Decade 1990–2000: Labour, Culture, and Society in Post-Apartheid South Africa*. Pretoria: Unisa Press, 2010.

Sitas, Ari. "Marikana." *New Coin* 49, no. 1 (2013): 36–38.

Shelley, Percy Byshe. "A Defense of Poetry." In *A Defense of Poetry and Other Essays*, ed. J. M. Beach, 31–54. 1840. Reprint, Austin, TX: West by Southwest, 2012.

Simmel, Georg. *Philosophy of Money*. Trans. Tom Bottomore and David Frisby, with Kathe Mengelberg. London: Routledge, 1978 [1907].

Simmel, Georg. "The Stranger." In *The Sociology of Georg Simmel*. Trans., ed. and intro. Kurt Wolff. New York: Free Press, 1950 [1921]).

Singer, Linda. "Sex and the Logic of Late Capitalism." In *Erotic Economy: Sexual Theory and Politics in the Age of Epidemic*, ed. Judith Butler and Maureen MacGrogan, 34–61. New York: Routledge, 1993.

"Sinkhole Causes Water Chaos." *Carletonville Herald*, August 8, 2016. https://carletonvilleherald.com/7616/sinkhole-causes-water-chaos/.

"Sinkhole Threat." *Rand Daily Mail*, September 24, 1963.

"Sinkholes Answer Likely Soon." *Rand Daily Mail*, May 29, 1963.

Skota, T. D. Mweli. "Prince Gwayi Tyamzashe." In *African Yearly Register*, 104–5. Wits Historical Research Papers, Series C, ZA HPRA A1618-C2_01.

Skota, T. D. Mweli. "T. D. Mweli Skota Papers." In *The African Yearly Register*, 130–1974. Wits Historical Research Papers, Accession No. A1618.

"Slimes. The Cost of Treatment. The Probable Financial Results." October 17, 1896. *African Review* 9 (October–December 1896): 122–12.

Sohn-Rettel, Alfred. *Intellectual and Manual Labor: A Critique of Epistemology*. Atlantic Highlands, NJ: Humanities, 1978.

Solomon, Rayman L. "The Politics of Appointment and the Federal Courts' Role in Regulating America: U.S. Courts of Appeals Judgeships from T.R. to F.D.R." *American Bar Foundation Research Journal* 9, no. 2 (Spring, 1984): 285–343.

Solomons, Ilan. "Government to 'Amend and Relax' Legislation for Small-Scale Miners to Combat Illegal Mining." *Mining Weekly*, March 24, 2017.

Sontag, Susan. *AIDS and Its Metaphors*. New York: Farrar, Strauss and Giroux, 1988.

Sontag, Susan. *Illness as Metaphor*. New York: Farrar, Strauss and Giroux, 1978.

"South African Chamber of Mines Re-Named: Minerals Council of South Africa." *Mining Review*, May 23, 2018. https://www.miningreview.com/top-stories/sa-chamber-mines-renamed-minerals-council-south-africa/.

South African Insurance Association. "Annual Review," 2019.

South African Labour Bulletin. "Mine Struggles in the Carletonville Region." Digital Innovation South Africa portal, University of KwaZulu-Natal, 1985, 19–20. https://disa.ukzn.ac.za/sites/default/files/pdf_files/LaJul85.0377.5429.010.008.Jul1985.15.pdf.

South African National AIDS Committee. "HIV and AIDS and STI Strategic Plan for South, 2007–2011."

"South African President Deploys Army to Tackle Illegal Mining." *Daily Maverick*, November 9, 2023.

Sparks, Allistair. "S. African Township Gangs: Murder and Firebombing in the Cause of Freedom." *Washington Post*, January 5, 1990.

Spender, Stephen. "Beethoven's Death Mask." In *Collected Poems, 1923–1953*, 27. New York: Faber and Faber, 1946.

Spillers, Hortense. "Mama's Baby, Papa's Maybe: An American Grammar Book." In *Black, White and in Color: Essays on American Literature and Culture*, 203–29. Chicago: University of Chicago Press, 2003.

Spivak, Gayatri Chakravorty. "Can the Subaltern Speak?" In *Can the Subaltern Speak: Reflections on the History of an Idea*, ed. Rosalind C. Morris, 237–91. New York: Columbia University Press, 2010.

Spivak, Gayatri Chakravorty. *Critique of Postcolonial Reason: Toward a History of the Vanishing Present*. Cambridge, MA: Harvard University Press, 1999.

Spivak, Gayatri Chakravorty. "Feminism and Critical Theory." In *The Spivak Reader*, ed. Donna Landry and Gerald McLean, 53–74. 1985. Reprint, New York: Routledge, 1996.

Spivak, Gayatri Chakravorty. "Supplementing Marxism." In *An Aesthetic Education in the Era of Globalization*, 182–90. Cambridge, MA: Harvard University Press, 2012.

"The Start of the Tragedy." *Rand Daily Mail*, September 12, 1973, 2.

Steedman, Carolyn. "Something She Called a Fever: Derrida, Michelet, and Dust." *American Historical Review* 106, no. 4 (2001): 1159–80.

Stein, Gertrude. *Brewsie and Willie*. New York: Random House, 1946.

Stein, Gertrude. *Paris, France*. 1940. Reprint, New York: Liveright, 1996.

Stein, Gertrude. *Writings and Lectures*, ed. Patricia Meyerowitz. New York: Penguin, 1971.

Stein, Gertrude. *The Geographical History of America, Or the Relation of Human Nature to the Human Mind*. In *Writings 1932–1946*, ed. Catherine R. Stimpson and Harriet Chessman. New York: Library of America, 1998.

Stemmet, Farouk. *Golden Contradiction: A Marxist Theory of Gold, with Particular Reference to South Africa*. Aldershot, UK: Avebury, 1996.

"Striking Miners Go Home." *Rand Daily Mail*, September 6, 1973, 2.

Suttner, Raymond. *The ANC Underground in South Africa*. Johannesburg: Jacana, 2008.

Switzer, Les. "The Beginnings of African Protest Journalism at the Cape." In *South Africa's Alternative Press: Voices of Protest and Resistance, 1880–1960*. Ed. Les Switzer, 57–78. Cambridge: Cambridge University Press, 1997.

Tau, Poloko. "'Hola GP, Hola.'" *Independent Online* (IOL), South Africa, March 20, 2009. http://www.iol.co.za.

"The Taung Children." *Sowetan*, October 16, 2007.

Tema, Sophe. "5m Technical High School Is Handed Over." *Rand Daily Mail*, June 26, 1984.

"Testimony of Mr. Labouchere." In *Papers on the Political Situation in South Africa, 1885–1895*, ed. Charles Leonard, 368–71. London: Arthur Humphreys, 1903.

Terreblanche, Sampie. *Lost in Transformation: South Africa's Search for a New Future Since 1986*. Johannesburg: KMM Preview, 2012.

Thabane, Motlatsi. "Marashea Gangs in South Africa. Review of Gary Kynoch, *We Are Fighting the World: A History of the Marashea Gangs in South Africa, 1947–1999*." *Journal of Southern African Studies* 32, no. 3 (2006): 629–31.

Thakali, Thabiso. "Finance Minister Has a Sting in his Tail." *Cape Argus*, December 13, 2015.

Thatcher, Margaret. "Speech to Conservative Women's Conference," May 21, 1980. Accessed July 12, 2024: https://www.margaretthatcher.org/document/104368.

Thema, R. V. Selope "Dingane a Senzangakana (Dingane of Senzangakhona)" *Abantu-Batho*, December 16, 1920. In *The People's Paper: A Centenary History and Anthology of Abanto-Batho*, ed. Peter Limb, 442. Johannesburg: Wits University Press, 2012.

Therborn, Goran. *What Does the Ruling Class Do When It Rules?* London: New Left, 1978.

Thomas, Kylie. "A Better Life for Some: The LoveLife Campaign and HIV/AIDS in South Africa." *Agenda: Empowering Women for Gender Equity* 62 (2004): 29–35.

Thomson, R. J., and D. B. Posel. "Burial Societies in South Africa: Risk, Trust, and Commercialisation." Paper presented to the Actuarial Society of South Africa, Annual Convention, 2003.

Thompson, Alex. "Incomplete Engagement: Reagan's South Africa Policy Revisited." *Journal of Modern African Studies* 33, no. 1 (1995): 83–101.

Thornton, Robert. "*Zamazama* 'Illegal' Artisanal Miners, Severely Misrepresented by Press and Government." *Extractive Industries and Society* 1 (2014): 127–29.

Tilly, Charles. "War Making and State Making as Organized Crime." In *Bringing the State Back In*, ed. P. B. Evans, D. Rueschemeyer, and T. Skocpol, 169–91. Cambridge: Cambridge University Press, 1985.

Tlhabi, Redi. *Beginnings and Endings*. Johannesburg: Jacana, 2012.

Tobias, P. V. "Apartheid and Medical Education: The Training of Black Doctors in South Africa." *Journal of the National Medical Association* 72, no. 4 (1980): 395–410.

Transvaal Chamber of Mines. *Correspondence Relating to Conditions of Native Labour Employed in Transvaal Mines.* Johannesburg: TCM, 1904.

Transvaal Chamber of Mines. "A Descriptive and Statistical Statement of the Gold Mining Industry of the Witwatersrand." Annexure to the Thirteenth Report of the Transvaal Chamber of Mines for the Year 1902. Johannesburg: TCM, 1902.

Transvaal Chamber of Mines. *Gold in South Africa.* Johannesburg: TCM, 1969.

Transvaal Chamber of Mines. *The Gold Standard. Report of the Proceedings at a General Meeting of the Transvaal Chamber of Mines held on Friday, 13th November, 1931. Mr. John Martin in the Chair.* Johannesburg: TCM, 1931.

Transvaal and Orange Free State Chamber of Mines. *In the Common Interest: The Story of the Transvaal and Orange Free State Chamber of Mines.* Public Relations Series No. 94. Johannesburg: TOFS Chamber of Mines, 1967?

Trollope, Anthony. *South Africa.* Ed. J. H. Davidson. 1878. Reprint, Cape Town: Balkema, 1973.

Tshitereke, C. "GEAR and Labour in Post-Apartheid South Africa: A Study of the Gold Mining Industry, 1987–2004." PhD diss., Queen's University, 2004.

Tunce, Loyiso. "The Dynamics of Mining Towns: The Case of Khutsong Township, Carletonville." Master's thesis, University of Witwatersrand, School of Architecture and Planning, 2016.

Turner, Richard. *The Eye of the Needle,* new and expanded edition, intro. and ed. Rosalind C. Morris, with essays by Tony Morphet. Calcutta: Seagull, 2015.

Turrell, Robert Vicat. *Labor and Capital on the Kimberley Diamond Fields, 1871–1890.* London: Institute of Commonwealth Studies, 1987.

Turrell, Rob. "Kimberley: Labour and Compounds, 1871–1888." In *Industrialisation and Social Change in South Africa: African Class Formation, Culture and Consciousness, 1870–1930,* ed. Shula Marks and Richard Rathbone, 45–76. London: Longman, 1982.

Twain, Mark. *Following the Equator.* New York: Doubleday and McLure, 1897.

Tyamzashe, Gwayi. "Life at the Diamond Fields. August 1874." In *Outlook on a Century. 1870–1970,* ed. Francis Wilson and Dominique Perrot, 19–21. Cape Town: Lovedale Press and Spro-cas, 1973.

UNITAID. "South Africa to Introduce State-of-the-Art HIV Treatment." Press Release. November 17, 2019.

U.S. Geological Survey. "What Is Fool's Gold?" Accessed May 1, 2019. https://www.usgs.gov/faqs/what-fools-gold?qt-news_science_products=0#qt-news_science_products.

Uthini Research. "Project Usizi: Management Report." G:ENESIS, August 2004.

van der Merwe, Schalk Daniël. "The Dynamics of the Interaction Between Music and Society in Recorded Popular Afrikaans Music, 1900–2015." PhD diss., University of Stellenbosch, 2015.

Van Eeden, Elize. "The Effect of Mining Development on the Cultural Experience of the Carletonville Community." *South African Journal of Cultural History* 12, no. 1 (1998): 75–89.

Van Eeden, Elize. "So Long, Gold Mines, Long Live Industries? A Case Study of Carletonville's Battle for Economic Survival." *South African Journal of Economic History* 12, nos. 1–2 (1997): 103–27.

van Helten J. J., and Y. Cassis. *Capitalism in a Mature Economy: Financial Institutions, Capital Export and British Industry, 1870–1939.* Aldershot: Edward Algar, 1990.

van Niekerk, H. J., and I. J. Van der Walt. "Dewatering of the Far West Rand Dolomitic Area by Gold Mining Activities and Subsequent Ground Instability." *Land Degradation and Development* 17 (2006): 331–52.

van Kessel, Ineke. *Beyond our Wildest Dreams: The United Democratic Front and the Transformation of South Africa.* Charlottesville, VA: University of Virginia Press, 2000.

van Onselen, Charles. *New Babylon, New Nineveh: Everyday Life on the Witwatersrand 1886–1914.* Cape Town: Jonathan Ball, 1982.

Verhoef, Grietjie. "Nationalism and Free Enterprise in Mining: The Case of Federale Mynbou, 1952–1965." *South African Journal of Economic History* 10 (1995): 89–107.

Vilakazi, Benjamin Wallet. "Ezinkomponi" [On the Mine Compounds], rev. trans. F. L. Friedman. In Francis Wilson, *Labour on the South African Gold Mines, 1911–1969*, 190–94. Cambridge: Cambridge University Press, 1972.

Vilakazi, Benjamin Wallet. "Ezinkomponi" [On the Mine Compounds]. Trans. A. C. Jordan. Bantu Treasury Series No. 3, 115–19. https://disa.ukzn.ac.za/sites/default/files/pdf_files/asjan57 .17.pdf.

Vinson, Robert Trent. "Garveyism, *Abantu-Batho* and the Radicalisation of the African National Congress during the 1920s." In *The People's Paper: A Centenary History and Anthology of Abanto-Batho*, ed. Peter Limb, 282–97. Johannesburg: Wits University Press, 2012.

"Vital Pointer to Trends in the Transkei." *Rand Daily Mail*, November 17, 1963.

Wittgenstein, Ludwig. *Philosophical Investigations*. Trans. G.E.M. Anscombe. London: Blackwell, 2001 [1953].

"The Voice of South Africa's Young Generation: 'Go Underground and Organize.' New African Talks to TEBELLO MOTAPANYANE, Secretary General of the Banned South African Students' Movement," *New African* (December 1977): 1188.

von Schnitzler, Antina. "Performing Dignity: Human Rights and the Legal Politics of Water." In *Democracy's Infrastructure: Techno-politics and Protest After Apartheid*, 168–195. Princeton, NJ: Princeton University Press, 2016.

Vorster, Hendrik. "Sinkhole Swallows Family." *Rand Daily Mail*, August 3, 1964.

"We May Have Bungled Wages, Mine Chief Admits." *Rand Daily Mail*, September 13, 1973, 1.

Weber, Max. "Politics as a Vocation." In *From Max Weber: Essays in Sociology*, trans. and ed. H. H. Gerth and C. Wright Mills, 77–128. New York: Oxford University Press, 1946 [1919].

Weber, Samuel. *Benjamin's Abilities*. Cambridge, MA: Harvard University Press, 2008.

Weber, Samuel. *Mass Mediauras. Form, Techniques, Media*. Stanford, CA: Stanford University Press, 1996.

Welles, Albert H. "Patents of Interest to Chemists." *Journal of the American Chemical Society* 15 (1893): 180–81.

Wells, Julia C. *We Now Demand: The History of Women's Resistance to Pass Laws in South Africa*. Johannesburg: Wits University Press, 1993.

"West Driefontein Gold Mining Company: Outlook for Development and Production." *Rand Daily Mail*, November 10, 1949.

"West Witwatersrand Areas, Ltd. Oppressive Level of Taxation. Exhaustive Review of Company's Financial Position." *Rand Daily Mail*, November 14, 1946.

"West Wits Chairman on Prospects of Higher Price of Gold." *Rand Daily Mail*, November 27, 1952.

"West Wits Income Continues to Grow." *Rand Daily Mail*, November 29, 1963.

"Western Deep Levels: Further Comment by Mr. G. Langton." Business Mail, *Rand Daily Mail*, March 22, 1979, 15.

"Westonaria Bid for Hospital." *Rand Daily Mail*, February 1, 1963, 3.

"What Shall We Do?" In *The People's Paper: A Centenary History and Anthology of Abanto-Batho*, ed. Peter Limb, 455–56. Johannesburg: Wits University Press, 2012.

"What the Ball Was Like: From a Woman's Point of View." *Johannesburg Times*, June 22, 1895.

Wilhelm, Peter. "Like a Troubled Dream: *A Man Called Sledge*." *Rand Daily Mail*, May 25, 1971.

Williams, Brian, Dirk Taljaard, Catherine Campbell, et al. "Changing Patterns of Knowledge, Reported Behaviour and Sexually Transmitted Infections in a South African Gold Mining Community." *AIDS* 17, no. 14 (September 2003): 2099–107.

Williams, Raymond. *The Country and the City*. London: Chatto and Windus, 1973.

Williams, Raymond. "Dominant, Residual and Emergent." In *Marxism and Literature*, 121–27. Oxford: Oxford University Press, 1977.

Wilson, Francis. *Labour in the South African Gold Mines*. Cambridge: Cambridge University Press, 1972.

Witwatersrand Chamber of Mines. "Articles of Association." In *Eighth Annual Report*, 1896, v–xii.

Witwatersrand Chamber of Mines. "Labour Returns, 1895." *Annual Report*, 1895, 180.

Witwatersrand Chamber of Mines. "Memorial: Presented to the Volksraad." *Annual Report*, 1895, 180.

Witwatersrand Chamber of Mines. "Return of Stores Consumed for the Year, 1895." *Annual Report*, 1895.

Witwatersrand Chamber of Mines. "Treatment of Rand Ores." *Annual Report*, 1895, 162–63.

Witwatersrand Native Labour Association. "Annexure A." *Report of the Board of Management for the period ended December 31, 1945*.

Wolpe, Harold. "Capitalism and Cheap Labour-Power in South Africa." *Economy and Society* 1, no. 4 (1972): 425–56.

"Women's Suffrage Bill: Protest of Bantu Women." *Umteteli Wa Bantu*, April 9, 1921, 3.

World Bank. "Poverty on the Rise in South Africa." August 22, 2017.

"World Gold Rush Still On, but Paper Boom Possible." *Rand Daily Mail*, August 11, 1971.

"Yakal' Inkhomo." *Chimurenga Chronic*. Accessed December 26, 2023. https://chimurengachronic.co.za/yakhal-inkomo.

Žižek, Slavoj. *The Sublime Object of Ideology*. New York: Verso, 2009.

Zondi, Nompumelelo. "Three Protagonists in B. W. Vilakazi's 'Ezinkomponi'" (On the Mine Compounds)." *Literator* 32, no. 2 (August 2011): 173–87.

Zundkler, B. *Zulu Zion and Some Swazi Zionists*. London: Oxford University Press, 1976.

Films and Videos

British Pathé. "Deep Shaft Sets Record—South Africa." (ID: 1595.4) Newsreel film, 1959.

de Witt, Lewis, dir. *Joe Bullet*. Written by Tonie van de Merwe. Produced by Leon Glenn, Tonie van der Merwe, and Martin Wragge, 1973.

Morrow, Vic, and Giorgio Gentili, dir. *A Man Called Sledge*. Written by Vic Morrow and Frank Kowalski. Produced by Harry Bloom, Dino de Lauretis, Carl Olsen, 1970.

Neo Makiri, Omphile, and Bafana Lecwamotse, dir. *16 Khuts*. Executive Producer Bhabile Mithani. Neo Influence and the Khutsong Literary Club, 2017. https://www.youtube.com/watch?app=desktop&v=thmZJHGZ3Kk.

Penny Penny ft Rafiki. "Goldbone." Composed by Gezani E. Khobane/Gorden Netshikweta/Julius Dlamini. Written by Penny Penny and Rafiki. Penny Penny Publishing. Accessed February 8, 2022. https://www.youtube.com/watch?v=NEPN9ExVx6E.

Ziman, Ralph, dir. *Gangster's Paradise: Jerusalema*. Written by Ralph Ziman Produced by Ralph Ziman and Tendeka Matatu, 2008.

INDEX

display value, 27–28, 83, 102, 107, 139, 264,
409–10, 496, 508, 524n48; and youthful
aesthetics of desirability, 429
disposability, 410, 425, 435, 527n39
Dlamini, Jacob. *See* nostalgia
documents: lack of, 123–25, 127, 133; as object
of desire, 29, 501; as pass cards, 92, 153; as
source of recognition, 123. *See also* pass laws
dolomite. *See* Witwatersrand: geology of
domestic labor, 116–18, 133, 154, 261, 285;
dehumanization of, 208–9; on farms, 222;
figure of, 189; growth of, 160, 475; and
middle class household economies, 257,
283; unpaid and women's union activity,
302; wages of, comparative, 117; and zama
zamas, 480
domestic violence. *See* sexual violence
dream image, 282, 473, 478, 518; of lawfulness,
501; as prognostication, 182
dreamwork, 148, 178
dumps (of mine tailings): as evidence of
underground excavation, 176; as markers
of landscape, 175; as sites of violence, 177;
as sources of construction material, 175–76
dust, 1–2, 10, 129; as archival medium, 116–17;
as domestic worker's bane, 116–118; as
environmental element in Johannesburg,
118, 129; extraction of gold from, 175; as
figure of dispersion, 118; red, associated
with sinkhole, 178, 507; as source of lung
affliction, 120, 123, 492; and theatrical
light, 118
dynamite: monopoly on, 94, 97–98, 530n40;
use by zama zamas, 482

Eckstein, Hermann, 81. *See also* Wernher,
Beit and Eckstein
Economic Freedom Fighters (EFF), 449, 456, 459
Edura fabric store, 388–98. *See also* Muslim
community of Carletonville
Eighteenth Brumaire of Louis Napoleon, The
(Marx), 317–19, 468. *See also* Marx, Karl;
Spivak, Gayatri Chakravorty
encryption, literary narrative as, 203–5.
See also Derrida, Jacques; survivance
Ethiopianism, 150–51, 544n68
ethnicity: commonalities between, 318;
and conflict in Khutsong, 396, 408;
corporatization of, 478; and gangs, 350,
361, 448; and job categories, 226–27, 344,
555n39; organization of urban space and,

241, 253; related to colonial governance,
217; and social typification, 331; and
xenophobia, 397, 408, 481. *See also*
Apartheid; tribalism
event: *arrivant*, 3; as that which did not occur,
180–81; and time/temporality, 5
excrement/shit, and racialization, 46–49
Ezinkomponi (On the Mine Compounds,
Vilakazi), 8, 195–96, 204, 320

Fanakalo: as lingua franca of the mines, 325;
and mistranslation; and new unions,
304–5; used at Marikana, 458–59; 581n14
Fanon, Frantz: and armed struggle, 355; on
inaccessibility of precolonial authenticity,
392; and Mannoni, 147–48; and N.
Chabani Manganyi, 263; on political
education, 414
Far West Rand Dolomitic Water Association,
184
fashion: and abstraction, 108; advertised in
local newspapers, 70; and commodity
consumption, as displacement of desire;
413, 428–29; and commodity values, 113;
and culture industries, 260; and gold
jewelry, 287; and industrial exhibition,
110–13; and prostitution, 286; as up-to-
dateness, 497; and women as bearers of
emblematic values, 109. *See also* Stein,
Gertrude
Fassie, Brenda, 365–67, 382, 413
fate, 2, 5, 25, 28, 57, 187, 189, 484; in fatalism,
422, 477
Faust (Goethe), 77–78, 80, 108
Fenves, Peter, 330, 411–13, 429
fetish. *See* fetishism
fetish-character. *See* fetishism
fetishism, 23, 40, 108, 203, 393, 529n15;
accusation against Africans, 113, 429,
538n81, 563n62; and the archaic, 111;
associated with vice, 47; Benjamin's
theory of, 108, 209; and capitalism, 105,
179, 232; of commodities, 76, 108, 412,
489; and education, 390, 394, 407; of
finance, 393; of gold, 23, 25, 27, 61, 207,
492, 510; Flaubert's warning about, 408;
and law, 321, 331; of money, 105, 412; 505;
and pass laws, 157; of the political party,
382; and sexual economy, 108, 279, 291,
294, 425, 428; of technology, 115, 179; of
waste, 99

rape: as experience of migrant women,
125–27, 133, 480; as figure of colonization,
290; in marital ritual, archaic, 498; as
political violence, 374–80; as reason for
seeking police protection, 504; reported in
Soweto riots, 314; and women in mining,
494, 559n3; zama zamas accused of, 504–5.
See also sexual violence

Rhodes, Cecil: and Beit, 83–84; and British
South Africa Company, 108; and brother
Frank, 108, 536n37and de Beers, 129; and
deep level mining, 98; and Jameson Raid,
83, 98, 106, 533n105, 536n37; as Mason, 107

real estate: development as remediation of
mines, 51; fungibility of land as, 244;
values affected by sink holes, 184, 190. *See
also* advertisements

recognition, 123–25, 133. *See also* documents

redemarcation, 20; protests against, 20, 347–48,
391, 394–408; ANC policy regarding cross-
border municipalities, 340, 394, 398–99

refugees, in Bloemfontein, 154. *See also*
Arendt, Hannah

Rhodes Must Fall (movement), 472, 513

Rivonia Trial, 181, 387

roads: as locus of pass patrols, 124, 126; as locus
of prostitution, 260; as locus of protests,
315, 348, 500; names of, as historical traces
and political signifiers, 57; as object of
scavenging by zama zamas, 514–16

Rukeyser, Muriel, 5, 14, 123, 477

rural areas: abundant harvests in, as reason
for labor shortage on mines, 138; access
to education in, 470; carceral, 212; as
category opposed to the urban, invented
in the township, 215–20, 225–26, 325;
integration with urban populations
under ANC cross-border policy, 394,
398; Khutsong township hostility toward,
396–37, 406; low incomes of, 141; as object
of attachment and locus of "traditional
masculinity," 434; origin of migrant
workers, 35–36, 92; presumptive political
conservatism of, 316; society in Boer
republics, 66; and tribalism in Chamber
of Mines discourse, 228–29 (*see also*
tribalism); village communities recoded
as, 199, 215; women as signifiers of, 492

scarcity, 94; artificial, 143

Schapera, Isaac, 38, 140

secret: underground highways imagined as,
206; destroyed in telling, 206; logic of
Apartheid exposed in materialist analysis,
232; HIV status as, 433

sefela, 36–38

segregationism: in Apartheid cinema, 289;
differentiated from Apartheid, 174,
553–54n28; and healthcare services, 417;
in pre-Apartheid era, 128, 153–54, 168, 224,
231, 259; and radicalization in utopian town
planning, 152, 252; unaddressed by TRC, 381

separatism, racial: as aesthetic principle
linked to cyanide, 18, 115, 149, 211;
as Apartheid policy, 33, 128; in pre-
Apartheid era, 132; as mania in witchcraft
and political violence, 350. *See also*
segregationism

sexual economy. *See also* Singer, Linda;
stabilization

sexual violence, 35–76, 431; coded as domestic
violence, 274, 377. *See also* rape

sharecropping and farm tenancy, 222, 224,
234, 238, 387, 457. *See also* feudality

Shaw, George Bernard, 72

Siegel, James T., 349–50, 503, 566n47

silicosis and related lung diseases, 9, 48, 118,
202, 218, 278

silver: and colonization in the Americas, 72;
in Marx's theory of money, 71, 73–76, 79;
mines featured in *Bonanza*, 269; mines
in Ilmenau, 17; and moon in monetary
myth, 283; and other currencies, 267; in
Prussian state monetary system, 532n73.
See also bimetallism

Simmel, Georg: and mythology of science,
113; theory of sacrifice as basis of value,
72, 391; theory of stranger, 36, 524n4

Singer, Linda, 423–40, 444

singing, during strikes, 461–63

sinkholes: contemporary, 211; creation of
Carletonville Herald, 179, 183; dewatering
as cause of, 10, 184–85, 199, 202, 205, 388;
Die Briels's song about, 179; evictions
from Bank and, 388; explanations for,
202; as figure of investment loss and
unpayability, 178–79; as geological
phenomena, 183; investigations into, 190;
likened to cave, 185–86, 202; and myths
about, 178–81; of 1907, 190–93; of 1964, as
covered in media, 182–89, 193. *See also*
Carletonville; Green, Michael Cawood

League (ANCYL); gangs; generation; HIV/AIDS: youth perception of; Soweto: students uprising in

zama zama: discourse of luck versus effort, 2, 486–87; as gamblers, 56–57, 484; as hard-working, 51; laughter of, 486–90; learning practices of, 121–123; meaning of term, 3, 176; mechanization and, 499; practices of, 482–83; previous employment of, 480; state opposition to, 488, 499–505; relationships to ancestors,

484–86, 497; relationship to parental generation of, 497–98; women in, 492–95

Zionism: and Christian churches in South Africa, 128, 163–65; Garveyism likened to, 547n36; and Jewish nationalism in Palestine, 540n10. *See also* Ethiopianism

Zoutpansberg, 62, 130, 150, 155, 541n15

Zuma, Jacob: in Ayanda Mabula's art, 472; inquiry into corruption of, 455; speech of, 41–54

Printed and bound by CPI Group (UK) Ltd, Croydon, CR0 4YY

23/04/2025

14660942-0004